Wales since 1939

Martin Johnes

Manchester University Press

Manchester and New York

distributed in the United States exclusively
by Palgrave Macmillan

Published by Manchester University Press
Oxford Road, Manchester M13 9NR, UK
and Room 400, 175 Fifth Avenue, New York, NY 10010, USA
www.manchesteruniversitypress.co.uk

The publisher acknowledges the financial support of the Welsh Books Council.

Distributed in the United States exclusively by
Palgrave Macmillan, 175 Fifth Avenue, New York,
NY 10010, USA

Distributed in Canada exclusively by
UBC Press, University of British Columbia, 2029 West Mall,
Vancouver, BC, Canada V6T 1Z2

British Library Cataloguing-in-Publication Data
A catalogue record for this book is available from the British Library

Library of Congress Cataloging-in-Publication Data applied for

ISBN 978 0 7190 86663 *hardback*

ISBN 978 0 7190 86670 *paperback*

First published 2012

Typeset in Perpetua by R. J. Footring Ltd
Printed in Great Britain
by TJ International Ltd, Padstow

This book is dedicated to my daughters, Bethan and Anwen,
in the hope that they will grow up to realize that Wales matters
but that there are other things that matter more.

Contents

Figures and tables

Figures

Tables

Acknowledgements

Thanks are due to the following people for their help with sources, leads and ideas: Duncan Bush, Gillian Clarke, John Conibear, Lewis Davies, Andrew Edwards, Rebecca Edwards, Neil Evans, Neil Fleming, Gwenno Francon, Roger Granelli, Ralph Griffiths, Richard Johnes, Bill Jones, Sarah L. Jones, Daryl Leeworthy, James Mabbett, Mass Observation, George McKechnie, Christopher Meredith, Louise Miskell, Steffan Morgan, Adam Mosley, John Osmond, Rachel Pick, Elain Price, Steve Smith, Wyn Thomas, Peter Wakelin, Paul Ward, Chris Williams, Daniel Williams and Nick Woodward. I am especially grateful to Huw Bowen, Peter Stead and Gareth Williams, who read the whole text, and to Ralph Footring, who drew the maps and was a thorough and eagle-eyed copy-editor. The book could not have been started let alone finished without the remarkable Heather Moyes, who keeps my life and me on track.

Further resources

For full details of the sources used, links to websites referenced, and for further reading, resources and notes please visit www.hanescymru.com.

Note on the use of place-names

Where places have different official names in English and Welsh, the English form is used (thus Caerphilly rather than Caerffili). Where Anglicized place-names have been dropped at some point since 1939, the modern Welsh form is used regardless of the period being discussed (thus Llanelli rather than Llanelly). 'The Valleys' refers to the industrial valleys that stretch from east Carmarthenshire to west Monmouthshire (see map overleaf). This area is loosely equivalent to the south Wales coalfield and, despite never being officially defined, the term was widely used. 'Rural Wales' is generally used in the text to signify the 1974–96 counties of Dyfed, Gwynedd and Powys (see map overleaf) but might also include the large rural tracts in parts of Clwyd and Glamorgan. Where Wales is referred to in the text it includes the county of Monmouth, whose legal status as part of Wales was a little ambiguous before 1974 (hence the contemporary term, not used here, 'Wales and Monmouthshire'), even though it was a Welsh county for all political and administrative purposes. The counties of Wales were reorganized in 1974 and 1996 and the book uses whichever name was in existence in the period being referred to. Y Fro Gymraeg refers to the Welsh-speaking heartland. The precise area denoted by the term diminished over the period but it is generally taken to mean those parts of the rural west and north where Welsh was the dominant language.

The counties of Wales: above, pre-1974; left, 1974–96.

Abbreviations used in endnotes

CDH	*Caernarvon and Denbigh Herald and North Wales Observer*
CJ	*Carmarthen Journal*
CW	*Contemporary Wales*
DWHS-1	John Williams, *Digest of Welsh Historical Statistics, vol. 1* (Cardiff, 1985)
DWHS-2	John Williams, *Digest of Welsh Historical Statistics, vol. 2* (Cardiff, 1985)
DWHS-3	John Williams, *Digest of Welsh Historical Statistics, 1974–96* (Cardiff, 1998)
DWS	*Digest of Welsh Statistics*
HC Deb	*House of Commons Debates* (*Hansard*)
LDP	*(Liverpool) Daily Post*
NA	National Archives
NAW	National Assembly for Wales
NLW	National Library of Wales
Pl	*Planet*
SWE	*South Wales Echo*
SWEP	*South Wales Evening Post*
WAG	Welsh Assembly Government
WHR	*Welsh History Review*
WL	*Wrexham Leader*
WM	*Western Mail*

Introduction

CAPT JOHN ROBERTS: All this play-acting about Wales doesn't matter, boy. Wales is just another country like any other.
MORGAN (quietly): It isn't to me, Pa. I've made it my world.

After the Funeral, in Alun Owen, *Three TV Plays* (1960), 103

ANYONE CROSSING THE BORDER from England into mid Wales during the 1930s or 1940s would probably not have noticed that they had entered a different country. There were no signs offering a welcome to Wales. Before they had reached Wales they might have already travelled through villages with names like Craigllwyn or Llanyblodwell or passed a chapel in Oswestry where services were held in Welsh. Yet, when one traveller asked a road sweeper where the border was, he was told that the front wheels of his car were in Wales and the back ones in England. There was no marker but the sweeper knew all the same. Moreover, he was offended when the traveller asked if he was Welsh because of his 'sing-song' accent.[1] The invisible border was thus real enough. A 1943 history book even suggested that a newly arrived visitor in Wales would quickly notice 'a certain twilight stillness of antiquity refusing to be bustled even by the roar of bombers and Spitfires'. For this author, Welsh antiquity was embodied by its timeless mountains. He acknowledged the existence of coalfields but pointed to how these were concentrated in the one county, a county, he could have added, that was rather hard to get to from the north and west. Rather than seeing Wales in the industrial districts, where the majority of people actually lived, he thought that it was in the 'small white farmhouse' that the 'true book of the country's traditions' could be found.[2] For all its blurred borders, this was how many people in and outside Wales imagined the nation: rural and beautiful but at odds with the modern world, a place connected to England but different.

Over the next sixty odd years this was a Wales that disappeared, something which became a source of both regret and relief. So too did the other Wales, the Wales of the coalfield that was so often dismissed in the more quaint pictures of the nation but that was itself also a powerful image of Welsh nationality. What stepped into the void left by the passing of those two traditions was less apparent. There was a National Assembly that gave Wales some form of statehood, but only a quarter of citizens had voted for it to come into being. Fewer people now spoke Welsh but fewer also denied they were Welsh. The majority chose to call themselves Welsh before British but were still more interested in the television, books, politics and football that happened on the other side of the border. There remained deep regional tensions and it was still easier to travel eastwards to England than north or south to the other half of Wales. But, when someone did head east, the English border was now clearly marked on most roads. Indeed, travellers reaching England by motorway were even welcomed with a sign in Welsh.

This book is a history of that complex and contradictory nation. It is a history of what Wales meant to people and what the implications of those sentiments were. It is also a history of the people of Wales, of who they were and how they lived. The place called Wales and the idea called Wales were not always quite the same thing and tensions over what the nation was and might be are central to the book. The questions of national identity may rarely have been central to people's lives but they matter and form a backbone of this book.

It covers the seventy-year period that followed the outbreak of the Second World War. The division of history into periods is always a rather arbitrary exercise. World wars provide more obvious bookends than most events but 1939 remains a rather artificial starting point because a new generation did not suddenly come into being in that year. Throughout the 1940s there were people whose memories stretched back to the middle of the nineteenth century. They were Victorians who had not read about the industrialization of Wales but rather who had witnessed and been part of it. There were Edwardians around too, still scarred by the Great War, while the inter-war depression remained a powerful personal memory for many well into the 1970s. Considering any period thus requires an understanding of what came before it. The outbreak of the Second World War may be a less conventional divider than 1945 but any consideration of the post-war period cannot escape the legacy of that war. It continued to affect everything, from social and economic policy, to the landscape and people's personal lives. It also reaffirmed how Welsh and British identities were intertwined, enhancing many people's sense of belonging to both nations, a theme which did not go away. The end of any period is no more straightforward. This book ends in approximately 2009, at the start of what appears to be a public spending crisis and further constitutional change. Future developments may well lead the recent past to be seen very differently from my take on it but such is the hazard of writing contemporary history.[3]

The seven decades that followed the war were a period of remarkable change. The economy floundered between boom and bust, traditional communities were transformed and the Welsh language and other aspects of Welsh culture were undermined in a globalizing world. Wales was deeply divided by class, language, ethnicity, gender, religion and region, categories that all shifted in meaning significantly. Its people grew wealthier, healthier and more educated but they were not always happier. Wales developed a more assertive identity of its own and some of the apparatus of a nation state. Indeed, while so much modern British history is, rightly or wrongly, dominated by the theme of decline, quite the opposite could be said of Wales. In many ways this was a period when Wales was remade from an idea into something more tangible. Yet Wales remained deeply integrated with England. Even after devolution, Westminster continued to directly govern much of Welsh life. The Welsh economy was so entwined with the rest of the UK that it could be questioned whether it existed at all. Economic links across the border meant personal links too. In 2001, there were 598,800 people born in England living in Wales, a fifth of the entire population. There were also 616,000 people born in Wales living in England.

Much of what happened to Wales was far from unique. Wales' pluralism – in terms of regional diversity, population and what the nation meant to that population – was common to most, if not all, nations. The pressures of industrial decline and economic change, the reconfigurations of class, gender and communities, and the pleasures and pains of family, consumption and popular culture were all experiences that could be found across the UK. Despite these shared experiences and the perpetual sense of Britishness within Wales that they helped create, Wales remained a powerful idea or state of mind that could exert a deep emotional pull. This existed on both a personal and a collective level, but Wales' material existence was less certain. When Wales is dissected or deconstructed, beyond institutions, only the Welsh language makes the nation different to England. Even then, Welsh speakers had strong common experiences with people in England, based on other dimensions to their lives, such as the type of community they lived in, what they did for a living and what they did for fun. Some find reducing Wales to an idea, a state of mind, or an 'imagined community' as academics put it, a little insulting; it implies that Wales is somehow not real. I would argue quite the opposite. It was precisely because Wales was a state of mind that it was so important. National identity was not something that was imposed on the Welsh people by history. People chose to be Welsh and they also chose what that meant to them.

Of course, amid the pressures of living, the calls of the nation were rarely high in anyone's priorities beyond a few for whom nationhood was an all-consuming concern. Nor was being Welsh to the exclusion (and perhaps more significant than) other identities and mindsets. Indeed, the differences between the people of Wales could be much greater than the similarities between them. Thus, to some extent, by placing different classes, different regions and different ethnic groups within the covers of one book called 'Wales', I am putting up borders where they did not exist and playing my part in making that nation exist as something more than an abstract concept. But everyone in Wales still knew they lived in Wales. A nation is not made just because historians write about it.

A lot happened in post-war Wales and it would be impossible to write about it all. There is thus, inevitably, a considerable amount of selection in what is included. I have tried to cover what I think is most important to the history of the idea of Wales and the history of the Welsh people. Culture and cultural representation come into that but those who want to find out about classical music, literature, theatre and art will be disappointed. Popular culture is better represented but more for what it tells us about wider things than for its own sake. Although the emphasis is more social history, the book inevitably has much on politics too. What parties did and how people voted affected everyday life and thus cannot be ignored any more than the state of the economy can. However, in dealing with politics I have been guided by my loose theme of national identity. Thus nationalists get more attention than their electoral fortunes maybe deserve and Liberals might feel short-changed. Finally, my choice of themes has also been influenced by where Welsh experiences were in some ways different from those in the rest of the UK.

I hope that this book matters for three reasons. The recent history of Wales tends to get rather marginalized within wider British history or sometimes ignored completely. That is partly because there is not a significant body of research on post-war Wales for those working on surveys of Britain to draw upon.[4] It is partly because Wales accounts for only around 5 per cent of the British population and thus probably seems rather marginal to historians from across the border. But British history has to consider what Britain actually is: a multicultural nation of nations that are themselves diverse places. Wales should not just be ignored or condemned to a few comments on nationalism. Understanding Britain means understanding its margins.

Secondly, if Welsh history is to come closer to the realities of the lives of its subjects it needs to look not just at the world of political parties and institutions but at more mundane topics too. History needs to address not just the uniqueness of Wales but the diversity of the Welsh people. It needs to look at events and parts of ordinary life that had no specifically Welsh dimensions but impacted on Wales nonetheless. Welshness has existed and still exists within the British state and culture, making Britishness not something external to Wales but part of Wales. A history of Wales that does not acknowledge Britain is deeply misleading.

The book also, I hope, says something for contemporary Wales. It shows that not all politicians are cynical and self-serving. It shows that individuals fighting for what they believe in can change the world they live in. It shows that the diversity of Wales no more undermines the concept of a Welsh nation than diversity undermines any nation. It shows that being part of Britain is not a threat to being Welsh or the survival of Wales. It shows that the social and economic gains of the last seventy years that improved life have been greater than the losses. It shows that devolution matters, as a recognition of the Welsh nation at the very least. There is much wrong with Wales in the early twenty-first century but there is more that is right. Many historians, quite rightly, shy away from claiming that the past has lessons for the present but if there is one thing that can be learnt from the recent history of Wales it is that we should appreciate how far the nation has come, both materially and as something that exists as more than an idea.

The book begins with chapters dedicated to the Second World War and the period of Labour government from 1945 to 1951, periods singled out because they witnessed rapid and profound changes. It then moves on to look at the 1950s and 1960s, with chapters that explore the emergence of an affluent society (chapter 3), the impacts on youth (chapter 4), class and community (chapter 5), and rural society and the associated 'Welsh way of life' (chapter 6). That leads on to the theme of national identity in the 1950s and 1960s, the subject of chapter 7, and the emergence of a more politicized sense of nationalism, examined in chapter 8. Nationalism owed something to how some disillusionment with the Labour Party had emerged by 1970, and the decline of that party's Welsh hegemony and the associated industrial retreat are the subject of the next chapter. What this meant for national identity into the 1980s forms the subject of chapter 10, while chapter 11 looks at how the Conservative governments of 1979–97 tried to rebuild Wales. Chapter 12 explores the significant social transformations that happened from the 1970s onwards against this backdrop of political and economic change. The next chapter examines the countryside in the same period, while chapter 14 switches back to a chronological view, with an examination of Wales under devolution.

In 1999 Wyn Roberts, a former Welsh Office minister, complained in his diary that history was being rewritten 'to make devolution the climax of our achievement.... Historians are a mercurial lot, slavishly interpreting the past to please those who dominate the present.'[5] It is difficult not to see devolution as a climactic event, something more than just a by-chance conclusion to this book. There may be some disillusionment with what it has delivered but it is an affirmation of Welsh nationhood. Recognizing that does not require a bending of the past to please the present. But it would be nice if the present paid more attention to the past. It might then better realize what it should complain about and what it should be grateful for.

Notes

1 H. V. Morton, *In Search of Wales* (1932), 16–17.
2 R. Davies, *The Story of Wales* (1943), 7–8.
3 For further reflections on this see M. Johnes, 'On writing contemporary history', *North American Journal of Welsh Studies*, 6:1 (2011), 20–31.
4 For an overview of the historiography of twentieth-century Wales see M. Johnes, 'For class and nation: dominant trends in the historiography of twentieth-century Wales', *History Compass*, 8:11 (2010), 1257–74.
5 Lord Roberts of Conwy, *Right from the Start: The Memoirs of Sir Wyn Roberts* (2006), 341.

1

'The waging of war.' 1939–45

> The waging of war has filled the valleys with work and wages. Boys swagger in the streets with pocketfuls of money. Omnibuses crowded with women and girls rumble to and fro between the scattered mining villages and the concentrated munition factories. The tide of migration has turned. The little houses of the hospitable miners are filled with English children from the 'blitzed' towns over the Border. The expulsive power of a new experience has dimmed the memories of the nineteen-thirties. The sufferings of enforced idleness have given place to the horrors of bombing and burning.
>
> Thomas Jones, October 1941[1]

> The war, bad as it is in many ways, has been the making as well as the breaking of many. Young chaps that nobody had much use for in peacetime have helped to save their country from Hitler's gang. Now our Gwen, instead of looking after those well able to look after themselves, is going to serve her country. What is there wrong in that?
>
> Jack Jones, 'Wales marches on', radio broadcast, 1941[2]

IN PONTYPOOL a twenty-five-year-old advertising canvasser spent the last days of August and the first of September 1939 working, deploring local traders for cutting down on advertising in a time of crisis and arguing with people about who was to blame for the impending war. He noted in his diary that such arguments were becoming more spiteful, perhaps because of people's nerves. He made blackouts for his windows but also spent a lot of time in pubs, where he found little comfort because the constant talk of war annoyed him. People worried about the future, being called up and having to house evacuees. He had other problems too. His girl from down the valley had not written all week, a married woman wanted to go blackberrying with him and he wondered whether the stories of 'easy availability' during wartime were true. He was also avoiding listening to the radio, afraid he might hear a news bulletin announcing that war had started. Determined to occupy himself, he spent the morning of Sunday 3 September 1939 repairing his bicycle, meaning he missed Chamberlain's announcement that Britain had declared war on Germany. When he found out from a friend, they went for a walk and discussed giving up their jobs to have some fun before being called up. Then they went to church to hear what the vicar had to say about the war. It was crowded with women and old men; he was one of the few young men there.[3]

It was unsurprising that people were worried. It was little more than twenty years since the Great War had ended, a conflict in which three-quarters of a million members of the British armed forces had been killed. Forty thousand of them had been Welsh. Technological developments meant that this war threatened far higher numbers of casualties, and not just in the armed forces. The government estimated that 600,000 British civilians might die in bombing in the first two months of a conflict. Thus when war broke out, a man from Aberystwyth remembered: 'It cast a gloom everywhere.... One began to feel, as perhaps they hadn't in previous generations, that now you were in the front line'.[4] Yet, for all the memories of past horrors and the promise of future ones, there was little serious opposition to the decision to declare war. Nazi aggression in Europe was obvious and the conflict was widely believed to be a just one. Upon war's outbreak, an editorial in the *Western Mail* proclaimed grandly:

> The things against which we are fighting – 'brute force, bad faith, injustice, oppression and persecution' – all must be overthrown if we are not to be plunged back into the barbarism of the dark ages.... We are fighting neither for territory nor vengeance, neither for Danzig nor Poland, but to preserve values which transcend our purely national interests, values shared by all civilised humanity – for liberty, freedom, democracy, the reign of law, justice between nations, and against the most monstrous eruption of brute force in the history of the world.[5]

This was also the line peddled in the propaganda of the government, the BBC and the press; it was also true. There were other reasons to support the war. After the long, depressed years of the 1920s and 1930s, rearmament had already begun to bring some prosperity back to Wales' shattered economy. Steel and coal were now needed and many young men were finding regular employment for the first time in their lives. But older heads remembered what had happened after the last war. Conflict might bring jobs and better wages but they were unlikely to outlast the emergency. And a global war was a hefty price to pay for simply having a job.

Thus while there was none of the patriotic fervour that had greeted the start of the Great War, there was an immediate willingness on the part of many to do their bit. On the day war was declared, hundreds gathered outside the recruitment offices in Cardiff only to find they were shut. One man dryly remarked, 'Still what can you expect in Wales. Nothing opens on a Sunday.'[6] In the following weeks thousands enlisted rather than waiting to be called up. In Glamorgan alone, 52,000 people volunteered during the war's first month for what became the Home Guard.[7] Yet much simply carried on as before. In November 1939 a young Cardiff woman wrote to her friend: 'I remember when War was declared I thought it strange that practically every-thing went on as usual, you know milk-man, baker, fish-man all coming to the door as usual. Yet I guess if we didn't it wouldn't be British would it?'[8]

IN SEPTEMBER 1939 the poet Dylan Thomas wrote to a friend that he wanted to get something out of the war but put little in. He wrote to another that he was eager to secure something before 'conscription, and the military tribunal, & stretcher-bearing or jail or potato-peeling or the Boys' Fire League. And all I want is time to write poems.' But beneath his commitment to his personal safety and comfort were more fundamental doubts. In another letter he asked: 'What have we got to fight for or against? To prevent Fascism coming here? It's come. To stop shit by throwing it? To protect our incomes, bank balances, property, national reputations? I feel sick. All this flogged hate again.'[9] This mix of personal and political concerns was typical, although few would have shared Thomas' interpretation. Most Welsh people enlisted with a sense of resigned inevitability, aware that they had little choice but knowing that, in some abstract way, it was the right thing to do. This sense of resignation meant that once in the forces it was very easy for soldiers to become preoccupied by the mundane realities of everyday life. One Welsh Guardsman recalled that the talk in the military huts ranged from

> sex to the absolute bloody awful life of the British Soldier and then inevitably to the schemes for 'working your ticket', i.e. being thrown out as unfit for duty. Schemes like holding the little finger of the right hand just over the barrel of a 2" mortar and getting it blown off were discussed and discarded, the impact might blow the lot off, and in any case, the loss of a little finger was considered too trivial, there were many cases of soldiers with three

> fingers. Threatening the Sergeant Major with a bayonet, and many similar enterprises were all discarded. Surprisingly all this talk did no harm at all to the general moral[e] and discipline. Quite the opposite in fact, it kept the dream alive to beat the system, now that would be something![10]

That such talk did not damage the willingness to fight was evident in the sacrifices made by the armed forces throughout the conflict. But it was not the great moral and political issues that made troops do this. Comradeship sustained people, not political ideals. People fought to survive, for their mates, for the ordinary things in life. After learning of his brother's death, Cardiffian Brian Baker wrote to his father, 'I have seen enough of this world to realise what home means. No Pop, I'm going to settle down at some job or other, and see if we cannot make up a little of the loss of Ron to each other. I would like to take up golf, and perhaps we can manage a little car between us … we could have some grand times eh?' Brian was killed on active service two years later.[11]

Unlike in the Great War, the armed forces made no effort to keep local people together. Instead, recruits were sent to whatever units needed the skills or bodies. This meant that thousands of Welsh men and women ended up fighting and dying alongside other Britons. A few were angry at not being in Welsh units but a Merioneth man in the South Lancashire Regiment was probably more typical when he wrote in his memoirs that 'the army was the army, and it hardly made any difference which badge I was given'.[12] For those who were fighting, the constant danger created a powerful bond between them that transcended any differences arising from different cultural backgrounds but this does not mean that individuals' Welshness was subsumed beneath a wider Britishness. The forces created an awareness of the diversity of Britain. A Welsh member of the Women's Royal Naval Service recalled, 'I don't think I'd ever heard of a Scouse person or a Geordie until I joined up. Then, suddenly, all these different accents all around you. A lot of people didn't know my accent. I'd be asked what part of Scotland I came from. Or Ireland – was I north or south?'[13] Many men and women spent their war being known by everyone as Taff or Taffy, making their nationality central to who they were. Welsh was also spoken and tolerated in the forces. The *Western Mail* even thought it had been used to 'deceive the Germans on the Western Front and confound the Japanese in the swamps and jungle of Burma'.[14]

The biggest demand for labour came not from the armed forces but from the industries that sustained the war effort. To combat the existing unemployment, six Royal Ordnance factories were set up in south Wales. The largest was at Bridgend, which employed 35,000 at its peak. Over the course of the war, there were 130,000 men and women employed in Wales in entirely new jobs created by the war effort, making everything from explosives and torpedoes to trucks, parachutes and radars. Such jobs ended the poverty of the 1920s and 1930s. Wages rose faster than living costs and there were substantial overtime opportunities too. In Britain as a whole, average earnings increased by 80 per cent, while prices rose by only 60 per cent. War also brought prosperity to Welsh agriculture, perhaps for the first time ever. There were directives and regulations to obey but farmers' incomes rose substantially, as did those of their labourers. The war thus brought a more materialistic culture to rural communities because the profits that could be made out of farming were greater than in the days when there was little reward for innovating or working longer hours. Indeed, the wealth accumulated by many farmers allowed them to purchase their farms.[15]

Miners too found themselves in demand again, although many, still resentful of their treatment during the depression, saw the war as an opportunity to escape the dirty and dangerous world of the pit. The coal industry moved from having thrown tens of thousands of unwanted men on the scrap heap in the 1930s to a serious labour shortage, as 25,000 Welsh workers left the industry between 1938 and 1941.[16] The loss of French and Belgian coalfields to the allied war effort in 1940 compounded the problems and, with the supply and price of coal being badly managed, the government took control of the industry in 1942. The effect was quickly felt as Welsh miners were sent off to English coalfields, where shortages were more acute. Mining was made a reserved occupation, exempting its employees from military service, whether they liked it or not, and leaving only the Home Guard for those who wanted to contribute more directly to the defence of the country. Coal's labour shortage also led to the introduction of the Bevin Boys in 1943, where one in ten eighteen-year-olds were drafted into mines rather than the forces, something not popular with the draftees, who felt denied their opportunity to fight abroad, or with the existing miners, who feared for local jobs. Nonetheless, the introduction of English workers from all kinds of backgrounds into the hard world of the south Wales coalfield furthered the sense that the war was a shared experience for the whole of Britain.

Other parts of Wales were also enjoying visitors, as troops, workers, children and government departments were moved away from the bombs. Around 200,000 people moved to Wales from England in 1939–41. Some of these were previously exiled Welsh men and women but others were unofficial evacuees looking for work in a safer part of Britain. The *National Geographic Magazine* was told by one man that Wales had become 'little old England's refuge room' and by 1941 the Welsh population was back to almost where it had stood at the onset of the depression twenty years earlier.[17] Clashes of lifestyle were inevitable, despite the classes run in rural towns to enable interested civil servants and other incomers to learn Welsh. Catholics from Liverpool found themselves in Nonconformist north Wales, upset to be denied both their church and pub, a case of 'Bohemian Ideals versus the Puritan ethic' as one newspaper put it.[18] A senior police officer in Carmarthen similarly complained that female evacuees and war workers from England were 'teaching local women to drink'.[19] Bangor perhaps got the biggest shock when the BBC's Variety Department was relocated there. One newspaper noted that the city 'lost its innocence overnight with one trainful of actors'. But it grew to tolerate the 'painted women' and bohemian men and enjoyed the local concerts and constant need for studio audiences.[20]

Some people saw black men for the first time when Americans were stationed in rural and industrial communities. The GIs came with food, gum, stockings and money to spend in the pubs, which made them very popular among children and young women reared on diets of American films and glamour. Many were housed with local families, officers with the middle classes and the ranks with the working classes. This created both a sense of shock among the Americans at British living standards – which were twenty-five years behind America according to one soldier who stayed in the Rhondda – and a sense of gratitude for how they were treated. This was evident in this letter home from a New Jersey private billeted with a Treorchy family:

> These people were very kind, after all their food is very scarce. Their house is very small but they enjoy life. They are not like the ordinary type of English people. You remember I always disliked the English. The distinction is they are Welsh. People here are all coalminers or factory workers. They were the hardest hit in the early 30's. There is not much entertainment here just a few movies and churches, stores and each bar is called a Pub. That means a place where people gather to drink a few pints of beer and talk.... The mountains here are high and barren. There is not much of anything here compared to home. The thing that makes most of us come back though is that people were so kind and willing. They gave us the key and let us do as they would have their own sons do.[21]

Nonetheless, there were tensions. Some objected to having to take soldiers in and, more commonly, local young men resented the competition for girls from the more exotic and better-paid Americans.

It was the movement of women and children that was to have the most impact and cause the most controversy in Wales. Land girls from across Britain were sent to Welsh farms, where some endured a difficult and isolated war, although others enjoyed the work and camaraderie. Women were also encouraged into factories across industrial Wales, where the local male population was simply not large enough to sustain such ventures. Some did not want to leave their own district and others had husbands who pressurized them into staying at home. 'She's not going! Let bloody Mrs Churchill go and make munitions', the husband of one volunteer told a labour exchange.[22] But from March 1941 all women aged between eighteen and forty-five were required to register with their local labour exchange, giving notice of their work situation and domestic and family responsibilities. Conscription into factories and the services for women in their twenties then began at the start of 1942, with those who were unmarried being eligible to be transferred anywhere in Britain. In 1943 conscription was extended to women up to fifty, although those with domestic responsibilities or children under fourteen were exempt. That year, 55 per cent of Welsh war workers were female, the highest percentage of anywhere in Britain. This development was all the more significant given the narrow range of jobs open to women in Wales before the war. In 1939, there were just 94,000 insured women workers in Wales; by 1944 there were 219,000. This meant that the female labour force had grown by 133 per cent in Wales, whereas in Britain as a whole the growth was only 30 per cent. Men, however, still dominated the workforce, although between 1939 and 1944 the number of insured male workers in Wales did fall from 602,000 to 480,000.[23]

Like men, women were brought into the war effort by a mix of compulsion and ideological and practical motives. There was patriotism in the factories and women were sustained by the knowledge they were doing something that would contribute to victory. But a stronger motive was the desire to earn money and factory work paid well.[24] Given that it was usually the wives who had borne the burden of running a home when their husbands were on the dole during the depression, some women were acutely aware of the benefits of an extra wage and of the importance of saving for the future. Others, however, took less long-sighted views. One female munitions worker recalled, 'Whereas before, regarding clothes, you had a best thing and you didn't put that on during the week, now all that changed. You lived for the day because you didn't know what was going to happen. We'd never seen such money.'[25] That sense of living for the moment was evident in the growth in the marriage rate in Wales, which rose by 28 per cent between 1938 and 1940.[26]

Despite the extra money, the experience of working was not always positive for women. Leaving home could be traumatic, especially for Welsh speakers sent to England. Munitions work could turn hair and skin yellow, while some blondes went green. The hours in factories were long, the commuting tedious and the work monotonous. Many still had domestic commitments and finding time for shopping became a particular cause of complaint. There were accusations that the children of factory workers were being fed from tins and not being disciplined. Some husbands were annoyed too after they found they could no longer expect dinner on the table when they got home. Other men who struggled to find work due to ill-health resented the employment of women and there was indignity among some miners who discovered that they were earning less than their wives or daughters.[27]

The drinking and sexual antics of the munitionettes and women in general became a particular concern. An alarmist piece in the *South Wales Echo* spoke, no doubt with some exaggeration, of teenage girls as young as fourteen haunting places where troops were stationed to such an extent that they took business away from prostitutes, of servicemen's wives being 'anybody's meat' and of Cardiff in the blackout being full of couples having sex in doorways and alleys.[28] There was certainly a rise in the number of women in pubs and increased extramarital sex. The illegitimacy rate in Wales more than doubled from 3.9 per cent in 1938 to 7.9 per cent in 1945. Yet the fact that over 90 per cent of children were still born in wedlock suggests that premarital sex was never quite the epidemic that some made out. Mass Observation certainly thought that men exaggerated the impact work had on female drinking, overspending and sexual behaviour. Some of the worry can be put down to an underestimation of what had been happening before the war but much of the concern was individual incidents being inflated by commentators and observers into a general trend.[29]

Despite the accusations of frivolity, drinking and sexual irresponsibility that munitionettes had to face, many women found war work an enriching personal experience that developed their confidence and independence and raised their expectations of home life after the war. But the war did not bring female emancipation.[30] Most significantly, domestic responsibilities remained paramount in women's lives and aspirations. Indeed, during the war there were more women in Britain who were housewives than there were in the military and paid employment combined. Among these women there was a stoic view of their role, based on coping and surviving with the restrictions of wartime and even a degree of angst and guilt that they were not contributing to the war effort in a more direct and obvious way. Nonetheless, when voluntary, full- and part-time work are taken into account, some 80 per cent of married women directly assisted the war effort.[31]

Some of this voluntary work included taking in evacuees. To avoid the chaos and disruption of a mass migration of people from urban centres, the government had drawn up plans for an official evacuation of children to parts of Britain unlikely to be targeted by German bombers and most of Wales, including the industrial valleys, was designated a reception area. The 'phoney war' and the reality of sending one's children away meant that only about a third of the evacuees Wales had been designated to take ever arrived. Nonetheless, around 110,000 children were estimated to have been received by the Welsh counties, including some evacuated within Wales. The majority, 33,000, went to Glamorgan but 10,000 were sent to both Carmarthenshire and Caernarfonshire. Not all the children stayed or arrived at once and evacuation was an ongoing process rather than a sudden flood.[32]

In Ferryside, near Carmarthen, Londoners reputedly refused to leave their bus because the village was too quiet.[33] A far more serious problem faced those children who found themselves placed with people whose English was very poor. Even where Welsh-speaking hosts had good English, young children's trauma at being sent away from their parents was still compounded by their sense of being in a foreign land. One Liverpool girl found the language frightening and even thought she had been sent to witches after entering a home with a large cauldron on a fire. Another Liverpool girl recalled, 'We all thought we were going abroad because we didn't know anything about Wales really ... my friend said I wonder if they've got foreign money'.[34] Those evacuated within Wales experienced cultural shock too. An evacuee from Swansea to north Pembrokeshire recalled:

> Here was a world of woods and cwms, green fields and dingles, and strange, dark men speaking Welsh. This was a far cry from the shabby streets and blitz-debris of Swansea. There, I had shared a bed with my two brothers, gone shoeless, and lived at times on dry toast and dripping. But my evacuee days at Brohedydd brought me knowledge of another life – fresh country food, a room of my own, and the green beauty of the countryside.[35]

Some children found themselves in families more than happy to accept the financial and social burden, and they were even kitted out in new 'Sunday best' to wear to chapel. Genuine emotional bonds developed between evacuees and their hosts and some stayed on to live in Wales permanently. When, in 1945, a trainload of evacuees left Carmarthen, two boys shouted out 'Cymru am byth!' (Wales forever). On their departure, the local paper looked proudly at what had been done for the evacuees, not just housing them but loving them, even reforming some of them of their thieving. It was, said the paper, 'Welsh hospitality at its best'.[36]

The recipients were not always so enamoured of their new charges. There were fears of germs, lice and disease being brought into the countryside from English slums. Some Liverpool girls' first taste of Welsh hospitality was a bath in disinfectant, having their heads shaved and their clothes burnt. In March 1940, the Merioneth medical officer inspected every mother and child from Liverpool and found most were in a 'verminous condition'. In Llanrwst locals were so angry that the Women's Voluntary Service feared rioting. It was not just the physical state of the children that worried people but their moral condition too. Buckley Urban District Council received complaints that the evacuees were not only 'filthy' but 'not observing the ordinary decencies in the houses' either. Given such situations, some people had to be forced to accept evacuees by the authorities.[37]

In communities with large numbers of evacuees, the incomers tended to be taught separately from the local children, sometimes in a separate building but often in different shifts at the local school. Such arrangements could mean, in the words of one evacuee in Aberystwyth, 'we didn't mix much with the locals, it was them and us'.[38] But where evacuees were more scattered there was more intermingling of children from the two different linguistic cultures. In areas that were overwhelmingly Welsh-speaking, the evacuees tended to be assimilated and *The Times* thought they were showing a 'surprising eagerness' to learn the language, even entering local eisteddfodau with 'zest'.[39] Where the linguistic culture was more balanced, evacuees tipped the balance to English, with local children succumbing, as a 1953 report put it, 'to the glamour and romance of acquiring the stranger's language'.[40] Saunders Lewis, the former president of Plaid Cymru, spoke for many nationalists when he called evacuation 'one of the most horrible threats ... to the life of the Welsh nation that has ever been suggested'.[41] Yet such views found little support and thousands of people, most quite voluntarily, opened their homes to help children who otherwise would have been in mortal danger from bombing. Evacuation thus brought together people from different regional, class and linguistic backgrounds in a way that really had no precedent. Although the resulting tensions were as much about rural and urban differences as nationality, evacuation did make both English and Welsh people aware of the traditions, standards and way of life of the other and reinforced not just a sense of shared Britishness but also of the cultural diversity that existed within that Britishness.

PEOPLE TOLERATED BEING conscripted into the forces or factories, taking strangers into their home and even fighting and killing because there was a fear that their own lives and way of living were under threat. This was especially true in the spring of 1940 when, after the fall of France, the threat of invasion was very real. Leaflets were issued in both English and Welsh telling people what to do 'If the Germans come'. Suddenly the barbed wire and concrete erected on beaches meant something. One woman remembered of her childhood at this time: 'Every night I'd look under the bed to see if Hitler was there. If he wasn't there I would get into bed and lie on my back. I didn't dare go onto one side or the other in case Hitler came from the back and stabbed me.'[42] Another woman remembered of rural Carmarthenshire that even the 'meekest, most God-fearing chapel deacon was all for sharpening the pitchforks against the marauding Germans'.[43] Victory in the Battle of Britain delayed the threat of invasion but it did not crush it and in the autumn of 1940 a new peril emerged with the intense bombing of London, something which led to increased evacuation to Wales.

Bombing also put Wales on the frontline. Cardiff was the first town to suffer badly and over the course of the war 33,000 houses in the city were damaged, over 500 demolished and 355 civilians killed. But it was Swansea that suffered the most intense attack when a three-night raid in February 1941 destroyed half the town's centre. The fires turned night into day and could be seen for miles, adding to the impact of the horror. Some 30,000 bombs were dropped, 575 business premises burnt out, 282 houses demolished and 11,084 damaged. At least 227 people were killed, thirty-seven of them under the age of sixteen.[44] An Air Raid Precautions (ARP) warden noted in his diary that he saw 'streams of people' coming from the bombed area, 'mainly women and children, carrying all sorts of parcels, suitcases, bundles, some wheeling perambulators. It bore some resemblance to the pictures one had seen of refugees in Poland, France etc.'[45] At the height of the Swansea blitz, when asked where her husband was, one woman replied, 'He is in the army, the coward'.[46] The docks and industrial works of Cardiff and Swansea made them obvious targets but there was danger elsewhere too. Ordnance factories, oil installations, mining towns and even rural communities were bombed in orchestrated attacks, but also by lost planes or those just eager to lose their cargo. Even quiet Caernarfonshire saw five deaths from bombing over the course of the war. In April 1941, twenty-seven people lost their lives in a raid on Cwmparc in the Rhondda; six of them were children, including four evacuees. A miner recalled of seeing the coffins: 'That's when you realised there was a war on'. In total, 984 people were killed and 1,221 seriously injured in bombing raids on Wales.[47]

The impact of these attacks on civilian morale was a key concern for the government. At one level, people faced the danger with real courage. In a letter to her boyfriend, a Cardiff woman reported, matter of factly, that 'some German property "dropped"' on her street, 'doing an awful lot of damage'. Although there were scratches, bruises and some upset, 'everybody in the street were real bricks, they can certainly take it'.[48] After the second night of intense bombing in the Swansea blitz, the BBC reported from the town:

> there are the usual smiles; even those who have lost friends and relatives are not really depressed and their stories are told in a subdued manner but with a sense of pride ... the only effect on the spirit of the people has been to raise it higher than ever.... I saw some elderly men and women running through the streets clutching small cases and parcels in their hands. These were all they had left in the world. Many of them raised their hand and gave us a cheery greeting.[49]

This did not go down well among the vast majority, who were feeling nothing of the sort and resented being made to feel that they had 'fallen short of some ideal standard' of taking it with stoicism. The Ministry of Information told the BBC that broadcasts from blitzed towns should cease if they could not eliminate such mistakes.[50] An ARP warden overheard a woman say, 'I would rather sleep in a field tonight than go through last night again'. Mass Observation noted privately that in Swansea people were shaken but they 'put a good face on things'.[51] A good face did not mean brushing aside the bombing as if it were a minor irritant; it meant helping each other and having the ability to cope and not give up. Across Britain, Home Intelligence felt there was an impression that 'if London can take it, so can we'. The Ministry of Information reported that in Glasgow there was a new sense of partnership with English blitzed cities. There is no reason to believe that the same was not true of bombed towns in Wales. But people wanted the shared suffering to be recognized. In 1940, Home Intelligence reports noted increasing criticism in Wales that it was not always mentioned in raid reports.[52]

Yet the terror of bombing and the fear of invasion should not be exaggerated. After a raid in March 1941, just a month or so after the worst attacks on south Wales, Mass Observation noted that people were self-consciously laughing about not going to the shelters and that during daytime no one seemed to take cover on hearing the sirens but instead made light and half-joking comments such as 'Here he is again'. A different atmosphere could be found where there was not an immediate and obvious danger; in these areas the experience of war could be rather more mundane. Even around Cardiff docks Mass Observation found little war talk and interest. As one barmaid put it, 'We don't seem to notice the war much down here'.[53] Probably more typical was a twenty-three-year-old woman who worked as a statistician in a Monmouthshire engineering works. She wrote in her diary in May 1940, the month when Germany invaded France, 'This has been such a wonderful spring and the trees are so lovely, and, in spite of the war, I've enjoyed it all immensely'. Nonetheless, she was worried about being locked up in a Nazi concentration camp for owning left-wing books and wondered whether, if defeat was going to come, it would be better to surrender early to avoid the slaughter. The raids on Newport and Cardiff were near enough for her to see and sometimes get caught up in. At times she felt 'rather as though I was living in a film'.[54]

BOMBING, RATIONING, CONSCRIPTION, the loss of a son or husband – all these trials and tribulations fell on rich and poor alike, creating the idea of a 'people's war', something promoted by both the propaganda of the day and popular memory since. Yet sacrifices were not even and there was some resentment and dissatisfaction with how the burden was being shared. Those with money could access the black market, which lost any strong sense of illicitness, or eat out rather than use up rations. For those in rural areas, especially farmers, rationing was much easier to supplement and circumvent. Workers in heavy industries were the most dissatisfied with rationing, with 42 per cent in one survey saying it was not enough to keep them fit.[55] Old social cleavages lived on through the war. Women in factories reported divides, not just between management and the shop floor but between common sorts and 'tidy' girls, who could be shocked by the language and conversation matter of their fellow workers. Some British-born black seamen in Cardiff were in demand after a period of being excluded from work but others still found gaining employment difficult, despite the labour shortages. Bombs were far more likely to fall on working-class inner-city districts than middle-class suburbs. This meant that the solidarity the blitz created was more within working-class communities rather than between the classes.[56] Even that working-class solidarity should not be overstated, as evidenced by the looting of bombed-out houses, something two labourers were sentenced to six months in prison for in Swansea in 1941. Indeed, crime itself increased significantly during the war, partly fuelled by a general shortage of goods. The number of recorded indictable crimes in south Wales rose by 84 per cent between 1939 and 1945, with violent crimes against property rising by nearly 150 per cent.[57] But the sense of solidarity was more than mere rhetoric and to relegate it to myth is to distort what people felt at the time. A Cardiff woman remembered: 'The community was absolutely marvellous. It was a time of rationing and shortage of food but everybody rallied round'.[58] During the bombing of Cardiff and Swansea private householders opened their doors to friends, relatives and strangers who had had to leave their own homes, easing the burden on official help. Mass Observation even claimed that residents in Swansea seemed to show a greater self-reliance than many people in English towns.[59]

War thus did not eradicate social differences but it did create something of a common purpose. This helped people cope with the daily struggle, not least for food. Shortages were both profound and everywhere, and queuing and imaginative cooking became necessities, something which was faced with varying levels of good humour and competence. Furthermore, there was a genuine levelling of eating habits between the classes.[60] The middle classes were introduced to new foods like dried egg and lost touch with old ones like oranges and bananas. Imported fruit had never been especially widespread in either industrial or rural inter-war Wales. In depressed districts women had always struggled to feed their families because of a lack of money; as a Monmouthshire housewife remarked in 1942, 'We've been rationed here for years'.[61] What rationing, better wages and full employment did was ensure a fair share for all. Indeed, nutrition levels seem to have gone up during the war.[62]

In 1941 George Orwell claimed that the poor and rich were increasingly reading the same books, watching the same films and listening to the same radio programmes.[63] The BBC was certainly central to the idea of a nation united behind the war effort. It became quite consciously, as one historian put it, 'an avid propagandist for the "British nation"' and tried to use the wireless to maintain national unity and to help people cope with the fear and anxiety the conflict generated. There were certainly broadcasts – like the news (which three-quarters of the population heard at least once a day) and popular shows like *ITMA* – that did win mass audiences but much of the BBC's output went unheard by the vast majority of the population. Indeed, not everyone even had a radio, while others struggled against the scarcity of batteries. But, thanks to better wages and the hunger for news, the number of radio licence holders in Wales rose from 405,954 in 1939 to 490,000 in 1945, while many others listened in factories, shops and pubs.[64]

Much of the propaganda was actually heavy-handed and the audience rather resistant to it. Early Ministry of Information outputs had rather grandiose ideas of national character and destiny that were as alien to industrial England as they were to industrial Wales. Furthermore, people could be annoyed by the BBC's use of 'England' where it meant 'Britain'. Even the Welsh news unit was prone to call Britain 'Lloegr'. A Welsh resident of Sheffield wrote to his local newspaper about the BBC's conflation of the two countries: 'Is the war being fought by English people only and to safeguard their interests only?' In 1940 the Ministry of Information formally told the BBC not to use 'England' when it meant 'Britain' because it caused 'irritation among the minorities'. But it was 1942 before the BBC issued a ruling to such an effect. Of course, such semantic insensitivities perhaps mattered little in the context of a war for the future of humanity and in image and word 'England' was still evoked by the BBC.[65]

At the beginning of the war the BBC decided to stop broadcasting in Welsh. Given that the 1931 census had recorded 97,932 monoglot Welsh speakers, an English-only service undermined the BBC's claim to be a voice for the whole of Britain. After some internal wrangling, by the end of 1939 the Corporation was broadcasting, on average, some two hours and fifteen minutes a week in Welsh, partly in order to counteract 'the subversive tendencies' of Welsh nationalists. This was half the pre-war output and the content was mostly news, talks, children's programmes and religious services but Welsh's vocabulary was extended as words were developed for concepts like 'ration' and 'air raid'. Although the programmes were welcomed by Welsh speakers, the BBC's hierarchy in London worried about the content, and the controller of home broadcasting was anxious that it 'did not make for national disunity'.[66] This was unlikely, since the news had little Welsh content and was essentially just a shortened and translated version of the BBC's main news. Items in Welsh were, however, broadcast to the whole of Britain rather than on the local frequency used before the war. For many outside Wales this was their first encounter with the language, marking, in the words of one historian, 'one of the more curious examples of the way in which the war amplified the plurality of Britishness'.[67] In 1947 the *Welsh Review* concurred, noting that although broadcasting in Welsh had infuriated 'millions of monoglot English listeners … it was some acknowledgement even during a total war that Wales is distinct and different from England. What were the 300,000 Welsh in the Allied Forces fighting for, if not for the right to be themselves?'[68] Welsh-language programmes were part of the BBC's efforts to depict the war as a conflict to preserve a familiar way of life from an alien foreign force by broadcasting items that reflected the diversity of ordinary life in Britain, something which cemented the trust people had in the Corporation.[69] This philosophy also ensured a place for English-speaking Wales on the airwaves, although there were concerns in Wales about the exaggerated and overly traditional way in which Welsh life, accents and idioms were portrayed. Nor did Welsh accents win over English audiences but again they marked a coming together and recognition of the diverse British nation.[70] This diversity was apparently something of a surprise to some English people. In discussing evacuees learning Welsh, the *Daily Mirror* felt it had to point out that in parts of Wales Welsh was the primary language of social interaction and some people's English was poor or even non-existent. 'To every native of that charming little country', the paper told its readers, 'English, Scots and Irish visitors are just as much foreigners as French folk'.[71]

Although there was scepticism surrounding the more obvious items of propaganda, the BBC was a trusted source of continuity in times of trouble. There is nothing to suggest that its attempts at generating a common sense of purpose were not as effective in Caernarfon as they were in Chelsea. J. B. Priestley was one of the most effective broadcasters. In 1940, he told the listening nation:

> just now we're not really obscure persons tucked away in our offices and factories, villas and back streets; we're the British people being attacked and fighting back; we're in the great battle for the future of our civilisation; and so instead of being obscure and tucked away, we're bang in the middle of the world's stage with all the spotlights focused on us; we're historical personages.[72]

It was hard not to be inspired by such rhetoric. Listening to Churchill's broadcasts similarly gave people a feeling of being 'part of a great nation on an heroic enterprise'.[73] One Rhondda woman remembered of her Liberal, Welsh-speaking mother: 'She listened enthralled to his war oratory, often weeping tears of pride to be British'.[74] Writer Caradoc Evans noted: 'When Winston Churchill denounces Germans we are glad we are not Germans. Faint hearts he strengthens and the timid man he makes into a warrior.'[75] Even Churchill's sending of troops to Tonypandy after riots in the town in 1910 was, according to one historian, 'temporarily forgiven if not forgotten'.[76]

Like the wireless, the cinema could successfully encourage British unity only if it recognized differences rather than created an illusionary sameness. Fictional and documentary films thus acknowledged Britain's class and regional diversities at the same time as depicting the British as a stoic, heroic and resourceful people. This was evident in productions like *Millions Like Us* (1943), a heroic but tension-filled picture of the struggles, dilemmas and hardships shared by the different kinds of British people. Its characters included Gwen, a Welsh factory girl in England, whose, according to the film's press book, 'wise-cracking remarks hide a kind heart'. *The Silent Village* (1943) showed the Nazi occupation of a Welsh village where unions, strikes and the Welsh language were banned and, after the assassination of a local German official, the men were executed while singing 'Hen wlad fy nhadau'.

The local teacher's Welsh medieval history lesson and exhortations that the children should not forget their language was further evidence that the Britain the Welsh were fighting for had its own nuances.[77] However emotive such films were, the cinema was primarily an urban experience. In very rural districts going to the pictures was largely limited to the young and even then only infrequently. Furthermore, the images of the upper-class heroes of some British war films did not always go down as well in Wales as they did in England.[78] But the pictures still played a crucial role during the war and one that extended beyond propaganda for the war effort. Films of all genres offered escapism and for some there were times in the war 'when Chicago seemed more real than Dan y Graig itself'.[79]

Despite the propaganda of the cinema and the BBC, after the tide of the war turned in 1942 and the fear of invasion and bombing ebbed, some people took remarkably little interest in the conflict's political and military dimensions. In 1943, Mass Observation found that in factories people's interest in the war was sustained by how it impacted on their personal lives and not through the fortunes of the fighting itself. If a woman was working very long hours and could eat at a works canteen then she could have an 'almost complete lack of war feeling'.[80] A young diarist employed at a Monmouthshire engineering works wrote of her disapproval of the typists who were 'unconscious of the war', workmen who were unabashed when their faulty valves caused aircraft parts to be scrapped and young men who simply saw conscription as an inevitability, like going to school. The war may have gradually become normalized into the routines of daily life but a weariness of the sacrifices it demanded still helped bind people together. Tiredness, ill-health and the strains of balancing war work and domestic responsibilities all took their toll and caused significant levels of absenteeism among women workers. In January 1942 nearly a quarter of female workers' hours at the Bridgend ordnance factory were lost due to unaccountable absences.[81] Despite the good wages, the weariness and grumbles were exacerbated by what miners' leader Arthur Horner called 'the most drab and sordid existence, with nothing to do and nowhere to go except work'.[82] One female munitions worker recalled: 'The problem was, we were earning more money, but we didn't have anything to spend it on! We couldn't buy clothes, we couldn't buy sweets, and if you went into the pub – which you wouldn't do – you'd be judged, you just couldn't.'[83]

The combination of war weariness and a new bargaining power was bad news for labour relations in the coal industry. The leadership of the labour movement was committed to supporting the war effort and trade union representatives were brought into war planning at a local and regional level. But on the shop floor and at the coalface there were tensions, despite miners' strong commitment to helping the war effort. Miners were dissatisfied with their long hours and pay, especially when young women could earn more working in a factory and enjoy facilities like canteens and tea breaks.[84] Tensions were exacerbated by legal prosecutions against miners for petty offences such as lateness, even when it was caused by the bus service. Some were just bitter at the whole climate of the period and one miner recorded in his autobiography: 'Intimidation and fear, sanctimony and cant were everywhere. Fifth columns, pimps in office, Britain's aristocracy shipping their children overseas, ration cheating, MI5 round up of Rhondda Italians, the blitzing of towns, these were the slush of War.'[85] Against this background, there were 514 stoppages in the south Wales coalfield between September 1939 and October 1944. Among this number were the unofficial 1942 and 1943 pit boys' strikes by a disaffected youth, stuck underground because of the Essential Work Order but earning less than the men whose jobs they were doing. In 1943, the writer and miner Bert Coombes noted in a broadcast that many of his young peers in the larger towns were bitter about conditions, distrustful of officialdom and often had little respect for older workers and community institutions. He put this down to their having grown up in a period of idleness and misery.[86] More sympathetically, a miners' agent from the Swansea valleys noted the pit boys' strikes were as much a revolt against the 'conditions of life during the war' as about wages: 'you went to the pit, came out of the pit, and that was the end of the bloody day for you'.[87] In the spring of 1944, some 100,000 Welsh miners struck over wages. They won a healthy minimum wage but dented their reputation as patriotic workers.

Compounding the weariness and further undermining the façade of national unity was the fact that people were beginning to think about what would happen after the war. Mass Observation found a general fear among miners in Blaina and Nantyglo that unemployment would return after the conflict was over. Munitions workers also expected a return to pre-war conditions, realizing that their industry was temporary.[88] In 1942 the Ministry of Information released a film entitled *Wales, Green Mountain, Black Mountain*. Over footage of unemployed men in the Valleys, Dylan Thomas recited a melancholy poem that asked viewers to remember the victims of the depression, before declaring that it would never 'happen again'. The Ministry of Information's Welsh Office wondered if Thomas should have written it, since his London residence meant he was not a 'real' Welshman.[89] But the film struck a chord. Across Britain what kept many going during six hard years of war was the thought that it would lead to a better world. Yet there was never any guarantee and, as *The Times* noted in 1943, 'Wales faces the future with hope and fear. Will history repeat itself?'[90] People's fears for the future were exacerbated by the fact that unemployment never completely disappeared during the war, especially in the Valleys, which did not have the space to build large munitions factories and where transport was often too expensive for people to travel far to work. Moreover, many elderly and disabled ex-miners there were simply not fit enough to find work. In May 1940 there were 13,319 unemployed miners in Wales and the sight of them on street corners was a bitter reminder of what had once been and what might be again.[91]

NOT EVERYONE IN WALES supported the war. The mass unemployment of the inter-war years had created pockets of significant support for the Communists, who found themselves in a difficult position after the Soviet Union allied itself with Germany in 1939. Arthur Horner, the Communist president of the South Wales Miners' Federation, resisted the demands of the Comintern and endorsed the war on its outbreak. However, he was outvoted in his party and, until Germany's 1941 invasion of the USSR, the British Communists denounced the conflict as an imperial war. There were a few sceptics within the Labour Party too. S. O. Davies, the MP for Merthyr, was deeply uneasy about his party's coalition with the Tories and the government restrictions on political expression and action. He was determined that the freedom and well-being of those inside Britain should not be forgotten amid what he saw as the profiteering of a capitalist war waged in the name of democracy.[92]

More visible than the socialist opposition were the Welsh nationalists, whose arguments for peace drew upon both Nonconformist traditions of pacifism and fears for the future of Wales. Although Plaid Cymru had only some 2,000 members in 1939, it enjoyed significant support among the Welsh-speaking intelligentsia and a public profile since three party members were imprisoned after a politicized trial for setting alight an RAF bombing school in 1936. Professor J. E. Daniel, president of the party from 1939, claimed that the war was 'a clash of rival imperialisms from which Wales, like the other small nations of Europe, has nothing to gain but everything to lose'. He rejected both the view 'that this war is a crusade of light against darkness' and 'the right of England to conscript Welshmen into her army'.[93] Gwynfor Evans, a future party leader, was even suggesting in private that a German victory might be better for Wales.[94] One historian has claimed, rather dubiously, that Plaid Cymru sent an official delegation to Berlin in 1940 to offer support for a Nazi England in return for an independent Wales. Hitler did not take up any supposed offer.[95] As the obvious threat of Nazism deepened, Plaid Cymru refrained from appearing overtly hostile to England and instead concentrated on protecting Welsh interests. By June 1940 Daniel was maintaining that a Welsh nationalist 'will not fight for England, but neither will he fight against her. What he wants is to be is acknowledged by her.'[96] From within Plaid Cymru's ranks, the Undeb Cymru Fydd (New Wales Union) was formed and the group had twenty-two branches across Wales by 1943.[97] It worried that the crisis and British propaganda were drawing people away from feeling Welsh and it was particularly concerned by the movement of English speakers into and Welsh speakers out of Wales. It also protested against the symbolic issue of the requisitioning of Welsh land by the military. In 1940, the War Office appropriated 40,000 acres on Mynydd Epynt (Breconshire), meaning that 219 people were ejected without full compensation or explanation, and a pub, school and church were closed. It was one of the last Welsh-speaking communities in the county and, to one minister, this was a conscious attempt to 'destroy our nationality'.[98] A farmer complained, 'They drove us into the mountains and now they are driving us from the mountains, like dogs with no place to go.'[99] But despite the protests there was little that could be done. Indeed, the county secretary of the National Farmers' Union warned that 'outsiders' were trying to make political capital out of the issue and he helped ensure that not a single family was willing to resist the clearance. By the end of the conflict, 10 per cent of the Welsh land surface was under the control of the War Office. Such losses gave a physical face to a wider process, which was at least a century old, of the erosion of the Welsh language and traditional Welsh culture. But with the sudden upheavals of war, the fate of Welsh-speaking Wales suddenly seemed more urgent and more real. The outside world was impinging on Wales as never before. Even chapels were less popular as longer working hours, including on Sundays, and perhaps a loss of faith in a time of suffering drew people away from these bastions of Welshness. Nonetheless, Nonconformism was still a powerful influence, something only too clear when Carmarthen magistrates refused the town's pubs an extension to celebrate VE Day.[100]

The war proved deeply divisive for Plaid Cymru and the Welsh-speaking intelligentsia that was its constituency. Many nationalists were deeply hostile to Nazism and members of Plaid Cymru did serve in the armed forces. Because of his alleged anti-Semitism and fascist sympathies, Saunders Lewis, Plaid Cymru's founder, became a target for opponents of the party and an embarrassment to some of its supporters. Indeed, it seems that outright opposition to the war was a minority position among the Welsh-speaking intelligentsia. This was evident in the 1943 by-election for the University of Wales seat, when Saunders Lewis was roundly defeated by the Liberal candidate, W. J. Gruffydd, a professor of Celtic languages. Yet supporting the war did not mean people were unconcerned about its potential impact on Welsh culture and Gruffydd himself remarked that 'England can win the war and Wales can lose'.[101]

Plaid Cymru complained that the 'English government' did not have the right to conscript Welshmen but that government did recognize Welsh nationalism as grounds for conscientious objection. However, the two tribunals that covered Wales did not always put this into practice. Of the mere two dozen or so who refused to serve on nationalist grounds, around half ended up in prison, with the rest being fined. Those who refused to undertake war work on religious grounds were treated more fairly, especially when compared with the official hostility such men had faced during the First World War. A few, like Gwynfor Evans, were given unconditional discharges and exempted from even industrial war work. The tribunal looking after north Wales rejected 9 per cent of applications but in south Wales the figure was 54 per cent, illustrating a lack of uniformly implemented standards. By the end of August 1944 in Wales, just forty-seven men and twenty women had been imprisoned for failing to undertake war work. The Home Office had even pressurized local authorities in Cardiff and Swansea to reinstate employees dismissed for refusing to sign declarations of support for the war.[102] Over the course of the whole war, there were 2,920 registered conscientious objectors in Wales. This was a greater proportion of the population than in England or Scotland but it was still a clear mark that the overwhelming majority supported the war. That sympathy meant public attitudes to opponents of the war were less forgiving than official attitudes. Gwynfor Evans recalled that he received more kindness than overt hostility but his father had 'spy' and 'traitor' painted on his van and shop windows.[103] Four Plaid Cymru activists were nearly lynched when they walked about and taunted soldiers during the playing of 'God save the King' on Aberystwyth promenade in 1941. They were saved from the crowd when the police arrested them for a breach of the peace.[104]

The fact that public opposition to war was allowed at all was, according to one historian, 'a vindication of the oft-repeated claim of Britain's propaganda that this was a war fought for tolerance, freedom and democracy'.[105] At one level this is correct but it seems likely that had Welsh nationalism been regarded as a genuine threat to the war effort then it would have been treated more harshly. The British secret services certainly monitored

Plaid Cymru and its publications. But only six party members were on a list of potential traitors in Wales to be arrested immediately in the event of an invasion. The state's view was evident in 1944, when the Regional Commissioner in Cardiff reviewed complaints that the newspaper *Baner ac Amserau Cymru* was hostile to the war effort. After consulting MI5, it was decided not to take action, 'principally on the grounds that the activities of the Welsh Nationalists, though objectionable, were comparatively trivial' and that the publicity that would arise from suppressing the paper would only help nationalist feeling to grow. Even in 1940 MI5 had placed little importance on the nationalists and it concluded that there was no evidence that they or their publications were having any adverse impact on the war effort. The Nazis, however, had different ideas and even tried Welsh-language propaganda broadcasts and to recruit nationalists as spies. The broadcasts were short-lived after the Celtic studies academic in Germany overseeing the operation struggled with the colloquial Valleys Welsh spoken by the prisoner of war chosen to make the transmissions. The Nazis' idea of using Welsh spies was, though, exploited by the British secret services, who employed Welshmen as double agents and even concocted a Welsh Nationalist Aryan World Movement to dupe the enemy.[106]

PLAID CYMRU'S OPPOSITION to the war was never in any way representative of what the majority of Welsh people thought. The party did win a quarter of the vote in a Caernarfon by-election in April 1945 and 16 per cent in a by-election in Neath three weeks later but these were at a time when the war was all but over and thoughts were firmly turning to the future. Most people in Wales were British nationalists rather than Welsh nationalists. Just as the shared experience of mass unemployment had sustained a powerful consciousness of class that cut across local, regional and national identities within inter-war Britain, the shared experience of war did much the same for a British identity and the Welsh people perhaps felt more British during the Second World War than at any other time during their history. Despite continuing tensions and inequalities, that sense of solidarity also cut across gender and class lines in a war where everyone was 'in it' together. Fundamental to this was an acute fear of the enemy, the state's mass mobilization of its citizens and the way the news and popular entertainment were dominated by the 'shared national predicament', a predicament that ran from the danger of death to the deprivations of everyday life.[107] Moreover, war meant people in Wales travelled more, listened to the radio more and had more contact with the English, as even the most remote

Welsh villages gained inhabitants from elsewhere in Britain. Psychologically and physically the British nation came closer together during the war.

Nonetheless, Plaid Cymru's concern and feeling for Wales were indicative of a sense of Welsh national identity that extended far beyond cultural and political nationalists and which seemed to have been exacerbated by the experience of war. Contact with England and the English promoted a sense of Welshness as well as Britishness. In 1943 a soldier returning to Wales after three years away on active service wrote that the war had made the Welsh realize that they had 'a country, a people, a culture and a tradition *different* from England's to fight for. There is a new wave of national feeling about among our people. There is, in truth, a Welsh renaissance.'[108] On the occasion of the first 'Welsh day' at the House of Commons, a *Western Mail* editorial claimed that 'Never before have the people of Wales cherished their language and traditions more fervently'. Similarly, W. J. Gruffydd told the Commons that the wartime prosperity and influx of people had not harmed Welsh culture but stimulated it.[109]

A Welsh day at the Commons was a government concession after it had refused the demands from local authorities, MPs, the press, churches and trade unions for a Welsh Secretary of State. These demands were driven by a belief that a more Welsh-orientated method of government would avoid a repeat of the inter-war economic problems and that it would also be a worthy recognition of Welsh nationality. Nonetheless, the petitioners also argued that the creation of a Welsh Office would strengthen British unity and they were keen to stress Welsh loyalty to the British state and empire.[110] The strength of specifically Welsh feeling during the war meant there were discussions within the government over how Wales could be bound to the British state. Thanks partly to the lobbying of David Lloyd George and a 365,000-signature petition, the Welsh Courts Act was passed in 1942, which allowed the Welsh language to be used in court proceedings where English would put a defendant or witness at a disadvantage. In practice, some judges already allowed this but campaigners felt the legislation's failure to give everyone an absolute right to use Welsh was a betrayal.[111] Following concerns from government minister Herbert Morrison that Wales' attachment to its history and culture might be used to foster anti-British discrimination among those who felt politically neglected, there was discussion of giving Princess Elizabeth some form of Welsh title, such as Duchess of Wales. When that fell foul of the Palace, who were reluctant to give her new public duties, there was discussion of making her a patron of the Urdd, although the Palace turned that down too, concerned at the number of pacifists within the Welsh-language youth organization.[112]

If anyone from the government had visited the 1944 National Eisteddfod they would not have worried about Wales. The festival, the first full one since the start of the war, had a distinct international flavour, with performances from other Allied countries. Welsh and British flags flew alongside each other and there were many attacks on separatism in the presidential speeches.[113] This popular interweaving of Britishness and Wales was also evident on less organized occasions. After news of the Japanese surrender came through, a crowd of several thousand gathered in Tonypandy's main street and sang 'Land of hope and glory', while a reporter recorded that he must have sung 'Hen wlad fy nhadau' a hundred times over the VE holidays.[114] The *Western Mail*'s celebration of VE Day clearly showed Wales' dual sense of nationality. At one level, it celebrated how the British had contributed something very real to the future of the world, telling its readers that they had served a 'humane and righteous cause'. But it also published a page looking proudly at what the Welsh had contributed to the victory at home and abroad.[115] To readers of the article, it was evident that the Welsh had fought, worked and died for a greater cause, and many had sung while doing it. Similarly, a north Wales housewife wrote in her local paper, 'I was proud of our small Welsh nation too. The B.B.C. do not always give us full credit, but yesterday and the previous day, Wales came forward in its true colours. What was more befitting for the Welshman than to sing the hymns of his forefathers in his days of exultation and rejoicing.' Megan Lloyd George MP told an Anglesey eisteddfod that the Welshmen who had fought were 'worthy successors of the heroes of Wales, such as Llewelyn and Owain Glyndŵr, and others who fought not only for the independence of Wales, but of nations as well'.[116] In the aftermath of the war the London press celebrated Welshness too. The *Daily Mirror*, for example, proudly told the story of prisoners of war in Thailand who each week held a meeting of a Welsh society:

> In the heart of Thailand jungle there rose the voices of the choir of the dying men, the old songs of Wales.
>
> Slowly they sang them, 'Land of my Fathers' and the hymns Welsh miners sing.
>
> Men who would never again see the valleys and towns of Wales, men almost too exhausted to speak, took up the refrain.
>
> And some died singing.[117]

Such stories represented how the people of Britain had been fighting, not just to defeat Nazism, but for their own homes and their own traditions too. People had fought for their Britain, whether that meant the mountains of

Snowdonia or the side streets of Splott. As historian Angus Calder points out, the idea and use of 'us' in propaganda was widely accepted but it was interpreted in different ways by different audiences. As he puts it, for 'the miners it meant the miners; [and] for the working class it meant the working class'.[118] The war was a British one but Britain meant many different things and Wales was as much a part of it as anywhere else.

When David Beaty Cos returned to his home village of Trefor after five years as a prisoner of war in Germany, children gathered flowers and sang 'Hen wlad fy nhadau' and 'Calon lân'. He was carried shoulder high through the village to a party at his home behind a banner saying 'welcome home to the hero'. It was such personal occasions that marked the real significance of the end of the war, and not its nuances of nationality. Wales may not have been physically destroyed like so much of Europe, the Welsh may not have suffered the collective horrors endured by civilians in eastern Europe, but the conflict was a powerful and emotional experience. It was something that marked people, physically and emotionally, for the rest of their lives. While the war was hated, it was paradoxically an event which gave people a sense of purpose and to which many wanted to contribute. A female airframe fitter from Cardiff recalled that the war 'was an experience that in some ways enriched my life, if only for the many loving and human characters I encountered'.[119] Those too young to take part could even feel cheated. One Welsh servicewoman recalled, 'I know it's awful but I didn't want the war to end until I was old enough to join up. I just wanted to do something.'[120] Yet some women ended up bored by the menial tasks they found themselves doing in the forces. Richard Burton felt his peaceful two years in the RAF had given him nothing but some time to read and enjoy himself.[121] In contrast, one injured Welsh soldier recorded, 'One night when my leg was gangrenous, the orderly gave me a shot of morphia and I felt myself nodding and smiling. And there was no more jungle, no Japs, no screams, no difficulties at home, no nothing.'[122] For those who had seen active service, the war was deeply traumatic, costing their youth, their innocence and their lives. Of the 50 million the war left dead, some 15,000 were Welsh. They had made the ultimate sacrifice, for both their nations.

Notes

1 Foreword to Eli Ginzberg, *A World Without Work* ([1942] 1991), xxvi.
2 Quoted in M. A. Williams, *A Forgotten Army: Female Munitions Workers of South Wales, 1939–1945* (2002), 62–3.
3 Mass Observation, Diary 5161, 29 Aug. to 3 Sep. 1939.
4 Quoted in P. Carradice, *Wales at War* (2003), 5.

5 *WM*, 4 Sep. 1939.
6 *SWE*, 5 Sep. 1939.
7 *WM*, 9 May 1945.
8 Quoted in M. Cragoe and C. Williams (eds), *Wales and War: Society, Politics and Religion in the Nineteenth and Twentieth Centuries* (2007), 195.
9 P. Ferris (ed.), *Dylan Thomas: The Collected Letters* (1985), 408, 410, 415.
10 A. R. Lewis, 'Working his ticket', at www.proprose.co.uk.
11 Quoted in Cragoe and Williams, *Wales and War*, 197.
12 W. Griffith, *The Welsh* (1950), 184. See also S. Roberts, *Tocyn Dwyffordd* (1984).
13 Quoted in Carradice, *Wales at War*, 98.
14 *WM*, 9 May 1945.
15 National Industrial Development Council of Wales and Monmouthshire, *Wales and Monmouthshire* (1954), 19. S. Fielding, 'The good war: 1939–45', in N. Tiratsoo (ed.), *From Blitz to Blair: A New History of Britain since 1939* (1998), 37. A. D. Rees, *Life in a Welsh Countryside: A Social Study of Llanfihangel yng Ngwynfa* ([1950] 1996), 145, 30.
16 H. Francis and D. Smith, *The Fed: A History of the South Wales Miners* (1998 edn), 396.
17 *National Geographic Magazine*, 85:6 (1944), 751–68.
18 *Daily Mirror*, 28 Feb. 1942. C. Williams, N. Evans and P. O'Leary (eds), *A Tolerant Nation? Exploiting Ethnic Diversity in Wales* (2003), 19.
19 Quoted in G. E. Jones and D. Smith (eds), *The People of Wales* (1999), 205.
20 J. Davies, *Broadcasting and the BBC in Wales* (1994), 134.
21 B. Morse, *A Moment in History: The Story of the American Army in the Rhondda in 1944* (2001), 94.
22 Quoted in B. Roberts, 'The "budgie train": women and wartime munitions work in a mining valley', *Llafur*, 7:3–4 (1998–9), 146.
23 Williams, *A Forgotten Army*, 2. B. Thomas (ed.), *The Welsh Economy* (1962), 30.
24 B. Roberts, 'A mining town in wartime: the fears for the future', *Llafur*, 6:1 (1992), 82–95, 87. Williams, *A Forgotten Army*, 63–4, 71. D. Beddoe, *Out of the Shadows: A History of Women in Twentieth Century Wales* (2000), 115.
25 Quoted in Carradice, *Wales at War*, 81.
26 Calculated from *DWS*, 5 (1958), 4.
27 Roberts, 'A mining town', 87, 88. Beddoe, *Out of the Shadows*, 115–16. Williams, *A Forgotten Army*, 162–6.
28 *SWE*, 8 Sep. 1943.
29 *DWS*, 5 (1958), 4. Roberts, 'The "budgie train"', 151. Williams, *A Forgotten Army*, ch. 4.
30 Williams, *A Forgotten Army*, 263.
31 J. Purcell, 'The domestic soldier: British housewives and the nation in the Second World War', *History Compass*, 4:1 (2006), 153–60. S. Kingsley Kent, *Gender and Power in Britain, 1640–1990* (1999), 313.
32 Ministry of Education, *Place of Welsh and English in the Schools of Wales* (1953), 20–1. J. Davies, *A History of Wales* (1993), 600.
33 N. Evans, 'Immigrants and minorities in Wales, 1840–1990: a comparative perspective', *Llafur*, 4:5 (1991), 11.
34 Carradice, *Wales at War*, 112. D. Griffiths, 'Leaving Liverpool', at www.bbc.co.uk/wales/mid/sites/ww2/pages/dorothy_griffiths.shtml.
35 B. Johnson, *The Evacuees* (1968), 130.
36 M. L. Parsons, *'I'll Take That One': Dispelling the Myths of Civilian Evacuation, 1939–45* (1998), 126, 67. H. Walstow, 'Evacuation to Aberdare during World War Two', *Llafur*, 7:2 (1997), 23–31. *CJ*, 29 June 1945.
37 Parsons, *I'll Take That One*, 14, 119, 195, 197. Evans, 'Immigrants and minorities', 11.
38 W. Troughton (ed.), *Aberystwyth Voices* (2000), 77.
39 *The Times*, 9 Sep. 1940.
40 Ministry of Education, *Place of Welsh and English*, 21.
41 Quoted in R. Weight, *Patriots: National Identity in Britain, 1940–2000* (2003), 71.
42 Quoted in Carradice, *Wales at War*, 46.

43 Siân Phillips, *Private Faces: The Autobiography* (1999), 38.
44 *Cardiff, 1889–1974: The Story of the County Borough* (1974), 67. *WM*, 9 May 1945. J. M. Morris, 'Morale under air attack: Swansea, 1939–1941', *WHR*, 11 (1983), 358–87.
45 Diary of ARP warden Basil Radford, West Glamorgan Archives, D/D Z 416/2.
46 Quoted in Davies, *A History of Wales*, 597.
47 J. O'Sullivan, *When Wales Went to War, 1939–45* (2004), 3. Carradice, *Wales at War*, 44.
48 Pat Cox to John Leversuch, 22 May 1941, Glamorgan Record Office, D/D Xgc 263/4/4.
49 Quoted in I. McLaine, *Ministry of Morale: Home Front Morale and the Ministry of Information in World War II* (1979), 128.
50 Quoted from Mass Observation in Peter Lewis, *A People's War* (1986), 95. McLaine, *Ministry of Morale*, 129. Morris, 'Morale under air attack'.
51 Diary of ARP warden Basil Radford. Mass Observation, File report 591, 26 Feb. 1941.
52 Angus Calder, *The Myth of the Blitz* (1992), 127, 130, 126.
53 Mass Observation, File reports 602, 9 Mar. 1941, and 788, 16 July 1941.
54 Calder, *The Myth of the Blitz*, 134–6.
55 I. Zweiniger-Bargielowska, *Austerity in Britain: Rationing, Controls and Consumption, 1939–1955* (2000), 73, 75.
56 Williams, *A Forgotten Army*, 72–3. St Clair Drake, 'The "colour problem" in Britain: a study in social definitions', *Sociological Review*, 3:2 (1955), 197–217. M. Sherwood, 'Racism and resistance: Cardiff in the 1930s and 1940s', *Llafur*, 5:4 (1991), 56. Fielding, 'The good war', 36.
57 D. J. V. Jones, *Crime and Policing in the Twentieth Century: The South Wales Experience* (1996), 67.
58 Quoted in Carradice, *Wales at War*, 39.
59 Mass Observation, File report 591, 26 Feb. 1941. Pat Cox to John Leversuch, 8 Jan. 1941, Glamorgan Record Office, D/D Xgc 263/4/1.
60 Zweiniger-Bargielowska, *Austerity in Britain*, 39.
61 Quoted in Jones and Davies, *People of Wales*, 202.
62 I. Gazeley, *Poverty in Britain, 1900–1965* (2003), 134–9.
63 George Orwell, 'The lion and the unicorn' (1941), 407.
64 Davies, *Broadcasting and the BBC*, 138–9.
65 Weight, *Patriots*, 53. Davies, *Broadcasting and the BBC*, 129. N. Hayes and J. Hill (eds), *'Millions Like Us'? British Culture in the Second World War* (1999), 305.
66 Davies, *Broadcasting and the BBC*, 125, 129, 133. G. H. Jenkins and M. A. Williams (eds), *'Let's Do Our Best for the Ancient Tongue': The Welsh Language in the Twentieth Century* (2000), 327.
67 Weight, *Patriots*, 53.
68 *Welsh Review*, 6:2 (summer 1947).
69 Hayes and Hill, *'Millions Like Us'?*, 62–92.
70 H. Thomas, 'The Welsh voice', *Welsh Review*, 4:2 (June 1945), 130–4. S. O. Rose, *Which People's War? National Identity and Citizenship in Wartime Britain, 1939–45* (2003), 221.
71 *Daily Mirror*, 28 Feb. 1942.
72 Broadcast, 8 Sep. 1940.
73 Weight, *Patriots*, 35.
74 M. Parnell, *Block Salt and Candles: A Rhondda Childhood* (1991), 149.
75 J. Abse (ed.), *Letters from Wales* (2000), 310.
76 K. O. Morgan, *Rebirth of a Nation: Wales, 1880–1980* (1981), 296.
77 J. Fox, 'Millions like us? Accented language and the "ordinary" in British films of the Second World War', *Journal of British Studies*, 45 (2006), 819–45. D. Berry, *Wales and Cinema: The First Hundred Years* (1994), 191–5. J. Richards, *Films and British National Identity: From Dickens to Dad's Army* (1997), ch.4.
78 Rees, *Life in a Welsh Countryside*, 107. P. Miskell, *A Social History of the Cinema in Wales, 1918–1951: Pulpits, Coal Pits and Fleapits* (2006), 126–7.
79 A. Richards, *Dai Country* (1973), 28.
80 Hayes and Hill, *'Millions Like Us'?*, 22.
81 Calder, *The Myth of the Blitz*, 134–6. Williams, *A Forgotten Army*, 128.

82 Quoted in Francis and Smith, *The Fed*, 407.
83 Quoted in Williams, *A Forgotten Army*, 208.
84 Roberts, 'A mining town', 86.
85 R. Berry, *History Is What You Live* (1998), 89.
86 Francis and Smith, *The Fed*, 398. B. L. Coombes, 'Bitter idleness' (1943), in P. Hannan (ed.), *Wales on the Wireless* (1988), 102.
87 Quoted in S. Bloomfield, 'The apprentice boys' strikes of the Second World War', *Llafur*, 3:2 (1981), 53–67.
88 Roberts, 'A mining town'.
89 A. Lycett, *Dylan Thomas: A New Life* (2003), 206.
90 *The Times*, 15 Feb. 1943.
91 *HC Deb*, 2 May 1940, vol. 360, c. 872. *The Times*, 1 Apr. 1940.
92 R. Griffiths, *S. O. Davies: A Socialist Faith* (1983), ch. 6.
93 *WM*, 5 Aug. 1940, quoted in Morgan, *Rebirth of a Nation*, 257. *Welsh Nationalist*, 8:10 (Oct. 1939) and 8:5 (May 1939).
94 R. Evans, *Gwynfor Evans: Portrait of a Patriot* (2008), 68.
95 Weight, *Patriots*, 49.
96 *Welsh Nationalist*, 9:6 (June 1940).
97 *The Times*, 19 Feb. 1943.
98 H. Hughes, *An Uprooted Community: A History of Epynt* (1998), 98.
99 Quoted in J. Davies, 'The fight for Preseli', *Pl*, 58 (1986), 6.
100 Evans, *Gwynfor Evans*, 64–5. Jenkins and Williams, *'Let's Do Our Best'*, 234. Williams, *A Forgotten Army*, 159. *CJ*, 11 May 1945.
101 A. O. H. Jarman, 'Plaid Cymru in the Second World War', *Pl* (1979), 21–30. Jenkins and Williams, *'Let's Do Our Best'*, 262.
102 K. O. Morgan, *Modern Wales: Politics, Places and People* (1995), 107–13. Williams, 'In the wars', 199. Beddoe, *Out of the Shadows*, 125.
103 Gwynfor Evans, *For the Sake of Wales* (2000), chs 6 and 7. Evans, *Gwynfor Evans*, 89–90.
104 Weight, *Patriots*, 57–8. *Welsh Nationalist*, 10:12 (Dec. 1941). P. Madgwick, N. Griffiths and V. Walker, *The Politics of Rural Wales: A Study of Cardiganshire* (1973), 60.
105 R. Mackay, *The Test of War: Inside Britain, 1939–45* (1999), 103.
106 I. Wynne Jones, *Hitler's Celtic Echo* (2006), ch. 2, 83. Meeting of the Regional Commissioner, Cardiff, 22 July 1944, NA, 45/25484. M. Howard, *British Intelligence in the Second World War, Vol. 5: Strategic Deception* (1990). C. Andrew, *The Defence of the Realm: The Authorized History of MI5* (2009), 249.
107 Hayes and Hill, *'Millions Like Us'?*, 301–2. Weight, *Patriots*, 48.
108 *Wales*, 1 (July 1943).
109 *WM*, 17 Oct. 1944.
110 Weight, *Patriots*, 51–2.
111 J. G. Jones, 'The national petition on the legal status of the Welsh language, 1938–1942', *WHR*, 18:1 (1996), 92–124.
112 See NA, HO 144/22915, and Jones, *Hitler's Celtic Echo*, 34–6.
113 K. Bernard, *Visible Welshness: Performing Welshness at the National Eisteddfod in the Twentieth Century*, PhD thesis, Swansea University (2004), ch. 6.
114 *WM*, 16 Aug. 1945 and 11 May 1945. *LDP*, 9 May 1945.
115 *WM*, 8 May 1945.
116 *CDH*, 11 and 25 May 1945.
117 *Daily Mirror*, 13 Sep. 1945.
118 A. Calder, *The People's War: Britain 1939–1945* (1992), 138.
119 *CDH*, 25 May 1945. H. H. Price, 'Experiences in World War II', *Llafur*, 6:1 (1992), 113.
120 Quoted in Carradice, *Wales at War*, 93.
121 Beddoe, *Out of the Shadows*, 122. D. Jenkins, *Richard Burton: A Brother Remembered* (1994), 61.
122 *In the Green Tree: The Letters and Short Stories of Alun Lewis* ([1948] 2006), 126–7.

2

'The spirit of reconstruction.' 1945–51

As we enter 1946 with a Labour government in power pledged to introduce great and sweeping reforms, the air is charged with the spirit of reconstruction. Coming soon are a great social insurance scheme to banish want, coupled with family allowances and higher compensation for injured workers, long-looked for nationalisation of the mining industry, a broader and better education system, a comprehensive national health service, more houses.... The horizon looks bright; we walk into this New Year full of hope of better times to come.

Aberdare Leader, 5 January 1946

I had the feeling that we in Britain and the people of Europe were at the beginning of the transition from one way of life to another.... The world now seemed to be in the melting-pot out of which it would become unrecognizable to many. After some hundreds of years future Trevelyans and Toynbees would tell posterity what was happening to us now in 1946, when me and my family didn't seem to count for much.

Jack Jones, *Give Me Back My Heart* (1950), 72

VICTOR IORWERTH LEWIS from Cardigan was on his way to Denmark with the Pembrokeshire and Cardiganshire yeomanry when the war finished. After six years in the army, it was 'a great shock to the system … it felt as if you'd been made redundant'. When he got home he found it 'very difficult to settle down to civilian life' but got through it thanks to 'the blessing of a good wife'.[1] Others were not so fortunate. The traumatic memories of conflict and the emotional distance caused by physical separation created difficult situations. Some men returned to children who did not know them and wives who had been unfaithful or were unwilling to relinquish the control they had enjoyed over the home during the war. Inevitably, not all marriages survived and the number of divorced women in Wales rose from 628 in 1931 to 4,935 in 1951. In a 1956 Welsh-language novel about a soldier who leaves his family, one woman claimed 'If a man steals or drinks or chases women, the war always gets the blame', while another thought 'war has certainly made people more shameless. Plenty of these things happened before, but people hid them.' Neither had much sympathy for what the husband might have been through in the forces.[2] Those who had not fought had their own demons to face. Some were dogged with guilt for not having served when their friends had died for their country. A short story claimed: 'Somehow they weren't real men and were seen to be what they were, as dodgers'.[3]

Outside the home things were not always any easier for returning service personnel. Civilian jobs could be very mundane and some found themselves in subordinate positions after having commanded troops through the terrors of war. Worse was the threat of not finding a job at all. The acute wartime fears that peace would bring a return to the depression and misery of the 1930s deepened as the wartime economy wound down. In Wrexham, after the closure of a munitions factory, unemployment rose from 444 in June 1945 to 4,940 six months later, a figure higher than before the war. By February 1946, unemployment had hit 10 per cent in Wales.[4]

It was the fear that this could happen that had made the Labour Party's promise that socialism could change the very basis of society so appealing. The promise also seemed realistic now that the war had shown that state action could both eradicate unemployment and raise living standards. The chance to make that a reality came at the 1945 general election. One north Wales newspaper thought that, in Caernarfonshire,

> Wales is the central issue.... What is most gratifying is that this concentration on Welsh problems is no vote-catching stunt. It springs rather from an inner conviction that, whatever party is victorious, it will be no victory for Wales unless its economic and cultural life – aspects which are only too frequently being separated – is guaranteed.[5]

But most people did not vote for the good of Wales but the good of themselves and that meant a party that would put the ordinary working man and woman first. Labour thus took 58.1 per cent of the Welsh vote and twenty-five out of thirty-six Welsh seats, making seven gains. It had majorities of over 20,000 in nine seats and in Llanelli James Griffiths won by more than 34,000 votes, giving him Britain's second largest majority. The mammoth majorities in industrial districts were hardly a surprise, as many of those seats had been Labour since early in the century, but in the coastal towns there was evidence of a shift in opinion. In Cardiff, a professor of industrial relations, a school teacher and a naval officer won three seats for Labour. People were voting for change and the sense of optimism was real and palpable. Some electors cried with joy on hearing the result and James Callaghan, newly elected in Cardiff South, felt 'Nothing was impossible. We were unconquerable.'[6]

But not everyone welcomed Labour's promised sweeping reforms and the uniformity of the desire for change and the faith placed in the party should not be exaggerated. In Rhondda East, Harry Pollitt, general secretary of the Communist Party of Great Britain, lost by just 972 votes. This was partly a personal vote but it also showed that there were pockets of people who wanted more radical change than Labour promised. At the other end of the political spectrum, the Tories were far from entirely unpopular, taking four seats and 23.8 per cent of the Welsh vote. Even in Aneurin Bevan's Ebbw Vale constituency they won 19.9 per cent of the vote. The Liberals won six seats in rural Wales, although in Pembroke their majority was 168 and in Merioneth it was just 112. These seats did, nonetheless, show the continuing influence of older notions of what had once been Nonconformist radicalism but was now simply conservatism. In rural Llanfihangel-yng-Ngwynfa (Montgomeryshire), the Liberal candidate's mild socialism severely shook old radicals, who were worried by his calls for land nationalization and unenthusiastic about his desire to bring modern luxuries like bathrooms and cinemas to the area.[7] Those who had not voted Labour thus faced the future with apprehension, as much because of the uncertain and perilous economic and social climate as because the party of the workers was in power. The conservative *Western Mail* accepted that the people had spoken but said that it would have preferred a socialist experiment in more stable times.[8]

It was not Welsh votes that put Labour into power but Welshmen were central to the party's plans for a safer, securer and wealthier future. Aneurin Bevan was in the cabinet as Minister for Health and Housing and five other Welsh MPs were in junior government positions, including James Griffiths, who was responsible for National Insurance. At the heart of the new government's programme was the welfare state, which promised health, education and work for all to curb the excesses of the free market that had shattered Britain's industrial districts between the wars and exacerbated the country's social and economic inequalities. Indeed, for Griffiths and Bevan, the commitment to these policies was a direct result of their personal experience of unemployment in the inter-war Valleys. For many historians the welfare state has come to be seen as the golden achievement of any British government, a rebuilding of society against all the odds. The Labour administration of 1945–51 certainly laid the basic foundations of government social and economic policy until the advent of Thatcherism. But it has also been interpreted as a time of missed opportunities, a period when the government failed to modernize the economy and instead overstretched meagre resources with the demands of an expensive welfare state and delusions of keeping Britain a world power on the international stage.[9]

AT THE END of the war, people's immediate concern was somewhere to live. The pre-war housing stock was in a dire state. Over 60 per cent of homes in many of the mining valleys in 1951 had no fixed bath, while 28 per cent of houses in Glamorgan did not have their own piped water or kitchen sink and almost a quarter of households had to share a toilet with another. Aside from lacking basic facilities, many homes were not just cold and damp but actually wet. In south-west Wales at the end of the 1940s, somewhere between 5 and 10 per cent of houses were deemed suitable only for demolition, while another 15–30 per cent had only a short remaining useful life or were in need of major repairs. Only 35–40 per cent of houses were thought satisfactory. Similarly, in rural counties over half of houses were in need of major repairs and around one in ten of the local stock was classified as unfit for habitation.[10] Even finding a house could be difficult, especially in Cardiff and Swansea, where the bombing had exacerbated shortages. The scale of the problem was evident in Maesteg, a town of 23,000 people at the 1951 census, where there were a thousand families on the housing waiting list in 1948. Families ended up living in single rooms in relatives' or strangers' homes. This overcrowding was worse in Wales than in England. In 1949 the average household in south Wales comprised 3.42 persons, whereas in Britain as a whole it was 3.18 and in London 3.07. Prefabricated homes were erected, some 7,000 in Wales by 1949, to cope with the shortages.[11] They are now fondly remembered by some but they could be rather shabby. One woman complained of her Swansea prefab: 'The doors are ill-fitting, windows draughty and the base on one side is crumbling.' Doctors told her she had to move for her health but she was unable to go back to a house that she actually owned because the council had let it during the war when it was vacant and now refused her tenancy of her own home.[12] Others were even less fortunate, ending up in unheated and leaky army huts while they waited for something better: 'It was terrible. I went in one night to my little boy, [in] the part that was supposed to be a bedroom, and the oil cloth was floating on the floor with water.'[13]

Rent controls stopped the market forcing prices out of control but material shortages limited the government's ability to ease the housing crisis. It gave priority to public housing and, between April 1945 and the end of 1951, 49,678 new houses were completed in Wales, 87 per cent of which were built by local authorities.[14] These new council houses gave people space to breathe, eat, bathe and just live, and it was thus unsurprising that those lucky enough to get one could feel as though they had been left a 'big fortune' and that it was 'a dream come true'.[15] But the supply of new housing in Wales lagged far behind both people's needs and aspirations and the rate of building in parts of England. Fewer houses were completed in Wales in 1950 and 1951 than had been in 1937 and 1938.[16] In 1950 there were still 15,000 families on Cardiff's housing waiting list.[17] Such people had little choice but to share with other families or live in houses that were unsuitable for human habitation.

If housing was a gaping hole in the government's clothing, the National Health Service was the jewel in its crown. One historian has called it 'one of the finest institutions ever built by anybody anywhere'.[18] A few contemporaries were initially less enamoured. The Service opened in 1948 in the middle of the Berlin crisis and amid concerns about the impact Marshall aid would have on Britain's independence. The *South Wales Evening Post* thus noted that 'Britain's first day under a comprehensive National Health Service and social security system has dawned in a world that is most sadly in need of international security'.[19] Others had more basic concerns, leading an editorial in a Pontypridd paper to ask

> Some people complain about the cost of the new social services, but while to many people the 4s 7d stopped weekly out of their wage packets may seem a heavy penalty, is it too much to pay for safeguards that will eliminate from lives what has been described as 'the corroding anxiety of insecurity'? No longer will the ordinary worker dread the financial effects of illness or unemployment for the days when they meant dire poverty and hardship in the home will pass.[20]

Even general practitioners, often hostile in England, were more enthusiastic in Wales.[21] Most of the hospitals of Wales were simply in too poor a condition for any serious opposition to their nationalization.

Conditions which people had lived with for years, not least poor teeth and eyesight, were now rectifiable and demand was immediately higher than anyone had anticipated. Seeing the doctor was no longer a last resort; poor eyesight or bad teeth were no longer things to endure without treatment. By June 1954, 1.8 million pairs of glasses had been issued by the

NHS in Wales.[22] Thousands of lives became immediately better but some of the NHS's benefits were less obvious. The physical appearance of people who went from having no teeth to properly fitted dentures was improved, boosting their self-confidence. Subsidized wigs were available, leading to miners becoming the biggest customers of a large wig manufacturer in Swansea. There was also a degree of keeping up with the Joneses or simply exploiting what could be had for free now in case of a future emergency or an abolition of the Service. People built up stores of medicine and some even took bandages to make curtains because of a shortage of more conventional materials. In more rural communities, doctors and hospitals were still sometimes mistrusted and a last resort after traditional old beliefs and medical cures had failed.[23] But in towns, with expectations raised, new complaints emerged about the accessibility of services. In 1951 one letter writer from Prestatyn complained that people were not being admitted to hospitals, that doctors had become distributors of paperwork, that there were long queues at chemists and that it was 'much safer in Korea than in Rhyl on a Sunday afternoon'.[24] Given the huge demand, the NHS proved to be hugely more expensive than first estimated. In its first two years it exceeded its budget by nearly 40 per cent. In Wales, with its elderly population and long reliance on industries that harmed their workers, the financial cost was particularly heavy. There were estimated to be 5,000 unemployed ex-miners in south Wales with lung disease. In 1952 an x-ray population survey found that nearly half of working miners in Rhondda Fach had pneumoconiosis and almost one in five had its most deadly form. No wonder then that expenditure on social services in Wales in 1952 was 33 per cent higher in Wales than in the UK as a whole.[25]

BEFORE 1944 SECONDARY EDUCATION beyond fourteen was only for those who were bright enough to win scholarships or those whose families had enough money to support them. The 1944 Education Act, passed by the wartime coalition but largely enacted and embraced by Labour, changed all this by introducing a tripartite system of free education. Those who passed the 'eleven-plus' entrance exam, a mixture of composition, arithmetic and essay writing on topics as inspirational as 'washing day' or 'our bonfire', were sent to grammar schools.[26] Those who failed were put in secondary moderns or, occasionally, technical schools. The latter were meant to support local industry but they were dogged, especially in Wales, by an image of inferiority. In 1951 there were just twenty technical schools in Wales, catering for 3 per cent of secondary school pupils.[27] Instead, the new education system was dominated by the division between grammar schools and secondary moderns. There was no attempt at educational egalitarianism. The public schools and universities were left untouched. Although working-class children intelligent enough (or coached well enough) to pass the eleven-plus were given the opportunity of a free education that could get them into university and up the social ladder, those who failed it were relegated to what was widely regarded, often quite rightly, as a second-rate education.

There was some opposition from Labour-controlled local authorities to the division of children into different kinds of education. Other Welsh councils objected because certain small village schools had to close after their numbers fell because children were now having a separate secondary education. Wales actually already had a relatively high number of county (secondary) schools because of local authorities' historic reverence for education. With these schools becoming grammars, it became generally easier to pass the eleven-plus in Wales than in England, simply because there were more grammar school places to fill. In England the proportion attending grammar school could fall as low as 10 per cent in some areas and rise as high as 45 per cent in others. The average seemed to be around 25 per cent. In Wales, however, the proportions at grammar schools varied from 35 to 45 per cent.[28] Furthermore, the popular importance placed on education meant more pupils in Wales stayed on in school past the age of fifteen. In 1953, 12.6 per cent of seventeen-year-old boys and 11.6 per cent of seventeen-year-old girls were still in school in Wales, whereas in England and Wales as a whole the figures were 7.0 and 6.5 per cent.[29]

The grammars modelled themselves on English public schools. Boys and girls were usually separated, masters wore gowns, Latin was taught, prefects ruled the roost and everyone was organized into houses. According to historian Peter Stead, the system introduced by the 1944 Act meant that 'a significantly large minority of Welsh working-class children most of whom were under fifteen were being given an education that would in a later era be perfectly acceptable at undergraduate level within an American state university'.[30] Other products of the system also look back fondly on their education. Carwyn James, the son of a miner and a rugby coach, remembered his 1940s grammar school: 'the lingering impression I have is one of belonging to one happy family. The staff were counsellors and friends, skilful, patient and wise disciplinarians. I feel that the school reflected the local coal mining community with its intense respect for learning. A warm, close community where everyone knew everyone else. Snobbery was anathema to all, and anyone who tried it on, was soon cut down to size.'[31]

Yet the grammar schools also had significant problems. Those who did not want to go to university could feel ignored by their teachers and dismissed as 'an unintelligent lout'.[32] The best boys tended to be pushed towards classics and the arts rather than engineering or the sciences. One pupil at Ebbw Vale Grammar from 1946 to 1953 remembered the annual prize giving and academic awards at the eisteddfod: 'I watched with envy as the parade of budding poets and essayists walked on stage to receive their prizes. There was never an award for the most creative physics experiment or the most poetic mathematical formula written in Welsh.'[33] Some felt 'the whole world of industry was a closed book' to many teachers.[34] Such an emphasis meant the much-celebrated Welsh education system actually did rather little to meet the needs of local industry and it was no wonder that so many of the most able products of grammar schools left Wales altogether. Indeed, part of the whole reason for 'the Welsh veneration for education' was precisely because, as one short story put it, the 'road out of the pit led through a school book'.[35] It was an education system that helped individuals but made less of a contribution to the economic needs of Wales.

Teachers may remember that within the grammars it did not matter what job a child's father had but education created a different social fissure that one historian has called the 'sharpest social divide' in post-war Wales.[36] Children at a town grammar kept themselves to themselves and avoided 'village boys'. A journalist from Carmarthen recalled, 'In a working-class childhood there were always faces that, because of the eleven-plus, disappeared as abruptly as in any totalitarian state, so if you met them afterwards, either you or they were embarrassed, not knowing how to react.'[37] The eleven-plus thus became a major event in children's lives. Its results were published in the press and closely scrutinized by locals. Those who did not pass were often regarded as failures, destined for a life of manual work and even subject to nicknames such as 'town scrubbers'. The secondary moderns they were put in had fewer resources and employed teachers unable to find jobs in the grammars. By 1960 teachers in such schools could be found remarking that one of their biggest tasks was helping children overcome the 'psychological trouble' that resulted from failing the eleven-plus.[38] The secondary modern curriculum was more practical than academic, concentrating on the basics and handicrafts. Whereas over half of grammar pupils stayed to do A-levels, most children left secondary moderns at fifteen and very few went on to university.[39] Thus how children performed in an exam at the age of eleven played a major part in determining the course of their future lives. Indeed, children were coached for the exam and thus the division of children into those likely to pass or not could begin well before eleven. Moreover, despite the route to social mobility it could offer, the exam also exacerbated traditional class barriers. In larger towns, living in working-class districts lessened people's chances of making it to grammar school. In Swansea at the start of the 1960s, 30 per cent of children went to grammar schools, while 46 per cent went to the secondary modern (with the rest at new comprehensives). Yet in the relatively deprived working-class district of St Thomas, only 17 per cent made it to the grammar school, while 77 per cent ended up at the secondary modern. Studies in England also suggested that working-class children secured fewer places than might be expected and the 1944 Act was perhaps of most benefit to middle-class families, who would have had to pay fees under the old system.[40]

Yet the educational divide created in 1944 was not as straightforward as it first seems. For girls, of whom less was often expected and less could be achieved in the wider world, where a choice of husband rather than career was usually seen as the key to social destiny, the benefits of passing the eleven-plus were less decisive. Nor were grammars always quite what they were made out to be. Cowbridge Grammar was described by a teacher there in the 1950s as 'cheerful chaos'. He noted the spasmodic discipline and how poor some of the teaching was in the sciences.[41] Because more children went to grammar school in Wales than in England, there were simply not enough middle-class openings for all of them when they left. A survey of selected rural Welsh districts showed that of 308 children who left grammar schools in 1951, only 61 went on to university or training college, whereas 136 (including 32 boys) went into occupations of 'limited prospects' such as shop work, domestic service and routine clerical jobs.[42] Thus passing the eleven-plus was no guarantee of a middle-class career. In rural Wales the impact of the divide was also less stark because the population was just too small to support a genuine two-tier system. Many schools shared a building and classes were combined in the first two years of secondary education. Such practical issues meant that in 1949 Anglesey opened Wales' first comprehensive, in Holyhead, one of the very first in Britain.[43]

Grammar school children were not always appreciative of their position. One seventeen-year-old, for example, was acutely aware that as a grammar school girl she was subject to the injustices of teachers but her contemporaries were now adults with 'jobs and steady boy-friends or fiancés'. They stayed out 'until midnight' and smoked. 'One was even expecting a baby and had got married.'[44] Similarly, a 1950s Flintshire girl remembered that, rather than looking down on secondary modern children, 'we envied them for knowing how to be outsiders and as we grew older we aped their style:

caps and berets balled up in pockets, greased and lacquered quaffs of hair, secret lockets and chains with rings on them under their shirts'.[45] The 'New Jerusalem' never quite worked in practice how it was meant to.

AT PENALLTA COLLIERY before dawn on 1 January 1947, men and boys stood around the pithead waiting for the floodlights to be switched on. There were some wives there too, complete with sleepy children brought to see a day they were not meant to forget. A band played and the miners sang 'Hen wlad fy nhadau' and 'God save the Queen'. Speeches were made about past strife and new beginnings; one speaker shouted 'private enterprise has had it!' There were tears and cheers. A notice was erected that said 'This colliery is now managed by the National Coal Board on behalf of the people'. Such 'almost eisteddfodic occasions' were repeated around the south and north Wales coalfields.[46] One paper said of the miners in the Amman valley that morning: 'one could sense a new feeling among them, a sort of expectation, as though they were looking for something better in the future. It was a day for which the miner had longed for 40 years.' Nationalization thus had a symbolic dimension, in that it promised security and status for the future, rather than the miseries and sense of inferiority of the past. Many managers welcomed it too, knowing that the huge investment needed to modernize and save the industry was not going to come from any source but the state. Of course, not everyone was quite so jubilant. The Conservative-leaning *Western Mail* quoted a miner saying 'What does it matter who I get the coal for? All I am concerned about is getting a day's pay for a day's work and it taking it home to the missus.' But such voices were in the minority. Nationalization was something to celebrate and a north Wales miner greeted his under-manager that day with a simple 'we are in charge now'.[47]

No one expected a complete revolution or a utopia from nationalization, just better conditions and an enhanced role for the union. A five-day week, pensions and paid holidays were quickly implemented; wages also gradually rose, making the miner the best-paid industrial worker by the start of the 1950s.[48] The new pithead baths that were gradually introduced enabled miners to head home clean and were, especially for the wives who had to bathe their husbands and sons, 'a massive, massive change'.[49] But there were still significant challenges ahead. The war may have raised wages and the public esteem of the miners – although there was some perception outside Wales that miners were overpaid – but the conflict did little to solve the industry's structural problems.[50] Even in the late 1940s the South Western Division of the new National Coal Board (NCB) was making losses. There were some 134,100 men employed in coal mining in Wales in 1948 but many were still shovelling coal by hand and washing at home in tin baths. Modernization was slow and the closure of some of the smaller and most outdated pits was inevitable, although the workers there were found jobs at other collieries. Indeed, with young men becoming reluctant to enter the industry, there was a labour shortage and Italian and Polish labour had to be imported. Fuel shortages placed added pressure on miners to raise output in the interests of the nation. At a rally in Pontypridd, the Board's chairman even resorted to urging women to encourage their men to make even greater efforts in the interests of coal production.[51]

In the NCB's very first year, one Welsh commentator was speaking of 'Disillusion over the difference between the golden promise of nationalization in theory and its drab performance in actuality'. He pointed to a housewife who, thinking she now part-owned the nation's coal, said she was rather surprised she had to pay for it.[52] Within the industry, bureaucracy became a source of complaint and there was resentment over the compensation paid to the former owners. There was also a lack of faith in some of the higher officials. Much of this was down to the fact that, despite a sprinkling of recruits from the National Union of Mineworkers (NUM), most of the new officials had held similar positions in the old private coal companies. This led to claims that the Board was 'the same old firm dressed up in a new suit'. What nationalization did do was lead to a change of atmosphere within the industry, from one where workers were in fear of managers to one where the latter tried to seek the consent of the labour force. Power still lay with the bosses but the workers were treated with respect.[53] Relations between the union, which now had access to the highest levels of government, and management also improved significantly but the involvement of union officials in the running of pits placed a barrier between them and the men. Thus, when tensions emerged over pay, conditions, the behaviour of officials and the way mechanization was changing production patterns, strikes were inevitable. In 1949, there were 131 stoppages in the Swansea area alone. Significantly, eighty-eight of these did not even have the backing of the local branch of the union and just five had the support of the union's district level. It was no wonder then that the NUM had begun to fear that its position was being undermined. Grassroots anger increased as thirty-four pits in south Wales closed in the NCB's first three years. In north Wales two of the eight collieries that existed in 1948 had closed by 1952.[54] In 1951 the NUM lodge at Wern Tarw (near Bridgend) issued a leaflet protesting against the transfer of men to another colliery. It complained of the systematic 'murder' of collieries by an NCB trying to establish itself and rather than providing 'the pay and other conditions in the industry to attract sufficient Welsh lads, the Board is trying to solve its man power problem by closing collieries (Cilely), by transferring miners, and by introducing Italian labour'.[55] Whereas before 1939 it had been having a job at all that mattered, the war and the new atmosphere had raised miners' expectations. The heady feeling of the first day of nationalization had quickly become a distant memory. So too, perhaps, had the realization of how far the status, conditions, wages and security of miners had come in such a short time.

Coal was, of course, not the only industry nationalized. There was much sense in taking over the Bank of England in order to facilitate interest rates being used as a tool to fight unemployment but nationalization also created large bureaucracies of doubtful democratic qualities. Around 170 small private transport and haulage companies in Wales were nationalized, despite there being no obvious need to remove ownership from local concerns.[56] Steel was privatized in 1953 but in a gradual incremental process that was to last ten years and that had little immediate impact. In north Wales just the fear of nationalization in the slate industry led to an abeyance in capital investment in at least one quarry, thus helping to keep the industry outdated and in retreat.[57] Gas and electric services had previously been controlled by elected local authorities but were now removed from local control through nationalization, in the hope of making them more efficient and creating a more rational system. The new system may have been more efficient but it did not always meet the needs of those it was supposed to serve, especially in rural areas, where a dispersed population meant that building new infrastructure was very expensive. In 1950, the president of the Carmarthenshire Association of Parish Councils complained that the South Wales Electricity Board did not look after rural interests; it spent millions on advertising to townspeople but failed to get electricity to parts of the countryside. In Radnorshire in 1950, up to 80 per cent of houses occupied by agricultural and other workers were without electricity.[58] The provision of piped water and sewerage was often far worse. The 1949 meeting of the National Federation of Women's Institutes heard from a Denbighshire housewife how her village had to use an uncovered well for its drinking water that collected debris and into which passing motorists threw rubbish. She was cheered when she announced 'It's all wrong that hundreds of British families still live under these primitive conditions'.[59]

The bureaucracy of nationalization and planning reflected practical rather than cultural considerations. There were Welsh 'regional' boards for health, gas and town and country planning but not coal, electricity, the Post Office and the railways, where operational practicalities took precedent over any recognition of national or regional homogeneity. Thus the clearly defined south Wales coalfield was even lumped together with the Forest of Dean and Somerset in the creation of the South Western Division of the NCB. There were vocal complaints from politicians inside and outside the Labour Party that there should be more of a Welsh dimension to planning and policy. W. H. Mainwaring MP (Labour, Rhondda East) argued in 1946: 'There is a growing conviction that, in present government circles, Wales does not count as a nation, that at best it is a province of England, with little or no claim to its special development'.[60] There was clear support among Welsh MPs for a Secretary of State for Wales, not because the post would be a symbol of Welsh nationhood but rather because it would help prioritize Welsh needs within government. As Nigel Birch MP (Conservative, Flint) put it in the Commons, 'I simply do not believe that Wales would have gone through what she has gone through if she had had a Minister in this House to speak for her'.[61] However, the government was not willing to consider it. Englishman Herbert Morrison, the Deputy Prime Minister, had suggested that a Welsh Secretary of State would lead to overly complex government administration, negate efficient central planning and suffer from a lack of competent Welsh civil servants.[62] Aneurin Bevan, in particular, was a formidable opponent to anyone who advocated any form of Welsh devolution or any separate Welsh way of doing things. At the 1944 'Welsh day' at the House of Commons he had spoken against the idea that there were uniquely Welsh problems or solutions, and asked how the problem of rearing sheep on Welsh mountains differed from the problem of rearing them on Scottish mountains. Bevan's antipathy was mixed up with a degree of unease about what role the Welsh language might play in government. In 1946 he told the Commons:

> What some of us are afraid of is that, if this psychosis is developed too far, we shall see in some of the English speaking parts of Wales a vast majority tyrannised over by a few Welsh speaking people in Cardiganshire ... and the vast majority of Welshmen would be denied participation in the government of their own country.[63]

But even Bevan eventually conceded support for a Welsh Secretary of State after seeing in 1959 how much James Griffiths believed in it.[64] To combat Tory promises of a Ministry for Welsh Affairs, the Council for Wales and Monmouthshire was founded in 1948, with its nominated members tasked with advising the government on all matters relating to Wales. The civil service had initially advised the government that such a body would be either a 'dead letter or a dilatory nuisance' and in many ways both proved true. Its chair, Huw T. Edwards, a north Wales union leader, was bright, listened to and well respected but the Council had no actual power and ended up as a very vocal but frustrated talking shop (see chapter 8).[65]

It was no surprise that the government was not willing to grant more of a Welsh dimension to decision making. The government itself, and Prime Minister Clement Attlee in particular, were very traditional and the war had reinforced constitutional conservatism. The House of Lords, the monarchy and other symbols of traditional privilege were left untouched. But there was also little popular appetite for radical change, whether that meant reforming the basic political system or establishing Welsh political institutions. Instead, within Wales there was a powerful sense of solidarity with the wider British labour movement, a sense that was epitomized by the South Wales Miners' Federation voting in 1945 to dissolve itself and become part of the new National Union of Mineworkers. It was Britain that had won the war and it was on a British scale that reconstruction needed to happen. The nationalized industries, the unions and the welfare state thus became part of what one historian has called the 'mundane architecture of Britishness'.[66] They symbolized the British nation and people's popular attachment to it. Thus, as Welsh nationalists were only too aware, the economic and social transformations of British life were further tying Wales into the British system.[67] Indeed, it was through British systems that the labour movement thought Wales would gain a better future. As a Labour Party policy statement claimed in June 1945: 'True freedom for Wales would be the result and product of a Socialist Britain, and only under such conditions could self-government in Wales be an effective and secure guardian of the life of the nation'.[68]

FOR ALL THE HOPES placed on nationalization, the government, unions and wider population knew that the Welsh economy had to diversify if it was to be strengthened. The needs of the war economy had cemented the importance of heavy industry and by 1946 a third of all workers in industrial south Wales were employed in coal or steel. To put all Wales' economic eggs in one basket was to risk catastrophe again. The war had at least created a labour force, men and women, experienced in factory work and the government began a programme of regional aid designed to attract manufacturing, light industry, metalworking and engineering to Wales and other previously depressed areas. At a time when private firms found it very difficult to get licences to build premises in locations of their own choosing, there were new factories being built in Wales ahead of demand, and loans and tax concessions for companies wishing to take up tenancy. By 1949, 179 new factories had been built in Wales, 112 by the government, meaning companies looking to expand in the new peacetime economy often had no alternative but to come to a designated development area, and south Wales was the closest one to the preferred destinations of the Midlands and London.[69] By the 1950s the trading estate at Treforest was employing 20,000 people and there were similar vast estates in Bridgend, Hirwaun and Swansea. The Welsh economy was thus finally diversifying. Potato crisps and toys were being made in Swansea, nylon in Pontypool, stockings in Dowlais, rubber in Brynmawr, televisions in Hirwaun and light bulbs and washing machines in Merthyr. In 1951 the *South Wales Industrial Review* claimed that there had been a second industrial revolution.[70] Three years later the National Industrial Development Council of Wales and Monmouthshire was stating that 'Wales has a brighter outlook than at any time in the present century. A great reconstruction has taken place.' It claimed that companies were queuing to get into Wales, seeking the labour and building facilities that were lacking in London and the Midlands.[71]

Behind such upbeat proclamations lay problems. The Welsh economy was reliant on the support not just of the British state but of the American one too, as the Marshall plan propped up British wealth. Moreover, the fullest ambitions of reconstruction were not being met. The 1945 Distribution of Industry Act was supposed to create 123,000 jobs in south Wales but by July 1949 it had made only 79,000. In south-west Wales just 47 per cent of the target had been met.[72] The high-profile successes in attracting English firms into Wales disguised the reluctance of others because of the preconceptions and realities of life in Wales. Teddington Controls, for example, found its key workers were disinclined to move from Sunbury to a new factory in Merthyr because of the 'below standard accommodation and the educational facilities'. It complained that the 'rail services were bad and the roads not good'. It took two and a half hours to get to Bristol by train and three and a half by car, unless the ferry at Chepstow was used, but that was hourly, crowded and did not take reservations. When new factories did come there could be local resentment if imported workers were given priority for housing. In 1951 a 'turbulent and malicious mob' invaded local-authority offices in Loughor in protest at the council giving a house to the foreman of a new factory. There was also some feeling that the new factories were obscuring the lack of traditional skilled jobs for men. The NCB had its own gripes, fearing that too many factories would make it hard to recruit workers to mining.[73]

By 1950 there were just 22,000 unemployed people in Wales and most were unfit to work because of age or disability.[74] But falling unemployment and economic reconstruction hid the disruption a shifting economy was causing for individuals. There may have been jobs in both the coal and the metal industries but the older and inefficient mines and works were being closed and people had to relocate or face inconvenient commutes if they wanted to stay in the industries. Given that the poor state of local transport was causing even local people problems in getting to work, the prospect of being relocated could give rise to anger. One miner from Hengoed complained that he and others who worked the afternoon shift were not able to get home easily: 'I myself, having been home two weeks with flu and bronchitis through having to walk half a mile to the nearest bus stop from the colliery, and waiting about at the end of the queue for the last bus to our village, a mile and a half away, we find at 10.30 p.m. the queue is made of half-drunks, picturegoers, dance hall riff-raff, and we who have been sweating our guts out at the coal face are left to shiver in the bitter cold and hear the bus conductor say – "Sorry, only three or four" as the case may be. Those types of pub crawlers can get home, but we miners have to walk through the torrents of rain or snow storms across the fields over the mountains to get home about 11.30 p.m., or near mid-night, and then perhaps we have to return in the morning to perform some special job.'[75]

At least in the industrial valleys there were jobs to commute to. In rural areas, there was a strong feeling that economic reconstruction was not just leaving them behind but destroying the local culture too. In 1946 the War Office announced plans to use 500,000 acres, around a tenth of the Welsh landmass, for military purposes. A retired naval officer appealed to *The Times*: 'Leave us something of our birthright. To those who are Welsh this Wales is most dear and it is so small and yet so lovely. Can we be spared this last crushing blow to our national life?' Saunders Lewis thought that the issue would decide the fate of the Welsh language.[76] The strongest opposition came in the Preseli mountains (Pembrokeshire), where a 'battle' was waged against the planned requisition of 16,000 acres and 105 complete farms for a tank range. While local authorities to the south saw the financial benefits, within the affected area the opposition feared the impact on Nonconformity, local culture and the Welsh language. One campaigner argued: 'To us, the mountain is the bread of life, and is a holy sacrament. Our lives are woven into its essence. If we lose the mountains nothing will remain but "snobbery" and "chip" shops.' A local minister suggested that the War Office put the range in the Valleys, which were 'so full of aliens and so dead'. Moreover, militarism was an anathema to many Nonconformists and, in an era of the atomic bomb, tanks and guns all seemed rather obsolete. In the face of vocal opposition and plans for non-violent resistance, the Preseli scheme was withdrawn and the requisitioning across Wales was reduced to 57,000 acres but even that upset pacifists and nationalists.[77]

The government placed much hope in the potential for forestry to help arrest the economic problems of upland Wales. The Forestry Commission promised to bring permanent jobs to rural communities, stimulating local trade, arresting the economic and cultural problem of depopulation and contributing to wider reconstruction of the British economy. In 1949 the Commission estimated that it would be employing 4,000 workers in Wales by 1951 and it promised that it was making every effort to recruit local men. Jobs never materialized in the numbers promised but forestry did bring new work to rural north and west Wales, where there were few other opportunities. Yet many forestry workers, especially the superintendents, were English and in 1953 it was estimated that only 20 per cent of trainees in the industry were Welsh.[78] Despite the fact that forestry helped stem depopulation, the Welsh-language press and literature saw it as another threat to the future of Welshness because it brought in English workers, dislocated Welsh-speaking farmers and desecrated the landscape with alien and angular blocks of quick-growing coniferous trees that did not change with the seasons. A Breconshire farmer complained in 1950 that 'Year by year, piece by piece, vast tracts of Welsh agricultural land are taken out of production to satisfy the cravings of the tree worshippers and the guns-before-mutton brigade'. He claimed that if this continued, the wood would be able to be used for the coffin of the Welsh nation.[79] The number of acres under Forestry Commission trees increased from 88,600 in 1946 to 281,568 in 1965, transforming the appearance of many upland areas. This did, at least, enable farmers to sell uneconomical land for inflated prices and people's willingness to sell meant that only once did the Commission try to use its powers of compulsory purchase in Wales. Tenant farmers, however, found themselves being given notice after their landlords sold up, and the clearance of sheep to make way for forestry was an upsetting experience for some whose families had worked the land.[80] Forestry was thus another example of how government economic policy failed to create the full prosperity it promised but instead introduced another industry that was heavily reliant on public subsidies and at odds with what some local people wanted.

The state also tried to help rural communities (and ease food shortages) by directing agriculture, although it never seriously considered the nationalization of land. In the late 1940s there were new subsidies, notably for hill farmers, and the 1947 Agriculture Act guaranteed minimum prices for the fat-stock, milk and eggs that dominated Welsh agriculture. Indeed, in 1948 the state was spending the same on supporting farming as it was on the new NHS. Two years later average farm incomes were six times their pre-war peak. One consequence was that farmers could afford more machinery, which reduced the need for local labour and undermined the wider rural economy. As before the war, old estates continued to be sold off, and their manor houses knocked down, continuing the growth in owner-occupied farms, although tenants often just swapped a financial obligation to a landlord for one to a bank manager. During the war just over a third of farms were owner-occupied but by 1970 this had increased to nearly 64 per cent.[81]

Agriculture's reliance on the state and the proliferation of small, family-based farms engendered a sense of insecurity. A 1953 report noted in rural Wales the existence of a 'sense of discouragement born of the harsh memories of the inter-war years and the want of confidence in the future'.[82] Such fears culminated in 1955 in the creation of the Farmers' Union of Wales, a breakaway from the National Farmers' Union, which was felt to be dominated by large English farmers who were not paying adequate attention to Wales.[83] In urban Wales too, despite jobs being plentiful, the memory of the inter-war depression ensured that the fear of unemployment never went away. However, the expanded National Insurance system meant that being on the dole or being too ill to work were not as financially devastating as they once had been. Moreover, National Insurance now covered dependants too and was supplemented by a National Assistance scheme which provided a means-tested safety net for all. None of this eased the fear of unemployment but it did at least make it easier to cope with when it happened, even if inflation did quickly eat away at the value of the benefits paid.[84]

Men's fears about unemployment were reinforced by the growth of the female workforce during the war. With the return of servicemen looking for work, there were social pressures on women to return to the domestic sphere, something which many but not all were happy to do. One Welsh woman remembered,

> The war changed people's outlook. It brought them out of themselves, I think. After the war look how many women carried on working. Before the war very few married women went out to work, and if they did, it would only be a little cleaning job or something. They got used to it during the war. I suppose they'd got used to the money and a bit of freedom.[85]

But women who carried on working faced a degree of social opposition. In Aberdare in October 1945, for example, where there were 1,500 unemployed and plans for a new trading estate with a 70 per cent female workforce, a local councillor declared, 'This was not what our boys fought for: to place the responsibility of earning money on the women while the men are on the dole'. The number of insured women workers did fall, from 219,000 in 1944 to 158,000 in 1946. But the rise in manufacturing was creating new opportunities for women on production lines and female employment never fell back to its pre-war levels. In 1948 there were 105,201 women employed in the south Wales development area; in 1938 there had been 54,712. Despite these advances, in 1951 only a quarter of women in Wales were in paid employment. Moreover, those who were working earned less than men doing the same jobs, regardless of their class. The 1944 Education Act had failed to guarantee equal pay for female teachers, although it did at least abolish the bar on married women teaching. But more often women did not do the same jobs and were stuck in unskilled work in factories, shops and catering. In 1948 average female wages were just over half those of men.[86] But this was simply not an issue of any real concern or controversy. Men and women were clearly pigeonholed into roles. In Glyn Ceiriog (Denbighshire) an anthropologist noted that women who ran businesses without the help of men gained no sympathy, female doctors were distrusted, women at public meetings were mocked and those few who entered pubs would be greeted by silence and stares. It was unsurprising then that some women would go to a pub when visiting the local town but not in their own village. After the first flushes of love, husbands and wives in the village socialized separately and local associational groups were demarcated by gender.[87] Women's subsidiary role was also reflected in rural areas by the way that most wives switched to the chapel denomination of their new husband. When standing for Parliament in East Flintshire in 1950, Eirene White had to explicitly tackle voters' doubts about her gender by pointing in election leaflets to her Oxford education and experience in journalism and the film industry.[88] Traditional gender roles were also reinforced by the welfare state. National Insurance was payable only by those in work, thus leaving housewives dependent on their husband's contributions. The new family allowance payments were given directly to the mother but this was only after a fight by female MPs.

Within families, however, at the level of the ordinary housewife and mother, gender relations were not always quite so unequal. At the Red Lion in Blaina, there were men who drank heavily but also those who brought their wife along on a Saturday night and others whose drinking was curtailed by their partner being in charge of the weekly pay packet. Actress Siân Phillips (born 1933) remembered of her Carmarthenshire childhood: 'Men were deferred to, made much of, "tended" to, even referred to sometimes as "The Boss" but I was aware that I lived in a matriarchy. Women balanced the books, paid the bills, made the decisions and when necessary ran their small farms and businesses alone.'[89] Another Welsh woman remembered of the early post-war years:

> I was a bit – felt more equal somehow – in my own right as I wasn't just a housewife. I was able to do other things as well – think for myself. After all, I'd had to do all the thinking for four and a half years on my own, and bring up my children on my own, and then suddenly your husband comes back and he's telling you what to do again.... God, you've managed for four and a half years without him and done very well, so you're coming now to the routine which we did resent a bit. He thought he was right and you knew you was right, because you'd proved it over the last four and a half years.[90]

Such self-belief and confidence may not have brought a gender revolution but its impact on individuals' own sense of who they were mattered all the same.

IN INDUSTRIAL DENBIGHSHIRE one travel writer noted in 1949 that the owners of small traditional houses had 'geranium pots for defiance' in their front windows. They were sometimes wrapped with green or yellow crepe paper but this had faded from the sunlight and stained from regular watering.[91] The late 1940s and start of the 1950s were a period of austerity, when moments of brightness seemed few and far between and even pots of flowers could struggle to bring a bit of colour. The long-term significance of the welfare state and programme of nationalization obscures the frustrations people felt in this period, when the New Jerusalem was not all that apparent. As well as the lurking fear of unemployment, the cost of living was becoming a real concern. Between 1938 and 1950 retail prices rose by 85 per cent, undermining the gains in wages in the same period and limiting the increase in real earnings to 28 per cent.[92] For all the free healthcare available, other things seemed to be getting worse. A global shortage of grain led to the introduction of bread rationing in July 1946, something which the government had strongly resisted during the war for fear of harming morale. Meat rations were also significantly reduced in 1951, after the failure to secure new supplies from Argentina. Despite the apparent equality of rationing, it was still the working class that was hit hardest, since those with some money could eat in restaurants rather than use up their rations. Bread was not freely available again until July 1948; it was 1949 before people were free to buy whatever clothes they wanted and 1950 before canned and dried fruit, chocolate biscuits, treacle, syrup, jellies and mincemeat came off the coupon. Sweets and sugar rationing did not end until 1953. Food was not the only thing in short supply. The waiting lists for housing were still intolerably long into the 1960s and in the hallowed NHS some people were waiting over a year for a pair of glasses. In 1948 an Aberystwyth newspaper could even be found wondering whether Britain could maintain its current level of population and whether mass emigration was the only solution to the economic problems.[93] A bitterly cold winter in 1947, which saw up to twenty-four inches of snow and twenty-foot drifts, exacerbated both shortages and the sense that things were not right. Some remote communities had to be supplied by air. When the snow thawed it caused flooding. Maybe a million sheep died, threatening the very livelihood of farmers. As one Llangynidr farmer put it, 'it was cold, you know; terrible cold. I don't want to see anything like it again.'[94]

Compounding a sense of frustration and fear was the deteriorating international situation. The war had given people an interest in the events of the wider world and a sense of how their own fortunes were connected to international developments. As an alderman told a meeting of the Swansea Labour Association in 1952, 'The World was now a small place'.[95] It also seemed a frightening place. War broke out in Korea in 1950 and a conflict with the USSR was widely believed to be a very real, if not immediate possibility. The Soviet Union had once been revered in south Wales as an example of the socialist dream come true and there was much popular sympathy for the sacrifices made by ordinary Russians during the war, but it was now emerging as an aggressive state, as keen to boost its own power as the imperialist countries it hated. What made this all the more terrible was not just the recentness of the last war but the emergence of the atomic bomb.

Among the middle classes, shortages and government controls on so many aspects of life in the home and in the workplace caused significant resentment and created a sense that people were being stripped of their authority and dignity. The *Holyhead Mail* attacked the government for subjecting people to the 'soulless monster' of the state.[96] Similarly, an editorial before the 1950 general election in the *Carmarthen Journal* bemoaned 'A misguided decision of the electorate to keep the Socialists in power for another five years would mean not only a continuance and extension of the policies which have already served us so ill, but a further invasion by the Executive of rights and freedoms which our forbearers fought to win'. It complained about nationalization, 'the soaring price of coal, the costly confusion in our transport services, the bill we have to foot for an army of inspectors and pen-drivers' and people being treated 'like little children unfit to think or act for themselves'. Labour had not, it thought, delivered the promised 'land of plenty'.[97] Such sentiments would have been quite at home in suburban southern England but they could be found across Wales. A Caernarfon newspaper's editorial said that it could not see that Wales had received 'any benefits whatsoever' from socialism. It went on, 'In all directions we hear nothing but universal complaint. The people, generally speaking, are sad and dejected. Everybody finds it a mental and physical struggle to make ends meet.'[98] In the 1950 general election a Conservative stood in Merthyr for the first time in forty years; he won over 6,000 votes.

The smaller size of the Welsh middle class made the impact of these complaints far less profound but their salience in England meant that Labour's majority fell from 146 to six at the 1950 general election. Some twenty months later the Conservatives and their allies won a majority of seventeen. In Wales the Tories took Cardiff North in 1950 and Barry and Conwy in 1951. In the latter year they raised their share of the Welsh vote to 30.8 per cent (compared with 23.8 per cent in 1945 and 27.4 per cent in 1950). This might have been almost half the figure for Labour but it meant that the Conservatives gained 154,600 Welsh votes between 1945 and 1951 and it demonstrates how far Wales was from being a monolithic Labour-voting place. In Ebbw Vale the local Conservative Party claimed 70 per cent of its supporters were miners, steelworkers and their wives, while its chairman was a works foreman. After the 1951 election, a Cardiff housewife told the *Western Mail*, 'About time too! I feel a different woman altogether now', while another from the working-class district of Ely said, 'I'm going straight home to clean out the larders and make room for some decent food at last'. The paper concluded that many Labour supporters shared in the general feeling of fresh air that the result represented. If that was true, it was far from a universal feeling. One labourer remarked that he had 'given up all hope' and expected some of the social services to be done away with.[99] In Aberdare, Neil Kinnock, then just nine, watched his grandparents cry when Labour lost power. Labour actually won 146,600 more Welsh votes in 1951 than in 1945. That rise owed much to how rural constituencies were turning away from the Liberals. Labour won Merioneth and Anglesey, as the Liberal share of the Welsh vote fell from 14.9 per cent in 1945 to 7.6 per cent in 1951. This shift was rooted in Labour's promises of rural economic development and its now more vocal sympathy for traditional Welsh culture but it also marked how Welsh politics was falling into the same two-party system that characterized England.[100]

The Times claimed the solid Welsh Labour vote in 1950 was the result of bitter memories.[101] In industrial areas Labour politicians were certainly still making speeches that called upon people to remember the miseries of the

1930s and contrast them with the present-day blessings of full employment, wage packets and the nourishment of their children.[102] The trauma of those memories meant that the Labour vote was more instinctive than thinking. In 1951 a Swansea newspaper complained that several local Labour candidates were 'institutions with a public that yields unquestioning allegiance' and that the party had no ideas but instead had 'the stubborn loyalty of a host of followers, with whom the vague term "Labour" has become a cult, an obsession, but can still be defined in effect as the pursuit of a sectional self interest to the blind exclusion of all considerations of expediency or practicability'.[103] The party's active membership was of course nowhere near the level of its support in elections. In 1952 the average membership of Labour constituency parties in Wales was 1,110, compared with 1,426 in Britain as whole. In 1952 in Swansea East, the industrial zone of the town, Labour actually had more female than male members. Local party membership was just 706, whereas the Labour vote in that constituency in the 1951 election had been 32,790.[104]

Historian Kenneth Morgan has suggested that Labour's hold on Wales was a victory for 'the old values. It was based on the communal solidarity of the pit and the choir and the co-op and the Workers' Educational Association' and its leaders had outlooks shaped by 'past experience'. But Labour's victory also gave 'socialist values and historic images a new infusion of life'.[105] There was something of a spirit of modernization, of updating the economy, the function of the state and the quality of people's lives. That was evident in the modernist architecture of some schools and factories, with their clean straight lines and plentiful glass, all paid for by the state.[106] But there were distinct limits to how much change people wanted. They sought more comforts and security but they also wanted the basic structures of their worlds to remain. As a sociologist noted of urban south-west Wales, people wanted stability; they were satisfied with much of the status quo and had some antipathy towards government's attempts to diversify industry where that might upset the pattern of local life. The lack of radicalism was evident in the evaporation of support for the Communists, something fuelled by the emerging cold war. The Communist Party had lost Rhondda East only by 972 votes in 1945 but in 1950 Labour won a 22,182 majority in the constituency. In 1952 Communist campaigners in Flint were physically attacked and driven from the town, with the police having to block off the railway station to protect their escape. Labour itself was socially conservative and its support owed as much to that as to its political agenda. At least 15 per cent of chapel leaders in the Swansea region also held positions of responsibility in trade unions.[107]

People's fear was that too much change would undermine their local community, whether that was the small rural village or the urban community grouping based around pit, pub and pulpit. The strength of that community should not be underestimated. It was perhaps most evident at the miners' welfare halls that stood proudly in every mining centre. This was clear in one 1954 travel book, where the travellers look at the programme of events at a miners' hall in the Rhondda:

> There was to be a Shakespearean performance by a travelling company under the aegis of the Arts Council. Several concerts were promised, two of them with international artistes. A Drama Contest Week was announced, and quite a number of amateur play productions. An Eisteddfod, too, and a Brass Band Contest. Other posters and smaller notices advertised evening classes in first aid, economics, trade-union history, and English literature; meetings of the Miners' lodges, and of other trade-union branches; political party meetings; and, twice a week, cinema shows. One notice indicated there was a library within.
>
> 'There's always plenty doing in the Rhondda,' said Mr Thomas proudly. 'And if there's nothing there for you,' he added, laughing and pointing to the hoarding, 'there's always boxing, football, whippets, and choir-practice.'[108]

Community was also strong in rural Wales. In 1950 Alwyn Rees published a study of Llanfihangel-yng-Ngwynfa, an upland rural parish in Montgomeryshire. It painted a picture of an introspective community living a simple life to which agriculture, religion, the Welsh language and close social networks were central. It was based on fieldwork undertaken during the war but much of the way of life described could easily have pertained to the nineteenth century or even earlier. People lived in scattered stone cottages and farmhouses that centred on a hearth. Families were the central units of society, with a strong sense of responsibilities between generations. In echoes of medieval customs, sons who married had to set up elsewhere and were eliminated from inheriting the family farm. This was to pass to the youngest son but not until his father was too old and his brothers had left. He was unable to marry while his mother was alive, to ensure she was not displaced in her own home. Communal leisure was still determined by the farming calendar and families depended on home-grown foods. They often had pictures of Lloyd George, Gladstone or Nonconformist preachers on their walls. People's ties to their community were bound by a complex web of family relationships that closed out outsiders and which Rees called 'clannishness'. It gave individuals a sense of belonging and security and acted as a check on violent or instinctive behaviour, which, rather than just alienating one person, would alienate a whole body of neighbours. Yet the kinships rarely came together except for funerals and weddings, which consequently were important community events. On the horizon was the threat of urbanism, with its 'disintegration into formless masses of rootless nonentities', but for now the parish retained its traditional culture, untouched by the language and worries of the modern world.[109] No wonder then that commentators so often talked of a 'peasant culture' in rural Wales and a traveller in Cardiganshire could say of an old woman he met: she was 'not of this age; she walked straight out of the age of peasants and wood burners'.[110]

In the early post-war years, people in rural and urban Wales were thus caught between looking forward and looking back. They wanted to preserve their traditions and their communities, but they also feared a return to the harsher economic times that had helped make those communities. They wanted jobs, security and modern comforts but they knew that economic and material progress had its social costs, whether that was undermining community, the Welsh language, religion or gender relations. Wales was far from alone in this. Across Britain there was the idea of what some historians have called a 'return to the future', the twin currents of a desire for modernity alongside the retention of tradition.[111] This contradictory culture owed much to the widespread pessimism about the future that was rooted in the everyday problems and inconveniences of life in austerity Britain and in the international tensions brought about by the emerging cold war and atomic age. As the writer of a travel book about Wales noted in 1948, 'It seems to me that we are looking ahead at a blank space, at nothing, and feverishly trying to get there before the nothing turns into something pretty grim'.[112] No wonder then that people sought entertainment wherever they could get it. Mass Observation recorded that workers in Blaina drank to escape the pits, steelworks and 'depressing atmosphere of a small mining town'. Sporting attendances reached new highs, as did the popularity of going to the pictures. Maybe half the population went regularly to one of Wales' 352 cinemas in search of a cheap, familiar, escapist and exciting night out.[113]

The sense of insecurity has meant that the record of the 1945–51 Labour government has been better appreciated by historians than it was by contemporaries. In many ways this was the golden era of British government. Out of the physical and emotional ruins of war, a welfare state was built that genuinely made people's lives better, safer and more secure. It was not just the workers who benefited but the middle classes too, especially those who had struggled and sacrificed to afford the education and healthcare that the workers simply went without. The NHS, National Insurance and lesser known reforms such as family allowances, better pensions and compensation for industrial injuries were remarkable achievements and a testament to what governments can do. But it was only the long-term perspective that was to make that obvious. For those who lived through the first post-war years, life was too often hard, dour and frustrating, while their memories and expectations had been shifted and distorted by the horrors, sacrifices and hopes that the war had created.

There were, of course, failures too and there was certainly no social revolution, despite much of what had remained of Wales' upper class disappearing, as high taxes led them to sell off estates, demolish houses or make donations to the people, such as the Marquis of Bute's gift of Cardiff Castle in 1947. Private education was not abolished, meaning that people who could pay had access not only to what was often a better education but also to a world of social networks that reinforced privilege and social stratification. Meanwhile, the bulk of working-class children were left in schools that were openly thought of as second class, condemning them to remain firmly at the bottom of the social ladder. The government commissioned nuclear weapons as well as schools, hospitals and homes. The establishment stayed much as it was, with its members simply accepting the welfare state as a sign of the times that they could live with as long it was not too expensive and they retained a large say in its running. Such attitudes meant that Britain was possibly, as the leading historian of the era put it, 'the most settled, deferential, smug, un-dynamic society in the advanced world'.[114]

The limits of the government's desire for change led Aneurin Bevan to resign from the cabinet in 1951, following the plans to introduce dental and ophthalmic charges in order to pay for a new programme of rearmament, something he regarded as an attack 'on my Health Service'.[115] He won little support in the Welsh Labour Party or with trade unions, which further illustrated the limits of social and political change in the years after the war. Bevan never returned to power but it was his Health Service that was the most successful and enduring legacy of the post-war reconstruction. For all the limitations on change, there was at least, in the reassuring visits to doctors, in the free medicines, in the new hospitals, something created that did resemble a New Jerusalem. And better times were on the horizon as the shortages gradually eased, restrictions were lifted and the economy began to boom, fed by the pent-up demand for consumer goods. In December 1953 an estimated 250,000 people poured into Cardiff to watch Wales play New Zealand at rugby or go on a Christmas 'spending spree'.[116] It was also the first time that a rugby international in Cardiff had been televised. Wales even won. A new age of affluence was dawning.

Notes

1 V. I. Lewis, 'Action in El Alamein', at www.bbc.co.uk/wales/mid/sites/ww2/pages/iori_lewis3.shtml.
2 K. Roberts, *Y Byw Sy'n Cysgu* (1956). Published in translation as Siân James, *The Awakening* (2006), 15.
3 G. Williams, *A Life* (2002), 60. A. Richards, *The Former Miss Merthyr Tydfil* (1976), 162.
4 E. Watkins, *The Cautious Revolution* (1951), 116. B. Thomas (ed.), *The Welsh Economy* (1962), 30–54.
5 *CDH*, 15 June 1945.
6 J. Callaghan, *Time and Change* (1987), 64.
7 A. D. Rees, *Life in a Welsh Countryside: A Social Study of Llanfihangel yng Ngwynfa* ([1950] 1996), 157–60.
8 *WM*, 27 July 1945.
9 C. Barnett, *The Lost Victory: British Dream, British Realities, 1945–1950* (1995).
10 T. Brennan and E. W. Cooney, *The Social Pattern: A Handbook of Social Statistics of South West Wales* (1950), 68–9. Council for Wales and Monmouthshire, *Memorandum by the Council on Its Activities*, Cmd 8060 (1950), 29.
11 T. Brennan, E. W. Cooney and H. Pollins, *Social Change in South-West Wales* (1954), 41. D. Beddoe, *Out of the Shadows: A History of Women in Twentieth Century Wales* (2000), 144–5.
12 *Daily Mirror*, 15 Feb. 1949.
13 BBC Wales, 'Wales yesterday'. Formerly at www.bbc.co.uk/wales/history/sites/wales yesterday/pages/1940s.shtml.
14 *DWHS-2*, 89.
15 New tenants quoted in M. A. Williams, *A Forgotten Army: Female Munitions Workers of South Wales, 1939–1945* (2002), 254.
16 *DWHS-2*, 89. For comparisons with England see Council for Wales and Monmouthshire, *Memorandum by the Council on Its Activities*, 30.
17 *The Times*, 9 Feb. 1950.
18 P. Hennessy, *Never Again: Britain, 1945–1951* (1993), 143–4.
19 *SWEP*, 5 July 1948.
20 *Pontypridd Observer and Free Press*, 3 July 1948.
21 K. O. Morgan, *Modern Wales: Politics, Places and People* (1995), 187.
22 Beddoe, *Out of the Shadows*, 149.
23 *All Our Lives*, BBC Wales, 10 Feb. 1995. National Industrial Development Council of Wales and Monmouthshire, *Wales and Monmouthshire* (1954), 97. C. Hughes, *A Wanderer in North Wales* (1949), 172, 174.
24 Undated Mar. 1951 clipping from NLW, Huw T. Edwards papers, file F5.
25 R. Lowe, *The Welfare State in Britain since 1945* (2005), 186. *The Times*, 9 Mar. 1951. H. Francis and D. Smith, *The Fed: A History of the South Wales Miners* (1998 edn), 440. J. Davies, *A History of Wales* (1993), 621.
26 1957 Glamorgan eleven-plus examination paper reproduced at www.abgs.org.uk/11-plus/index.htm.
27 G. E. Jones and G. W. Roderick, *A History of Education in Wales* (2003), 152.
28 Jones and Roderick, *A History of Education in Wales*, 148, 154. H. Hopkins, *The New Look: A Social History of the Forties and Fifties in Britain* (1963), 150. P. Hennessy, *Having It So Good: Britain in the Fifties* (2006), 75.
29 G. L. Rees, *Survey of the Welsh Economy*, Commission on the Constitution research papers (1973), 50.
30 P. Stead, *Richard Burton: So Much, So Little* (1991), 98.
31 Quoted in A. Richards, *Carwyn: A Personal Memoir* (1984), 48.
32 *WM*, 27 Nov. 1969.
33 R. Sullivan, 'Blue and gold: Ebbw Vale County Grammar School', at www.evcgs.co.uk/Reminiscences.html#Eric.

34 *WM*, 27 Nov. 1969.
35 Richards, *The Former Miss Merthyr Tydfil*, 57.
36 P. Cobb, *At Cowbridge Grammar School, 1949–66* (2001), 70. P. Stead, 'Popular culture', in T. Herbert and G. E. Jones (eds), *Post-War Wales* (1995), 109.
37 C. Hughes, *The Civil Strangers* (1949), 16. B. Rogers, *The Bank Manager and the Holy Grail* (2003), 257.
38 Cobb, *At Cowbridge Grammar School*, 6, 97. *Aberdare Leader*, 6 Aug. 1960.
39 Jones and Roderick, *A History of Education in Wales*, 150. D. Sandbrook, *Never Had It So Good: A History of Britain from Suez to the Beatles* (2005), 422.
40 Margaret Stacey, *The Human Ecology of the Lower Swansea Valley* (1962), 116. K. Wilson, 'Education and opportunity', in F. Carnevali and J. Strange (eds), *20th Century Britain* (2007), 360.
41 Cobb, *At Cowbridge Grammar School*, 97–8.
42 Council for Wales and Monmouthshire, *Second Memorandum by the Council on Its Activities*, Cmd 8844 (1953), 46.
43 Jones and Roderick, *A History of Education in Wales*, 148, 183. D. Rubinstein and B. Simon, *The Evolution of the Comprehensive School, 1926–1966* (1969), 46–7.
44 M. Parnell, *Plateux, Gateaux, Chateaux* (1997), 19.
45 L. Sage, *Bad Blood* (2000), 147.
46 *Daily Mirror*, 2 Jan. 1947; T. Blackwell and J. Seabrook, *A World Still to Win: The Reconstruction of the Post-War Working Class* (1985), 71. *Welsh Review*, 6:1 (spring 1947).
47 B. Jones, B. Roberts and C. Williams, 'Going from the darkness to the light: South Wales miners' attitudes towards nationalisation', *Llafur*, 7:1 (1996), 96–100. K. Gildart, *North Wales Miners: A Fragile Unity, 1945–1996* (2001), 28.
48 Gildart, *North Wales Miners*, 23. A. Horner, *Incorrigible Rebel* (1960), 198–200. Francis and Smith, *The Fed*, 438.
49 Miner quoted at BBC, 'Wales yesterday', formerly at www.bbc.co.uk/wales/history/sites/walesyesterday/pages/1940s.shtml.
50 W. Wilkinson, *Puppets in Wales* (1948), 29. Francis and Smith, *The Fed*, 395.
51 *DWS*, 4 (1957), 20. *Pontypridd Observer and Free Press*, 10 July 1948.
52 *Welsh Review*, 6:1 (spring 1947), 57.
53 Francis and Smith, *The Fed*, 437. *Blue Scar* (1949), dir. Jill Craigie. H. Francis and K. Howells, 'The politics of coal in south Wales, 1945–48', *Llafur*, 7:1 (1996), 74–85.
54 Brennan *et al.*, *Social Change*, 83. Gildart, *North Wales Miners*, 50–5. Francis and Smith, *The Fed*, 445, 442. L. Jones, 'Coal', in B. Thomas (ed.), *The Welsh Economy* (1962), 110.
55 *Wern Tarw Where Next?* (1951), leaflet reproduced in Francis and Smith, *The Fed*, 443.
56 National Industrial Development Council, *Wales and Monmouthshire*, 178.
57 J. Lindsay, *A History of the North Wales Slate Industry* (1974), 300.
58 *CJ*, 29 Sep. 1950. Brennan and Cooney, *The Social Pattern*, 73–4. Council for Wales and Monmouthshire, *Memorandum by the Council*, 37–44.
59 *Daily Mirror*, 15 June 1949.
60 Quoted in J. G. Jones, 'The attitude of the political parties towards the Welsh language', in G. H. Jenkins and M. A. Williams (eds), *'Let's Do Our Best for the Ancient Tongue': The Welsh Language in the Twentieth Century* (2000), 263–4.
61 *HC Deb*, 28 Oct. 1946, vol. 428, c. 370.
62 The Administration of Wales and Monmouthshire, 23 Jan. 1946, NA, CAB 129/6.
63 *HC Deb*, 17 Oct. 1944, vol. 403, cc. 2311–13; *HC Deb*, 28 Oct. 1946, vol. 428, c. 401.
64 R. Griffiths, 'The other Aneurin Bevan', *Pl*, 41 (1978), 26–8.
65 K. O. Morgan, 'Power and glory: war and reconstruction, 1939–1951', in D. Tanner, C. Williams and D. Hopkin (eds), *The Labour Party in Wales, 1900–2000* (2000), 179. G. Jenkins, *Prif Weinidog Answyddogol Cymru: Cofiant Huw T. Edwards* (2007).
66 L. Colley, 'Britishness in the 21st century' (8 Dec. 1999), at www.goabroad.net/users/resourcefiles/2007/April/123/admingroup/148285bc39e30e1210604483.pdf.
67 See for example D. J. Davies, 'The welfare state', *Welsh Nation*, Jan. 1950.

68 Quoted in Jones, 'The attitude of the political parties', 263.
69 G. Humphrys, *South Wales* (1972), 27, 59. G. Manners, 'A profile of the new south Wales', in G. Manners (ed.), *South Wales in the Sixties* (1964), 47.
70 Quoted in Morgan, 'Power and glory', 177.
71 National Industrial Development Council, *Wales and Monmouthshire*, 15, 21.
72 Brennan and Cooney, *The Social Pattern*, 35.
73 Quoted in T. Rowlands, *Something Must Be Done: South Wales v Whitehall, 1921–1951* (2000), 183, 169. *SWEP*, 9 Feb. 1951. Brennan *et al.*, *Social Change*, 57.
74 Council for Wales and Monmouthshire, *Memorandum by the Council on Its Activities*, 6–7, 10.
75 Quoted in D. Kynaston, *Austerity Britain, 1945–51* (2007), 195.
76 *The Times*, 10 Feb. 1947. R. Evans, *Gwynfor Evans: Portrait of a Patriot* (2008), 111.
77 *Baner ac Amserau Cymru*, 25 Dec. 1946 and 5 Feb. 1947. Welsh Nationalist Party, *Havoc in Wales: The War Office Demands* (1947). R. Griffiths, *S. O. Davies: A Socialist Faith* (1983), 151–2. J. Davies, 'The fight for Preseli', *Pl*, 58 (1986), 3–9.
78 *Rural Wales*, Cmd 9014 (1954), 9–10. Forestry Commission, *Forestry in Wales* (1949). Ministry of Education, *Place of Welsh and English in the Schools of Wales* (1953), 20.
79 *Y Cymro*, 19 Sept. 1947. K. Bohata, *Postcolonialism Revisited: Writing Wales in English* (2004), ch. 4. *CJ*, 13 and 27 Jan. 1950.
80 G. Ryle, *Forest Service: The First Forty-Five Years of the Forestry Commission of Great Britain* (1969), 299. R. A. Jones (ed.), *Hyd Ein Hoes: Lleisiau Cymru* (2003), 21.
81 L. James, *Warrior Race: A History of the British at War* (2001), 704. D. A. Petty, *The Rural Revolt That Failed: Farm Workers' Trade Unions in Wales, 1889–1950* (1989), 208. *DWHS-1*, 239.
82 Council for Wales and Monmouthshire, *Second Memorandum*, 48.
83 A. Butt Philip, *The Welsh Question: Nationalism in Welsh Politics, 1945–1970* (1975), 268–71.
84 N. Timmins, *The Five Giants: A Biography of the Welfare State* (1995), 14–18.
85 Quoted in P. Carradice, *Wales at War* (2003), 149.
86 Beddoe, *Out of the Shadows*, 132–3, 139, 142. Thomas, *The Welsh Economy*, 30, 32.
87 R. Frankenberg, *Village on the Border: A Social Study of Religion, Politics and Football in a North Wales Community* (1957), 51–7.
88 E. Davies and A. D. Rees, *Welsh Rural Communities* (1962), 228. N. Evans and D. Jones, '"To help forward the great work of humanity": women in the Labour Party in Wales', in Tanner *et al.* (eds), *The Labour Party in Wales*, 229.
89 D. Kynaston, *Family Britain 1951–57* (2010), 130–1. S. Phillips, *Private Faces: The Autobiography* (1999), 25.
90 Quoted in N. Charles, 'Women: advancing or retreating?', in R. Jenkins and A. Edwards (eds), *One Step Forward? South and West Wales Towards the Year 2000* (1990), 84.
91 C. Hughes, *A Wanderer in North Wales* (1949), 108.
92 I. Gazeley, *Poverty in Britain, 1900–1965* (2003), 132–3.
93 *CJ*, 27 Jan. 1950. *Welsh Gazette*, 1 July 1948.
94 *The Times*, 3 Apr. 1947. Wilkinson, *Puppets in Wales*, 38.
95 Swansea Labour Association, *46th Annual Report and Statement of Accounts for the Year Ending Dec. 31st, 1952*, 5.
96 Brennan *et al.*, *Social Change*, 187. M. Jones, *A Radical Life: The Biography of Megan Lloyd George, 1902–66* (1991), 210.
97 *CJ*, 8 Jan. 1950.
98 *CDH*, 9 Mar. 1951.
99 *Picture Post*, 16 Aug. 1952. *WM*, 27 Oct. 1951.
100 R. Harris, *The Making of Neil Kinnock* (1984), 30. A. Edwards, 'Answering the challenge of nationalism: Goronwy Roberts and the appeal of the Labour Party in north-west Wales during the 1950s', *WHR*, 22:1 (2004), 126–52. J. G. Jones, 'The Liberal Party and Wales, 1945–79', *WHR*, 16:3 (1993), 326–55.
101 *The Times*, 16 Feb. 1950.
102 See for example the report on Jim Griffiths in *The Times*, 9 Feb. 1950.
103 *SWEP*, 24 and 27 Oct. 1951.

104 I. McAllister, 'The Labour Party in Wales: the dynamics of one-partyism', *Llafur*, 3:2 (1981), 79–89. Swansea Labour Association, *46th Annual Report*, 4.
105 Morgan, 'Power and glory', 186.
106 J. Alfrey, 'Schools of architecture', *Heritage in Wales* (2002), 18–21.
107 Brennan *et al.*, *Social Change*, 108, 82, 104. Gildart, *North Wales Miners*, 42.
108 D. Raymond, *We Go To Wales* (1954), 167.
109 Rees, *Life in a Welsh Countryside.*
110 For example Sir F. Rees, *The Problem of Wales* (1950), 14. Wilkinson, *Puppets in Wales*, 138.
111 B. Conekin, F. Mort and C. Waters (eds), *Moments of Modernity: Reconstructing Britain 1945–1964* (1999), 1.
112 Wilkinson, *Puppets in Wales*, 11–12.
113 Kynaston, *Family Britain*, 175–6. P. Miskell, *A Social History of the Cinema in Wales, 1918–1951: Pulpits, Coal Pits and Fleapits* (2006), 26, 39. M. Johnes, *A History of Sport in Wales* (2005), 71.
114 Hennessy, *Never Again*, 435.
115 Quoted in K. O. Morgan, *The People's Peace: British History since 1945* (1992), 102.
116 *SWE*, 19 Dec. 1953.

3

'The hard times are finished.' The coming of affluence, 1951–64

South Wales likes to spend. It has never had money before. It has waited a long time. It is determined to enjoy.

Observer Magazine, 30 October 1966

'Me and Clare Beynon were born at the wrong time; two wars and poverty, that's all we've enjoyed.'

'Give over, Ma. We've always had food on our table.'

'You don't know what it cost to put it on the table.'

Comfortably by the fire, Beynon said, 'I reckon the hard times are finished.'

'Sure they are. Gone for ever,' Miskin said.

'Ah! For ever's a long time. People have long memories. I have a few myself.'

Ron Berry, *Hunters and Hunted* (1960), 32

IN JULY 1957 Prime Minister Harold Macmillan gave a speech in Bedford that has come to define the age of affluence. It has actually received far more attention from historians than it ever did from contemporaries, who were more taken with how it marked a strong vein of caution that historians tend to forget. Macmillan said,

> Indeed, let's be frank about it: most of our people have never had it so good. Go around the country, go to the industrial towns, go to the farms, and you will see a state of prosperity such as we have never had in the history of this country.
>
> What is beginning to worry some of us is 'Is it too good to last?' For, amidst all this prosperity, there is the problem that has troubled us – ever since the war. It's the problem of rising prices.

Commenting on the speech, the *Western Mail* agreed that 'there has never been a period of such prosperity shared by almost all sections of the community'. But it warned that individuals had their part to play in maintaining that and the paper used the speech to attack politically motivated strikes, which acted as 'a blow at the country's prosperity'.[1] Macmillan's speech and the reactions to it capture the dominant mode of the period of Conservative governance from 1951 to 1964. Living standards did rise but without ever really creating a full sense of security. The transition from austerity to affluence was gradual, slow and not universally shared. Even rationing of food did not end completely until July 1954. One historian has suggested:

> For many people living in the mill towns of Yorkshire, among the mining valleys of south Wales or beside the shipyards of the Clyde, life in the late fifties went on as it always had, a weary routine of little money and hard work.... These were places where the affluent society was little more than a mirage.[2]

Throughout the 1950s much did seem the same in industrial Wales. The landscape was scarred and the housing was often appalling. Some common sights, such as babies being carried in woollen shawls or coal being delivered in horse-drawn carts, would not have been out of place in the Victorian age. Macmillan's key phrase was 'most of our people'; poverty did not disappear. But it did lessen and the aspirations and expectations of those who did not fully share in this affluence rose too. For the whole of the working class, the 1950s and early 1960s were in no way comparable to the miseries of the 1920s and 1930s. The coming of luxuries such as televisions and washing machines to ordinary homes provided a symbolic and tangible sign that life was better. Economic and moral insecurities never disappeared by any stretch of the imagination but the welfare state did take the sting out of illness and unemployment. Most significantly, being out of work was quite simply rarer. The hardships of the 1930s and the age of austerity were ebbing away. Life was changing and people knew it.

AT THE HEART of the age of the affluence was an economy of near full employment, where manufacturing continued the growth that had begun under Attlee's government. This growth may have been based on the absence of space and labour in the Midlands and southern England, and it may have been despite some firms and managers being weary of Wales and complaining of the high transport and telephone costs brought about by Welsh locations, but it was central to Wales sharing in the good times of the

1950s. Between 1951 and 1964, 6.5 per cent of all new factory building in the UK took place in Wales and the boom was most evident at the five huge industrial estates at Treforest, Bridgend, Hirwaun, Fforestfach (Swansea) and Wrexham, which by 1958 were home to 60,000 workers. The manufacturing explosion was based on supplying consumer goods to the newly affluent population. Newport, for example, had factories making ladders, cakes, toys, hearing aids, pins, knitting needles, corsets and sweets, and the *Western Mail* concluded in 1958 that 'Wales can make anything'.[3] Such products may not have sounded as impressive as good-old-fashioned coal and steel but they were in demand and some factories were as big as traditional industrial works. British Nylon Spinners near Pontypool employed 5,000 people, while 2,000 made washing machines at Hoover in Merthyr. After a slowdown in the economy, new government powers were introduced in 1958 to assist industry in development areas. This led to the opening of a new series of major factories, such as Hotpoint in Llandudno, Revlon in Maesteg and Rover in Cardiff. In 1935 there had been 88,000 people in south Wales employed in (non-metal) manufacturing. By 1968 the figure was 210,000. Manufacturing was now employing nearly twice as many people in south Wales as the coal and metal industries combined.[4] Other new industries were also developing. Milford Haven emerged as Britain's largest oil port in the 1960s and in 1964 there were over 20,000 people employed in the chemical industry in Wales. In 1963 *The Times* called the economic redevelopment of south Wales 'one of the great success stories of the last thirty years'.[5]

But manufacturing did not offer the Welsh economy or Welsh workers long-term security. State support, whether through grant aid, loans or the building of factories, underpinned the sector's growth, making it potentially vulnerable to shifts in government policy. The growth was also dominated by external firms expanding or relocating in Wales. Of 34,200 manufacturing jobs created in Wales from 1960 to 1965, only 11,700 came from companies that had been based in Wales before 1945. Branch factories of companies based elsewhere were also always going to be vulnerable and of the 279 firms from outside Wales that opened branches there between 1945 and 1960, 46 per cent had closed by the end of 1965.[6] The continued opening of factories and talk of a manufacturing revolution also disguised redundancies and short-term dislocations. Full employment was always more political rhetoric than economic reality. Unemployment in Wales was, though, less than 3 per cent throughout the early and mid-1950s and reached its lowest point in July 1955, when it fell to 1.4 per cent. There were also 13,300 unfilled vacancies in Wales at the time, almost the same as the number of people out of work.[7] But the late 1950s saw the British economy slow down and unemployment became a political issue again. In 1958 Megan Lloyd George MP claimed that 'Many of the old signs, all too well known in the valleys, are coming back – the anxious, drawn faces, the queues at the employment exchanges'.[8] Unemployment in Wales was up to nearly 4 per cent, compared with just over 2 per cent in Britain as a whole. In December of that year there were 4,543 men in Wales (18.7 per cent of the total unemployed) who had been out of work for over a year. By September 1963 the unemployment rate had dropped again, to 3 per cent (or some 28,990 people), but this disguised some regional problems. It remained at 7.1 per cent in Anglesey, 6.6 per cent in Milford Haven and 5.2 per cent in Rhondda.[9] The low national figures also obscure the personal tragedy, depression and sacrifices of those who were out of work. Indeed, it was perhaps worse psychologically to be out of work at a time when relatively few were than it was when being on the dole was a common experience.

Many of the long-term unemployed of the 1950s were miners who had left the industry because of health problems as the industry contracted. By the 1950s it was clear that the National Coal Board (NCB) had brought better safety, wages and conditions to Wales' most important industry but it had not eradicated the old problems of overcapacity and inefficiency. In Menna Gallie's 1962 novel *The Small Mine*, one miner reflects, 'You used to say nationalisation would cure all evils, didn't you, Steve, but it's made a few of its own, all right'. The hopes and dreams had faded, to be replaced by new grumbles and fears over jobs. In the modernized pits, according to the same novel, 'nationalisation was felt to be almost synonymous with mechanisation and the skilled, proud craftsmen of colliers felt demoted, like bits of wheels, lengths of chain; men had become man-hours'.[10] Miners thus increasingly felt undervalued and looked down upon by society and were often eager to leave the industry. One former miner even claimed in 1966 that the job was 'a social stigma, like the Caste system in India'.[11] In 1961 there were 1,100 vacancies in mining in the Rhondda and Pontypridd area and a local paper was wondering if labour should be imported in the form of European displaced persons still in poverty after the war. Pay was also an issue. Between 1948 and 1959 the average real wage of British miners did rise by 16 per cent. But in 1952 average wages for colliery workers in south Wales were 12s 3d less than they were for British miners. This difference had increased to 22s 10d by 1959. By then, miners' earnings had also been hit by fewer overtime opportunities and an end to Saturday shifts, all caused by a downturn in demand for coal.[12] Older problems remained too. In spite of modernization, it could still be a deadly occupation. Over the course of the 1950s, 823 men were killed in accidents at Welsh coal mines. Explosions at Six Bells (Abertillery) in 1960 and at Cambrian (Clydach Vale) in 1965 killed forty-five and thirty-one men respectively. There were also more mundane reminders of the hazards of mining. Silicosis was a particular problem in south Wales because of the quality of the coal and the lack of anti-dust measures. In 1949 one observer noted, 'you see a great number of men walking idly with grim, sullen faces and with a genuine grievance'. A youngster rightly remarked that such men were 'walking propaganda against recruitment for the pits'.[13]

Oil was growing in importance as a source of industrial power and even in the domestic market those people who could afford it were beginning to show a preference for forms of heating than did not leave coal's black tinge on the wallpaper. In 1950 the South Western Division of the NCB had sold over 2 million tons of coal to the railways. By 1970 it was selling them just 13,000 tons. Its sales to industry had fallen from 4.3 million tons to 0.75 million tons. There was thus a need to cut back on the number of pits if the industry was to be profitable and thirty-two pits shut in the south Wales coalfield between 1951 and 1958. Between 1948 and 1958, the number employed in coal mining in Wales fell from 134,100 (14.6 per cent of the insured labour force) to 119,600 (12.9 per cent).[14]

The running down of the coal industry did not bring significant political protest in the 1950s because there were other jobs to go to. Shorter hours, less strenuous work and the availability of canteen meals all made working in a factory an attractive alternative to mining. Factory jobs also opened up leisure opportunities, because men could go straight from work rather than having to go home first to eat and wash. But there were downsides too. In the Swansea area in the early 1950s there was sneering about 'dolls-eyes' factories' because jobs there were not regarded as men's work, a feeling reinforced by factory wages often being lower than in mining. One ex-miner, now working in a toy factory in Swansea, told the *Western Mail* in 1958: 'I am very happy here. But I would sooner be in the pit if I was young and fit. You know, with the boys.'[15] A Pontypool MP whose constituency included many factories thought that the men in them were 'condemned to the anomie of the modern factory which for some becomes endurable only with the relief of absenteeism, of periodic flights into illness or, perhaps more salutary individually although socially disastrous, of aggressive strikes'.[16]

For most of the 1950s people could choose whether to put up with the less sociable comfort of factory work or the hardships, camaraderie and better money of the mines. But, with an economic slowdown meaning that the supply of coal exceeded demand and making other jobs harder to find, the NCB announced a new round of pit closures in December 1958. South Wales was especially hard hit; old class tensions were awoken and the local branch of the National Union of Mineworkers (NUM) complained: 'For the displaced miners, dole and poverty; but for the old owners of these mines, compensation and interest beyond the value of the pits they owned, which the Coal Board will continue to pay although the pits may be closed.'[17] The union, however, also feared doing anything that might give the Conservative government an excuse to end nationalization.[18] Individual miners, meanwhile, were disillusioned enough with a career underground and believed there were still enough alternative options to mean that there was no strike against the closures. By 1962 the number of mines in south Wales had more than halved from its 1948 total of 203. That year there had been 134,100 people employed in coal mining in Wales. By 1962 there were 97,200.[19]

The older parts of the metal industry also faced cuts in the name of modernization and rationalization. Between 1945 and 1965 over thirty iron, steel and tinplates works were closed. The *Guardian* thought that in 1961 the millmen in Pontarddulais had 'the strange dignity of a race that know they are doomed to extinction'.[20] In 1957 the mayor of Llanelli claimed that west Wales was facing one of the biggest crises in its history because of the lack of employment for redundant metal workers and the migration of technically able men. Youngsters wanting apprenticeships in skilled industries were being compelled to move to the Midlands because of a lack of local opportunities. Henry Brooke, the Minister for Welsh Affairs, had to warn a meeting in the town about the dangers of pessimism. He argued there was no large-scale unemployment and that new industrialists would not come if they thought people in west Wales were gloomy about the future.[21] While older metal works were closing, newer ones were opening thanks to the demand for steel to make motor cars and food cans. Llanwern steelworks opened in 1962 and employed 3,500, while Port Talbot, opened in 1951, had 18,000 employees by 1962, making it Europe's largest integrated steelworks. With other major steelworks at Shotton, Cardiff and Ebbw Vale, Wales had 29 per cent of the UK's steel capacity by 1964 and around 70,000 steelworkers.[22] Steelworks were far from pleasant places. One man wrote of starting employment at Ebbw Vale: 'The place was huge, shambling, spectacular, filthy and frightening. Only more filthy and more frightening than I had thought possible.'[23] But the pay more than compensated. By the 1960s some other industries were struggling to find staff because of the high wages in the steel industry.[24] Indeed, the money was so good that Port Talbot was nicknamed 'Treasure Island' and there were stories of bricklayers with Jaguars and a man who sold his two shops because he could make more money as a labourer. At one of the clubs in the town, bar takings in 1965 were £117,000 and the committee room was fitted with leather and steel chairs and a thirty-foot mahogany table. 'People won't have the old stuff anymore. They want the best', remarked the club's chairman. The town even had its own casino.[25]

Steelworkers were not the only ones whose pay packets were growing. Average real earnings in the UK increased by 47 per cent between 1948 and 1965. There were, however, regional variations within that picture. In 1962 the average personal income in Wales was £375, compared with £452 in the UK as a whole.[26] These figures are skewed by the fact that fewer people in Wales were in employment, mostly due to the high disability rate left by the coal industry. In 1962, only 70 per cent of Welsh males aged fifteen and over were in paid employment, compared with 77.5 per cent in Britain as a whole.[27] When male manual workers are looked at alone, a more favourable picture emerges. In 1962, their average weekly wage in Wales was 315s 8d, compared with a UK average of 312s 10d. Only in the Midlands and the south of England were male manual wages higher than in Wales. In Scotland they were 285s 11d and in Northern Ireland the figure was just 246s 6d. Family incomes were also rising, as more women went out to work thanks to the growing number of opportunities in the factories. Wales, however, lagged behind in this development. In 1962 only 28 per cent of Welsh women aged fifteen and over were in paid employment, compared with 39 per cent in Britain as a whole. A 1960 survey in Swansea suggested that just 7 per cent of married women with children under fifteen years had full-time jobs.[28]

Thus, as a society, average incomes in Wales lagged behind those in England, but for those men who did work, especially if their wives did too, the 1950s and early 1960s were good times. When average Welsh incomes are compared with those of the 1930s and 1940s rather than those in other parts of Britain, which is what, after all, many people at the time would have actually done, then the period seems all the more comfortable. In such a climate it was no surprise that consumer expenditure in Wales rose from £524 million in 1953 to £821 million in 1962, some £135 million more than if the increase had been at the rate of inflation.[29] For the middle classes consumerism was nothing new but its extension to the vast majority was a remarkable social development. A 1953–4 survey estimated that consumer spending on recreation in Wales, as in Britain as a whole, had doubled since the late 1930s. Yet incomes and expenditures varied significantly. The survey suggested that the poorest families were spending less than 2 per cent of their expenditure on household goods, whereas some better-paid families spent over 10 per cent. Perhaps the survey's most significant finding was that those families earning less than £8 a week were spending more than they earned. Even then, 'semi-luxuries' like biscuits, frozen vegetables, fruit and eggs were beyond the reach of those on the lowest incomes.[30]

By the mid-1960s it was becoming clear that the Welsh economy still had significant problems. Above all, despite the growth of manufacturing and the prosperity of steel, too much of Wales was still dominated by heavy industry, something which continued to worry economists and politicians. In 1961 over a quarter of the male labour force worked in mining, quarrying, engineering and metal manufacturing. The NCB remained south Wales' largest single employer and supported, directly or indirectly, 28 per cent of the region's labour force.[31] In 1964 consultants were pointing out that the steel industry in Wales was overstaffed by maybe as many as 9,000 people. Two years later it was recommended that the works at Brymbo, Ebbw Vale, East Moors, Briton Ferry, Llanelli and Gowerton be phased out.[32] Industrial development remained strongly dependent on external investment, to the extent that there was even some feeling that entrepreneurship was alien to Wales and that Welsh culture, with its emphasis on education and the influence of chapels, had given the professions more status than business.[33] Some of the new manufacturing concerns were also encountering problems as the general economic outlook grew bleaker and firms began to feel the transport costs of being located far from English markets.[34] One of the biggest blows came when ICI closed its Dowlais plant in 1962 to relocate to Severnside. People were still leaving in search of work and, between 1961 and 1966 alone, 58,530 economically active people moved out of Wales.[35] The Conservatives concluded in 1964 that the image of Wales was not helping:

> It is time we Welshmen killed the myth of Wales as a land of slag heaps, populated by wild men in cloth caps and mufflers, unredeemed save by the enthusiasm for rugby football and song. It would be as well if more Welsh authors would face up to the fact that their homeland has changed in the last half century and realised that it is neither as anachronistically quaint nor as materially repulsive to executives and their wives as their sentimental portraits would lead one to believe.[36]

Yet when Wales is looked at as a whole, when its economic diversification is considered, for all the rundown of its traditional industries and the fragility of its manufacturing base, it is difficult not to conclude that under the Conservative governments of 1951 to 1964, economically at least, Wales had indeed never had it so good. In 1951 Welsh unemployment had been twice the UK average. By 1964 it was one-and-a half times the British figure.[37]

The fact that unemployment was still higher in Wales than in Britain as a whole meant there was no general sense of security. Nor had poverty disappeared but, for the majority, affluence was replacing austerity.

PERHAPS THE SUREST sign of affluence was the purchase of what officials called consumer durables. The 1950s and early 1960s was the period that first saw the television, washing machine, refrigerator and vacuum cleaner reach working-class homes. The domestic consumption of electricity in Wales more than doubled between 1949 and 1957, with around 187,000 homes gaining electrical power for the first time.[38] Before anyone thought of anything as fancy as a washing machine, there was electrical lighting to get. Simply being able to flick a switch and have light, even in daylight, was its own joyous mark of better times. The length of people's leisure time was extended, even if just for activities like reading, and in some homes previously dark hallways and landings suddenly became places that could be lingered in rather than just passed through. For some, the arrival of electricity in their village created a 'thrill to know that we were modern, at last!'[39] It was no wonder that the connection of one Anglesey village was celebrated with a ceremony that consisted of the reading of a poem and the switching on of lights, kettles and other appliances all at once, to gasps of admiration. Not everyone, however, could understand what they were receiving and some people, afraid of the new technology, would only switch on the light to find a match for a lamp. Electricity also created worries about cost, which limited both people's use of lights and the number of rooms they were installed in. Some families had electric lights in the parlour, which was used only on Sundays, but none in the kitchen, the busiest room.[40] Only as the novelty gradually wore off did people become more comfortable with using the lights without thinking about the cost.

Cost also limited people's take-up of other consumer durables and working-class purchases were reliant on the availability of hire-purchase agreements. Rising wages and the desirability of the things that could be bought did see the pre-war fear and distaste for personal debt dissolve as people strove to share in the new age. But there was always caution. As one housewife remembered, 'We did not rush out to buy electric appliances immediately, money was scarce in those days – we had to weigh the pro's and con's before we ventured out to the shops'. Oral evidence from rural areas suggests that, after lighting, an electric iron was people's first priority because it was relatively cheap, made light of the old work of heating an iron in the fire and avoided getting iron marks on the laundry. Despite the rarity of carpets, vacuum cleaners were the next priority, no doubt drawing upon the importance placed on the respectability of cleanliness. Then came the mains-operated wireless, which saved the need to trudge into town to recharge batteries.[41]

Although it was women who benefited the most from the new labour-saving devices, it was usually men who had the decision over whether a purchase should be made. This was clear in a 1950 South Wales Electricity Board newspaper advertisement in which a husband was depicted saying, 'You wouldn't catch me going down on my knees to clean carpets but I don't mind lending a hand with a vacuum cleaner occasionally.... It certainly gives my wife more time to spend with me and the youngsters.'[42] Both parties may have had something to gain from the purchase but the drudgery of the housewife's life did not end with a vacuum cleaner or washing machine. The cleaning still had to be done and, regardless of what new electrical goods they owned, domestic chores still filled married women's days, or, if they worked, their evenings. One Aberdare housewife remembered,

> the standards you are expected to live up to promptly expand with every increase in amenities. Once you have carpets on the floor, you have to keep vacuuming them. Once you have acquired a twin tub washing machine, because it is less laborious, the sheets and everything else get changed much more often and that makes more ironing.[43]

Furthermore, not every appliance saved that much time. The first washing machines were remarkable enough for women to sit watching the clothes whirl around, but early models were difficult to use, requiring tubs to be filled and emptied with a hose and leaving clothes in a heavy tangled knot. Nonetheless, technology moved on and by 1961 advertisements could declare 'Jump for joy! Washing drudgery has vanished with the new automatic washing machines.'[44] Women may have filled their days with more housework but it is difficult to deny that the advertisements were right: domestic chores were made easier by electrical appliances.

The ownership figures for appliances show that the consumer-durable revolution was far from complete even by the end of the 1960s (table 3.1). Moreover, its reach was even more limited in Wales than in the UK as a whole. The clear difference between Wales and the UK in refrigerators and telephones, which were less essential items, was unsurprising with disposable incomes in Wales being around 10 per cent lower than the UK average throughout most of the 1960s. But, whatever the differences between Wales and the rest of Britain, given that in 1952 only 11 per cent of UK households had owned a television, 6 per cent had a fridge and just

Table 3.1 Percentage of households with durable goods, Wales and UK, 1964 and 1969

	Wales 1964	UK 1964	Wales 1969	UK 1969
Car	40	37	41	45
Central heating (full or partial)	1	7	17	25
Washing machine	55	53	64	63
Refrigerator	23	34	50	60
Telephone	19	22	21	32

Source: Rees, *Survey of the Welsh Economy, 47. Abstract of Regional Statistics, 2* (1966), 53.

10 per cent had a washing machine, the subsequent spread of consumer goods was a remarkable development.[45]

In choosing which appliances to buy, families would often be guided by what their neighbours owned and a degree of competition developed. In the early 1950s sociologists in industrial south-west Wales were noting that the best-paid workers spent money on carpets and furniture that were as much for show as utility.[46] Some found this new world of consumerism distasteful and denied that it existed in their communities. Leo Abse MP (Labour, Pontypool) argued of Welsh miners:

> Having bought his own terraced house, or continuing to rent it for a very small sum, and having amply furnished its small rooms and perhaps bought a modest car, his needs cease. He has his beer and his brisket and that suffices. He has the imprudent rationality to consider it droll to work merely in order to keep up with the Joneses: indeed the Joneses within a tight mining community are his cousins, and they will join him in the miners' club wanting no more than he.[47]

But more convincing was a man who actually lived among the Joneses on a Swansea council estate:

> there's plenty of showing off – you know the sort of thing, beautiful curtains on the windows but nothing on the bed. If anybody does a bit of decorating or buys something new, they leave the lights on with the curtains open to make sure the neighbours get a good look. And the palaver with the dustbins when they are put out on the pavements for collection on a Tuesday morning is quite a sight – all the best tins, or bits of expensive vegetables or chicken bones or whatever, stuck prominently on the top where the neighbours can see how well off the family is, or pretends to be. And then every Monday, though nobody admits to it of course, we have the Battle of the

> Washing Lines. I tell my wife she buys all this fancy nylon underwear just to stick it out on the line to give the neighbours something to think about. If one of them has something new, particularly something for the kids, the others are matching it on the line by the following Monday.[48]

The degree of keeping up with the Joneses was evident when it came to buying electric ovens. With people fearing the cost of electricity, some still used their old ovens after having bought an electric one. Others used their new purchase as a store cupboard at first or even kept it in the parlour because there was nowhere in the kitchen to put it. When women did begin using their electric ovens they found it opened a new world of cooking. With controlled temperatures, suddenly new delights like sponge cakes were possible. But electric ovens were particularly expensive, meaning that by 1961 just 30 per cent of British homes had one. As late as 1968, the *Guardian* was noting that black ranges with coal ovens and brass knobs were common in the homes of Welsh farmers and miners, that bakestones and even the occasional spit were still being used and that simple, traditional and economic dishes were the normal fare.[49] That was probably especially true in rural areas. One resident of Cwm Rheidol (Cardiganshire) remembered of the 1950s:

> You lived off the pig and the vegetable plot because you had no choice. So it was *cawl*, bacon broth, every day for dinner. It was certainly a healthy diet compared with all the over-refined shop foods. Home-made bread and butter, buttermilk to drink, oatmeal porridge, fresh eggs and vegetables – it was wholefood with nothing taken out and no chemicals added, as people would see it now. But then it just seemed dreary and people longed for all the unhealthy tinned foods and shop cakes and processed cheese, because they were treats, a break from the monotony of home-produced fare.[50]

An anthropologist working in a north Wales village concluded that because people there thought of themselves as poor they did not try to compete with each other for the more expensive goods such as electric stoves and carpets.[51]

The slow penetration of the new affluent society was further evident on Welsh high streets. In 1960 there was not a single laundrette in the west Wales towns of Ammanford, Carmarthen, Llanelli, Neath, Pontardawe and Port Talbot. In Swansea there were 207 butchers and 279 confectioners but no licensed restaurants, just two carpet/linoleum shops and a single coffee/milk bar, places often heralded or lamented as a symbol of the new age. The town also had thirty-four branches of the Co-operative Society but only two supermarkets.[52] Supermarkets were one of the most popular markers of change and affluence in the 1950s and 1960s. In Llanelli, the Station

Road Co-operative store became self-service in 1950, one of the first shops in Wales to adopt this American system. Once people grew accustomed to the idea of serving themselves, the path was paved for supermarkets and, in 1958, the Co-operative opened one in Llanelli, claiming it was Wales' first purpose-built supermarket and the 'Most modern and hygienic food store in the Principality'. As well as frozen food, it also sold whole chickens barbecued in a glass oven in the store itself. Supermarkets served wider catchment areas than the highly localized small shops they were ousting and this led to new commercial battles within towns for custom. In 1965–6, Llanelli also gained a Fine Fare and a Tesco store of 4,500 square foot, with 100 feet of refrigerated cabinets, eight checkouts and sixty staff. It opened with a four-page advert in the local press which promised 'Best for less and it's all under one roof' and claimed that Tesco supermarkets were a 'revolution which is making life easier and happier for shoppers'. On Fridays the store was open until eight o'clock to cater for women who worked and wanted to do something with their Saturdays beyond shopping.[53] For many women such changes were indeed a revolution that saved time and traipses up and down high streets and broadened the fares they could cook for their family. But it also made shopping a less personalized and sociable experience. The neighbourly chat with a storekeeper who knew you and your likes was fading away, striking another blow against the traditional conceptions of community. The number of grocers and provisions dealers in Wales fell by 2,386 (23 per cent) between 1961 and 1971. The biggest victim was perhaps the Co-operative Society, which saw nearly half of its 1,297 Welsh shops close between 1966 and 1971. But, as with all the symbols of affluence, the shift to self-service stores was slower in Wales than in southern England and small independents still dominated the high streets. In 1971, there were 23,457 independent shops in Wales compared with 2,848 branches of chain stores.[54] No wonder then that even a Cardiff woman can remember: 'For all that I lived in a busy, modern capital city my first visit to a supermarket was to one in Ilfracombe, Devon in 1968. How strange it was to push the wire trolley around and to hunt on shelves for what we wanted!'[55]

Visiting places like Ilfracombe was becoming more common because of the rise of the motor car. The number of licensed cars in Wales increased from 90,200 in 1948 to 221,600 in 1958 to 537,300 in 1968 and most gave their owners a sense of freedom and independence. The problems of getting around meant that car ownership was higher in rural areas. In urban areas public transport was better and shopping and leisure facilities much closer; this made owning a car in towns in the 1950s and early 1960s more of a source of leisure and a status symbol than a practicality. Indeed, at the start of the 1960s there were some industrial communities where the roads were simply in too poor condition to actually drive a car on.[56] By 1962, whereas there were twenty-one cars per 100 people in Radnor and nineteen in Montgomery (the highest figures in Wales), there were only ten in Glamorgan and eight in Merthyr (the lowest). This was a time when the British figure was fourteen. By 1970, a similar picture remained. The British figure had risen to twenty-one cars per 100 people, and the Radnor figure to thirty-one and Montgomery to twenty-nine. In Glamorgan the new number was eighteen and in Merthyr fifteen.[57]

This growth in car ownership created new social problems. In small rural towns, with their narrow streets, parking facilities were utterly inadequate and became a staple of complaint and discussion in the local press. Elsewhere, congestion was becoming a significant problem on main roads that passed through towns. Newport, Queensferry and Port Talbot were particular traffic bottlenecks. In 1960 there were, on average, around thirty-three vehicles crossing a bridge in Newport every minute on the main route between south Wales and England, double the figure six years earlier. In peak hours the rate was more than fifty-six vehicles a minute. Such levels of traffic also, of course, disturbed the peace and caused air pollution.[58] On housing estates, meanwhile, which had not been designed with the thought that every home might need somewhere to put a car, there were complaints about the nuisance caused by neighbours parking or even washing their cars.[59] The rise in car numbers also hit the profitability and thus provision of bus services, which created a new form of social exclusion for those without access to a car. The number of passenger trips in Cardiff fell from 105 million in 1948–9 to 77 million by 1964 and 45 million by 1973.[60] In large towns, passenger numbers remained sufficient for the services still to be provided, but in rural areas many were closed, literally cutting off some people in remote villages (see chapter 6).

The route from Wales to south-west England was a narrow twisting road with a one-way bridge over the Wye at Chepstow; getting to the Midlands involved navigating the country lanes of Monmouthshire. Within Wales, east–west traffic was hampered by inadequate and narrow roads that went through the centres of towns. Combating these problems was seen as central to supporting the Welsh economy. Ambitious plans were drawn up in the 1940s but it was not until the mid-1960s that major new roads were opened. Most significant were the Severn Bridge (which opened in 1966 and cut the journey from south Wales to London by up to two hours), the Port Talbot section of what became the M4 (1966, cutting the journey from Swansea to Cardiff by up to an hour) and the Heads of the Valleys A465 (1964, improving links with the Midlands).[61] The impact of such roads was not just to make it easier to get around Wales but also to open up its economy to England, encouraging investment from outside firms. They were also symbolic statements of the modernization of Wales. Although its full impact would not become apparent until the motorway network was complete, the Severn Bridge in particular became an icon of modernity, standing proud and sleek above the river. One man remembered it was 'tremendous to drive over that bridge.... It was like something out of the movies.'[62] Yet other roads were more problematic than iconic. Port Talbot's motorway brutally dissected the town, while in Conwy a new bridge brought vehicles into the middle of town and ruined the view of the castle.

Of all the symbols of modernity and affluence it was television that had the furthest reach and the biggest impact on people's daily lives. Television broadcasting began in Wales in 1952 but by then there were already 12,000 Welsh television licence holders tuned in to fuzzy pictures from Birmingham. Thousands more bought their first sets to watch the coronation in 1953 and, by September of that year, there were 82,324 Welsh licence holders. Basic sets, however, were not cheap, costing around £70 in 1952, when the average manual weekly wage was less than £5. This expense led to some people spending whole evenings watching through the windows of television shops. It also added a new dimension to socializing, as adult friends and family dropped in to watch, sometimes even when only the children were home.[63] But prices did fall and sets were made more affordable by hire purchase. Consequently, the numbers watching mushroomed. By 1959 half of Welsh households had television licences and more probably owned televisions. By 1969, 92 per cent of Welsh households had a set. The growth would have been quicker had it not been for reception problems in upland areas, something which caused significant resentment. At the start of 1953 some 300,000 people in Wales were unable to receive satisfactory signals. By 1958, although 92.4 per cent of the Welsh population (compared with 98.8 per cent of England) could receive television pictures, more than half of people in Pembrokeshire, Merioneth and Radnorshire could not.[64]

The 'box' was spellbinding and the television became the new spiritual and physical focus of the living room or parlour, which itself was becoming known as the lounge in more sophisticated families. The best programmes were enough to make people in rural areas forget viewing the television was like 'trying to watch through a heavy shower of snow'.[65] By the start of the 1970s one survey suggested that 97 per cent of British adults were watching twelve hours or more of television a week. Television was also responsible for the 1950s and 1960s fashion for knocking through the front and middle rooms in Welsh terraces, as people tried to create a larger room to watch in. People's horizons were expanding too and sociologists in Swansea noted that local gossip no longer focused just on family, neighbours and locals who got 'into the papers' but now included monarchy and film stars.[66] Inevitably, community activities suffered from the competition. Cledwyn Hughes MP (Labour, Anglesey) was told at a sparsely attended meeting during the 1959 general election: 'The village still supports you but everybody now has television.'[67] Television also caused fewer rural people to travel to the cinema, dances, sport and other public occasions in the way they once had, while some librarians in the 1950s blamed a decline in book borrowing on the rise of the 'box'. The biggest casualty, however, was the cinema, whose number in Wales fell from 350 in 1950 to 100 in 1975.[68] The widespread closures in the 1960s and 1970s left small towns such as Abergavenny without a cinema at all, while bigger towns lost their neighbourhood cinemas, leaving just the larger central picture houses.

A few, of course, did not want television at all, fearing it would bring immoral scenes into the home and disturb mealtimes, that it would distract their children from their studies and adults from their work, or even because it was felt to be somewhat common.[69] Intellectuals were particularly scathing, especially after the launch of commercial television (which reached Wales in 1958) with its quiz shows, films and adverts for brighter teeth and whiter whites. In 1963 a survey of south Wales women found that many felt that advertisements treated women as if they were 'morons'. They wanted more romances to be screened and were uncomfortable with the sex, crime and violence shown.[70] Raymond Williams, a Cambridge don and the son of a Pandy railway worker, claimed television was 'an anti-culture, which is alien to almost everybody, persistently hostile to art and intellectual activity … [and] given over to exploiting indifference, lack of feeling, frustration and hatred'.[71] But this was narrow-minded, especially in an era when the BBC took its public service mantra exceptionally seriously. Television may have changed family routines and leisure activities but broadcast hours were limited to prevent addiction and there was strict self-regulation of anything likely to offend the majority. The early years of television may not have been overly intellectual but for most people they were entertaining.

NEW CONSUMER GOODS needed places to be put and housing marked both the most significant gains and the limits of the age of affluence. Promises to build more houses had been central to the Conservatives' victory in the 1951 general election and they did make it a priority when in government. In England the house-building boom was led by the private sector, but in Wales it was first driven by local authorities before a rapid growth in private building in the 1960s. In total, 121,503 houses were completed in Wales in the 1950s, 76 per cent of which were built by local authorities. In the 1960s another 167,960 were finished, 49 per cent of which were local-authority built. Despite such huge numbers, the rate of house building was still slower than in England. Between 1951 and 1969, on average, 53.8 homes were built each year per 10,000 people in Wales, but in Britain as a whole the figure was 64.8. Things were not helped by the fact that 38,738 unfit houses in Wales were closed or demolished between April 1945 and the end of 1969.[72] Thus, throughout the 1950s and 1960s, there remained a significant housing shortage in Wales. There were even 487 families in Wales still living in hutted camps in 1956. The shortage was clearly evident in Swansea, where, at the start of the 1960s, there were some 6,000 families on the council-house waiting list and 18 per cent of married people were having to share their home with others. What this could mean was illustrated by a house in Aneurin Bevan's constituency in 1959: a family of four were sharing one room, another couple and their teenage daughter slept in the main bedroom and a man lived in the box room.[73]

Even at the start of the 1970s only 35 per cent of Welsh housing had been built after 1944, whereas in England the figure was 38 per cent and in Scotland it was 42 per cent.[74] These averages disguise the extent of the ageing stock in some Valleys towns, where basic housing had been erected quickly and cheaply during the industrial growth of the nineteenth century but still remained in use. In 1965, in Merthyr 55 per cent of housing was over ninety years old. Old houses were usually cold, dark, damp and lacking in basic facilities, a world away from the glossy images of 1950s magazines. In 1965 some 3 per cent of Welsh households, representing up to 75,000 people, did not even have electricity or gas. In 1961, in the East Glamorgan and Monmouthshire valleys 43 per cent of houses had no fixed bath. Even in the coastal towns of Cardiff, Swansea, Bridgend and Port Talbot the figure was 24 per cent.[75] Rural Wales was no better. Forty per cent of homes in mid-Wales in 1964 had no fixed bath, 28 per cent had no inside toilet and 35 per cent had no hot-water tap. Even in 1966 nearly 15 per cent of Welsh households had no hot-water tap, over 28 per cent had no inside toilet and some 95,000 people were living in homes that had no toilet at all, even one shared with another household.[76] Some houses could not be upgraded, even if the resources existed, and were instead condemned. In 1955, 40,048 of the 748,919 homes in Wales were deemed unfit for human habitation (5.3 per cent). One of the worst towns was Merthyr, where 16.3 per cent of homes were classified unfit.[77] One such house was home to a family in Blaenllechau. It was literally falling down and had holes in the roof that were so big the family had to sleep on the floor because the bedding was wet through from the rain.[78] The cramped nature of many houses was not helped by people's reluctance to use their whole house. For many, especially those without televisions, the back kitchen of a small terraced house was still the hearth, with the parlour 'reserved for death and courting'.[79] The general reliance on coal fires in the main room exacerbated conditions by leaving soot everywhere. One woman remembered of her 1950s north Wales home: 'We did everything in one room and that was the room with the fireplace in it.... The fireplace not only heated you, it boiled your water, it cooked your food, it was where you had your bath, it was the main hub of the house.'[80]

However much the litany of housing statistics undermines the idea of an age of affluence, they do not necessarily portray how the inhabitants felt about such homes. For the younger generation aspirations were growing but older people had lower expectations. They could object to their homes being labelled slums and oppose attempts to demolish them. One elderly Swansea woman declared, 'They say these houses aren't fit for human occupation just because there isn't a bath. How do they think we have managed for the last seventy years?' A resident of Cardiff docks remembered, 'They told us Tiger Bay was a slum. We didn't know it was a slum, and it wasn't.' A Swansea councillor claimed that many condemned houses were actually 'little palaces'.[81]

The continuing problems also disguise the progress that was made. Improved housing contributed to notifications of tuberculosis in Wales falling by 60 per cent between 1948 and 1961.[82] At the start of the 1950s, less than half of Welsh households had a fixed bath, less than a third had their own sink or stove and 15 per cent did not even have access to a shared outside toilet. However, by 1966 two-thirds of all Welsh households had a fixed bath, an inside toilet and a hot-water tap. This was less than the figure of 72 per cent for England and Wales as a whole but it still represented significant progress. The house-building programme also reduced overcrowding and in Glamorgan the average household size fell from 4.01 in 1931 to 3.11 in 1966.[83] Although some forwent their opportunity of getting a new local-authority house because the rent was more than they paid for their existing unmodernized homes, the houses built were highly desirable and clearly different from older, undeveloped properties.[84] By 1966, 30 per cent of the Welsh population lived in local-authority properties, which generally meant bigger houses, as well as gardens, garages and more space between neighbours.[85] On an estate in Llanrumney on the edge of Cardiff, families who had moved from the inner city in the early 1960s constantly spoke of the fresh air 'out here'.[86] Yet the new estates also created concerns about whether they replicated the community of the old working-class areas that people were moving from (see chapter 5).

Rising affluence also enabled owner occupation in Wales to grow from around 30 per cent in 1950 to 48 per cent in 1963.[87] Despite the long-term financial security it could offer, owning a home was not always thought desirable when there was good-quality public housing. Some feared the debt and the responsibility; as one new bride in Swansea said at the end of the 1960s: 'I don't want my own house. I don't believe in spending the best years of my life with a mortgage round my neck.'[88] Homeowners in industrial areas also had a sense of insecurity as many ninety-nine-year leases on properties built in the Victorian boom approached their end. New legislation in 1950 won people two years' protection upon the expiry of a lease but many still feared a sudden hike in rents or demands for repairs from the owners of the land on which their houses were built. Not until the 1967 Leasehold Reform Act did many homeowners find a sense of security.

Whether they were rented or owned, the homes of the majority were slowly changing. The typical traditional terraced houses were transformed over the course of the 1950s and 1960s by the introduction of televisions, carpets, sofas, small extensions for a bathroom, electric goods and tiled kitchens. As well as becoming more comfortable, they were becoming more vibrant too, with the spread of the do-it-yourself movement and the fashion for bright colours and swirly patterns. People had the time and money to make improvements and there were women's magazines, which sold in their millions across Britain, to help people know what to buy, what was fashionable and how to keep a house. Such was the desire for a bit of colour that there were even more budgies than dogs in 1950s Britain.[89] In the lower Swansea valley, people's satisfaction with their home was noted by social investigators: 'They add bathrooms and modernise kitchens, put in new grates, hang paper, paint inside and out and generally take a good deal of pride in their homes'.[90] In an Alun Richards short story one woman looks proudly at her new bathroom with its pink bath, hand towels, mat and toilet cover and 'luxury of luxuries, a separate shower attachment'. She remembered 'what it was like not to have a proper bathroom and she thought her coloured suite a whiz and no mistake.... It was the most hallowed room in the house.'[91] It was in such rooms that the age of affluence could genuinely be found, but when such luxury was appearing in ordinary working-class streets it must have made the resentment of some of those left behind in houses without a bathroom or even a watertight roof all the more heartfelt.

Affluence may not have been universal but it did change life for everyone, if only in the sense that their own material poverty became more obvious as their neighbours bought a washing machine. The days when whole working-class communities were poor were over.

BY THE MIDDLE of the 1960s Wales was a world where some of the working class had pink luxurious bathrooms, and electric lighting and television had reached nearly everyone who wanted them. It was a world where the mood was 'garish' and tastes were 'flashy'.[92] But other symbols of affluence remained out of many people's reach and a significant minority of Welsh homes did not own a washing machine, half did not have a fridge and a majority did not have a car, a phone or central heating. Thus the age of affluence, if marked by consumer goods, did not reach everyone but it did make significant inroads into Welsh life and its symbols were coming to be expected by the young, even if they could not afford them. In 1966, a welfare office in Cwmbran reported that people were 'struggling to adapt to modern society'. Suddenly confronted with new and significantly more expensive housing they overstretched themselves with goods bought on hire purchase and fell behind on those payments and the rent.[93]

Older people, who had grown up with deprivation, probably tolerated being excluded from the comforts of affluence better than the young. This was maybe a good thing since, with high rates of employment, old age had become the most common cause of poverty in Britain, a condition which, in 1964, 5.5 per cent of the UK population were calculated to be living in.[94] The welfare state, of course, meant the poverty of the 1950s and 1960s was not as dire as the poverty which the elderly had known in their youth but the new welfare system was not the straightforward safety net that it first seems. Its payments were more static than wages and, in an era of rising prices, the living standards of the old fell further behind the rest of the working class. In 1964 one Dowlais pensioner wrote to her local paper:

> With regard to people alone – the dead hand of loneliness usually goes hand in hand with poverty. A television set, for example, would help to break the monotony of life for many such people – but for the majority the cost prohibits such pleasures. We all have the greatest sympathy with the starving millions abroad, but if we cannot see justice done in our own sphere of influence how can anyone hope to set matters right over which we have little or no control.
>
> By all means let us strive together for the national good, but let us hope that all shall share in the national prosperity.[95]

In Monmouthshire it was reported in 1966 that some pensioners were not eating properly because of the price of food and that they still associated the idea of receiving help from the welfare state with the poorhouse.[96] In the rural north the welfare system, with its complex rules and regulations, was looked upon as rather arbitrary, 'welcome but not to be relied on'. Furthermore, those uncomfortable with the English language would sometimes not see a doctor or claim benefits they were entitled to, although others might plead linguistic ignorance to gain advantage in their dealings with officialdom.[97] Nor did the welfare state eradicate industrial Wales' long-term health problems. These extended beyond industrial diseases. Infant mortality rates in the Glamorgan and Monmouth valleys were 39 per cent higher than the England and Wales average in 1951–5 and 35 per cent higher in 1956–60. Even in 1966–70 they were still 25 per cent higher.[98] The death rate for tuberculosis in Wales had fallen from 548 deaths per million people in 1948 to 116 in 1958. This was a testament to the effectiveness of the welfare state but it still did not change the fact that, in 1958, 335 people in Wales died from a disease that was rooted in poor living conditions.[99] In the age of affluence, pockets of poverty clearly remained.

In 1961 a Lloyds bank advert in a Rhondda paper captured what young families were coming to expect. It asked a man hanging wallpaper what he did for his family: had he started buying a house, bought a second-hand car, hire-purchased a washing machine and opened a bank account?[100] Whether he had or not, if he looked outside his front door what he saw was a world that still bore the physical and mental scars of the past, that had changed little since the war and that again undermined the idea of affluence. One 1949 observer described the mining valleys as 'shady and shabby, covered in dust, fumes, rubbish, with wires and wheels, broken timber and steel, mud and bleak houses dominated by the blind and turpid tips and the awesome pit-gear'.[101] Worse was Landore in Swansea, described in 1949 by one student as 'an industrial wasteland' that was 'camouflaged in acid green and toxic yellow'.[102] The surrounding Tawe valley was still in 1961, in the words of two sociologists, a 'vast and bleak landscape ... of abandoned tips and derelict factories weathered into gaunt and grotesque shapes: a blasted heath covered with the debris of Victorian capitalists'. Building debris was lying around, abandoned houses were left to fall down and rubbish was even accumulating on the new housing estates.[103] Parts of north Wales were not much better. In 1947 a traveller to Corris found himself 'plunged into the gruesome, derelict slate-quarry industry, into a dead, lugubrious world of mountains of dead, grey-black rocks'. Some cottages were empty shells, with trees growing inside them, and some slate roofs were even patched with canvas or corrugated iron. It was a 'monstrous and melancholy tragedy'.[104] A resident of Blaenau Ffestiniog described the town in the 1960s:

> Slate tips dwarf the houses and shops; sheep walk down the middle of the High Street, past Woolworths and the Co-op, to graze in chapel grounds and front gardens or knock over and feed from dustbins in back alleys; decaying sheds and quarry machinery rusting on green hillsides complete a unique urban landscape.[105]

Even Wales' beaches were suffering from oil pollution. This was all not just a matter of aesthetics. Women had to fight to keep homes clean in polluted towns where dust blew in from tips and unmade roads. Moreover, these landscapes were not just places in which people lived. They were mindscapes too, shaping and containing people's perceptions of the worlds they lived in. However comfortable your home, however many consumer durables you owned, this was the kind of world that surrounded the majority of the Welsh people and it was one that reminded them of the past, of hungrier, leaner times, making the age of affluence a fragile one. Yet this did not mean that people looked upon themselves as simply living in an ugly world. People on the sides of the lower Swansea valley were proud of their expansive view across the scarred, polluted land below.[106] A poet summed up in a 1943 radio broadcast:

> We who were born in these valleys know too well that our homes are not among the beautiful places of the earth, but we have, nevertheless, a shrewd idea that there are worse places in the world to live in.
>
> After all, it is not so much the landscape itself that matters. The essence of the thing is often in its associations. Even the old slag-heaps themselves are more than mere slag-heaps to some of us. They are for ever associated with generations of our people who gave so much of their blood and sweat in years gone by. And at present we unconsciously feel that they are part and parcel of our daily lives.[107]

Those associations were a signal of both how far people had come and how incomplete the transformation of affluence was.

Historian Kenneth Morgan has argued that the general tone of the decade from 1951 to 1961 was buoyancy.[108] But the fragility and limited reach of affluence meant that, although people's expectations were raised and they were aware of how much life had changed, there was never a general sense of security in this period. In rural north Wales ordinary people still thought of themselves as 'the poor Welsh country people'.[109] Industrial workers had their fears too. A reporter noted in 1952 that the memory of the depression acted as a brake on how prosperous steelworkers in Ebbw Vale lived, encouraging saving rather than lavish spending.[110] The sense of insecurity in towns with new factories was reinforced by a feeling that consumer products like washing machines were dependent on an unsteady market and others, like toy cars or stockings, were dependent on fashion. There were other things to worry about too; as one 1957 short story put it, 'I've been afraid of too many things. Bailiffs, bosses, dreams, neighbours, new holes.'[111] Even the fruits of affluence brought their own worries and one miner complains in a 1968 novel: 'I can't afford to lose work.... We're paying for the house, the furniture, the telly, every-bloody-thing's on tick!'[112] There were also new social problems rooted in affluence, such as youth crime (see chapter 4) and community disintegration (see chapter 5), as well as less pressing issues such as the emergence of tooth decay among children, caused by a growth of sweet eating. A widespread sense of insecurity was furthered by technological developments such as computers and robots, which, encouraged by the futuristic images in television shows like *The Avengers* and *Doctor Who*, people feared would reduce the need for manual and clerical workers.[113] More than 2,000 people even killed themselves in Wales over the course of the 1950s, presumably because of a lack of love, work or hope.

Most worryingly, the threat of nuclear war continued to be never far away, as the USSR tightened its grip on eastern Europe and the Americans developed a siege mentality towards communism. In 1955 the Labour candidate in Aberavon told his constituency party:

> I find there is no feeling of security amongst the people in foreign affairs not even with the Hydrogen bomb behind us. From a psychological point of view the Hydrogen bomb is most disturbing. There is also a vague feeling that we are living in a phoney economy. An economy that is partially and mainly based on armaments production is bound to be a phoney economy.[114]

A series of international crises – such as the Soviet interventions in Hungary and Czechoslovakia – all created the impression that communism was a threat to world peace and the future of the human race. One student from Tylorstown wrote in his diary during the Cuban missile crisis, 'We live from day to day'.[115] Most people remembered the horrors of the Second World War and many remembered the First World War too. A nuclear conflict, however, would be a completely different affair. In 1953 civil servants estimated that three 'Nagasaki type' bombs might be dropped on Wales in the event of a war with the USSR. Assuming evacuation plans worked, they calculated (or guessed) that some 26,000 people would still be killed in Cardiff, Swansea and Newport. The total death toll in Britain would be over

1.3 million. These were the earliest days of the nuclear threat, which grew and grew as nuclear arsenals gained in size and strength. By the late 1960s RAF Valley, RAF Brawdy, Cardiff and Swansea were thought to be the likely Welsh targets in a nuclear attack, while Brecon was also considered a possibility since it had been mooted as a centre for a regional government in any future war. It was no wonder then that people were frightened. A Gallup survey in 1958 showed that 80 per cent of people thought that less than half the British population would survive a nuclear attack.[116] In a 1962 novel one miner remarks:

> 'people are so bloody daft, mun, it's frightening.… Makes you feel so small, like. But it's no good thinking about it, I suppose; we're helpless; us ordinary chaps, we don't count no more. Not in this world.'
>
> 'Change the subject, Steve, here's the missus with my tea. If you start her off about the bomb, we'll have 'sterics here.'[117]

Such feelings of helplessness led to the formation of the Campaign for Nuclear Disarmament (CND) in 1957. Over 1,000 people attended a public meeting in Aberystwyth in 1958 to form a Welsh council for CND. Its first official event in Wales came in 1959, with a mass rally in Rhyl, where the vice principal of Bala-Bangor Theological College claimed, 'Britain could be completely destroyed in under twenty minutes.… Although a handful of people might survive in the event of an attack they would certainly be barbarians and the human story would have to start from scratch again.'[118] Such a threat compounded the existing danger the Welsh way of life was in and a pamphlet produced for a CND rally in 1961 tried to raise support by declaring in Welsh that nuclear weapons were a threat to the very existence of the Welsh nation and language. CND drew upon support from a wide spectrum of people, especially those with nationalist, socialist and religious sympathies, but quite how many people agreed with Britain disarming while the Soviets still kept their weapons is harder to gauge. When a prominent anti-nuclear meeting was held at the university in Aberystwyth in 1958, only one of some twenty-five professors was prepared to support it, with another expressing a preference for 'being fried alive' to being subject to the Soviets. When another anti-nuclear rally was held by the town's war memorial a year later, ex-service personnel were upset enough for the British Legion to scrub the steps afterwards.[119] Despite the support CND found among trade unionists and churches and chapels, it remained something of a middle-class movement and relied heavily on the support of students and intellectuals. As one historian has pointed out, CND never 'seized the imagination of the majority', who worried about a nuclear war but not enough to 'devote their lives to a crusade against it'.[120] But that does not change the fact that the nuclear threat was another, and very significant, factor that undermined people's sense of security and well-being.

THE INSECURITIES PEOPLE FELT, tempered by rising prosperity, were evident in how they voted. Labour won 57.6 per cent of the Welsh vote at the 1955 general election, 56.4 per cent in 1959 and 57.8 per cent in 1964. In contrast, the Conservatives, who emphasized how they had brought a 'new era' of prosperity and prized Wales' language and culture, won 29.9 per cent (1955), 32.6 per cent (1959) and 29.4 per cent (1964).[121] Geoffrey Howe, standing for the Tories in his native Aberavon, told a party meeting before the 1955 election that in the last year 'the people of this country built more houses, earned higher wages, saved more money, spent more money and ate more food than at any time in their history'. He told the local press that in his canvassing of mining districts he found that 'Many confirmed Labour supporters could find no fault with what the Tory government had done'. Despite the insecurities felt, such arguments were not without foundation and even had a limited effect. Howe never won Aberavon but in 1955 he secured 30.5 per cent of the vote and in 1959 he won 27.6 per cent. The problem his party faced was as much historical as about whether people felt affluent or insecure during the 1950s. Howe recalled getting a friendly welcome across the constituency, even in local mining villages. His family was well known locally and the most frequent greeting he received was 'Pity you're on the wrong side, boyo'. He explained this by claiming that locals thought 'Conservatives to be born complete with horns and cloven hooves'.[122] But Howe's solid vote in a working-class constituency (which was far from alone) did show that, despite the majority's commitment to Labour, some people's attitudes were beginning to shift in the age of affluence.

Historian Andrew Walling has noted that in industrial Wales voting Labour in the 1950s was 'a way of life, passed on from one generation to the next'. There were, however, more positive reasons to vote Labour. The party was promising higher public expenditure and investment in economic development, a modernizing agenda that would bring jobs.[123] In 1963 Prime Minister Sir Alec Douglas-Home had condemned the Labour Party in a speech at Swansea, claiming 'Their Luddism belongs to the nineteenth century, their vocabulary to the twenties and their economic planning ideas are a hangover from the days of post-war shortage and rationing'.[124] The problem was that in Swansea and other parts of Wales such ideas were still needed because the days of plenty were not being shared by all. But the fact that there was clearly some affluence meant that Labour was also caught between accusing the Tories of not delivering prosperity to everyone and denouncing what did exist as fool's gold.[125] Furthermore, the party also had organizational problems that suggest, whatever people might have felt about the long-term prospects of the economy, the general tone of the 1950s was not bad enough to warrant political activism on the part of many voters brought up in a Labour tradition. In both urban and rural Wales, Labour Party membership was falling. In Newport it collapsed from 3,294 in 1950 to under 1,000 in 1964.[126] In 1955 Llanelli MP James Griffiths recorded in his diary that the party was the victim of

> the success of our policies from '45 to '51 – and of the Tories' behaviour in refraining from making frontal attacks on the Welfare State. There was no widespread grievance. Full employment, overtime, increased earnings – all this outweighed the increase in the cost of living.[127]

After that year's general election, the Labour agent in Aberavon complained, 'It's not like it used to be in the old days. The enthusiasm and fire of General Elections seems to have been quenched. Far too many people seem to take too much for granted.'[128] One young miner in a 1966 novel summed up the view of many: 'I'm not politically minded. All I know is I slave for five shifts up in the Druid, and if I could get out of it, I would.'[129] Trade unionism, meanwhile, was slipping from discussing big principles to smaller issues such as the right to smoke in the toilets. In the north Wales coalfield younger miners in the 1950s, who had not known the hardships of the pre-war years, were not as active in the union or Labour Party as their older workmates, but they remained committed to the ideals of the party.[130] Past poverties, present problems and future anxieties were still prevalent enough to secure the majority of working-class votes for Labour but the general raising of living of standards was enough to ensure that that support was something less than the radical mass movement of the past. Rather than being politically active, people were more likely to garden, do odd jobs around the house, have a quiet pint and watch some television.

DOMINIC SANDBROOK HAS suggested that Britain in the 1950s was 'one of the most conservative, stable and contented societies in the world'.[131] There were certainly places in Wales where life was secure and introverted. One literary resident of the Cardiff suburb of Whitchurch complained that it was

> nothing much, a sad coffin of the Tory Macmillan culture of meretricious hollowness [where] … life is too banal and humdrum to accommodate thoughts of calamity of any shape or form.… I believe that even the use of words like love or God in conversation, and the plea for colour tolerance, are considered extreme, sufficient to disperse the company completely.[132]

Across Britain, the rises in living standards were strongest among those on higher incomes, people who lived in places like Whitchurch. The rest of Wales was generally more prosperous than ever before but it remained poorer on average than England. In 1964 the gross domestic product of Wales was 88 per cent of the figure for the UK and lower than that of every English region (although higher than that of either Scotland and Northern Ireland).[133] Even by Welsh standards of affluence, there remained people who were removed from the good times. Those who did not get a new house, a washing machine or a new job were increasingly resentful of it. Those with decent wages and decent jobs were never entirely confident of keeping them, especially if they were old enough to remember the austerity of the 1930s. They were right to worry. With over a quarter of the workforce still employed in metal and mining, the Welsh economy was still fragile. It may have diversified but it was still lacking in the big growth industries of the period that fed English affluence.[134] And then there was the ever-present shadow of the nuclear bomb. Wales, like the rest of Britain, may have been better off, stable and socially conservative, but it was not content.

Notes

1 *WM*, 22 July 1957.
2 D. Sandbrook, *Never Had It So Good: A History of Britain from Suez to the Beatles* (2005), 178.
3 R. Lewis, *Wealth for Wales* (Conservative Party, 1964), 11. *Board of Trade Journal*, 10 Jan. 1958. *WM*, 4 July 1958.
4 G. Humphrys, *South Wales* (1972), 133, 76.
5 Lewis, *Wealth for Wales*, 9. *The Times*, 2 Mar. 1963. See also *Guardian*, 2 Mar. 1963.
6 G. L. Rees, *Survey of the Welsh Economy*, Commission on the Constitution research papers (1973), 56, 58.
7 *Report on Government Action in Wales and Monmouthshire 1955–56*, NA, LAB 43/252.
8 M. Jones, *A Radical Life: The Biography of Megan Lloyd George, 1902–66* (1991), 302.
9 *DWS*, 5, 1958 (1959), 26, 30. Lewis, *Wealth for Wales*, 15.
10 M. Gallie, *The Small Mine* ([1962] 2000), 9, 116.
11 R. Berry, *Full Time Amateur* (1966), 69.
12 *Rhondda Fach Observer, Leader and Free Press*, 29 Apr. 1961. L. Jones, ‘Coal’, in B. Thomas (ed.), *The Welsh Economy* (1962), 106–7.
13 *DWS*, 10, 1963 (1964), 38. F. Zweig, *Men in the Pits* (1949), 103.
14 Humphrys, *South Wales*, 116. Jones, ‘Coal’, 93. B. Thomas, ‘Post-war expansion’, in Thomas (ed.), *The Welsh Economy*, 37.
15 T. Brennan, E. W. Cooney and H. Pollins, *Social Change in South-West Wales* (1954), 50.

Wales Can Make It: The Success Story of Our New Industries (booklet of reprints from *WM*, 1958).
16 L. Abse, *Private Member* (1973), 25.
17 Quoted in H. Francis and D. Smith, *The Fed: A History of the South Wales Miners* (1998 edn), 449.
18 A. Horner, *Incorrigible Rebel* (1960), 192, 221–2.
19 G. Humphrys, 'The coal industry', in G. Manners (ed.), *South Wales in the Sixties* (1964), 88–89. *DWS*, 1 (1954) and11 (1964).
20 Humphrys, *South Wales*, 41. *Guardian*, 29 Dec. 1961.
21 *SWEP*, 9 Dec. 1957 and 4 Jan. 1958. *WM*, 23 July 1957.
22 Lewis, *Wealth for Wales*, 5. J. England, *The Wales TUC: Devolution and Industrial Politics* (2004), 8.
23 *Arcade*, 5 (9 Jan. 1981).
24 D. Holding and T. Moyes, *History of British Bus Services: South Wales* (1986), 57.
25 Humphrys, *South Wales*, 12. *Observer Magazine*, 30 Oct. 1966. R. Fevre, *Wales Is Closed: The Quiet Privatisation of British Steel* (1989), 21.
26 I. Gazeley, *Poverty in Britain, 1900–1965* (2003), 161. E. Nevin, A. R. Roe and J. I. Round, *The Structure of the Welsh Economy* (1966), 7.
27 Rees, *Survey of the Welsh Economy*, 32. Figures exclude self-employed.
28 Lewis, *Wealth for Wales*, 21–2. C. Rosser and C. Harris, *The Family and Social Change: A Study of Family and Kinship in a South Wales Town* (1965), 78.
29 Nevin *et al.*, *The Structure of the Welsh Economy*, 25.
30 Ministry of Labour, *Report of an Enquiry into Household Expenditure in 1953–54* (1957). J. Parry Lewis, 'Income and consumers' expenditure', in Thomas (ed.), *The Welsh Economy*, 167.
31 Calculated from census classifications. Humphrys, 'Coal industry', 75.
32 C. Baber and L. Mainwaring, 'Steel', in K. D. George and L. Mainwaring (eds), *The Welsh Economy* (1988), 214.
33 Humphrys, *South Wales*, 30.
34 See for example B. M. Brunt, *The Contemporary Economic Problems in Merthyr Tydfil* (1972).
35 Rees, *Survey of the Welsh Economy*, 144. In the same period, 49,540 economically active people moved into Wales.
36 Lewis, *Wealth for Wales*, 29.
37 *Ibid.*, 10, 14.
38 *DWS*, 5 (1958), 56.
39 Quoted in M. S. Tibbott, 'Going electric: the changing face of the rural kitchen in Wales, 1945–55', *Folk Life*, 28 (1990), 70. C. Hughes, *The Civil Strangers* (1949), 40. M. Francis, 'Cwato dan Ford', in H. Wyn (ed), *Mam-gu, Siân Hwêl a Naomi: Hanes a Hudoliaeth Bro Maenclochog* (2006), 431.
40 D. Beddoe (ed.), *Changing Times: Welsh Women Writing on the 1950s and 1960s* (2003), 88. Tibbott, 'Going electric', 66.
41 Tibbott, 'Going electric', 65.
42 *CJ*, 29 Sep. 1950.
43 Beddoe, *Changing Times*, 145.
44 S. Phillips, *Private Faces: The Autobiography* (1999), 73. D. Beddoe, *Out of the Shadows: A History of Women in Twentieth Century Wales* (2000), 146. *Rhondda Fach Observer, Leader and Free Press*, 18 Nov. 1961.
45 Rees, *Survey of the Welsh Economy*, 118. A. Sampson, *The Anatomy of Britain* (1965), 622.
46 Tibbott, 'Going electric'. Brennan *et al.*, *Social Change*, 102.
47 Abse, *Private Member*, 30.
48 Rosser and Harris, *The Family and Social Change*, 83–4.
49 Tibbott, 'Going electric', 68. *Guardian*, 11 Oct. 1968.
50 N. Jones, *Living in Rural Wales* (1993), 121.
51 I. Emmett, *A North Wales Village: A Social Anthropological Study* (1964), 19–21.

52 'Marketing information: Swansea and south-west Wales', section VIII of *Scanning the Provinces* (4th edition), Northcliffe Newspapers (nd), 4–7.
53 K. J. Evans, *The Secret History of Llanelli Co-operative, 1895–2000* (2000), 298–322.
54 Calculated from Department of Industry, *Report on the Census of Distribution and Other Services 1971, Part 3 Area Tables Wales* (1975). *The Times*, 9 Mar. 1959.
55 A. McCulloch at 'Your 1960s: shopping', at news.bbc.co.uk/1/hi/magazine/6707573.stm.
56 *DWS*, 16 (1970), 92. M. Stacey, *The Human Ecology of the Lower Swansea Valley* (1962), 32.
57 Rees, *Survey of the Welsh Economy*, 70.
58 J. H. Richards, 'Transport', and B. Thomas, 'Conclusion', in Thomas (ed.), *The Welsh Economy*, 144, 199.
59 See for example *Denbighshire Free Press and North Wales Times*, 30 Apr. 1960.
60 Holding and Moyes, *History of British Bus Services*, 78–9.
61 Humphrys, *South Wales*, 97–102.
62 *A Promised Land*, HTV broadcast, 29 Apr. 2004.
63 *Daily Mirror*, 26 June 1952. Beddoe, *Changing Times*, 30. Francis, 'Cwato dan Ford', 431.
64 J. Davies, *Broadcasting and the BBC in Wales* (1994), 199–201. Rees, *Survey of the Welsh Economy*, 47. Complaints about poor television reception in parts of Wales, NA, BD 24/200.
65 L. Ebenezer, *Cae Marged* (1991), 85.
66 D. Sandbrook, *White Heat: A History of Britain in the Swinging Sixties* (2006), 376. Davies, *Broadcasting and the BBC*, 258. Rosser and Harris, *The Family and Social Change*, 1.
67 Lord Cledwyn, 'Wales: yesterday and tomorrow', lecture at National Eisteddfod, Bro Colwyn, 1995, 5.
68 Council for Wales and Monmouthshire, *Report on the Rural Transport Problem in Wales*, Cmnd 1821 (1962). M. Benbough-Jackson, *Cardiganshire* (2007), 131. J. Davies, *A History of Wales* (1993), 635.
69 See for example R. Berry, *Hunters and Hunted* (1960), 174.
70 *South Wales Argus*, 5 Apr. 1963.
71 Quoted in Sandbrook, *Never Had It So Good*, 390–1.
72 Calculated from *DWHS-2*, 88. Rees, *Survey of the Welsh Economy*, 45.
73 *Wales and Monmouthshire: Report of Government Action for the Year Ended 30 June 1956*, Cmd 9887 (1956). Rosser and Harris, *The Family and Social Change*, 62. A. Walling, 'The structure of power in Labour Wales, 1951–1964', in D. Tanner, C. Williams and D. Hopkin (eds), *The Labour Party in Wales, 1900–2000* (2000), 206.
74 Rees, *Survey of the Welsh Economy*, 44. *Welsh House Condition Survey 1968* (1969).
75 Transcript of Welsh Grand Committee, second sitting, 24 Mar. 1965, 'Mid-Wales development and depopulation', c. 81. Humphrys, *South Wales*, 26.
76 Rees, *Survey of the Welsh Economy*, 44–5. D. W. Drakakis-Smith, 'Substandard housing in Welsh towns', in H. Carter and W. K. D. Davies, *Urban Essays: Studies in the Geography of Wales* (1970). *Sample Census 1966: England and Wales, Housing Tables Part 1* (1968), 148.
77 Calculated from Ministry of Housing and Local Government, *Slum Clearance (England and Wales)*, Cmd 9593 (1955), 51.
78 *Rhondda Fach Observer, Leader and Free Press*, 14 Jan. 1961.
79 Gallie, *Small Mine*, 15.
80 Quoted in M. Akhtar and S. Humphries, *The Fifties and the Sixties: A Lifestyle Revolution* (2001), 78.
81 Rosser and Harris, *The Family and Social Change*, 266. A. Llwyd, *Black Wales: A History* (2005), 156. *SWEP*, 20 Oct. 1961 and 15 May 1962.
82 Calculated from *DWS*, 11, 1961 (1962), 11.
83 *Census 1951 England and Wales: Housing Report* (1956), 63. Rees, *Survey of the Welsh Economy*, 46. Humphrys, *South Wales*, 104.
84 Rosser and Harris, *The Family and Social Change*, 62, 64, 66. Emmett, *A North Wales Village*, 37.
85 Calculated from *Sample Census 1966: England and Wales, Housing Tables Part 1* (1968), 125.

86 L. Brito, 'Staying power', in *Cardiff Central: Ten Welsh Writers Return to the Welsh Capital* (2003), 47.
87 G. Harbour, 'Housing', in George and Mainwaring (eds), *The Welsh Economy*, 64.
88 D. Leonard, *Sex and Generation: A Study of Courtship and Weddings* (1980), 225.
89 M. Stephens, 'A small house in Meadow Street', *Pl*, 105 (1994), 81–6. H. Hopkins, *The New Look: A Social History of the Forties and Fifties in Britain* (1963), 333.
90 Stacey, *The Human Ecology*, 31.
91 A. Richards, *Dai Country* (1973), 108–9.
92 C. Hughes, 'Charm of the past in a changing Wales', *Times Literary Supplement*, 16 Aug. 1957.
93 *South Wales Argus*, 21 May 1966.
94 Gazeley, *Poverty in Britain*, 172–8, 184. On the rediscovery of poverty see Donnelly, *Sixties Britain*, ch. 9.
95 *Merthyr Express*, 11 Jan. 1964.
96 *South Wales Argus*, 21 May 1966.
97 Emmett, *A North Wales Village*, 80, 34.
98 J. T. Hart, 'A forgotten war', in P. H. Ballard and E. Jones (eds), *The Valleys Call* (1975), 184–99.
99 *DWS*, 5, 1958 (1959), 12.
100 *Rhondda Fach Observer, Leader and Free Press,* 4 Mar. 1961.
101 Zweig, *Men in the Pits*, 43.
102 Quoted in Z. Leader, *The Life of Kingsley Amis* (2006), 241–2.
103 Rosser and Harris, *The Family and Social Change*, 42. Stacey, *The Human Ecology*, 27.
104 W. Wilkinson, *Puppets in Wales* (1948), 175.
105 I. Emmett, 'Blaenau boys in the mid-1960s', in G. Williams (ed.), *Social and Cultural Change in Contemporary Wales* (1978), 87.
106 *The Times*, 22 Jan. 1952. Stacey, *The Human Ecology*, 21, 24, 34.
107 I. Davies, 'Valleys' (1943), in P. Hannan (ed.), *Wales on the Wireless* (1988), 55–6.
108 K. O. Morgan, *The People's Peace: British History, 1945–1990* (1990), 194.
109 Emmett, *A North Wales Village*, 17.
110 *Picture Post*, 16 Aug. 1952.
111 M. Jones, *Life on the Dole* (1972), 65–6. G. Thomas, *Selected Short Stories* (1984), 67.
112 R. Berry, *Flame and Slag* (1968), 88.
113 *Monmouthshire County Council, 1888–1974* (1974), 115. Sandbrook, *White Heat*, 45–6.
114 *Glamorgan Gazette*, 6 May 1955.
115 John Morgans, *Journey of a Lifetime* (2008), 112 (diary entry, 23 Oct. 1962).
116 P. Hennessy, *The Secret State: Whitehall and the Cold War* (2002), 128–9, 164–7. Sandbrook, *Never Had It So Good*, 273.
117 Gallie, *Small Mine*, 11.
118 Meeting to form Welsh Council, Aberdare, 20 Sep. 1958, NLW, CND Cymru papers, A5. *LDP*, 16 Sep. 1959.
119 CND Welsh Council, 'An all-Wales rally', 20 May 1961, NLW, CND Cymru papers, A5. M. Davies, 'Bertrand Russell in Aberystwyth', *Pl*, 103 (1994), 76–80.
120 Sandbrook, *Never Had It So Good*, 274.
121 'A new era for Wales', Conservative Party election leaflet, 1959.
122 *Port Talbot Guardian*, 6 May 1955. Undated *SWEP* clipping 1955, NLW, Lord Howe of Aberavon papers, FACS 1007. Geoffrey Howe, *Conflict of Loyalty* (1994), 28–9.
123 Walling, 'The structure of power', 193.
124 Quoted in Sandbrook, *White Heat*, 9.
125 J. Tomlinson, 'Economic growth, economic decline', in K. Burke (ed.), *The British Isles since 1945* (2003), 65–6.
126 Walling, 'The structure of power', 202–3.
127 J. Griffiths, *Pages from Memory* (1969), 142.
128 Undated clipping from *SWEP*, 1955, NLW, Howe papers, FACS 1007.

129 R. Berry, *Full Time Amateur* (1966), 33.
130 Brennan *et al.*, *Social Change*, 5. K. Gildart, *North Wales Miners: A Fragile Unity, 1945–1996* (2001), 36.
131 Sandbrook, *Never Had It So Good*, 31.
132 J. Tripp, 'Living on the strip', *Pl*, 44 (1978), 33.
133 Gazeley, *Poverty in Britain*, 161–3. Rees, *Survey of the Welsh Economy*, 114.
134 G. Manners, 'A profile of the new south Wales', in Manners (ed.), *South Wales in the Sixties*, 59.

4

'Promiscuous living.' Youth culture and the permissive society, 1951–70

> It seems that the present-day problem of delinquency and moral standards is seriously complicated by the efforts to shock or [an] unhealthy obsession with sex.... Our young people are not given the opportunity to realise that unhappiness and sorrow can result from promiscuous living.
>
> Representative of the Townswomen's Guilds in South Wales, 1963 [1]

> Perhaps the most surprising thing about the permissive society in Wales is that it does exist.
>
> *Western Mail*, 20 June 1969

IN SEPTEMBER 1956 Bill Haley's film *Rock Around the Clock* was released across Britain. It awoke the media to a bewildering and shocking new craze called rock'n'roll. A family doctor told readers of the *South Wales Echo* that the film was horrible, 'an uncouth bedlam of sound' that revolved around the 'abuse of decent musical instruments and the debasement of music itself'. He was particularly shocked by the effect it had on the audience: 'They clapped, howled, hissed, yelled. They got out of their seats and performed horrid contortions all over the place. Not content with this, they smashed up seats, tore fire extinguishers from places and generally ran amok.' This was symptomatic, he maintained, of youth the world over in a 'neurotic age', with its easy money, poor discipline, misguided education and lax morals.[2]

In Newport, identified by a cinema company as 'a likely trouble spot', the fears surrounding the film meant that police were put on standby and the film opened on a Monday rather than at the weekend. After the Newport audience inevitably created the now 'ritualistic' trouble, an editorial in a local paper reflected that those authorities that had banned the film had made the right decision. It put the behaviour down to parental laxity and mistaken kindness with young children.[3] Yet, while some were agonizing over what jiving teenagers meant, others were less anxious and the Welsh press also published articles pointing out that the ripping of seats and teenage violence were actually nothing new. Indeed, nor was there trouble everywhere and the secretary of a Cardiff youth club congratulated both teenagers on their behaviour and a cinema manager who had told the audience that they could jive as long as they did no damage and no one got on stage.[4]

The contrast with the stark, formal world of the chapel could not be more obvious. Everything, from the sound and the clothes to the sheer exuberance of the music, was new and captivating. Even in rural villages, teenagers tried to imitate Haley's kiss curl. One trainee priest had to wear his drainpipe trousers under his normal ones to avoid the condemnation of his landlady when he went to see the film in Aberystwyth. He changed on the bus. When Haley played a concert in Cardiff in 1957 there were 60,000 requests for tickets. The queue to get in was more than a quarter of a mile long and, when a nearby music shop put on some rock'n'roll records, those queuing began to dance in the street. The theatre manager proclaimed he had never seen anything like it in his twenty years in the business.[5]

Haley actually turned thirty-one in 1956 and was perhaps a little old to be the teenage icon he was, but he was soon followed by more glamorous, better-looking and more musical heroes, the most significant of whom was, of course, Elvis Presley. 'The King' was handsome, musical, very cool and integral to making popular music more than just entertainment. Meic Stevens, later a singer himself, remembered being simply amazed on hearing Presley's 'Heartbreak hotel'. He never heard anything like it and asked 'what the hell music is that'?[6] For teenagers, Elvis was the voice of defiance and they copied his hair and clothes. The impact of rock'n'roll was thus not just about the music: it was about growing up, maturing sexually and coming to terms with who you were and who you wanted to be. A Newport man born in 1943 thought he was on his 'way to being a missionary' but then 'I heard Little Richard, Chuck Berry and then Elvis, [and] everything changed'.[7] For girls, crushes on Elvis and others could be deeply intense and personal, much more than simply being about looks or the music. In such a world the traditional dances that had been so popular during the war seemed staid and people found themselves waiting for the band to finish so they could dance to the rock'n'roll records that were played in the interval.[8]

Historian Eric Hobsbawm has claimed that 'Suez and the coming of rock-and-roll divide twentieth century British history'.[9] In fact, youth culture, and concern about it, had much older roots but its importance, profile and impact did explode in the 1950s.[10] Rock'n'roll was more than just another teenage craze. It was to become not only a big business but a symbol of how far the age of affluence was changing life, for good or bad. It was the beginning of a revolution in popular culture that was to mark the second half of the twentieth century. This revolution belonged to the young. Their apparent self-confidence was obvious in their dress and music, and that engendered an association between youth, rebellion and a breakdown in public behaviour and morality. The 1950s and 1960s were thus an era when teenagers in particular became a topic of social comment and social concern.

INTEGRAL TO THE ATTRACTION of rock'n'roll was that it was American. The cinema already ensured that the USA, with its tough gangsters, beautiful dames and Wild West cowboys, held a glamorous appeal for young people.[11] This was evident in how American phrases began to pepper both Welsh and English, to the annoyance of many purists. As early as 1942, a *Daily Mirror* reporter had noted teenagers in a Caernarfon cinema speaking Welsh until one remarked of the actress on screen: 'Say, boys, ain't she sure a hot momma, eh?' It was the only English they spoke all conversation.[12] Among English speakers in the south, the meeting of cultures could be just as blunt, as one 1955 novel illustrated: '"Where'd you blow in from? What is this?" he asked in Welsh-American; then, reverting engagingly to Welsh-English: "Bloody terrible head I've got, man. Fell over. Spewed too … *Ach-y-fi*, eh?"'[13] Over the course of the 1950s television too meant that 'America was scorched and burnt' into the consciousness of teenagers, as one of them later put it.[14] An anthropologist noted in 1964 that for the young in the Welsh countryside, 'Films, radio and television bring the world of big towns near, familiar and unfrightening', making it easier for them to decide to move away from their rural communities. Even for adults, American images were aspirational, a sign that affluence could be real and more rewarding than its British equivalent.[15]

The perceived impact of cinema and television was much more than just raising people's aspirations and widening their horizons. In 1963 a lady from Brynmawr complained: 'Far too frequently we see films showing scenes where young people are flouting authority and the law is treated with disrespect and brutality. We read almost daily of bank robberies, post office hold ups by masked men and of small shopkeepers being beaten up.' She felt this was the 'aftermath of many films on television and that the young hooligans who roam our own streets with coshes and bicycle chains are imitation of these films and plays'.[16] Crime did become a significant social concern in the 1950s and 1960s, exacerbated by the attention the press lavished on it. There were some well reported gruesome murders to fuel both people's curiosity and horror. In 1953, for example, a St Clears farmer and his wife were beaten to death with a hammer by a nephew who wanted the farm and money.[17] Beyond such newspaper stories, there was more definite evidence of rising crime. Indictable recorded crime in Wales increased by 60.5 per cent between 1949 and 1959 (compared with 46.9 per cent in England and Wales combined) and by 160.2 per cent between 1959 and 1969 (compared with 120.3 per cent in England and Wales). At one level such statistics were evidence of a more effective or interventionist police force and a greater willingness of people to report offences, but they also marked a real rise in crime. What worried people most about this was the increase in violent offences. In 1949, there were just 292 indictable offences of violence against the person known to the police in Wales. By 1959, there were 920 and in 1969 there were 2,029. By this measure, violent crime had risen by 595 per cent in twenty years. The blame for rising crime was often attributed to people's standards having changed during the war, when shortages led many to turn to the black market, petty theft and minor abuse of regulations and coupons. But affluence was contributing too. The typical person and home had more things that could be stolen and there was, according to the chief constable of Glamorgan at least, a class of person who now expected luxuries and would turn to crime to get them. This was evident in the figures for breaking and entering in Wales, which rose from 3,996 in 1949 to 6,151 in 1959 and 17,542 in 1969.[18]

Of all the causes of crime, the most popular culprits to blame were the young. Across the UK, the behaviour of first Teddy boys and then mods, rockers and young people in general became the topic of much consternation and was widely regarded as a symbol of collapsing moral standards. In 1948, of persons found guilty in Wales of indictable offences 22.5 per cent were aged between fourteen and twenty-one. In 1958 the figure was 31.5 per cent and in 1968 it was 40.8 per cent.[19] The press certainly dwelled upon incidents that suggested youth violence was a significant problem. On Guy Fawkes night 1965, for example, 200 youths in Cardiff were said to have thrown bricks at firemen answering a call, perhaps made for that purpose, while in Penarth 300 youths smashed the windows of shops, restaurants and hotels.[20] After two nights of pitched battles between youths from Caerphilly and Cardiff in the summer of 1966, an editorial in a local paper worried about the threat of '"gangster" combats'. It noted rather sensationally:

> so many youngsters today have cars, motor-cycles, scooters and other forms of transport that they can descend swiftly on any district and explode into frenzied action.... Those of us who are parents have a further duty; we

> must exercise greater control over our teenage children and make them realise how senseless and dangerous these outbreaks of mass hysteria are. If we cannot stamp out savage unruliness by precept and example, then the courts will have to mete out condign punishment to teenagers who act like gangsters and hoodlums. Teenage mob violence must be stopped![21]

Even in a small town like Blaenau Ffestiniog, fights became so common in the mid-1960s that the local dance was closed down. There were different youth groups in the town, such as rockers and mods, but people knew each other too well for there to be gangs or any serious or sustained fighting. Local skinheads did travel to Pwllheli and Rhyl armed with razor blades but, despite the occasional fight, much of such behaviour appears to have been threat rather than substance. Although much of the violence might not actually have been particularly serious, disorder was becoming an increasing concern in rural towns. In 1958 Carmarthenshire and Cardiganshire Police Authority heard complaints of hooliganism and rowdyism on Saturday nights throughout its area but especially in Carmarthen, where some people thought it was not safe to walk through certain streets at night. Most of the trouble was after closing time and licensees conceded there was a 'minority of hooligans' who descended upon the town. But trouble was not just the preserve of teenage gangs. In 1965 some Cardiff hotels considered closing for rugby internationals because of the vandalism they were witnessing. One reported that after a Wales–England game it had had its chandeliers ripped down and 5,000 glasses broken, not to mention people urinating in the lounge and a male striptease.[22]

Why youth crime was on the up is not straightforward. There was a perception that the instability and excitement of war, as well as the increased number of broken homes in the wake of the conflict, had unsettled many young people.[23] But the kind of tough masculinity that led teenage boys and young men to fight had older roots. Being physically strong had always mattered to working-class men because it helped them earn a living. The fathers of teenagers in the 1950s and 1960s had often been able to prove their own masculinity in the war or in heavy industry. Their sons did not have the first opportunity and were increasingly less likely to have the second. But traditional masculinity still mattered to them and the singer Tom Jones, the son of a miner, recalled fighting to prove his toughness because it was suspect when he sang solo in the chapel.[24] Inevitably, alcohol was to blame for much of the trouble. Affluence was good news for pubs and clubs and the 1960s saw many drinking institutions undergo renovations and expansions to meet increased demand. People had certainly always fought after having too much to drink but now young people could afford to drink more and pubs did not seem too concerned about enforcing age restrictions. Certainly in Carmarthen, the police in the 1950s were complaining that drinking was increasing, especially among the under-thirties.[25] Studies in Swansea in the late 1960s suggested that boys and girls typically had their first alcoholic drink with friends when aged thirteen or fourteen, while boys often began to drink heavily at fifteen or sixteen, when they could get away with it in pubs. Drinking was thus an integral part of teenage socialising and it marked a rite of passage of its own. In 1956 a young woman complained to the *Carmarthen Journal* that it was no wonder that drinking was on the increase given the lack of facilities locally for school leavers. 'So', she appealed, 'get out of those bath-chairs, councillors, and try and remember that you, too, were young once'.[26] Even when alcohol was not involved, the social lives of the young increasingly showed the disdain that rock'n'roll encapsulated for older notions of respectability. This was evident at a youth club in Kenfig Hill in the early 1960s, which took place in a chapel. Pews were pushed to the side and a record player brought in and set to full volume. The local teenagers 'brought our 78s, and taught each other to jive before snogging and smoking in the dark rooms and cellars adjoining the vestry'.[27] The young may have always misbehaved and questioned authority but doing so in a chapel was surely a sign of changing times.

The affluence that enabled the young to drink so much was a cause for concern in itself. Living at home with rising wages and a relatively healthy job market meant that the young were well placed and well able to enjoy their youth. By the early 1960s teenagers had an average of wage of £10 per week, of which some 70 per cent was disposable income. The affluence and hedonism of teenage life were evident in a study of fifteen- to seventeen-year-olds in the lower Swansea valley, who were all earning 'good money' in the steelworks in the early 1960s. Twenty-nine per cent of them went out, to the cinema, pubs, dances and sports, seven nights a week and another 58 per cent went out four or five times a week.[28] The affluence of the young was also evident in the importance they were able to place on fashion and being of the moment. Welfare hall cinemas complained that when they were unable to get hold of the big films until months after release the pictures lost their 'glamour' and 'the winner of today becomes a very ordinary picture'.[29] Indeed, the young now expected to be able to enjoy themselves. In 1961 a man from Cardigan wrote to the *Western Mail* to complain about young people. He spoke of 'immoral commercialism' and young people's belief in their right to have 'plenty of spending money'. He compared their position with the condition of disabled ex-servicemen and spoke of the 'jungle of conscienceless affluence, in which the Prime Minister and his fellows think we "Never had it so good"'. Similarly, a letter to the *South Wales Argus* in 1963 complained that the young were 'squandering' what the older generation had 'scraped and struggled to save during the depression years on American records and suits at cabinet minister prices'.[30]

Complaints that affluence was hurting rather than helping the youth were common and fuelled by how visibly different youth culture was becoming from what preceded it. The sight of 'macho, sweaty, gum-chewing Teddy boy clones with string ties and sideburns' might excite girls of the same age but to the older generation it was bewildering, precisely as it was meant to be.[31] A miner born in 1945 remembered:

> We used to wear Teddy Boy trousers to work, and the older men used to really have a go at us. 'What's the world coming to,' you know, 'how ridiculous you look'. It was an era where you were [*sic*], you stood out in many ways – probably the first of young people to really stand out and take on the challenge of adults.[32]

As a young male character noted in a 1962 novel, it was worth getting drunk just to annoy your mother.[33] Even in the early 1950s sociologists noted that young people, especially women, were clashing with their parents over issues like drinking and smoking. Their high spirits were evident in public places, even on Sundays, and, while such behaviour was not unique to Wales, its perceived novelty there was thought to cause more acute personal disputes and anxiety than elsewhere.[34] Some parents were certainly shamed or embarrassed by their children's haircuts and clothes. In Blaenau Ffestiniog long-haired men were even thought to be 'literally sick in the mind, perverse and in need of treatment'.[35] Pupils were sent home from school for wearing winkle-pickers and one Cardiff headmaster complained in 1963, 'There is such a lot that lacks taste today'.[36] But such things were ultimately presentational issues that were unlikely to undermine society, as the more measured were well aware. One woman recalled her friend coming back to Wales from London with white boots and 'masses of eye make-up, including false eyelashes and painted-on eyelashes underneath, and white lipstick'. Inspired, she went to London herself and bought a 'white PVC mac with black buttons from Miss Selfridge'. Rather than being shocked, people kept making jokes about her looking like a lollipop lady.[37] A male quarry worker remembered, 'People made remarks about our long hair – were we trying to be women and so forth, but quite a lot of us worked in the quarry and so from the other men the antagonism couldn't be that great. They judged us by what we did, not what we looked like. They took the mick out of us for our hair, yes, but we did the same work.'[38]

The fact that the generation gap was not always as wide as the contemporary press or popular memory sometimes suggested is reinforced by the fact that most teenagers did not look or behave outlandishly in the 1950s and 1960s. As common as drinking beer, if not more common, was drinking coffee, studying, reading, playing sports, watching television and going to the pictures. Some teenagers were even praying. But most of all they were listening to music, something which was associated with the idea of rebellion and youth even for people who still dressed like their mothers or fathers. Sandbrook argues that Britain at the end of the 1950s was still a world of 'anglers, knitters and amateur footballers'.[39] That was still true a decade later but even for the studious and the 'square' the mental horizons of being young did change in the 1950s and 1960s. Even if teenagers knitted or played football rather than go to dances or fight, they could still listen to rock'n'roll and the invention of cheap transistor radios, bought or homemade, allowed them to do so in bed or in their own rooms, free from family disapproval, even on the Sabbath. The fact that, before the launch of BBC Radio 1 in 1967, the stations playing rock'n'roll were 'pirate' stations added to the sense of rebellion that simply listening could engender. Not every teenager was committing crime, wearing their hair long and drinking to excess, but it was becoming the norm to question received values and just be conscious that being a teenager was different to being older. This was evident in young people's attitudes to Welsh choirs. *The Times* remarked in 1968 that 'To those young ones who are not musically-inclined the choir is an old-fashioned institution of mums and dads; to those who are, it is an enemy rather than a friend because of its self-satisfied repertory, an obsolete barrier to the things they want to hear'. Starved of young people, by the end of the decade choirs were said to be closing 'rather faster than the pits'.[40]

Male teenagers of the 1950s and early 1960s also had a distinct period and sense of being young enforced on them by the knowledge that it would be curtailed at eighteen by national service. In later years conscription would be called for to mould young people but what it actually did was create a sense of abandonment for those waiting to be called up. National service postponed the responsibilities of adulthood and created a breathing space for some fun between the enforced disciplines of school and call-up. The National Service Act, seen as a necessity for national security rather than an exercise in character building for young men, meant that from 1949 all eighteen-year-old males had to spend eighteen months in the forces, a period extended to two years during the Korean War. Even once that period was up, these men still had to spend the next four years in reserve, ready to be called upon in a national emergency. Initially, opposition was more serious in Wales than elsewhere. Over 700 Welsh organizations, including churches, trade union branches and young farmers' clubs, passed resolutions that branded conscription 'an injustice to Wales'. Twenty Welsh MPs voted against the National Service Bill's second reading. The only Conservative MP in Britain to vote against it was Colonel Price-White (Caernarfon Boroughs), who did so on his constituents' wishes. The opposition was rooted in reasons as diverse as the potential impact on industry, Welsh nationalism, Nonconformist pacifism and even fears that young men would be exposed to drink.[41] Yet, after the initial controversy of its introduction, there was little real opposition to peacetime military conscription, even when troops saw active service in Malaya, Cyprus and Kenya. As the newspaper *Y Faner* put it, parents would not see 'much harm' in a year's 'military disciple' for eighteen-year-old boys.[42]

National service continued until 1963 and some 5,000–6,000 Welshmen entered the army every year. Just as they had been during the war, these young men were lifted out of their communities and forced to live, work and fight alongside their peers from across Britain, creating a sense of both difference and unity. Wyn Roberts, the son of an Anglesey minister but educated at Harrow, found himself with a host of Geordies, of whom he hardly understood a word except for the swearing.[43] Welsh recruits were told by the army to describe themselves on their registration forms as 'British (Welsh)' and informed that Welsh should not be listed when they were asked if they could speak a foreign language. Yet enlistment tests did cause some embarrassment among recruits with a poor command of English. A third of recruits were allocated to the Welsh Brigade but the rest were scattered across the forces. Miners and agricultural workers could be exempted and some young men in mining areas did decide to go down the pit to avoid military service.[44] But national service was a chance to see something of the world and experience life beyond the confines and constrictions of close Welsh communities. Indeed, drinking and sex, or at least seeking those pleasures, defined the period of service for many. Nonetheless, one signalman recalled, 'My service taught me self-confidence, taught me comradeship, understanding of my fellowmen, discipline and appreciation of my home and parents. I returned to Caernarvon a very responsible adult.'[45] The experience, though, changed others so much that their ambitions grew and they left Wales forever. But it could also be a frustrating time that had no obvious function and seemed merely to put wider life on hold. One Welsh soldier recalled, 'It was always like that, preparing for a war we never went to. Not that we were particularly keen to see foreign parts where the bullets were flying.... Boredom was worn like a second skin.' Discipline could be harsh and the army was run through with the hierarchies, mores and snobberies of the English class system, which engendered a sense of apprehension among Welsh people who became officers. Others hated the dull work, the enforced haircuts and the 'monstrous crushing of individuality, and its habitual whim of sending young men to some unpronounceable place to get killed by strangers'.[46] A government committee claimed in 1955 that most men regarded their service 'as an infliction to be undergone rather than a duty to the nation'. As a novel of the time noted, 'He said he joined the Army to get out of the mines, but now he can't wait to get back'.[47]

THE STATE'S INSISTENCE on national service thus helped create the idea of 'the teenager'. Older adults reinforced that by giving it official recognition and looking to make money from the concept through promoting and selling dances, teenage clothing and the like. For those who stayed on in education or were working but not yet tied down by marriage and children this teenage culture extended into their twenties. Its acceptance was shown by the fact that by 1960 many local papers had teenage pages and popular music columns. Jukeboxes had been put in many cafés and some local eisteddfodau had introduced modern music categories. Yet how music and youth culture would develop still remained unclear. A Cardiff shipworker who played in a rock'n'roll band said in 1961, 'it's very popular up to now. But now the trend seems to be for ballads and slower numbers. Also numbers which are a lot more musical even. I think that's the thing of the future.'[48] At the start of 1963, a weekly fashion, film and music page in the *Wrexham Leader* announced that country and western would continue in its ascendancy on the music scene. That year was to see the paper proved very wrong when four lads from Liverpool took the music scene by storm and revolutionized the whole standing of youth culture. The Beatles played nine gigs in Wales in their short touring career and Beatle-mania was as strong there as anywhere. Crowds queued for hours to see them. Boys began to dress like them. Girls, as a newspaper noted of a 1964 Cardiff concert, 'clasped their faces, they moaned with delight, they bounced on their chairs with joy, they screeched, they waved, they yelled, cried, whistled, swooned, laughed, shouted, went wild'. A fourteen-year-old from Newport who saw the band in 1963 remembered, 'Being a good grammar school girl, I had decided beforehand that although I loved the Beatles, especially George, I wasn't going to do any screaming. However, when they appeared on stage, all that was forgotten and I screamed along with the rest. It was a magical time.' Although many wondered how long it would last, by 1964 the centrality of the Beatles to mainstream culture was such that the *South Wales Echo* made their return from the USA the front-page headline and the paper issued a sixteen-page supplement to mark the release of their film *A Hard Day's Night*, a film seen by some 50,000 in Cardiff during its first week of release. The band was still, of course, a minority taste but to some this was all evidence that the country was heading in the wrong direction. After an appearance by the Beatles in Llandudno, a letter in a local paper complained of 'the unbelievable display of mass hysteria'.[49] A letter to the *Wrexham Leader* in 1963 said that the young had been 'brainwashed by the commercial pop kings of the disc world'.[50] Teachers and hairdressers worried about the long hair that the band was encouraging in boys and a Colwyn Bay headmaster reflected, 'I will not be surprised if historians refer to our time as the age of lowering standards'. There were letters of complaint in the Welsh press after the band were awarded MBEs in 1964. After Lennon claimed that the Beatles were more popular than Jesus, a letter in the *South Wales Echo* argued that the comments were juvenile but worried that if people thought, read and listened to the Beatles more than Jesus then 'it is ourselves, our society and our country we should feel sorry for, and not John Lennon'.[51]

The Beatles were not the first pop band and they had their contemporaries playing the pubs and clubs of Wales. One such band was Llanelli's the Corncrackers. Their guitarist, Deke Leonard, remembered of the club committees:

> They didn't understand this new fangled, rock'n'roll razzmatazz but their younger patrons demanded it, so they had to provide it, but that didn't mean they had to like it. They regarded all bands as the spawn of Satan, somewhere, on the social scale, between arsonists and child-molesters.

His band found itself harangued by committees for being too loud in its music and too sexy in its dancing.[52] Nor was such music just an urban phenomenon. Dances and concerts were held in halls in small rural towns too, leading to complaints about noise and bad language. One paper declared in 1969: 'You can laugh, but there IS a teenage "scene" in Montgomeryshire! There is always some kind of action or a dance going on in one of the villages or towns in the county. The main problem is getting to know where and when and how good these events are going to be.' Teenagers in the county did, however, find it difficult to buy the latest clothing trends locally. As hippy attire became fashionable things became a bit easier, as improvising, tye-dying and jumble sales all became sources of being 'cool'.[53] One sociologist even suggested that a lesser proportion of teenagers in small rural Welsh towns were 'square' or conventional than in large English cities.

Teenage behaviour, dress and speech were very public performances and in smaller rural places, where everyone knew one another, all the young were quickly touched by any new styles that emerged, making it harder for parents to exert older values and styles in the way they might in a larger and more diverse urban setting. For those who were different in rural Wales, youth culture could help in unexpected ways and Jimmy Hendrix's coolness made life easier for a teenager from the only black family in Llandudno.[54]

A woman who was a student in the late 1960s explained the pull of the new youth culture in rural Wales by asking, 'What else is there to do in Aberystwyth in the middle of winter but men and drink and the odd little puff of grass?'[55] People in places like Aberystwyth had actually begun to combine new and older cultures, again creating a source of generational tension. In 1958 in Aberystwyth a national festival of arts organized by a young farmers' club, for example, included penillion singing, skiffle and rock'n'roll. There was even screaming in an Urdd eisteddfod after a duet by teenagers influenced by the Beatles and the Everly Brothers. They were disqualified for not being in the tradition of the eisteddfod. Skiffle was also banned from the National Eisteddfod in 1957, with the archdruid claiming it was not music but 'rubbish'.[56] Another row followed in 1965, when John Rowlands finished runner-up at the National Eisteddfod with the novel *Ienctid yw 'Mhechod* (*Youth Is My Sin*), which featured the first detailed description of sexual intercourse in Welsh. It did not help that it was between a minister and a middle-aged woman whose mother lay dying upstairs. Such work was part of a wider British literary trend for challenging conventions through often gritty fiction. While this kitchen sink genre tended to be written by young working-class men, the most remarkable Welsh-language novel of the period came from a middle-aged journalist at the *Daily Telegraph*. Caradog Prichard's *Un Nos Ola Leuad* (*One Full Moon Night*, 1961) was inspired by his Edwardian childhood in Bethesda and painted a picture of a community beset by murder, suicide, sexual abuse and mental illness. It was a complex read but it set a marker that writing in Welsh could be ambitious and radical and showed that Welsh-language culture was shedding some of its puritanical chains.

Another sign of change came in 1967, when a pop band appeared on the National Eisteddfod main stage for the first time. Y Blew were a group of Aberystwyth students and featured Gwynfor Evans' son on bass guitar. They criticized Dafydd Iwan, a contemporary who sang Welsh protest songs reminiscent of Bob Dylan, saying he appealed to the patriotic but what were needed were 'groups prepared to twist and shout in Welsh'.[57] At the same eisteddfod, the archdruid denounced drinking and singing in nearby pubs, but to little effect. For Iwan and other Welsh-speaking students, the National Eisteddfod itself was gradually becoming a focal point for an alternative form of youth culture that involved much drinking, poked fun at the Welsh establishment and Welsh traditions but still retained a deep loyalty to Wales. Such modern trends offered some hope for the future of the Welsh language, which was clearly finding a place in the new cultural forms of the young. By the end of the 1960s there were some twenty-five groups and singers making records in Welsh, while *Helo Sut Dach Chi* (*Hello, How Are You*, BBC radio) and *Disc a Dawn* (*Disc and Talent*, BBC television) meant there were dedicated Welsh-language pop programmes, even if the latter did often just involve commissioned translations of English hits.[58]

Such developments were important because they undermined how some young people saw being Welsh and speaking Welsh as uncool. In her study of mid-1960s Blaenau, a Welsh-speaking mod told Isabel Emmett: 'We were anti-Welsh because Welsh people were square, Wales was square. You couldn't be with it if you were Welsh.'[59] Emmett also found twenty-something shop assistants and office workers in a rural village whose first language was Welsh but who self-consciously removed themselves from local culture. They cultivated English accents, followed magazine fashion advice and wanted to marry 'rich Englishmen'. They even sometimes spoke English among themselves. But she also noted that many of the local teenagers 'want to learn to jive; they like to go to the cinema; they listen to popular record programmes on the radio; they like to wear "teen-age" clothes. But they all feel the pull of the Welsh culture; are proud of their own language and generally prefer to speak Welsh.'[60] Taking on styles, fashions and music from America or England thus did not undermine everyone's sense of being Welsh. While some felt constricted by Wales and left, there were others content to be consciously Welsh mods, rockers or hippies. In doing so they updated Wales and Welshness, setting the foundations for a rise in more formal recognitions of the Welsh nation. Indeed, the realization of the need for Welsh-language culture to evolve if it were to survive meant that the backlash against youth culture, and all it was associated with, was never quite as widespread in Welsh-language circles as it sometimes was elsewhere.[61]

IT WAS THE FACT that some young people were having and openly talking about sex that was the greatest social concern around youth culture. It is difficult to know how much extramarital (or indeed intra-marital) sex was actually taking place in the 1950s and 1960s and how much pleasure people derived from it. A 1940s sociological study of London suggested a lack of knowledge and expectation towards sex among married women and concluded that, for most, sex was 'not rapture but routine'. The clitoris was often misunderstood or even unknown to many 1950s married couples.[62] For those not married, the fear of being seen as 'soiled goods' or getting pregnant, compounded by many girls' rather hazy knowledge of the facts of life, limited sexual activity. Nonetheless, on reviewing contemporary surveys, one historian has concluded that during the 1950s at least half of British adults had had sex before marriage.[63] There is little to suggest anything different in 1950s and 1960s Wales. One short story captured some of the confused nuances of Welsh teenage romance, with a girl worrying that a boy would put his tongue in her mouth in order to make her sleep. He would then, her friend had told her, pull down her underwear and give her a baby. It was, she was told, a boy's place to try and a girl's place to refuse.[64] In rural areas, children might have a better idea of biology from farm animals. One Caernarfon woman, born in 1943, recalled an 'enormous amount' of sexual play during her childhood. Of her teenage years she remembered people doing everything except actual intercourse. Others in the 1950s had a rule of 'anything above the belt but nothing below'.[65]

In the 1950s such things remained hidden from public discussion. Only in the 1960s did sex become the subject of open debate. Part of the opening up of the public profile of premarital and extramarital sex was due to wider events. The 1963 Profumo affair, where the Defence Minister had to resign after lying to the Commons about an affair with a prostitute who had also slept with a Russian agent, shocked and titillated in Wales as it did across Britain. But the controversy was more about the hypocrisies of the ruling class than the existence of extramarital sex. A columnist in *Welsh Farm News* was put out at the parallel drawn by an angry Tory MP between the scandal and the sexual behaviour of farmyard animals, maintaining that farm animals were not hypocritical, liars or partial to prostitutes.[66] If the open discussion of sex had its coming-of-age moment, it was the 'not guilty' verdict delivered in November 1960 to Penguin Books on a charge of obscenity for publishing *Lady Chatterley's Lover.* Outside religious circles, there was little support for the suppression of the book. A Methodist bookshop in Cardiff refused to stock it but the *Western Mail* welcomed the verdict, declaring that 'With the extension of mass education and the development of good taste, society should be able to determine more and more for itself what it will, and will not, accept'. When the book hit the shops of Cardiff it was sold out by the middle of morning. Young girls were particularly keen to read it and one seller told the press, 'You should have seen them. All giggling away. Bold as brass some of them, blushing like mad the others. But they all wanted the book.' One reporter watched a girl go into a shop and say, 'I want that book, the dirty one – you know, Lady Chatterley something'.[67] A copy was purchased by Swansea library but it was available only on request; young female assistants were not allowed to handle it and older female staff were allowed to refuse to do so. Libraries in Cardiganshire refused to stock it all.[68]

What such events also did was run into a wider current of concern at changing sexual habits, something that would only increase with the invention of the idea of the swinging sixties. Throughout the 1960s the Welsh press was prone to talk of a 'social malaise' caused by a decline in religious values, the impact of the media and poor sex education. Extramarital sex obviously ran contrary to chapel morality and some even thought that promiscuity was at odds with Welsh values.[69] But it existed all the same. One young Welshman told a television reporter in the mid-1960s about trying to pick up girls for sex at dances: 'If you try really hard and you're not particular you usually end up alright'.[70] A 1965 enquiry into the sex lives of Cardiff schoolboys found a relationship between sexual activity and lack of religious attendance. Nonconformity, however, retained a clear influence on public affairs and notions of proper conduct. Through the 1960s there was no sex education allowed in Swansea and the town's university was the last in England and Wales to introduce mixed-sex halls of residence (1974). Two medical officers at the university in Aberystwyth were sacked in the late 1960s for refusing to divulge to the college authorities the details of students who had become pregnant. Students' freedom was further curtailed by an 11 p.m. curfew in most halls of residence, with harsh penalties for breaking it. Cardiff Council, meanwhile, banned the showing of X-rated films on Sundays from 1963 until 1969 for fear of harming public morals, despite the fact they were allowed in other Welsh towns and in the capital during the rest of the week.[71]

No wonder then that some found Wales stifling. As one Swansea girl said of her late teens, 'In 1963 I left Wales to sample Swinging London. I was young, up for it, and my hormones were racing. I was looking for fun and freedom.'[72] Yet there was also some realism in popular attitudes which sidestepped religious condemnation. A study of rural Llanfrothen at the start of the 1960s noted that tolerance was shown towards unmarried mothers which meant they did not have to feel they had to leave home to have their baby because of the local shame and embarrassment. They were still gossiped about and censured by the chapels but the study argued that most people did not generally regard premarital sex as wrong and even suggested that it was more common in rural areas. Many local marriages certainly took place after conception and few couples were willing to have the dates of both marriage and birth recorded in the chapel books. Further credence for such ideas came from the fact that in 1959 all but four of the thirty-nine English counties had homes or hostels for unmarried mothers, whereas in Wales only Glamorgan did.[73] As early as 1949–51, of births to married mothers under twenty in Wales 69.2 per cent happened between zero and eight months after their marriage. For those between twenty and twenty-four it was 26.8 per cent.[74] Whatever the tolerance of premarital sex, the idea that 'nice girls didn't' remained strong and sexual knowledge was still often confused and fragmented in the 1960s. School sex education was rudimentary, more concerned with discouraging sexual behaviour than educating people about it. While the benefits of better sex education for reducing pregnancy were acknowledged, there was also a strong fear that it would encourage promiscuity.[75]

There were practical difficulties that discouraged premarital sex. Simply finding somewhere to do it could be difficult and extramarital intercourse generally took place outside, in places such as mountainsides or back alleys. There was also, of course, the question of contraception. The introduction of the pill in 1961 was never quite the revolution that some have made out, at least not until the 1970s and 1980s. Some historians stress how difficult it could be for unmarried women to get the pill but Pick's recent research refutes this. Technically, it was not until 1967 that general practitioners would prescribe the pill to unmarried girls and even then most required some form of reassurance or proof of a commitment to marriage or at least a stable relationship. In practice, however, doctors' attitudes were more diverse and could be considerably more liberal. Oral evidence shows that even girls dressed in school uniform and without steady boyfriends could be prescribed the pill by some doctors.[76] Perhaps more of a hindrance than the attitude of doctors was the fear of asking in the first place, especially in small close-knit communities. When one Swansea mother found out that her engaged daughter was on the pill in the late 1960s she did not speak to her for a week.[77] Attitudes were slowly changing, however. The *Western Mail* claimed in 1968 that the issue of family planning 'is no longer one of the morals of the young. It is the morality of whether it is better to dispense with lies and deceit in order to allow the honest handling of a complex human problem.'[78] Nonetheless, by the end of the 1960s nearly half of Welsh local authorities were still not providing a full family planning service. By then maybe 10 per cent or more of women in Wales were on the pill. One of them remembered: 'You felt it was expected of you to have sexual relations on the first date really, and you felt you were damned if you didn't and damned if you did. And, in hindsight, rather than liberalising women and freeing them up, I think it entrapped them more.' Another concluded that women's 'new found sexual freedom had merely increased the pool of available crumpet'.[79]

In 1969 the *Western Mail* interviewed young people from across Wales about their attitudes and found strong support for sex outside marriage but little evidence of rampant promiscuity. A twenty-year-old student in Cardiff spoke for many when she concluded, 'Now that the risk of unwanted children is virtually over, there is no reason for not having sex when you are single. But I don't believe in free love. Love becomes obliterated that way.' An RAF serviceman from Cardiganshire was blunter: 'Sex before marriage? Sure. The bird might be frigid. You don't want a bird that's no good in bed, do you?' Not all the young men were so blatant. A twenty-year-old farmer's son from Johnstown said, 'Sex before marriage is all right if you love the girl. If you don't, it's wrong. Romance means everything to me.' Some young people were very traditional about marriage and a twenty-year-old trainee teacher from Caernarfon told the reporter firmly, 'If you have a conscience you won't go to bed with a fellow before marriage – however right the papers make it seem'. There was also evidence of both double standards and traditional worries. A nineteen-year-old female clerk from Pontypridd summed up, 'A boy is a hero if he goes to bed with a girl – but the girl is called a whore. It isn't easy to be virtuous today.... The idea that all young people know all about sex is quite wrong. Many of my friends worry about the first night of marriage.'[80]

Thus it seems that premarital sex in stable relations was on the up but promiscuity was the habit of a minority. A British survey suggested that at the end of the 1960s around a quarter of men and two-thirds or more of women were still virgins when they married, which either means that a lot of men were boasting or a third of unmarried women, and no doubt some wives too, were seeing to the needs of three-quarters of unmarried men. As one historian concluded of the 1960s, 'Far from being especially wanton, then, most young people led extremely boring sex lives; far from storming the barricades of moral repression, most of them spent their evenings in front of the television.'[81] That did not stop the Welsh press dwelling upon reports of venereal disease (VD) to decry contemporary morals. VD statistics for Wales were first published in 1970 and they showed that the number of cases was 6,632, an increase of nearly 74 per cent since 1966. This was a steep rise but it was still hardly a widespread problem. The number of illegitimate births in Wales rose from 1,683 in 1960 to 2,983 in 1969. But even this figure was lower than the 3,261 illegitimate births in Wales in 1945. In 1969, the year of the so-called summer of love, 93 per cent of Welsh births were still legitimate.[82] A quick marriage was the obvious reason why most births were legitimate but abortion was available in hospitals before the procedure's partial legalization in 1967 if the mother's life was in danger. In practice, though, this often came down to whether a woman could afford to pay for private medical assessment and care. After 1967 there were concerns that abortion's new availability would encourage promiscuity but, in 1970, of the 3,031 notified abortions in Wales, 1,765 were actually had by married women.[83] Thus the statistics again do not suggest the rampant and careless promiscuity that is often imagined of the 1960s.

Because tales of sex, drugs and violence did not always match the reality, youths themselves could feel ill-treated and stereotyped by the media. As one twenty-year-old female ceramics student in Cardiff noted, 'The popular image of young people today is sex, drugs, pop music. But I've yet to meet anyone here who takes drugs. A few smoke marijuana, but none, as far as I know, is on hard drugs.' In 1969 the *Western Mail* investigated the idea of a permissive society by interviewing over 100 young people of twenty-one years and under from across Wales about a series of issues. What emerged was a picture of growing freedoms but a far more conservative group than might be imagined. A nineteen-year-old secretarial student from Machynlleth said she liked 'to shock people with the things I wear, and to make people stare at me. Although I give the impression of not caring about anything, in fact I do worry about being responsible.' An apprentice mechanic in Dolgellau felt that the young were not treated seriously and not allowed to become part of the community: 'Just because we've got long hair we are dismissed outright by older people.' The reported summed up,

> The most overwhelming impression gained from speaking to young people about their attitudes to politics is their feeling of isolation, their feeling that their ideas and opinions will not alter the behaviour of those in power.... The young people we spoke to were, almost without exception, engrossed in their personal problems, their own image, their friendships, their education, and destiny. They displayed a scepticism, which sometimes verged on the frankly cynical, when asked their views on established institutions such as marriage and the political world.

The paper concluded that, given how the young are condemned and dismissed, 'the wonder is that there are so few dropouts from our smug society'.[84]

This is not to say that some of the excesses of youth culture in the 1960s did not hit Wales. There were, after all, over 6,000 cases of VD in Wales in 1970. Even at the start of the 1960s there was, in Cardiff at least, something of a scene for art students, with drugs, parties and a café on Queen Street full of 'loose schoolgirls looking for sexual adventures, petty thieves, quasi-intellectuals, young guys on the make as the well as the hip cool beatniks'.[85] This scene remained hidden from most people's attention but by the end of the decade the press was writing about bands that covered the stages of clubs with flowers, took drugs and exhorted their audiences to 'freak out'. The *Herald of Wales* described one concert:

> In the middle of the dance-floor some kissed while others kept their eyes fixed intently on the strangely-clothed group. One well-educated and half-naked boy wearing coloured beads and bangles told me that he saw nothing wrong in making love when and where he pleased. His girlfriend agreed.

Some of the audience saw flower power as a religion; others took drugs to find their true selves and dressed in beads and flowers to 'counteract the hard, tough reputation of the male'.[86] In 1974 a total of 578 people were found guilty of drug offences in Welsh courts. Most had been using cannabis but forty cases related to LSD, twenty-six to cocaine and ten to heroin. Nor was this just an urban phenomenon. Rural Wales proved a popular destination for those seeking to 'drop out' from mainstream society and a sociologist in Blaenau Ffestiniog noted how, despite class differences, such figures inspired local youths.[87] It was when people saw their children being influenced in such ways that concerns about the permissive society were at their deepest. Then it was something more than just a story in the papers or on television. People's own families became microcosms of wider tensions. A mother from Merthyr thought of the 1960s as 'screaming' rather than 'swinging', 'as I yelled at the family to cut down the volume on the transistor, screeched in despair as the Rolling Stones were played for the umpteenth time on the record player and squawked my head off at teenagers about getting their hair cut'.[88]

EVERY GENERATION WORRIES about the behaviour of those who are younger than it and on the surface the young, whether they lived in the same house or were just seen on television, seemed to be ever deteriorating. Much of this was moral panic rather than an objective understanding of what was happening. Even crime, the most serious problem and something that was certainly escalating, never quite deserved the hysterical reaction sometimes found in the press. What such press coverage did do was help bring into the mainstream of life what had begun as the culture of teenagers and people in their early twenties. This process was clearest in pop music, which by the 1970s was at the very centre of popular culture and could be heard everywhere from cafés and pubs to even some churches and eisteddfodau. Some of the bands were growing up too, producing more serious, artistic music rather than the simple tunes of the 1950s and early 1960s. That was clearest in the case of the Beatles, who in the process became national institutions and won the artistic approval of parts of the establishment, even if their psychedelic phase bewildered many previous fans. In 1966–7, Pontypridd's Tom Jones, whose gyrating was once so shocking, was selling over a million copies in the UK of the ballad 'Green, green grass of home', an emotional song which appealed more to housewives than to teenagers.[89] Such developments were perhaps not surprising, since pop music's first generation was now itself settling down. Someone who had been fifteen in 1957 when Elvis had his first number one in Britain was twenty-eight by 1970 and probably married with children.

It is easy to overstate the pervasiveness of pop music. In 1958 Welsh-language newspaper *Y Cymro* still felt it had to explain to its readers what a jukebox was.[90] Even in the 1960s there were alternatives that were immensely popular among the young. In October 1965 the *Sound of Music* entered its seventh month in Cardiff cinemas, becoming Wales' longest-running film. Nearly half a million had watched the film in the city's main cinema, with it not being uncommon for people to have seen it thirty or more times. Indeed, one Cardiff woman claimed to have seen it 150 times. A cinema manager told the press that for some people the film had become a 'way of life'. He noted, 'It's a family story. It's got a universal appeal. It's an acceptable story with a little bit of humour affecting members of a family, and a large family at that. It has a romantic angle and, of course, there is the wonderful music.' By 1975 the film's soundtrack had sold more copies worldwide than the Beatles' best-selling two albums combined. Its pretty melodies and conservative tale of a loving family simply had a wider reach than anything now remembered as characteristic of the swinging sixties.[91]

The popularity of the *Sound of Music* with all ages owed much to the fact that it was a love story. Love was still an ideal to aspire to for most people. The physical and emotional rewards of a relationship could provide a bedrock of stability on which people's lives could be built, making so many of the financial and physical hardships of life tolerable. As one novel about a 1950s miner put it, 'Away from Liz he felt dull, the spice seemed to have gone out of things. Rugby, work, the pub, they were all a jumble of colourless incident.' Yet much of this went unsaid. Indeed, to articulate it could be regarded as sentimental or even unmanly. In the same novel, when the relationship breaks up the distraught miner thinks that people would not understand: 'To them it was a bit of an affair between a couple of youngsters who didn't know their own minds and were full of romantic nonsense. Perhaps they were right. Perhaps there were more serious problems in the world, like war and starvation and the rest. But they meant nothing to him. All he cared about was Liz, and that was over.'[92]

The fact that most young people still felt like this at the end of the 'swinging sixties' meant that much of the reaction to the promiscuity that did exist was misplaced. In 1970 the women's page of the *Western Mail* looked back at the 1960s and asked: 'Were they really permissive? No, of course not.... All we did during the sixties was discard our mock modesty.... Let us look at them as a time when free speech became a little nearer being free and sex became the acknowledged way of conceiving babies.' But that openness was significant change in itself and the fact remained that unmarried couples sleeping together or short skirts on teenage girls were no longer quite the scandals they had once been. There was what another writer in the *Western Mail* called a 'quiet revolution' in morals. Although she could have probably made the same comment of much of provincial Britain, 'Wales is permissive', she concluded, 'but not quite so permissive as some other places'.[93] That revolution may have started with teenagers, but it trickled upwards too, encouraging some older people to challenge received wisdoms and codes of behaviour, a process that was, of course, reinforced by the young themselves growing older.[94] Perhaps the most important facet of this revolution was not the sex that preoccupied commentators but wider freedoms. One woman thought in 1969 that changing manners meant that females could now ask others about the price of their dresses and even 'use four-letter words in mixed company, if you know your listeners. The most shockable, apparently, are older men.'[95] The middle aged and elderly did indeed struggle to accept changing values. A former miner remarked in 1966, 'God strike me dead, but the introduction of women to clubs and pubs is terrible. It's two drinks and two packets of fags and the kids going without. If my grandmother could come back and see the women drinking in the Swansea pubs she'd go mad.'[96] One woman recalled being asked to leave a Cardiff pub in 1966 because her skirt was too short. Such attitudes meant the revolution arrived more like a tortoise than a hare but it arrived all the same, bringing less deference and less acceptance of the status quo. At Aberystwyth, students may have worn gowns to formal meals and lectures but they still went on strike in 1964 after having permission refused for a student bar in the university.[97] They won. This may not have been the barricades of student revolt in France but in rural Nonconformist Wales such small things could feel like an earthquake.

Notes

1 Quoted in R. Pick, *A Moral Revolution? Reporting the Welsh Experience of the Swinging Sixties*, MA thesis, Swansea University (2008), 18.
2 *SWE*, 13 Sep. 1956.
3 *SWE*, 10 and 18 Sep. 1956. D. Sandbrook, *Never Had It So Good: A History of Britain from Suez to the Sixties* (2006 edn.), 459–60.
4 *SWE*, 14 and 11 Sept. 1956.
5 L. Ebenezer, *Cae Marged* (1991), 85–6. *WM*, 19 Jan. 1957.
6 *Dragon's Breath*, BBC Radio Wales, episode 2 (2001).
7 Ebenezer, *Cae Marged*, 86–7. N. Upham, 'Your 1950s: fashion and leisure', at news.bbc.co.uk/1/hi/magazine/6683883.stm.
8 L. Sage, *Bad Blood* (2000), 194. T. Jones, in *Dragon's Breath*, BBC Radio Wales, episode 2.
9 Quoted in P. Hennessy, *Having It So Good: Britain in the Fifties* (2007), 491.
10 D. Fowler, *Youth Culture in Modern Britain, c.1920–c.1970* (2008).
11 For memories of such images see P. Stead, 'By the light of the silvery moon', *Pl*, 116 (1996), 35–43.
12 *Daily Mirror*, 28 Feb. 1942.
13 K. Amis, *That Uncertain Feeling* ([1955] 1975), 206.
14 D. Beddoe (ed.), *Changing Times: Welsh Women Writing on the 1950s and 1960s* (2003), 21.
15 I. Emmett, *A North Wales Village: A Social Anthropological Study* (1964), 139. D. Bush, 'Lash LaRue and the River of Adventure', *Pl*, 130 (1998), 75–84.
16 *South Wales Argus*, 5 Apr. 1963.
17 B. Hinton, *South Wales Murders* (2008).
18 *DWS*, various volumes. Home Office, *Recorded Crime Statistics 1898–2004/05*, formerly at rds.homeoffice.gov.uk/rds/pdfs/100years.xls. D. J. V. Jones, *Crime and Policing in the Twentieth Century: The South Wales Experience* (1996), 79, 82.
19 Calculated from *DWS*, 17 (1971), 33.
20 *WM*, 8 Nov. 1965.
21 *Rhondda Fach Leader*, 8 July 1966.
22 I. Emmett, 'Blaenau boys in the mid-1960s', in G. Williams (ed.), *Social and Cultural Change in Contemporary Wales* (1978), 90–3. *Welshman*, 17 and 31 Oct. 1958. *SWE*, 22 Jan. 1965.
23 Jones, *Crime and Policing*, 79.
24 *Daily Mirror*, 5 Dec. 1966.
25 See the complaints of a Rhondda minister about underage drinking being rooted in youths having too much money, *SWE*, 4 Sep. 1956. *CJ*, 10 Feb. 1956.
26 D. Leonard, *Sex and Generation: A Study of Courtship and Weddings* (1980), 76, 79. *CJ*, 17 Feb. 1956.
27 H. Marks, *Señor Nice: Straight Life from Wales to South America* (2006), 8.
28 M. Akhtar and S. Humphries, *The Fifties and Sixties: A Lifestyle Revolution* (2002), 43. Leonard, *Sex and Generation*, 77.
29 Executive member of Welfare Cinema Association, 1956, quoted in S. Moitra, 'Between class culture and mass culture: south Wales miners' institutes and the cinema after 1945', Industrial History, Industrial Culture: Representation, Past, Present, Future, conference, Swansea University, Sept. 2008.
30 *WM*, 19 June 1961. *South Wales Argus*, 10 Apr. 1963.
31 V. Gregg, 'Sapphic passions: from a Welsh closet to London and lesbian lust', in C. Merriman (ed.), *Laughing, Not Laughing: Women Writing on 'My Experience of Sex'* (2004), 44.
32 BBC Wales, 'Wales yesterday', formerly at www.bbc.co.uk/wales/history/sites/walesyesterday/pages/1950s.shtml.
33 J. Edwards, *Dechrau Gofidiau* (1962), 16.
34 T. Brennan, E. W. Cooney and H. Pollins, *Social Change in South-West Wales* (1954), 5.
35 Emmett, 'Blaenau boys', 97.
36 Quoted in D. Jones, *The Beatles and Wales* (2002), 12.

37 A. Pressley, *Changing Times: Being Young in Britain in the '60s* (2000), 23.
38 Quoted in Emmett, 'Blaenau boys', 91.
39 Sandbrook, *Never Had It So Good*, 146.
40 *The Times*, 1 Mar. 1968. *South Wales*, winter 1968–9.
41 R. Griffiths, *S. O. Davies: A Socialist Faith* (1983), 150–1. L. V. Scott, *Conscription and the Attlee Governments: The Politics and Policy of National Service, 1945–51* (1993). *Welshman*, 8 Feb. 1952.
42 Sandbrook, *Never Had It So Good*, 287. Quoted in R. Evans, *Gwynfor Evans: Portrait of a Patriot* (2008), 115.
43 Lord Roberts of Conwy, *Right from the Start: The Memoirs of Sir Wyn Roberts* (2006), 28.
44 Council for Wales and Monmouthshire, *Third Memorandum by the Council on Its Activities*, Cmnd 53 (1957), 119–20, 123, 126. *Guardian*, 28 May 1956.
45 Quoted in Sandbrook, *Never Had It So Good*, 432.
46 J. Tripp, 'Farewell to a shambles', *Pl*, 28 (1975), 22, 23. A. Richards, *Carwyn: A Personal Memoir* (1984), 83–5.
47 Quoted in Sandbrook, *Never Had It So Good*, 431. D. Lodge, *Ginger, You're Barmy* ([1962] 1982), 61.
48 *SWE*, 19 Jan. 1957. *Face of Wales* (film, 1961).
49 Jones, *The Beatles and Wales*, 12, 49, 18, 34, 19, 40, 27.
50 *WL*, 22 Nov. 1963.
51 Jones, *The Beatles and Wales*, 35–8, 56, 72.
52 D. Leonard, *Maybe I Should've Stayed in Bed? The Flip Side of the Rock'n'Roll Dream* (2000), 81.
53 *Montgomeryshire Mercury*, 31 and 17 Oct. 1969.
54 Emmett, 'Blaenau boys', 89–90. H. Williams (ed.), *The Century Speaks: Voices of Wales* (1999), 42, 57.
55 Translated from R. A. Jones (ed.), *Hyd Ein Hoes: Lleisiau Cymru* (1999), 67.
56 M. Dewe, 'In them long hot summer days', *Pl*, 130 (1998), 52. Williams, *The Century Speaks*, 103. S. Hill, *'Blerwytirhwng?' The Place of Welsh Pop Music* (2007), 58.
57 Quoted in *Arcade*, 20 (7 Aug. 1981).
58 *Observer*, 13 Aug. 1967. *WM*, 1 Feb. 1968.
59 Quoted in Emmett, 'Blaenau boys', 92.
60 Emmett, *A North Wales Village*, 40–1.
61 Emmett, 'Blaenau boys', 98–100. K. J. Bernard, *Visible Welshness: Performing Welshness at the National Eisteddfod in the Twentieth Century*, PhD thesis, Swansea University (2004), ch. 5.
62 E. Slater and M. Woodside, *Patterns of Marriage: A Study of Marriage Relationships in the Urban Working Classes* (1951), 145. L. A. Hall, *Sex, Gender and Social Change in Britain since 1950* (2000), 155.
63 *Welsh Way of Life: Sex and the Century*, BBC1 Wales, 30 Oct. 2006. D. Sandbrook, *White Heat: A History of Britain in the Swinging Sixties* (2006), 457.
64 J. Edwards, 'Only for a walk', in M. Stephens (ed.), *A Book of Wales* (1987), 53.
65 Williams, *The Century Speaks*, 40. Beddoe, *Changing Times*, 164.
66 *Welsh Farm News*, 22 June 1963.
67 *WM*, 3 Nov. 1960. *SWE*, 7 and 10 Nov. 1960.
68 C. Haste, *Rules of Britain: Sex in Britain, Word War I to the Present* ([1992] 2002), 181. *Welsh Way of Life: Sex and the Century*, BBC1 Wales, 30 Oct. 2006.
69 Pick, *A Moral Revolution?* For a fictional representation see A. Richards, *The Former Miss Merthyr Tydfil* (1976), 176.
70 *Welsh Way of Life: Sex and the Century*, BBC1 Wales, 30 Oct. 2006.
71 Pick, *A Moral Revolution?*, 14, 62, 63, 48. Leonard, *Sex and Generation*, 28.
72 Gregg, 'Sapphic passions', 46.
73 Emmett, *A North Wales Village*, ch. 8. In contrast, there is a sense of shame among some family members in Jane Edwards' novel *Dechrau Gofidiau* (1962), after a young unmarried woman from north-west Wales gets pregnant and does not know who the father is.
74 J. P. Lewis, 'Population', in B. Thomas (ed.), *The Welsh Economy* (1962), 183.

75 Pick, *A Moral Revolution?*, ch. 3.
76 D. Beddoe, *Out of the Shadows: A History of Women in Twentieth Century Wales* (2000), 150. Pick, *A Moral Revolution?*, 59, ch. 3.
77 Leonard, *Sex and Generation*, 28.
78 Quoted in Pick, *A Moral Revolution?*, 54.
79 J. Davies, *A History of Wales* (1993), 641. BBC Wales, 'Wales yesterday', formerly at www.bbc.co.uk/wales/history/sites/walesyesterday/pages/1960s.shtml. Beddoe, *Out of the Shadows*, 150.
80 *WM*, 25 Nov. 1969.
81 G. Gorer, *Sex and Marriage in England Today* (1971), 30. Sandbrook, *White Heat*, 465.
82 Calculated from *DWS*, 17 (1971), 30, 14.
83 Beddoe, *Out of the Shadows*, 151. Calculated from *DWS*, 17 and 18 (1971 and 1972).
84 *WM*, 24 and 28 Nov. 1969.
85 M. Stevens, *Solva Blues* (2004), 87.
86 Quoted in Leonard, *Maybe I Should've Stayed in Bed?*, ch. 25.
87 *DWHS-3*, 281. Emmett, 'Blaenau boys', 90–1.
88 Beddoe, *Changing Times*, 266.
89 C. Larkin, *Virgin Encyclopedia of Popular Music* (2002), 674–5.
90 *Y Cymro*, 18 Sept. 1958.
91 *WM*, 23 Oct. 1965. Sandbrook, *White Heat*, 389–90.
92 A. Haines, *The Drift* (1974), 107, 114.
93 *WM*, 2 Jan. 1970 and 20 June 1969.
94 See for example Emmett, 'Blaenau boys', 97.
95 *WM*, 27 Nov. 1969.
96 *Observer Magazine*, 30 Oct. 1966.
97 Pick, *A Moral Revolution?*, 21. *The Times*, 25 Apr. 1964. P. Hannan, *The Welsh Illusion* (1999), 60.

5

'A new society.' Class and urban communities, 1951–70

> [A] new world and a new society are coming into being as a result of the industrial renaissance of South Wales. Even the democratic class structure of Wales is changing. It is losing its homogeneity and uniformity. . . .
>
> Goronwy Rees, 'Have the Welsh a future?', *Encounter* (March 1964)

> 'Things is a lot different down in these valleys now, isn't it, from what it was before 1945, when Sam by here and me was kids. Isn't that right Sam?'
>
> 'Well, aye, of course. No money in the pubs in them days, when blokes didn't have the price of a pint from one week to the next.'
>
> 'Are you thinking of promoting yourself to Liberal, or what, Joe Jenkins?'
>
> 'Don't be daft, mun, Steve.'
>
> 'I thought you was going snobbish for a minute and turning traitor. Your old grandfather would spin in his coffin if he thought you'd do that.'
>
> 'Is it snobbish to vote Liberal then?'
>
> 'Of course it is; middle-class Liberals is, for blokes with cars and washing machines.'
>
> 'Well, I'm saving up for a car and Mam's already got a washing machine, and you can't accuse us of being middle-class, for God's sake.'
>
> 'Aye, there you are, see, I told you things was different. All our symbols have gone to hell. It was much easier to talk sense about politics before, indeed to God. I know I've got to be mad at somebody, but who the hell is my enemy, boy?'
>
> Menna Gallie, *The Small Mine* ([1962] 2000), 10

WHEN ANEURIN BEVAN died in 1960 there was an outpouring of grief and admiration in Wales for a man who had fought for his people. The *South Wales Echo* declared, 'it is as a rebel, a great orator and a man of courage that his name will live in history. That, too, is why the Welsh are especially proud of him.' The landlady of a pub near Tredegar where Bevan drank and where his portrait hung on the wall said, 'He never changed you know. He was always one of the boys. They would all die for him here. To run Nye down is worse than running down a member of the family.' She noted approvingly that he always refused to have a 'posh' glass for his beer, instead preferring to drink from the same handleless mugs as everyone else. But the reality was that Nye had moved onwards and upwards. He no longer lived in the Valleys but on a farm in Buckinghamshire that had cost him £15,000 and where he kept cattle, pigs and poultry and employed farm hands. There he also drank in a local pub, which again had his picture in the bar. In that pub he preferred to talk about farming than politics. His will was worth £23,481, the equivalent of £405,000 at 2008 prices. Bevan's political beliefs had moved on too. He had often been at odds with union power within the Labour Party but in the last years of his life he could be found supporting nuclear weapons and on the right of the party. On Bevan's death, the *Western Mail*, a paper which he derided, celebrated the way he saw that the attitudes of the 1930s were not relevant in the 1950s.[1]

Yet most of the Welsh celebrations of Bevan's life were rooted in the 1930s rather than the 1950s. They were celebrations of a Wales rooted in industrial labour and which consisted of poor working-class communities with deep talents but no pretensions. This was a Wales born partly of reality but also partly of what Kingsley Amis called 'those phony novels and stories about the wry rhetorical wisdom of poetical miners, all those boring myths about the wonder and the glory and the terror of life in the valley towns'.[2] The most phoney of these novels was Richard Llewellyn's *How Green Was My Valley* (1939), a sentimental and romantic tale of a Valleys family where 'mam' ruled the roost, miners sang hymns to and from work, and life was good before English immigrants and industrial discord undermined the community and its prosperity. It was a vision that betrayed both the labour movement and historical accuracy but it was immensely popular nonetheless and the film version could bring entire Welsh cinema audiences to tears. This popularity owed much to the strength of community the book and film portrayed, an ideal also evident in Wales' cinematic contribution to the Festival of Britain. *David* (1951), a documentary centred on Ammanford, described that mining community as 'more a family than a town'.[3]

Beneath the veneer of romanticism there was a grain of truth. In the early post-war years urban industrial communities were tight-knit and introspective. As an unromantic 1960 mining novel put it: 'We live in a small village and everybody knows as soon as you're constipated there and everybody cares about you. P'raps they hate your guts or maybe they love you mad, but whatever they feel, they care.'[4] Academics saw it too. Sociologists argued that the industrial region around Swansea consisted of strong communities with a semi-rural outlook. The chapels, unions and political associations there had overlapping leaderships and strong codes of respectable behaviour, giving the area in distinctive way of life and culture.[5] A study of a 1950 Llanelli street showed that three-quarters of the residents had been born either in the street or within half a mile of it; 69 per cent of the inhabitants had lived there for more than twenty years. The newcomers were men from other parts of the town who had married local girls or young couples who had bought a house there. Three-quarters of the men worked in heavy industry and 93 per cent of the street spoke Welsh fluently, while the others understood a little of the language. Although a few men had white-collar jobs, nearly everyone on the street considered themselves working class.[6]

According to historian Dai Smith, the late 1940s were the 'last authentic years of that distinctive culture'.[7] Many people were moving up the social ladder thanks to educational achievement, better wages, increased consumerism and new housing, ending the old idea of a working class united by poverty. Manual job opportunities were increasingly dispersed as older mines and industrial works closed down and were replaced by factories elsewhere. This all undermined the physical, social and emotional unity of the urban working-class communities that was celebrated in film, fiction and academia and it meant that, running parallel with the progress of affluence, was a sense of uncertainty and decline. By the 1970s social scientists could talk of life in the Valleys being 'unstructured and purposeless' without the solidarity of close-knit places of living, play and worship.[8] This was not unique to Wales. Commentators like Richard Hoggart were writing passionately of the changes that the English working class were undergoing, as their traditional world of neighbourliness and communal work was transformed in the affluent economy. In Wales, however, the matter was complicated because traditional working-class communities and their culture had been central to the making of the modern nation and their fading was seen as another nail in Wales' coffin. As one old north Wales miner remarked in 1966: 'No doubt about it, lad, Rhos is getting more and more like Lancashire every day'.[9]

IN 1953 THE *LIVERPOOL DAILY POST* noted perceptively, 'the prosperity of the two-and-a-half million who live in Wales today seems to corrode the nation's life as poverty never did'. It gave the example of a tinplate worker from Llanelli who moved to a new estate in Port Talbot to be nearer his new work. There he was removed from the old chapel activities that he used to take part in in the evenings. He had a 'lovely place … bathroom, electric fire, everything. But no chapel, no choir, not even a pub. So there's Rhys bach – money in his pocket but no roots. Television but no oratorio. And all Wales is gradually going where Rhys is now.'[10] A significant minority of the working class remained in what can only be described as poverty but there was a widespread belief that the affluence that Rhys and others were enjoying was creating a working-class lifestyle that resembled the individualistic lives of the middle classes. In fact, this was a process that began before the affluence of the 1950s. One miner noted in 1949 of the increased bus provision in the Valleys: 'You can move freely for a few pence and get any amusement you want outside the village'. This though, he thought, had brought a decline in choirs, drama societies, poetry and musical clubs.[11] Such trends increased in the 1950s. This was clearly evident in sport. Cardiff City Football Club saw its average attendance tumble from 37,871 in 1947–8 to 10,587 in 1964–5. In a world where you could go shopping, for a spin in the car or just sit in your armchair in front of the box, standing on a cold terrace, even if it was with all your mates, was simply less appealing to much of football and rugby's traditional audience. Cold pews were not much more attractive and emptying chapels were another sign that the traditional communal activities that were so central to community life were fading away (see chapter 6). Meanwhile, the miners' welfare halls, once a powerful symbol of the vitality and self-sufficiency of working-class life, were becoming sites of entertainment rather than community institutions. Their libraries were being sold off to raise funds or make way for a club that centred on drinking, dancing and bingo. In the first decade after the war, the halls hosted opera, bands, art exhibitions, choirs, drama and even ballet. In 1970, just eight people turned up to the annual general meeting of the Pontarddulais Institute. The hall had been reduced to two nights of cinema a week, two nights of bingo and the occasional pantomime and jumble sale. All the staff except the manager had to be made redundant and in 1970 even its cinema came to an end, another victim of the coming of television to ordinary working-class homes.[12]

Despite the improvement in working-class material conditions that allowed people to buy televisions, the general pattern of economic development added to a sense that traditional industrial communities were being undermined. Where factories were built in the Valleys, their management usually chose to live elsewhere, breaking down the ability of places of employment to create coherent communities.[13] But the new employment opportunities being created in Wales were not concentrated in the locations where the older coal mines and metalworks were being closed. Employers preferred developments on the coastal belt, where transport links were better and local amenities more congenial for any incoming management and specialist labour. This meant a lack of local employment opportunities for people in the south Wales Valleys, leaving many ordinary workers with a choice between commuting or relocating. By 1966 there were over 35,000 people working in Cardiff who did not live there. More than 2,000 of them lived in the Rhondda and, by 1971, 37 per cent of the employed Rhondda population worked outside the area. Even Swansea became an exporter rather than an importer of labour, thanks to the growth of the steel industry in nearby Port Talbot. Some 2,000 steelworkers travelled there from Swansea every day.[14]

Commuting was time consuming and expensive. A pipe fitter in the Rhondda, for example, complained that he had to get up at 4.30 a.m. to get to work in Barry and that he did not arrive home until 7.30 p.m. It was thus not surprising that many people moved in order to be closer to their new places of work. Between 1951 and 1970, the south Wales coastal belt had an estimated net gain of 38,200 people through migration. In the same period, the central and eastern valleys of south Wales had an estimated net loss of 83,000 migrants.[15] One Rhondda newspaper noted that many young people had 'set their face resolutely against coal mining careers' and were leaving because there were simply not enough alternative employment opportunities locally. But it was not just jobs that was driving people out of the Valleys. Some people simply wanted to live somewhere more attractive or with better amenities.[16] Others went because, in the words of one commentator,

> they disliked the cohesiveness and closeness of the community, the traditional social and moral attitudes held by their parents and grandparents, and because in old Rhondda at least – to depart from well established social rules, to ignore well ingrained social conventions or simply to be different was to run the risk of being regarded as deviant. Many of those who left wished to be free of conventions and this necessitated being free of the Rhondda.

Rhondda's population fell from 111,389 in 1951 to 88,972 just twenty years later. In 1921 over 162,000 had lived there, which meant that Rhondda's population had nearly halved within the living memory of its oldest residents. It was also now much easier to make this break because the welfare state meant that people were less on reliant on their families for support.[17] Indeed, more might have gone had family connections and the cost of housing in more affluent areas not acted as barriers. As one fitter in his twenties from the Amman valley put it, 'I'd like to go somewhere like Kent or Surrey, lovely places and plenty of work, but the wife would never go from here and leave her mother.' A study of migrants from that valley suggested most people wanted to move as short a distance as possible and 83 per cent had stayed in Glamorgan. They were significantly more satisfied with employment, amenities and housing in their new areas but missed friends and relatives.[18] Sociologists studying the industrial areas around Swansea in the early 1950s also found that people were extremely attached to their local communities and that 'an offer of new houses three miles away is interpreted as a plan for "uprooting people from the land of their birth"'.[19] When, in 1949, Ted Jones, a leader in the National Union of Mineworkers, was offered the chairmanship of the Miners' Welfare Commission he refused after his wife, according to the government minister who made the offer, 'almost had hysterics at the prospect of leaving North Wales and moving so far up in the economic and social scale'.[20]

Even if people were not leaving their town, they were often moving within it in search of better housing, which further contributed to the breakup of old communities. Slum clearances meant they did not always have much choice in this. Between 1954 and 1969, 92,352 people in Wales were moved as a result of the demolition or closure of their former homes. The docks area of Cardiff alone lost 10,000 people between 1961 and 1971, a quarter of its population.[21] Such movements were often accompanied by a sense of frustration as people literally watched their communities being torn down. They worried about where they were being moved to and about losing contact with friends, and they resented homes that they had brought up families in and had struggled to buy being labelled slums. One woman from Cardiff's docklands, who was watching the demolition around her but had not yet moved on herself, told filmmakers with a sense of exasperation: 'What can you do?'[22]

The dynamics of this increasingly mobile population were evident in Swansea. Industrial developments were bringing people into the town from across south Wales and beyond. Its population grew from 160,988 in 1951 to 173,355 in 1971. By the early 1960s, a quarter of the population had not been raised in the town and 13 per cent had been raised outside Wales. Within Swansea, those who could afford it were moving away from the industrialized, polluted and disfigured east towards the western suburbs and the beauty of Gower. Others were leaving the neighbourhoods they grew up in for wherever in the town they could get a council home. At the 1961 census, 28 per cent of people in Swansea had lived in their house for less than five years and 9 per cent for less than a year. Indeed, had more housing been available, then the breakup of older communities would probably have been swifter. In an extensive sociological study of the town, over a third of people indicated their desire to move, a feeling that was strongest among people under thirty and weakest among those over sixty. Careers and housing aspirations meant that on two middle-class Swansea estates in the mid-1960s 54 of 120 households did not expect to be living there in five years' time. In working-class areas aspirations were less definite. The cost and time of travelling to work meant there was some reluctance to move 'out Gower way'. One elderly working-class man remarked, 'the boys usually follow their wives off to wherever they are from. A girl doesn't want to be far from her mother, not unless the husband has a very good job of course and they have to follow the job'. People also still had a loyalty to their local neighbourhood. Moving west within Swansea was seen as social progress but old loyalties meant this could sometimes be a source of embarrassment rather than pride. Requests for council houses showed a preference for the nearest 'nicer' area rather than the nicest areas by Gower.[23]

The closure of old industries and the movement of people created a strong sense of change and sometimes anger among those left behind. Sports and social clubs, once symbols of the community, struggled and aged as young people moved away. The changes were also evident in the landscape, as new housing estates and factories appeared on the edge of towns and older heavy works stood idle, no longer spreading their noise and smoke over neighbouring communities. On the death of one old miner in Llanharan in 1959, the local paper remarked, 'The demise of the collieries saw the passing of many of these outstanding characters and personalities. So much so, that it can be truthfully said that the Llanharan of today has sadly lost its true identity.' When a local pit closed three years later, an ex-collier told the press, 'We have relied so much on the [colliery] hooter that Llanharan will not be the same with so much peace and quiet. It will alter the traditional colliery life of the village, although I suppose we will get used to the change in time.'[24] In a 1968 novel the wife of one miner remarks of her village after the pit closed: 'It's depressing since all the life has gone. Our street alone – why it's full of old people. You can hear them coughing at night.'[25] That same year, a retired Monmouthshire miner wrote in the *Western Mail* after another colliery closure: 'There is nothing to mourn about. The young can move on and start afresh. We who stay will, no doubt, linger on until some official will come and condemn our houses. And so we'll be rehoused somewhere. It is nothing to us old 'uns really. No one can hurt us much more. But a village will die!'[26] Even where a local colliery stayed open, there was still a sense of frustration in the surrounding community because there was always the threat of closure, while the job itself was increasingly regarded as not just dangerous but poorly paid too.

Falling populations in traditional industrial centres meant falling local taxation revenues and this reduced the ability of local authorities to provide amenities. Health and education services were being concentrated in larger centres of population, reinforcing the sense of marginalization in smaller communities. Government economic policy did not help, as it concentrated on the largest industrial estates outside the central valleys and promoted growth in the more accessible Cwmbran and Llantrisant. Exasperated, the chairman of the local council in Blaenavon complained in 1962 that 'We are being planned out of existence'. The town had lost 13.9 per cent of its population in ten years as people moved to new jobs further down the Valleys and to the new town at Cwmbran (see below). When the government then planned to develop Llantrisant into a town of up to 145,000 people, it met with opposition from MPs and most of the local district authorities in south Wales, who feared the impact on their own economies. One alderman accused Glamorgan County Council, which supported the plans, of trying to kill off the Rhondda.[27] Studies in the Rhondda at the start of the 1970s found an anomic population that felt a lack of leadership, a nostalgia for the past and a sense of not belonging and anti-authoritarianism. Absenteeism was high, as were occurrences of psychosomatic illness. An unemployed girl from Merthyr told a writer, 'People think we live in caves down here.'[28] Delegates at a 1973 conference about the future of the Valleys reported that people there felt deeply stigmatized and apathetic. They listed the problems of their communities:

> Vandalism, industrial closures, unemployment, poor housing, bad urban planning, large estates with no sense of belonging, withdrawal of locally based essential services, having to travel to register complaints, remote central government, decision-making away from the people, lack of civic pride, pollution, run-down of social amenities.[29]

In 1974, Mid Glamorgan County Council's education director wrote bluntly to the Secretary of State for Wales: 'The Valleys are dying.'[30]

In many ways the governments of the 1950s and 1960s did give up on the Valleys. Industry was being encouraged to come to Wales but there was no state insistence on it being located in the places where it was needed most.[31] This was evident in the faith government placed in the idea of new towns. Cwmbran, which lies on the north–south route from the eastern valleys to the coastal belt, was designated a new town in 1949, when it had a population of around 12,000. Its primary aim was to reduce the travelling that was taking place in the area by providing homes for existing workers. It was planned around five residential neighbourhoods, each with its own social, retail and educational facilities. One architectural survey described them as 'neat and pleasant, yet without being particularly daring or modern'.[32] There was also a large town centre, designed to offer pedestrianized covered shopping and, what was thought by its planners to be its biggest asset, up to 4,000 parking spaces. The town had a population of 35,000 in 1965, was growing by 2,000 a year and had a target of 55,000.[33] Cwmbran differed from most of the new towns in that it was based on a reasonably large pre-existing settlement but, with a ring road, no high street and a design that emphasized the car, some complained that the town lacked a heart or soul.

Cwmbran suffered from comparisons with the old ideal of Valleys communities. Similarly, one young Rhondda housewife told the press in 1965, 'I don't want to go down to the Vale to live. It holds nothing for me. It is cold and has no character.'[34] That was also a complaint about many of the new housing estates that were being built in this period, despite their better-quality housing, public spaces and dense designs that were supposed to enhance community. A lack of room on the valley floors meant that some estates were built on steep hillsides and even moorlands up to 1,000 feet above sea level. The Penrhys estate, on the ridge between the two Rhondda valleys, was inspired by Italian hill settlements but did not have an Italian climate and there was some difficulty in getting people to move to and stay on such developments. A lack of facilities such as shops and pubs did not help the new estates. In 1958 residents of the Pentre Maelor estate at Wrexham complained that they had to travel five and a half miles to get to a shop. The author of a report on regenerating the Rhondda claimed the new housing estates lacked 'any sense of locality'. He pointed to the Rhiwgarn estate, which, he claimed, was not the Rhondda or Wales. For him, putting semi-detached houses in the Rhondda would destroy it.[35] New estates were not helped by the points system used to allocate council housing. This meant that the estates had an over-representation of single parents and large families with low incomes. Thus the people most in need of help were all together in remote estates, where providing support was more difficult and local amenities such as shops, pubs and clubs were least accessible.[36] Despite the fabric of homes being better than the traditional terraces, the seeds were being sown for a future calamity.

High-rise housing was proving particularly problematic, even though few such blocks were built. A 1967 survey found that 84 per cent of the people moved into a fifteen-storey block in Butetown (Cardiff) would prefer to live somewhere else and 30 per cent wanted to move out immediately. Half the residents of the 195 flats said they could tolerate living there but only reluctantly. The flats had been built in 1964 as part of the slum clearances in the docks area and nearly three-quarters of occupants said they had not chosen to live in them. The local authority had decided to build flats only because many locals had not wanted to leave densely populated Butetown. Elsewhere, where the population density was much lower, it had built houses. The dissatisfaction was strongest among parents, who were afraid of their children falling down the stairs or even out of windows. The street was felt to be too far away for children to play in and even the local director of education called the flats cages for children. Other common complaints concerned the 'hospital atmosphere' of the entrance halls, families dropping rubbish out of the windows, a lack of facilities to dry clothes and trouble with the lifts. Two-thirds of people also complained of noisy neighbours and there was a general sense of being cut off and a disappearing community spirit.[37]

The social integration of those in such new housing developments became a topic of social and political comment across Britain. There were alarmist reports of illness in new towns and psychiatrists began to talk about 'Crawley neurosis', where housewives struggled to settle in the lonely new estates and towns. As historian Harry Hopkins put it in 1963,

> A lifetime of 'slipping around the corner' to pub and club was abruptly broken off. Mum – miles away now – couldn't 'pop in' for a cup of tea and a natter. Sitting on the doorstep to watch the world go by was 'not done'. In any case, all one would have seen would have been a row of front doors, brightly painted, neat – and closed.[38]

People did seem to miss the neighbourliness and complained about the costs of the new housing. The popularity of television soap opera *Coronation Street*, which began in 1960 and quickly drew very large audiences, may have owed something to sentimental nostalgia for the old-style communities. By 1970 people were reluctant to move to Plas Madoc, a new estate in Wrexham, because the housing crisis was easing and people were becoming more selective. The local paper reported that people did not want to be 'uprooted from their own neighbourhood to live on a large estate where they lose their identity and sever close community ties'.[39] But community was not absent on the new estates. Harry Hopkins noted that, in time, people did settle and, even if the patterns of life on them remained different, the new estates were not without their own society as people got to know their neighbours. Indeed, sociological studies in comparable English housing estates suggested that most people were far happier in the modern conditions that they had moved to.[40] As long as it was affordable, cleaner, larger and more modern, housing was perhaps worth the sacrifice of old-fashioned communities. But older traditions had not died out. On two middle-class estates in Swansea, just over half the 120 husbands who lived there came home from work for their lunch.[41]

People may have been more dispersed but they still retained maps of mental connections that crossed geographical boundaries, extending beyond the new estates and helping keep alive a wider sense of community. As one resident of Swansea put it, that town was really 'a string of villages tied together with gossip'. Family was fundamental to this and it continued to be influential in how people both thought of and lived their lives, even if it was spread out over a wider geographical area and, with more women working, less important in day-to-day life than for earlier generations. In a survey of Swansea 54 per cent of married women has seen their mother in the last twenty-four hours and another 27 per cent had in the last week. There was mutual benefit to such contact, as parents gave practical support, not least with childcare, which enabled daughters to work, and adult children helped ageing parents with domestic chores and care. Some married men even had tea at their mother's every day, while some older parents visited their children every evening to watch television. Tensions and quarrels were, of course, common, especially over behaviours and burdens of care, and it was a common complaint of the elderly that the young did not look after them the way they used to look after their own elderly relatives. But the Swansea survey concluded that family was still at the heart of society and, amid a mobile population, this ensured some sense of community, even if it was not central to deciding where in the town people lived.[42]

Yet the importance and accessibility of family also harmed the emergence of a sense of community on the new estates. This was evident in a study of two middle-class housing estates in west Swansea, which showed clear differences between locals and non-locals. Locals had extended families in the town and were thus not reliant on neighbours for help and support, whereas the non-locals placed much greater investment in day-to-day contact with their neighbours, who helped at times of illness and with babysitting, laying drives, patios and so on. This ability of locals to call on family rather than neighbourly support created a clearly felt sense of division. The locals were referred to as 'the Welsh', even though many of the non-locals were also from Wales. The wife of one engineer put it thus: 'They don't really want to get to know you, have you noticed that, it's as if you are unwelcome in their country, no I don't mean that, they are just different and they keep themselves to themselves … they just don't join in like the rest of us'.[43] People were especially interested in the occupations of other people on the estates and keen to understand their place in their respective hierarchies but unlike the issue of being local this did not structure social relations. There was, of course, contact between the locals and non-locals, not least when they lived next door, but the social division was real and felt.

It was older people who were most concerned at the changes. They were a living link with an older way of life; their generation spanned the movement from the countryside to the towns at the end of the nineteenth century. What is now distant history was then living memory. The Wales of their childhoods had gone or was going and they were uncertain of the implications of the new world of hire purchase and supermarkets, of trading estates and colossal steel mills.[44] They resented the appearance of betting shops on the high streets and the emptying of the chapels and were deeply suspicious of the newness of the affluent society. In 1960, a Swansea man in his seventies remarked:

> I don't want to go back to that [poverty], but I do think we've lost a lot too when I look at the way the children seem to live, hardly ever seeing one another except when they meet here at their Mam's and hardly knowing who their neighbour is. Tell you the truth I wouldn't like to live with any one of them. We lived all together in the old days in Morriston – now they all seem to live in worlds of their own.

The sociologists who were told this story reported that the old seemed 'bewildered and confused by the social revolution of the last generation or so, and filled with nostalgia for the friendly, familiar, stable, familial atmosphere of the past'. But, significantly, they also concluded that 'the young seem less sentimental'.[45] For them the new living standards had raised expectations and weakened the appeal of older aspirations to get on in the union or chapel. Instead, thought other investigators in south-west Wales, money now mattered more.[46] Poverty had created the communal and tight-knit culture of the working class and it was affluence that was killing it, even if only by driving people away in search of it or making them resentful of what they had not got.

AFFLUENCE ALSO UNDERMINED another Welsh ideal, the classless society.[47] In rural communities the sense that class was an alien concept was particularly strong and instead people believed in a homogenous, Nonconformist, Welsh-speaking society. In industrial Wales the shared experiences of religion and work were thought to have created communities with little social distinction within them and that were united in their loyalty to the Labour Party and trade union movement. Indeed, because the Labour Party was the local establishment, it was quite possible to be a manual worker and someone of significant local importance. Moreover, the value placed upon education and cultural achievement meant that it was, as one Welsh actress remembered, 'dangerous, certainly unwise, to assume that a working-class person was uneducated or illiterate'.[48] The appearance of equality was added to by the way regional accents disguised social differences in a way that was far rarer in England.

Despite this widespread belief that Wales was classless, there was certainly a consciousness of class at the beginning of the post-war period. One study of miners in 1949 claimed:

> The great majority of miners are not politically minded, but all of them have an enormous – I would say overwhelming – class consciousness. Even the least intelligent, who has only a dim picture of the world and events, and who can scarcely think for himself, knows one thing: that he belongs to a separate class of men, who earn their living by working with their hands, and whose interests are served by the unions; and nothing that has happened or could happen can shake this belief. He does not read political, social and economic books, and in most cases his definitions of socialism are naïve; but he knows one thing – that he is a worker belonging to a class which has been oppressed for centuries, and which must always be on its guard to get a fair deal – which he is not likely to get by arguments, by sympathy or charity, but only by the strength of the whole body of the working class, by its physical and organised power.[49]

For the Welsh miners, by and large, the target of that class consciousness was not a local or Welsh middle class but an external one that lived elsewhere. It did nothing to diminish the idea that Wales itself was classless. Yet, in both rural and industrial areas, economic status clearly mattered and the myth of classlessness disguised the tensions and divides that existed within communities, tensions and divides the pulls of the modern world were exacerbating.

On a broader British platform there was some feeling that traditional class boundaries were collapsing and the working class was undergoing embourgeoisement by its affluence. Political scientists began to talk of 'class hybrids', skilled workers who were 'working class by occupation and culture, but middle class in terms of income and lifestyle'.[50] Both the Conservative and Labour Parties consequently tried to portray themselves as classless (while simultaneously portraying the other as class based). In a world where large parts of the working class were affluent and its most able members socially mobile, while much of the middle class were committed to the consensus around welfare, the old class basis of politics was no longer quite so sure. Yet when social scientists tested these assertions they found clear evidence that people still believed that a two-class system existed and the vast majority knew their position within it. Other surveys showed that people, especially the middle classes, thought a three-class system existed.[51] Inequalities were still obvious within society, not least in who was running the country. Cultural markers of class, such as manual work, accent, leisure habits and dress, also remained. Social mobility may have confused and blurred the boundaries but they clearly still existed.

This was true of urban Wales too. The rhetoric of classlessness was perhaps as much about trying to make Wales appear different to England as it was a genuine reflection on the situation in Wales. When people examined Wales on its own terms, rather than in comparison with England, then it was clear that class existed. To outsiders the Valleys may have seemed 'in effect one and the same place, a series of interchangeable villages peeping out between the tips through a persistent drizzle' but to people raised there the local loyalties and local divisions were significant. Thus a small mining village like Aberaman had, in local eyes, 'a posh part'. Even within the mines there was a clear pecking order, with face workers at the top and surface workers and contractors at the bottom. In traditional urban communities the middle class was getting smaller as it became easier for people in such occupations to commute from more 'attractive' areas. In 1966 in the central valleys, professional workers, employers and managers made up just 6 per cent of economically active and retired men.[52] However small the middle class was, class tensions were certainly known within industrial communities. There was a clear resentment of 'Tin pot officials, people who sit in offices all day, who'd just faint if they got their hands dirty' as one mining novel put it.[53] When a factory in Ammanford closed in 1958 the blame locally was put on 'school teachers and clergymen', in the belief that the residents of large semi-detached houses opposite the factory had prevented it from getting planning permission to expand.[54] A readership survey for the *Western Mail* in 1962 estimated that 11 per cent of Wales was middle class (compared with nearly 15 per cent for Britain as a whole). Official attempts as classifying the population showed that Wales had a lower proportion of professional and skilled workers than Britain but a higher proportion of intermediate, semi-skilled and unskilled. In a 1960 extensive survey of Swansea only 1 per cent of people did not know what class to allocate themselves to, while 59 per cent chose 'working class' and 31 per cent 'middle class' (figures similar to surveys in England). Many respondents were well aware of the simplicities of the two-tier system but, as the two social scientists responsible concluded, class was 'hazy' but 'very real' in people's minds and lives.[55]

For most people in the Swansea survey, class seemed to be a complex mix of behaviour, wealth and perception. It showed clear differences in taste and behaviour. The papers people read, the holidays they took, what they eat and drank, the music they liked and what they watched on television all helped mark where people were situated or imagined they were. The sociologists drew up a table to illustrate the 'rough cultural dichotomy' and argued that 'most people fall, by and large, one side or the other of this great cultural divide'.[56] In the working-class column were bingo, football pools, holiday camps, coach tours, hire purchase, pop music, ITV, bowls, mild and the *Daily Mirror*. In the middle-class column were premium bonds, private holidays, motoring, budget accounts, 'good' music, BBC, golf, bitter and the *Daily Mail*. Similarly, when the *Western Mail* asked people in Wales who the middle class were, they were identified by their accent, clothes, hair and tastes, with one housewife summing up that it was 'anyone who doesn't play bingo'.[57] Even in less prosperous industrial towns, where cultural tastes perhaps diverged less significantly, material differences still acted as a loose indicator of class. Thus, as one short story put it, 'the family were what might be called very lower middle class. That is to say, they ran to a new second-hand car every five years and were the first in the street to have a fully automatic washing machine with spin dryer.'[58]

Cultural tastes were fundamental divisions because they were public and tangible affirmations of status, wealth and difference in a world where social mobility had blurred the old boundaries of occupation and family roots. A collier's son who had a Cambridge education, a profession and a home in Gower remarked, 'It's education and speech and general style of living that counts nowadays – not just money or family background'. These blurring of boundaries created opportunities for people to imagine their position in the social hierarchy rather differently to how outsiders might see it. Twenty-three per cent of manual workers in Rosser and Harris' Swansea survey described themselves as middle class and 32 per cent of non-manual workers as working class. Thus a forty-one-year-old male nurse who lived on a council estate claimed 'Swansea has the usual three classes – working, middle and kidding themselves'.[59] A further complication was that income alone was no longer a marker. In the early 1960s some Welsh factory and steel workers were earning £30 a week, more than many of those in professional occupations. The Swansea study also acknowledged that there were many people, probably more than a third of the population, who fell somewhere in-between the working and middle classes, as a result of how the profile of their occupations, family backgrounds, education and cultural tastes did not neatly fit into either class. This was partly because social mobility was not just a matter of moving upwards. In the study of Swansea, 5 per cent of the sample were men in artisan jobs but whose fathers had been in managerial or professional occupations. This was only a little less than the 8 per cent of managers and professionals whose fathers had been artisans. Most people did not move up or down. Fifty-six per cent of the sample were artisans whose fathers had been artisans.[60]

Social mobility centred on education. Beyond teaching, there was little work in the Valleys that required much of an education, which meant that the better the education boys and girls received, the more likely they were to leave the area or go on the dole. Despite the fact that education and university degrees were unlikely to solve the problems of an industrial town, out of a mix of idealism, pragmatism and snobbery, they were widely esteemed in all Wales. Collections were held for local children going off to university and letters after a name were seen as so important that 'all the village and the neighbours talk about Tom B.A., or Caradoc B.Sc.'[61] Even Welsh-speaking children brought up with stories of the English oppression of the Celts could find themselves under parental pressure to move up in the English world of class and language. It worked and bright children made heroes of barristers and scholars 'who'd come up from NOTHING, mind'.[62] The desire to see people get on was often rooted in experiences of having to graft. Rugby international Mervyn Davies, the son of a Swansea welder, remembered that the 'greatest demand' his parents placed on him was that he pass the eleven-plus:

> They gave me no choice. If I was going to get anywhere in life, if I wanted to avoid a dirty, dangerous future, if I wanted to get well away from the acrid smoke of the smelters' yard or the blackness of the mine, then I would have to 'think' my way out. My father didn't want either one of his boys toiling away like him.[63]

Such attitudes were so common that the Rhondda president of the National Union of Teachers complained in 1960 that people were putting too much emphasis on education, saying 'We're not all cut out for "white collar" jobs or to achieve the ambitions of snobbish parents'. In 1958 a councillor in Ammanford complained, 'Some women will do anything to get their children in so she can say "My child is in a grammar school." With all these promises of a bicycle if they pass, by the time they get to the examination they are nervous wrecks, and it is all because of parental snobbishness.'[64]

Many blamed women for it, but snobbery was common in industrial communities. It underpinned the culture of 'keeping up with the Joneses' that drove forward the spread of consumer goods (see chapter 3). It was also entwined with the emphasis placed on public conduct. One historian claims the key divide in Barry (a place he called 'the quintessential small British town') in the late 1940s and early 1950s was not between the middle and working classes but between 'unskilled labourers and those working-men who prided themselves on traditional artisan values' of respectability. Fiction certainly shows that within industrial communities individuals could think of others as 'not their kind of people'.[65] One man remembered of his 1940s childhood in Treforest 'we were, in short, a *tidy* family, and we boys were not allowed to forget it'. A woman in Merthyr remembered her life being controlled by the ethics of her extended family, and any 'sign of abandonment on my part was crushed with a simple "What would the neighbours think?"'[66] Gossip was important everywhere and acted as a social sanction. An English woman who ran a catering business in Wales complained that people threw rubbish over the wall at the back of their houses, concerned only that the front was tidy. And yet being too open about that snobbery was widely regarded as poor form. The son of a miner who becomes a university lecturer notes in one 1960 novel that 'going up in the world for us is a rude thing to say, it means going snobby, getting stuck up'. Nonetheless, his mother lived on 'my bit of glory' because her son is 'getting on in the world'.[67]

Snobbery reached its peak among the bourgeoisie, the better-off members of the middle class, or the *crachach* as they were called in Welsh, a people found in the larger towns and more rooted in the English upper middle class than in the Welsh popular culture around them. While some members were caught up in a tight constricting respectability, others sought something more glamorous, even bohemian. All had their own snobberies. One short story suggested there were clubs where people were proud to have 'no Jews, bookies or inspectors of taxes'.[68] John Fulton, principal of the university in Swansea until 1961, objected to his professors and lecturers appearing together on the same radio broadcasts. He likened it to officers mixing with men. He was a socialist but he sent his sons to Eton. Yet an academic at Swansea was told by a local, 'We don't mix with people from the university. They have second-hand prams and their children pick things up from the floor.' One Swansea woman who cleaned a dentist's home in the town was angry at her 'Lady Muck' employer and the local teachers who thought themselves superior to the dinner ladies.[69] Kingsley Amis, another academic at Swansea from 1949 to 1961, captured this world in his 1955 novel *That Uncertain Feeling*. The hero, a librarian son of a miner, says of what he saw as the local upper class: 'why couldn't they stay Welsh? Why had they got to go around pretending to be English all the time?' Yet, to the actual English upper class, the *crachach* could seem quite different. A review of the book in *Tatler* called them 'staggeringly common'.[70]

After his election as Ebbw Vale MP in 1960, Michael Foot claimed that:

> The people of industrial Wales are proud of their working-class tradition, proud of their working-class achievements and still as proud as ever of *being* working class. Against this rock all the prissy values preached by the BBC, all the tinsel tuppenny-halfpenny ideas filtered through television, all the snobbery and smug complacency associated with a Tory-directed affluent society beat in vain.... Men and women still believe that it is better to live in a real community than to set before themselves the idea of rising out of their class.[71]

He was right that class was alive in people's minds, even if precisely what they meant by class was unclear, but wrong that there was no aspiration to escape its lower rungs. Even if they did not articulate it that way, class for most people was an idea, a description and a label rather than a sociological and closed category. It was more about where you were rather than where you came from. But where people were was changing and the affluence and social mobility of the 1950s and 1960s showed that moving beyond the working class was possible and that raised people's hopes of doing precisely that. Owning a washing machine and seeing your children gain a profession were realizable dreams that encouraged snobbery and fragmented the mental unity of the working class, exacerbating the process begun by the decline of religion and communities centred on a single workplace. For some English commentators this represented the embourgeoisement of the working class but that was a misleading idea. There may have been something of a convergence with middle-class lifestyles but there was not assimilation. Differentials of income and cultural taste remained. Owning a washing machine did not make someone middle class. More importantly, not everyone even owned a washing machine. Thus the most significant thing affluence did to the class structure of Wales was not to dissolve the gap between the workers and the middle class but to blur its boundaries and increase the differences within the working class. People were only too aware of that and their preoccupation with status meant, if anything, that class became more not less important in affluent Wales.

NOT EVERYONE IN WALES was Welsh. The number of people in Wales who were born in England rose from 360,688 in 1951 to 415,305 in 1971. Some of this was down to Welsh residents using maternity hospitals in Chester and Shrewsbury but there was also a migration of English people into both urban and rural areas. Between 1961 and 1966 alone, nearly 55,000 people were estimated to have moved into south Wales from England (with nearly 67,000 moving the other way).[72] Most of the industrial developments of the 1950s and 1960s were by companies based in England and they brought with them their own managers and technical staff. This meant that most middle and senior managers were English. Not all came enthusiastically. As one chemist who settled in Swansea put it, 'We were more than dubious at first … we expected [it] to be very drab and "How Green is my Valley"'.[73] Such fears were generally dispelled by living away from the immediate area where they worked. Thus steel executives at Port Talbot tended to live away from the industrial environment, choosing places like Gower and Porthcawl. Factory management also often lived in more desirable areas than the industrial districts where government support had meant their factories were located.[74] There is nothing to suggest they met any real anti-Englishness but if there was resentment of English management it would have been entangled with class tensions. However, their presence did perhaps reinforce the connections in people's minds between the English language and social status.

It was not just middle-class English people who were moving into urban Wales. The recurring labour shortages within the coal industry and pit closures in the north of England led to miners arriving in north Wales from Lancashire and Yorkshire. A newspaper described the Point of Ayr colliery in 1968 'with its 150 Joneses, its contingent of Lancashire lads, its Jamaicans, Spaniards and Germans' as a 'happy colliery'. The English were welcomed but there was a sense of difference evident in some anti-English camaraderie and banter in the pubs and under ground, and in the way their children continued to be thought of as English years later. That sense of difference owed something to the English miners having different terms for tools and being less involved in local cultural activities such as the male voice choir. The incomers themselves complained of the lack of a 'working-class culture' and even took coach trips back to Lancashire to visit clubs, while their wives felt isolated in places where shops and entertainment were now a poor bus service away rather than within walking distance.[75] Yet despite the sense of difference, there is little evidence to suggest there was any significant ethnic tension, perhaps because the similarities with the English in-migrants far outweighed the sense of difference. Similarly, judging by the size of their majorities, the electorate of mining constituencies like Ebbw Vale were quite happy to accept English people with few local connections as their Labour MPs.

England, of course, was experiencing its own immigration and the 1950s and 1960s saw the movement of people from the Commonwealth become a political hot potato. Overt racial prejudice was generally frowned upon but there were clearly popular prejudices and imagined differences between black and white. After Enoch Powell's infamous 1968 warning that immigration would lead to 'rivers of blood', a local paper in Pembrokeshire, an almost entirely white county, asked whether their new Conservative candidate would 'stand up for Mr Powell and say that he was right'.[76] He did not but the paper's views were in accord with wider opinion polls that suggested that over 70 per cent of the British population agreed with Powell. Tensions had already turned into violence at the Notting Hill riots of 1958. In their wake an editorial in the *South Wales Echo* claimed that the trouble was not representative of white opinion but just thugs looking for easy fun. Nonetheless, it went on: 'There IS disquiet about the number of immigrants allowed into Britain from the colonies, and some new policy has been required for some time. The Government must seriously review this basic problem of easy immigration.'[77] The paper was probably in tune with its readers here but there was no large-scale immigration into its catchment area. Wales simply did not have enough jobs or cheap housing to attract Commonwealth immigrants in great numbers. In 1966 there was just an estimated 12,810 people born in the Commonwealth and living in Wales.[78]

Cardiff did, however, have a long-established immigrant community in Butetown, where some 80 per cent of the 6,000 inhabitants were not white. One visitor in the 1950s remembered, 'It was like a foreign country – the people dressed in seafaring clothes, boiler suits, saris, Arabian robes and the brightly coloured clothes of Africa and the West Indies'.[79] This ethnically mixed community had developed at the start of the twentieth century and was sometimes held up as an example of racial tolerance. In 1951 *The Times* reported,

> Cardiff may be described as the coloured man's paradise in Great Britain. In no other city are the coloured people so much a part of the community as in this South Wales city, and nowhere else is there evidence of so much friendliness between them and their white fellow citizens.

But the perception of tolerance came from the fact that the black population was actually, as *The Times* later acknowledged, 'exceptionally isolated' from the rest of Cardiff.[80] The *Picture Post* noted in 1950 that 'partly by race prejudice, partly by repute, partly by the queer conformation of the place they live in, they are cut off from the ordinary life of the city, and trapped in what is the nearest thing to a ghetto we have in this free land'. Butetown was an urban slum and other Cardiffians thought it a dangerous and disreputable place and were often very unwilling to socialize or work with blacks. As a Somali seaman put it,

> Outside here, they believe we've got horns under our hats. We've got some of the worst bastards and some of the best people, same as everywhere. But if I go up into town, say to the pictures, why, man, everybody looks at me as I left some buttons undone.

There was also a crime problem, notably when it came to prostitution. One sympathetic black writer claimed in 1954, no doubt with some exaggeration, that 'quite often' at cafés, some of which were covers for brothels, a 'knockout drop' would be added to drinks and the recipient would wake up with empty pockets in a nearby lane. Such beliefs meant that the area attracted much unwanted attention. Outsiders were not popular, claimed the *Picture Post*: 'Too many of them act as if they are afraid they'll be knocked on the head, or else are rude to the girls, or ask the boys if they can read and write.'[81]

In the 1960s, amid growing ethnic tensions in England and the United States, Wales actually seemed rather peaceful. The *Western Mail* concluded in 1967 that although people were becoming more aware of racial questions, south Wales was 'nowhere near the brink of racial trouble'. There were then some 8,000 'coloured people' in Cardiff and another 1,000 in Newport. The paper put down the 'considerable success' in integration in employment, housing and religion to the fact that some black people were third or fourth-generation immigrants, which provided a stabilizing influence it felt was not found in many other towns. Housing conditions were improving and, although some of the black population had now been moved to other working-class parts of Cardiff, 73 per cent of people living in Butetown had been asked to be rehoused there. But beneath the *Western Mail*'s congratulatory headlines there were hints of tensions. Butetown and its population remained physically and socially isolated from the rest of the city. Only six girls from what the *Western Mail* termed 'immigrant families' had jobs in shops in the city centre and more would not apply because they feared rebuff. The paper suggested that racial difference was still plentiful enough that, 'presented with a tinder box, [it] could flare up into trouble'.[82]

If Cardiff lacked racial tolerance then there was little hope for other parts of Wales experiencing their first taste of overseas immigration. In 1969 residents in Baneswell in Newport objected to plans for an old warehouse to be used as a mosque, fearing it would lead to more Pakistanis moving into the area, depressing house prices. After a letter in the local press accused local residents of intolerance, one wrote in to say it was nothing to do with prejudice but locals felt their area was being classed as a slum and they were being forced to accept what better areas would not. In 1965 such attitudes were further evident when a black electrician from Liverpool who worked in Broughton (Flintshire) had his deposit returned after he tried to buy a house in a new estate near his workplace. The owner of the building company told the local press:

> I am awfully sorry for this gentleman. I would be quite happy to live next door to him but we are business men. We have more than £100,000 tied up in this estate and cannot afford to have property left on our hands. We had to ask ourselves if prospective buyers would be prepared to live on the same estate as coloured people.... If we allowed coloured people in there might be twenty or thirty families within no time. Then how would we stand?

There was some outrage at the news but beneath this was a more subtle prejudice that was based not on individuals but on a fear of being overrun. As one local housewife told a reporter, 'I have no objection to one coloured person coming but what I am afraid of is that they may bring more.'[83]

IN THE 1950s and 1960s change seemed to be everywhere in working-class Wales. People from England or even further afield were moving in. Young people were moving out, to new estates, new towns or even England. Traditional communities, where families and relations lived near each other and neighbours had similar jobs and incomes, were fragmenting. Occupations, wages, values, beliefs were all diversifying. Work itself was becoming more mechanized. The chapel was falling away as a local centre and leisure was becoming less 'cultured' and more domesticated, as homes became both more comfortable and, thanks to television, more entertaining. But homes were not even permanently occupied by women anymore, as more and more females found jobs to supplement family incomes in order to keep up with the neighbours and pay for hire-purchase agreements.

The old found these changes bewildering. Those younger people who were not fully sharing in the benefits of affluence were not happy either. Nor were some people outside working-class culture. Poet John Tripp described Port Talbot in 1970 as a

> restless wilderness. The basis of social life in this industrial insult are the packed working men's clubs, offering solidarity, mutual moral support for eternal grievances, mindless bingo and endless supplies of alcohol. In a way it is the end of the world, the place to which the greed, cynicism and insensitivity of our century has brought us.

He bemoaned that the inhabitants were not happy and endured boredom in return for a regular payslip. 'They have clubs and bingo, beer and skittles, a beach nearby with candy-floss and fish and chips. But they all look as happy as the inhabitants of "Coronation Street".'[84] The historian Kenneth Morgan similarly wrote, 'In place of the old class militancy, that fierce industrial culture associated with the miners' clubs, welfare halls, and the WEA [Workers' Educational Association], there was a shallow proletarian capitalism based on drinking clubs, bingo halls, and cheap holidays abroad'. He added: 'Everywhere, life seemed more conformist, more impersonal. The neighbourliness of old communities gave way to the alien impersonality of housing estates or commuter suburbs. Much of the vital culture of the Welsh heartland disappeared with them.' However, Morgan also conceded, 'It ill behoved middle-class critics to disparage the quality of life of working-class people enjoying the amenities of a more secure existence for the first time and revelling in its comforts.'[85] The real tragedy of the social changes that affluence brought was not what it did to working-class culture but the fact that not everyone shared in its material benefits.

In England, the bemoaning of the gradual passing of an old working-class culture owed much to people who had actually left it behind themselves through social mobility. They did not like a world they had left behind changing but they made no effort to go back there themselves.[86] Moreover, in England and in Wales the extent of change and the embourgeoisement of the working class were exaggerated. Firstly, the idea of the traditional homogenous urban world was mythologized by the nostalgia of those who had left and a determination to paint industrial Wales as a place apart. Secondly, while the majority of people were certainly better off, poverty remained and middle-class incomes rose too, thus preserving a gap. Finally, class remained a very real if rather hazy barrier. The extended reach of consumer goods may have reduced their power to signify social status but there were other signifiers of class. The papers people read, the holidays they took, what they eat and drank, the music they liked and what they watched on television all helped mark where people were situated. Some people certainly imagined they were higher up the social ladder than they really were and, thanks to some well paid skilled manual jobs or the benefits of a grammar school education, another group were somewhere 'in-between' the two classes, often with incomes like the middle class but the cultural tastes of the working class.

To what extent this undermined the cohesion of communities depends on how cohesive they were in the first place. Where there were now differences in income there had before been differences in religious belief and public behaviour. Knowing all your neighbours and working in the same place as them did not necessarily make a better society. You only need a small number of helpful neighbours or relatives to make life easier. In the past, as one observer pointed out, 'the close mesh of kinship and the friendship networks and the fact that everybody knew everybody else occasionally degenerated into spitefulness, jealousy, backbiting and into the stigmatising of certain families that did not observe neighbourhood standards and community values'.[87] Such happenings did at least recede, something which itself probably contributed to the growth of promiscuity which also partly characterized the 1960s. It also set the basis for the disappearance in urban areas of something people called 'the Welsh way of life', a culture rooted in the chapel, speaking Welsh and Sunday observance. The idea of class and knowing your neighbours did survive affluence but the Welsh way of life was to prove much weaker.

Notes

1 *SWE*, 7 July 1960. *South Wales Weekly Argus*, 9 July 1960. *WM*, 7 July 1960.

2 K. Amis, *That Uncertain Feeling* ([1955] 1975), 96.

3 J. Richards and D. Sheridan (eds), *Mass-Observation at the Movies* (1987), 245. K. Howells, 'After the strike', *Pl*, 51 (1985), 6–11. D. Berry, *Wales and Cinema: The First Hundred Years* (1994), 161–6, 246–8.

4 M. Gallie, *Man's Desiring* (1960), 50.

5 T. Brennan, E. W. Cooney and H. Pollins, *Social Change in South-West Wales* (1954).

6 D. K. Rosser, 'The decay of a Welsh-speaking street community: migration and its residual effects', *CW*, 3 (1989), 119–35.

7 D. Smith, *Wales: A Question for History* (1999), 163.

8 H. Carter, 'The crisis of the valleys and its challenge', in P. H. Ballard and E. Jones (eds), *The Valleys Call* (1975), 32.

9 R. Hoggart, *Uses of Literacy* (1957). K. Nurse, *Footsteps to the Past: A Welsh Quest* (1998), 81.

10 *LDP*, 3 Aug. 1953. 'Bach' is a term of endearment that translates as 'little'.

11 F. Zweig, *Men in the Pits* (1949), 110.

12 S. Moitra, 'Between class culture and mass culture: south Wales miners' institutes and the cinema after 1945', Industrial History, Industrial Culture: Representation, Past, Present, Future, conference, Swansea University, Sept. 2008. H. Francis, 'Survey of miners' institutes and welfare hall libraries, October 1972–February 1973', *Llafur*, 1:2 (1973), 93–9.

13 D. Massey, *Spatial Divisions of Labour: Social Structures and the Geography of Production* (1984).

14 G. Humphrys, *South Wales* (1972), 92, 94. W. K. D. Davies, 'Towns and villages', in D. Thomas (ed.), *Wales: A New Study* (1977), 202. C. Rosser and C. Harris, *The Family and Social Change: A Study of Family and Kinship in a South Wales Town* (1965), 75.

15 *WM*, 11 Mar. 1967. Calculated from G. L. Rees, *Survey of the Welsh Economy*, Commission on the Constitution research paper (1973), 137–40.

16 *Rhondda Fach Observer, Leader and Free Press*, 19 Nov. 1961. Humphrys, *South Wales*, 91

17 D. Reynolds, 'Planning a future for Rhondda's people', in K. S. Hopkins (ed.), *Rhondda: Past and Future* (1974), 249–50, 251.

18 S. W. Town, *After the Mines: Changing Employment Opportunities in a South Wales Valley* (1978), 22. T. Rees, 'Population and industrial decline in the south Wales coalfield', *Regional Studies*, 12:1 (1978), 69–77.

19 Brennan *et al.*, *Social Change*, 6.

20 P. M. Williams (ed.), *The Diary of Hugh Gaitskell, 1945–1956* (1983), 156.

21 *DWS*, 16 (1970), 29. W. T. R. Pryce, *Housing and the People: An Introduction to Problems and Policies in the City of Cardiff* (1976), 10.

22 B. Dumbleton, *'Help Us, Somebody': The Demolition of the Elderly* (2006), 75–7. H. Jones and C. Bellinger (dirs), *After Many a Summer: The Changing Face of Tiger Bay* (1968).

23 Rosser and Harris, *The Family and Social Change*, 47, 66, 8. C. Bell, *Middle Class Families: Social and Geographical Mobility* (1968), 22, 37. M. Stacey, *The Human Ecology of the Lower Swansea Valley* (1962), ch. 3.
24 Quotes from T. J. Witts, *A Time of Tears: Llanharan and Brynna, the Story of Two Mining Villages Where Coal Reigned Supreme at the Turn of the Century* (2000), 119, 122.
25 R. Berry, *Flame and Slag* (1968), 172.
26 *WM*, 3 Feb. 1968.
27 *The Times*, 17 Apr. 1962 and 18 May 1971. *Rhondda Observer, Leader and Free Press,* 29 Jan. 1965.
28 Reynolds, 'Planning a future', 258–9. M. Jones, *Life on the Dole* (1972), 86.
29 P. H. Ballard and E. Jones (eds), *The Valleys Call* (1975), 43, 41.
30 K. S. Hopkins, 'A letter to the Secretary of State for Wales', in Hopkins (ed.), *Rhondda*, 269.
31 G. Manners, 'A profile of the new south Wales', in G. Manners (ed.), *South Wales in the Sixties* (1964), 62.
32 J. B. Hilling, 'Architecture', in M. Stephens (ed.), *The Arts in Wales, 1950–75* (1979), 155.
33 Cwmbran Development Corporation, *Town of Opportunity: Cwmbran New Town and the Trader* (1965) and *Cwmbran New Town: A Brief Account of Its Objectives and Developments* (nd).
34 *WM*, 11 Oct. 1965.
35 Humphrys, *South Wales*, 105. *WL*, 24 Oct. 1958. *WM*, 11 Oct. 1965.
36 Reynolds, 'Planning a future', 260.
37 *WM*, 7 Nov. 1967.
38 D. Sandbrook, *Never Had It So Good: A History of Britain from Suez to the Beatles* (2005), 124. M. Young and P. Willmott, *Family and Kinship in East London* (1957). H. Hopkins, *The New Look: A Social History of the Forties and Fifties in Britain* (1963), 326–7.
39 C. Vereker, J. B. Mays, E. Gittus and M. Broady, *Urban Redevelopment and Social Change: A Study of Social Conditions in Central Liverpool 1955–56* (1961). K. Roberts, *The Working Class* (1978), 75. *WL*, 13 Feb. 1970.
40 Hopkins, *The New Look*, 327. Sandbrook, *Never Had It So Good*, 124–5.
41 Bell, *Middle Class Families*, 131.
42 Rosser and Harris, *The Family and Social Change,* 1, 219, 152–4, 269. Rosser, 'The decay of a Welsh-speaking street community'.
43 Bell, *Middle Class Families*, 136–7.
44 A. Richards, 'Disappearing Wales' (1963), in P. Hannan (ed.), *Wales on the Wireless* (1988), 153–4.
45 Rosser and Harris, *The Family and Social Change*, 12, 60.
46 Brennan *et al.*, *Social Change*, 7–8.
47 See for example J. Morgan, 'Two faces for a Welshman' (1961), in Hannan (ed.), *Wales on the Wireless*, 3.
48 S. Phillips, *Private Faces: The Autobiography* (1999), 269.
49 Zweig, *Men in the Pits*, 15.
50 B. Harrison, *Seeking a Role: The United Kingdom, 1951–1970* (2009), 209.
51 D. Cannadine, *Class in Britain* (1998), 144–55.
52 P. Hannan, *The Welsh Illusion* (1999), 23–4. K. Gildart, *North Wales Miners: A Fragile Unity, 1945–1996* (2001), 48. Humphrys, *South Wales*, 204–50 (Maesteg, Orgmore and Garw and Rhondda Urban Districts).
53 A. Haines, *The Drift* (1974), 154.
54 Town, *After the Mines*, 68.
55 *WM*, 11 Sep. 1962. Rees, *Survey of the Welsh Economy*, 12. Rosser and Harris, *The Family and Social Change*, 86, 110. Sandbrook, *Never Had It So Good*, 34.
56 Rosser and Harris, *The Family and Social Change*, 114.
57 *WM*, 11 Sept. 1962.
58 A. Richards, 'The drop-out' (1973), in J. Davies and M. Jenkins (eds), *The Valleys* (1984), 95.
59 Rosser and Harris, *The Family and Social Change*, 113, 92, 83–4.

60 *WM*, 11 Sept. 1962. Rosser and Harris, *The Family and Social Change*, 93–99, 102.
61 Jones, *Life on the Dole*, 78. C. Hughes, *A Wanderer in North Wales* (1949), 147.
62 D. Beddoe (ed.), *Changing Times: Welsh Women Writing on the 1950s and 1960s* (2003), 240–1. Phillips, *Private Faces*, 96.
63 M. Davies and D. Roach, *In Strength and Shadow: The Mervyn Davies Story* (2004), 28.
64 *Rhondda Fach Observer, Leader and Free Press*, 24 Dec. 1960. *Welshman*, 17 Jan. 1958.
65 Rosser and Harris, *The Family and Social Change*, 82. P. Stead, 'Barry since 1939: war-time prosperity and post-war uncertainty', in D. Moore (ed.), *Barry: The Centenary Book* (1985), 457. A. Richards, *Dai Country* (1973), 155.
66 M. Stephens, 'In John Jones's country', *PI*, 82 (1990), 19. Beddoe (ed.), *Changing Times*, 264.
67 Letter in *Wales*, 47 (Dec. 1959). M. Gallie, *Man's Desiring* (1960), 91, 150–1.
68 Richards, *Dai Country*, 213.
69 Z. Leader, *The Life of Kingsley Amis* (2006), 240, 354. Rosser and Harris, *The Family and Social Change*, 83.
70 Amis, *That Uncertain Feeling*, 208. Leader, *The Life of Kingsley Amis*, 355.
71 Quoted in M. Jones, *Michael Foot* (1994), 252.
72 Rees, *Survey of the Welsh Economy*, 142. South Wales was here defined as Glamorgan, Monmouth, Carmarthen and Brecon.
73 *Guardian*, 18 Feb. 1965. Bell, *Middle Class Families*, 31.
74 Bell, *Middle Class Families*, 12.
75 Gildart, *North Wales Miners*, 44, 105–7.
76 N. Crickhowell, *Westminster, Wales and Water* (1999), 12.
77 D. Sandbrook, *White Heat: A History of Britain in the Swinging Sixties* (2006), 643. *SWE*, 3 Sept. 1958.
78 *Sample Census 1966: Commonwealth Immigration Tables* (1969), 2, 8.
79 M. Stevens, *Solva Blues* (2004), 80.
80 *The Times*, 11 Jan. 1951 and 25 May 1959.
81 A. L. Lloyd, 'Down the bay', *Picture Post*, 22 Apr. 1950. L. Constantine, *Colour Bar* (1954), reproduced in J. Proctor (ed.), *Writing Black Britain: An Interdisciplinary Anthology* (2000), 64, 67.
82 *WM*, 27 July 1967.
83 *South Wales Argus*, 1 and 4 July 1969. *Flintshire Leader*, 29 Oct. 1965.
84 John Tripp, 'The monster in Glamorgan', *PI*, 1 (1970), 38–40.
85 K. O. Morgan, *Rebirth of a Nation: Wales, 1880–1980* (1981), 319, 347, 325.
86 T. Blackwell and J. Seabrook, *A World Still to Win: The Reconstruction of the Post-War Working Class* (1985), 88–90.
87 Reynolds, 'Planning a future', 250.

6

'Life among the hills.' The Welsh way of life, 1951–70

> Even today, therefore, if you wish to see the real Welsh people in their natural surroundings you must (like the prophets of old) look once again to the hills. There you will find them in their isolated farmsteads, surrounded by their families and their flocks and herds, speaking their native language, singing the hymns of their beloved nonconformist chapels. They will always find time to listen in to the broadcasts of the National Eisteddfod or a *cymanfa ganu* amidst the latest news of stock prices and the fortunes of the Milk Marketing Board. The fact is that in spite of modern innovations the essential fortunes of Welsh life among the hills have continued with little change for nearly 2,000 years.
>
> E. G. Bowen, in *The Land of the Red Dragon* (1969)

> This afternoon, Helen – went to the Birleys. For cocktails, Harri! Can you imagine that? Cocktails in Wales on a Sunday afternoon. Of course they're English, the Birleys.... There was this professor there – from Bangor. You should have seen his suit, Helen! Talked about wine all the time. My word, haven't things changed in this old country! When we were girls all the professors – even the scientists – did local preaching and supported the temperance movement. Now it's all that *Nuits St George* and the best year for *Beaujolais* with them.
>
> Stead Jones, *The Ballad of Oliver Powell* (1966), 32–3

ON 9 NOVEMBER 1953 a thirty-nine-year-old poet named Dylan Thomas collapsed and died. Although his health had been ruined by drink and his confidence racked by self-doubt, he was probably the most famous Welshman of his generation. He also encapsulated the ambiguities and uncertainties surrounding Wales and Welshness. His own father had consciously not passed on the Welsh language to his son, despite naming him after a figure from medieval Welsh literature. Thomas himself mocked

Welsh nationalism in a 1940 story in which a group of earnest nationalists search for 'seditious literature', proclaim 'Heil, Saunders Lewis!' and drink parsnip wine.[1] Nonetheless, the man who said 'Land of my fathers? My fathers can keep it' was emotionally entwined with Wales and another of his sayings was 'One: I am a Welshman; two: I am a drunkard; three: I am a lover of the human race, especially of women'. He also depicted Wales in his work, most famously in *Under Milk Wood* (1954), a portrayal of life in an eccentric village with promiscuous, drunken, mad and even murderous inhabitants. The play was immediately and widely popular for its humour and characterization. When it was performed in Swansea in the late 1950s, there were even audible 'Amens' in the audience after the Rev. Eli Jenkins spoke. But in Welsh literary circles the reception was quite different. In Eli Jenkins and his neighbours critics saw not a celebration of Wales but a mockery. The play was attacked as 'nonsense' and 'sordid and obscene'. A senior BBC official decided it was unfit for the Welsh Home Service and it was banned by a Cardiff Empire Games committee who thought it 'not truly representative of Welsh life'. There were attempts to have Thomas removed from a list of writers recommended overseas by the British Council.[2]

In 1964 the writer Gwyn Thomas wrote of his namesake Dylan: 'He was a sort of living revenge on all the restrictions and respectabilities that have come near to choking the life out of the Welsh mind.'[3] Those restrictions and respectabilities were integral to what many people regarded as the Welsh way of life, a culture rooted in Nonconformity, the Welsh language and public morality. Its origins were rural but the movement of people in the nineteenth century had also implanted it in urban areas, where it often transcended linguistic divisions and became an important symbol of how Wales was different to England. By the 1950s it was a way of life that was in retreat before the forces of affluence and modernization, and the hostility that Dylan Thomas often met among the Welsh intelligentsia owed much to a wider defensiveness that this cultural change was generating. Their frustration at what was happening was compounded by the way Thomas and so many of his fellow Welshmen and women were consciously turning their backs on all traditional Wales stood for. In urban Wales in the 1950s and 1960s that happened to such an extent that the Welsh way of life all but disappeared. Increasingly, it was the countryside that people regarded as the real Wales.

Anyone looking for the traditional Welsh way of life could find it in *Shepherds of Moel Siabod*, a 1967 television documentary about a farming family in Snowdonia. It depicted people with a simple lifestyle, bound to a harsh but beautiful landscape. There were glimpses of modernity in a television in the house and a Land Rover outside, but otherwise the family was living in a world that might as well have been a million miles away from the swinging sixties. The family lived mostly off bacon and eggs, dressed shabbily, read the Bible and had a social life that revolved around the chapel. The grandmother and a teenage son struggled to speak English, while the children disliked school and showed little inclination to do anything with their lives except farm.[4] While the majority of the audience probably gawped at the backwardness, there were no doubt some who warmly welcomed the evidence that the Welsh peasantry lived on. But any satisfaction would have been curtailed by the knowledge that beneath the timeless pictures was a rural society that was under severe external pressure. The young were leaving in droves, not least because mechanization in agriculture and the decline of traditional industries like slate quarrying meant there were few jobs. Religion, once at the heart of rural life, was being undermined by the secularism and alternative attractions of a modern age, an age that itself was making people less tolerant of the impoverished conditions characteristic of rural communities. Old traditions like blacksmithing and fishing with coracles were in danger of disappearing. The landscape was changing with the appearance of electricity pylons and power stations. Even 'parish talk and local opinion' were being replaced by the influence of television. Welsh monoglots were literally passing away. A Liberal peer asserted at the 1962 Montgomeryshire by-election that all around was 'the spectacle of a dying rural community.'[5]

With the coming of sewers, clean water, new houses, a village hall and a school canteen, a shopkeeper at Llanelltyd (Merioneth) noted in 1952 that the village had seen more developments in a year than it had in the last century. Such modernization, of course, brought benefits but the elderly looked back at the world of their childhoods and noted that hardly any of it now survived.[6] The nostalgia for the old peasantry was captured in D. J. Williams' *Hen Dŷ Ffarm* (1953), an evocative portrayal of his family history in Carmarthenshire, tinged with a despair at the erosion of this way of life. Williams complained of the 'moral turpitude and soul-rotting materialism' of the Welsh people. 'It is a sign of the present disregard of the values of our national life and of their deterioration', he complained, 'that so many Welsh people take more interest in the pedigree of their dogs and of their milking cows than in their own mothers' and fathers' descent and history'.[7]

WHILE SOME COMPLAINED that rural life was changing, others remained unhappy that some of the benefits of the modernization seen elsewhere in Britain were not reaching them fast enough. The state of rural housing was a particular problem. In 1950 a third of dwellings in some rural parishes were said to be empty or even in ruins, while another third were deemed unfit for habitation according to modern standards. In Cardiganshire and Montgomeryshire in 1953 some 80 per cent of the population were using earth or pail closets for toilets. There were local variations; in 1955 in Holyhead, 796 of the 3,005 houses in the area were unfit for human habitation, but in Betws-y-Coed there were no houses at all in that condition.[8] Local authorities' house-building programmes were slower to rectify problems in rural areas than they were in urban areas. In 1965, while one in four houses in Glamorgan and one in three in Monmouthshire had been built since the war, the figure was one in seven in Radnorshire and Merioneth. That year, one in six houses in Radnorshire and one in twelve in Merioneth still had no piped water; in contrast in Glamorgan the figure was one in seventy-five and in Monmouthshire one in fifty.[9] Even where a new house was built in a rural village, it was not always possible to connect it to modern services and the continuing lack of electricity in many villages was a particular gripe, despite the vast progress made over the course of the 1950s. Provision was slowest in the most westerly counties and a few remote villages were still not connected to the national grid in the 1960s. Isolated houses and farms were even worse off. In 1956, 40 per cent of Welsh farms did not have mains electricity. Some had their own generators but others continued to make do with paraffin lamps. By 1964 electricity had reached some 85 per cent of farms and many of the remainder were unconnected only because some farmers were reluctant to pay the cost and were wary of change.[10] One writer claimed in 1949 that the thrift of north Wales farmers often evolved into 'meanness' and 'a low standard of living to achieve the ambition of a fat bank balance'. They forsook modern furniture, food and clothes to save money. In Llanfihangel-yng-Ngwynfa (Montgomeryshire) one farmer had piped water installed to his cowshed in the 1950s but not to the house. Such attitudes were clear in a 1956 novel where an elderly farmer remarks: 'People today think the millennium has dawned if they have hot water and a bathroom. The only time you need hot water is on pig-killing day.'[11]

There was also a lack of jobs in rural communities. Agriculture was undergoing profound changes, as the mechanization of farms reduced both the need for labourers and the extent to which farmers relied on helping each other. The number of male agricultural workers thus fell from 92,510 in 1931 to 45,130 in 1971. This diluted the importance of agriculture to the rural economy, something evident in Montgomeryshire, where the share of the workforce occupied in agriculture fell from 50 per cent in 1931 to 32 per cent in 1971.[12] Yet, for farmers themselves, things were improving.

Electricity, tractors and machinery reduced the physical slog of farming, giving people more free time and easier lives. A shift from traditional breeds to Friesian cows in the 1950s improved milk yields and thus incomes. In Pembrokeshire, for example, milk production more than doubled between 1946 and 1956. Although uptake was initially slow, upland farmers could make use of new grants towards the cost of improving farm houses, outbuildings and installing water and electricity supplies. Agricultural subsidies, meanwhile, offered an invaluable degree of security in an uncertain industry; in 1958–9, Welsh farmers received nearly £14 million from the government.[13] But, for the small upland farms, government support was still not enough and, in the 1960s, 45 per cent of hill farmers still earned less than a typical farm worker's wage. The more successful and ambitious farmers, however, started buying up neighbours' land and the number of farms in Wales fell from 55,134 in 1950 to 36,184 in 1970. Although they brought returns, buying land, stock and machinery usually required borrowing money and the bank manager thus became an important figure in many farmers' lives, someone to whom they went 'in fear and trembling'.[14]

Rural Wales' other significant industry was slate. Demand was strong because of the boom in house building and yet the quarries in Caernarfonshire and Anglesey remained in terminal decline. Their machinery was outdated and they found it difficult to recruit skilled labour as many workers who had left the industry during the war never returned. By 1951 the slate industry was employing just 3,059 men, more than 4,500 fewer than it had in 1939. The danger and difficulties of working in the quarries dissuaded younger men from joining the industry and fathers could be reluctant to see their sons follow in their footsteps. In 1952 the manager of one quarry said 'I could employ 200 men but can only get 27'.[15] The labour shortages speeded up the closure of the smaller quarries but a more serious problem was that builders were switching to cheaper tiles and the industry lost around half its workforce in the 1950s.

The decline of agriculture and slate contributed to the fact that, by the late 1950s, parts of rural Wales had some of the worst unemployment problems in the UK. By December 1958 unemployment reached 9.2 per cent in Caernarfonshire and 12.5 per cent in Anglesey, at a time when it was 4.2 per cent in Wales as a whole and just 2.4 per cent in Britain. Moreover, even those with jobs were often badly paid. In 1957 the average income per head of population in mid-Wales was £132, compared with £172 for Wales as a whole, £182 in rural England and £228 in England as a whole. In 1966, 74 per cent of incomes in Cardiganshire were below £1,000 per annum, whereas the figures for the UK and Wales were 57 and 66 per cent respectively.[16]

Faced with such conditions, many people simply decided to move away, just as so many of their forefathers had. Between 1871 and 1961 the population of the five counties that made up mid-Wales had fallen by nearly a quarter but the decline gathered pace in the decade after 1951. In 1957 Goronwy Roberts MP (Labour, Caernarfonshire) remarked, 'At the moment the situation is awful. Every week, and almost every day I hear about people leaving.... Hunger drives them out of Wales.'[17] Merioneth and Radnor were the worst hit, losing 7.6 per cent of their population between 1951 and 1961. With a small amount of in-migration into some counties and an increase in the birth rate, such figures disguised the extent of migration. Between 1951 and 1961 nearly 10 per cent of the population of Radnor migrated away, while it was estimated that mid-Wales had lost nearly 6,000 people aged under sixty-five through migration.[18] The falls did slow in the decade after 1961, when mid-Wales lost 1.9 per cent of its population, compared with 3.8 per cent in the previous ten years. But there remained pockets where depopulation was at staggering levels. The Talyllyn parish (Merioneth), for example, saw its population fall by 23.7 per cent between 1961 and 1971.[19]

The popular emphasis on education exacerbated the loss of population since, in the words of one sociologist, '"getting on" inevitably meant "getting out"'. His 1950s study of one village found that, of the twenty-four pupils from the local primary school who had gone onto grammar school between 1933 and 1940, none still lived in the community and only six were still in the county. After the closure of some small schools in the 1944 reorganization of education, even just attending school could take children away from the local community and into neighbouring towns, where they became increasingly urbanized in outlook.[20] Over half the grammar school children in late 1940s Tregaron wanted to leave the village, and among pupils aged fourteen to eighteen this rose to 73 per cent. A 1964 report claimed that some people in mid-Wales thought 'success and migration are synonymous – and that that those who stay are not quite "with it"'.[21] Nationalists blamed teachers for glamorizing England as the place to 'get on' and as the home of kings, soldiers, poets and other famous people, while nothing was done by this 'anglicised education system to awaken their pride in Wales or their desire to serve her'.[22] This was a little unfair; there were simply not enough suitable jobs in rural communities for all those leaving grammar school. A Cardiganshire solicitor remarked in 1971 that by educating young people 'you make certain that they will not get work in the county'.[23]

Despite unemployment, depopulation could make finding labour very difficult. In Pembrokeshire some farmers had to transport in workers from up to eight miles away. Finding a wife could be even harder. Teenage farmers' sons were resigned to having to marry town girls because all the farmers' daughters had had enough of rural life and wanted to move away. One rural woman concluded, 'A wife is as indispensable to a hill farmer as a horse, and not nearly so easy to find. So news of a young farmer's forthcoming marriage would be greeted with a buzz of excitement and envy. "Where did he get hold of *her,* then?"'[24] The falling population also created a vicious circle where private enterprises struggled and local authorities had declining revenues to provide the better facilities that might help keep people. In 1953 there were sixteen schools in Cardiganshire that had fewer than twenty pupils and thus it was unsurprising that the county shut seven primary schools between 1952 and 1960. In 1961 there were two schools in the county that did not even have electricity. Infrequent bus services and the distance to a doctor, a cinema or good shops all mattered more in the post-war era than they once had. The decline in amenities was evident in Montgomery, which in the mid-1960s had no bakers, auctioneers or solicitors, whereas it had had seven of these businesses in the 1890s. Similarly, while there were five footwear establishments and two bakers in Llanidloes in 1964–5, there had been a total of twenty-five in the 1890s.[25]

The decline of Llanidloes and Montgomery owed much to their proximity to Shrewsbury and Hereford, which the motor car had now put in easy reach for the rural villages that these Welsh towns had once served. Despite the constant complaints about the state of rural roads, the car had a huge impact on many rural lives, reducing their isolation and opening up the options for entertainment. But it also hit rural communities by making buses and the railways increasingly uneconomical. Bleddfa (Radnor) epitomized the problem. In the early 1950s there were forty return bus services a week from the village to neighbouring towns and villages. Ten years later the village's population of some 100, including more than twenty pensioners, had none and around a quarter of residents had no alternative means of transport to leave the village.[26] In an age of affluence, there were people in rural Wales with no means to reach a local library, surgery or even a shop.

The 1963 Beeching inquiry responded to the impact of the car on rail lines by proposing drastic closures. Welsh local government, trade unions and political groups feared the cuts would result in 'irreparable damage' to Wales' social and economic life, exacerbating unemployment and depopulation and hitting trade and commerce. However, as early as 1951, only six of the twenty-four stations in Breconshire had an average of more than five passengers using a train and five stations had an average of less than one passenger per train. By the time of its closure, one of the lines in Breconshire was costing the taxpayer £400 a year for every passenger who used the service. The 'Beeching axe' saw 190 stations and sixteen lines close in Wales, while another six lines had services reduced. As the Welsh Office concluded, Wales was 'particularly hard hit' but it was not being singled out: it just had a lot of little-used lines.[27] Indeed, things might have been worse. The closure of the Aberystwyth to Shrewsbury line had been mooted and the mid-Wales line that linked Shrewsbury and Swansea might have gone too but for the fact that it passed through six marginal constituencies.[28] But that did not change the feeling that railway cuts were dealing rural Wales yet another harsh blow.

IN A 1956 NATIONALIST NOVEL, two exiled quarrymen argued that the Nantlle valley was 'one of the worst examples of the neglect and misgovernment of Wales and its people'.[29] Rural Wales was never a priority for government development policies because the falling and sparse population meant that the total number of unemployed people was actually relatively low, while the cost of improving amenities in rural communities was prohibitive. Successive administrations did, however, seek to develop the economic base of small towns. Tourism was one area of obvious potential. The general growth in prosperity meant that holidaying in Wales was growing rapidly. This was evident from the number of visitors to Caernarfon Castle, which rose from 120,900 in 1957 to 223,900 in 1961. By 1961 tourism was worth £50 million to the Welsh economy (compared with the £114 million coal was worth), with over 4 million people taking holidays there, including 200,000 from outside the UK. Most went to the north, although around a fifth of visitors visited only Llandudno and Rhyl. Caravan parks, which offered the working classes a cheap holiday, began to change the face of parts of the coastline. By the mid-1960s there were an estimated 40,000 caravans in Wales on over 1,000 sites.[30] Such developments added to wider concerns about the conservation of Wales' natural beauty, something which had already led to the creation of national parks in the Brecon Beacons, the Pembrokeshire Coast and Snowdonia in the 1950s. Despite its growth, tourism had its own problems. The development of overseas package holidays meant that relatively affluent holidaymakers did not have to chance the Welsh weather. The growth of working-class motoring in the 1960s, meanwhile, was a mixed blessing. On the one hand it made the Welsh mountains more accessible but it also made it easier to visit and then go home again without actually spending the night. The impact on hotels was significant, as was evident in Aberystwyth, which had ten seafront hotels in 1945 but just one by 1960. Wales also seemed slow to wake up to the economic opportunities tourism offered. In 1962 a writer in *Welsh Farm News* concluded that some north Walian hotels did not apparently want custom; he had failed to find anywhere that did afternoon tea.[31]

A 1963 official report concluded that tourism could not drastically change the rural economy or stop depopulation.[32] The employment that tourism supported was small scale and low paid and thus successive governments were more interested in developing manufacturing. Typical of the efforts to achieve this was the Mid-Wales Industrial Development Association, which was formed in 1957 and marketed the huge district under its remit to industrialists on its low cost, government financial support, available space, a stable labour force and natural beauty. It did enjoy some success, attracting small manufacturing and engineering ventures; by 1965 it had helped create around 1,000 jobs. But the new light industries could be a mixed blessing. In the north-west, the managers of slate quarries worried that factories would tempt workers away in search of better wages. Furthermore, to the concern of some, developments were achieved with English capital and brought in English managers and craftsmen, enhancing the status of the English language.[33] However, rural Wales was unattractive to employers because it lacked a large workforce and its population was dispersed. To combat this, planners seemed obsessed with the expansion of existing towns and the creation of new ones. Among the ideas floated in the mid-1960s were a 'sub-metropolis', based on Aberystwyth, of 250,000 people and a new town of 70,000 at Caersws (Montgomeryshire).[34]

The plans to develop Caersws were attacked by farmers who feared a loss of land and labourers, racists who feared an influx of black and Asian immigrants and nationalists who feared it would accelerate wider processes of Anglicization. Even less ambitious schemes faced problems. In 1967 state plans were drawn up to expand Bala from a population of 1,500 to 10,000. All the local authorities accepted the idea, except Penllyn Rural District Council, which felt it would be detrimental to the area's natural beauty and harm both the tourist trade and social and cultural life. The Mid-Wales Industrial Development Association was not impressed and argued that 'narrow aesthetic or cultural concerns' should not hold back economic development. In a referendum held by Merioneth County Council on the plan 55 per cent of voters (on a 90 per cent turnout) accepted development that allowed the population to grow to 3,500 but rejected the options of more expansion or none at all. Yet when plans were announced for the first advance factory there was renewed local opposition, with many arguing that it was at odds with the town's character and would bring in outsiders and activities such as drinking and gambling that should not be part of a

Welsh Nonconformist community. In the end, the scheme was never fully implemented and Bala was no longer identified as a potential growth town.[35]

Concerns for traditional rural Welsh culture were central to such objections. The demographic and economic problems of rural Wales were hardly unique and were being faced across the British countryside, but in Wales the national element added a different dimension and vocabulary to the problem. Rural Wales was at the heart of traditional conceptions of Welsh nationhood. It was the home of the *gwerin*, the semi-mythical and romantic Welsh-speaking peasantry who were intertwined with their land and nation by their history, religion and occupation.[36] There was believed to be an integral link between the land itself, the language and the nation. The rhetoric of Plaid Cymru between the wars had suggested that Welshness was often understood in geographical terms and that eliding of physical and mental worlds continued. One writer noted in 1948 that for most people the meaning of Wales would be 'in some corner of a field, a pool under a rock, in a bare-sheep walk or a cottage folded in a gulley, in a hard road trodden by the feet of our father and their father before them; some private place that can never engage a general admiration'.[37] Rural sites and landscapes could, however, conjure shared memories of people and events from history. The mountains of Snowdonia were the last refuge of the independent Welsh in the face of medieval invaders. In Nevern churchyard (Pembrokeshire), a yew tree stood that was said to weep blood (actually a red sap) until the local castle was ruled by the Welsh again. Such sites helped people imagine and connect to their nation. One writer looked upon the hills and mountains and experienced 'the feeling of Wales', a landscape imbued with an ancient history and where now 'the last British people resist but passively the penetration of the English influence into their lives, speech and culture'.[38] Thus plans that might bring in outsiders or alter the landscape were seen as a threat to the nation and the intelligentsia who dominated the nationalist movement in the 1950s reacted to them with hostility.

The local working class was not always impressed by such reactions. In 1951, after sit-down protests against further land requisition plans for the military at Trawsfynydd, a police report claimed that there was no evidence of local sympathy, while the *Western Mail* thought there was 'acute' feeling in the village because 200 local people were employed at the existing military camp.[39] Similarly, while much of the Welsh-speaking establishment was against nuclear power stations in Snowdonia, many working-class locals saw an opportunity for jobs. Thus, the newspaper *Y Faner* claimed in 1958 that if plans for a power station were allowed to proceed, 'we might as well bury all beauty under piles of rubble and place pylons on the top as a monument to the blindness of our generation'. But locals marched in favour of it, with banners declaring 'Bread before Beauty' and 'Pylons before Poverty'.[40] Increasingly, such tensions developed a national twist to add to the intra-Welsh class tensions. Proposals for hydropower schemes in Snowdonia drew strong opposition in England from those wanting to prevent a 'massacre of the mountains'. Welsh people, however, argued that there was nothing beautiful about unemployment and depopulation.[41] Goronwy Roberts, a local Labour MP, felt that those who opposed industrial developments in Gwynedd were outsiders who only holidayed in Wales. He told the Commons, 'They tend to regard Snowdonia as a kind of Red Indian reservation, set aside for tired Manchester stockbrokers.... Our duty is to see that human nature as well as nature has a chance of survival.'[42] A new hydropower plant was built in Gwynedd, as were two huge concrete nuclear power stations, which were described in one architectural survey as 'disconcerting and awesome in their raucous and spine-chilling disregard for their surroundings'.[43] The local economic impact was as significant as their mark on the landscape but they did not eradicate unemployment. The skilled jobs tended to go to outsiders and even the construction led to labour being imported. Indeed, by attracting people to the area, the projects added to the number of unemployed when construction came to an end.[44]

THE RURAL SOCIETY that the more romantically minded wanted to protect from power stations, new towns and Anglicization was a society tied together by kinship, religion and the Welsh language and free from the divisions of class and snobbery. The reality of rural life was, of course, always more complex. It was often pointed out that the Welsh language does not have a traditional word for 'class', but it does allow the articulation of status through the use of the formal *chi* and informal *ti* (for 'you'). These were, in rural communities, remembered one man, 'social weapons of the utmost power and pierced the very soul. The presumptuous and worthless were put in their place at once with one judicious use of the "Ti", and they wilted under it. Into it were packed as the occasion demanded, rebuff, contempt or insult.'[45] Such linguistic games illustrated that status clearly mattered, even if there was not an immediately apparent class system. In rural communities money remained central to deciding people's local status and judgements of what made a good marriage. Thus the appointment of a new bank manager was still front-page news in the local paper and his biographical details were told to all. Even within chapels, divisions of education, occupation and wealth were reflected in the organization of family pews. As one sociologist concluded, 'Becoming rich brings prestige so long as one does not behave as though one were rich'.[46]

Islwyn Ffowc Elis' *Cysgod y Cryman* (1953), the most popular Welsh-language novel of the 1950s, clearly depicts a rural world where class mattered. Set in Montgomeryshire, its central characters, a prosperous farming family, are deeply concerned with their public reputation and good name. This was rooted in public conduct but also, very clearly, in their wealth. There are, however, suggestions in the book that Labour's reconstruction programme was undermining the traditional class system. A farm labourer is convinced that 'the day of "the gaffers" was over' and reminds his angry boss of that by speaking back to him. The novel also illustrates how the limited industrial activities of rural areas had helped create something resembling a proletariat. Following a conversion to communism, the family's eldest son decides to join a road gang, to be among the workers:

> Their humour was all about lavatories, women's underwear and farmyard filth, all peppered with the usual adjectives. They sat in judgment on the ministers and deacons of Llanaerwen's chapels and were down on everyone who didn't earn his living with pick and shovel. This, thought Harri, is The People, the intelligent and immortal People, over whose virtues the book-Socialists drivel from their ivory towers. It would do them good to spend a day in the company of The People, clearing snow on the back road between Llanaerwen and Caerllugan.[47]

There were, however, distinct limits to class consciousness among the people of rural Wales. The number of branches of the National Union of Agricultural Workers in Wales rose from 142 in 1947 to 212 in 1950, but membership fell back again after Labour lost power and by 1960 just 10 per cent of the Welsh agricultural labour force belonged to a union. Farmers' and labourers' sons were educated together in local schools and shared the same cultural background, muting the class structure of society.[48] Anthropologists argued that high personal qualities could raise people above their occupation in terms of local status. Moreover, the nature of life in a small town, where people lived near each other and their social relations overlapped, restricted social stratification. In the words of one rural anthropologist: 'Social intercourse leads constantly to integration'.[49]

Within such interactions, the traditional idea of kin remained important in the rural Wales of the 1950s and 1960s. Only a quarter of the Welsh-speaking households in late 1940s Aberporth (Cardiganshire) had no relations there, a figure which would have been lower if it were not for emigration.[50] The large turnout at weddings and funerals was the most obvious outward sign that these extended families mattered but kin was more than just a matter of turning up to events. A sociologist in the Vale of Glamorgan found that many elderly women there knew of six generations and between 200 and 500 dead and living relatives, usually knowing at least details of residence, marriage and occupation. Locals spoke of 'real Vale people' and newcomers who could not be identified by their family connections were often treated with suspicion. Until an incomer married into a local family, it was difficult to be accepted into the community. But the number of incomers was on the increase and people were moving into the Vale in search of both a rural lifestyle and social mobility and status. By 1960 around 40 per cent of the Vale's population were not born locally.[51]

The Vale was near Cardiff and ideal for middle-class incomers to commute from. In more isolated rural communities, the numbers of incomers was much smaller, creating a more introspective dynamic to life. In the early 1960s there were five hamlets in the remote upper part of the parish of Trefeurig (Cardiganshire). Although there were just 173 people in the area, there was a general store, a school and four chapels. Most of the houses had not been modernized and local employment opportunities were dominated by agriculture and forestry, meaning there was little to keep the young. There was not a single person with a professional occupation living in the parish and 47 per cent of the workers were in unskilled positions. Without a good bus service, access to Aberystwyth, the nearest town, was difficult and less than a quarter of the housewives went there for a weekly shop and less than a fifth of the population visited weekly for entertainment. Little wonder then that the population was ageing and falling. Yet many still felt that it was in such rural communities that the real Wales lay, not least because 91 per cent of residents there spoke Welsh. As a sixty-year-old Blaenau Ffestiniog quarryman told the *Observer* in 1966, 'this is the proper old country, this Wales. And we're proper Welsh.'[52]

Outsiders in this 'real Wales' were marked out not just because of their lack of local ties, which was not always even true, but also often because of salaried positions, an inability to speak Welsh or membership of a church rather than a chapel. None of these alone was enough to distinguish people as strangers but the combination reinforced a clear sense of difference, even though local people and outsiders happily mixed.[53] As early as 1948 concern was being expressed about English (and Polish) people buying Welsh farms. Cheap land coupled with rising affluence saw this trend continue. The land may have been of poorer quality than in England but people preferred the status and satisfaction of owning bigger farms. Not all in-migrants, however, came to work. The MP for Caernarfonshire noted that in-migration was doing little for rural renewal because it was not the young who were moving in. He complained in 1958: 'As the native Welsh leave their cottages the English immediately buy them. But these are middle aged people. Professionals or those who have retired. They have no children or their children have grown up.'[54] Far worse for rural communities was when people did not live all year round in the houses they bought, thus undermining the local economy and services. In 1965 twenty-seven of the forty-eight houses in Llangrannog (Cardiganshire) were empty in the winter. It was no wonder that buses from the village had fallen from eighteen a week in 1950 to three in 1965.[55]

One Carmarthenshire observer thought the English who came to farm arrived without 'any rooted prejudice' against the Welsh or the Welsh language and that they did not try to form their own groups. He found they had settled happily, appreciated the help of their neighbours and that a local church put on a monthly English-language service for them. Other community groups, such as the parish council and the local Women's Institute, were also switching to English to accommodate newcomers. One English person living in north Wales remarked that the English were always liked, as long as their manners were not 'too awful'.[56] But they were still regarded as English. It was indeed the attitude of the incomers that decided the extent to which they were accepted. After the Welsh-speaking Cardiffian Goronwy Rees was appointed principal of the university in Aberystwyth in 1953, he faced a variety of prejudices and gossip because he wore suede shoes and white socks, did not pay his bills, mixed with homosexuals and drank in pubs. Nor was his wife exempt: she was looked down upon for being English and liking big cars but not coffee mornings. In his inaugural lecture he told of his surprise at how little things had changed: 'Wales seems to lie like a ship becalmed, waiting for some fresh breeze which will bring it once more under full sail'. For those university intellectuals who wanted to save traditional Wales these were not welcome words.[57] Rees was forced out his job in 1957.

His downfall owed much to gossip, something so endemic and powerful in small rural communities that it regulated behaviour and could ruin lives. A character in a 1955 novel remarked that gossip was the 'chief industry' of a small rural town: 'If they put as much energy into their work they'd all be millionaires'.[58] Kate Roberts' novel *Y Byw Sy'n Cysgu* (1956) depicted a woman who is abandoned by her husband and then seems to feel even more crushed by the knowledge that people are talking about her. She distances herself from a man she likes because of gossip and eventually moves away to a remote farm. A study of Glyn Ceiriog (Denbighshire) in the early 1950s argued that such gossip had an important social function. The community strove to avoid open conflict and 'strangers', people from outside the village, were brought in to judge competitions and take on positions of leadership in local organisations where existing rivalries might be awoken if a local person were in charge. Instead, locals used gossip to air grievances without creating open and public rifts that would undermine the village. Such gossiping, the study argued, strengthened the sense of local community, as quarrels became part of a shared experience that made people into villagers. Nonetheless, the idea of tight-knit rural communities was belied by the fact that a football club and the local carnival both collapsed in the village, as people were unable to cross the divides of religion, language and personality in dealing with the demands of running these activities.[59]

Social interaction was central to the sense of community in villages like Glyn Ceiriog but the changing economic base of rural Wales was undermining it. In-migration, commuting, television, the mechanization of farms, not to mention the volatile question of secularization, were all creating a rural society that was less cohesive and less dependent on neighbours for help and entertainment. An old man's autobiography noted in 1972,

> It is no longer the close-knit society that it was; there is not now that interdependence of cottage on farm, farm on cottage, and one farm on another. All that people need nowadays they can get for money, and, as they have the money, they prefer it that way. Farm servants now form a group of their own, and the tendency is for farmers to do the same; the cottagers, often working ten to twenty miles away, and earning good wages, are entirely independent of the farms. So independent and self-contained is every family to-day that it could, if it wished, live like families in big towns, without knowing its next door neighbour.[60]

Even where neighbours did help each other in remote communities, the rise of the motorcar meant they did not have to stay long and there was a decline in traditional hospitality. One anthropologist noted that the time wives had spent on entertaining was now replaced with menial tasks around the farm.[61]

IN 1947 THE WRITER John Cowper Powys argued that the Welsh were 'the most profoundly Christian' ancient race on earth.[62] Whatever the hyperbole of that statement, the importance of Christianity ran beyond spiritual matters; for many people religion, and especially Nonconformity, was intimately entwined with their nationhood, leading one minister to claim that secular Welshness was 'almost a contradiction in terms'. Welsh was often referred to as the language of heaven and another minister remarks in a 1960 novel: 'I always think a little Welsh prayer carries a bit more weight before the throne of Grace'.[63] No wonder, then, that one historian of religion has concluded that chapel culture was 'virtually synonymous' with Welshness.[64] Nonconformity had, after all, been central to the maintenance of a sense of Welsh nationhood over the past two hundred years. The chapels had given the Welsh language a social status denied to it in other realms of the modern commercial world and they bred a sense of difference to England, with its class-ridden hierarchy of the Anglican Church. Moreover, the 1881 Welsh Sunday Closing Act, the product of Nonconformist influence within the Liberal Party, had not only affirmed Welsh nationhood by giving Wales its first unique piece of modern legislation, it also meant that Nonconformity touched the lives of those who were not religious, by shutting the pubs on Sundays and creating an atmosphere where work or play on the Sabbath was unacceptable.

In 1950, half the Welsh population was formally attached to a church or chapel. Actual attendance at services did not match this but when this figure is compared with the 24 per cent of the UK population who were members of a Christian church then Wales seems a very devout, or maybe a very conservative, place. Religious attendance was strongest in rural communities. In late 1940s Aberdaron, a small village based on farming, fishing and tourism, 30 per cent of men and 38 per cent of women went to chapel twice or more on a Sunday, whereas only 11 per cent of men and 3 per cent of women never went, and some of these were still nominally members. Adults who had stopped attending still sent their children to Sunday school, although perhaps for some peace and quiet as much as any religious aspirations. In 1950 in Ponthenri (Carmarthenshire), 110 out of 134 local children went to Sunday school.[65]

With membership extending far beyond the reach of any secular organization, the impact of the chapel upon daily life in rural communities was unsurprisingly strong in the immediate post-war period. One journalist argued in 1958, 'the strain of the chapel philosophies still infuses Welsh country life, and gives it a flavour totally lacking from the easy-going apathy of modern English society'.[66] On farms and at quarries, chapel membership and attendance could be a requirement of employment, leading one Blaenau Ffestiniog quarryman to recall that quarry owners used religion 'to keep us down'.[67] In industrial areas too, middle-class chapel leaders enjoyed respect and prestige among non-chapel-attending socialists and even communists did not attack the chapels for fear of losing members. Christianity was at the heart of widely held community values such as neighbourliness, hospitality and obligation to family. Furthermore, concerts, singing, eisteddfodau, literary competitions and even young people's quizzes and games were held under the auspices of the chapel, giving religion a secular as well as a spiritual function. The chapels also curtailed other activities and there was a strict sense of Sabbatarianism that decried ball playing, reading of non-sacred texts or even whistling on a Sunday. The closure of pubs was, of course, central to what was known as the Welsh Sunday and even chapel wine was often non-alcoholic. Such was the influence of Nonconformity that one anthropologist found no dancing and very little gambling or drunkenness in a wartime study of Llanfihangel-yng-Ngwynfa (Montgomeryshire). Sunday observance was relaxing in rural areas in terms of reading the Sunday newspapers and listening to the radio but something like hanging washing on the line or even going to the beach was still seen as wrong, while the wearing of Sunday clothes in public remained important. Indeed, even hanging out washing too early on a Monday was avoided for fear of raising suspicion that it had actually been done on the Sunday.[68]

Anthropologists working in the late 1940s noted a schism between believers and non-believers and the use of terms like *pobl y cwrdd* (people of the religious meeting) and *pobl y dafarn* (people of the pub) or *bois y pop* (boys of the beer). Such ideas influenced social interaction and friendships. They were, in the words of one anthropologist, 'a social classification based upon fact and upon the values of the community, a differentiation locally recognized both in conduct and speech'. He estimated that 60 per cent of Aberporth (Cardiganshire) belonged to the chapel group, with the remainder in the pub grouping. This system of social classification was partly related to economic positioning. The chapel people valued prestige jobs (which a third of them held), were thrifty and 88 per cent of them owned their homes. In contrast, most of the pub people were manual workers and only 46 per cent of them were homeowners. Significantly, the chapel group admired 'getting on', even if that involved leaving the village, and they were disproportionably represented among the rural emigrants. Their emphasis on education and social mobility was thus the seed of the decline of their own culture at home. Another divide noted by some observers and contemporaries was between church and chapel and, indeed, between the different kinds of chapels. Wyn Roberts, the son of an Anglesey minister, was warned by his mother during the war, 'Never tangle with those church people. They're not like us.' In Glan-Llyn (Merioneth) an anthropologist noted that where people shopped and how they voted in local elections were determined by religious denominations.[69]

Despite the emphasis placed upon by these divides by some academics of the time, they were more nominal than absolute and there were clear overlaps between the adherents of church, chapel and pub. All had the same emphasis on kin and some people did drink and pray, although they might feel that they had to sneak into pubs via the backdoor. Religious rivalries might surface at times of other tensions in village life but they were generally understood by locals in terms of nominal ritual and practice rather than belief or values. Denominations intermarried, socialized with each other and supported one another's social events. Some people even changed sects when they moved house, in order to worship somewhere closer to their new home. Even the difference between church and chapel was more a matter of family tradition than belief or behaviour. Despite Anglicanism's historic image, rural churches were full of Welsh speakers and those committed to Welsh culture. There were no significant differences in levels of drinking, gambling and dancing between church and chapel and they had similar moral codes. Thus religious differences generally counted for little in day-to-day social life and the main difference was that the chapels were exclusively Welsh-speaking, whereas the church was not. Furthermore, single moral lapses, such as the odd drink or fathering or mothering an illegitimate child, did not write off a person's respectability provided their conduct was otherwise acceptable. Chapels might still turn people out for such activities but only for a period of time. Gossip faded and, provided people were discreet and there was no obvious impact upon a community, then social lepers were not created. Thus, despite the area's strong Nonconformity, 10.2 per cent of births in Merioneth in 1950 were illegitimate, the highest rate of any county in Wales or England.[70]

The limited actual impact of the divide between sects and the religious and the non-religious was rooted in the small scale of community life. Local economies and villages were simply too small to support two independent cultures and ways of life. Religion might divide but neighbourliness and everyday life united. Work in particular brought people together, regardless of whether they felt more at home on a pew or at a bar. Activities like sheep shearing or bringing the hay in were impossible without the help of neighbours. A study of Llanfrothen (Merioneth) between 1958 and 1962 illustrated the complex nature of village life. There, everyone respected and paid lip service to the chapel code, meaning that drinkers expected deacons to live better lives, blasphemies were still regarded as bad, hymn singing could be found everywhere from the pub to the milking parlour, and even those who did not attend chapel were wary, even afraid, of openly working on a Sunday. Yet the religious ethos was also broken, although it was generally done with a great deal of pretence, turning a blind eye and play acting to help save face and reconcile actual behaviour with the chapel code. Thus, rather than there being two distinct ways of life, based on chapel and pub, there was instead a culture where religion mattered but was often not actually practised and a common sense of community and Welshness bound people together, smoothing over the religious divides.[71]

AS THE 1950s AND 1960s PROGRESSED, the biggest challenge religion faced was not denominational differences but growing secularism. As Lewis Valentine complained in 1954, Welsh-speaking Wales was becoming more 'irreligious every year'.[72] In a climate where religion was in decline, it made little sense to make too much of denominational differences. The sense of decline in Nonconformity was particularly strong because of its previous ascendancy. Not untypical was Capel Bethel in Bont Dolgadfan (Montgomeryshire). In 1900 it had 262 members but by 1950 membership was 111. Such figures disguised actual attendance at services. In 1966, for example, Hen Gapel in nearby Dôl-fach had 340 members but only a third of them were regular worshippers.[73] Moreover, the large number of places of worship meant that Nonconformist congregations could be as small as a dozen and the Anglican church often had the largest congregation of any single place of worship in a community. The vibrant public life associated with churches and chapels, such as debating societies and eisteddfodau, was also in retreat, and even ceasing completely in some rural places, as it had done in many urban communities before the war. Within rural communities, the emergence of groups like the Women's Institute (WI), Workers' Educational Association (WEA) and Mothers' Union were all signs of how chapels were losing their centrality in local life.[74]

By 1966 regular chapel attendance in the Cardiganshire town of Aberaeron was down to 25 per cent of the population and regular church attendance to another 20 per cent. This still outstripped urban attendance: a 1960s survey in Swansea showed that less than a quarter of people had been to a religious service in the last week. Nonetheless, in England and Wales as a whole the comparable figure was around 14 per cent.[75] Those who were going were increasingly old and female, which hardly filled people with hope for the future. A Swansea man remarked, 'it's the women that keep them going – sisterhood mainly. It's not so much a *family* affair as it used to be'.[76] Similarly, a 1962 mining novel noted that on a Sunday morning most fathers were in bed with the *News of the World* while mothers were in chapel, 'comparing notes on the finery of the scrubbed, singing children'.[77] By the 1970s a survey in Cardiganshire was suggesting that only 17 per cent of people under twenty-four years old attended church or chapel regularly, whereas 58 per cent of those over sixty-five did. The faster rate of decline in urban Wales was further evident in 1972, when 37 per cent of weddings in north and central Wales were civil services, compared with 43 per cent in Glamorgan.[78]

The decline in attendance was nothing new and perhaps what shocked people most was how, in the twenty-five years after the war, people began openly to question the public morality religion imposed. This was most evident when it came to the matter of the Welsh Sunday. For many this was a symbol of national difference but it was increasingly regarded by some as anachronistic after a war for personal freedom and in a new era of state socialism. A letter in the Pontypridd press in 1948 called for the Sunday opening of pubs and cinemas, declaring: 'We have had enough of restrictions and regulations since 1939. We all deserve a little relaxation now, and let everyone please themselves what they do with their spare time.' In 1968 a west Walian who had moved to Barry wrote: 'I carry with me always the feeling of having escaped from the closed minds and narrow attitudes with which I grew up and with which I associate the Welsh way of life'.[79] As such letters suggested, it was in urban areas that the traditional influence of Nonconformity was under greatest pressure. The local authorities in the more cosmopolitan coastal towns of the south were the first to overcome some of the restrictions of the Welsh Sunday, by holding referenda on cinema opening. Swansea voted for opening in 1950 by just 2,908 votes but when more Anglicized Cardiff followed suit in 1952 the majority was 34,393, even though less than half the electorate turned out. Yet even in the 1960s Cardiff City Council refused to let X-rated films be shown on a Sunday. In the industrial valleys, the restrictive influence of Nonconformity on officialdom was longer lasting and a 1950s Sunday there remained a day with few options for fun. One Maesteg woman remembered of that decade's Sundays: 'the streets were silent as no children played except for those of the disreputable or the damned'.[80] But the older generation, raised in more austere times, was dying off or retiring from positions of influence, while the disreputable and damned simply did not think of themselves that way and were growing large enough in number for change to be inevitable. Nonetheless, it was still not until 1960 that the local authority in Aberdare – where, according to the local press, the 'Welsh Sunday is rigidly maintained in outward semblance at least' – decided to open children's play areas on a Sunday.[81] By 1968 the Football Association of Wales was allowing competitive soccer on a Sunday for the first time and Glamorgan County Cricket Club played its first Sunday match.

In rural Wales change was much slower and it was not with too much exaggeration that Gwyn Thomas remarked in 1958 that there were still places 'where the only concession to gaiety is a striped shroud'. But even here the erosion of the Welsh Sunday was clearly evident by the end of the 1950s and some chapel services were even being rearranged to avoid clashing with favourite Welsh-language radio programmes.[82] In 1959 there were complaints in the local press from a resident of Denbigh that the town was 'fast becoming a Sunday Bedlam':

> What people coming home from chapel or church on a Sunday morning find is a couple of youngsters selling Sunday papers from door to door, shouting to each other on top of their voices, with their newspapers very often flying about.... On a Sunday evening again, it is not unusual to hear a crowd of young people walking about the streets, singing sloppy songs, and even shouting the place down during service hour. Now it is not sanctimony but ordinary decency and respect for those who still believe in Sunday observance, that calls for different behaviour to this brand of modern vulgarism on the Lord's Day.

The determination to preserve the Lord's Day led Penllyn Rural District Council to vote in 1960 against allowing fishing and boating on a Sunday on Bala lake. Seaside resort Colwyn Bay did not open its cinemas on Sundays until as late as 1967.[83] Such moves brought the Welsh Sunday into conflict with the needs of tourism. This was clear in 1966, when a Lancashire visitor to north Wales wrote to a newspaper asking for a 'brighter Sunday'. Some locals, incomers and tourists responded by claiming the quietness and lack of facilities were a blessing, not a drawback, but generational change was evident too. A 'Billy Bach' complained that teenagers had nothing to do on rainy Sundays. He was particularly concerned by the enforced absence of jukeboxes and summed up:

> To the councillors, magistrates, police officials and others in authority, I would like to say this – the year is 1966; man is conquering space and the whole concept of life is changing swiftly. It is time that we, the residents of Anglesey and Caernarvonshire, got ourselves into 2nd gear and pressed for the abandonment of Victorian thinking by the people who 'represent' us and ask ourselves: is it a sin to enjoy life?

Some people's answer was visible in another report in the same paper that year. Half a dozen members of an Anglesey choir were sacked for going to a pub during a meal stop on a trip to a local eisteddfod. Some of the women complained of the smell of beer from the stage and said the choir had been shamed.[84]

Drink was at the heart of the battle to protect the Welsh Sunday. To Sabbatarians, the closing of the pubs was central to upholding God's sanctity but a Rhondda MP complained in 1961 that being able to drink on a Sunday was a 'civic right' that was being granted to the English but not the Welsh. Urban public opinion was clearly shifting and by the late 1950s even the Archbishop of Wales was in favour of the Sunday opening of pubs. A large study in Swansea in 1960 suggested that 56 per cent of the middle class approved of Sunday opening but only 40 per cent of the working class did.[85] The distancing of the middle class from Sunday abstention meant there was clear political pressure for change and the government's decision to reform the opening hours of pubs in England provided an opportunity for Welsh Sunday opening to be addressed. Conscious of the recent furore over the flooding of the Tryweryn valley (see chapter 8), Conservative ministers were keen to avoid the image of an English government imposing change on Wales and the 1961 Licensing Act legislated for Sunday opening referenda in Wales. Despite fears of the confusion a local pattern might create, the government rejected the idea of a national poll and instead decided to let counties make their own decisions. There were complaints that Wales was being divided and the *South Wales Echo* even claimed it would lead to more drink-driving as people travelled to 'wet' counties. But the government was thinking about Welsh opinion, particularly rural opinion, in its decision, and noted the serious objections to the idea of a national referendum in which the urban areas could swamp the rural opposition to Sunday opening.[86]

This is precisely what would have happened when, at the 1961 referendum, 453,711 people voted for Sunday opening and 391,123 against. The organization of those votes into county referenda, however, meant that the pubs now opened on Sundays in the south, where the bulk of the Welsh population lived, while eight counties in west and north Wales all remained dry. The resulting map gave the impression of a Wales divided into opposing factions but the voting statistics suggested a greyer picture, with significant numbers supporting the losing side in all counties. In Glamorgan 40 per cent voted against opening, whereas in Merioneth 24 per cent voted for it. Nor was it quite the emotional issue that many supposed. As the vote approached, a Rhondda paper concluded that 'by-and-large Mr and Mrs Public are not especially concerned either way'.[87] The turnout was just under 47 per cent in Wales as a whole. It peaked in Merioneth at 65 per cent – a figure higher than might be expected in a local election but lower than at a general election – and troughed in Newport at 34 per cent. Although turnout was significantly higher in Welsh-speaking rural areas, where Nonconformity was still strongest, there was no overwhelming majority in any area, either for or against the measure.

The result, however, did mean that people no longer had to cross the English border for their Sunday pint, although many in the west and north still faced a long drive if they wanted one. Nothing, though, changed in Llanymynech (Montgomeryshire), where the Lion straddled the English border. The pub's bar was in England and thus wet but the lounge was in Wales and in a county that voted to stay dry. Those who wanted a Sunday drink in the lounge had to wait until after the 1968 referendum. That vote showed the influence of Nonconformity was clearly retreating. The turnout was just under 30 per cent and new majorities for Sunday opening were secured in the most Anglicized parts of rural Wales: Pembrokeshire, Montgomeryshire and Denbighshire. This left only the Welsh-speaking heartlands dry. There were 186,438 fewer votes cast against closing than in 1961. Some of these lost opponents must have died in the intervening period but others may have drifted away from religion or ceased to believe that the issue mattered enough to vote on.

This was all more significant than just the issue of whether you could buy a drink on the Sabbath. There were, after all, 1,360 clubs in Wales, many of which served alcohol on a Sunday, and their membership extended to maybe 60 per cent of the male population. Instead, the referenda were, in the words of a *Times* editorial, a vote 'for and against a certain type of Welshness, of which Sunday closing is both an ingredient and a symbol'.[88] Some regarded Sunday closing as one of the things that made Wales different and consequently an attack on it was an attack on Welshness. They thus defended it not so much because they thought it important in itself but because of what it represented. Moreover, the referenda of 1961 and 1968 allowed people to take a stand in defending Welsh culture without getting into the more problematic and divisive areas of self-government or the compulsory use of the Welsh language in public life. The results were thus upsetting to some not because they allowed people to drink on a Sunday but because they were seen to symbolize the Anglicization of swathes of Wales.[89]

Yet Sunday opening was as much a product of the decline of the chapels as it was of a decline in the type of Welshness that the chapels represented, and secularization was something that was happening across Europe. One historian has argued that the 'Welsh did not revolt against Christianity, rather did they slip from its grasp'. For another, Nonconformity was killed off 'essentially by television and the family motor car'.[90] Certainly, watching a western in an armchair or taking a spin in the car made a cold pew seem less appealing but neither interpretation quite captures the nuances of what was happening. Chapels suffered as some people turned away from Welshness and the Welsh language. One gloomy tract celebrating the tercentenary of religious separatism reflected that Nonconformity's Welshness, once so central to its strength, had become a weakness in an age of Anglicization.

Others had lost their faith during a horrific world war. Old traditions were being challenged in a modernizing world and there was less willingness to accept the mystery of the afterlife. The Bishop of Llandaff noted in 1961 that the Anglican Church was not hated but had simply become irrelevant to people.[91] That irrelevance was rooted in religious institutions' failure to engage with the social issues of the day beyond drinking and gambling. The president of the Swansea Free Church Federal Council, for example, argued in 1952 that they had been 'peculiarly dumb on such subjects as education, housing and playing fields for children'.[92] Indeed, it could be suggested that it was religion that was turning away from the people, rather than the other way round. In a 1968 radio programme about Welsh teenagers, all the participants said that they saw religion as rather old fashioned and cut off from modern life. As a farmer's son put it, religion was too concerned with non-attenders not going to heaven; it was 'far too much to the book and not half enough to life'.[93] Chapels were increasingly seen as dour and their harsh morality out of kilter with the age. In the late 1960s, when a new young minister in Llanidloes tried to introduce more music into services he was accused of pandering to the young by turning worship into concerts and was told that it would 'not be enjoyed'.[94] The fault of the chapels themselves was even more evident when it is considered that there was not a straightforward decline of religion *per se*, with both Catholicism and Anglicanism showing some signs of growth in the 1950s. At Easter 1945 the (Anglican) Church in Wales had given communion to 155,911 people. By 1962 this figure had risen to 182,864. The Church was working at modernizing its services and liturgy. But it too would be caught up by social changes. By 1974 Easter communions were down to 135,228.[95]

The extent of this decline was not as apparent as it might have been because of the hold religion still had on public conduct in rural areas, even if people's sense of guilt increasingly did not stop them reading the papers or doing housework on a Sunday. Nonetheless, a 1955 survey of one 'strong' Congregational chapel in south-west Wales illustrated how religion was losing its grip on people. Forty-four per cent of the 324 members did not attend services, blaming ill-health, fatigue, disagreements with other members and being weary of constant requests for money. But other reasons given included not deriving any benefit from services or even non-believing. Of those who did attend, sixty-two said they did out of habit, thirty-four 'for the sake of the children' and twenty-seven out of respect for the minister. Across Wales, however, not believing in God remained the realm of a minority. In an extensive 1960 survey of Swansea less than 2 per cent of people said they were atheists or agnostics, although it was more than six months since 49 per cent of the sample had attended a religious service. In Cardiganshire in 1971, while only 37 per cent of respondents to a survey said they attended church or chapel once or more a week, just 23 per cent never did and claimed no membership of any religion. Nor should the power of faith be underestimated for those who had it. One student minister wrote in his diary in 1962: 'Although we were only 8 in a dilapidated, huge, old, ramshackle ice cold building, God's Spirit was there. They are a warm, human group of God's people.'[96]

GORONWY REES REMARKED in a radio broadcast in 1953, 'What is surprising is the permanence and persistence of the Welsh way of life and belief, an intense cultural and intellectual conservatism which shows itself sometimes in almost Chinese reverence for what is established and sanctified by custom'.[97] That Welsh way of life, however, was much more than an abstract concept. It meant that there were rural children and old people in the 1950s for whom English was a 'strange and foreign' language. It meant that there was considerable emphasis placed on kinship, community responsibilities and being seen to be respectable. In 1954 social scientists reported the story of a teacher in the Swansea region who sought to begin divorce proceedings, only to be warned by the local education authority that a scandal would not be good for his career. He stayed in his unhappy marriage, rarely speaking to his wife.[98] That story is a testament to the power of religious belief over the lives of both communities and individuals. By the end of the 1960s such a scandal would have been unlikely, because religion's impact on public conduct had lessened in both rural and urban communities, just as religious attendance itself was in severe decline. Whereas once chapels had brimmed with people praying, now their pews were sparsely populated. The new idols of the young sang songs about girls, not God, and even older people were increasingly driven by the material rather than the heavenly. Indeed, the Swansea teacher's decision to stay in an unhappy marriage was motivated by his desire to get on in his career rather than to follow the sanctity of marriage. For believers, the growing secularism of society meant that humanity was turning its back on God. The tragedy of this was more than just spiritual. Going to church or chapel, following its social codes, attending its social functions and believing in God were shared experiences that bound people together and helped create communities. The lack of hope for the future of the churches and chapels echoed a lack of hope for rural communities, since both seemed to be being deserted by the young and left behind by the forces of modernization.

Indeed, the empty pews were both a product of and a cause of the decline of rural life. Moreover, for many believers, religion and the Welsh Sunday were entwined with Welshness and what made Wales distinctive. By the late 1960s that way of life was clearly on its last legs in urban areas. In rural communities it had more vitality but even there it was in retreat as the young left, the chapels emptied and more and more people used Sundays as a day of pleasure rather than worship and rest. Wales, or at least one kind of Wales, was coming to an end. Eleven years after the broadcast in which he expressed surprise at the continuance of the Welsh way of life, Goronwy Rees wrote an article that asked whether the Welsh had a future at all.[99] While some bemoaned the transition, others just got on with their lives and embraced the greater liberty it brought.

The debates over the Welsh way of life were not just about Wales. They were also about modernization; as one writer noted in 1958, sometimes 'the essence of Welshry is simply old-fashionedness'.[100] The debates thus reflected a wider anxiety in middle-class England about liberalization and social change, as the world moved forwards into what was referred to as the 'jet age' or the 'space age'. The moral, political and economic decline of Britain often seemed something of a highbrow obsession and in 1963 America's *Newsweek* commented that the British were 'wallowing in an orgy of self-criticism as relentless as the one which swept the US after the launching of the first *Sputnik*'. After the debacle of Suez, there was a clear sense that Britain was losing its political and economic place and influence in the world. At the same time, Americanism was undermining British identity and traditions, while a combination of the unions and management were stifling innovation in industry. For some in England, this engendered a sense of nostalgia for the Empire and old order. But for others, 'American culture was the very model of glamour, classlessness and modernity, promising a brave new world of affluence'.[101] Similarly, in Wales, progress and modernization created a strong sense of nostalgia for the old world of the Welsh peasantry among some, but for others they were a welcome change that promised not just the freedom to have fun on a Sunday but also a better job and a better home. By the start of the 1960s it seemed that modernization would win. The *Observer* concluded in the 1966 that

> The fight looks hopeless. It is amateur against professional, old against new, the chapel against bingo, an operatic society challenging the telly, parish pump politics defying centralised power, community or anonymity, and a choice of a village with three shops, two buses a day, no running water and a shortage of jobs and marriage partners, or a modern town.

The vice-chairman of Wales' Economic Council told the paper, 'Within my lifetime the concept of Wales will cease to exist. A lot of people would say there wasn't much substance in it now.'[102]

The loss of traditions, young people and services from rural Wales was bemoaned but it actually drew little concrete action. It was only once English-speaking outsiders began to move into Wales, actually helping stem off depopulation, that the dynamics changed. At first the numbers were small enough for them to be absorbed with little trouble but once the movement grew the reaction was much stronger. An early sign of that came in the area around Llanfrothen and Croesor in Snowdonia, where landowner Sir Clough Williams-Ellis, famous for his surreal creation at Port Meirion, encouraged bohemian friends from the English intelligentsia to settle in what became nicknamed 'the Greenwich village of Wales'. Isabel Emmett, who moved there, found locals expected 'English people to be rich, aloof and a bit crazy.... Behaviour which would not have been condoned in a local woman, such as drinking in the pub with the men, was accepted as understandable in me.' She carried out an anthropological study in the area between 1958 and 1962 and argued that the English–Welsh fault line was fundamental to local social relations and how people conceived of themselves. Central to this Welsh pride was a strong sense of belonging to a Welsh-speaking rather than English community. Even teenagers did not forget their Welsh songs, despite an interest in American films and music. The profound sense of difference to the English which defined the community took two forms. The first was actual contact with English people, whether they were visitors to the community or incomers who held posts like headteachers, magistrates and matrons. Yet many actually got on well with English individuals and thus this was more a sense of difference than antagonism. However, the second was a sense of the English as an outside imperial force, governing local people, imposing a foreign tongue and sending minions such as police officers, tax collectors and river bailiffs to impose rules. The fact that English was the language of officialdom created embarrassment, resentment and humiliation among people not comfortable in that language. There was thus a moral code in the community that led people to seek to cheat the alien English system in something resembling a deeply felt partisan war. Acts like poaching were widely popular and seen as a resistance to English officialdom and a sign of Welshness. But this sense of alienation from English officialdom drew not just on nationhood and language but on a sense of class too. Although people were not very conscious of being part of a wider British working class, Emmett thought that Welsh nationalism was at least partly an expression of class antagonism.

The local gentry were seen as English, even though they were from Welsh families, while the rulers of Wales were judged to be English corporations and English-speaking individuals. The English were generally regarded as upper class and the Welsh as classless. Emmett summed up:

> The frequent presence of English visitors and the constant presence of anglicized landlords and English people with top jobs, make Llan people very aware of their Welshness, and what permits the presence of apparently contradictory elements in their values system is the fact that all elements in it are Welsh. In the presence of the enemy, Welshness is the primary value; deacon and drunkard are friends, old schisms become unimportant.... You are either Welsh and in that case in the fight; or you are trying to be English in which case you are on the other side.[103]

At this time, the historian Eric Hobsbawm lived near Llanfrothen for part of the year. For him, the incomers and locals were 'two entirely different and barely overlapping species'. They were divided not just by language but also by class and lifestyle and he thought the locals were increasingly 'turning inwards' in order to defend their own culture. He concluded that the area 'was an unstable and unhappy place full of underlying tension. It found expression in a growing, resentful and sometimes rancorous anti-English feeling.'[104]

The rate of people leaving rural Wales means such views underestimate the pull of England and 'getting on' in the wider world. Rural Wales remained far removed from might be regarded as the mainstream living standards and ideas of the 1960s. Some areas could not even receive a clear television picture. The very type of Welshness that many wanted to preserve was what many of the young were moving away to escape from. But what was happing in and around Llanfrothen was a sign for the future. Increased contact with English people and a sense of class-based deprivation would feed a stronger sense of nationhood. Central to that was the realization that the Welsh language was under threat in the rural communities of north and west Wales. By the 1970s even those hostile to nationalism could regret and be shocked at the pace of change they were witnessing: English people were moving in and a pint could not be asked for in Welsh in the local pub; 'it seems odd somehow', said one man.[105] Language was what made the rural question different in Wales than in England. It was also moving to the centre stage of the debates surrounding Welshness. As the Welsh way of life faded away, the language became the battleground. What was once the automatic forum through which that life was lived was now itself fighting for survival.

Notes

1 D. Thomas, 'Where Tawe flows', in *Collected Stories* (1984), 186.
2 J. Ackerman, *Welsh Dylan: Dylan Thomas's Life, Writing and His Wales* (1997), 29, 27. J. Harris, 'Popular images', in M. W. Thomas (ed.), *A Guide to Welsh Literature, Vol. VII: Welsh Writing in English* (2003), 216–17.
3 Quoted in J. Harris, 'The war of the tongues: early Anglo-Welsh responses to Welsh literary culture', in G. H. Jenkins and M. A. Williams (eds), *'Let's Do Our Best for the Ancient Tongue': The Welsh Language in the Twentieth Century* (2000), 460.
4 *Shepherds of Moel Siabod*, BBC2, 5 Nov. 1967.
5 R. Jones (ed.), *Cofio'r Cymro* (2007), 46. C. Hughes, *Portrait of Snowdonia* (1967), 14. J. G. Jones, 'Emlyn Hooson's parliamentary debut: the Montgomeryshire by-election of 1962', *Montgomeryshire Collections*, 81 (1993), 127.
6 *Y Cymro*, 21 Nov. 1952. J. Davies, *Atgofion Bro Elfed* (1966).
7 D. J. Williams (trans. W. Williams), *The Old Farmhouse* ([1953] 1987), 57, 88.
8 Welsh Agricultural Organization Society, *Rural Wales: A Yearbook of Welsh Agricultural Co-operation, 1950–51* (1952), 35. Council for Wales and Monmouthshire, *Second Memorandum by the Council on Its Activities*, Cmd 8844 (1953), 49. Ministry of Housing and Local Government, *Slum Clearance (England and Wales)*, Cmd 9593 (1955).
9 Transcript of Welsh Grand Committee, second sitting, 24 Mar. 1965, 'Mid-Wales development and depopulation', cc. 82–3.
10 Draft white paper on rural Wales, 1956, NA, CAB 129/85. R. J. Moore-Colyer, 'Lighting the landscape: rural electrification in Wales', *WHR*, 23:4 (2007), 72–92.
11 C. Hughes, *A Wanderer in North Wales* (1949), 79. Llanfihangel Social History Group, *A Welsh Countryside Revisited: A New Social Study of Llanfihangel yng Ngwynfa* (2003), 148–9. K. Roberts, *Y Byw Sy'n Cysgu* (1956), published in English as S. James (trans.), *The Awakening* (2006), 117.
12 *DWHS-1*, 97. A. Howkins, *The Death of Rural England: A Social History of the Countryside since 1900* (2003), 165.
13 D. W. Howell, 'Farming in Pembrokeshire, 1815–1974', in D. W. Howell (ed.), *Pembrokeshire County History, Vol. IV: Modern Pembrokeshire, 1815–1974* (1993), 101. Moore-Colyer, 'Lighting the landscape', 90. A. Martin, 'Agriculture', in B. Thomas (ed.), *The Welsh Economy* (1962), 85.
14 Howkins, *The Death of Rural England*, 166. *DWHS-1*, 238. *Welsh Farm News*, 28 Jan. 1961.
15 *Wales and Monmouthshire. Report of Government Action for the Year Ended 30th June 1956*, Cmd 9887 (1956). J. Lindsay, *A History of the North Wales Slate Industry* (1974), 299–300. A. J. Richards, *Slate Quarrying in Wales* (1995), 185.
16 B. Thomas, 'The unemployment cycle', in Thomas (ed.), *The Welsh Economy*, 64. Committee on Depopulation in Mid-Wales, *Depopulation in Mid Wales* (1964), 10. P. J. Madgwick, N. Griffiths and V. Walker, *The Politics of Rural Wales: A Study of Cardiganshire* (1973), 168.
17 A. Edwards, 'Answering the challenge of nationalism: Goronwy Roberts and the appeal of the Labour Party in north-west Wales during the 1950s', *WHR*, 22:1 (2004), 141.
18 *Depopulation in Mid Wales*, 3, 79. G. L. Rees, *Survey of the Welsh Economy*, Commission on the Constitution research paper (1973), 11.
19 G. C. Wenger, *Mid-Wales: Deprivation or Development* (1980), 141.
20 J. L. Williams, 'Some social consequences of grammar school education in a rural area in Wales', *British Journal of Sociology*, 10:2 (1959), 128. Council for Wales and Monmouthshire, *A Memorandum by the Council on Its Activities*, Cmd 8060 (1950), 37.
21 D. Jenkins, E. Jones, T. Jones Hughes and T. M. Owen, *Welsh Rural Communities* (1960), 106. Mid-Wales Industrial Development Association, *Mid Wales: Its Problems and Prospects* (1964), 5.
22 D. J. Davies, 'Rural depopulation', *Welsh Nation*, Mar. 1953.
23 Madgwick *et al.*, *The Politics of Rural Wales*, 176.
24 *Cardigan and Tivyside Advertiser*, 11 Jan. 1966. *I Myself*, BBC Radio, 11 Mar. 1968. D. Beddoe (ed.), *Changing Times: Welsh Women Writing on the 1950s and 1960s* (2003), 142.

25 W. G. Evans, 'Education in Cardiganshire, 1700–1974', in G. H. Jenkins and I. G. Jones (eds), *Cardiganshire County History, Vol. III* (1998), 540–69. C. R. Lewis, 'The analysis of changes in urban status: a case study in mid-Wales and the middle Welsh borderland', *Transactions of the Institute of British Geographers*, 64 (1975), 49–65.
26 Council for Wales and Monmouthshire, *Report on the Rural Transport Problem in Wales*, Cmnd 1821 (1962), 12.
27 Breconshire County Council, *County Development Plan: Report of Survey* (1954), 71. Railways in Wales, NA, PREM 11/4596.
28 K. O. Morgan, *Rebirth of a Nation: Wales, 1880–1980* (1981), 329.
29 I. Ffowc Elis, *Yn Ôl i Leifior* (1956), published in English as M. Stephens (trans.), *Return to Lleifior* (1998), 58.
30 Council for Wales and Monmouthshire, *Report on the Welsh Holiday Industry*, Cmnd 1950 (1963), 118, 11. D. Phillips, 'The effects of tourism on the Welsh language', in Jenkins and Williams (eds), *'Let's Do Our Best'*, 530.
31 Morgan, *Rebirth of a Nation*, 331. *Welsh Farm News*, 7 July 1962.
32 Council for Wales and Monmouthshire, *Report on the Welsh Holiday Industry*.
33 Mid-Wales Industrial Development Association, *Industrious Mid-Wales: A Record of Progress and Achievement* (Aberystwyth, nd). Welsh Grand Committee, second sitting, 24 Mar. 1965, 'Mid-Wales development and depopulation', col. 65. Edwards, 'Answering the challenge', 145. Ministry of Education, *Place of Welsh and English in the Schools of Wales* (1953), 22.
34 Economic Associates, *A New Town in Mid Wales* (1966). P. R. Mounfield, 'Aberystwyth: growth point?', *Town and Country Planning*, 34 (1966).
35 Mid-Wales Industrial Development Association, *Mid Wales '68: Eleventh Annual Report* (1968), 7–8. Wenger, *Mid Wales*, 16.
36 P. Morgan, 'The Gwerin of Wales: myth and reality', in I. Hume and W. T. R. Pryce (eds), *The Welsh and Their Country: Selected Readings in the Social Sciences* (1986), 134 –52.
37 G. Jones, *A Prospect of Wales* (1948), 30–1.
38 R. M. Lockley, *Wales* (1966), 13–14.
39 NA, HO 45/25484. *Daily Telegraph*, 3 Aug. 1951; *WM*, 1 Oct. 1951.
40 Translated from *Y Faner*, 13 Nov. 1958. Evans, *Gwynfor*, 186. G. Edwards, 'Mudiad y di-waith Dyffryn Nantlle, 1956–1960', *Llafur*, 5:1 (1988), 29–36.
41 *The Times*, 21 Apr., 20, 21 and 27 June 1950.
42 Edwards, 'Answering the challenge', 140.
43 J. B. Hilling, 'Architecture', in M. Stephens (ed.), *The Arts in Wales, 1950–75* (1979), 164.
44 J. Lovering, *Gwynedd: A County in Crisis* (1983), 34. I. Emmett, *A North Wales Village: A Social Anthropological Study* (1964), 135–8.
45 D. Parry-Jones, *Welsh Country Upbringing* (1948), 137.
46 *CJ*, 27 Jan. 1950. Jenkins *et al.*, *Welsh Rural Communities*, 110, 233.
47 M. Stephens (trans.), *Shadow of the Sickle* (1998), 15, 91, 217.
48 D. Pretty, *The Rural Revolt That Failed: Farm Workers' Trade Unions in Wales, 1889–1950* (1989), 209–10. D. Parry-Jones, *My Own Folk* (1972), 54.
49 Jenkins *et al.*, *Welsh Rural Communities*, 232–4, 90. R. Frankenberg, *Village on the Border: A Social Study of Religion, Politics and Football in a North Wales Community* (1957), 12.
50 Jenkins *et al.*, *Welsh Rural Communities*, 10–11.
51 J. B. Loudon, 'Kinship and crisis in south Wales', *British Journal of Sociology*, 12:4 (1961), 333–50.
52 *Observer Magazine*, 30 Oct. 1966.
53 Frankenberg, *Village on the Border*, ch. 2.
54 *Y Cymro*, 26 Mar. 1948. Parry-Jones, *My Own Folk*, 135. Edwards, 'Answering the challenge', 141.
55 E. Hooson and G. Jenkins, *The Heartland: A Plan for Mid Wales* (1965), 7.
56 Parry-Jones, *My Own Folk*, 135–6, 138. *Wales*, Dec. 1959.
57 J. Rees, *Looking for Nobody: The Secret Life of Goronwy Rees* (1994), ch. 9.
58 E. Humphreys, *A Man's Estate* ([1955] 2006), 132.

59 Frankenberg, *Village on the Border.*
60 Parry-Jones, *My Own Folk*, 92.
61 A. D. Rees, *Life in a Welsh Countryside: A Social Study of Llanfihangel yng Ngwynfa* ([1950] 1996), 166–7.
62 J. C. Powys, *Obstinate Cymric: Essays, 1935–47* (1947), 173.
63 Madgwick *et al.*, *The Politics of Rural Wales*, 69–70. M. Gallie, *Man's Desiring* (1960), 145.
64 D. D. Morgan, *The Span of the Cross: Christian Religion and Society in Wales, 1914–2000* (1999), 208–9.
65 *WM*, 30 Jan. 1950. P. Hennessy, *Having It So Good: Britain in the Fifties* (2007), 125. Jenkins *et al.*, *Welsh Rural Communities*, 166. *CJ*, 21 Apr. 1950.
66 J. Morris, 'Welshness in Wales', *Wales*, 1 Sep. 1958, 14.
67 I. Emmett, '*Fe godwn ni eto*: stasis and change in a Welsh industrial town', in A. P. Cohen (ed.), *Belonging: Identity and Social Organisation in British Rural Cultures* (1982), 175.
68 T. Brennan, E. W. Cooney and H. Pollins, *Social Change in South-West Wales* (1954), 98–9, 105. Jenkins *et al.*, *Welsh Rural Communities*, 202–3, 14, 43–4. Rees, *Life in a Welsh Countryside*, 127. Llanfihangel Social History Group, *A Welsh Countryside Revisited*, 145.
69 Jenkins *et al.*, *Welsh Rural Communities*, 1–63, 239, 231. Lord Roberts of Conwy, *Right from the Start: The Memoirs of Sir Wyn Roberts* (2006), 10.
70 Llanfihangel Social History Group, *A Welsh Countryside Revisited*, 111. Frankenberg, *Village on the Border*, 17, 58. Jenkins *et al.*, *Welsh Rural Communities*, 239, 231–2, 166. Rees, *Life in a Welsh Countryside*, 114–15, 158. Emmett, *A North Wales Village*, 76–92, 103.
71 Emmett, *A North Wales Village*, ch. 8.
72 Quoted in translation in D. D. Morgan, 'The Welsh language and religion', in Jenkins and Williams (eds), *'Let's Do Our Best'*, 388.
73 Morgan, *The Span of the Cross*, 206. M. Rees (ed.), *Llanbrynmair yr Ugeinfed Ganrif* (2005), 342, 319.
74 Rees, *Life in a Welsh Countryside*, 118. Jenkins *et al.*, *Welsh Rural Communities*, 174–5.
75 M. L. Davies, 'A small town community in mid Wales: an introductory study', in H. Carter and W. K. D. Davies (eds), *Urban Essay: Studies in the Geography of Wales* (1970), 188. C. C. Harris, 'Churches, chapels and the Welsh', *New Society*, 21 (21 Feb. 1963), 19.
76 C. Rosser and C. Harris, *The Family and Social Change: A Study of Family and Kinship in a South Wales Town* (1965), 11.
77 M. Gallie, *The Small Mine* ([1962] 2000), 86.
78 Madgwick *et al.*, *Politics of Rural Wales*, 66–67, 77. Diane Leonard, *Sex and Generation: A Study of Courtship and Weddings* (1980), 221–2.
79 *Pontypridd Observer and Free Press*, 3 July 1948. *WM*, 26 Feb. 1968.
80 *WM*, 27 Sep. 1952. Beddoe (ed.), *Changing Times*, 122.
81 *Aberdare Leader*, 9 July 1960.
82 *Punch*, 18 June 1958. E. Phillips, *The Reluctant Redhead* (2007), 118.
83 *Denbighshire Free Press and North Wales Times*, 26 Dec. 1959 and 30 Jan. 1960. *WM*, 1 Feb. 1968.
84 *CDH*, 1, 8, 15 July and 17 June 1966.
85 *Rhondda Fach Leader*, 19 Nov. 1961. A. Road, *Newspaper Dragon* (1977), 39. Rosser and Harris, *The Family and Social Change*, 107.
86 *SWE*, 1 Nov. 1960. K. O. Morgan, *Modern Wales: Politics, Places and People* (1995), 318. Cabinet conclusions, 25 Oct. 1960 and 8 Nov. 1960, NA, CAB 128/34.
87 *Rhondda Fach Leader*, 4 Nov. 1961. *The Times*, 10 Nov. 1961.
88 *The Times*, 30 Oct. 1961, 8 Nov. 1968 and 10 Nov. 1961.
89 B. Mitchell, *Law, Morality and Religion in a Secular Society* (1967), 34–5. H. Carter and J. G. Thomas, 'The referendum on the Sunday opening of licensed premises in Wales as a criterion of a culture region', *Regional Studies*, 3 (1969), 61–71. *Baner ac Amserau Cymru*, 14 Nov. 1961.
90 J. Davies, *A History of Wales* (1993), 643. P. Stead, 'Popular culture', in T. Herbert and G. E. Jones (eds), *Post-War Wales* (1995), 117.

91 Morgan, *The Span of the Cross*, 209, 196.
92 *SWEP*, 16 May 1952.
93 *I Myself*, BBC Radio, 11 Mar. 1968.
94 J. Morgans, *Journey of a Lifetime* (2008), 181.
95 Morgan, *The Span of the Cross*, 189, 197–8, 254. G. Simon, *Then and Now: A Charge* (1961), 31.
96 Morgan, 'The Welsh language and religion', 388. Rosser and Harris, *The Family and Social Change*, 122, 127, 128. Madgwick *et al.*, *The Politics of Rural Wales*, 66–7. Morgans, *Journey of a Lifetime*, 112.
97 G. Rees, 'Coming back' (1953), in P. Hannan (ed.), *Wales on the Wireless* (1988), 180.
98 T. G. Williams (ed.), *Hunaniaeth Gymreig* (2004), 94. Brennan *et al.*, *Social Change*, 188–9.
99 G. Rees, 'Have the Welsh a future?' *Encounter*, Mar. 1964.
100 Morris, 'Welshness in Wales', 15.
101 Quoted in D. Sandbrook, *White Heat: A History of Britain in the Swinging Sixties* (2006), 54. D. Sandbrook, *Never Had It So Good: A History of Britain from Suez to the Beatles* (2005), 540, 224.
102 *Observer Magazine*, 30 Oct. 1966.
103 Emmett, *A North Wales Village*, xiv, 12–13, 22.
104 E. Hobsbawm, *Interesting Times: A Twentieth Century Life* (2002), 238, 242, 244.
105 Madgwick *et al.*, *The Politics of Rural Wales*, 113.

7

'A cottonwool fuzz at the back of the mind.' Language and nationhoods, 1951–70

> I always associated Welshness with quarrelling committees, with things going wrong, little political men with vested interests and families of unemployable nephews screwing money and jobs out of the State for their own special, personal causes. And the Language that nobody spoke in the towns, unless it was to get on in the BBC or Education. Of course, I remembered the more emotive things, hymns at football matches, those great spasms of emotion that swept across the terraces at football grounds, waves of feeling and piping tenor voices, patterns of song as intricate as a folk weave, but meaningless in terms of my present. Welshness was like a cottonwool fuzz at the back of the mind because Wales was always round the corner where I lived. Men remembered it beerily when the pubs closed, or at specially contrived festivals – somebody's pocket and kudos again. We had come to be the St. David's Day Welsh. . . .
>
> Alun Richards, *Home to an Empty House* (1973 [2006]), 243

> But there has also been a lot of co-operation and of fighting together, of suffering and grieving together, of feeling shame, pride and joy together. . . . If Britishness is an illusion, it is a very powerful illusion. . . .
>
> Translated from A. D. Rees, 'Cenedl ddauddyblyg ei meddwil', *Barn*, 29 (Mar. 1965), 129

IN 1958 LORD RAGLAN, the seventy-three-year-old lord-lieutenant of Monmouthshire and president of the governors of the National Museum of Wales, wrote an article which claimed that, in general, Welsh was the language of the illiterate. He maintained that it was used for 'three undesirable purposes, to conceal the results of scholarship [into traditional Welsh literature], to try to lower the standards of official competence [by requiring it for jobs where it should not be needed] and, worst of all, to create enmity where none existed'. Welsh was thus a 'moribund language' with no usefulness. He concluded, 'It will be a happy day for Wales when that language finally takes its proper place – on the bookshelves of the scholars'.[1] The article caused a furore among the Welsh establishment, with Raglan being called everything from a fool, to a Nazi and a communist. But Raglan found his defenders too. An RAF officer from New Quay took the opportunity to declare the language 'melodious gibberish'. The *Birmingham Post* argued that the anti-Raglan brigade were 'grown men dressed in nightshirts and reciting mediocre verse of their own composition in an incomprehensible language'. Another writer dismissed those seeking to remove Raglan from his position at the National Museum as 'faceless zombies who mastermind many lucrative jobs in Wales, and as far as possible impose their attitudes in the University Colleges, the BBC, the TWW [television station], education committees of local authorities, the Welsh section of the Arts Council, the Chapels and all the rest of it'. Parts of the Welsh-speaking establishment that made up this 'gang of bigots and nepotists' were actually less hysterical, noting, for example, that the thousands who professed to cherish the language but did nothing about it were a greater threat than Raglan.[2]

This was far from a unique incident. Despite the Welsh language being everywhere in Wales in the form of place-names, those who promoted its use often met with bemusement or even hostility. In 1957 there were complaints about a letter posted in Cardiff with the address in Welsh that eventually arrived in Colwyn Bay with 'Try foreign section' and 'Not known in China' written on it. When Welsh names were chosen for new urban estates in the 1950s and 1960s there was often resentment among locals. A woman writing in the *Daily Post* in 1954 summed up what many thought would and should happen: 'our Welsh language, having fulfilled its purpose and controlled by inexorable laws of the universe, must in this technological age, just fade away'.[3] Newspaper *Y Dydd* concluded that the Raglan affair had 'given voice to the secret wish of many people in Wales. Perhaps it will be a good thing if it focuses us to face up to the question and to decide whether we want to be Welshmen or not.'[4] The answer to that question depended on what was meant by being Welsh. If it meant the rurality and restrictions of the Welsh way of life, then many were quite content to leave Welshness behind. Similarly, if it meant speaking Welsh at the expense of getting on in life, then the answer was also negative. But that did not mean there was a desire not to be Welsh. A historian noted in 1971:

> English-speaking Welshmen are, as a rule, not apologetic about their Welshness or without pride in it. They are conscious of an amalgam of many traits which shade them off from the English or the Irish or the Scots: a separate

> history, a prevalent radicalism in religion and politics, a dislike of class distinctions and snobbery, a warmth and ebullience of temperament, a deep attachment to their own kin and locality, a love of singing and rugby football, and the like. They often view with keen regret the decline of the Welsh language and confess, a little ruefully, that they wish they could speak it.

But, significantly, he also noted: 'in general, they have not been willing to think of their Welshness as the determining factor of their political or cultural allegiance. A large majority of them, indeed, have hitherto judged it to be largely irrelevant to the most serious social and political issues.'[5] A columnist in the *New Statesman* thought that for most working-class Welsh people nationalism was associated with 'the Wales that their ancestors left behind 150 years ago – with coracles, harps, women and tall hats, and sturdily independent small farmers. Undeniably this Wales still exists and most urbanised Welshmen view it with affection.' The *Observer* similarly thought that many older Welsh people had a kind of schizophrenia, caught between 'their dreams of the past and a present dominated by their ubiquitous neighbours'.[6] That schizophrenia spun around like a loose pendulum over the 1950s and 1960s but the gradual growth of Welsh education and a Welsh media, alongside the decline of the traditional Welsh way of life, were reweighting its trajectory in a way that would free Welshness from some of the chains of the past, allowing a more modern and populist Welsh identity to emerge.

THE HOSTILITY TO ATTITUDES such as Raglan's was born out of the knowledge that the Welsh language was in decline. Every ten years the census provided incontrovertible proof of this (table 7.1). The number of monoglot Welsh speakers fell from 97,932 in 1931 (4.0 per cent of the population of three-year-olds and above) to 41,155 (1.7 per cent) in 1951 and 26,223 by 1961 (1 per cent). Not speaking English was becoming something for young children and the old, although there were still nearly 16,800 people of working age in 1951 who spoke only Welsh. Moreover, in an era where 'all the machinery of English bureaucracy is at work, where mothers get their free milk, infants watch their Andy Pandy, farmers complete their Whitehall questionnaires', it was rather remarkable that there still were some tens of thousands of people who did not speak English, not immigrants from the Commonwealth but British citizens, born and bred.[7]

The strength of the language was clear in the fact that there were remote parishes in the rural north-west where nearly everyone spoke Welsh. Llanrhaeadr-ym-Mochnant (Montgomeryshire) was just six miles from the

Table 7.1 Percentage of Welsh speakers, recorded by county, 1931–71

	1931	1951	1961	1971
Anglesey	87.4	79.8	75.5	65.7
Brecon	37.3	30.3	28.1	22.9
Caernarfon	79.2	71.7	68.3	62.0
Cardigan	87.0	79.5	74.8	67.6
Carmarthen	82.3	77.3	75.1	66.5
Denbigh	48.5	38.5	34.8	28.1
Flint	31.7	21.1	19.0	14.7
Glamorgan	30.5	20.3	17.2	11.8
Merioneth	86.1	75.4	75.9	73.5
Monmouth	6.0	3.5	3.4	2.1
Montgomery	40.7	35.1	32.3	28.1
Pembroke	30.6	26.9	24.4	20.7
Radnor	4.7	4.5	4.5	3.7
Wales	36.8	28.9	26.0	20.8
Total number of Welsh speakers	909,261	714,686	656,002	542,425

English border but still over 80 per cent Welsh-speaking in 1961. Nonetheless, the number of communities where over 80 per cent of the population spoke Welsh fell by nearly a third during the 1960s. There were other reasons to be pessimistic about the language's future. In 1961 only 13 per cent of three- and four-year-olds spoke Welsh but 37 per cent of those aged over sixty-five did. Further south, a much starker picture was emerging. In Radnorshire there were just 657 Welsh speakers, of whom only fourteen spoke no English. As early as 1950, a survey estimated that only 4 per cent of pupils in Rhondda spoke Welsh. It was no surprise then that the percentage of Welsh speakers there fell from 29 per cent in 1951 to 13 per cent in 1971. By then, 37 per cent of people aged over sixty-five in Rhondda spoke Welsh but only 4 per cent of ten- to fourteen-year-olds. Even on the western edge of the industrial region there were significant falls. In Neath, for example, Welsh speakers made up 44 per cent of the population in 1951 but only 26 per cent in 1971. The consequence in many industrial communities was that local eisteddfodau ended and choirs and chapels switched to English.[8] A culture was fading away.

The causes of the decline were clear enough. The physical barriers of distance and geography that had kept the language isolated but safe were now beginning to collapse. One novelist bemoaned in 1961,

> The English language is not just the medium of school instruction for seven hours each day, but a ubiquitous voice throughout the day on radio, in newspapers, and on the television screen. Wales is no longer a haven beyond the mountains, but an open playground for hordes of motorists and cyclists and hikers, and an experimental field for the Government's technology. The teeth of her defensive mountains have been drawn, her valleys drowned by the English, and the innards of her rural society ripped out. She now stands naked before the world.[9]

Modernity was not just bringing English into 'Y Fro Gymraeg' (the Welsh-speaking heartlands), it was also making it harder to live life entirely through the medium of Welsh. Although new vocabulary was being developed, a 1952 education report expressed fears that the language was 'struggling for the mastery of the complexities of modern life, and in many parts of the country it is in grave danger of degenerating into a patois'.[10] It was perhaps the broadcast media that were the most serious threat. In 1945, 65 per cent of Welsh households had radios, but by 1952 the figure was 82 per cent. Some of the programming came from Wales but the radio was a common British experience. The most listened to station, as it was everywhere in the UK, was the Light Programme and its best comedies, quizzes and dramas could attract half the British population, Wales included. A prominent Plaid Cymru member called the radio 'the greatest murderer yet of the Welsh way of life' and the party complained that the media were bringing both the English language and English tastes into Welsh-speaking homes and communities. Such fears grew with television but were also mixed with a general snobbishness that somehow a cinema in the home was lowbrow and rather common. Saunders Lewis, dramatist, novelist and founding member of Plaid Cymru, typically warned in 1951 that the television 'could totally destroy all culture'.[11]

The Anglicizing influence of the media was not straightforward. Children might watch films in English but they could still enact gangster and cowboy games in Welsh.[12] Nonetheless, the cinema, television, radio and rock'n'roll all gave English a glamour that Welsh could not match. In the 1950s, when there was Elvis Presley or even Cliff Richard on the radio, speaking Welsh could seemed dated, old fashioned and even embarrassing. This was especially true in much of industrial Wales, where Anglicization processes before the war had already aged Welsh in young people's minds and entwined it with the chapels and their restrictive culture. One novelist born in 1929 looked back upon his Valleys youth where Welsh was 'the language of *old* people and those young people who spoke it were in some ways freaks, either every recent immigrants from the rural areas of Wales or, often, the sons and daughters of non-conformist ministers who maintained stubborn oases of Welshness which seemed somehow comic and countrified to outsiders'.[13] But even in rural areas some young Welsh speakers took to talking English among themselves. A 1947 survey found that in Caernarfonshire primary schools 72 per cent of pupils could speak Welsh but only 51 per cent habitually played in the language. Among girls in Tregaron (Cardiganshire) in the late 1940s there was a preference for being taught in English and they used English in the playground, seeing it as urbane and sophisticated, although the boys preferred using Welsh.[14] In areas where English predominated, children from Welsh-speaking homes could feel different to their peers and thus want to hide their linguistic background. This was not surprising when Welsh-speaking children at grammar school in Wrexham in the 1940s had to endure jokes from teachers about being savages.[15]

Other forces were at work too, reducing both opportunities to speak Welsh and the number of people actually able to do it. In urban communities the movement of people in search of work and better amenities was not only breaking up the old communities, it was also undermining the Welsh language. In Swansea, sociologists found evidence that the speech of people changed when dispersed from Welsh-speaking industrial valleys to new council estates across the borough, where English was the dominant language. This compounded the older trend whereby some working-class Welsh speakers raised their children in English, especially if they had married an English monoglot. According to a 1950 Ministry of Education survey, across Wales just 70 per cent of children aged five to fifteen spoke Welsh where both parents did, a mere 6 per cent did where only the father alone spoke Welsh and 11 per cent did where the mother alone spoke Welsh. Even in Caernarfon, only 91 per cent of children in the survey spoke Welsh where both parents spoke the language, 19 per cent did where only the father spoke Welsh and 43 per cent did where only the mother did. In Glamorgan just 42 per cent of children with Welsh-speaking parents could speak Welsh and a mere 7 per cent where only the mother spoke Welsh.[16] It was thus very clear that parents were not always passing the language on to their children. This was not simply an omission but was done in the belief that they were helping their offspring. One woman from near Criccieth (Caernarfonshire) recalls Welsh-speaking parents in the 1950s lobbying their local school not to teach Welsh: 'It's no use in business', they proclaimed, 'it only holds the children back'.[17] In Llanfrothen (Merioneth) in the late 1950s some people did exaggerate their lack of English skills because if they could not understand the language they could not be expected to comply with official regulations. Yet even there, having good English was deemed socially useful, especially in dealing with officialdom, and it conferred some status on people.[18] At the start of the 1950s the parents of Mervyn Davies, a future rugby international, decided to stop speaking Welsh in their Swansea home. They were, in the words of their son, 'a solid working-class Welsh breed, chapel-goers all', but they wanted to help their sons achieve at school. At the time of their decision, Davies was unable to speak any English at all.[19] Within such families the Welsh language could, in the words of one novelist, 'have the status of a pet, reserved for occasional greetings', Sundays and keeping things 'from the children'.[20] A sociologist noted that in the industrial Amman valley of the early 1970s, a mining community where some 80 per cent of people spoke Welsh, the language was used by many people simply because it was their first language and not out of a conscious effort to preserve it or recognize Welsh culture.[21] Once it is remembered that for many Welsh speakers the language lacked any ideological meaning, then their willingness to stop speaking it, whether temporarily to avoid being rude to non-speakers, or more permanently to help their children, is quite understandable.

Among the rural working class, the loyalties to the Welsh language were stronger. Isabel Emmett's picture of Llanfrothen at the start of the 1960s as a Welsh-speaking people waging a guerrilla war against the forces of Englishness (see chapter 6) probably overplays the politicization of the Welsh language among the working class, perhaps unsurprisingly given that it was conducted in a community experiencing an unusual level of English middle-class immigration. The Caernarfonshire MP, however, did argue in 1956 that 'people in Arfon cherish their language'.[22] Speaking Welsh certainly defined such people in a world that was dominated by the English language. But in 1971 a Welsh-speaking councillor in Cardiganshire went as far as saying that local people's Welsh and Welshness meant 'nothing at all to them'.[23] Even if they did cherish it, as in urban areas, speaking Welsh was not first and foremost a political act. Outside language campaigners, there was little evidence of a resentment of English's status as the official language of most of public life. The newspaper *Yr Herald Cymraeg* argued in 1962–3 that most people in Welsh-speaking areas preferred to do official business in English, 'the more important of our two languages'.[24] Just 7 per cent in a 1971 Cardiganshire survey thought the future of the Welsh language was the area's most serious problem, while 79 per cent of people did not pick it at all from a list of problems from which they were asked to nominate the issues they were most concerned about. In contrast, more than three-quarters chose rising prices.[25] An early 1950s study of Glyn Ceiriog (Denbighshire) argued that villagers valued Welsh. They were flattered when English people wanted to learn it 'but rather resentful at their success'. They also had 'a half-suppressed feeling that English is more "educated", and they fully recognize the economic importance to learning to read and write good English'.[26] Such attitudes were shared by the working class across rural Wales.

The cause of the language was not helped by the barrier between the Welsh-speaking working class and elite Welsh-language culture. For all the clichés of a working class embroiled in poetry, literature and history, much of Welsh literary culture was beyond the masses, in terms of either interest or language. As one grammar book points out, literary Welsh 'is no-one's native language' but its success as the medium of literature engendered 'a sense of inferiority' among 'ordinary Welsh speakers' whose colloquial language was 'neglected and relentlessly disparaged' by the elite.[27] Many Welsh speakers thus preferred to write and read in English.[28] A villager in Aberdaron in the 1960s remembered that the vicar, the poet R. S. Thomas, used to come into 'the village shop and insist that they used the proper Welsh words like *eiryn gwlanog* for peach. People just used to stare at him, they'd never heard of such a word.'[29] At the start of the 1950s the average sale of a book in Welsh was 2,000. The town librarian at Bangor thought in 1966 that only 'the elderly and a few children' read books in Welsh anymore. There was little in the way of Welsh popular fiction and the Cardiganshire librarian called for 'good rubbish' to be published in order to attract people to reading in Welsh.[30] Newspapers were more widely read. An English-language newspaper in north Wales suggested that people bought the Welsh-language press 'not from patriotism, not from concern for the Welsh language, but because Welsh is their natural language and because these papers give them the news and the information and the reading that they want'.[31] Yet in 1969 the various Welsh-language current affairs periodicals and papers had circulations of just 47,000 between them.[32] Indeed, the 1971 census, the first to look at literacy rather than just speech, showed that just 73 per cent of Welsh speakers aged fifteen and over could write the language, while 84 per cent could read it.

WHILE SOME WERE turning their back on speaking Welsh, a few were turning their back on being Welsh altogether. The language, Nonconformity and the Welsh way of life all created the idea that Welshness was somehow out of date. One south Walian student at university in Aberystwyth found most Welsh speakers 'pretty narrow, chapel-driven, clannish, old fashioned and a little more than somewhat dull'.[33] Some of the images of Wales in popular culture did not help. Characters like Dai and Twm, the two naïve miners in the Ealing comedy *Run for Your Money* (1949), and Jones the Steam, Dai Station and Evans the Song in *Ivor the Engine* (1959–64, and 1976–7) all reinforced an impression that the Welsh were a rather comic people. No wonder then that some were keen to play down their Welshness. One of the easiest ways of doing this was 'speaking nice', by avoiding the grammatical oddities of Welsh English and dropping or moderating the Welsh accent. The *Observer* claimed in 1966 that elocution lessons were thriving in Wales, with people eager to lose their accent.[34] Grammar schools tended to soften people's accents into what was sometimes called the 'cultured Welsh voice' epitomized by the likes of Richard Burton and Dylan Thomas. Even a secondary modern schoolboy might try to 'hide his Cardiff Market vowels with a nasty lah-di-dah copied off Welsh B.B.C. announcers'. Part of this was snobbishness, but it was also pragmatism. The English had a particularly strong view of the Welsh as backward and thus assimilating and getting on often required becoming less Welsh. In 1950 one woman was told by her Cambridge teacher-training college, 'it would be wise if you got rid of that boring Welsh accent'.[35] Even those from wealthy backgrounds could face the contempt of the English class system. Future Conservative cabinet member Michael Heseltine endured snobbery at Oxford in the 1950s because he came from Swansea and his father managed a steelworks.[36] If anyone needed an example of how dropping a Welsh accent could help you get on then they had only to look at Roy Jenkins, the miner's son from Abersychan who became a Labour Home Secretary and Chancellor of the Exchequer. He never played up or even made reference to his background. When it was suggested that Jenkins was lazy, Aneurin Bevan said 'No boy from the valleys who has cultivated that accent could possibly be lazy!'[37]

The exodus of the ambitious from Wales might itself be interpreted as indicative of a lack of patriotism. In 1964 the press in north Wales certainly wondered why so many students preferred to study in England after it was announced that, of the 540 new students at Bangor that year, only ninety were from Wales. The answer lay in the narrow range of opportunities for professional and management jobs anywhere in Wales. This was especially true in rural areas, where there was nothing remotely close to enough professional jobs to meet the needs of grammar-school graduates.[38] One academic who left looked back: 'It hardly occurred to any of us that we should make a career in Wales.... What was left in Wales seemed narrow, petty-bourgeois and hypocritical.'[39] In such a context there was little point getting too flustered about being Welsh. This ambivalence towards Wales was as much about class as nationality, and it had much in common with the difficulty working-class grammar-school products from the north of England had in assimilating into the middle-class worlds their occupations could place them in. In a 1960 novel by the Welsh writer Menna Gallie, a working-class south Walian who goes to work in an English university feels awkward with the girls there because 'It's where you come from, not where you're going that counts'. They are 'posh' and 'don't know our patterns; they have a dining-room, and they don't call their best room the parlour and keep it for death. They have drawing-rooms and only drink coffee or cocktails in them.'[40]

Others reacted differently. A Blaenau Ffestiniog man remembered of the mid-1960s: 'I was ashamed of being Welsh. But when I went to art college the students there were so middle class, that started me coming back to being Welsh.'[41] With the rise of icons like the Beatles, coming from a working-class background was becoming fashionable in the middle of the 1960s. Wales had its own self-consciously working-class hero in Tom Jones. In 1966 he told the press that he was earning a couple of thousand pounds a week but still had to wipe his feet and take his turn bringing the coal in when back home. Like the contemporary Welsh-language pop singers (see chapter 4), such figures encouraged the young to take more pride in being Welsh by modernizing that identity's associations. This also led to émigrés playing up their Welsh accent after years of trying to suppress it.[42] Some grew nostalgic about the community they had left behind. A short story of the time captured this:

> Like so many South Walians who leave home in their teens and never really return except on holiday, Barton retained a warm, myth-inspired image of a tumultuous valley community whose pre-war qualities of a shoulder-to-shoulder empathy caused him to think of it with nostalgic glow as a special world-defeating place.... [He] retained the exile's enchantment with a never-never land, and nothing would shake it.[43]

Yet, for all the pride émigrés were finding in their Welshness in the 1960s, there was little hope of many of them returning. In 1970 the Mid-Wales Industrial Development Association wrote to 160 Welsh societies across the UK to tell them of the developments taking place in the area in the hope of enticing some to return. Just two societies replied. One magazine complained in 1971 that London was 'full of Welsh who still sing the praises of Wales and the Valleys – but never return expect for a fleeting hour or two, once or twice a year.... They will sing "Land of my Fathers" at the Albert Hall, so long as they are never seriously asked to serve that land'.[44]

Within Wales itself some regions had a rather marginal sense of being Welsh. The historic weakness of the Welsh language in south Pembrokeshire meant some locals denied they were Welsh at all, despite living in one of the most westerly parts of the country. In 1947 one traveller said he was told 'almost at once' after arriving in Milford Haven, 'We are English here'.[45] Along parts of the English border, admitting to being Welsh was unfashionable and even farmers might deny their family was Welsh-speaking. In Flintshire Maelor, a small rural area protruding into England, people in the 1950s had, according to one woman there, 'little national feeling, rather a sense of stubbornly being *where you were* and that was that'. In 1963 the local council there even threatened to try to become part of England because it feared Welsh being pushed in the area in the event of a reorganization of local government.[46] In parts of Monmouthshire some residents insisted that they already lived in England. The county was Welsh for all legal and administrative purposes but it had traditionally occupied a somewhat ambiguous position, which led to the phrase 'Wales and Monmouthshire' being used for clarity in many official arenas. The objection of some residents to this was evident in a 1963 letter from Newport to a local paper which complained that organizations like the South Wales Electricity Board and Wales Gas Board had been trying to convince Monmouthshire it was Welsh:

> Even the G.P.O. are now trying to do the same, selling stamps of the Welsh type. I agree that they also sell the English type, but you have to ask for these or they pass the Welsh ones off on you.
>
> It is time Monmouthshire people stepped out and demanded their rights to be classed as English, before we are all classed as Taffs.[47]

The replies showed that not all agreed but the feeling was strong enough that when the local council put up signs on the border saying 'Welcome to Wales' they were 'tarred and feathered, defaced with paint and even removed'. In the 1950s Newport grammar school solved the dilemma by celebrating both St David's and St George's Day.[48]

Even when parts of Wales did regard themselves as Welsh there was no guarantee that the rest of Wales would accept them as such. The northern coastal towns, with their caravan parks and Lancashire holidaymakers, were summed up in one book as having nothing 'which could by any stretch of imagination be called characteristically Welsh'.[49] A Rhondda woman remembered being told by a shopkeeper on a trip to Pwllheli (Caernarfon) in the late 1940s that she was 'an English girl' because she did not speak Welsh. Indignantly, she replied that 'I'm as Welsh as you! More Welsh in fact because I'm from *South* Wales which is much more important than up here.'[50] Kingsley Amis claimed southerners thought northerners 'primitive, rustic, also sly and treacherous, rather like the stock English view of the Welsh in general'.[51] Even for Welsh speakers in the south the psychological gap with the north was substantial. A traveller was told by a Senny Bridge farmer in 1947:

> those people up in North Wales are terrible! … They won't look at you, they are that unfriendly. They think so much of themselves, nobody's good enough for them.… They think they're more Welsh, the true Welsh, the only Welsh, more aristocratic, or something. And they speak differently from us. I can hardly understand a word they say. Round here we are friendly, and can be friendly with anyone. If you are going up there, you'll have a terrible time.[52]

Northerners, in contrast, complained that the south dominated images of Wales. Thus one woman bemoaned that whenever she met people in England they made allusions to choirs, mining and rugby.[53] But given that Cardiff to London by train was three hours, whereas it took a whole day to get to Caernarfon from Cardiff, it was hardly a surprise that the gulf between north and south was vast.

The regional divisions that beset Wales were clearly evident in attitudes to Cardiff. In 1945 a request from proud councillors in Cardiff that it be recognized as the capital city was rejected by the government because there was no unanimity on the issue. In 1950 the Council for Wales and Monmouthshire decided to revisit the issue and it received claims from Aberystwyth, Caernarfon, Cardiff and Llandrindod Wells. The Council, however, concluded there was widespread support for Cardiff's claim, even in the north. Caernarfon was unimpressed and its town clerk reiterated that his town 'stands supreme as a living symbol of all that is best in the Welsh way of life'.[54] In contrast, Cardiff's Welshness was open to debate, questioned by even some of its own residents. The writer Bernice Rubens, who grew up there in the 1930s and 1940s, recalled: 'Cardiffians were an ambivalent people, nervous and with an unsure identity'. To the city's residents the adjective 'Welsh' could be derogatory, signifying something backwards, a world of 'Shonnies' and 'Boyos'. This did not mean that they did not regard themselves as Welsh but Cardiff was different, neither quite English nor Welsh.[55]

The Conservatives' creation in 1951 of the Minister for Welsh Affairs, with an office in Cardiff, was a major step forward, since it made the city a seat of governance. The government in London, however, remained cautious because it perceived a lack of agreement in Wales and felt Cardiff would simply evolve as a capital as more government work was concentrated there.[56] But the pressure for a formal capital remained amid fears that Welsh nationhood needed bolstering as the Welsh way of life faded. In 1954 the decisive move happened when Welsh local authorities voted overwhelmingly to propose Cardiff as capital. While Cardiff got 134 votes, it is instructive that Caernarfon received eleven, Aberystwyth four and Swansea one, with large authorities like Monmouth, Montgomery, Newport, Denbigh and Anglesey declining to support anyone. Despite this, a senior civil servant called it 'an almost startling degree of unanimity for Wales'. Caernarfon, Cardiff's main competitor, accepted the vote, and the government, after checking with the Queen and deciding not to raise the issue of whether capital status referred to Wales or Wales and Monmouthshire, concurred. Cabinet was briefed:

> The question of a capital is one of prestige for the people of Wales, and to refuse recognition to Cardiff would undoubtedly give great offence. Although an announcement might stimulate a demand for further devolution of functions – which would not be out of harmony with the Government's policy – there would be little risk of encouraging pressure for Welsh independence, or for the appointment of a separate Secretary of State for Wales.[57]

To avoid giving the decision too much importance, the announcement was made in a reply to a written question in Parliament.

Capital status did not create much feeling for Cardiff. One writer claimed in 1964 that the city was 'little more than a name' to those who lived in mid and north Wales. Even for those who were nearer there was often scepticism and a sense of difference. A 1958 letter to the *South Wales Echo* from someone in Merthyr complained that he came to Cardiff a few times a year and found the people 'stuck up and distant'. He could sit in a pub for a whole evening without anyone speaking to him and found that people reacted with incredulity when they heard him speak Welsh. In 1958 a reporter remarked, 'A foreigner could spend a week in Cardiff or Penarth and think himself still in England'.[58] No wonder then that a man who spent his teens in the city in the early 1970s recalled, 'it seemed that I was living in a kind of Welsh-flavoured England'. He supported Wales fanatically at rugby but felt different to the Welsh speakers he encountered; 'we knew in our heart of hearts that we were "not really Welsh"'.[59] Yet part of the ambivalence towards Cardiff was as much to do with its size and urbanity, and the complaints of unfriendliness were echoes of provincial attitudes to metropolitan centres everywhere. For the young, the city did have some glamour. A Rhondda schoolgirl in the early 1950s thought it 'a grand, romantic city'. It had a 'Lord Mayor, ancient castle and TWO railways stations, where the porter, ticket collector and station master weren't the same man. It had elegant, smooth trains instead of swaying, jolting buses and restaurants with palm court orchestras in them – a place far posher and more awesome than Porth or even Pontypridd.'[60]

IN MYTHOLOGY THE LANGUAGE was driven out of places like Porth and Pontypridd by an English education system that punished children for speaking their mother tongue. The education system was indeed heavily Anglicized but it was also many children's only direct contact with the Welsh language in the 1950s. How much Welsh was taught varied across the country. In Glamorgan it was the policy of the local authority that all primary school children be taught Welsh for at least six lessons a week, while in Caernarfonshire a minimum standard of efficiency in both languages was expected by the age of eleven. In contrast, in Merioneth the principal concern of the council was for children to become fluent in English.[61] At secondary level, local authorities left individual schools to develop their own policies. In 1946 a little over 40 per cent of grammar-school pupils took Welsh as a subject at some stage in their education but in only ten out of 151 such schools was it compulsory. Welsh was not taught at all at twenty-four grammar schools, while the rest offered it as an option, which required the dropping of another language such as French or Latin. While some preferred to drop Welsh for something which they saw as more useful, others took it as a 'soft option' because their school entered them for exams designed for learners rather than native speakers.[62] In 1951, whereas 997 children were taking English Higher School Certificates, 555 were taking French and 249 were taking Latin, just 189 were taking Welsh.[63] This was two years after the Welsh Department of the Ministry of Education had issued a report calling for Welsh culture to be made the background of education because 'In no other way can the pupil grow to the full height of his Welsh citizenship, and bring his own contribution to a British, European, and finally a world citizenship and culture'.[64] A 1953 report from the same department advocated that all children be taught in Welsh and English according to their ability, with a second language being introduced in primary school.[65] Such calls did encourage some teachers to pay more attention to Welsh history and culture and led local authorities to give more funding to the teaching of Welsh. But provision for the language throughout the 1950s and 1960s remained limited. Too often it involved learning verbs and passages by heart; a woman who attended a grammar school in Porth in the early 1950s remembered: 'we could all recite several poems in Welsh despite having a minimal idea of what they meant but could scarcely string together three words of the language'. At the male grammar school in her town, boys wishing to do a language in the sixth form were divided on the basis of their father's occupation. Middle-class children were put into French and working-class children into Welsh.[66]

In 1939, parents who were concerned at the Anglicization of Aberystwyth, especially with the arrival of evacuees, set up a private school to teach the whole curriculum through the medium of Welsh, marking the beginning of a new trend which extended into the state sector after the war. By 1950, fifteen official Welsh-medium primary schools existed, educating 996 children. This figure had risen to thirty-six by 1962 and forty-one by 1971, embracing some 5,000 pupils.[67] Most of these schools had come about as the result of pressure from middle-class parents and were often operating on a distinctly small scale, using spare classrooms and even chapel vestries.[68] But they also created a demand for Welsh-medium secondary education and, in 1956, Rhyl's Ysgol Gyfun Glan Clwyd became Wales' first such school. A second opened in Pontypridd in 1962 and by 1970 there were six Welsh-medium secondary schools. They were, however, in areas where the Welsh language was weak. In the 'Fro Gymraeg', the urgency to preserve the language that underpinned the pressure for Welsh-medium education was much weaker because Welsh was still spoken in the community. Many primary schools there did most of their teaching in Welsh but without ever being formally designated as a Welsh-medium school. At secondary level, while pupils' grasp of English was improving in the lower years, some Welsh was used to teach all subjects but by the third year instruction in English was the norm. In Merioneth, Caernarfonshire and Anglesey during the 1950s only twelve secondary schools taught formally in Welsh, and then only for religious education.[69]

In a Welsh-language secondary school in Rhyl in the 1960s and 1970s, English, like swearing, became a language of the dissidents and rebels. In the wider town, speaking Welsh marked children out as different, not always to their pleasure. The parents were consequently often more radical in their Welshness than their offspring.[70] Elsewhere, there could be a deep hostility among some parents to teaching through the medium of Welsh or even teaching any Welsh at all. A flurry of letters on Welsh-language education in one south Wales paper suggested that the subject was tinged with 'bitterness and racial prejudice'. There were comparisons with South African apartheid and accusations of segregation in Pontarddulais, where parents were alleged to have told their offspring not to play with children who were not at the

Welsh-medium school.[71] How far the antagonism extended on both sides of the argument should not be exaggerated. In a survey for a 1967 government education report, 45 per cent of parents saw no positive advantage to their children learning Welsh but only 10 per cent were openly hostile to their children being taught the language. A Welsh-medium headmaster in Pontypridd argued in 1974 that many rural Welsh speakers regarded Welsh 'as a second rate language of use only for the Eisteddfod, the chapel and for talking about the weather. They see no future for it as a language of education.' He was right that some did think in such ways but in the 1967 survey only a quarter of Welsh-speaking parents saw no advantage for their children knowing the language.[72] The official report for which that survey was conducted advocated that primary school children be taught in their mother tongue, but with full opportunities, especially in Anglicized areas, to learn the second language. In response, there was a slow increase in the teaching of Welsh across Wales. Anglesey went furthest and designated schools by language but still allowed parents to opt out of having their children taught Welsh as a second language.[73] Pockets of hostility remained and a Welsh-speaking GP in Aberystwyth told the press in 1969 that the county council's plans to increase teaching through the medium of Welsh were 'racial discrimination' and would destroy the town's growth. But the *Holyhead and Anglesey Mail* probably summed up the majority view: 'The difficulty is to do everything possible to preserve the Welsh language and to treasure it, and at the same time not to use it to the detriment of English, with all that can mean to the careers of boys and girls in these modern days.'[74] Whatever the importance of the developments in Welsh-language education in the 1950s and 1960s, it could only go so far in protecting the future of the language. A defender of education policy in Denbighshire, where children were taught in their first language but also taught the second language, was quite right when he pointed out that the future of the Welsh language and its associated culture 'is absolutely dependent upon the willingness of the parents to speak Welsh in the home'.[75] In the late 1960s the fact remained that some 20 per cent of children from Welsh-speaking homes did not speak Welsh themselves.[76] But the fact that in schools the language was taught at all, that English-language eisteddfodau were common and that St David's Day was widely celebrated all helped reinforce the idea in children's heads that they were living somewhere different to England. They might not remember much, maybe any, Welsh but they knew they were living in a country with its own distinct language.

It was not just the education system that was reminding the Welsh that Wales existed. Although not all of Wales could receive it, Wales did have its own popular Home Service radio station, where home-made programmes in both languages dominated the evening schedules in the 1940s and 1950s. However, it did little to present a more modern view of the Welsh language. In 1950 some 70 per cent of the religious programming made in Wales was in Welsh, while 70 per cent of the variety programming was in English. The distance between the management of the BBC in Wales and what its audience wanted was evident in 1947 when it decided that place-names should be pronounced in Welsh, even where people who actually lived there used an Anglicized form. This upset inhabitants of places like Merthyr and Porthcawl, who suddenly found their 'r's being rolled and their vowels sounding very different. In 1951 usage reverted to what was generally accepted in the locality. As it was intended to, Welsh-language radio was, however, beginning to show north and south that they had common interests, despite differences in dialect. There were also the first signs of modern programming, such as *Galw Gari Tryfan*, a detective series for older children that began in 1952 and convinced some teenagers that Welsh could still be relevant to their lives. Sports broadcasting in Welsh was also popular, although it had required the invention of Welsh terms for rugby positions. However, there were also fears throughout the 1950s that Welsh-language radio programmes were leading people to tune to other regions and thus undermining the unity of Wales. A 1948 survey suggested that 29 per cent of listeners in Wales tuned in on a fairly frequent basis to the English rather than Welsh Regional Home Service.[77]

This began to matter less in the 1950s as radio faced the challenge of television. On 1 March 1953 the first television programme entirely in Welsh was broadcast; predictably, it was a chapel service. That year also saw a BBC competition to devise a Welsh word for 'television'. Like radio, Welsh-language television was initially dominated by religious and literary matters and it did little to draw the young and disillusioned to the language. This narrowness owed much to how little could be broadcast in Welsh. In the last quarter of 1955 the BBC was broadcasting a monthly average of two hours forty minutes of Welsh-made television in English and one hour twenty-five minutes in Welsh. On average there was not even one adult programme every week in Welsh. The limited output was rooted in the technical problems of transmitting to Wales. South Wales shared a transmitter with the English south-west and parts of the Midlands, while the north shared broadcasts with the north-west. The problems this would cause quickly became apparent after the first feature programme in Welsh, a 1953 documentary about a Merioneth bibliophile, drew complaints from England, despite the fact that it replaced only the test card. To avoid this problem and annoying English monoglots within Wales, Welsh-language programming was largely banished to late hours. The 'toddlers' truce', a cessation of broadcasting in England between 6 and 7 p.m. to allow younger children to be got to bed, did, however, offer a slot that could be used to ensure some Welsh on primetime television. But when the truce ended in 1957 the only way of broadcasting primetime programmes was by replacing English ones. The BBC in London was reluctant to agree to this and Welsh-language programmes, totalling two hours a week by 1958, were thus again concentrated at inconvenient times.[78] Plaid Cymru, not unreasonably, was deeply unimpressed with the whole situation. It thought the Welsh broadcast media would 'dismiss a world catastrophe in a sentence but report at length on activities of a purely parochial nature'. This made the BBC in Wales more like a local paper than a national daily. World affairs, science and the arts could thus only come to Wales, the party argued, via the filters of English fashion and taste.[79]

The arrival of commercial television changed the situation. The quality of most of the programming was not to everyone's tastes, with the service heavily reliant on American comedies to attract large audiences, but the new channel was organized on a regional basis and, when Television Wales and West (TWW) began broadcasting to south Wales and the West Country in January 1958, it put out around three hours twenty minutes a week in Welsh.[80] Parts of north Wales could receive Granada from the English north-west but had to wait until the launch of Wales (West and North) Television (WWN) in September 1962 for their own station. WWN enjoyed significant support from the Welsh-speaking establishment and it claimed to be committed to serving Wales rather than personal profit. It broadcast nearly eleven hours of Welsh material (in both languages) a week. The commercial channels took forward Welsh-language television, with magazine-style programmes that contained items on song, food and conversations with Welsh figures. This was a more accessible Welsh-language culture than anything shown on the BBC but the programmes were still concentrated at off-peak times because of the need for advertising revenue. Indeed, in north Wales some people continued to watch Granada simply because reception was better. Under the financial pressure of low advertising revenue, producing its own ambitious programming and coping with the technical problems of broadcasting to a mountainous region, WWN collapsed in early 1964 and had to be taken over by TWW. Its failure showed, according to the *Western Mail,* that home-grown programmes were not adequate replacements for westerns.[81] A new transmitter opened in 1964 which allowed TWW to make separate broadcasts to the west of England. Its programming in Welsh increased to six hours a week, although this annoyed English monoglots in

Wales as much as it had in England. In 1967 TWW lost its ITV franchise to Harlech, a company which promised to do more for Wales. Its region, however, still included the west of England and commercial television continued to juggle the needs of the two audiences.[82]

The new commercial rivals to the BBC enabled its Welsh hierarchy to exert pressure on London for more Welsh-language programmes to maintain the Corporation's perceived place at the heart of national life. The BBC was thus soon showing current affairs programmes and documentaries on Welsh life, as well as commissioning Welsh-language plays, dramas and talks, all making it the key patron of Welsh-language writing. An emphasis on traditional aspects of Wales did remain but this was at a time when television also ignored much of working-class English culture.[83] An editorial in the Rhondda local press worried about how English-speaking Wales was being looked after and represented, complaining about 'the superfluity of stories revolving around the coal-pit, the chapel, the muffler, dai-cap and dreary poverty'.[84] Despite such concerns, pressure within the BBC bore fruit when Wales finally got its own television service in February 1964. Most of the content of the new BBC Wales channel was initially the same as that of BBC1 but there was nearly nine hours of home-produced material a week. By 1972 this had increased to twelve hours, seven of which were in Welsh. Again, the new channel illustrated how divided Wales was. There were complaints that people could not receive it because the signal was not strong enough; others were unhappy because the new service was all they could receive. The biggest bone of contention remained the fact that some Welsh-language programmes were broadcast at peak time. Alun Oldfield Davies, the BBC's controller for Wales, told a 1964 protest meeting at Aberystwyth: 'I cannot understand how any reasonable person can possibly imagine that, out of a total of fifty viewing hours a week, seven hours of Welsh programmes constitute an "outrage", an injustice or a form of dictatorship'. The BBC, however, still had to promise that popular programmes like *Z Cars* would not make way for programmes from Wales. Even then the complaints did not go away. Technological developments in the late 1960s meant that aerials could no longer automatically receive broadcasts from both England and Wales, meaning people had to choose where to tune their aerials to. Where people could receive an English signal, a majority seemed to be tuning into it. In 1969 the Welsh edition of the BBC's listing magazine *Radio Times* was selling 70,000 copies, whereas 96,000 copies of other regional editions were being sold in Wales.[85]

Broadcasting thus became entangled with people's attitudes to language and nationality. For the cultural establishment it offered an opportunity to unite the disparate parts of Wales and reinforce the role of the Welsh language in everyday life.[86] There was some success in this. The daily news television outputs from Wales were popular and helped develop some kind of shared national outlook. On the radio *Good Morning Wales*, which began in 1963, had 350,000 listeners by 1968, 15 per cent of the population, and a higher proportion than its UK equivalent, *Today*. A Welsh-language version, *Bore Da*, was launched in 1969 and had up to 150,000 listeners. Such developments have led historian John Davies to argue that Wales could be defined as an 'artefact produced by broadcasting'.[87] In 1961 Sir Ifan ab Owen remarked of a generation who had grown up with the broadcast media but without the memories of war and depression that fostered the importance of the British state: 'It may be that today's youth are more conscious of the nationhood of Wales than we were. Ours was a simple love of Wales; for them Wales is something very real.'[88] But there were still distinct limits to this. The Welsh media did not stop some young people seeing being Welsh as uncool, at least before being working class became fashionable in the mid-1960s. Moreover, not only were English-speaking viewers being turned away by programming in Welsh, but 27 per cent of the Welsh population in 1969 could not receive the BBC Wales signals even if they wanted to.[89] The most popular programmes remained those produced outside Wales. In the middle of the 1950s *The Archers*, which combined both human interest and agricultural stories, was listened to by nearly half the Welsh population.[90] On television *Coronation Street*, advertised by Granada as 'life in an ordinary street in an ordinary town', began in 1960 and soon became immensely popular because it depicted a life recognizable in urban Wales too. The *Wrexham Leader* concluded its success was 'because to most people it was more than a slight reflection of their own lives'. The Labour Party even had to avoid canvassing when the show was on.[91] Thus, on the one hand, television and radio did help bring the Welsh language into the modern world and underpinned a common sense of Welshness that crossed regional and linguistic divides. Yet, at the very same time, it also brought out those divides, annoying some viewers by restricting the viewing options when Welsh-language programmes were on and pushing people further from the idea of Wales when they tuned into English transmitters, whether out of choice or simply in search of a better signal.

The broadcast media also reinforced Wales' Britishness. They spoke to the audience as fellow Britons and helped generate shared hopes and fears, interests and outlooks and thus flagged up and sustained Wales' place in a culture beyond Wales. This process was reinforced by the reach of the London press. In the late 1950s it was estimated that the *News of the World* alone was read by 58 per cent of the south Wales population. A 1961 survey suggested that 21 per cent of adults in Wales read the *Western Mail* (the main south Wales morning daily) and 7 per cent the *Liverpool Daily Post* (the north Wales equivalent) but 38 per cent read the *Daily Mirror*, 28 per cent the *Daily Express*, 18 per cent the *Daily Herald* and 15 per cent the *Daily Mail*. Even in Welsh-speaking Tregaron (Cardiganshire) in 1946, where nearly every home took a daily paper, 180 homes bought London titles, compared with 139 taking the *Western Mail*. There, the *Western Mail*'s Conservative politics were unpopular and its sales were based on its coverage of Welsh news.[92] Thus, like television and radio, newspapers sustained a sense of both Welshness and Britishness in the 1950s and 1960s. At least in their reading, watching and listening tastes, the majority seemed more drawn to thinking at a UK rather than Welsh level but that might just be because what was on offer from across the border tended to be more entertaining.

THE POPULAR PRIDE in Britishness was evident in 1953, when the nation celebrated the coronation of Elizabeth II. In Caernarfon most shops put up special displays in their windows and nearly every street had a children's party, although many were held in garages because of the threat of rain. There were also a twenty-one-gun salute, open-air dances, fireworks and a public bonfire in the town. The council ran a competition for the best-decorated street and gave out souvenir mugs and Bibles to children, who were allowed to choose which language they wanted theirs to be in. There were special services in churches and chapels and the town vicar gave a public address saying that Caernarfon had always been loyal and was tied to the Royal House by kinship and history. Families with televisions held parties and invited the neighbours in to watch. A television was installed in a local hall for pensioners. There was nothing unusual about any of this and some within Plaid Cymru were disappointed that the Welsh 'lost their heads as completely as anyone'. But such attitudes brought a rebuke from Saunders Lewis for being 'sour-nosed' and it was the party's policy that Elizabeth would be Queen of Wales if the nation ever achieved dominion status.[93] If there was any doubt about the popular commitment in Wales to the monarchy, it was killed when the Queen and Prince Philip made a two-day visit as part of their coronation tour of the UK. The *Western Mail* estimated that maybe a million people saw them on the southern part of the tour. It reported, 'Everywhere they went a tide of cheers coming from afar like the roar of an incoming sea beat about their open car, and everywhere, even on the tops of lonely mountains, there were people to wish them blessing on their way.'[94]

The coronation celebrations were not just an uncomplicated demonstration of Britishness. They were also evidence that people's sense of Britishness was interwoven with a sense of Wales. Two letter writers complained to a Caernarfon newspaper that there was no Welsh emblem on their coronation mugs. The editorial of that paper gushed, 'Wales has ever been loyal to those who have ascended to the throne, and has contributed to its majestic greatness since the ascension of the Tudors and the first Elizabethan era, and has during this festive week joined with as much enthusiasm as any other nation in the Commonwealth'. Celebrating the coronation no more diminished Welsh nationhood than it did Canadian or Australian nationhood.[95] When the Queen announced at the 1958 Empire Games in Cardiff that her son would be invested as Prince of Wales there was further evidence that Welshness and Britishness sat comfortably together in the popular imagination. A witness in the stadium recalled men and women crying with emotion. The *Western Mail* decided that for the Welsh 'it was a symbol of their country's new renaissance – in keeping with the happy signs they saw all around them of an ever-increasing prosperity, of a growing consciousness of their cultural inheritance'.[96]

Such popular royalism explains why one woman remembers having her Brownie badges publicly ripped off by the Brown Owl in the late 1950s after refusing to take a pledge to the Queen.[97] But an emotional Britishness was not just limited to royalty; it was also evident when Winston Churchill died in 1965. Prime Minister Harold Wilson told the country, 'our nation mourns the loss of the greatest man any of us have ever known'.[98] People did indeed mourn. Although a strike by south Wales busmen was a contributory factor, Cardiff was described on the day of his funeral as a 'ghost town', with shops shut as a mark of respect. Of those in the city centre, many watched the funeral on televisions in shop windows.[99] But perhaps the clearest evidence of the respect for Churchill came from the Rhondda, where he had not enjoyed the best of reputations because of his decision to deploy troops there after the 1910 Tonypandy riots. This was part of local folklore and had become exaggerated into the tales of cavalry charges and soldiers firing upon unarmed miners. In fact, the troops arrived after the riots and enjoyed a peaceful stay. Nonetheless, the story was strong enough for a television company to send a film crew to the Rhondda on Churchill's death and for the local MP to write a piece in the press pointing out the truth of 1910. The scenes in Rhondda seemed no different to anywhere else. The local paper reported 'a general air of sadness as our people join in the worldwide mourning for the death of the greatest statesman of our time'. There were tributes paid in churches, chapels and pubs. Some shops even put draped photographs of him in the window. Whatever had happened fifty-five years earlier was beyond the living memory of most people. What they knew was the Churchill who had led the country during the war and a period that saw austerity give way to some affluence. A Rhondda paper concluded, 'We salute him, believing that this earth is a happier and better place because he passed this way'.[100]

The idea of the British nation standing together that Churchill epitomized was, however, slowly unravelling in the changing international world. Successive Westminster governments were determined to keep the UK an influence on the world stage but its people were less certain of the wisdom of this. This was evident when troops were sent to fight in the Korean War (1950–3). The Welsh poet Waldo Williams refused to pay his income tax in protest and ended up being declared bankrupt, having his furniture seized and twice spending time in prison as a result. For Williams, national service meant that young Welshmen were being ordered to maintain another nation's imperial rule.[101] Another opponent of the war was S. O. Davies, Merthyr's Labour MP. Like Williams, he received little support for his stance and was attacked by the *Western Mail* for the 'sort of pacifism which has caused many wars'.[102] Such strong responses were out of line with public opinion. Despite the huge cost of the war, napalm bombing, the mass murder of civilians and the death of over 1,000 British troops, the public reaction was muted. This led Waldo Williams to conclude that people had become so weak and ignorantly dependent on the state that they did not question its actions.[103]

After the Second World War, public opinion in Britain was once again turning towards introspection but its focus was shifted outwards again in 1956 by the Suez crisis, a moment that was to become a watershed in Britain's swing in orientation from Empire to Europe.[104] Opinion polls showed that British popular opinion was deeply divided on the rights and wrongs of the situation. A teacher at Cowbridge grammar school in the 1950s and 1960s remembers that whereas Vietnam, Korea and African nationalism had little impact on pupils and staff, the Suez crisis evenly polarized opinion, causing 'actual hostile wrangling, which went far beyond the scale of a school debate. I suppose we all recognised the seizure of the Suez Canal as the stroke which effectively killed off the ailing British Empire, a demise that some really cared about and others scorned.'[105] The aftermath of the crisis coincided with a by-election in the Liberal seat of Carmarthen. At its beginning an editorial in the local paper had declared that Egypt's President Nasser was learning that 'If you hit a Britisher once he smiles. If you hit him a second time, he turns away. If you hit him a third time, he kills you.'

Local public opinion was less sure. Plaid Cymru's candidate denounced the government's action as 'the criminal continuance of the London imperialist policy', while the Liberal candidate openly supported the decision to intervene. Labour's agent thought that many working-class voters did too and wanted his party's campaign to concentrate on the price of milk. However, Labour's Megan Lloyd George ignored the advice, attacked Suez and won a 3,000 majority. But perhaps most telling was the letters page of the local paper at the outbreak of the crisis. No one wrote in about Suez but there was barrage of correspondence about five-leaf clovers.[106]

Thus, even at times when British foreign policy was the subject of public debate, there was still much ambivalence towards external affairs. This was further evident in popular attitudes towards the British Empire. One historian has claimed that most people 'simply knew very little' about the Empire 'and cared even less'.[107] No main political party tried to make electoral capital out of promising to wind the Empire down. Election pamphlets like that of S. O. Davies in 1945 (which declared that 'No nation can enjoy full freedom as long as it keeps others in bondage') were rare. Surveys did suggest, however, that while specific knowledge of the workings of the Empire may have been vague, many people did hold opinions on it. There was clear knowledge of the role the Empire had played in supporting Britain during the Second World War and a widespread acknowledgement that greater freedom would have to be given to the colonies.[108] In Cardiff, immigrant communities held independence parties when their homelands gained their freedom. But it was political reality, not popular sentiment, that drove decolonization. Holding on to colonies that did not want to be colonies would be expensive, difficult and even dangerous. By the start of the 1960s popular opinion in Britain was slowly becoming uncomfortable with the harsh nature of imperial governance in Kenya and Nyasaland. The Empire was becoming an embarrassment rather than a source of greatness.[109] But even then it was never a significant political issue and the Empire's end was remarkably uncontroversial. No serious politician argued for its continuation; there was no popular movement supporting or rebelling against the independence being bestowed to former colonies. This ambivalence towards the Empire also perhaps owed something to a growing awareness that Britain's imperial past was not quite so glorious. For the Welsh, one important moment in this process was the film *Zulu* (1964), a hugely successful celebration of the 105 soldiers from the South Wales Borderers who held off 4,000 Zulu warriors at Rorke's Drift in 1879. At one level, the film was another reminder of how Wales and Britain were intertwined. It was certainly laden with Welsh accents and references. The men sang 'Men of Harlech' while under attack, reminisced about home and experienced tensions with English upper-class officers. But while the film flagged Wales' role in the Empire and celebrated the bravery and valour of its troops, it was no piece of imperial jingoism. The men's near-suicidal stand was not depicted as a glorious military operation but as the result of the bloody mindedness of the commanding English officer.[110] With such people in charge of the Empire it was perhaps time to move on.

The Empire did, however, have ramifications for the popular understanding of contemporary Wales. Some Welsh people drew positive parallels between the diversity of different nationalities in the Empire and Britain itself. Others saw the same parallel in a negative way. In 1968 a cartoon in the *Daily Express* depicted two thick-lipped black Africans skipping away from Prime Minister Harold Wilson with bags of money, while an official told him that there two more Prime Ministers of 'emergent nations' waiting, 'demanding the usual' – at the door were the leaders of Plaid Cymru and the Scottish National Party with placards declaring 'Money for Wales' and 'Money for Scotland'.[111] In 1956, a Welsh officer stationed in Germany wrote to a magazine:

> Was it wrong for a great country like India, with its own languages, religion and way of life, to strive for self-determination and later attain it? … like India, Wales is a nation in its own right, with a language, heritage, culture, way of life and a contribution to the world all of its own.[112]

Such viewpoints lend credibility to Tom Nairn, who has drawn links between the breakup of Empire and the emergence of nationalist parties in Wales and Scotland. Keith Robbins, in contrast, sees the parallel developments as coincidental.[113] What is certain is that both contemporaries in and outside Wales saw connections, even if they were not of cause and effect. The spread of decolonization even frustrated Welsh nationalists and revealed something of their own racial assumptions. One 1954 Plaid Cymru publication noted that 'The black folk of the Gold Coast have already reached a stage of self-government which puts them ahead of Wales'. As late as 1972, at the National Eisteddfod the presidential address bemoaned the lack of support Welsh people gave to their own nation while supporting 'freedom for semi-primitive tribes in the far reaches of the earth'.[114] In contrast, with the Nazi atrocities of the Second World War in such close memory and a new era of international cooperation in the west, nationalism seemed unsavoury to many people. As a character in a 1969 novel remarked, getting worked up about Wales when men were going to the moon and countries were no longer self-sufficient just seemed a remnant of the past.[115]

MOST PEOPLE IN WALES in the 1950s and 1960s had some sense of being British. That national identity was rooted in the popularity of the British media, the memory of the war, the safety net of the welfare state and nationalized industries and a popular pride in royalty. These were all, by and large, tangible realities in people's lives. Moreover, the migration of the inter-war years, where nearly half a million people left the economic turbulence of Wales, and the continued attraction of England to the socially and economically ambitious after the war meant that family ties increasingly spread beyond Wales. An extensive 1960 survey of Swansea suggested that half the people had relatives elsewhere in Britain. In the north-west, people in the late 1950s travelled to Manchester, Liverpool, Ireland or even the Isle of Man for sports events, holidays or just to see the sights.[116] To rural old men, London may have been somewhere 'so very far from everywhere' but for younger generations it was not that far at all.[117] The decline of the Empire had not undermined this Britishness because the Empire had never enjoyed that much popular support or interest in the first place. The cold war, however, kept alive the wartime sense that there were common enemies that threatened the whole British people, a people that included family members who had moved away. When individuals considered international relations and the world beyond they did so in relation to their own lives and the cold war was relevant only because it threatened themselves and their families. The National Union of Mineworkers thus may have involved itself in international campaigns but Welsh miners voted not to accept into the pits Hungarian refugees from the Soviet oppression because of fears about their own jobs.[118] There is nothing surprising about this. Even if television news was bringing pictures of international events into people's living rooms, they were still abstract compared with the reality of everyday existence. Similarly, feelings of being Welsh and/or British were real but they were part of the background to people's lives rather than at the forefront of their mental existence.

The precedence of the everyday over the external world was evident at the celebrations of Elizabeth II's coronation in Glyn Ceiriog (Denbighshire). Plans by the male-dominated coronation committee for a village tea were abandoned after objections from the women that it would be too much work for them. There was controversy at the final of the village's coronation football tournament over ineligible players and a sending off. The pitch was invaded and the visiting team left the field, refusing to play on. At the coronation fancy dress competition, English immigrants to the village were chosen as judges because no local could be trusted not to exploit, or be suspected of exploiting, his or her ties with entrants.[119] Thus no national celebration could usurp the more mundane realities of everyday life. The primacy of the local in people's mental world was further evident in a 1959 survey of Welsh housewives that showed that readership of local newspapers was higher than that of the nine national morning papers combined.[120] Reading one of the local newspapers in the 1950s and 1960s shows a world of court appearances, funerals, weddings, dog and flower shows, arguments in the local council, public lectures, town and village sports clubs, and perennial complaints about parking, unemployment and housing. This was the world that people lived in. Thus the talk in pubs was, to quote one drinker:

> about horses and racing, about miners going back to farming, clay pigeon and racing pigeon, of the endless honour of miners' children at school, university and all kinds of places, of greyhound and whippet, the rhubarb and the sweet peas, rugby and cricket, the choir and the pools, fishing and shooting and mushrooms, eisteddfodau, television and the beer, and cars too now.[121]

Where the nation did impinge on that local world – such as on international day or at an eisteddfod – it did so within the context of localized concerns such as the pride in the local boy getting his cap or the hope that the winning poet would be from the north or the south. Similarly, significant international events, such as the Vietnam War, the assassination of Kennedy or the moon landing, might generate some temporary excitement but they quickly faded amid more mundane day-to-day concerns. For most people, the wider world of Wales, Britain and the globe was a background to more prosaic concerns and being Welsh, like being British, was a 'given', obscured somewhere amid the noise of daily life.

For those who spoke Welsh this was less true because their daily life often revealed how the language and its associated culture were in decline or perhaps even holding them back. But the resulting sense of Welshness was, as sociologists noted in Cardiganshire, still a 'diffused and unfocussed sentiment' that found life in a loose sense of difference. In a 1971 survey of the county, 76 per cent of respondents said that the Welsh way of life was different to England and 53 per cent that Welsh people were very different to the English. Only 14 per cent disagreed with the suggestion that it was annoying for a Welsh person to be called English, whereas 37 per cent thought the English tended to 'walk around acting as if they own the place'.[122] Most of the wider English-speaking majority also shared this unfocused but proud sense of Welshness, something perhaps encouraged by economic insecurities creating a loose political sense that somehow Wales was not being fairly treated by the British government. In 1966, two-thirds of respondents to one national survey described themselves as Welsh rather than British, while 70 per cent said it was important to preserve the Welsh language and customs.[123] In Cowbridge grammar school only a minority of boys knew the words to the Welsh national anthem and the boys never spoke Welsh beyond a few expletives and tags that everyone knew. Nonetheless, they all wore leeks and daffodils on St David's Day and supported Wales enthusiastically at rugby.[124] Typically, Howard Marks, born in 1945, does not remember being aware of any Welsh–English hostility during his youth in a Welsh-speaking home in the Glamorgan mining village of Kenfig Hill. At school he had learnt about Glyndŵr's revolt and a subsequent history of friendly relations and had heard nothing from adults to suggest otherwise. The enemy in comics and games were the Japanese or Germans. But he was aware of differences: 'The Welsh could sing better, but not the songs that I liked. The English had glamour and sex, while the Welsh had chapels and sheep. The English were better footballers.... The Welsh were good at rugby.'[125]

It was perhaps at sport that a popular sense of Welshness came out most forcibly. As Wilf Wooller, a former cricketer and rugby player, put it, 'If ever Wales is to be unified it will not be by our councillors and politicians who have failed lamentably. It will be by Sport.' Sport certainly crossed the boundaries of class and belied the lack of confidence in Wales that some noted. At Cardiff Arms Park rugby stadium were to be found 'professional men, labourers, artisans and civil servants – a classless society drawn together only by the love of the game'.[126] Like St David's Day – celebrated at most schools with cawl, Welsh cakes, daffodils, leeks, sometimes a halfday holiday and often an eisteddfod – sport was a rare public celebration of Welshness that was not rooted in using the Welsh language. For people in English-speaking areas, sporting internationals encouraged and developed an awareness of being Welsh. A Wrexham man remembered of his youth in the late 1940s and early 1950s: 'It was on the packed "Kop" that we became true Welshmen'.[127] Indeed, the BBC's Welsh management hoped that sports coverage would convince many south Walians to tune into the new BBC Wales television service rather than an English region. Coverage from London was less sympathetic of Welsh identity. In 1949 the *Daily Mirror* received a letter from a Cardiff lady complaining that the sports commentators at the BBC spoke while the Welsh anthem was being played. Other such slights to Wales could also bring out a pride in being Welsh. The flooding of the Tryweryn valley was a powerful example (chapter 8) but there were other, more fleeting controversies too. In 1951 *The Times* received a letter complaining there was no Welsh flag being flown at the Festival of Britain exhibition in London. It concluded, 'One does not need to be a Welsh nationalist to wonder why this is so.'[128]

Those who were nationalists, however, despaired at how unfocused Welsh identity was and at how large numbers of Welsh people were consciously rejecting the language they considered its core. The writer Ned Thomas argued in 1971 that educated Welsh speakers saw in the working class of south Wales a lack of dignity and values: they were 'people who have lost a culture and gained only a higher standard of living'. As Thomas himself noted, this could be condescending and patronizing but even he spoke of a 'shattered cultural background' in the south and the humiliation of losing your own language, especially when it contained spiritual resources that could help people face economic hardships.[129] But it was not just the working classes of the industrial south who were losing the Welsh language. The rural working class may have spoken Welsh but they were not politicizing or prioritizing its use. This meant that there was the danger that, as the number of Welsh speakers in rural communities declined, those who could still speak the language might find it easier to switch to English in all aspects of daily life and the disintegration of Welsh-speaking Wales would be complete.

In 1957 Islwyn Ffowc Elis published the novel *Wythnos yng Nghymru Fydd* (A Week in the Wales That Will Be), the story of a man who makes two journeys from 1953 to the Wales of 2033. The first was to a prosperous, Christian and independent Wales. Everyone was fluent in Welsh and people preferred speaking their mother tongue. There was low crime, full employment and industry was run by cooperative units. Furthermore, hats were tipped to ladies, few drank or ate meat, sunshine was imported, Cardiff City played beautiful football and there was a statue of Saunders Lewis in the centre of Cardiff. Wales had even put a man on the moon. But in his second journey the nation had been renamed Western England and Welsh had died out. There were street gangs and an oppressive government that relied on a secret police. Half the nation was now given over to forestry and towns like Aberystwyth had become streets of 'steel and concrete flats, pubs, chip shops, saloons, dance halls and gambling dens'. The time traveller manages to get an old woman to recite a little of a Welsh psalm before she reverts back to English and her eyes dim. The hero bemoans: 'I had seen with my own eyes the death of the Welsh language'. The political message of the novel was clear when the hero weeps 'out of rage at my own generation that let the pigs come in and smash it up. I was sure that heaven would not forgive the Welsh, nor me either, for selling their heritage so cheaply.' At the novel's conclusion he is told by a scientist that which Wales comes to be in 2033 depends on him 'and your families and friends, and their families and friends, from Holyhead to Cardiff. You Welsh, and you only, have the choice.'[130]

Commissioned by Plaid Cymru, it was an unsubtle novel but its basic message was quite right. It was up to the Welsh people whether the Welsh language would survive or not. Yet whether the will for survival existed remained doubtful and that had ramifications for the wider nation. One writer recorded in 1950: 'It is not easy for a Welshman to-day, especially if his memory goes back beyond this century, to feel optimistic about the future of his country'.[131] But the growth in the teaching of Welsh at school and the rise of the Welsh media were sowing the seeds of a more prominent sense of Welsh nationality among those growing up in the 1950s and 1960s, a generation who were also too young to remember how the British state had saved Wales from the traumas of the war and mass unemployment or to know the stranglehold imposed by the chapels on individual liberties. That process was helped along by how youth culture led to 'provincial' and working-class cultures becoming fashionable from the mid-1960s. Slowly, being Welsh was coming to mean something more modern than an old-fashioned way of life. However, the reaction to suggestions that Welsh mattered at anything more than a sentimental level could still be hostile enough that people began to question whether the nation would survive. Among the educated Welsh-speaking establishment there was despair and frustration but their sons and daughters were of a different generation, one that still shared their parents' cultural attachment to Wales but combined it with the radicalism and confidence of youth and in the 1960s they led a new movement that would try to save Wales and the Welsh language. It did not always go down well with their compatriots but it slowly eroded the idea that Welsh and Welshness were old fashioned.

Notes

1 Lord Raglan, 'I take my stand', *Wales*, 2 (Oct. 1958), 15–18.
2 Janus, 'The writing on the wall?', *Wales*, 44 (Sep. 1959), 13–20.
3 *WM*, 17 July 1957. *Observer Magazine*, 30 Oct. 1966. *LDP*, 15 Feb. 1954.
4 *Y Dydd*, 14 Nov. 1958.
5 Republished in G. Williams, *Religion, Language and Nationality in Wales* (1979), 147.
6 *New Statesman*, 22 July 1966. *Observer*, 20 Apr. 1975.
7 J. Morris, 'Welshness in Wales', *Wales*, 1 (Sep. 1958), 16.
8 Ministry of Education, *Place of Welsh and English in the Schools of Wales* (1953), 37. *Arcade*, 12 (Apr. 1981). J. W. Aitchison and H. Carter, 'The Welsh language, 1921–1991: a geolinguistic perspective', in G. H. Jenkins and M. A. Williams (eds), *'Let's Do Our Best for the Ancient Tongue': The Welsh Language in the Twentieth Century* (2000), 49. S. Rhiannon, 'The fight for Rhymney', *Pl*, 70 (1988), 11–16.
9 I. Ffowc Elis, *Fy Nghymru I* (1961). Reproduced in English in M. Stephens (ed.), *Illuminations: An Anthology of Welsh Short Prose* (1998), 90.
10 Welsh Department, Ministry of Education, *The Curriculum and the Community in Wales* (1952), 5.

11 J. Davies, *Broadcasting and the BBC in Wales* (1994), 182, 184–5, 173. D. J. Davies, 'Rural depopulation', *Welsh Nation*, Mar. 1953. Report by Plaid Cymru for committee on broadcasting, nd, NA, 25/59. *Report of the Broadcasting Committee, 1949*, Cmd 8116 (1951), 158.
12 B. M. Davies, 'Y llwynog dan y gwydr', *Barn*, 275 (Dec. 1985), 467–8.
13 A. Richards, *Carwyn: A Personal Memoir* (1984), 29–30.
14 J. R. Webster, *School and Community in Rural Wales* (1991), 189. D. Jenkins, E. Jones, T. Jones Hughes and T. M. Owen, *Welsh Rural Communities* (1960), 102, 105.
15 R. A. Jones (ed.), *Hyd Ein Hoes: Lleisiau Cymru* (2003), 16–17. K. Nurse, *Footsteps to the Past: A Welsh Quest* (1998), 58.
16 C. Rosser and C. Harris, *The Family and Social Change: A Study of Family and Kinship in a South Wales Town* (1965), 133. Ministry of Education, *Place of Welsh and English*, 38.
17 D. Beddoe (ed.), *Changing Times: Welsh Women Writing on the 1950s and 1960s* (2003), 137.
18 I. Emmett, *A North Wales Village: A Social Anthropological Study* (1964), 33.
19 M. Davies and D. Roach, *In Strength and Shadow: The Mervyn Davies Story* (2004), 18–20.
20 G. Thomas quoted in Richards, *Carwyn*, 29.
21 S. W. Town, *After the Mines: Changing Employment Opportunities in a South Wales Valley* (1978), 23–4.
22 Quoted in translation in A. Edwards, 'Answering the challenge of nationalism: Goronwy Roberts and the appeal of the Labour Party in north-west Wales during the 1950s', *WHR*, 22:1 (2004), 134.
23 P. J. Madgwick, N. Griffiths and V. Walker, *The Politics of Rural Wales: A Study of Cardiganshire* (1973), 183.
24 Quoted in translation in R. Smith, 'Journalism and the Welsh language', in G. H. Jenkins and M. A. Williams (eds), *'Let's Do Our Best'*, 296–7.
25 Madgwick *et al.*, *The Politics of Rural Wales*, 91, 174.
26 R. Frankenberg, *Village on the Border: A Social Study of Religion, Politics and Football in a North Wales Community* (1957), 32.
27 G. King, *Modern Welsh: A Comprehensive Grammar* (2003), 2.
28 Frankenberg, *Village on the Border*, 32. Cf. Jenkins *et al.*, *Welsh Rural Communities*, 101.
29 B. Rogers, *The Man Who Went West: The Life of R. S. Thomas* (2007), 230.
30 *Report of the Committee on Welsh Language Publishing*, Cmd 8661 (1952), 2, 14. *CDH*, 15 July 1966. R. G. Jones, 'Welsh literature since 1914', in Jenkins and Williams (eds), *'Let's Do Our Best'*, 414.
31 *CDH*, 15 July 1966.
32 A. Butt Philip, *The Welsh Question: Nationalism in Welsh Politics, 1945–1970* (1975), 65.
33 M. Stephens, *A Semester in Zion: A Journal with Memoirs* (2003), 123.
34 *Observer Magazine*, 30 Oct. 1966.
35 M. Gallie, *Travels with a Duchess* ([1968] 1996), 10. Beddoe, *Changing Times*, 77.
36 M. Crick, *In Search of Michael Howard* (2005), 56–7, 61.
37 A. Sampson, *The New Anatomy of Britain* (1971), 52. Quote from D. Sandbrook, *White Heat: A History of Britain in the Swinging Sixties* (2006), 317.
38 *CDH*, 30 Oct. 1964. J. L. Williams, 'Some social consequences of grammar school education in a rural area in Wales', *British Journal of Sociology*, 10:2 (1959), 126.
39 T. Conran, '*Poetry Wales* and the second flowering', in M. W. Thomas (ed.), *A Guide to Welsh Literature, Vol. VII: Welsh Writing in English* (2003), 224.
40 M. Gallie, *Man's Desiring* (1960), 150–1.
41 I. Emmett, 'Blaenau boys in the mid-1960s', in G. Williams (ed.), *Social and Cultural Change in Contemporary Wales* (1978), 92.
42 *Daily Mirror*, 5 Dec. 1966. Beddoe, *Changing Times*, 246.
43 A. Richards, *Dai Country* (1973), 20–1.
44 Mid-Wales Industrial Development Association, *Mid Wales,'70: 13th Annual Report* (1970), 23. *South Wales Magazine*, summer 1971.
45 W. Wilkinson, *Puppets in Wales* (1948), 22.

46 P. E. Mayo, 'The importance of identity', in O. Davies and F. Bowie (eds), *Discovering Welshness* (1992), 35. L. Sage, *Bad Blood* (2000), 5. *WL,* 2 July 1963.
47 *South Wales Argus*, 3 Apr. 1963. *WM*, 27 Oct. 1965. C. Williams, 'Monmouth – Wales or England?', in H. V. Bowen (ed.), *A New History of Wales: Myths and Realities in Welsh History* (2011), 89–96.
48 *The Times*, 3 June 1963. J. Humphries, *Freedom Fighters: Wales's Forgotten 'War', 1963–1993* (2008), 23.
49 W. Griffith, *The Welsh* (1964 edn), 48.
50 M. D. Parnell, *Plateux, Gateaux, Chateaux* (1997), 156.
51 K. Amis, *Memoirs* (1991), 130.
52 Wilkinson, *Puppets in Wales*, 83.
53 Letter in *Wales*, 46 (Nov. 1959).
54 Huw T. Edwards, NA, BD24/6. Letter from Caernarfon town clerk, 26 Apr. 1951, NA, BD 23/219.
55 B. Rubens, *When I Grow Up* (2005), 69. D. Bush, 'Lash LaRue and the river of adventure', *Pl*, 130 (1998), 75–84.
56 Briefing note, 15 Nov. 1951, NA, BD 24/6.
57 NA, BD 23/219, BD 24/10. Briefing note for cabinet discussion, 8 Nov. 1955, BD 24/10. Cf. PREM 11/11081.
58 Griffith, *The Welsh*, 51. *SWE*, 2 Sep. 1958. Morris, 'Welshness in Wales', 13.
59 O. Davies, 'Welsh hills', in Davies and Bowie (eds), *Discovering Welshness*, 75.
60 M. D. Parnell, *Snobs and Sardines: Rhondda Schooldays* (1993), 97.
61 Ministry of Education, *Place of Welsh and English*, 32–3. Webster, *School and Community in Rural Wales*, 192.
62 Welsh Department, Ministry of Education, *Bilingualism in the Secondary School in Wales* (1949), 8–9, 23.
63 Ministry of Education, *Place of Welsh and English*, 27.
64 Ministry of Education, *Bilingualism in the Secondary School in Wales*, 5.
65 Ministry of Education, *Place of Welsh and English*, 1.
66 Parnell, *Snobs and Sardines*, 146, 187.
67 Webster, *School and Community in Rural Wales*, 189. Ministry of Education, *Place of Welsh and English*, 35. W. G. Evans, 'The British state and Welsh-language education, 1914–1991', in Jenkins and Williams (eds), *'Let's Do Our Best'*, 361, 363. G. E. Jones and G. W. Roderick, *A History of Education in Wales* (2003), 187.
68 Central Advisory Council for Education (Wales), *Primary Education in Wales* (1967), 221.
69 Evans, 'British state and Welsh language education', 365. *Primary Education in Wales* (1967). Webster, *School and Community in Rural Wales*, 192.
70 E. Owens, 'The strange Welshness of Rhyl', *Pl*, 135 (1999), 64–8.
71 Rosser and Harris, *Family and Social Change*, 113. *SWE*, 4 Sep. 1956.
72 Central Advisory Council for Education (Wales), *Primary Education in Wales*, 236. G. Humphreys, 'What are we?', in P. H. Ballard and E. Jones (eds), *The Valleys Call* (1975), 76.
73 Webster, *School and Community in Rural Wales*, 196. Jones and Roderick, *A History of Education*, 176–9.
74 *Observer*, 19 Jan. 1969. *Holyhead and Anglesey Mail*, 28 Nov. 1958.
75 *Denbighshire Free Press and North Wales Times*, 21 May 1960.
76 Central Advisory Council for Education (Wales), *Primary Education in Wales*, 238.
77 Davies, *Broadcasting and the BBC*, 194, 197, 163, 187–8, 271, 162, 183.
78 Davies, *Broadcasting and the BBC*, 204, 209, 203, 218. *County Herald*, 20 May 1953.
79 Report by Plaid Cymru for committee on broadcasting, nd, NA, 25/59.
80 Davies, *Broadcasting and the BBC*, 220.
81 *Baner ac Amserau Cymru*, 6 Feb. 1964. I. G. Evans, 'Drunk on hopes and ideals: the failure of Wales Television, 1959–1963', *Llafur*, 7/2 (1997), 81–93. J. Medhurst, '"Wales Television – Mammon's Television"? ITV in Wales in the 1960s', *Media History*, 10:2 (2004), 119–131. *WM*, 20 Feb. 1964.

82 J. Medhurst, '"Servant of two tongues": the demise of TWW', *Llafur*, 8:3 (2002), 79–87.
83 Davies, *BBC and the Broadcasting*, ch. 5.
84 *Rhondda Fach Observer, Leader and Free Press*, 4 Mar. 1961.
85 Davies, *Broadcasting and the BBC*, ch. 6. Butt Philip, *The Welsh Question,* 70. *WM*, 20 Feb. 1964. J. Medhurst, "You say a minority, Sir, we say a nation': the Pilkington Committee on Broadcasting (1960–62) and Wales', *WHR*, 22 (2004), 109–36.
86 Alun Oldfield Davies, writing in *Y Ddinas*, 10/8 (May 1956).
87 Davies, *Broadcasting and the BBC*, 323, backcover.
88 Quoted in G. Davies, *The Story of the Urdd* (1973), 291.
89 Butt Philip, *The Welsh Question*, 70.
90 Davies, *Broadcasting and the BBC*, 235.
91 D. Sandbrook, *Never Had It So Good: A History of Britain from Suez to the Beatles* (2005), 400. *WL*, 2 July 1963. N. Evans and D. Jones, '"To help forward the great work of humanity": women in the Labour Party in Wales', in D. Tanner, C. Williams and D. Hopkin (eds), *The Labour Party in Wales, 1900–2000* (2000), 231.
92 A. G. Jones, *Press, Politics and Society: A History of Journalism in Wales* (1993), 235, 220. *Readership Survey of Wales* cited in Butt Philip, *The Welsh Question*, 67.
93 D. J. Davies, *Towards Welsh Freedom* (1958). R. Evans, *Gwynfor Evans: Portrait of a Patriot* (2008), 145–6. *Y Ddraig Goch*, 25 (1953), reproduced in English in M. Stephens (trans.), *Illuminations: An Anthology of Welsh Short Prose* (1998), 71.
94 *WM*, 9 July 1953.
95 *CDH*, 29 May and 5 June 1953.
96 *WM*, 30 June and 21 June 1961.
97 Jones (ed.), *Hyd Ein Hoes*, 13.
98 Quoted in Sandbrook, *White Heat*, xiii.
99 *SWE*, 30 Jan. 1965.
100 *Rhondda Observer, Leader and Free Press*, 29 Jan. 1965.
101 J. Nicholas, *Waldo Williams* (1974). *Baner ac Amserau Cymru,* 20 June 1956. W. Williams, 'Brehniniaeth a Brawdoliaeth', *Seren Gomer*, summer 1956.
102 R. Griffiths, *S. O. Davies: A Socialist Faith* (1983), 195. K. O. Morgan, 'Power and glory: war and reconstruction, 1939–1951', in Tanner *et al.* (eds), *The Labour Party in Wales*, 185.
103 C. MacDonald, *Britain and the Korean War* (1990). D. W. Davies, 'Waldo Williams, "In two fields", and the 38th parallel', in T. R. Chapman (ed.), *The Idiom of Dissent: Protest and Propaganda in Wales* (2006), 50.
104 D. Sanders, *Losing an Empire, Finding a Role: An Introduction to British Foreign Policy since 1945* (1995), 8.
105 A. Thompson, *The Empire Strikes Back? The Impact of Imperialism on Britain from the Mid-Nineteenth Century* (2005), 210. P. Cobb, *At Cowbridge Grammar School, 1949–66* (2001), 95–6.
106 *CJ*, 10, 24, 31 Aug. 1956. M. Jones, *A Radical Life: The Biography of Megan Lloyd George, 1902–66* (1991), 278–88.
107 Sandbrook, *Never Had It So Good*, ch. 8, quote from 303.
108 Griffiths, *S. O. Davies*, 147. Thompson, *The Empire Strikes Back?*, 208–9.
109 A. Llwyd, *Black Wales: A History* (2005), 171. Thompson, *The Empire Strikes Back?*, 212–15.
110 D. Berry, *Wales and the Cinema: The First Hundred Years* (1994), 266–7. J. Richards, 'Imperial heroes for a post-imperial age: films and the end of empire', in S. Ward (ed.), *British Culture and the End of Empire* (2001), 128–44.
111 K. J. Bernard, *Visible Welshness: Performing Welshness at the National Eisteddfod in the Twentieth Century*, PhD thesis, Swansea University (2004), 346. *Daily Express*, 22 July 1968.
112 *Y Ddinas*, 10/8 (May 1956).
113 T. Nairn, *Breakup of Britain* (1981 edn). K. Robbins, *History, Religion and Identity in Modern Britain* (1993), 283, 290.
114 H. Edwards, *What Is Welsh Nationalism?* (1954 edn). *Guardian*, 10 Aug. 1972.
115 P. Ferris, *The Dam* (1969), 30.

116 Rosser and Harris, *The Family and Social Change*, 51. Emmett, *A North Wales Village*, 92.
117 H. Clwyd, *Defaid yn Chwerthin* (1980), reproduced in English in Stephens (trans.), *Illuminations*, 165.
118 H. Francis and D. Smith, *The Fed: A History of the South Wales Miners* (1998 edn), 429. *SWE*, 15 Jan. 1957.
119 Frankenberg, *A Village on the Border*, 43, 121, 53.
120 Jones, *Press, Politics and Society*, 338–9
121 W. Jenkins, 'The story of "Yr Hen Dafarn"', *Welsh Outlook*, 1 (Apr. 1965).
122 Madgwick *et al.*, *The Politics of Rural Wales*, 104, 85, 92.
123 A. Edwards and D. Tanner, 'Defining or dividing the nation? Opinion polls, Welsh identity and devolution, 1966–1979', *CW*, 18 (2006), 57.
124 Cobb, *Cowbridge Grammar School*, 72–3.
125 H. Marks, *Señor Nice: Straight Life from Wales to South America* (2006), 86.
126 W. Wooller, 'Rugby: prospects for the season', *Wales*, 1 (Sep. 1958). L. H. W. Paine, 'The Arms Park', *Wales*, 39 (Apr. 1959).
127 Nurse, *Footsteps to the Past*, 59. M. Pill, *A Cardiff Family in the Forties* (1999), 122–3.
128 NA, BD24/201. *Daily Mirror*, 22 Nov. 1949. *The Times*, 17 May 1951.
129 N. Thomas, *The Welsh Extremist* ([1971] 1973), 117, 113.
130 Translated from I. Ffowc Elis, *Wythnos yng Nghymru Fydd* ([1957] 1993), 130, 141, 143, 152–3.
131 W. Griffith, *The Welsh* (1950 edn), 185.

8

'Nationalists of many varieties.' 1951–70

In that part of Wales lived nationalists of many varieties – writers of letters to the *Western Mail* and the *Welsh Nation*, authors of tracts about Welsh water and Welsh mutton, Baptist ministers who sprinkled their sermons with sly jokes about the English, rural councillors with *Cymru* badges on their cars, young farmers who liked a bit of fun with petrol and a Union Jack.

Paul Ferris, *The Dam* (1969), 133

None can deny that these days it is exciting to live in Wales. There is the sense of participating in a drama in which the end is hidden.

Letter to *Western Mail*, 2 February 1968

IN 1949 A YOUNG ACTOR called Richard Burton made his screen debut in a film about plans to flood a Welsh village in order to supply Liverpool with water. As *The Last Days of Dolwyn* unfolds, it is revealed that Lord Lancashire, the wealthy English peer behind the scheme, did not actually know the village was inhabited and the blame passes to his Welsh agent. The story thus becomes one of personalities rather than the politicized tale of class and nationality that the actual history of reservoir building in Wales maybe deserved. When plans emerged from Liverpool City Council in the 1950s to build another reservoir in Wales the response was anything but apolitical. Liverpool initially favoured a site in Montgomeryshire but anticipated opposition because it included the historic home of a famous hymn writer. Instead, it chose Tryweryn, on the basis that, of the possible locations, this would cause the least public opposition. Building a reservoir in that valley meant the removal of six farms and the village of Capel Celyn, with its forty residents, school (with nine pupils), burial ground and post office. Another ten farms would also lose land.[1] The villagers claimed they found out about the plans only when surveyors arrived there. They were naturally upset but the scheme angered many others too. A Welsh-speaking community was being destroyed (or at least moved) to provide water for an English city that seemed deeply reluctant to discuss it with the people whose homes it was taking. It was easy to see the project as another piece of the English imperialism that was killing the Welsh language and way of life. Iorwerth Peate, a prominent nationalist and curator of traditional Welsh life, claimed the flooding was part of the 'gradual murder of the Welsh national personality by various forces from beyond the Dyke'.[2] Led by nationalist activists, a campaign against the plans began. Its most poignant moment came in November 1956, when nearly the entire village marched in Liverpool bearing placards that asked the city to save their homes and reminded it of how the village had taken in evacuees from Merseyside during the war. Gwynfor Evans, the Plaid Cymru leader, told Liverpool City Council that Capel Celyn was 'in the middle of, perhaps, the most cultured part of the whole of Wales. These people have values apart from material values.' But appealing the case of 'poets and singers' was not going to win when the city thought it needed water. The council voted by ninety-four to one to flood Tryweryn and a bill was introduced into Parliament to facilitate that.[3]

Conservationist groups did not oppose the decision, even thinking that the marshy landscape might be improved by the reservoir. But those in Wales who saw the landscape in human rather than aesthetic terms were outraged. The Ministry for Welsh Affairs received 680 letters of protest, some of which even threatened violence.[4] The minister responsible for Welsh affairs during the parliamentary bill's first stages was Gwilym Lloyd George. That Wales was being despoiled by the Welsh-speaking son of perhaps its greatest national hero deepened the anger. One letter he received trusted he would 'not sell Wales and be a traitor', while another declared 'Wales' destiny is in your hands. For the sake of everything, Sir, and for the sake of your family name, save us.' A Wrexham preacher just asked, 'I wonder what your father would say about it?' A letter from Swansea summed up the dominant tone of the complaints received by the government: 'We in Wales are fighting to the last ditch to defend our language and our culture. We dread to think that a power like Liverpool Corporation has the freedom to walk into our country and steal our water and our land in this tyrannical way.'[5] The natural beauty of the area, the question of human rights and the economic future of Wales were also recurring themes and many of the complainants stressed that they were not nationalists. Some even drew parallels with opposition to communism or pointed to God's judgement.

Other groups had more specific concerns, such as what it would do to salmon fishing on the river Conwy. Many trade union branches also voiced their opposition in a forgotten dimension to the affair. It took place against a backdrop of rising unemployment and there was much concern that the transfer of water to Liverpool would hamper future industrial development in north Wales, perhaps by attracting companies to Merseyside that might have otherwise come to Wales, had the reservoir's resources been kept there. But even such concerns, though not motivated by concern for the Welsh language or the community being drowned, were still understood within the context of Welsh resources being taken by England. Indeed, for all those not personally affected, the key issue was the fact that the flooding was being imposed on Wales and that awoke the normally unfocused sense of popular Welshness. One woman told a journalist that she would not have minded so much had the water stayed in Wales 'but it's all going to England, don't you understand?'[6]

In Parliament few English MPs and lords seemed to give much weight to arguments based on either the rights of individuals or Welsh culture. They preferred to look at the collective British good. As an English lord put it, 'After all, Wales is just one part of these islands'.[7] The government, however, did acknowledge the validity of the cultural arguments but also concluded that they were exaggerated. The minister's briefing for the bill's second reading noted that Welsh culture would be affected but that 'the community is very small and it is doubtful whether less social damage would be done on any alternative site. The intensity of the objection is a reflection of the sensitivity of "Welsh Wales" to the tremendous "foreign" pressure on its culture. It is a feeling which, for tactical reasons alone, needs to be respected.'[8]

No matter how much contemporaries and national mythology portrayed Tryweryn as a valley flooded by the uncaring English authorities against the wishes of Wales, the reality was more complex. At the Liverpool Corporation bill's first reading, thirty-five of the thirty-six Welsh MPs voted against it. But the Labour figures who campaigned against the flooding also understood Liverpool's need for water and tried to combat the anti-Englishness that was emerging in the affair. They pointed to the benefits of the flooding: new modernized housing would replace much older stock, while the reservoir would also serve the needs of proposed local nuclear power stations, all objectives that Plaid Cymru also supported. David Llewellyn (Conservative, Cardiff North), the only Welsh MP in favour of the measure, argued that opponents did 'an ill service to Welsh culture by suggesting that its survival depends on sub-standard houses, a dog-in-the-manger attitude to untapped resources, and a callous indifference to the prosperity of Merseyside, where there are far more Welshmen than in the whole of Merioneth'.[9] Nor was opposition in Wales either as widespread or as sustained as is often made out. Campaigners claimed that only 3 per cent of people in the Bala area had refused to sign the petition. Yet Plaid Cymru worried that its campaign was meeting apathy; Bala Town Council itself declined to support it, while Merioneth County Council did so only on a second vote and then it was close decision. There were those in the surrounding area who saw the issue as a waste of time and Capel Celyn as 'an unremarkable, unromantic back-water'. As the legislation passed through Parliament, opposition petered out. Only twenty-seven Welsh MPs voted against its second reading, with the rest abstaining. By the third reading just twenty voted in opposition. Denbighshire County Council and other organizations withdrew their objections, leaving Merioneth County Council and a parish council as the only formal objectors. After the legislation was passed, Plaid Cymru's calls for a strike of support by miners and steelworkers got nowhere.[10] One man who had farmed in the valley for over fifty years wrote to the government: 'So much is said about this Valley by people who do not know anything about the place'. He complained that many of the members of the Capel Celyn defence committee were outsiders and Plaid Cymru members who did not know the conditions that locals had been living in. He had a clear sense of the community's decline. When he had been at Capel Celyn school there were fifty pupils there. Now there were fewer than ten. He saw how many farmhouses had become unfit for habitation and how the land had declined because of flooding and forestry planting. Whether this farmer represented local views is unclear but it certainly shows that the community was not united in outright opposition. The government was also told by a local trade union representative and justice of the peace that 'many of those affected by the dam did not really regret it, but did not like to say so in view of the pressure from the Nationalists'.[11] The village defence committee had ended up being run by outsiders because of a lack of volunteers from within the community. The villagers had had to be persuaded by the Plaid Cymru leadership to protest in Liverpool itself. They did not expect to be listened to as, in the words of one farmer's wife, they were just 'a few village people from Wales' who did not speak English well. By 1957 Gwynfor Evans was being told by an adviser that 'the vast majority' of Tryweryn residents were 'more than satisfied' with the compensation and were 'satisfied for the scheme to proceed'.[12] After all, many had the opportunity to move to the new modern homes that so many in rural communities were leaving in search of. Moreover, as the government later concluded in an internal review of the episode, since people were being rehoused only three and a half miles away their Welsh culture should be strong enough to withstand the move. By the end, to some dissent within the party, even Plaid Cymru's hierarchy had accepted the inevitable and had shifted to trying to keep some of the wealth in Wales by proposing that the construction be done by Welsh workers and a new water board established to run it with representatives from local government in Liverpool and Wales. When the reservoir was built, the *Wrexham Leader* at least was impressed; noting the use of natural stone rather than concrete, the paper decided the dam was 'a new wonder of Wales'.[13]

IN BRIEFING THE BRITISH EMBASSY before Gwynfor Evans visited the USA, the Ministry for Welsh Affairs concluded:

> It is difficult to decide how far the widespread agitation over the Tryweryn issue was due to the influence of the Welsh Nationalists. Many people who were not members of the party felt very keenly on the issue and this showed that the emotional reaction which causes some people to become party members is felt in a lesser degree by a much wider circle of Welshmen. It showed also that Welsh nationalist feeling can be inflamed more easily than might be supposed.[14]

But what was becoming clear was that the emotional reaction had only a limited electoral impact. By the end of the 1950s Plaid Cymru did not appear to have advanced much since 1950, when it had won 17,580 votes in the general election. At the 1959 general election, the first after the Tryweryn affair, the party took over 20 per cent of the vote in both Caernarfon and Merioneth. It also secured 17 per cent in Rhondda West, showing that there were people outside Welsh-speaking areas who were voting nationalist. Yet, overall, the party secured just 77,571 votes, 5.2 per cent of the Welsh total. The Tryweryn affair had in many ways struck discord among nationalists rather than inflaming them. The failure to take any decisive action against the flooding brought deep criticism of Gwynfor Evans' leadership of the party. Some even called him a traitor.[15] Evans himself was always more of an idealist than a strategist but he was trying to broaden the party's focus. Tryweryn, however, reinforced the notion that Plaid was a party for the Welsh-speaking countryside. Its own research in the 1950s showed that voters thought the party too right wing, too middle class and too hostile to English-speaking Wales. The party struggled to change this image, not least because it did not have access to party political broadcasts. In the mid-1950s the BBC had intended introducing 'regional' party political broadcasts and extending them to all parties that put up three or more candidates in Wales. However, the Conservative government, after confirming that the Labour

Party agreed with its position, refused to allow such a move. In 1958 the *Sunday Times* claimed that the odds against Plaid Cymru 'ever becoming a serious political entity are infinite'.[16] But Tryweryn was a clear warning shot that Welsh patriotism could easily be inflamed.

Fears about the economic future in the late 1940s and early 1950s had also created demands within the Labour Party for some official recognition of distinct Welsh needs and a distinct Welsh identity. In an acknowledgement that Wales did at least exist as an economic, administrative and cultural unit, the Council for Wales and Monmouthshire had been set up in 1949 as a non-elected advisory body to the government. It came under the chairmanship of Huw T. Edwards, a Caernarfonshire trade unionist whose profile through the 1950s saw him dubbed the 'unofficial prime minister of Wales'. Looking back in 1958, a civil servant argued that the Council had probably been intended as 'relatively meaningless sop' but Edwards' personality had seen it gain a good deal of importance. Through the 1950s the Council did keep up the pressure on the government to create a Welsh Office and Secretary of State, framing its demands more in terms of effective government than national recognition. The Council was taken seriously by government but Edwards resigned in 1958 after it became apparent that a Secretary of State would not be introduced.[17] The government interpreted the Council's demands as a desire for parity with Scotland but feared that, should that be granted, Scotland might demand further devolution. Given that Wales was operating under the same legal system as England, the government foresaw that any Secretary of State would have to follow different policies to England in order not to make the position superfluous. This, it feared, would be difficult to explain and would lead to inequalities that would be especially manifest in the Marches, where social and economic ties crossed the border. It also worried about the costs and administrative complexity of forming yet another department and feared controversy over the position of Monmouthshire, which it regarded as an English county but one that by tradition would have to be included in Welsh administration.[18]

There was some popular support for devolving selected powers from London. In 1956 the Parliament for Wales campaign presented a petition with 240,652 signatures, representing some 14 per cent of the Welsh electorate. Gwynfor Evans estimated that 80 per cent of the people asked had signed it. This was the culmination of a six-year campaign that had included leading figures from Labour, the Liberals and Plaid Cymru. But it won no sympathy with the government or most of the press. The Cardiff Labour MP George Thomas thought the Welsh people needed saving from themselves, while David Llewellyn, a Tory MP in the same city, even drew parallels between the campaign and *Mein Kampf*. The lack of specificity in the campaign's claims probably made it easier to collect signatures but the internal disagreements within the campaign over what Wales' problems actually were and how a parliament would solve them undermined its political influence. At the end of 1956 one of the leading figures in the campaign reflected, 'All the petition's papers are now in cardboard boxes, one on top of each other, rotting through dampness'. The campaign did help raise the profile of Plaid Cymru and was another step towards the gradual construction of a proto-Welsh state but ultimately its failure marked a widespread satisfaction with the status quo. This was clear when the south Wales area of the National Union of Mineworkers voted against the campaign, fearing it would undermine the UK bargaining position of the union.[19]

The Tryweryn revolt, the reports of the Council for Wales and Monmouthshire and the Parliament for Wales campaign may not have secured their immediate objectives but cumulatively they encouraged government to take specifically Welsh interests seriously. In 1958 civil servants anticipated that Plaid Cymru could grow if Welsh feelings were 'handled tactlessly' and if there was a fusion between the party and elements within Labour that were 'more Welsh than Socialist'. The key to avoiding this, they felt, lay in persuading Wales that the government was taking its economic welfare seriously and in dispelling the 'widespread notion that people in England neither know nor care whether the Welsh and Welsh culture fare well or ill'.[20] Seven months earlier the Prime Minister had told his cabinet,

> There is a general feeling among Welsh people that their particular interests are not receiving the attention which they should and we shall need to be specially careful and sympathetic in our handling of Welsh affairs at the present time if we are to prevent the Welsh Nationalist movement from gaining ground.[21]

In response to pressure from Welsh MPs for a Secretary of State for Wales, the Conservatives had already introduced a Minister of Welsh Affairs in 1951, a post held by an existing cabinet member with a different portfolio. Although the Minister did not have a government department, the position did ensure there was someone within the cabinet with a specific remit to look after and act on Welsh interests. The first holder was the Home Secretary, Sir David Maxwell Fyfe, a Scottish lawyer, who tried to defuse criticism that he was not Welsh by claiming that one of his ancestors had led an army from Scotland which tried to join Owain Glyndŵr. He proved the worth of the post by shelving unpopular forestry and military plans for Welsh land.[22] Although there were still the occasional controversies –

such as the government's 1960 appointment of someone who did not speak Welsh as national governor of the BBC in Wales – there were significant signs of increased sensitivity to Wales. In 1958 a Festival of Wales was held under the government's auspices. It culminated in the holding of the Empire Games in Cardiff and the announcement by the Queen that Charles would be made Prince of Wales. The introduction of county rather than national referenda on Sunday opening in 1961 was a concession for rural Wales, as was the main mid-Wales railway line's survival of the Beeching axe.[23] The government began giving financial support for the publishing of Welsh-language school books in 1954, and the 1959 Eisteddfod Act allowed local authorities to support financially the National Eisteddfod. In 1958 a new steel development went to Llanwern rather than Scotland after anger in Wales that the construction of the Forth Bridge had been given priority over a bridge across the Severn, despite the Minister for Welsh Affairs arguing the Severn's case to combat the 'wide and deep distrust of the Government's attitude towards Wales'.[24] Cardiff was made the official capital of Wales in 1955 and four years later government pressure on Buckingham Palace led to the Red Dragon being declared the official national flag.[25] These Conservative concessions were the result of external pressure on the party but they also show how the existence of a Minister for Wales and then sensitivity over Tryweryn increased the influence of Welsh interests in government. In contrast, internal pressure from Labour MPs, not least James Griffiths, led that party finally to commit itself to creating a Welsh Office and Secretary of State for Wales, a promise which it honoured when it returned to power in 1964. Not everyone in government was enamoured. In his diary Richard Crossman called the Welsh Office an 'idiotic creation' and 'completely artificial'.[26] There was also some concern in the north that Wales' voice in cabinet would actually diminish because the post meant Welsh affairs would be treated separately after England had been looked at. The Secretary of State would be 'a lone voice, and one can only hope for the best', one paper surmised. But one immediate benefit was felt. The new department took the importance of expanding the M4 far more seriously than the Ministry of Transport had done and plans were quickly put in place for a series of new sections that would open through the 1970s.[27]

DESPITE THE PIECEMEAL advances in the official position of Wales within government, there was, by the 1960s, a small but increasing minority within Wales who felt that constitutional politics had failed the nation. After all, as Gwynfor Evans himself later recalled, Tryweryn showed that 'even a united Wales was powerless'.[28] The arson of an RAF bombing school in Penyberth in 1936 by leading members of Plaid Cymru meant the party did have a history of direct action. Less spectacularly, in 1951 Plaid Cymru members blocked a road in protest at the siting of a military camp at Trawsfynydd, while complaints over Welsh-language broadcasting led to 151 people being summonsed for non-payment of radio licences in 1955.[29] At the start of the 1950s, led by a Swansea barrister, a somewhat more sinister group called the Welsh Republican Movement broke away from Plaid Cymru. They were suspected by MI5 of having firearms and explosives and links with the Communist Party. Most of their action was limited to burning Union Jacks but in 1952 they did try to blow up Fron aqueduct and a member was convicted of possessing explosives. But their muted approach was evident when plans to blow up the first post box to bear the initials ER were dropped because of the risk to life.[30]

Flirtations with explosives or road blocks won little support among most nationalists in the early 1950s but Tryweryn raised the stakes for a handful, leading to open discussion of extra-parliamentary action. In 1957 the editor of the *Western Mail* told the Minister for Welsh Affairs that 'the seeds of an Irish problem' had been planted. Two years later Plaid Cymru's leadership did briefly decide upon a course of non-violent resistance to the construction of the Tryweryn dam but then relented in the face of some internal party opposition.[31] In 1960 a Welsh-language newspaper published an anonymous article calling for a secret movement to fight for Wales and resist the government. It said that reasonable and constitutional argument had met with continued disrespect and reminded readers that the blood of medieval princes ran through their veins, before asking, can 'we leave the old nation to be murdered by men like Macmillan, Brooke and Brecon without striking a blow for it?'[32] Words turned to action when, in September 1962, two Plaid Cymru members vandalized an electricity transformer at the Tryweryn construction site, with the prior knowledge and approval of Gwynfor Evans. The following year explosives were used to damage the site itself and a pylon taking electricity there. Such actions put Plaid Cymru in a difficult position. Evans was left saying that he did not morally disapprove of all violence but that he did reject it as a political weapon. He tried to use the problem to his advantage when he told the Welsh Minister that he feared Plaid Cymru was being pushed towards violence by the indifference of the government. The government was certainly anxious to avoid the emergence of a militant splinter group and it worried that support for extremism was wider than the police claimed.[33] Violence, even if it was aimed at reservoirs rather than people, made many nationalists uneasy but more inspirational was the example of Eileen and Trefor Beasley of Llangennech. Between 1952 and 1961 this miner and his wife fought to receive a rate demand in Welsh from Llanelli Rural District Council, where all the councillors and much of the population spoke Welsh. They appeared in court sixteen times for non-payment of their English-language demands and had their property seized by bailiffs three times. But they were eventually sent a demand in Welsh.[34]

One man impressed by their actions was Saunders Lewis. He had been imprisoned himself for his part in the Penyberth arson of 1936. The fact that his trial was moved to England won him much sympathy but his hatred of socialism and desire for the Welsh people to return to the land contributed to the marginalization of Plaid Cymru, the party he had helped found in 1925. Furthermore, as an intellectual with a penchant for fast cars, good food, fine wine and bow ties, he was hardly a member of the Welsh peasantry. Thus he was quite right when he remarked in a 1961 television interview that his aim had been 'To change the whole course of Wales, and to make Welsh Wales something living, strong, powerful, belonging to the modern world. And I failed absolutely.'[35] But Lewis ensured himself a more meaningful place in history on 13 February 1962 with a radio lecture entitled 'Tynged yr Iaith' ('The fate of the language'), which warned that Welsh would 'cease to exist as a living language towards the beginning of the twenty-first century'. He argued that politics and economics were 'against the survival of Welsh. Nothing can change that fact except determination, will power, struggle, sacrifice and effort.' Success, he maintained, 'can only come through revolutionary methods'. Noting the example set by the Beasleys, he called for a wider unconstitutional campaign, with tactics such as not paying for licences available only in English. He anticipated 'a period of hate and persecution and strife' but thought the language's survival was the 'only political question deserving of a Welshman's attention'. Self-government before Welsh was an official language of administration would just hasten the language's demise. The rallying call was 'Go to it in earnest and without wavering, to make it impossible to conduct local authority or central government business without the Welsh language'.[36]

How many people actually heard the lecture is unclear. Lewis himself probably intended just to galvanize Plaid Cymru members and undermine Gwynfor Evans' strategy of constitutional politics. The lecture certainly annoyed Evans' allies. *Yr Herald Cymraeg* thought it 'hazy talk from the secluded study' about a language that had 'long since died' in much of Wales.[37] But the lecture did hit a nerve beyond Plaid Cymru, even though its dire predictions for the future of the language were hardly new. Even the *Western Mail* was sympathetic, noting how 'Economics, established practice and apathy' were against the language and if it was to be saved people had to 'spontaneously show more signs of wanting to preserve and expand its present use'.[38] Some were already doing that. At the start of 1962 a dispute began over the refusal of the legal service to issue a bilingual summons to a young Plaid Cymru member who was arrested for giving his girlfriend a lift on his bike's crossbars. Eleven days before Lewis' radio talk, a protest was held at an Aberystwyth post office where students plastered posters on the building with the hope of being arrested so they could refuse the English-language summons. When no one was arrested they did the same thing on a council building and the police station, before sitting down in the middle of a road bridge. Again, no one was arrested but the protest did attract the attention of newspapers and, against the background of Lewis' talk, the Home Office approved the future use of Welsh-language summonses. Inspired by this success and Lewis' rallying call, Cymdeithas yr Iaith Gymraeg (discussed further below) was formed in October 1962, a group that was to have a profound influence on Wales and which completely undermines historians' claims that the British student protests of the 1960s were ineffective and unimportant.[39]

Such protests, the lobbying of MPs and the Conservative government's general sensitivity to Welsh opinion after Tryweryn led to it setting up an inquiry in 1963 into the status of the language. David Hughes Parry, a Welsh-speaking law professor, was appointed as its chair because he was thought conservative and cautious. A permanent secretary at the Ministry for Housing, Local Government and Welsh Affairs summed up: 'we don't want to get landed with suggestions for a considerable enlargement of people's legal right to use the Welsh language'.[40] The inquiry found that Welsh was little used in central government, the health service or the nationalized industries and recommended legislation giving equal validity to the two languages in law and public administration. This meant that official forms should be available in Welsh where people wanted them. It also proposed that heads of government departments should have to speak Welsh so that public administration could cope.[41] A *Western Mail* editorial was unimpressed:

> under the guise of righting an ancient wrong a minority in Wales would be imposing on the majority an irrelevant and hampering burden. The Welsh language, as the tongue of the hearth and the living literature of our nation, must be helped in every way possible – but short of sacrificing sense and logic in the conduct of our public affairs.[42]

One member of the inquiry concluded that there was not 'opposition to the increased use of Welsh so much as nervousness at the prospect of change'. Welsh-speaking public servants were unsure if their command of the language was good enough to use in law or administration and some even doubted the language itself was flexible enough for such purposes.[43] Councillors supportive of the language, meanwhile, worried about the financial cost of giving Welsh equal legal status. In the weeks that followed, the *Western Mail* received little correspondence on the issue and concluded there was a general apathy.[44]

The general marginalization of Welsh cultural concerns from the popular political agenda was again evident at the 1964 general election, when twenty-one of the twenty-three Plaid Cymru candidates lost their deposits. Its general secretary had conceded that year that the party remained synonymous with the Welsh language, scarcely known and suffering from an image as old fashioned, puritan and wanting to turn the clock back. He accused Evans of being 'shy, weak, unimaginative, lacking in drive'.[45] At the 1966 general election Plaid won 8,000 fewer votes than it had in 1964. Shortly after that general election Megan Lloyd George, Carmarthen's Labour MP, died. This meant a by-election in the constituency that Gwynfor Evans lived in, at a time when the Labour government was enduring much criticism of its financial policies and having to cope with internal strife. Within the constituency there were concerns that local collieries and rural schools were threatened with closure, while farmers worried about small-business taxes. The Labour candidate was a shy north Walian who was perceived to be condescending, none of which endeared him to the local party and its supporters. Plaid Cymru, in contrast, fought an effective campaign, using different slogans and different linguistic emphases for its leaflets in the rural west of the constituency ('For a better Wales') and the industrial east ('For work in Wales'). Despite the circumstances, few anticipated a Plaid Cymru win and bookmakers were apparently offering odds of 2,000 to 1 on Evans taking the seat. Thus when he won, with a majority of 2,436, what was Plaid Cymru's first ever Westminster seat, there was considerable surprise. Outside the count, a crowd of 2,000 sang the national anthem and waved Welsh flags. The headline of the local paper declared 'Election of the Century – Plaid's Astonishing Win'.[46] Evans' nationalism was rooted in a deep personal patriotism but also a belief in the value of democracy and small communities. This, together with his personal dignity and lack of pretension, made him a genuinely popular figure with the electorate and young nationalists. When he took his seat in Parliament, the *Daily Mirror* described it as 'one of those highly-emotional occasions the Welsh do so well. All leeks and flags, hymns and chants as they invaded the capital by rail and coach.' The group sang the national anthem five times outside Parliament and gave Evans a reception with the 'fervour and enthusiasm they usually reserve for a winning try at Cardiff Arms Park (against England, of course)'. A porter at the House remarked, 'There's been nothing like it since the Beatles were here'.[47] Welsh nationalism had come of age and Gwynfor was its icon.

There was a positive reaction to the win and to Evans himself in much of England, not least among the right-leaning press, which saw it as a welcome blow to the government and a departure from old party politics. The *Daily Post* thought Evans' win would 'tickle the long-dormant sympathies of the suburban little Englander'.[48] In 1970 one English commentator looked back on the election as part of the trend of 'Orpington man', the ordinary voter who resisted the might of central government. The nationalist feeling was thus 'mere top-dressing, which provided the character and flavour of the movement without necessarily expressing the fundamental truth in what was affecting its supporters'. For this commentator, Evans' victory was evidence that ordinary people were feeling alienated and lost, with no control over events. In the wake of the election, a *Daily Express* cartoon showed people leaving a floundering ship called the UK in a lifeboat labelled 'independence for Wales', with James Callaghan, then Chancellor of the Exchequer, telling the captain, Prime Minister Harold Wilson, 'you can hardly blame them for wanting to take to another boat'.[49] The reactions in Wales were less sympathetic and drew on all the tensions that surrounded the Welsh way of life. Above all, nationalism was seen as a distraction from economic issues. A Caernarfon newspaper pointed to the economic situation, 'which shows up more vividly the irrelevance of what he represents. The peoples of Britain – all of us – stand or fall together'.[50] Gwynfor Evans noted in his maiden speech at Parliament that 'For many, the death of a nation and the awful waste of great moral and spiritual resources matter nothing as long as people are well fed, well dressed and well housed'. Perhaps afraid of what he stood for and its potential impact on their own base of support, some Labour MPs refused to speak to Evans or even look at him. Some of them feared any concession to the nationalists and were mistrustful of even their Welsh-speaking Labour colleagues.[51] One such colleague was Cledwyn Hughes, Secretary of State from 1966 to 1968. He tried to create an elected Welsh Assembly as part of a reform of local government but that was a step too far for many in Labour and there were fears in cabinet that it would encourage nationalism in Wales and Scotland and affect plans for English local government. Hughes was thus replaced by George Thomas, who was Secretary of State from 1968 to 1970 and seemed to have a virulent and paranoid hatred of nationalism and the Welsh language. He was particularly worried that the BBC and teachers were indoctrinating people and he complained to the Prime Minister in 1970 that the Corporation was 'firmly in the grips of Welsh nationalists' and that entertainment programmes were being used for propaganda.[52] The petty antagonism within Labour extended beyond MPs. When Gwynfor Evans was invited to speak on Welsh history at a Workers' Educational Association summer school in a local-authority building in Ferryside (Carmarthenshire), the Labour-controlled council insisted that the event be cancelled unless the invitation was withdrawn. The *Western Mail* was also hostile to Plaid Cymru and its news editor in the 1960s remembers that the paper actively 'sought to suppress the party's rise to prominence'.[53]

Such responses intensified in the late 1960s because the Carmarthen result seemed to open the floodgates for Plaid Cymru at a time when industrial communities were becoming deeply pessimistic about their future (see chapter 9). In the year after the by-election, the party claimed its membership had doubled and it started talking of winning eight seats at the next general election.[54] In 1967, amid concerns at rising unemployment, Plaid won 39.9 per cent of the vote at a by-election in Rhondda West, reducing a near 17,000 majority to just over 2,000. The following year in Caerphilly it reduced a Labour majority from over 21,000 to 1,874. James Griffiths, an MP since 1936 and Secretary of State for Wales from 1964 to 1966, had to be persuaded to stay on in Llanelli because of fears that the seat was vulnerable to Plaid Cymru's local candidate, the rugby coach Carwyn James. Suddenly, the Labour hegemony in Wales seemed under real threat. These votes owed much to dissatisfaction with the Labour government but the fact that large numbers of working-class voters were willing to turn to Plaid Cymru to make their protest was an indication that the sands were shifting and that popular patriotism could become political. But, among the masses, nationalism still had a long way to go. At the 1970 election the party contested every Welsh seat for the first time but twenty-five of its thirty-six candidates lost their deposits, while Gwynfor Evans was defeated by nearly 4,000 votes. Overall, Plaid won over 20 per cent of the vote in only seven constituencies and it secured only 175,016 votes (11.5 per cent) in Wales as a whole. Despite this failure to make any electoral gain, the party had at least shed something of its image of being only concerned with the language and traditional culture. It had also shown itself to be electable and put on the agenda serious discussion of whether Wales could be self-governing in any way. That all fed into the new sense of confidence among young Welsh people (see chapter 7). By 1969 a magazine could declare, 'Wales herself is today at the start of a renaissance. The old shell of introversion is being chipped away by a new generation of awareness. Slowly, but inevitably, the old barriers of resentment, insecurity and isolation are being broken. Self-assurance and national confidence is emerging at an entirely new level'.[55]

THAT CONFIDENCE WAS most evident in Cymdeithas yr Iaith Gymraeg (CyIG; the Welsh Language Society). Its membership was just 2,000 at its peak at the start of the 1970s; its most active members were students, 'young, long-haired, budding revolutionaries' in the words of one member.[56] Free tuition and grants that covered the cost of living meant the 1960s was a good time to be a student and those studying had both the time and resources to devote themselves to political activism. The expansion of higher education in the 1960s also brought Welsh people from north and south together on a scale hitherto unparalleled. Other forums of Welsh-speaking life, such as the Urdd, the National Eisteddfod and sporting internationals, also became far more accessible because of rises in disposable income and they offered places for the young to meet and feel a common identity that transcended regional differences. A group of friends from Blaenau Ffestiniog who went to Dublin to watch Wales play rugby recalled: 'There were these girls from Carmarthen – nurses and teachers – and we talked with them late into the evening. And we all felt it was great, do you understand? To feel there were people like us all over Wales and that we could get together like this.'[57] Such feelings underpinned the growth and success of CyIG. Despite the society's small numbers and narrow social base, its influence on Welsh public life and individuals' thinking about Wales was far greater. Edward Heath, the Tory leader, dismissed nationalism as 'flower politics for flower people' but the motives of the language movement (which Heath confused with nationalism) were far more serious and better thought out than the romantic idealism of hippies.[58] There was a sense of urgency in the society because it believed that the Welsh language was 'in dire peril of its life'.[59] Furthermore, when Saunders Lewis articulated in *Tynged yr Iaith* the sense that the language was at the heart of Wales and Welshness he was speaking for a great many, probably the vast majority, of Welsh speakers. Not all would have claimed that you had to speak Welsh to be Welsh but Welsh speakers' own sense of nationality was intimately entwined with their mother tongue. Thus if the language was in danger then so too was their nation.After its first flurry of activity, CyIG held back on further direct action while the government's inquiry into the legal status of the Welsh language took place. But, by the autumn of 1965, civil disobedience had begun again, with people refusing to license their vehicles until they could do so in Welsh. In April 1966 Geraint Jones became the first member to be sent to prison after he refused to pay a fine for not having a taxed vehicle. That year, CyIG had rejected violence, at least partly out of political pragmatism, but it stepped up other forms of civil disobedience, such as sit-ins and vandalism. The media became a particular source of complaint; BBC radio, for example, was said to broadcast more hours in Arabic than in Welsh, leading to its studios and transmitters becoming targets. There were more humorous protests too, such as throwing paper aeroplanes down on the chamber of the House of Commons, gluing the locks of Conservative Party offices and jamming the telephone lines of utility companies. By 1976 a total of 697 individuals had appeared in court and 143 had been imprisoned for their part in the society's actions.[60]

Wilson's Labour administration, where a quarter of the cabinet was Welsh and four ministers spoke Welsh, reacted to the mounting tensions by passing the 1967 Welsh Language Act. The recommendation in the report of the Hughes Parry inquiry (see above) that Welsh speakers be given preference for jobs in central and local government was not implemented but the Act did give the two languages of Wales equal validity, although English had primacy if there was semantic dispute. It specified that 'further provision' should be made to allow people to use Welsh in 'official and public business'. But that provision was not defined or facilitated. The government did promise that Welsh forms would be issued where there was 'fair demand' but noted that this would not be done regardless of cost.[61] The Act thus meant that people could not insist on using Welsh in dealings with the state and it failed to introduce anything remotely resembling full bilingualism in public life. Campaigners were unimpressed and quite right that the abstract principle of equal status was of no consequence unless it was put into practice. Where government departments did respond to the legislation and requests from the public by translating forms into Welsh, the resulting documents still often had to be asked for, something which some working-class people were apparently reluctant to do for fear of drawing attention to themselves. CyIG also argued that if forms had to be asked for, then this was a kind of oppression, as it placed the person in a position of inferiority. The government was even accused of instructing that Welsh forms were not to be put on public display.[62] The Post Office initially refused to accept official Welsh Ministry of Transport motor licence applications and courts found themselves in difficult positions when people were prosecuted for refusing to re-license using the English forms. Nonetheless, by 1969 there were over 250 government forms available in Welsh, whereas there had been only eleven in 1964. This made the Act a milestone, even if the government received little praise or thanks from the language movement.[63] Indeed, the significance of its specification that all future legislation had to distinguish Wales from England was widely unappreciated, despite the fact that it marked an important advance in the official status of the nation. The Act ensured all future laws had to address rather than assume the existence of

Wales and it encouraged the use of Welsh where the will existed. But it was too shrouded in ambiguity and the disappointment led to the campaigns of CyIG gathering momentum at the end of the 1960s. Popular attitudes also remained sharply divided: a 1968 opinion poll conducted for the *Western Mail* found that just 52 per cent of people thought that all official forms and signs in Wales should be bilingual.[64]

In the wake of the government inquiry advocating equal status for Welsh, Machynlleth Urban District Council decided to make its information signage bilingual and contacted the Welsh Office about its plans. There were already signs that used Welsh to welcome people to all counties except Glamorgan and Flint and town signs were often bilingual in the north. But beyond that most public signage was in English only. Machynlleth's plans caused debates among civil servants over which translations of 'toilet' and 'car park' could be fitted on signs without pushing up the cost too much. They feared the issue was just about making a political point but were also unsure whether bilingual signage would help or hinder tourism and they worried it might affect the decisions of industrialists looking to relocate in Wales, by giving a 'constant reminder that one is not in England'. In the end, the Welsh Office simply decided to offer its suggested translations and keep out of the matter.[65] As more requests came in the Welsh Office continued its tactic of trying to defer the matter back to local authorities but, after George Thomas took over as Secretary of State in April 1968, its line hardened into demanding requests be made for each individual sign. In response, road signs became CyIG's main focus, with the tactic being to deface or remove English-languages signs. In Cardiganshire, over 100 were defaced in just one week in February 1969. The importance of bilingual signage was symbolic rather than practical. It perhaps did not matter greatly that Swansea was not signposted 'Abertawe' since few locals used that name for the city but the failure of road signs to call Cardigan 'Aberteifi' was more serious since that what was what most people in the area actually called the town.[66] In an abstract way, they were being dispossessed of where they lived.

Cartoons in the *Sun* joked about Welsh protestors not knowing what their own placards said and about vandals having such fun that they would be rather disappointed if home rule did ever come. But in Wales the reaction to the campaigns was more serious. A 1969 Welsh Office internal briefing note said that it wanted to further the interests of the language but was worried that the protests were 'achieving the exact opposite effect. The antics of recent months are scandalizing all shades of opinion and are beginning to create the impression that the Welsh language is the preserve of fanatics.'[67] In the same year, a *Western Mail* editorial called for the full force of the law to be used, claiming that the 'vast majority of Welshmen are heartily sick of these destructive and self-indulgent antics'. This came after an incident where a group of sign-painters had been caught by ten local men in Rhayader, who boarded the protestors' bus and knocked some of them out cold. A Cardiganshire survey suggested that only 19 per cent of Welsh speakers and 7 per cent of non-speakers thought that pulling down signs was sometimes justified as a form of protest. In Denbighshire some councillors wanted to know whether bilingualism would mean that English translations would have to be drawn up for Welsh place-names and another asked what, if pressure groups were going to be bowed to, would happen if Chinese or Pakistanis requested their languages be used.[68] By 1970 the state was using harsher powers to control the protests. There were arrests for conspiracy to destroy signs, people were imprisoned for heckling court cases and there were incidents of police brutality. Over 185 cases of criminal damage were brought. In contravention of the Welsh Courts Act, in 1969 a man was ordered to pay a three-guinea fee for a translator if he wished to give his evidence in Welsh. One Welsh-speaking magistrate even insisted on calling the prominent campaigner Dafydd Iwan 'David' in court.[69] In England the treatment was no better. In 1970 fourteen campaigners were sentenced to three months for contempt after demonstrating at the High Court against the imprisonment of one of their peers. Faced with such treatment it was little wonder that some protestors ended up hunger striking in their cells. One philosopher summed up that those who fought for the language 'suffer every sort of curse and disadvantage. They are accused on all sides – as dangerous, irresponsible romantics, traitors and supporters of narrow mindedness and disunity, bitter fascists, parochial, fugitives to the past and enemies of progress, and – above all – as anti-Christian, enemies of the Christian emphasis on the similarity and brotherhood of all men.'[70]

Increasingly the tensions became as much about a generation gap and attitudes to public standards. As one short story put it, 'Questions of Welsh nationalism affected him in the same way as a wholly English counterpart might be similarly provoked by encounters with advocates of illegitimate birth, CND or permissive television'.[71] A Caernarfon paper said the defacing of road signs revealed 'not only ignorance and failure to grow up, but also incivility and plain malice'. Such reactions crossed the linguistic divide. Glanmor Williams, a Welsh-speaking historian who became chairman of the Broadcasting Council for Wales, remarked in his 1968 diary: 'It must be great fun and give a deep sense of having struck "a blow for Wales" without any of the painful responsibilities of having to think out what the consequences of demands are'.[72] After protests at the BBC in 1968, the newspaper *Y Cymro* dismissed CyIG as 'a band of cantankerous, naive, noisy, negative, disorderly and unkempt youths whose sole aim is to destroy, to trade slogans, to insult everybody in authority and to intrude without consent on other people's properties'. The unease the society caused within parts of the Welsh establishment was unsurprising because the movement thought of itself as challenging not just English and British oppression but also the worst restrictions of Nonconformity and Puritanism. They quite consciously held their meetings in pubs; this drew criticism but it made a point.[73]

Protestors also clearly saw themselves as part of a wider global movement. They were inspired by Ghandi and Martin Luther King particularly but also the Czechoslovakian rising of 1968 and the 1969 student protests. A biography of King was one of the best-selling Welsh-language books of 1969; it claimed that, having being held down for centuries themselves, Welsh people could understand the oppression of black Americans.[74] In the USA, the spirit of youth and rebellion was encapsulated by Bob Dylan and Wales had its own version in Dafydd Iwan, the society's chair from 1968 to 1971. He was an architect by training and the son of a teacher and Nonconformist minister. Influenced by Dylan, he wrote scores of protest songs and became Wales' most famous campaigner and prison inmate. His lyrics had all the defiance of youth and called Wales 'to battle'. But Iwan also recalled there was always fun, comradeship and exhilaration in the campaign. That did not undermine its political significance – Iwan was acutely aware that they were fighting 'for the continuation of the whole nation' – but it did make it easier to carry out those protests.[75]

The controller of BBC Wales told his governors in 1972 that CyIG had 'a few hundred activists, a few thousand active sympathizers and a perhaps a hundred thousand passive sympathizers'.[76] Part of the anger that Iwan and others felt owed much to the fact that there was widespread sympathy for CyIG's cause but not its tactics. As Iwan pointed out with exasperation, sympathy was not enough to save the language. But there was active support for CyIG from parts of the Welsh-speaking establishment, not least because that establishment included their mothers and fathers. Older sympathizers paid fines and wrote letters of support to the press. When protestors appeared in court for criminal damage and the like, lenient fines became rather common. In 1972 two defendants, protesting at the paucity of Welsh-language broadcasting, pleaded guilty to using television sets without licences but were given absolute discharges by a Cardiff court. That same year a Swansea magistrate was forced from the bench after objecting to a fine imposed by fellow magistrates on a CyIG member and then paying that fine herself. When Iwan was imprisoned in 1970 for refusing to pay a fine, twenty-one magistrates contributed to a fund to have him released.[77]

The cause of the support of older members of the Welsh establishment was clear in the words of the philosopher J. R. Jones, who wrote of:

> the experience of knowing, not that you are leaving your country, but that your country is leaving you, is ceasing to exist under your very feet, is being sucked away from you, as if by an insatiable, consuming wind, into the hands and possession of another country and another civilization.... What we have on our hands is war ... the struggle of the conquered for their very existence, the struggle to save their identity from being trampled into oblivion.[78]

Quite simply, for Jones and many others, Wales would cease to exist as a distinct nation if the language was lost. This meant that neither the society nor direct action was exclusively a young people's forum. At one point there were three ministers on CyIG's senate. A few older people, like Sali Davies, who refused her pension because she could not apply in Welsh, endured considerable personal hardship for the language. Even the Women's Institute was becoming more radical and in 1966 its Parc branch was expelled from the national organization after members withheld membership fees because the forms were not available in Welsh. They formed their own organization instead, which quickly grew into a national movement for Welsh-speaking women called Merched y Wawr. In 1969, the magazine *Barn* led a successful campaign to secure bilingual tax discs and over 600 of its readers vowed not to display English discs. Of the 642 people involved in the campaign, 41 per cent were teachers and 28 per cent clergy or university staff.[79] The campaign was seen as a test of the government's attitude to putting the 1967 Act into practice. Initially, it claimed that Welsh discs were not technically possible because of the computer system. Internally, civil servants in the Welsh Office were frustrated at the way the Department of Transport was brusquely dismissive instead of showing that 'everything is being done to meet the legitimate requirement of those who are Welsh speaking'.[80] Eventually internal political pressure and the revolt of the Welsh-speaking establishment meant that Welsh discs were issued. Lobbying and quiet campaigning by the Welsh establishment also played their part in making advances for the language. In 1965, for example, the Urdd, a Welsh-language youth organization, failed to get its bank to accept bilingual cheques but the issue then reached a senior London official at Midland Bank who happened to be Welsh. His influence led to banks issuing and accepting Welsh cheques, although local branches could still be very stubborn on the matter.[81]

Whereas such pressure could work, responding to more militant tactics was not so easy. In 1970 the Secretary of State was advised by senior civil servants that he could not give in to road-sign protests since that was 'the way to anarchy and tyranny'. Although the Welsh Office was happy to allow local authorities to make their information signs bilingual, it did not want two languages on directional signs because it feared the presence of Welsh might distract drivers and endanger safety. It also worried about practical issues such as whether bilingual road signs meant making the text smaller (which it thought dangerous) or making the signs bigger (which it thought would annoy householders who had already complained about their size). It also anticipated complaints from small towns that were not currently allowed to appear on signs because of a lack of space. The Welsh Office was, however, seemingly happy for local authorities to drop the English versions of place-names if they wanted, something not even CyIG suggested.[82]

Local authorities were indeed making changes to information signs. Following a request from Merched y Wawr, Cardiff City Council decided to give ten central streets bilingual nameplates, even though they had only ever been known by English names, and to erect new bilingual signs welcoming people to the city. Some local authorities in strongly Welsh-speaking areas were also 'Cymricizing' their spellings in the late 1960s and thus Dolgelley officially became Dolgellau, Llanelly became Llanelli and Conway became Conwy. This was generally uncontroversial, thanks to some sensitive handling. In Llanelli, for example, there was no requirement that local businesses adopt the new spelling but it was already in use by some and quickly became accepted by the others.[83] Transitions were not always so smooth. Amid fears that it would be seen as giving into vandalism, Denbighshire County Council's roads committee voted by just one vote to introduce bilingual signs. The clerk to the council even complained that 'This has been brought about by the fact that you have anarchists in your community'. Despite being in a Welsh-speaking area, Aberystwyth Trades Council voted by a majority of one that bilingual signs were a waste of money.[84] Typically, the Welsh Office, now under Tory control after the 1970 election, tried to defuse such tensions with an inquiry into road (rather than information) signs. Ten of the thirteen Welsh counties told it that they were in favour of bilingual signs, although the objectors included Glamorgan, the biggest county. In contrast, only nine of the sixty-five urban district and municipal borough councils had passed resolutions in favour of bilingual signs. The inquiry noted that there was perhaps indifference 'in many quarters to the issue'.[85] The inquiry's committee itself was divided but the majority reported in favour of mandatory bilingualism on all traffic signs, mostly on the grounds of 'natural justice', with Welsh placed first. The estimated cost was more than £3 million and it was finance that held back support among some local authorities. After much hesitation, the Welsh Office ended up encouraging but not requiring local authorities to put Welsh on their road signs but requiring that English be given priority. Central and local government implementation of this was hit by the economic problems of the 1970s, by when CyIG's main attention had moved on to other issues, reducing the external pressure. Even Gwynedd County Council, which still wanted signs with Welsh first, ended up putting its plans on hold.[86]

THE OFFICIAL CEREMONY to open the Tryweryn reservoir in 1965 was a farce. The 400 guests were outnumbered by 500 protestors and were met with a barrage of booing and chanting. Fireworks were let off, someone tried to burn a Union Jack and stones were thrown at the platform, one of which struck the project's engineer. The official speeches had to be curtailed after the microphone lead was cut.[87] Among the protestors was a group of uniformed young men calling themselves the Free Wales Army (FWA). Over the course of the late 1960s the FWA not only paraded in public but also made outlandish claims about its size, equipment and readiness to wage guerrilla war. The leader of its twenty-odd members was William Julian Cayo-Evans, a horse-breeder who had been educated at an English public school and had served in Malaya during his national service. His patriotism (and his army's) was, however, both genuine and deeply felt. One member, a lorry driver from Bridgend, told *Y Cymro*, 'It is difficult for you who are born Welsh speakers to understand how much the language can mean to us who are born without it'. He got interested in the language after the eisteddfod at Port Talbot and coming across the saying 'A nation that loses its language loses its heart'.[88] The Army did have access to guns and some contact with the IRA but despite its grand assertions – which it fed obsessively to the media and ranged from having 7,000 members, dogs trained to carry mines and access to a nuclear bomb that could blow up the Severn Bridge – the FWA was more talk than action. Their one attempt to actually lay a bomb failed because they forgot to attach a detonator.[89]

What fed the publicity surrounding the FWA were its claims of responsibility for a series of explosions around Wales in the 1960s that were actually nothing to do with it. The real perpetrators went under the name of Mudiad Amddiffyn Cymru (MAC; Movement for the Defence of Wales) and they sought to 'reawaken the national consciousness of the Welsh'.[90] Their first actions had been two of the attacks on the construction site of the Tryweryn dam in 1963, attacks which led to a café owner and student being sentenced to twelve months in prison. The group's operations then escalated with the growing involvement of an army sergeant named John Jenkins, under whom MAC gained not only more technological knowhow but also a more sinister side, in that it was prepared to risk loss of life in the fight to save the nation. MAC was not just Jenkins, however, and the small handful of active members were supported by some fifty people who gave alibis, shelter and food.[91] The next incident was in March 1966, when there was an explosion at the Clywedog reservoir. That was followed by four more explosions in 1967–8 on pipelines and an aqueduct taking Welsh water to England. More threatening were the five bombs that were successfully set off at buildings, including the Welsh Office itself, in 1967–8. One of them, planted at an RAF station in Pembrey, seriously hurt a serviceman (although former MAC members continue to deny responsibility for this attack). The *Observer* thought it changed the attitude of many Welsh people, who had previously seen the bombs 'as a daring gesture, at worst an irresponsible prank'. The *Wrexham Leader* agreed: 'For a long time it was a game of fireworks which happened to give discreet satisfaction to the politically minded'. People came to their senses, the paper thought, when someone was hurt.[92]

The extremists put Plaid Cymru in a difficult position, especially since Labour did its best to associate the party with the violence. Despite the very strong sympathy for their objectives, there was a strong feeling within the party that both the language campaigners and the bombers were alienating potential support. Saunders Lewis did not help when he declared that any resistance to the building of dams, what he called an 'irresponsible violence on the land of Wales', was 'wholly just'. He told another reporter that his 'heart leapt' with news of every explosion.[93] Evans, in contrast, was forced into expelling FWA members from the party and into a series of condemnations of the 'vicious and degrading cult of violence'. He was, however, also suspicious that the British intelligence services were trying to undermine popular sympathy for Welsh nationalism and feared they were trying to create a sex scandal by laying 'honeypot' traps for him.[94] Following the explosion at the Welsh Office in 1968, he suggested publicly that British security services might be responsible, claiming there was an explosion every time an important election came up for Plaid Cymru. An editorial in the *Western Mail* took the theory seriously, noting the timing of many of the explosions, although the Home Secretary dismissed such accusations as 'ridiculous'. Special Branch was certainly watching ordinary Plaid Cymru members and there were more accusations that agent provocateurs were offering guns and explosives to students.[95]

The government had sought to prevent any escalation of either the violence or support for Plaid Cymru by looking for ways to placate and recognize the Welsh nation. This led to Swansea being made a city in 1969, despite it not meeting the criteria needed by English towns. The grand plan, however, was to use the Prince of Wales to remind people of their British loyalties. After much government badgering of the Palace, it was announced in May 1967 that Charles would be invested as Prince of Wales at Caernarfon Castle. There was derision in nationalist circles, encapsulated by a Dafydd Iwan song entitled *Carlo*, the Welsh for Charles and a popular name for a dog, which declared the Prince the best Welshman ever. Young people held sit-ins, hunger strikes and demonstrations; they complained that the event was a political stunt, a colonial imposition and a waste of public money. The Caernarfon press blamed nationalist teaching in colleges and on television for fostering such nationalism. A Wolverhampton man who farmed in north Pembrokeshire was threatened with legal action for keeping his children off from school, where he believed they were being 'indoctrinated' after being told a foreign prince was coming to Wales.[96] Plaid Cymru's leadership were more circumspect in their attitudes, fearing alienating its youthful supporters by endorsing the event or the wider population by opposing it. In the end its official line was to ignore the investiture as much as possible.

To offset the criticism, Charles was sent to university at Aberystwyth for a stint at learning Welsh. Despite a bomb-disposal specialist being stationed in the town and plenty of security officers mingling with the students, the university's principal expressed grave fears about the climate there and said he could not accept responsibility for the Prince's safety. Given the bombing campaign, Harold Wilson also wondered whether Charles's stay at Aberystwyth should be cancelled but MI5 advised him that the risk was 'more of a matter of personal embarrassment than of physical harm'.[97] As it turned out, crowds lined the streets every day to watch him walk from his hall of residence, while a protest by 'an ill-assorted gaggle of student anarchists and extreme Welsh nationalists' was repulsed by buckets of water thrown by other Welsh-speaking students.[98] Charles himself acted with dignity and said the right things. He told the BBC, 'I don't blame people for demonstrating like that.... I've hardly been to Wales, and you can't expect people to be over-zealous about the fact of having a so-called English Prince come amongst them'.[99] Indeed, Charles' determination to recognize the national question worried George Thomas enough for him to write to the Prime Minister with his fears that the Prince had come under too much nationalist influence at Aberystwyth. He suggested the Queen have a quiet word with her son.[100]

Violent threats from the FWA created an atmosphere tense enough in the build-up to the event for the editor of the *Western Mail* to insist on seeing all articles on the investiture and CyIG. George Thomas later claimed he was getting almost weekly threats to his life. Wilson was worried about the safety of the special train and wanted troops employed if necessary. The atmosphere forced action and the attorney-general decided that there should be prosecutions of those who wore uniforms and carried arms and explosives, to make a point.[101] The leading FWA members were arrested on public order and explosive charges and put on trial to coincide exactly with the date of the investiture. The boasts they had made to journalists proved their undoing when they were used as evidence. The day after the investiture, Cayo-Evans was sentenced to fifteen months; two other FWA members were imprisoned and another three given suspended sentences. The judge said the lenient sentences were because the defendants' motivation was a misguided love of Wales. That image was played up to when one of the imprisoned men told the judge, 'I will not forget Wales in my lonely cell. My prayer is for heroic men, and I pray [to] God he will grant them every strength to bring back Wales free from chains.' Saunders Lewis, not unreasonably, called the trial a 'cruel persecution' of 'harmless-romantic lads'.[102]

Evidence at their trial suggested the FWA was planning some sort of armed rising at the investiture. How real these plans were is unclear and there were numerous hoax calls around the event. Even the KGB discussed disrupting the investiture by blowing up a bridge and creating the impression that it was the British security services trying to discredit Plaid Cymru. The real threat was MAC, which had already that year caused four explosions at public buildings, tried to blow up a monument in Holyhead dedicated to the Prince of Wales and encouraged copy-cat incidents when a letter bomb was sent to a police officer. The group planned four bombs for the day of investiture, none of which was probably designed to kill Charles but all of which were potentially lethal. Indeed, two members of MAC were killed on the day before the investiture when the gelignite they were carrying exploded. On the day itself another bomb exploded harmlessly near the garden of the chief constable of Gwynedd. Four days after the investiture, a ten-year-old holidaymaker lost a foot after tripping on explosives planted in an ironmonger's yard that Charles had passed. Another bomb was left on Llandudno pier but failed to explode. In November 1969, John Jenkins and Frederick Alders, an aerial rigger and a key MAC member, were arrested. The following year Jenkins was sentenced to ten years in prison and Alders to six for causing explosions, conspiracy and possessing and stealing explosives. Although other perpetrators remained at large, this brought the MAC bombing campaign to an end.[103]

Despite the bombs, the investiture went ahead at Caernarfon Castle on 1 July 1969. Again, Charles said the right things, recognizing Wales' determination to protect its heritage and remain a nation. Crowds of 90,000 watched the royal procession to Caernarfon, far short of the 250,000 first anticipated. But the local press still gushed as their town became the 'central spot of Britain enacting an ancient ceremony in a brilliant way'. That ceremony cost the public purse £200,000 but there were optimistic promises of as much as £30 million in indirect benefits to the Welsh economy through tourism and advertising. The *Daily Mirror* thought Charles had 'triumphantly and spectacularly draped his ermine-trimmed mantle around the shoulders of a nation and received more than an affectionate hug in return'. A special magistrates' court to deal with any incidents on the day had to preside over only seven cases, two of which were for indecent exposure. Two men were charged with possessing offensive weapons (a sheath knife and a lump of lead), while three were charged with behaviour likely to cause a breach of the peace. Two of them had made V signs at the Queen as she passed in her carriage, after which the 'extremely angry and hostile' crowd turned on them. A sixteen-year-old was bound over for throwing a banana skin under the feet of the Household Cavalry.[104]

Opinion polls suggested that three-quarters of the Welsh population supported the event, although about a quarter of young people seemed to be hostile. The popular support was also evident in a backlash against the protestors. Dafydd Iwan received hate mail and was threatened in the street. The feeling against him was particularly strong in Welsh-speaking Wales. A letter to a Caernarfon paper called him a 'little tin god' and argued that he did not represent the youth of Wales, who 'are sick and tired of having the skeletons of long dead princes dug up and rattled before them until the dust from "dem dry bones" nearly chokes them'.[105] Some nationalists despaired at the popular support for the investiture and saw it as representative of a nation heading towards its own death. The *Argus* concluded that:

> the inbuilt tension cannot disguise the fact that for the vast majority of people in Wales the investiture is a joyful and memorable occasion. For the ordinary man and woman in the street the abstract political arguments are less imposing than the reality of a colourful ceremony involving a young prince and his family who, in the past week or two, have come to be more intimately alive and real thanks to film, photographs and interviews in the Press and broadcasting media.[106]

The fact that many businesses and schools gave their workers and pupils a day off probably did no harm to the event's popularity either.

DESPITE NATIONALIST CLAIMS that the investiture was a tool to impose Britishness on the Welsh, it was a Welsh event and a celebration of Welsh nationhood, even if firmly within a British context. The *Rhyl and Prestatyn Gazette* even claimed, 'Welshmen in general are discovering in themselves a new pride. The Prince of Wales has by his interest in things Welsh, his obvious desire to identify himself with us, brought to us a new sense of nationhood.'[107] But the event's popularity, like the low tally of votes for Plaid Cymru and the ambivalence towards to the campaigns of CyIG, showed that separatist nationalism still remained marginal to the dominant strand of Welsh public opinion. The debates over the political future of Wales and its language were mostly conducted among the middle class. Indeed, some sociologists speculated that the 'comparatively sophisticated argument' surrounding the language largely passed 'over the heads of the loyal Welshmen of the farming and lower manual working class'. Their study of Cardiganshire concluded that most people were neither romantic nor unrealistic about the possibilities for the language. Most had some concern with its future but were not political, disliked agitation and 'wish to live their lives in home, work or chapel, speaking the language they find it most convenient to speak'. Nationalism thus still faced considerable hurdles before it could grow among the mass of ordinary people. The memory of the Second World War also hindered Plaid Cymru. One Liberal activist in Cardiganshire remarked in 1971 that nationalism was 'forty years out of date' and associated with war and violence.[108] The uncertainty over the economic future of both rural and industrial communities did not help the party either. While there was always the danger, as happened in the mid to late 1960s, that economic fears might lead to an upsurge in Plaid Cymru votes in the short term, in the longer term they kept people wedded to the safety net that the British welfare state provided. This was evident when Plaid Cymru's share of the vote in Rhondda West collapsed from 39.9 per cent in the 1967 by-election to 14.1 per cent at the 1970 general election.

But attitudes were slowly changing. In 1958 an article in the periodical *Wales* dismissed nationalists as 'fellows more inclined to romanticism than realism' and their ideas as 'farcical'. The writer said he was proud to be Welsh but the Wales he wanted lay in the 'future' not 'the Druidical past'.[109] By the 1970s, while some people still held such attitudes, Plaid Cymru had developed a political base and was a serious force in Wales. Here it was both helped and hindered by the emergence of a violent strand of nationalism. While this may have alienated some potential supporters and increased the ire of parts of the Welsh Labour Party towards Plaid Cymru, it also forced the government to take nationalism seriously and do enough to placate it to ensure that violence did not spread. This contributed to the setting up in 1969 of a royal commission to investigate the possibilities of devolution. Some of the institutional straitjackets that had held Plaid Cymru back were also receding in a climate where nationalism had to be accepted. The Committee for Political Broadcasting, which Plaid Cymru and the Scottish National Party were both denied membership of, decided, without consultation, that for the 1970 general election the nationalist parties could have one five-minute broadcast on both television and radio on their national transmitters. Plaid Cymru pointed out that 10 per cent of the Welsh population could not receive Welsh television broadcasts and others tuned into English transmitters by choice. The Committee, however, decided that only parties which put up fifty candidates could receive UK-wide broadcasts, which immediately discounted Plaid since there were only thirty-six Welsh seats. Two academic commentators noted, 'even someone with no sympathy for the smaller parties could feel that they were treated less than courteously and fairly'. At the 1970 general election, twenty-five of Plaid's thirty-six candidates lost their deposits, but the party's overall vote had doubled since 1966 and it saved its deposit in every one of the six seats where more than 70 per cent of people spoke Welsh. The party was now firmly established as a viable political voice for Welsh-speaking Wales.[110]

Central to that was a developing feeling that the British state was not only not looking after Welsh interests but actively endangering the future of the Welsh language and nation. The flooding of Tryweryn was a powerful example but there were others to stoke people's resentment, such as the 1965 attempt by a factory in Blaenau to ban its workers from speaking Welsh. In a 1971 survey of Cardiganshire, 37 per cent of fluent Welsh speakers agreed that the Welsh people had suffered under English rule.[111] Such were the levels of mistrust of the British state that even an economically beneficial project like the Severn Bridge could come under attack because, in the words of one nationalist, Wales' 'political impotence … makes this improvement in communication a potential source of disintegration' for Welsh society.[112] Voting Plaid Cymru, especially in industrial areas, was also part of the same disillusionment with the direction and actions of the state that gave vent to English anger at immigration from the Commonwealth. Government was increasingly perceived to be distant from people's lives and needs. A small 1964 Welsh survey suggested that a third of people thought there was no or not much difference between the parties. A quarter said they had no or not much interest in politics.[113] Supporting a more localized party like Plaid Cymru was one response, even if it was taken up by only a minority of people.

The emergence of nationalism as a serious force may have offered some English monoglots in Wales a patriotic protest vote but most were less sure how to react. Nearly all deplored the violence once it became clear that was what it was, but, as with so much of youth culture, reactions to the language protests varied from outright hostility to bemusement. Yet the subsequent consequences of the rise of Plaid Cymru and especially CyIG did, very gradually, impact on how English monoglots thought about Wales. Dafydd Iwan was right when he wrote to the Secretary of State saying that the majority of people did not have much contact with the Welsh language and that the provision of bilingual forms would help close the gap between the two linguistic communities.[114] The provision of bilingual signs did the same. It reinforced what the media had begun to do regularly and what sport could do periodically: it reminded people that they lived in a different country, a country with distinctive needs and a distinctive identity. Even where people disagreed with the protests, it was impossible to ignore the fury surrounding the language issue. For some English monoglots, it helped generate a resentment that history had denied them the ability to speak the tongue of their nation; for others there was a fierce resentment that their inability to speak Welsh disenfranchised them in the job market or somehow implied that they were not properly Welsh.[115] But, whatever the reaction, Welsh nationality had become more than a matter of sentiment. The growing importance and profile of the Welsh language, extremism and Plaid Cymru in the late 1960s all created a greater consciousness of the fact that Wales was a separate country in the present rather than just the past. It created a consciousness that maybe this mattered on a political level. With time, the implications of this would become less controversial. And, in both its development and the government's concessions to it, it is difficult to escape the conclusion that both peaceful and violent direct action did far more than the ballot box to help the Welsh cause.

Notes

1 NA, BD 11/2975. For an overview of the affair by a resident see W. L. Jones, *Cofio Tryweryn* (1988), part 2.
2 I. Peate in *The Times*, 27 July 1957.
3 *Daily Mirror*, 22 Nov. 1956. *Guardian*, 22 Nov. 1956.
4 O. G. Roberts, 'Developing the untapped wealth of Britain's "Celtic fringe": water engineering and the Welsh landscape, 1870–1960', *Landscape Research*, 31:2 (2006), 130. *HC Deb*, 3 May 1957, vol. 572, c. 205.
5 The letters can be found in NA, BD 24/174.
6 J. Morris, 'Welshness in Wales', *Wales*, 1 (Sep. 1958).
7 M. Cunningham, 'Public policy and normative language: utility, community and nation

in the debate over the construction of Tryweryn reservoir', *Parliamentary Affairs*, 60:4 (2007), 627.
8 NA, BA 11/2975.
9 A. Edwards, 'Answering the challenge of nationalism: Goronwy Roberts and the appeal of the Labour Party in north-west Wales during the 1950s', *WHR*, 22:1 (2004), 137–9. *The Times*, 30 July 1957.
10 Letter, 17 Dec. 1956, NA, BD 24/174. R. Evans, *Gwynfor Evans: A Portrait of a Patriot* (2008), 164–7, 185. *Hansard* record of divisions.
11 Letter, 14 Dec. 1956, NA, BD 24/174. Briefing note, 20 Nov. 1956, NA, BD 11/2975.
12 Evans, *Gwynfor Evans*, 165–77, 179. This is not always accepted: see W. L. Jones, *Cofio Capel Celyn* (2007).
13 'Liverpool Corporation Act, 1957', NA, BD 11/2975. Evans, *Gwynfor Evans*, 192–3. *WL*, 28 Aug. 1964.
14 Briefing note, June 1958, NA, BD 25/59.
15 Evans, *Gwynfor Evans*, chs 6 and 7.
16 *New Statesman*, 22 July 1966. Evans, *Gwynfor Evans*, 128. Broadcasts (political), 1955–6, NA, PREM 11/1211. *Sunday Times*, 30 Nov. 1958.
17 R. M. Jones and I. R. Jones, 'Labour and the nation', in D. Tanner, C. Williams and D. Hopkin (eds), *The Labour Party in Wales, 1900–2000* (2000), 251. H. T. Edwards, 'Why I resigned', *Wales* (Nov. 1958).
18 See NA, CAB 129/85.
19 M. Jones, *A Radical Life: The Biography of Megan Lloyd George, 1902–66* (1991), 232. J. G. Jones, 'The Parliament for Wales Campaign, 1950–56', *WHR*, 16:2 (1992), 207–36. E. Chartte, 'Framing Wales: the Parliament for Wales campaign, 1950–1956', in T. R. Chapman (ed.), *The Idiom of Dissent: Protest and Propaganda in Wales* (2006), 75–96.
20 Briefing note, June 1958, NA, BD 25/59.
21 Memorandum by the Prime Minister, 29 Nov. 1957, NA, CAB 129/85.
22 *The Times*, 24 Jan. 1952. J. G. Evans, *Devolution in Wales: Claims and Responses, 1937–1979* (2006), 54.
23 Cabinet conclusions, 25 Oct. 1960, 8 Nov. 1960, NA, CAB 128/34. Note by Welsh Office, 31 July 1963, NA, PREM 11/4596. J. G. Jones, 'Spitting in the face of the Welsh people', *Pl*, 145 (2001), 83–93.
24 Memorandum by H. Brooke, 15 Nov. 1957, NA, CAB 129/90.
25 R. Weight, *Patriots: National Identity in Britain, 1940–2000* (2003), 279–83.
26 Evans, *Devolution in Wales*, ch. 3. R. Crossman, *The Diaries of a Cabinet Minister, Vol. I* (1975), 117.
27 *CDH*, 6 Nov. 1964. W. J. McCoubrey (ed.), *The Motorway Achievement, Vol. III: Building the Network* (2009), 538, 548.
28 G. Evans, *Fighting for Wales* (1991), 97.
29 Evans, *Gwynfor Evans*, 155.
30 MI5 file on Welsh Nationalist Party and Welsh Republican Movement, NA, HO 45/25484. *The Times*, 21 Oct. 1952.
31 Evans, *Gwynfor Evans*, 106–7, 135–7, 181, 190–1.
32 *Baner ac Amsersau Cymru*, 7 July 1960.
33 Evans, *Gwynfor Evans*, 220–1, 227–8. 'Welsh National Party (Plaid Cymru)', NA, BD 25/59.
34 E. Beasley, 'Papur y Dreth yn Gymraeg', *Y Ddraig Goch*, 31:3 (1959).
35 B. Griffiths, *Saunders Lewis* (1979), 123. Quoted in translation in A. R. Jones and G. Thomas (eds), *Presenting Saunders Lewis* (1983), 78.
36 E. Edwards (trans.), 'The fate of the language', *Pl*, 4 (1971), 13–27.
37 Evans, *Gwynfor Evans*, 217. *Yr Herald Cymraeg*, 19 Feb. 1962, quoted in R. Smith, 'Journalism and the Welsh language', in G. H. Jenkins and M. A. Williams (eds), *'Let's Do Our Best for the Ancient Tongue': The Welsh Language in the Twentieth Century* (2000), 295.
38 *Y Cymro*, 5 Dec. 1957. *WM*, 15 Feb. 1962.

39 D. Sandbrook, *White Heat: A History of Britain in the Swinging Sixties* (2006), 510.
40 Quoted in G. P. Davies, 'The legal status of the Welsh language in the twentieth century', in Jenkins and Williams (eds), *'Let's Do Our Best'*, 239.
41 Welsh Office, *Legal Status of the Welsh Language: Report of the Committee under the Chairmanship of Sir David Hughes Parry, 1963–1965*, Cmd 2785 (1965).
42 *WM*, 26 Oct. 1965.
43 G. Williams, *A Life* (2002), 125.
44 *CJ*, 3 Apr. 1964. *WM*, 9 Nov. 1965.
45 *CDH*, 23 Oct. 1964. Evans, *Gwynfor Evans*, 236–7.
46 Evans, *Gwynfor Evans*, 259–60. B. Levin, *The Pendulum Years: Britain and the Sixties* (1970), 159. *CJ*, 22 July 1966.
47 *Daily Mirror*, 22 July 1966. *CJ*, 29 July 1966.
48 *LDP*, 7 Aug. 1966.
49 Levin, *The Pendulum Years*, 166. *Daily Express*, 16 July 1966.
50 *CDH*, 22 July 1966.
51 Evans, *Gwynfor Evans*, 272. Evans, *Devolution in Wales*, 105–6.
52 V. Bogdanor, *Devolution in the United Kingdom* (1999), 163. G. Thomas to H. Wilson, 10 Feb. 1970, NA, PREM 13/3069.
53 G. Evans, *The Fight for Welsh Freedom* (2000), 147. J. Humphries, *Freedom Fighters: Wales's Forgotten 'War', 1963–1993* (2008), 33.
54 *North Wales Weekly News*, 21 Dec. 1967. *WM*, 6 Nov. 1967.
55 *South Wales*, winter 1968–9.
56 G. Miles in Jones and Thomas (eds), *Presenting Saunders Lewis*, 19. D. Phillips, *Trwy Ddulliau Chwyldro? Hanes Cymdeithas yr Iaith Gymraeg, 1962–1992* (1998), 63.
57 I. Emmett, '*Fe godwn ni eto:* stasis and change in a Welsh industrial town', in A. P. Cohen (ed.), *Belonging: Identity and Social Organisation in British Rural Cultures* (1982), 178.
58 Quoted in Levin, *The Pendulum Years*, 160.
59 Letter from D. Iwan to Secretary of State for Wales, 28 Apr. 1969, NA, BD43/139.
60 D. Phillips, 'The history of the Welsh Language Society, 1962–1998', in Jenkins and. Williams (eds), *'Let's Do Our Best'*, 479. Phillips, *Trwy Ddulliau Chwyldro*, 68.
61 *HC Deb*, 17 July 1967, vol. 750, cc. 1462–98.
62 Letter from D. Iwan to Secretary of State for Wales, 28 Apr. 1969. Minutes of meeting between Secretary of State for Wales and Cymdeithas yr Iaith, 3 May 1969, NA, BD 43/139.
63 Briefing for Secretary of State for Wales, 3 May 1969, NA, BD 43/139. Commission on the Constitution, *Minutes of Evidence V: Wales* (1972), 84. *Barn*, 57 (1967).
64 Commission on the Constitution, *Minutes of Evidence V: Wales*, 86.
65 NA, BD43/139.
66 *Cardigan and Tivyside Advertiser*, 28 Feb. 1969. N. Thomas, *Welsh Extremist* ([1971] 1973), 86. P. Merriman and R. Jones, '"Symbols of justice": the Welsh Language Society's campaign for bilingual road signs in Wales, 1967–1980', *Journal of Historical Geography*, 35 (2009), 350–75.
67 *Sun*, 31 Oct. 1968, 2 June 1969. Briefing note for Secretary of State, 30 Apr. 1969, NA, BD 43/139.
68 *WM*, 17 Feb. 1969. P. J. Madgwick, N. Griffiths and V. Walker, *The Politics of Rural Wales: A Study of Cardiganshire* (1973), 133. *LDP*, 8 Mar. 1969.
69 Phillips, 'The history of the Welsh Language Society', 474. 'Cymdeithas yr Iaith, the courts and the police', *Pl*, 12 (1972), 9–16. Commission on the Constitution, *Minutes of Evidence V*, 85. D. Iwan, *Dafydd Iwan: Cyfres y Cewri 1* (1981), 56.
70 J. R. Jones, 'Need the language divide us?' (1967), reproduced in translation in *Pl*, 49/50 (1980), 23–33.
71 A. Richards, *Dai Country* (1973), 131, 135.
72 *CDH*, 18 Apr. 1969. G. H. Jenkins, '"Am I walking a tightrope?" Religion, language and nationality', in G. H. Jenkins and G. E. Jones (eds), *Degrees of Influence: A Memorial Volume for Glanmor Williams* (2008), 153.

73 Quoted in translation in notes in NA, BD43/139. Iwan, *Dafydd Iwan*, 52.
74 T. J. Davies, *Martin Luther King* (1969).
75 Lyrics from 'I'r Gâd'. Iwan, *Dafydd Iwan*, 82, 48.
76 Quoted in J. Davies, *Broadcasting and the BBC in Wales* (1994), 294.
77 *Y Cymro*, 30 Apr. 1969. Davies, 'The legal status of the Welsh language', 236. M. Davies, 'The magistrate's dilemma', *Pl*, 12 (1972), 46–58. *The Times*, 5 Feb. 1970.
78 J. R. Jones, *Gwaedd yng Nghymru* (1970), reproduced in translation in M. Stephens (ed.), *A Book of Wales* (1987), 157.
79 M. Löffler, 'The Welsh language movement and bilingualism', in Jenkins and Williams (eds), *'Let's Do Our Best'*, 496–7. *Barn*, 77–83 (1969). A. Butt Philip, *The Welsh Question: Nationalism in Welsh Politics, 1945–1970* (1975), 246–7.
80 Internal note, nd, NA, BD43/139.
81 G. Davies, *The Story of the Urdd* (1973), 311.
82 Briefing note for Secretary of State, Dec. 1970, NA, BD 43/139.
83 *SWE*, 4 Mar. 1969. Cardiff Central Library, Cardiff Reports of Councils and Committees (1968–9), items 9144, 9332. *Llanelly Star*, 8 Jan. 1966.
84 *Denbighshire Free Press and North Wales Times*, 5 Feb. 1971. *WL*, 9 Feb. 1971. *Cambrian News*, 7 Mar. 1969.
85 R. Bowen (chairman), *Bilingual Road Signs*, Cmnd 5110 (1972), 26, 40.
86 *HC Deb*, 26 Jan. 1978, vol. 942, cc. 1805–16.
87 *WM*, 22 Oct. 1965.
88 Quoted in Thomas, *Welsh Extremist*, 116.
89 Humphries, *Freedom Fighters*, 50. The most notable examples of press coverage are: *Daily Telegraph* (colour supplement), 30 Aug. 1968, and *Town*, Dec. 1967.
90 J. Jenkins quoted in Humphries, *Freedom Fighters*, 108.
91 Humphries, *Freedom Fighters*, 67.
92 *Observer*, 15 Sep. 1968. *WL*, 24 Apr. 1970.
93 Quotes from Thomas, *Welsh Extremist*, 62, and G. Talfan Davies, *At Arm's Length: Recollections and Reflections on the Arts, Media and a Young Democracy* (2008), 53.
94 Quoted in Levin, *The Pendulum Years*, 161. Evans, *Gwynfor Evans*, 283, 296–7.
95 *WM*, 27 May 1968. *Guardian*, 14 Nov. 1968 and 7 Aug. 1973. P. Williams, 'Yr Heddlu Cudd', *Pl*, 12 (1972), 39–45.
96 J. Beckett, 'City status for Swansea, 1911–69', *WHR*, 21/3 (2003), 534–51. J. S. Ellis, *Investiture: Royal Ceremony and National Identity in Wales, 1911–1969* (2008). *CDH*, 11 July 1969. *Observer*, 29 Sept. 1968.
97 Ellis, *Investiture*, 195–6, 230. G. Thomas, *Mr Speaker: The Memoirs of Viscount Tonypandy* (1985), 119. Investiture of HRH The Prince of Wales: security arrangements, NA, PREM 13/2903.
98 E. L. Ellis, *The University College of Wales, Aberystwyth, 1872–1972* (1972), 325.
99 Quoted in T. Nairn, 'All manner of folks', *Pl*, 62 (1987), 8.
100 G. Thomas to H. Wilson, 22 July 1969, NA, PREM 13/2907.
101 Davies, *At Arm's Length*, 38–9. Thomas, *Mr Speaker*, 118. Investiture security arrangements, NA, PREM 13/2903.
102 *The Times*, 2 July 1969. Griffiths, *Saunders Lewis*, 122.
103 Investiture security arrangements, NA, PREM 13/2903. R. Clews, *To Dream of Freedom* (1980). Humphries, *Freedom Fighters*, ch. 11. A. W. Thomas, *Wales and Militancy, 1952–1970*, PhD thesis, Swansea University (2011).
104 Ellis, *Investiture*, 179, 242. *CDH*, 4 July 1969. *Daily Mirror*, 2 July 1969.
105 Ellis, *Investiture*, 239–40. Iwan on *Dragon's Breath*, episode 3, BBC Radio Wales (2001). *CDH*, 13 June 1969.
106 For example the poem 'I'r Farwolaeth' ('To the Death'), in G. Lloyd Owen, *Cerddi'r Cywilydd* (1972), 18. *South Wales Argus*, 1 July 1969.
107 *Y Cymro*, 6 Mar. 1969. Ellis, *Investiture*, 256.
108 Madgwick *et al.*, *The Politics of Rural Wales*, 111, 131, 217.

109 B. Hopkins, 'Patriots all', *Wales*, 4 (Dec. 1958).
110 D. Butler and M. Pinto-Duschinsky, *The British General Election of 1970* (1971), 204, 340, 402.
111 *Yr Herald Gymraeg*, 21 June 1965. Madgwick *et al.*, *The Politics of Rural Wales*, 73.
112 Letter to *New Statesman*, 5 Aug. 1966.
113 D. Tanner, 'Richard Crossman, Harold Wilson and devolution, 1966–70: the making of government policy', *Twentieth Century British History*, 17:4 (2006), 557. I. Crewe, N. Day and A. Fox, *The British Electorate, 1963–1987: A Compendium of Data from the British Election Studies* (1991), 182, 164.
114 Letter from D. Iwan to Secretary of State for Wales, 28 Apr. 1969, NA, BD43/139.
115 See for example a letter from a teacher in *WL*, 13 Feb. 1970.

9

'Black times.' The passing of Labour, 1966–85

'He said he's thinking of going down the pit.'
'He's a bloody luny, mun.'
'He's married with a kid.'
'Same thing.'
'The bloke nextdoor to him do work down there. He've been talking to him.'
'I don' think I'd do it' Jack said.
'Fair money see. Better than this place.'
'Would you do it?'
'No fucking fear.' ….
'He must want to be a fucking working class hero or something' Jack said.

Christopher Meredith, *Shifts* (1988), 141

I see the signs of black times everywhere I run.
I can't stand another day.
I gotta move away.

The Alarm, 'Father to son', from the album *Strength* (1985)

IN 1958 THE NATIONAL COAL BOARD (NCB) began tipping refuse near a spring on a hillside overlooking the village of Aberfan. There was no survey undertaken when the site was chosen. The spring was visible and on all local maps of the area but they had not been looked at. As the tip grew, the local authority made complaints to the NCB about the danger posed by coal slurry being washed down to the rear of the village primary school. The Board made assurances that the matter was in hand and the tip was safe. At 9.15 a.m. on 21 October 1966 the water-logged tip slid down the mountainside, engulfing a farm, houses and part of the school. Of the 144 people who were killed, 116 were children.

The Tribunal of Inquiry was appalled by the behaviour of the NCB and some of its employees, both before and after the disaster. It was particularly critical of Lord Robens, the NCB chairman, who had claimed that the spring underneath the tip had not been known about, a statement that was not retracted until Robens appeared in the final days of the two-month Tribunal, admitting that the Board had been at fault. The inquiry concluded: 'the Aberfan disaster is a terrifying tale of bungling ineptitude by many men charged with tasks for which they were totally unfitted, of failure to heed clear warnings, and of total lack of direction from above'. Nobody was prosecuted, dismissed or demoted. Robens' offer to resign was rejected by a government that thought he was the only man who could manage the decline of the coal industry and avoid strike action.[1]

The horror felt around the world at the tragedy led to a fund being set up to help the village. It raised £1.75 million (the equivalent of £24.4 million at 2008 prices) but accessing it proved awkward, causing a series of tensions between the village and the local authority that helped manage the fund. The council had already upset some people by sending a duplicated standard letter of sympathy to the bereaved. Parents were also angered when Aberfan pupils were at first relocated to a school at nearby Merthyr Vale which stood under a disused tip and gave a clear view of the cemetery where friends and relatives were buried, and travel to which involved crossing a busy road. The village wanted the remaining tips overlooking Aberfan removed because they were a constant reminder of what had happened and because of fears that the disaster could be repeated. The NCB claimed that it would cost too much. George Thomas, Secretary of State for Wales, told the Prime Minister that residents 'have worked themselves into an irrational state of mind on this issue'.[2] In August 1968 the government forced the disaster fund to contribute £150,000 to the cost of removing the NCB's remaining tips from above the village, tips which were in a condition and place that they should never have been, according to the NCB's own technical literature. Some people wrote to ministers to complain that this was inconsistent with the charitable objectives of the fund. The Charity Commission did not query whether the contribution was legal but it did ask the disaster fund to ensure that parents were 'close' to their children before making any payment to them for mental suffering. The disaster fund also ended up paying for the rebuilding of a chapel in Aberfan that had been used as a mortuary after the disaster. Its trustees pleaded with George Thomas to get the NCB to pay for it to be demolished and rebuilt because people could no longer bear to worship there. Thomas passed the plea on to Robens, who rejected it.[3]

The disaster and its aftermath showed the influence the NCB had over the government and over the local communities that it dominated. In places like Aberfan its economic importance was such that local authorities and residents found it difficult to challenge its decisions and power. But the NCB was also important emotionally in such communities, because it was the realization of the long-cherished dream of a mining industry owned by the people. The Labour Party held a similar position in working-class communities. At the general election seven months before the Aberfan disaster, Labour won thirty-two of the thirty-six Welsh seats, with 60.7 per cent of the vote. In thirteen constituencies its share of the vote was over 70 per cent and in three it was over 85 per cent. The fear of returning to a time before nationalization and the welfare state was central to winning those votes. One Labour address at the election claimed, 'We Merthyr people, with our memories of broken homes and broken hearts of those terrible days, do find it difficult to forgive the arrogance of those ignorant and pompous creatures who merely visit us to hope that they might fool us to vote for them'.[4] That year the historian Kenneth Morgan wrote of Rhondda West: 'to vote Labour was less a political act than a pledge of loyalty to your own communities, its memories, its values and its way of life'.[5] It was also a tradition passed down in families and some middle-class sons of miners regarded voting Conservative as a 'betrayal'. A columnist claimed in the *New Statesman* in 1966 that Labour could win at least half the Welsh seats with candidates who were 'polygamous, atheistic, alcoholic, and tone deaf'.[6] Thus what happened at Aberfan was a bitter disillusionment to such communities. As one bereaved parent later said: 'I was tormented by the fact that the people I was seeking justice from were my people – a Labour Government, a Labour council, a Labour-nationalised Coal Board'.[7]

AT THE TRIBUNAL S. O. Davies, the local MP, claimed that people's fears about the safety of the tips had not been pressed because of worries it might endanger the future of the local colliery. The Tribunal rejected this idea but the concerns for the future of collieries were very real. Labour's return to power in 1964 had done nothing to stop the programme of pit closures that had begun in earnest in 1959 because of a fall in demand for coal. The south Wales coalfield was particularly vulnerable because productivity there was far below the British average and the 1960s turned out to be devastating for the industry. In 1959 there were 141 NCB collieries in south Wales, employing 93,000 people. By 1969 there were just 55 collieries and 40,000 employees. The north Wales coalfield also lost half its workforce in the decade after 1962, leaving just two pits in the area. At the end of the 1960s, mining in Wales was employing 84,000 fewer people than it had in 1948.[8]

Given the wider sense of decline in Valleys communities and the coal industry's turbulent history, its rundown was remarkably peaceful. There were no major strikes or protests and one historian has even accused the miners of accepting the closures 'with remarkable docility and resignation'.[9] The leadership of the National Union of Mineworkers (NUM) was reluctant to strike for fear of undermining its influence with government and the consensus brought in with nationalization. At the grassroots, workers were apprehensive that strike action would simply hasten the demise of their own pit and they began to feel 'that the NCB are on top and the union exists in name only'.[10] There were actually few compulsory redundancies and many of the jobs were lost by pensioning off workers. When a pit closed, most employees had the option of a transfer to another colliery but this was not always popular. Long travel times, petty local bosses and new workmates and conditions unsettled people. Nor was there any guarantee that a transfer would be permanent as the pit closures gathered pace. One miner complained after his transfer:

> every night I used to pray that I would get badly injured so that I wouldn't have to go down again. Injury seemed the only way out. It was terrible, I was working with people I didn't know. None of my old butties were working with me. You get used to a colliery, you know which parts are dangerous and what to look for, you can feel when something is going to happen. At Cefn Coed it was strange, I didn't know anything.[11]

More and more people thus chose to leave the industry for safer, cleaner and, increasingly, better-paid jobs. Whereas between 1949 and 1957 wages had been on average 25 per cent higher in the coal industry than in manufacturing, by 1969 average manufacturing earnings were higher than in mining. A poem by a north Wales miner summed up: 'I look at my wage slip, And wonder why, They say coal's expensive, It must be a lie.'[12] Another miner remembers thinking, '"what the bloody hell am I doing working underground?" You're soaking in sweat all night, stripped to the waist. And I had to take pop bottles back to a pub to get the money back to have a bus fare to go to work.'[13]

The 1960s and early 1970s thus saw the ironic position of an industry that was shrinking but still finding it difficult to fill its vacancies. The NCB tried to appeal to the job's masculine status: there were advertisements on television and in the press that called for 'men with grit, guts, team-spirit' and promised them 'a job for life' and 'more money than ever'.[14]

While some former miners were tempted back because, according to the NCB, they missed 'the sense of companionship in mining', such campaigns struggled because people knew, either first hand or through their family, that the reality of mining was less glamorous.[15] One such person was Max Boyce, a poet and singer who worked underground for eight years and whose father had been killed in a colliery accident just before he was born. In a song as important to Welsh culture as anything written by Dylan Thomas or Saunders Lewis, Boyce reflected: 'they'll close the valley's oldest mine, pretending that they're sad, but don't you worry, butty bach, we're really very glad, 'cos it's hard, Duw, it's hard, harder than they will ever know.' The alternative may have only been 'counting buttons' in a factory but there would be tea and coffee breaks. He might not ever forget the camaraderie and laughing amid the fear but, with his cough to remind him of what had been, the song concluded that the mines had seen the last of him.[16] Like Boyce's comic tales of rugby expeditions, the song struck a chord and helped him become an immensely popular entertainer in both Wales and England. Yet Boyce was also criticized for 'shabby sentimentalism' and a 'maudlin fatalism' that trivialized what was worth protecting in Welsh society and diverted attention from economic and political crises. Some factories, after all, were poorly paid and skilled miners could see their wages halve.[17] Coffee breaks hardly made up for such a cut. But attacks on Boyce misunderstood the emotions that he communicated. The *Gwent Gazette* pointed out that Boyce was of the places he sang about; he knew the way of life he made jokes about, and 'we laugh because it's true'. When Boyce sang 'Duw, it's hard' in Ebbw Vale in 1974, the mood of the audience changed swiftly from laughter to silence. Fatalism did not change the attachment people felt to their colliery or occupation. Some men cried when their pit closed. They could also feel a sense of injustice, fed by the knowledge that there was still considerable coal left in many collieries and a suspicion that the NCB had deliberately tried to make some pits unprofitable so they could be shut.[18] But none of that changed how unpleasant the job was, something evident in the high rates of absenteeism, which averaged over 17 per cent in south Wales in the second half of 1966 and over 23 per cent in the Rhondda. A sociologist working in the Amman valley concluded that miners thought 'the best workmates' could be found in mines but that 'no one in his right mind' should ever venture into one, 'much less send his son'.[19] The injustice of the position aside, those miners who accepted what was happening and looked for safer and more comfortable jobs were just being pragmatic.

The state certainly appeared to have lost faith in the future of heavy industry in the Valleys. In 1967 the Welsh Office produced its first and rather optimistic blueprint for the future of the Welsh economy. It seemed to accept the decline of the coal industry as inevitable but without conceding any real hint of economic pain, although it did note the need to attract new industry to make fuller use of the available labour and create a greater choice of better jobs for those on low wages. The *Western Mail* was not overly impressed and thought the plan was too vague in outlining what would replace coal.[20] The lack of emphasis on coal was not surprising, even if the apparent unawareness of the scale of the needed economic restructuring was. In 1965 nearly half (48 per cent) of the Welsh workforce already worked in the service sector. Three years later there were 81,000 people in south Wales working in 'professional and scientific services', more than in both coal and metal production.[21] The Welsh economy had also become ever more reliant on state aid. The old government policies of grant aid, tax concessions and building factories continued. This was essential to making investment attractive because, as the *Financial Times* claimed, many people in England thought it impossible to walk around Wales 'without stumbling over lumps of coal or barking one's shins on a steel girder'.[22] In 1970 it was estimated that the government policy had directly helped create two-thirds of the 200,000 manufacturing jobs in south Wales. Such successes were not shared across all industrial Wales and it was proving much easier to attract industry to the north-east and southern coastal belt than it was to the Valleys. Even the government's plan to create 11,000 jobs by relocating state departments to Wales was concentrated on the coastal towns. The policy did, at least, create jobs, even if most were clerical and administrative and dominated by women. The Driver and Vehicle Licensing Centre opened in Swansea in 1965 and a passport office opened in Newport. During the 1970s Cardiff gained Companies House, a major income tax centre, an expansion of the Welsh Office and part of the Export Credits Guarantee Department. In preparation for decimalization, the Royal Mint was moved to the new town at Llantrisant in 1968, although only around a fifth of the 1,300 jobs there went to locals. The Welsh location was chosen over Cumbernauld, Runcorn and Washington and owed much to the preference of the existing Mint staff who were to be transferred. But they were not particularly happy with any of the locations because of what they perceived as a lack of amenities.[23] Llantrisant may have been better off than many places in the Valleys but the joke was still that the town was 'the hole with the mint'. Such perceptions meant that, in 1975, some 2,600 expected jobs were lost when British Rail reversed its decision to locate its western regional headquarters in Cardiff following opposition from staff in Bristol, Reading and London. Nonetheless, in the late 1970s, public sector employment still accounted for some 40 per cent of Welsh employment, with 15 per cent coming from nationalized industries, 16 per cent in the National Health Service and the rest in local and central government.[24]

State support for the Welsh economy became all the more important because of periodic turbulence in the 1970s global economy. One Merthyr man who had been out of work for four years said in 1971: 'Things are getting worse, aren't they? Everybody knows that. Firms closing down all the time, and nothing starting up. I used to go round looking for a job, but what's the point now?'[25] However, the wider British economy was still growing, which meant that in 1972 the North of England region (essentially Cumbria and the north-east) overtook Wales in terms of gross domestic product (GDP) per head. This left Wales as the poorest part of the UK (discounting Northern Ireland) for the rest of the 1970s and 1980s.[26] The year 1973 actually saw the start of a short boom but it quickly came to an end when political turmoil in the Middle East triggered an oil crisis. The dramatic rises in oil prices may have been good for the coal industry but they were disastrous for users of energy and they caused significant problems for the manufacturing that so much effort had gone into expanding in Wales in the 1950s and 1960s. Economic problems were then compounded when inflation exploded in 1975–6, growing so fast that some goods had doubled their price in just five years. Even teenagers could now swap stories about how much things used to cost. In 1975 there were over 17,000 redundancies in Wales and the Trades Union Congress concluded that maybe 10,000 school-leavers would not get jobs or on to training schemes, leading to increased delinquency, more petty crime, progressive frustration and maybe migration from Wales. Welsh GDP fell to 87 per cent of the UK figure and there were now approximately 100,000 fewer men in paid employment than there had been ten years earlier.[27] Many, especially in mining areas, had dropped out of the workforce through ill-health, meaning that the numbers classed as unemployed actually remained relatively low, rising from 38,400 (4.0 per cent) in 1970 to 63,200 in 1976 (5.2 per cent). Nonetheless, the state was spending 71 per cent more on sickness and invalidity benefits per head of population in Wales than it was in the UK as a whole and 97 per cent more on disability benefit. Wages and benefits also struggled to keep pace with inflation. By the late 1970s, while manual male wages in Wales were fractionally more than the British average (partly due to high wages in the steel industry), non-manual wages were just under 3 per cent lower than the British average. With fewer men and women working, household income in Wales in 1975 was just 85 per cent of the UK average, and lower than in every region except Northern Ireland. Although more people owned their own homes in Wales (around a third of households were owner-occupied), in 1970 the average personal wealth in Wales was 72 per cent of the British figure.[28] Thus, by the middle of the 1970s, the miracle of post-war affluence had well and truly faded and Wales had become the poorest part of the UK mainland.

Among those out of work there was real poverty. In 1973 the *Western Mail* noted that Cardiff's poorest families had to buy children's clothes on credit, paying as much as 50 per cent over the odds. One mother of ten in Tremorfa, whose husband was unemployed, complained she could afford meat only twice a week – chicken on a Sunday and mince on another day – and her family were enforced vegetarians the rest of the time, reliant on parcels of tins from her sister. She was ashamed that her children were poorly dressed but there was little alternative since the family was already in debt to money lenders. Entertainment was a few pints once a week for her husband and 60p a week for her bingo. The middle classes felt they were suffering too, as inflation ate away at their savings and their house prices and shares slumped. Trade unionists could strike in response and public sector workers were offered some protection by rises in government spending, but the well-off were left feeling vulnerable and shocked by the economic downturn.[29] The *Western Mail* ran another article in 1973 entitled 'The new poor of the middle classes'. It told the story an insurance inspector from Penarth with two children who was unable to save or afford many luxuries. He saw his financial situation as part of a wider social problem and told the reporter:

> But it's not just inflation. There just seems to be no future for the children here. All the fun seems to have gone out of life. You never see smiling faces. There's no fun or joy anywhere now.
>
> No one has pride in their work. Look at Cardiff, the streets are filthy, there's litter everywhere and all the walls are daubed with paint.
>
> Getting to and from the office took me half-an-hour to an hour and when I got there I couldn't find a place to park. Everything is a battle – getting to work, money, travel.
>
> There's an economic war going on and I don't want to be caught in the crossfire. You can see society breaking down.

He decided to move to Spain.[30]

THE ECONOMIC PROBLEMS of the early and mid-1970s meant that individual miners had fewer choices and were less willing to accept the erosion of their industry and wages. Tensions came to a head in 1972. By then there was a Conservative government again so the NUM felt more comfortable calling a strike. With support from other workers, notably in transport, and heavy picketing of power stations, the nation's coal stocks ran perilously low, forcing power cuts. After seven weeks on strike – facilitated by state benefits – the miners accepted an improved pay offer of nearly 20 per cent, more than double what they had initially been offered. It was a spectacular victory that many saw as revenge for the defeat of the 1926 miners' strike, something etched in the history of their families and communities. However, the better wages won were quickly eroded by rising inflation and continued losses in the industry made further contraction likely. After OPEC (the Organization of the Petroleum Exporting Countries) reinforced the demand for coal by tripling the price of oil in 1973, the miners' sensed an opportunity to assert their position and another national dispute began. With the supply of oil also under threat, coupons were printed in case petrol needed to be rationed and there were more power cuts, dimmed street lights and no television after 10.30 p.m. Most seriously, business was put on a three-day week in order to save power and there were redundancies at companies unable to function properly. Hairdressers claimed their trade was hit worst of all. They had power for only three hours a day in the week and five and a half hours on a Saturday. This made it difficult to do colouring, drying, bleaches and perms and they were cutting some people's hair by candlelight. A wig boutique in Cardiff reported that its sales were up 30 per cent. Despite the hardships being inflicted on everyone, the miners were unapologetic. One Rhondda miner told a reporter that if Prime Minister Edward Heath came to visit the colliery:

> We would go down the pit and walk two miles to the coalface, crouching down because of the low roof. His eyes would sting with the dust and he would think his brain was coming loose with the noise of the drills. He would see eat us sandwiches with filthy hands and hear about roof falls and he would get tired just watching us dig coal for seven hours in all that din and muck. Then I would say, 'Would you do it – the stinkiest job in Britain – for 31 quid a week takehome?'[31]

Regardless of the miners' plight, it was not with too much exaggeration that Heath told the nation it was facing a fight for survival; he called a snap general election, asking the electorate who was governing the country. Despite limited sympathy for the miners outside the coalfield, Heath lost the election, although his party did gain one extra seat in Wales, while Labour won 36,000 fewer Welsh votes than it had in 1970. The incoming Labour government gave the miners a 35 per cent pay rise. But this second spectacular victory failed to bolster the industry. Demand for coal continued to fall, particularly in south Wales, where pits were hit by a reduction in steel production. The increased wages meant that British coal became less competitive at a time of falling global coal prices. Imports of coal into Britain tripled in the late 1970s and the closure of collieries continued.[32]

The miners' victories of 1972 and 1974 represented the height of trade union power in Britain and helped usher in a period when the threat of industrial disputes seemed to become an almost constant backdrop to public life. Even the Welsh regional secretary of the Transport and General Workers' Union could recall that unions were 'inebriated' with the power they thought the miners' victories had given them.[33] The number of industrial stoppages in Wales in the 1970s peaked in 1977 at 263 but 1979 was the worst year for the sheer scale of disputes, when some 328,000 Welsh workers were involved in strikes. That year's strikes became famous for bringing a 'winter of discontent'. The strikes among local-authority workers did cause disruption, most visibly in the accumulation of uncollected rubbish, but the winter of discontent has been much mythologized and exaggerated; more days were actually lost to strikes in Wales the following year, after the Conservatives had taken power again (figure 9.1).[34]

Exaggeration aside, the unions increasingly, and not unfairly, became seen as an intransigent part of the political system. Amid fears that trade unionism represented some kind of radical left-wing revolutionary troop, surveys in Wales in the 1970s showed consistently that more than two-thirds of respondents felt unions had too much power.[35] But despite their influence

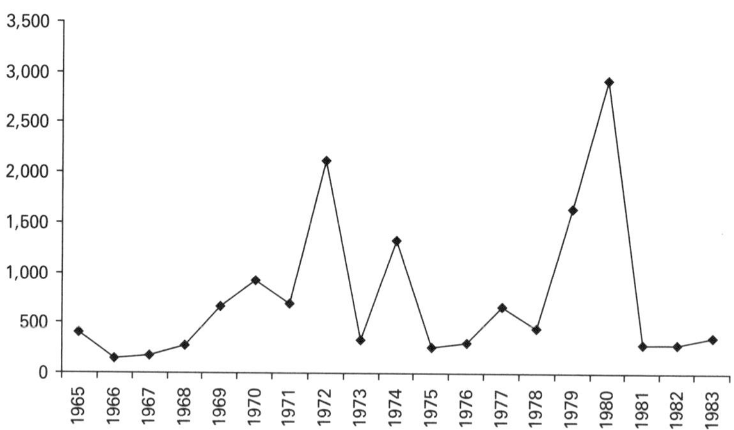

Figure 9.1 Working days lost in industrial stoppages in Wales (1,000s), 1965–83.

Source: *DWHS-1*, 166. *DWHS-3*, 149.

on government, the radicalism of trade unions should not be exaggerated. By the end of the 1970s there were in Wales nearly 650,000 members of unions affiliated to the Trades Union Congress but for most of these people trade unions were not about political power but about ordinary rights, wages and conditions. Moreover, the service sector in particular was under-unionized and some 383,000 Welsh employees were not members of a union in 1979.[36]

By striking, ordinary union members were simply reacting to the emerging economic chaos around them. Inflation hit 25 per cent in 1975 and if wages were to keep pace with prices there was a danger of mass unemployment and even national bankruptcy. To add to the persistent fears for coal, steel, once the bright hope of the Welsh economy, was now in trouble. Across the UK, the industry was running up heavy losses and facing increasing competition from overseas. It had not been helped by its complex history, being nationalized in 1951, denationalized in 1953 and renationalized in 1965. Welsh steel was expensive, and was produced in too many small and inefficient plants. Thus it was no real surprise when, in 1973, the British Steel Company (BSC) announced plans to shut all nationalized steelworks in Wales except Port Talbot and Llanwern. Nonetheless, the Secretary of State for Wales complained to cabinet that BSC was 'impervious' to the social and regional consequences of the potential loss of 17,000–18,000 steel jobs in Wales.[37] As unions, communities and local authorities campaigned against the closures, the plans were delayed but the state of the industry was indisputable. Labour's return to power in 1974 made no difference to that and arguments now revolved around timing. Despite being in the constituencies of the Secretary of State for Employment and the Prime Minister, production ceased at the main Ebbw Vale works in 1975 and at East Moors (Cardiff) in 1978. With the election of the Conservatives in 1979, the public subsidy of BSC was counting time, endangering the other plants. The *Western Mail* suggested in 1980 that 'The clouds over Welsh steel are nightmarish in their intensity, their shadows darken lives over the whole of the southern part of the country'.[38] That year Shotton steelworks closed with 6,400 redundancies, while Port Talbot shed 6,883 jobs and Llanwern 4,545. In 1973 BSC had employed 65,981 people in Wales. By 1983 the figure was just 19,199. Economists estimated that for every two jobs lost in Welsh steel, another was lost because of the knock-on effect on suppliers and other local industries.[39]

Redundancy payments in the steel industry were often large enough for some to buy their council houses and there were retraining schemes and 'make-up pay', where people who found new work at much lower wages could have it topped up to 90 per cent of their previous earnings for eighteen months. In Port Talbot some workers found themselves back in the steelworks, but this time as contractors earning less and with no security. But none of this helped people's long-term prospects or prevented the financial impact of losing a well paid job. Redundancy meant making sacrifices and less money for food, clothes and socializing, even if a new job was found. The wife of a redundant steelworker who had found new work noted in 1982: 'I never put the fire on if it's just me on my own here in the day, and we always have weak bulbs, and don't use the big light. I've got so I'll make a dinner out of anything. It'll be two corned-beef dinners, not two joints a week, and I do more cakes and big plate pasties. We've both cut down smoking, but without cigarettes we'd have killed each other.'[40]

The contraction of the steel industry was related to a deepening recession in the late 1970s and early 1980s, a recession then exacerbated by the Conservative government's monetarist policies, which kept interest rates high in order to keep inflation low, and its abandonment of any pretence that full employment was possible. These were, as one letter to the *Western Mail* put it, 'days of almost unmitigated economic gloom'.[41] Between 1978 and 1982 there were 176,939 redundancies in Wales. Manufacturing was particularly hard hit. The number of men employed in the sector in south Wales fell by over 60,000 (almost a third of the total) between 1973 and 1981, while 20,000 female manufacturing jobs (over 40 per cent of the total) were lost too. In 1971 a third of Welsh employees had worked in manufacturing; by 1981 this was down to a quarter. Less than half of the new factories opened between 1966 and 1971 were still open in 1984.[42] Unemployment hit levels not seen since the 1930s, which made the problems of the early 1970s seem relatively trivial. It peaked in 1986, at 13.7 per cent, although for men the figure was 15.9 per cent. This meant there were over 168,000 people registered as unemployed. That year 17.7 per cent of the male unemployed had been out of work for more than five years and 8.2 per cent had never had a paid job. The official statistics were also deflated by putting people on youth training schemes or paying them off with incapacity benefit. The percentage of adult men in the Welsh labour force who were economically active fell from 76 in 1979 to 69 just seven years later. By the mid-1980s just 37 per cent of Welsh households were headed by someone in full-time employment, compared with a UK figure of 45 per cent.[43] There were also many more married women looking for work than had registered as doing so because they had not paid enough National Insurance to get benefits. The extent of unemployment was evident in how even low-paid jobs were heavily in demand. In 1981, for example, a new Asda store in Swansea received 8,000 applications for 300 vacancies. The experience of unemployment was also much wider than the numbers of those out of work at any one time would suggest. In a 1981 survey of two districts in Newport, 21 per cent were unemployed but 30 per cent had been at some point in the previous two years and 45 per cent of households had had at least one member unemployed in the last two years. Two-thirds of sixteen- to nineteen-year-olds in the survey were out of work.[44] In 1982 one historian claimed that 'Rising around those who cling for their jobs to the state and service industries is a remorselessly growing underclass of permanently unemployed and wasted human beings and a generation of young people, in town and country, dumped like rubbish'.[45] Unemployment had certainly become a defining feature of the time and graffiti on the Severn Bridge declared 'Wales is closed'. Moreover, manual labour itself, once a defining feature of Wales, seemed to be in terminal retreat, declining from 61 per cent of economically active males in 1961 to 54 per cent in 1981. That year another historian remarked, 'Living in South Wales today can be an uncanny experience, especially if you're over 50, or an historian. It's almost like being a bewildered member of the cast in one of those post-holocaust movies. How the hell did we get here? Who zapped us?'[46]

It was not all doom and gloom. A Welsh Development Agency was set up in 1976 with a £100 million budget; it continued the old government policy of giving grants and loans and building factories. Between 1972 and 1984 Wales received £770 million in regional development grants, 17 per cent of the total paid in Britain. The European Economic Community (EEC) also emerged as an important source of funds, providing loans and support for building factories, roads and other infrastructure developments. Thanks to such support there were some high-profile new investments like a Ford plant near Bridgend, which was built by public money and opened in 1984, employing 1,800 people. The service sector also continued to grow. In 1965 it had accounted for 47.9 per cent of employment in Wales. By 1985 the figure was 64.4 per cent, although the statistical suggestion of growth was exaggerated by the decline of other sectors and many of the new jobs were only part-time.[47] This meant that there was a perception that jobs in the service sector were simply not as important as those in traditional industry. Rhodri Morgan, then South Glamorgan County Council's industrial development officer, had summed up the options in the face of steel closures: 'We don't want a pen-pusher's paradise'.[48] Such fears were exacerbated by the knowledge that unemployment, lower wages and higher numbers of people on social security meant that Wales remained the poorest part of mainland Britain. By 1984–5 the average UK household weekly income was £216, while in Wales it was £187. Average incomes in Wales were now higher than in the north of England but they were far behind the south-east of England, where average household income was £248. The impact of the recession was, of course, not shared equally across Wales. This was evident within Cardiff in 1981. The docks area of Butetown was suffering from 43 per cent male unemployment, while Ely, dominated by a huge council estate, endured a figure of 29 per cent. In contrast, leafy Radyr had a rate of just 4 per cent.[49] The steel towns were particular badly hit. The end of smoke blowing across the area was no compensation for unemployment hitting 30 per cent in Flint in the aftermath of Shotton's closure. Clwyd became Wales' unemployment black spot, with over 18 per cent of its workforce on the dole in 1982, the highest level of any Welsh county. In 1981 Clwyd's GDP was just 72 per cent of the UK figure, whereas for Wales as a whole it was 85 per cent.[50] Port Talbot had similar problems. In 1962 there had been over 18,000 employed at the town's steelworks. By 1984 this was down to 4,800. In 1982 BP announced 500 redundancies from its chemical works at adjoining Baglan, while nearby Llandarcy refinery lost 300 jobs in 1983 and the local council shed 200 full-time jobs in 1983–4. Three supermarkets, a cinema, a tax office and a medical centre also closed in Port Talbot in 1983. Two and a half years after the programme of redundancies at the steelworks, only 29 per cent of workers who lost their jobs had found another or become self-employed. The London media began to use the town as a symbol of the UK's recession, perhaps because they could catch a direct train there from London and still be home for dinner.[51]

At the beginning of the 1980s in industrial Wales there were tearful fears among the old of a return to the 1930s; among the young there was talk of 'anarchy, civil disobedience, a general strike, [and] violence'. In 1980 a Port Talbot steelworker, who preferred cricket to politics, told the press, 'it's a frightening thought what could happen. I don't think people will put up with deprivation nowadays and if it does arrive I think the reaction could be violent.'[52] Despite such threats, civil disobedience never emerged beyond a brief bombing campaign in 1980–2 on government and Conservative Party offices by tiny groups calling themselves the Welsh Socialist Republican Movement and the Workers' Army of the Welsh Republic. More common were angry demonstrations, although Nicholas Edwards, Secretary of State for Wales 1979–87, described them as 'never more than inconvenient and mildly unpleasant'.[53] Within the steel industry a thirteen-week strike in 1980 over pay and closures failed to win the support of other unions and ended with a whimper. During the industry's subsequent rundown steel-workers retained some pride in their work and were stimulated by the danger and virility of the 'mix of hot metal and sweat', but at the same time there was disaffection, alienation, cynicism and efforts to avoid work because of the forthcoming closure.[54] Their lack of radicalism also owed much to the good redundancy packages that were on offer. As the general secretary of the steelworkers' union said, 'How *can* you get workers, many of them in their fifties, some of them in debt, others needing a new car or new furniture or a holiday, to turn down huge sums of money and instead fight the employers with tough, sustained industrial and political action? The fact is, you cannot.'[55]

In several English cities the tensions did explode into violent riots in 1981. In their wake, the *Western Mail* interviewed unemployed youths in Cardiff. Many thought the same thing could happen there. There was a sense of antagonism towards the police and some sense of racial harassment. After the English riots, black and white youths did, apparently, try to draw police into the Cardiff docks area where they were to be ambushed with petrol bombs. The police did not follow and several thousand pounds' worth of damage to property was caused instead.[56] But this was a rare episode. In 1978 someone who had just lost his job wrote to the *Western Mail*: 'most people seem to treat unemployment like the weather. It hardly provokes more agitation than the fatalistic shrug of the shoulder when, not so many years ago, the prospect of well over a million people on the dole would have fed thoughts of revolution.' At a dole office in Cardiff he found

> over 60 people of all ages herded together, mostly on wooden benches, waiting their turn to be interviewed at a series of booths. At the reception desk was a notice which announced cheerfully that 'prompt attention' would be given to claimants. Later that day I understood the meaning of these words: over two hours' wait before you are seen – for young, old, mothers with their children.... The majority had already accepted the fact that they were second-class citizens, not deserving even the bare minimum of politeness or consideration.... [The staff's] glances across the counter were reminiscent of a farmer sizing up cattle.[57]

Rather than riot in response to such treatment and the poverty of being on the dole, most unemployed men stayed in bed late, did jobs around the house, gardened and watched a lot of television. But there was only so much DIY that could be done and materials cost money. The general worry and stress about finances and the future affected people's health and could create a sense of hopelessness.[58] The unemployed confessed to getting irritable, frustrated and bored; they felt looked down upon, inferior and embarrassed when they came into contact with people who were working, especially in situations where spending money was required. Local contacts were important in finding work, which meant that some men said they had to go out drinking in order to find a job. But more common was for the poverty of the dole to remove people from the networks of clubs and pubs that could offer some social support to help compensate for being out of work. Despite Norman Tebbit's suggestion as Secretary of State for Employment that the unemployed should get on their bikes and look for work, moving was a difficult choice because the cost of living was higher in more prosperous places and, as one unemployed man put it, 'I would rather be out of work at *home* where my friends and family are, than out of work in a place I don't know'.[59]

This support became more important because unemployment was increasingly becoming a matter of years. In 1981 one Welsh magazine noted that a prolonged period of joblessness

> begins to drive people down into spiralling poverty. Savings are eaten up completely. Clothes and shoes wear out and cannot be replaced. Consumer durables and other household assets, accumulated from many years of regular income, fall into disrepair and cannot be replaced. It is also the case that after two years of enforced idleness, the will to work can be seriously impaired and require rehabilitation.

Such prolonged economic circumstances placed pressures on marriages. Some unemployed men found some fulfilment in spending more time with their spouse and sharing tasks together but others found it hard to adjust to their wives being the breadwinner. In 1981 the South Wales Marriage Guidance Council reported that its number of clients had increased by nearly 60 per cent in the previous twelve months.[60] The impact of the recession was thus far worse than simply unemployment. A reporter noted of Maesteg in 1985: 'An air of decay envelopes the town, as tangible as the masonry which occasionally comes crashing down off some of the empty buildings in the street'. A man who remembered the depression of the 1930s told him, 'At least the public houses were open then'.[61] In the same year in Brynmawr, a Gwent town with 28 per cent unemployment if youth training schemes were discounted, a resident who also remembered the 1930s thought this depression was easier because it was not a matter of starvation anymore. A younger resident disagreed: 'It's worse now. Our expectations have been raised. We've got used to cars, foreign holidays, eating out. We've had the sixties. Why should we go back? I don't want to eat stew every day.'[62]

THE ARRIVAL OF THE 1980s had also brought little hope for the coal industry. With escalating costs and falling demand, the victory of 1974 had not stopped the rundown of the industry and from 1975 to the end of 1979 another eleven pits closed in south Wales.[63] After 1979, energy generation policy shifted towards nuclear power and legislation was passed to end operating grants for the NCB by 1983–4; the future of the whole coal industry seemed to be in danger. In 1981 Emlyn Williams, the president of the south Wales area of the NUM, called for 'a demonstration for existence' against 'the dereliction of our mining valleys'.[64] One Welsh miner wrote in 1983, 'we must realise that if we are not prepared to fight then we must be prepared to see Britain totally gutted of its basic industries and our communities smashed'.[65] Things looked particularly bleak in south Wales, where geological problems and a history of low investment meant that operating costs were very high. Only four of the twenty-eight south Wales pits were making a profit and the region was contributing a third of the NCB's total losses. The ever-declining wider economic picture was beginning to severely curtail the employment options for miners whose pits shut. In many mining towns unemployment was already over 20 per cent. Thus, when the closure of twenty pits and the loss of 20,000 jobs across the UK was announced, the NUM moved towards a national strike. Key to the escalation of the miners' reaction was the election of Arthur Scargill as NUM national president in 1981. This was the culmination of a 1970s battle between left and right which created deep divisions within the union. The fear of pit closures was drawing the rank and file of the union to its far-left leader but support for a strike remained muted. Only ten collieries in south Wales initially voted for strike action in March 1984 but as support for a strike grew in the rest of the British coal industry Welsh miners came round and a dispute began.[66]

One Crumlin miner remarked on the strike's eve: 'I'm against a strike. I just can't afford it. But once we're into it, well, it's a different matter then.'[67] To go against it would have been to go against union, community and workmates, all of which were important concepts in an industry that often felt undervalued and separated from wider society. These feelings quickly intensified as the state seemed to throw its entire resources against the miners. Benefits were denied to those on strike, picketers had their telephones tapped and their union's assets were frozen. With the government seemingly trying to starve the miners into submission, the strike quickly became one not just for the specific jobs under threat but for the future of the whole industry, the communities around it and the very right to have a union at all.

Support for the strike was stronger in south Wales than in any other part of Britain. After eight months only nineteen men had returned to work in south Wales. It was the only region with pits, six in all, that stayed completely 'scab free' until the very end, in March 1985, by when just 1,500 out of the 20,000 south Wales miners had broken the strike. The highest numbers of strike breakers were at collieries on the edge of coalfield, where mining was a less dominant force in the community. In north Wales, where mining communities were also less isolated, just 35 per cent of the workforce were on strike in the middle of November 1984, compared with 99.6 per cent in south Wales.[68] Beneath such outward unity, individual miners worried about debt, their homes being repossessed, the future and the ignominy of relying on food parcels. Only wives and children could receive social security payments and they had been much curtailed since the disputes of the early 1970s. The typical take-home pay of a south Wales faceworker had been £98 a week but some of their families now found themselves with £5 a week. Single miners could find themselves with literally no money coming in. Some families broke up under the pressures and all struggled to cope with the financial burden of a year without pay. There were even a number of suicides.[69]

It was such worries that had driven some back to work. Breaking the strike meant being seen to go against not just the community but the camaraderie and mutual trust among miners that made working underground both safer and more tolerable. 'Scabs' thus faced not only a cold shoulder but also at times physical violence and even their families were ostracized. Some were thought of as 'not from round here', as wife beaters or drug users. They had their houses picketed and pelted with missiles. Even their pets could be killed. A single miner who went to work at Garw Colliery was reputedly attacked with bricks, bottles and eggs by a 300-strong crowd of miners and their families.[70] There were seemingly different attitudes to men who returned to work after ten months and to those who had never struck, but for some miners 'a scab was always a scab'. After the strike was over there was still violence and death threats and it was little wonder that most strike breakers eventually moved out of south Wales.[71] The smaller number of 'scabs' did, however, mean that the strike was not as hostile in south Wales as in other coalfields. This was helped by Philip Weekes, the NCB's south Wales director and a cousin of the Labour MP for Merthyr. He did not want a trickle back to work and was much softer in his dealings with the NUM than most of his counterparts in England. So too were some police officers, who often came from the same communities as the miners. However, the increasing use of police from outside Wales led to rising tensions, while anger at police violence on English picket lines, many of which were visited by Welsh pickets, did carry back to Wales. As the strike dragged on, the tempers of both miners and police seemed to fray. The tapping of activists' phones, the constant stopping of their vehicles, and police using dogs, boasting about overtime pay and not wearing numbers did not help; nor did the violence that some miners met on the picket line and even in police custody.[72] Picketers sometimes gave as good as they got but the forces of the law and state were stacked against them.

The idea that the strike was about the future of communities meant that women were involved in unprecedented numbers. Their organization of food parcels and soup kitchens may have been within the confines of traditional gender roles but it ensured families could survive and was integral to keeping the strike going. Some women also took part in picketing and protested outside the homes of 'scabs'. Not all men were happy with this and women were not always allowed onto the picket lines or into meetings at miners' clubs. One novel noted how the involvement of women could be unsettling for their husbands: 'Jesus, she's like a different bloody woman. Always had more chops than a lamb, but about the usual things. You know, my drinking or time on the sick. Now she's around the place like Nye bloody Bevan.'[73] Women like that also had to endure sexist and sexual verbal abuse from the police. All of this intensified their realization of how women were often seen and their own sense of confidence, worth and unity. Many of the women who got involved were already active in local politics but for others it was a new experience. They might be pushed into it by the example of male members of their own family but they also drew on their own experiences and one activist from the Amman valley spoke of being 'hardened by looking after the kids and doing jobs round the house'. For some women the experience of being active in the strike was life changing, leading them to go on into work or education or simply receiving more help from their husbands with the housework. One miner's wife remarked, 'Before the strike he was a boss in a way, it's not like that now, any decisions we make equally, it's more like we're partners now than before, and the strike made that difference'. None of this, however, translated into a general feminist revolution. There was some animosity towards the middle-class feminist movement and concern that the involvement of outsiders would be detrimental to the central fight in support of the strike. As one woman summed up, 'We were fighting for our communities not just for women'.[74] Of course, not every miner's wife became active and many just worried about the financial and emotional strain on the family. In a novel about the strike one miner summed up, 'they're not all on action committees, you know. Mine just sees the bloody suite going back, perhaps even the telly next month.'[75]

Parts of the London media were deeply vitriolic in their coverage of the strike, labelling the miners thugs and bullies. In August 1984 in a UK poll 84 per cent of respondents thought the miners were using irresponsible methods, while 43 per cent said their sympathies were largely with the

employers and only 32 per cent with the miners. By the end of 1984 the percentage giving their sympathy to the employers had risen to 51 per cent. But wherever people placed their primary sympathy, there was never much taste for any idea of crushing the miners, who could hardly be dismissed as workshy or lazy in the way 1970s strikers in less arduous industries were. The Welsh media meanwhile were more sympathetic in their coverage.[76] Moral and financial support for the miners also seemed stronger in Wales than in many places, perhaps because of the centrality of mining to the Welsh self-image. Collections for the miners took place across Wales and there was considerable financial and moral support from groups as diverse as churches, nationalists, farmers and gay and lesbian campaigners. Some of this support was a way of demonstrating opposition to Thatcher's government and all it stood for. One poet, for example, celebrated how the strike was transforming villages from collections of people watching television to 'communities again', where meetings replaced the videos and fridge-freezers returned to the shops.[77]

Yet it is easy to exaggerate and romanticize the degree of wider support for the miners. The widespread sympathy that had existed for them was not really political but compassionate, a concern for the suffering and impossible situation fellow Welsh people found themselves in. Other unions gave financial but not physical support and, unlike in 1974, coal was still moved and used. One activist and historian of the strike complained that 'Old-fashioned trade union solidarity had, at best, been reduced to presentation turkeys at Christmas'.[78] Cooperation with Welsh steelworkers broke down after the NUM tried to prevent all coal deliveries to the industry, endangering the steelworkers' own jobs. Even the south Wales valleys were not quite as united as people liked to imagine. The wife of one striking miner in Treharris recalled, 'We were shocked when we went around the streets here, some people just didn't want to know'. A friend of hers pointed out how they had not seen one of their Labour councillors at all during the strike.[79] In Duncan Bush's novel *Glass Shot* a tyre fitter from Cardiff passes pickets while driving in the Valleys. To him they are 'woollybacks' and he slows down so they can stare at his car, before moving on through 'one more dirty-looking, Welsh, played out little village.... This isn't South Wales. It's Nineteen Five-Five.'[80] Even among the miners, only a minority were on the picket lines, while some worked throughout the dispute in other casual jobs, unwilling to break the strike but unwilling or unable to endure its financial hardships. This was hardly surprising: after all, the miners were actually fighting to protect jobs that many of them hated or at least did not want their sons to take up.[81]

On 30 November 1984 David Wilkie, a taxi driver, was killed after two miners dropped a slab of concrete from a bridge onto his car because he was taking a 'scab' to work at the colliery adjacent to Aberfan, a location that added to the horror. Many strikers saw their heart go out of their fight and public sympathy for the miners ebbed. With no power shortages (thanks partly to the misguided decision to call a strike in the spring) there seemed to be little hope of victory and distrust of the NUM's national leadership was growing among the rank and file. By 1985 the strike was collapsing in north Wales and other parts of Britain. There was a fear that the acrimonious trickle back to work would begin to reach similar proportions in south Wales, inflicting irrevocable harm on both communities and the union. The south Wales miners thus led a movement to bring the dispute to an end. After a year on strike, they returned to work in defiant marches that were meant to show that defeat had not killed the miners' unity. But in some places it had. At Point of Ayr in north Wales, the strikers' return was greeted with jeers.

After the strike, the coal industry collapsed at frightening speed. There was plenty of coal left but little political will to exploit it. Twelve collieries closed in south Wales within eighteen months of the dispute's end. The remaining pits received investment, improving productivity and moving the coalfield into an operating profit in 1986 for the first time since 1958.[82] But even then closures continued and recent investments were written off in what seemed to many people to be a vindictive retaliation by the government. Some miners even thought that management was deliberately taking bad decisions, to make a pit unprofitable and thus make closure possible. Abernant closed in 1988, just three years after the NCB invested £5 million in the colliery. It still had fifteen years' worth of coal left.[83] By 1987 there were just 10,000 miners and fourteen pits left in south Wales. By 1990 there were six pits and fewer than 3,000 miners. When Thatcher had come to power in 1979 there had been 27,000. On 1 January 1995 the British coal industry returned to private ownership. When the NCB had been created forty-eight years earlier it owned 203 collieries in south Wales; when it was disbanded it had just two.

There was little resistance to this final contraction; the miners had no fight left in them. Generous redundancy packages of up to £1,000 per year of service were particularly tempting given the large debts many had built up during the strike. Older workers could never have saved a sum like £30,000 in any other way and even younger ones could receive enough to buy their houses. However, the packages were sometimes on offer only for a period as short as forty-eight hours, which meant that fighting a closure would come at a huge personal financial cost. Miners thus, quite fairly, complained that a gun was being held to their head. Accepting transfers also became increasingly pointless as it became evident that all pits were threatened. One miner spoke for many when he remarked: 'I'm sick and fed up with the Coal Board and their tactics. After thirty-four years ... I don't want to work for the Coal Board ever again.'[84] Blaengarw closed in December 1985 and only fifty of the 600 workforce accepted a transfer to another colliery. After the last shift workers burnt an NCB flag.[85]

But there were other emotions too: 'I had a broken heart when the pit closed, it was like a wake, everyone was upset, people had sold furniture, lost houses. It was all gone washed away everything we'd fought for had been swept away ... there was nowhere for me to go'.[86] For those whose friends and relatives had lost their lives in the industry there was a strong emotional tie with a local pit, which made closure all the harder. A sense of family history reinforced the moral claim such ties engendered and a miner at Celynen North reflected: 'my grandfather sank this shaft, now I'm filling it in ... it took them two years to dig this shaft – by hand; it will take two weeks to fill it up'.[87] The sense of despair and inevitability about it all was captured by one Beddau miner who remembered that he was heartbroken, 'But I thought "well, what can we do about it?" It's the Tory policy to close everything and privatize it, and I thought, "Well, you can't do anything, it's been announced." Life still had to go on.'[88]

It was not easy to find another job, however, especially in a context where there were suddenly a lot of local people all looking for jobs at the same time. The closure of the Ynysybwl and Lady Windsor collieries were estimated by the constituency MP to have caused another 1,000 spin-off jobs to be lost and local unemployment hit 34 per cent.[89] It was easier for colliery electricians and the like because their skills were transferable but faceworkers had very specialist skills and a reputation for being disruptive. A survey of Markham colliery found that barely a third of those who lost their jobs when the pit closed in 1985 were in work eighteen months later. Boredom and missing the social side of work were seen as the worst costs of unemployment, with more than twice as many workers in the survey mentioning these costs than anxiety about money.[90] Many miners simply dropped out of the labour market, encouraged by a welfare system that made it relatively easy to claim incapacity benefit. The effect was that in some Welsh districts the percentage of people registered as permanently sick nearly quadrupled between 1981 and 1991. In 1991, of a sample of men who had been south Wales miners in 1981 (and who were still of working age) 45 per cent were in employment, 16 per cent were unemployed and 39 per cent were not seeking employment (mostly because they were sick or had taken early retirement). This made south Wales the worst-off region for both new employment and economic inactivity among former miners.[91] Even where work was found, wages were generally much lower than in the mines. A 1994 survey of former miners from Taff Merthyr (which closed in 1993) found that the average take-home pay of men who had found new employment outside the coal industry was £153; as miners their average pay had been £270.[92] With perhaps more than half of former miners not working and low wages for those who were, the hostility towards those who had broken the strike festered. In particular, arguments grew about Scargill's leadership of the strike and the role of NACODS, the officials' union (the National Association of Colliery Overmen, Deputies and Shotfirers), which had worked on to ensure the collieries remained safe and thus able to reopen when the strike was over.[93] With little obvious to look forward to, many people seemed stuck in the legacy of the strike.

THE MINERS' DEFEAT was a watershed in Welsh history but it was not quite the cataclysmic event that it is often portrayed as. The key decade for the decline of Welsh coal was not after 1984, when 22,000 jobs were lost, but the ten years after 1958, when 50,000 mining jobs went. By 1981 the proportion of Welsh employees working in mining and quarrying was just 3.8 per cent.[94] Mining had a symbolic importance but its economic importance to Wales as a whole had long since faded. Nor was the strike the cause of the end of mining: the culprits there were oil and gas. Thatcher's government simply applied the final fatal blow to an industry that had long been in terminal decline, although that hardly excuses the relish with which it seemed to do it. The strike was, however, the last gasp of an old kind of politicized working-class solidarity. Never again would a trade union try or even contemplate taking on the whole state. With the strike died any realizable dream of British working-class power. Despite a few believers, in student unions and trade union meeting rooms, class politics was dead. The NUM, and with it the whole concept of a working-class labour movement, was physically, financially and ideologically spent. Indeed, trade unions themselves lost rapid ground. New legislation meant that calling a strike could be done only after a ballot of members, while the appetite for a fight also seemed to ebb away (figure 9.2). The membership of unions affiliated to the Wales TUC fell from 649,000 in 1979 to 484,900 in 2002, a figure which represented just 40 per cent of Welsh employees.[95]

It was not just the unions that lost power and influence. The economic problems that hit the industrial heartlands in the 1960s and the whole

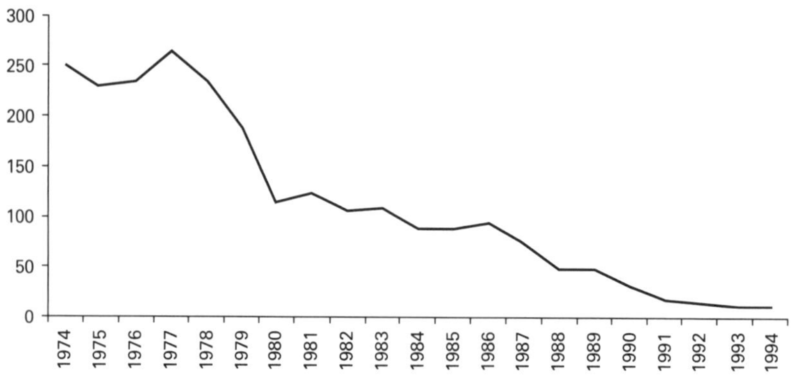

Figure 9.2 Number of industrial stoppages in Wales, 1974–94.

Source: *DWHS-3*, 148. This only includes disputes connected to terms and conditions of employment and stoppages involving more ten or more workers, except where the dispute lasted more than 100 days.

of Wales in the 1970s had already led people to lose faith in the Labour Party long before the strike. The resentment felt in Aberfan at how their community had been treated by Wilson's government had quickly extended to other parts of industrial Wales as the coal industry sank into terminal decline. There were significant tensions within the NUM over the government's actions and the loyalty demonstrated to Labour in return for nationalization began to fracture. The depth of that dissatisfaction was evident in the by-elections at Rhondda West (1967) and Caerphilly (1968), where Labour majorities of 16,888 and 21,148 were cut to 2,306 and 1,874 respectively. In 1967 one redundant miner declared: 'I'll never vote Labour again. What would I be voting for? A dead valley.'[96] After the Rhondda West by-election a pensioner from Treorchy who had switched to Plaid Cymru told the *Western Mail*, 'It was hard thing to do, but I feel that Labour closed down our pits, put men out of work without providing alternative jobs, and, being old-fashioned, I haven't forgiven them for what they did to our Welsh Sunday, by opening the public-houses. Don't use my name, I want to live in my peace with my neighbours.'[97] Those by-elections were protest votes and not repeated in general elections but from 1966 there was a clear decline in support for Labour (table 9.1). In 1966 in Wales 863,692 people voted Labour; in 1983 just 603,858 did. The party had lost over a quarter of million votes.

Table 9.1 General election results, Wales, 1964–83

	1964	1966	1970	1974	1974	1979	1983
Share of vote (%)							
Lab	57.8	60.7	51.6	46.8	49.5	47.0	37.5
Con	29.4	27.9	27.7	25.9	23.9	32.2	31.0
Lib	7.3	6.3	6.8	16.0	15.5	10.6	23.2
PC	4.8	4.3	11.5	10.8	10.8	8.1	7.8
Number of seats							
Lab	28	32	27	24	23	22	20
Con	6	3	7	8	8	11	14
Lib	2	1	1	2	2	1	2
PC	0	0	0	2	3	2	2
Winner	Lab	Lab	Con	Lab	Lab	Con	Con

The electorate was becoming increasingly aware of how, as one writer put it, 'unchallenged political power creates grubby nests where cosy improprieties fester'.[98] This was most evident in parts of local government, where nepotism and a lack of real democracy were a problem. There was some truth in the joke that councillors were 'not really in favour of local elections. They introduce an element of uncertainty into the council's business.' The problems of one-party rule had become obvious in Swansea, where rumours abounded in the 1970s that local councillors and officials were getting everything from international rugby tickets to trips to Amsterdam's red light district in return for favours. Such behaviour led the housing director and a former council leader to be convicted of corruption in 1977; both were sentenced to two years in prison.[99] Ultimately, such corruption was an extreme case but it added to people's lack of faith in local government and the Labour Party. Indeed, since the Profumo affair (see chapter 4), the popular respect for political parties and the establishment in general had been waning. Many felt worn down by the way society worked and no main party seemed to have the answers. In 1971 taxi drivers in Neath were said to moan about

> bureaucratic regulations that decreed one-way streets without consultation of street users. Of the schools 'system' that did not sufficiently consult the needs of parents. Of the social security 'system' that gives men so much reward for idleness that work hardly seems worthwhile. Of the Health Service 'system' that works so badly that people have to 'go private' and pay if they want operations.[100]

Academics studying Cardiganshire found that, for most people, 'politics is an unfamiliar and even distasteful activity'.[101] Although general election turnouts were holding up, Welsh surveys suggested that between 1970 and 1979 the proportion of people claiming a great deal of interest in politics had fallen from 31 to 15 per cent, while those saying they had not much or no interest in politics rose from 31 to 41 per cent. At the 1974 general election a Caerphilly housewife told a reporter, 'I've always voted Labour but I'm getting fed up with the big parties. Maybe I'll vote for Plaid Cymru – it may help to change things and the country needs a change.'[102] In 1973 Labour held 43 per cent of the seats on Wales' district councils; by 1976 it held just 29 per cent. That year Plaid Cymru took control of Merthyr Council, its first local-authority victory. As the birthplace of Welsh socialism, the symbolism was acute. The following year Labour lost 29 per cent of its Welsh county council seats, while the Tories doubled their number. In Mid Glamorgan and parts of the Gwent valleys it secured an average of 1,300 votes in each ward, compared with Plaid Cymru's average of 1,000.[103] Even in its heartlands, Labour was clearly in trouble.

The party did recover was from this low point but poor management of many local authorities was not its only self-inflicted wound. The Labour government of 1974–9 did little for its Welsh supporters and deeply upset some of them by trying to introduce devolution. At a UK level, deep rifts were emerging between the left and right wings of the party. Militants were never much more than a fringe in Wales but some of the more extreme ideas that began to emerge in the English Labour Party did not help its cause in Wales. Despite the talk of class conflict by senior Labour politicians and union leaders, there was little to suggest that the majority of working-class people anywhere in Britain were particularly radical. Antagonisms on the shop floor or refusing to cross another union's picket line were not the same as an ideological commitment to Marxism. Most workers were conscious of class but they were not class conscious in a political sense. Their commitment to the Labour Party was born out of a belief in the welfare state and a fear of the economic consequences of an uncontrolled free market. It was individuals and communities that mattered to most people and their active sense of being part of a working class often extended little further than voting Labour.[104] This was only too evident in the failure of the 1984–5 miners' strike to mobilize industrial support beyond that industry. It was also clear at the 1983 general election. An election survey suggested that in industrial south Wales three-quarters of voters thought that their personal position had deteriorated under Thatcher but only a quarter or so believed that Labour would improve their situation and less than a fifth saw Labour's

Michael Foot as the best leader of the main parties.[105] No wonder then that the Labour won 191,635 fewer votes in Wales in the 1983 general election than it had in 1979. It was outside the industrial heartlands that the Conservatives did best in Wales but in Pontypridd the Labour share of the vote fell to 45.6 per cent, in Torfaen to 47.9 per cent and in Wrexham to 34.3 per cent. In other words, more than half the voters of these formerly solid Labour communities were supporting other parties. Even in the Rhondda, more than 38 per cent of the votes were cast for parties other than Labour and the Tories actually won Bridgend. Not even those who were worst off were always voting for the party of the workers. A 1984 survey of skilled manual workers in Port Talbot, 40 per cent of whom had experienced some form of redundancy, found that only 60 per cent supported Labour.[106]

Much of the traditional commitment to Labour was historic, from people who had grown up before the Second World War, in an era when the party seemed to be the only one committed to the interests of the working class. Thus the fading of Labour support was partly just a matter of generational change; some of its most committed supporters were dying off. But voters were also becoming disillusioned with the structures that the party had put in place in 1945–51 to look after the working class. In 1974, surveys in Wales suggested that half of respondents did not think nationalization had been very important.[107] Even the welfare state was not always as popular as it once was. For some celebrants of traditional Wales, it was 'impersonal benevolence', the opposite of the traditions of 'friendship, love and mutual help' of the Welsh family. It had made Britain into 'a dull ordinary collection of human beings, cap-in-apprentices in the Welfare State'. Seventy-one per cent of people in a 1971 survey of Cardiganshire thought that the welfare state had made people lazy.[108]

The Labour Party itself was changing too. Whereas once Labour had been firmly a party of the people, its roots within local communities were dissolving. In 1959 there had been ten miners' MPs in Wales. Such figures had significant personal votes that lay above any consideration of party politics. Even a Conservative branch officer in Cardiganshire told academics in 1971 that he liked the local Labour MP, a local solicitor: 'I think I'll vote for him. I don't like his bloody politics though.'[109] But these politicians, deeply rooted in their communities and enjoying immense personal popularity, were in decline. By 1970 S. O. Davies (Merthyr) and Elfed Davies (Rhondda East) were the only MPs in Wales nominated by the NUM. By 1974 there were none. Instead, a new breed of Labour MP was emerging, who had grown up with the welfare state and enjoyed the social mobility it could offer. After a wave of retirements, three-quarters of the twenty-seven

Labour MPs elected in 1970 had professional backgrounds; twenty-one had been through higher education and as many as fifteen of them were either lawyers or teachers.[110] This was not to argue that they had no local connections. People like Labour leader Neil Kinnock were, after all, the sons of miners and had been raised locally, but their education had taken them out of those communities, however much they campaigned on local issues.

Those deserting Labour turned to a variety of alternatives. For a brief moment the Liberal–SDP Alliance was popular, taking nearly a quarter of the Welsh votes in the 1983 general election. Plaid Cymru was the obvious protest vote for those proud to be Welsh but its separatist policies were never going to win widespread support in industrial areas that were dependent on the British state for both jobs and social security. The Conservatives, meanwhile, were never as unpopular in Wales as folklore suggested. Even in 1966, the peak of the apparent Labour hegemony, the Tories still won 396,795 Welsh votes. In Rhondda West, one of the safest Labour seats in Britain, 1,955 people voted for the Cardiff doctor imported to be the Conservative candidate, not enough to secure the deposit but more than voted Communist and only 217 fewer than voted for Plaid Cymru.[111] The Welsh Conservatives were rooted in the middle class, a section of society that, through the 1970s, both grew with the development of the service sector and got increasingly angry at high taxes, union power and the general state of the country. This anger was evident in a letter to a Denbighshire paper that complained that 'No workmen have been pampered so much as these British dullards whose motto is more pay for less work'. A small-business owner in St Asaph said he voted Conservative in 1979 because he thought 'a powerful assertive attempt would be made to reduce, or contain, the power of a bureaucratic behemoth intent on domination'.[112] Before her election as Conservative leader, Margaret Thatcher said her priority would be regaining the ground her party had lost in Britain's industrial areas.[113] Fired up by the *Sun*, Wales' bestselling newspaper, the Conservatives under Thatcher did indeed win a sizable number of working-class votes thanks to the popular policy of selling council houses to tenants, Labour's uncertain defence policy, her stance over the Falklands and a desire to avoid any return to the disruption that unfettered union power could cause.

Labour remained Wales' largest party but it could no longer return rely on an automatic and emotional base of support. Neil Kinnock told a 1983 rally at Bridgend, 'If Margaret Thatcher wins on Thursday, I warn you not to be ordinary. I warn you not to be young. I warn you not to fall ill. I warn you not to get old.'[114] The fact that around half a million people in Wales still voted Conservative in 1983 and 1987 suggested that such rhetoric was falling on not a few deaf ears. Even Kinnock himself saw his majority decrease from over 20,000 to 14,380 in the election that followed his famous speech, a contest where there were little more than 100,000 votes between the Labour and Tory Welsh totals. As the economic turmoil deepened in the mid-1980s, Labour did win back some lost ground from the Alliance and Plaid Cymru, taking over 161,000 more votes in the 1987 general election than it had in 1983. But this, like its share of the vote, was still less than in 1979, while the Tories actually took more Welsh votes in 1987 than they had in 1983. Nonetheless, the commitment to Labour was apparently stronger in Wales than anywhere else in the UK. One small survey in 1987 suggested that 69 per cent of the working-class electorate in Wales voted Labour and 14 per cent voted Tory, whereas in the south of England only 30 per cent voted Labour, while 44 per cent voted Conservative.[115]

THE FACT THAT even 14 per cent of the Welsh working class were voting Conservative just a year after the post-war peak in unemployment illustrated how the fragmentation of the working class, which had begun in the 1950s with the retreat of workplaces where most local men were employed together, was continuing. By 1973 one Welsh novel was rejecting class as being 'as dated as TB'.[116] But people in the 1970s and 1980s still believed they lived in a class-based society, especially in areas where coal or steel continued to dominate the local economy. Even workers who were earning good wages still identified with the working class and were treated as workers at work. In the steel industry workers saw a class system, with the shop floor and some middle management drawn from the Valleys, while the upper management lived in rural conurbations and worked and ate separately in the day. This created a clear feeling of 'us and them'.[117] One historian remembers of growing up on a council estate in a mining community in the north-east in the 1970s and early 1980s:

> I was acutely aware of the importance of class divisions in Britain. A sense of 'them and us' pervaded every aspect of community life. This was most apparent in terms of education, the law and employment prospects. Large family gatherings, holidays in Blackpool, and a world that revolved around the pit, the pub and the betting shop, gave me a sense of a collective identity that I shared with other children. I soon realized that this identity was underpinned by class. To my family and others on the council estate, class was an uncomplicated term related to money and culture. It was a simple fact to all of us that the working class, 'us', had little money, while the middle and upper classes, 'them', had lavish amounts. Culturally we enjoyed

> popular music, action films, pubs, football and *Coronation Street*, while 'they' enjoyed opera, theatre, classical music and ballet.[118]

Such outlooks underpinned the success of and general sympathy for the miners' strikes of 1972 and 1974, but, with the ongoing decline of coal and steel, such experiences quite simply became less common. They also underemphasized the extent of divisions within such estates. Just because someone felt they were working class did not mean they felt the same as everyone else within the working class. For those members of the working class with jobs, disposable incomes were rising, giving access to what had once been luxuries like colour televisions and foreign holidays. Some people were buying their council homes, pushing them up the social scale, both practically and psychologically. This even allowed them to assert their individuality through something as simple as painting their front door a different colour to the local-authority standard. More and more people had non-manual jobs, which often paid less than skilled occupations in heavy industry but had something of a managerial image that could create a sense of difference. One Welsh sociologist thus talked of the emergence of a 'new working class', who lived a more privatized lifestyle in everything from DIY on bought council houses, to shopping at superstores rather than local shops, to watching videos rather than going to the pub or cinema.[119] The weakness of the Labour Party, a party built on the idea of common working-class interests, owed much to this fragmenting of that class.

The knowledge that Thatcher's Tories were winning working-class votes exacerbated the anger felt by some who were not sharing in the fruits of affluence. They may not have been rioting but Thatcher became hated in a way that no previous Conservative Prime Minister had. This was particularly evident during the 1984–5 miners' strike, when Thatcher was repeatedly and venomously referred to as 'her', 'she' or 'that woman'. The Alarm, a band from Rhyl, captured such anger in a 1984 song which cried 'You'd better look at what you have created and think of all the people who hate you'.[120] Yet rock bands like the Alarm were a minority taste. Far more popular in the 1980s were catchy pop songs that were an antidote to rather than a comment on hard times. New Romantics ruled the charts, while in Shakin' Stevens Wales had one of its most successful modern musicians ever, clocking up thirty-two top-forty records and enjoying success across Europe. Although he came from a deprived Cardiff council estate, his most popular songs were ditties about love, a green door, and Christmas. In this he was far more in tune with popular sentiment than those whose anger was politicized. Overt faith in the political system was becoming a thing of the past. Let down by and severed from the emotional pull of Labour, people in and out of work had more immediate and individualist responses to the economic collapse around them. By 1982, a survey was suggesting that 45 per cent of Welsh men were moderate or heavy drinkers. A *Western Mail* editorial argued in 1985: 'While toilet soap washes the outsides of millions, television soap washes their inner-selves – some would say unkindly, washes the mind clean of anything that resembles thought. True or not, the figures prove that it is what people want.'[121] More people in Wales watched a typical 1980s episode of *Coronation Street* than voted Labour in 1983 and even the party's 1987 vote failed to match the show's more popular storylines for popularity.[122]

In 1982 UK unemployment reached 3 million for the first time since the 1930s. Such a figure would have been seen as a political catastrophe before 1979 but popular values seemed to have changed. One reason was that rising property ownership made interest rates rather than unemployment levels the key public economic concern, a cultural shift that further undermined support for Labour.[123] The experience of the 1970s seemed to create a belief that inflation was a greater economic evil than unemployment and the growth in Conservative votes was a testimony to that. Nonetheless, through the 1980s there was widespread concern about the problem and UK surveys showed it was becoming less common to blame unemployment on the victims themselves, suggesting the Conservatives' notion of self-help and the responsibility of the individual was not fully accepted. The dominant belief was perhaps that people should work hard but if things did not go well it was not their fault. Yet few actually acted on their concerns for those on the dole and even many of the unemployed, including the miners after their defeat in 1985, seemed to accept their lot.[124] The inevitability of an economy that created inequalities and in which not everyone could find a job thus became accepted as an unpleasant truth in the 1980s. This new philosophy was a long way from the orthodoxies of the late 1960s and was as much a seismic shift as the collapse of the traditional Welsh industries.

Notes

1 *Report of the Tribunal Appointed to Inquire into the Disaster at Aberfan on October 21st, 1966* (1967), 25. I. McLean and M. Johnes, *Aberfan: Government and Disasters* (2000).
2 Draft minute from G. Thomas to H. Wilson, 23 July 1968, NA, COAL 73/5 and BD 11/3804.
3 McLean and Johnes, *Aberfan.*
4 Quoted in R. Griffiths, *S. O. Davies: A Socialist Faith* (1983), 256.
5 K. O. Morgan, *Modern Wales: Politics, Places and People* (1995), 290.
6 B. Khleif, 'Ethnic awakening in the first world: the case of Wales', in G. Williams (ed.), *Social and Cultural Change in Contemporary Wales* (1978), 108. *New Statesman*, 22 July 1966.

7 Unaccredited clipping, Merthyr Library, Aberfan Disaster Archive, D/17.
8 B. Curtis, 'The Wilson government and pit-closures in south Wales, 1964–70', *Llafur*, 9:1 (2004), 59–71. H. Francis and D. Smith, *The Fed: A History of the South Wales Miners in the Twentieth Century* (1998 edn), 452. K. Gildart, *North Wales Miners: A Fragile Unity, 1945–96* (2001), 62. G. L. Rees, *Survey of the Welsh Economy*, Commission on the Constitution research paper (1973), 126.
9 K. O. Morgan, *Rebirth of a Nation: Wales, 1880–1980* (1981), 318–19.
10 A. Burge and K. Davies, '"Enlightenment of the highest order": the education programme of the south Wales miners, 1956–71', *Llafur*, 7:1 (1996), 119. Francis and Smith, *The Fed*, 456.
11 Quoted in J. Sewel, *Colliery Closure and Social Change: A Study of a South Wales Mining Valley* (1975), 25.
12 S. W. Town, *After the Mines: Changing Employment Opportunities in a South Wales Valley* (1978), 38. Gildart, *North Wales Miners*, 110.
13 I. England, quoted in 'Wales in the 1970s', formerly at www.bbc.co.uk/wales/history/sites/walesyesterday/pages/1970s.shtml.
14 See for example *Rhondda Fach Observer, Leader and Free Press*, 8 July 1966.
15 *WM*, 24 Feb. 1970.
16 Max Boyce, *Live at Treorchy* (recorded 23 Nov. 1973).
17 K. Howells, in *Arcade*, 2 (14 Nov. 1980). Francis and Smith, *The Fed*, 456.
18 *Gwent Gazette*, 11 Oct. 1974. Gildart, *North Wales Miners*, 121. Town, *After the Mines*, 52.
19 M. Thomas, *The Death of an Industry: South Wales Mining and Its Decline, the Local Story in a Global Context* (2004), 106. Town, *After the Mines*, 37.
20 Welsh Office, *Wales: The Way Ahead*, Cmnd 3334 (1967). *WM*, 20 July 1967.
21 J. England, *The Wales TUC: Devolution and Industrial Politics* (2004), 9. G. Humphrys, *South Wales* (1972), 142.
22 *Financial Times*, 26 Nov. 1969.
23 Humphrys, *South Wales*, 61. Location of decimal factory and new Royal Mint, Memorandum by First Secretary of State and Secretary of State for Economic Affairs, 13 Apr. 1967, NA, CAB 129/129.
24 *Financial Times*, 29 Nov. 1976. G. Rees, 'Uneven development, state intervention and the generation of inequality: the case of industrial south Wales', in G. Rees and T. L. Rees (eds), *Poverty and Social Inequality in Wales* (1980), 202.
25 Quoted in M. Jones, *Life on the Dole* (1972), 135.
26 *Regional Statistics*, various volumes.
27 *WM*, 7 Jan. 1976. *DWHS-3*, 150, 26. Wales TUC Research Unit, *Unemployment in Wales: Problems and Prospects* (1975), 7.
28 P. Wilding, 'Income and wealth in Wales', in Rees and Rees (eds), *Poverty and Social Inequality*, 33–49.
29 *WM*, 15 Nov. 1973. A. Beckett, *When the Lights Went Out: Britain in the Seventies* (2009), 176–7.
30 *WM*, 13 Dec. 1973.
31 *WM*, 5 Jan. 1974. *The Times*, 10 Jan. 1974.
32 Thomas, *The Death of an Industry*, 169. K. D. George, L. Mainwaring, J. S. Shorey and D. R. Thomas, 'Coal', in K. D. George and L. Mainwaring (eds), *The Welsh Economy* (1988), 164.
33 P. Hannan, *The Welsh Illusion* (1999), 79.
34 *DWHS-3*, 148. Beckett, *When the Lights Went Out*, 496.
35 I. Crewe, N. Day and A. Fox, *The British Electorate, 1963–1987: A Compendium of Data from the British Election Studies* (1991), 292.
36 A. W. Turner, *Crisis? What Crisis? Britain in the 1970s* (2008), ch. 5. *DWHS-3*, 152, 137. England, *The Wales TUC*, 102.
37 Cabinet meeting, 20 Dec. 1972, NA, CAB 128/50/60.
38 *WM*, 3 Jan. 1980.
39 England, *The Wales TUC*, 53, 55. C. Baber and L. Mainwaring, 'Steel', in George and Mainwaring (eds), *The Welsh Economy*, 207.

40 L. D. Morris, 'Redundancy and patterns of household finance', *Sociological Review*, 32:3 (1984), 492–523.
41 *WM*, 4 Jan. 1980.
42 *DWHS-3*, 150. George and Mainwaring (eds), *The Welsh Economy*, 189, 26, 198.
43 *DWHS-3*, 141. Welsh Office, *Welsh InterCensal Survey 1986* (1987), 60. T. Rees, *Women and Work: Twenty-Five Years of Gender Equality in Wales* (1999), 10. C. C. Harris, 'Changing social conditions', in D. Cole (ed.), *The New Wales* (1990), 223.
44 J. Miller, *Situation Vacant: The Social Consequences of Unemployment in a Welsh Town* (1982), 10–14.
45 G. A. Williams, 'Land of my fathers', *Marxism Today*, Aug. 1982, 22.
46 Census profiles, excludes own account workers and agriculture. D. Smith in *Arcade*, 9 (6 Mar. 1981).
47 George and Mainwaring (eds), *The Welsh Economy,* 201, 233–61.
48 Quoted in Tom Forester, 'The moors murder', *New Society*, 9 Mar. 1971, 534.
49 C. Joll and S. Owen, 'Standards of living', in George and Mainwaring (eds), *The Welsh Economy*, 80. South Glamorgan 1981 census profiles.
50 *Guardian*, 8 Dec. 1980. *DWHS-3*, 142. Joll and Owen, 'Standards of living', 83.
51 R. Fevre, *Wales Is Closed: The Quiet Privatisation of British Steel* (1989), 23, 38–40. C. C. Harris, *Redundancy and Recession in South Wales* (1987), 15.
52 *Daily Mirror*, 14 Mar. 1980. *WM*, 3 Jan. 1980.
53 R. Griffiths, 'Resolving the contradictions between class and nation', in J. Osmond (ed.), *The National Question Again: Welsh Political Identity in the 1980s* (1985), 192–209. J. Osmond, *Police Conspiracy?* (1984). N. Crickhowell, *Westminster, Wales and Water* (1999), 33.
54 *Arcade*, 5 (9 Jan. 1981).
55 General secretary, Iron and Steel Trades Confederation, quoted in England, *The Wales TUC*, 55.
56 *WM*, 7 July 1981. *Arcade*, 20 (7 Aug. 1981).
57 *WM*, 17 Aug. 1978.
58 Harris, *Redundancy and Recession*, ch. 7. Miller, *Situation Vacant*, 56–7.
59 Harris, *Redundancy and Recession*, 132. P. Harris Worthington, 'Living without work', *PI*, 57 (1986), 82–96. Jones, *Life on the Dole*, 129–30.
60 *Arcade*, 32 (19 Feb. 1982). *WM*, 3 Apr. 1981.
61 *WM*, 28 Jan. 1985.
62 J. Davies, 'Brynmawr: then and now', *PI*, 51 (1985), 103.
63 Thomas, *The Death of an Industry*, 94–5.
64 Quoted in H. Francis, 'The valleys', in R. Jenkins and A. Edwards (eds), *One Step Forward? South and West Wales Towards the Year 2000* (1990), 112.
65 A. Evans, 'Coal in the 1980s and 1990s', *Moving Left in Wales*, 2 (winter 1983), 4.
66 S. Morgan, *Men on Strike: Masculinity and the Miners' Strike of 1984–5 in South Wales*, PhD thesis, Swansea University (2007), 82. H. Francis and G. Rees, '"No surrender in the valleys": the 1984–5 miners' strike in south Wales', *Llafur*, 5:2 (1989), 41–71.
67 Quoted in H. Francis, *History on Our Side: Wales and the 1984/5 Miners' Strike* (2009), 26.
68 A. J. Richards, *Miners on Strike: Class Solidarity and Division in Britain* (1996), 49, 109.
69 Francis and Rees, 'No surrender', 60. Morgan, *Men on Strike*, 255, 335. Thomas, *The Death of an Industry*, 220.
70 BBC Wales, *Week In, Week Out* (1984), online at www.bbc.co.uk/wales/history/archive/?theme_group=society_and_culture&theme=miners_strike&set=miners_strike. *The Times*, 6 Oct. 1984.
71 Morgan, *Men on Strike*, 301. Thomas, *The Death of an Industry*, 244.
72 For examples of the violence see J. Hunt, *From Despair to Where? Coal, Capital and the New Economy*, PhD thesis, Cardiff University (2004), 104–5.
73 R. Granelli, *Dark Edge* (1997), 37.
74 *Dora's Story* (Red Flannel Films, 1993). S. Morgan, '"Stand by your man": wives, women and feminism during the miners' strike, 1984–85', *Llafur*, 9:2 (2005), 59–71.

75 Granelli, *Dark Edge*, 20.
76 A. King, *British Political Opinion, 1937–2000: The Gallup Polls* (2001), 337. R. Vinen, *Thatcher's Britain: The Politics and Social Upheaval of the Thatcher Era* (2009), conclusion and 146. K. Howells, 'After the strike', *Planet*, 51 (1985), 6–11.
77 D. Bush, *Summer 1984*, in M. Stephens (ed.), *A Book of Wales* (1987), 11.
78 Francis, *History on Our Side*, 57. Richards, *Miners on Strike*, 134.
79 L. Dee and K. Keineg (eds), *Women in Wales: A Documentary of Our Recent History* (1987), 103.
80 D. Bush, *Glass Shot* (1991), 56, 59.
81 Vinen, *Thatcher's Britain*, 173.
82 George *et al.*, 'Coal', 166.
83 Thomas, *The Death of an Industry*, 261.
84 Richards, *Miners on Strike*, 212. Francis, *History on our Side*, 77.
85 *Radical Wales*, 10 (spring 1986).
86 Morgan, *Men on Strike*, 318.
87 Richards, *Miners on Strike*, 22, 32.
88 Quoted in M. Thomas, 'A colliery closure and the miner's experience of redundancy', *CW*, 4 (1991), 45–65.
89 *HC Deb*, 2 Mar. 1988, vol. 128, c. 1064.
90 V. Wass and L. Mainwaring, 'Economic and social consequences of rationalization in the south Wales coal industry', *CW*, 3 (1989), 161–86.
91 J. Morris, 'McJobbing a region: industrial restructuring and the widening socio-economic divide in Wales', in R. Turner (ed.), *The British Economy in Transition: From the Old to the New?* (1995), 64. E. Fieldhouse and E. Hollywood, 'Life after mining: hidden unemployment and changing patterns of economic activity amongst miners in England and Wales, 1981–91', *Work, Employment and Society*, 13:3 (1999), 483–502.
92 Valleys' Initiative for Adult Education, *Chasing the Dragon: Creative Community Responses to the Crisis in the South Wales Coalfield* (1996), 8.
93 Richards, *Miners on Strike*, 164–5.
94 McKenna, 'The overall level of activity', in George and Mainwaring (eds), *The Welsh Economy*, 26.
95 England, *The Wales TUC*, 82.
96 *Observer*, 22 Jan. 1967.
97 *WM*, 11 Mar. 1967.
98 A. Richards, *Carwyn: A Personal Memoir* (1984), 89.
99 C. Davies, *Welsh Jokes* (1978), 22. *The Times*, 31 May 1977.
100 *South Wales Magazine*, summer 1971.
101 P. J. Madgwick, N. Griffiths and V. Walker, *The Politics of Rural Wales: A Study of Cardiganshire* (1973), 230.
102 I. Crewe, N. Day and A. Fox, *The British Electorate, 1963–1987: A Compendium of Data from the British Election Studies* (1991), 164. *The Times*, 23 Feb. 1974.
103 D. Tanner, 'Facing the new challenge: Labour and politics, 1970–2000', in D. Tanner, C. Williams and D. Hopkin (eds), *The Labour Party in Wales, 1900–2000* (2000), 271. J. Osmond, *Creative Conflict· The Politics of Welsh Devolution* (1977), 128.
104 Gildart, *North Wales Miners*, 254.
105 Tanner, 'Facing the new challenge', 285.
106 Fevre, *Wales Is Closed*, 97.
107 Crewe *et al.*, *British Electorate*, 355.
108 C. Hughes, *Portrait of Snowdonia* (1967), 97, 153. Madgwick *et al.*, *The Politics of Rural Wales*, 128.
109 Madgwick *et al.*, *The Politics of Rural Wales*, 214.
110 I. McAllister, 'The Labour Party in Wales: the dynamics of one-partyism', *Llafur*, 3 (1981), 83.
111 Morgan, *Modern Wales*, 287–90.
112 *Denbighshire Free Press and North Wales Times*, 5 Feb. 1971. *LDP*, 9 Dec. 1980.

113 M. Garnett, *From Anger to Apathy: The Story of Politics, Society and Popular Culture in Britain since 1975* (2008), 48.
114 Quoted in M. Westlake, *Kinnock: The Biography* (2001), 208.
115 A. Heath, J. Curtice, R. Jowell, G. Evans, J. Field and S. Witherspoon, *Understanding Political Change: The British Voter* (1991), 108.
116 A. Richards, *Home to an Empty House* ([1973] 2006), 106.
117 *Arcade*, 5 (9 Jan. 1981).
118 Gildart, *North Wales Miners*, ix.
119 D. Adamson, 'Lived experience, social consumption and political change: Welsh politics into the 1990s', in G. Day and G. Rees (eds), *Regions, Nations and European Integration: Remaking the Celtic Periphery* (1991), 103–23. D. Adamson, *Class, Ideology and the Nation: A Theory of Welsh Nationalism* (1991), chs 7 and 8.
120 'Marching on', from *Declaration* (1984).
121 *DWHS-3*, 297. *WM*, 1 Feb. 1985.
122 This assumes an average audience of 15 million and that the proportion of people watching the programme was equal to the Welsh proportion of the UK population (4.9 per cent in 1981). The peak for *Coronation Street* in the 1980s was 26.6 million, in 1987, which might mean that 1.3 million people in Wales watched the show.
123 P. Clarke, *Hope and Glory: Britain, 1900–2000* (2004), 384.
124 I. Crewe, 'Values: the crusade that failed', in D. Kavanagh and A. Seldon (eds), *The Thatcher Effect: A Decade of Change* (1989), 244. Vinen, *Thatcher's Britain*, 132–3.

10

'Under an acid rain.' Debating the nations, 1970–85

> For me, one of the most striking developments is a growth of self-confidence; a willingness of the Welsh to be themselves. It is only now, in the last quarter of the twentieth century, that the bulk of Welsh people feel able to regard themselves as absolute equals with Englishmen, to squash the old and imposed inferiority and to stop apologizing for being Welsh. It has taken a long time and the cure is by no means complete and universal. But it is progressing steadily.
>
> Trevor Fishlock, *Talking of Wales* (1976), 13

> Some kind of human society, though God knows what kind, will no doubt go on occupying these two western peninsulas of Britain, but that people, who are my people and no mean people, who have for a millennium and a half lived in them as a Welsh people, are now nothing but a naked people under an acid rain.
>
> Gwyn A. Williams, *When Was Wales?* (1985), 305

FOUR MONTHS BEFORE his investiture, Prince Charles had attended the Wales *v.* Ireland rugby union international at Cardiff Arms Park. Since rugby was widely considered to be something of a popular Welsh obsession it was probably a deliberate part of the wider campaign to ingratiate Charles with the Welsh public. In its match report *The Times* noted, 'when the Prince of Wales came striding across the field in the sunshine, to his own tune, the crowd took him massively to their hearts and the singing of the national anthems was emotionally unrestrained'.[1] Here was the reconciliation of Wales' dual nationalities that the investiture was designed to promote. Wales won a bad-tempered game thanks to some artistry from their backs. The fly-half was one of Gwynfor Evans' constituents, Barry John, a player so talented and revered that he was to become known as 'The King'. His skills were sublime yet they seemed casually executed; they won him such adoration that women even curtsied to him. Wales won the Triple Crown that year, marking the beginning of the golden age of Welsh rugby. The backs in particular – players like John, Gareth Edwards, J. P. R. Williams, Gerald Davies and Phil Bennett – excited fans and journalists alike and drew parallels with the 'total football' played by the famous Dutch soccer sides of the 1970s. Wales won the Five Nations championship six times between 1969 and 1979, collecting three Grand Slams and six Triple Crowns in the process. It was a decade when, according to *The Times*, Welshmen expressed 'their tribal loyalty and some of their identity and surface nationalism' through the game.[2] Yet, in 1979, that tribal loyalty and identity seemed rather shallow when the Welsh electorate threw out a proposal to establish a Welsh Assembly and become a self-governing nation for the first time in their history. The recriminations began before the vote had even taken place.

Rugby (like football) had long since provided an alternative to such political bickering and it was coming to matter even more. A 1973 short story noted the importance of the local team:

> If the Welsh language was threatened, the coal industry staggering undermanned on its last legs, the Methodist chapels boarded up, the town Fifteen still retained the élan of old. They were a supreme in-group and the kudos attached to them was in no way diminished by the ravages of the sixties. Pop groups and cinema stars were outside figures, but the Fifteen, the boys, as Ronnie called them, remained local property and were regarded with tribal affection.[3]

Players in the 1970s remained local property and locally based because rugby union was an amateur game; unlike in football, there were no financial incentives to move to an English club. The players themselves were a mixture of English speakers and Welsh speakers and a combination of manual workers and the products of grammar schools; they were a reflection of the nation they represented. With industrial Wales in decline, the number of teachers, students, doctors and other public sector workers who played international rugby was increasing. Those who did start in heavy industry, like Phil Bennett, who began his working life in a steelworks, took advantage of their stardom and often moved on to more comfortable occupations, notably in sales. Welsh rugby actually interpreted amateurism rather liberally. Many smaller clubs made covert direct cash payments to their players to prevent them being lured away. When players did switch clubs, financial inducements were not uncommon. Similarly, expenses (for money foregone or spent while playing) could be very generous. There were even sponsorship deals for the star players from boot manufacturers. Some of the bigger teams refused to make financial transactions but, with the help of local firms, offered rewards in kind such as easy jobs, free cars and clothing. Rugby certainly opened doors for players in business and consultancy, where their fame was attractive to both employer and customer. People wanted to be associated with the best players, which meant that there were free meals, drinks and holidays to be enjoyed. John Taylor said of his fellow internationals, 'He will undoubtedly have better job prospects than his peers and will also enjoy the benefits of being a celebrity. Anything from suits to motor cars will be offered at trade prices and if he can stand the non-stop questions on the game, he will never have to buy a drink.'[4]

For the supporters drinking was an important part of match day but getting an actual ticket was never easy. Cardiff Arms Park itself became a Welsh Mecca, adorned on match days with red rosettes, leeks and daffodils, and ringing to the sound of the hymn 'Cwm Rhondda' and Max Boyce's 'Oggy-Oggy-Oggy, Oy-Oy-Oy'. Such behaviour upset some of the conservative older generation, as did the decline in the quality and range of hymn singing, but both players and spectators held the stadium and its acoustics in special affection. Winger Gerald Davies noted of the crowds in Cardiff: 'North and South Wales accents co-mingle, as do the Welsh and English languages. The nation is one today.'[5] The descent of people from across Wales to the National Stadium also contributed to a growth in the acceptance of Cardiff as the capital it had been declared in 1955. Lacking the apparatus of a nation state, sport was the only sphere where Cardiff actually provided the rest of Wales with something tangible to match its capital status. The impact of the national fifteen's victories went far beyond those watching in the stadium. With interest bolstered by a patriotic media that consciously saw the broadcasting of rugby as an 'instrument of nation-building', television enabled internationals to become national events that touched areas outside the game's historic hinterlands, notably in north Wales, traditionally a football area.[6] The move to colour broadcasting made the matches all the more vivid. For four Saturday afternoons a year, rugby seemed to bring much of Wales to a standstill, as it won the interest of even those for whom sport was a marginal aside at all other times. With the rise of more independently minded women with their own jobs, there were more females following and watching rugby too, although others took advantage of the fact that the shops were quiet on international days. Rugby, an important part of male popular culture in south Wales since the late nineteenth century, was now embracing a much broader social and geographical spectrum. It was becoming a genuinely national game.

Regular victories created a sense of confidence and even arrogance among Welsh fans, something that offended many English people within the sport. From the late 1960s, t-shirts celebrating the Free Wales Army were visible in the crowd, but it was the loud and routine booing of 'God save the Queen', the national anthem of both the English and the British, that was most the obvious sign of a concerted nationalism of sorts. Its playing could be justified at matches in Cardiff against England and Scotland, since it was the visitors' requested anthem, but its inclusion at clashes against France was less explicable. At such games, the spectacle of three anthems (Welsh, British and French) being played made no sense to many when there were only two teams playing. The booing of the British anthem quickly became an embarrassment and, from 1974, the Welsh Rugby Union (WRU) dropped it altogether for the visits of the French. There were problems at away games too. Everyone in Wales might have thought 'Hen wlad fy nhadau' was the Welsh national anthem but it had no official status and the other rugby nations were only slowly coming to recognize Wales' developing cultural nationalism. The anthem's inclusion for Wales' visit to Twickenham in 1968 appears to have set a precedent within Britain, while the French first played the Welsh anthem in Paris in 1971; yet at the end of the decade, and to much booing, they were still also playing 'God save the Queen' when Wales visited. Perhaps because of the booing of their anthem at Cardiff, the Rugby Football Union refused to allow 'Hen wlad fy nhadau' to played at Twickenham in 1974. In response, the WRU threatened to not allow 'God save the Queen' for future English visits. The RFU backed down and Welsh nationality was recognized.

Clive Rowlands, the Welsh coach from 1968 until 1974, held team meetings in the captain's small hotel room. Phil Bennett remembered,

> Wearing his Wales tie and pullover, Clive would pace the room, fag in hand, ranting and raving. He would demand you performed not just for yourself, but for your father, your mother, your long-lost aunt, the miners, the steelworkers, the teachers, the schoolchildren – in effect the whole Welsh nation. You were their representatives and you owed it to them to deliver. By the end of this sermon, some boys would be head-butting the walls and others would be crying their eyes out.

Such patriotic speeches could produce emotional displays on the pitch but they could only work so many times. Some stars became a 'little bored by all the nationalistic stuff'; others felt having to shout answers to rousing questions was a bit like being at the pantomime.[7] Yet all players spoke of their pride in donning the Welsh shirt and in 1977 Bennett was said to have rallied his team-mates before a match by declaring the English had 'taken our coal, our water, our steel: they buy our houses and live in them a fortnight a year.... Down the centuries these English have exploited and pillaged us – and we're playing them this afternoon boys.'[8] This may have helped raise the tempo of psyched-up sportsmen about to enter the field of play but it was not necessarily a political sentiment shared by the whole team. There were some players, like Ray Gravell, who idolized Owain Glyndŵr and for whom playing for Wales seemed to be a near-spiritual event. In contrast, J. P. R. Williams was the son of doctor, had been driven to primary school in his father's Rolls Royce and then educated at an English public school. He must have had rather a different understanding of what being Welsh meant.[9]

Yet such niceties did not matter in rugby, where, for fans and players alike, divided understandings of Wales were subsumed beneath the heady patriotism of the occasion, particularly when England were the opposition. The internationals provided thousands with, in the 1972 words of one historian, 'a fix of "Welshness"'.[10] That year Trevor Fishlock, *The Times'* Welsh correspondent, wrote that crowds at the Arms Park,

> swaying sparkle-eyed to the roared out anthem, are involved in a great communal experience, in the electric unity of tribalism ... many of them do not know the meaning of the Welsh words of the anthem that they learned parrot-fashion at school or chapel or on grandfather's knee. Yet there is an element in their singing of affirming their identity.[11]

Such reactions were part and parcel of the growing consciousness and pride in Welshness that emerged in the 1960s with the growth of political nationalism, Welsh broadcast media, Welsh-language teaching and the fading of associations with a repressive Nonconformity. Welsh patriotism had always been there in sport but the overtly confident, even aggressive edge to it was new. The widespread attention that Welsh successes achieved meant that, like bilingual road signs and the activities of language campaigners (chapter 7), rugby was part of the everyday 'banal nationalism' that helped sustain a sense of national identity among a disparate people.[12] It flagged up and reminded people of the existence of their nation and in doing so reaffirmed that nation, a nation that was often otherwise, for English monoglots at least, an abstract concept with little relevance in daily life. Furthermore, rugby glossed over the different meanings that the people of Wales attached to their nationality, enabling them to assert, maybe even understand, their Welshness in the face of internal division and the political, social and cultural shadow of England. This may not have created or reproduced a sense of national identity that pervaded all walks of life but it did contribute, in some intangible way, to Welshness being one of the identities that people saw in themselves. Quite simply, the successes on the rugby field in the 1970s did much to overcome the old insecurities that beset an English-speaking Welsh identity and to bring together the strands that had emerged in the 1950s and 1960s of a renewed sense of Welshness. However, those insecurities never quite disappeared and the dismantling of much of the traditional industrial base of Wales and the debacle of the 1979 referendum on devolution injected new life into old worries. By the 1980s talk of the death of Wales had resurfaced.

THE PATRIOTISM OF the rugby arena was music to the ears of political nationalists. The Arms Park on the day of an international provided an emotional opening scene for a Plaid Cymru party political broadcast at the October 1974 general election. Some nationalists saw the rugby glories as having the potential to inspire a national revival. In 1975 a poet wrote proudly in Welsh that Barry John would 'eradicate the scar of a shrivelled people.... Anyone who has known his genius can never grovel to foreign crowns.'[13] The confidence, even arrogance, that surrounded Welsh rugby was certainly in contrast to the earlier sense of inferiority that so many saw in Wales and it seemed to indicate something was changing. In 1975 a Plaid Cymru conference was told by the party chairman that Wales was at the beginning of a golden age, with the differences between Wales and England clearer than ever and hope and excitement for the future. In 1978 Trevor Fishlock claimed that rugby reflected 'the mood of modern Wales, the new confidence and pride in Welshness. It seems reasonable to relate the so-called golden age in rugby to the new awareness and the shaking off of old shackles.'[14] The new confidence was also evident in the lack of tolerance of external humour at Wales' expense. The BBC endured a barrage of complaints when *The Two Ronnies* parodied the Welsh anthem in 1977. The sketch was left out of the repeat. A greater consciousness of being Welsh was also evident in surveys; in 1979 one suggested that, when forced to choose, 57 per cent of the electorate labelled themselves Welsh but only 34 per cent British.[15]

Rugby was, of course, not the only source of a growing sense of Welshness in the 1970s. The reorganization of local government in 1974 gave new Welsh titles to counties formerly known by Anglicized names and a new generation of English speakers grew up whose Welshness was explicitly flagged by living in Gwent, Dyfed, Powys and Clwyd. The popular sense of Welshness was also becoming rooted in a pride in local communities, with their industrial heritage, sociableness, cultural traditions and distinct accents. Little of this may have been distinctly Welsh but people imagined it that way. It was also often fed by a sense of family history, where people knew that their grandparents or even parents had spoken Welsh.[16] The interest in the history and character of industrial communities increased because such places were in decline with the retreat of the coal industry and it was evident in the success of Llafur, a society formed in 1970 that brought together academics and ordinary people to celebrate, record and study Welsh working-class history. The loss of the Welsh language within families was thus gradually becoming a source of regret rather than a conscious choice. More positive attitudes to the Welsh language were also evident in 1977 when the WRU made the covers of its Five Nations match programmes bilingual and in 1978 when the Royal Welsh Agricultural Society did the same for its prize cards.[17] Like the WRU putting 'Dynion' on the doors of its male toilets, this was perhaps little more than tokenism but it was done nonetheless.

Another product of the resurgent popular Welshness was a growth in popularity of Welsh-medium education among monoglot English families. Some 80 per cent of children at Rhydfelen (Pontypridd), a school which had grown from eighty pupils when it opened in 1962 to 750 in 1973, came from homes where Welsh was not the norm. At the Welsh-medium primary in Barry the figure was over 90 per cent.[18] The attraction of Welsh-medium education may have been closely linked to people's aspirations for their children in the employment market and the numbers involved may have been small (there were fewer than 10,000 children in Welsh primary schools in English-speaking areas at the end of the 1970s) but they did impact on the sense of nationality of those who attended. A survey of sixth-formers in the mid-1970s suggested that the group with the strongest Welsh identification was found in Welsh-medium schools in predominantly English-speaking areas. There, 96 per cent chose Welsh before British as their nationality, whereas in English-medium schools in the same areas only 64 per cent did.[19] Learning Welsh also started to become popular in evening classes in the 1970s and the updating of the language's image was evident in the books that taught people about ordering beer and making comments about women's breasts in Welsh.[20]

The 1960s growth of specifically Welsh media that had contributed to people's sense of Welshness outside Y Fro Gymraeg also continued apace. The development of cheap VHF radio sets finally made the BBC's long-cherished idea of separate radio stations for the two languages of Wales possible. Radio Cymru launched in 1977, although a quarter of Welsh households were unable to receive it because of reception problems or simply because they did not own a VHF set. Radio Wales began in 1978 on the waveband vacated by Radio 4's move to long wave. Not was everyone impressed by these new national stations. There were complaints that Radio Wales was too southern, while the *Rhondda Leader* criticized the station for being 'pop and prattle'.[21] But it was another step towards a Welsh civil society and a popular culture that, while not always distinctively Welsh in its content, at least spoke with a Welsh accent. By 1982 over a quarter of Welsh adults claimed to listen to the station at least once a week. Audience research for the BBC that year suggested that the station, like BBC Wales and HTV Wales television, was more popular with those who identified themselves with Wales before Britain.[22]

The amount of Welsh on television was also slowly on the up, and totalling more twelve hours a week by 1971–2.[23] Some people watched simply because the programmes were in Welsh but most viewers were more interested in quality. A lot of the content remained rather traditional but there were some Welsh-language programmes that were both innovative and entertaining. The comedy *Fo a Fe*, which began on the BBC in 1970, was not only funny but caught and played on the rift and distrust in Welsh-speaking Wales between north and south, and literary, Nonconformist culture and a popular one more concerned with gambling and drinking. At its height the show was attracting almost 250,000 viewers, not far off half the Welsh-speaking population of Wales.[24] The soap opera *Pobl y Cwm*, first broadcast in 1974, was the other big success of Welsh-language television. It was credible, well written and did not moralize; it was also hugely popular. There was no equivalent English-language soap set in Wales. Had there been, then Welsh viewing tastes might not have been quite as dominated by programmes like *Crossroads* and *Coronation Street*. Nonetheless, both the BBC and HTV strove to ensure that television, not least in its coverage of news and sport, produced distinctly Welsh outputs through the English language. They received their share of critical acclaim but that did not change the fact that monoglot-English viewers' favourite programmes seemed to come from the other side of the border.[25]

It was thus unsurprising that the old insecurities could still be felt in 1970s Wales, whatever was happening on the rugby field. Fiction still talked about a Welsh sense of inferiority to England.[26] Rugby, the arena where this clearly did not exist, was not even as pervasive in Welsh life as it first seemed. In the north, football was more popular and the great Liverpool sides of the 1970s probably had as many north Walian followers as Welsh rugby did. Rugby was also, of course, a predominantly masculine arena, despite its growing female following. One woman from Mountain Ash pointed out in 1978, 'It is easier than you might imagine to live all your life in the Valleys and never see a rugger match – almost as easy as living in London and never running into a Beefeater'. For her, rugby was 'a background noise – a thing you hear men arguing about in trains and women complaining about in cafés'.[27] In 1979 an estimated 46 per cent of Welsh households tuned in to watch Wales play Ireland on one Saturday afternoon. In terms of viewing figures this was very impressive but it still meant that more than half the nation was doing something else.[28] That did not mean rugby that did not sustain and develop Welsh identity. The game may have been background noise to some people, but their inescapable awareness of the importance others placed on the game was still an affirmation that Wales mattered somehow.

There remained profound differences between the culture of English-speaking working-class communities and that of Welsh-speaking Wales. This was evident in the jokes of Grenfell 'Gren' Jones. His cartoons in the *South Wales Echo* and the *Western Mail* ran from 1968 until 1999 and were immensely popular, something to be collected and shared with friends and family. They were a story the south Welsh told about themselves, a story of a rugby-mad, self-deprecating people who wanted to get on but were community-rooted, a people proud to be Welsh but bemused by north Walians with their funny accents and funny language. Such an outlook formed the backbone of 1970s Welsh joke books – Plaid Cymru's small-holdings policy? 'Five acres and a Welsh-speaking cow' – although there was plenty of humour at the expense of the rugby-obsessed drunk misogynists of the south too. Beneath such jokes was a (not entirely unfounded) resentment that many Welsh speakers thought the working-class culture of south Wales was somehow not properly Welsh. In 1978 Leo Abse, the Labour MP for Pontypool, angrily told Gwynfor Evans that his constituency needed no lectures on nationality: 'we know how to express our Welshness in the front line of the Wales pack'. That to him was being Welsh, not 'retreating to the parish pump and becoming ancient Britons'.[29] Yet the culture of places like Pontypool could not even be seen, quite deliberately, during the 1970s at St Fagans, the Welsh folk museum located near Cardiff. The prejudices towards the south ran deeper than nationality and a letter to the *Daily Post* from Llangefni claimed that the majority in the south were 'Labour, Marxist, or Trotskyite' and 'of a rebellious mentality and strike-happy'. It concluded that south Walians were 'heavy drinkers' and 'their thinking must be befuddled as a consequence'. No wonder then that a 1977 article in *The Times* concluded that if the letters pages of the local press were to be believed then 'most Welshmen think most of their countrymen are either spendthrift, intolerant, extremist drunks, or pious kill-joy, extremist peasants'.[30] The exclusion of those who did not speak Welsh from some ideas of Wales fed the anger of those who still saw the language as 'a nuisance, a nonsense, an irrelevance, an imposition, even a kind of pollution'.[31] Such attitudes were certainly less common than in the 1950s and 1960s but just how widespread they continued to be is difficult to tell. Ron Davies remembered of his time as a councillor in the Rhymney valley that the Welsh language 'was something you were either "for" or "against"; there wasn't much room for neutrality'.[32] A survey for a devolution commission found that roughly three-quarters of respondents thought official things like forms and road signs should be bilingual but when it came to education attitudes were far more divided. Twenty-two per cent of respondents wanted teaching in Welsh abolished in all junior schools and 25 per cent in all secondary schools. Only 29 per cent thought the language should be taught to all children.[33] In other words, a majority accepted Welsh had a place but attitudes were divided on what that place should be. The split attitudes towards the language were clear in 1975 when Rhymney Valley District Council narrowly rejected changing the spelling of Caerphilly to Caerfili, following Welsh Office advice that where two similar forms of a place-name existed only the Welsh version should be used. Even in Gwynedd, the local council in Barmouth resisted pressure in the mid-1970s to adopt the Welsh version of the town's name (Abermaw). Other places still did not even want to be in Wales and in 1975 councillors in the border village of Llanymynech (Powys) lobbied the Post Office to have their county address changed to Shropshire.[34]

This was all more than petty prejudice. The deepening troubles in Northern Ireland provided a constant reminder in the 1970s of how nationalism could explode into violence. One writer called it a 'moral dilemma' that he, like many others, resented learning Welsh at school but felt sorry that the language was dying out. He saw a tension between state intervention and regulation and the need to allow moral freedom and choice.[35] The economic turbulence of the 1970s meant that people worried about whether separatism would bring further job losses. Jokes about lifeguards who could not swim but got jobs because they spoke Welsh were rooted in a real sense of disenfranchisement, marginalization and powerlessness. A Wrexham man told the government's devolution inquiry that a 'close-knit numerically small group of Welsh speakers [is] dictating policy upon important issues to the largely fragmented and disorganised non-Welsh speaking majority'.[36] Such attitudes were not helped when a Plaid Cymru councillor in the Cynon valley remarked in 1974 that Labour bred 'a race of school caretakers and educational welfare officers', while Plaid bred the professional classes. For one Labour councillor this confirmed his view that there was no difference between nationalists and Conservatives.[37]

Whatever some people thought about the economic advantages given to Welsh speakers, there was actually little sense of optimism in Welsh-speaking circles through most of the 1970s. By the middle of the decade the language campaigns that had helped unite so much of the Welsh-speaking community, at least over the cause if not the methods, had ebbed away. The deteriorating economic climate had diverted the media gaze and perhaps the attention of some young people. The first generation of protestors were getting older, settling down and probably less willing to contemplate prison. Victories over road signs, bilingual forms and the continued growth of Welsh-medium education had taken some of the sting out of the cause by ending some of the most visible impediments to the language, even though implementing the changes was rather slow. Across youth culture, idealism seemed to be being replaced by a cynicism and pessimism that thought little concrete change had actually come about from the wistful optimism of the 1960s. The language itself continued to decline and in the heartlands it seemed to be under a new threat from English in-migration (see chapter 13). There was a growing realization that the social mobility Welsh speakers were now able to enjoy, thanks to jobs at the BBC and other public bodies, was helping to kill rural Welsh-speaking communities by drawing talent to Cardiff.[38] During the 1970s the Welsh language's status and public profile may have been stronger than ever but it was like a long-forgotten historic building whose façade is suddenly refurbished and appreciated while its foundations continue to collapse.

Religion was part of the language's traditional foundations but that too was in decline. In one rural Clwyd parish some people were attending Welsh services specifically to support the language but others were not attending because they could not understand the Welsh used, while some older people did not go because they did not even want to admit they spoke Welsh.[39] Purists, meanwhile, complained about how young people increasingly used a slipshod form of language and even government forms in Welsh could be full of grammatical and typographical errors.[40] While some made conscious efforts to speak correct Welsh, other first-language Welsh speakers regularly employed English words and phrases, especially when speaking about occupations or hobbies such as motoring or football where there was no well established Welsh vocabulary. Even where easy and well known Welsh words existed they were not always used. Some people, for example, regarded using the word 'trydan' as pretentious because it was not coined until after the English word for electricity had passed into common usage in Welsh. Such behaviour led Gwynfor Evans to complain of a 'daily onslaught' of English into the language.[41] Yet those who were formally taught Welsh, as either a first or a second language, actually often had a greater awareness of standardized conventions than previous generations who had just learnt Welsh at home. This meant that some dialect forms were dying out, furthering the sense of loss among those who worried about the language.[42]

The reorganization of local government in 1974 did offer some opportunities to strengthen the position of the language. The new local authorities in Welsh-speaking areas began to pay serious attention to how they could provide a bilingual service. From its inception, Gwynedd County Council began designating primary schools where instruction would be through the medium of Welsh and non-Welsh-speaking children would be given intensive language lessons. In its other schools the two languages were to be given equal school time, while the mother tongue of Welsh speakers was given special attention. At Gwynedd secondary schools every pupil was taught Welsh until the end of the fifth year and the teaching of other subjects through Welsh was strongly encouraged. The council made all its documents bilingual, with Welsh given priority, and it tried to allow the public to use its services in the language of their choice. It had wanted Welsh to be the language of its internal administration, with any non-Welsh-speaking employees having to learn Welsh. This, however, drew criticisms from the trade union Unison and the Commission for Racial Equality and staff were allowed to work in whichever language they chose. Despite the council's aim of creating a bilingual society, old habits were hard to break and English remained the dominant language in internal administration.[43] Those at the receiving end of public services were not accustomed to officialdom in Welsh either. Some admitted to not understanding the vocabulary on Welsh-language forms, although they might still fill them in on principle, but only after checking the questions in English. The government estimated that just 1 per cent of driving licence applications made in Wales in 1975 were in Welsh. Despite serving a predominantly Welsh-speaking area, it was reported that a tax office at Bangor had received only seven requests for Welsh-language taxation forms from the 3,000 employers it dealt with. Elystan Morgan, the Welsh-speaking Labour MP for Cardiganshire, summed up in 1973, 'There is something bizarre in a situation where scores of young people defy the courts and go to prison, very often egged on by respectable middle-aged men who would rather remain academic militants, and where at the same time perhaps only a few hundred people avail themselves of the Welsh forms when they are ultimately published.'[44]

A NEW PERCEIVED THREAT to Welsh emerged from the question of Europe, which nationalists initially thought would be another superstate that would devour Wales in the way they thought Britain had. It was the declining importance of trade with the Commonwealth and the obvious economic success of the new and much nearer European market that had led Britain to apply (unsuccessfully) in 1963 and 1967 for membership of the EEC, then better known as the Common Market. French opposition put a stop to those applications but the issue again encouraged people to consider both Wales' and Britain's position in the world. This was not always easy. As a columnist put it in *Welsh Farm News* in 1962,

> I'm still no wiser than ever over this business of the Common Market, but as far as I can make out from what everybody tells me, we're going in. That does not mean that there will not be ceaseless argument, and if politicians can't agree in one language, I don't see how they can hope to agree in a large number of different languages.[45]

Britain finally joined in 1973, once the obstinate De Gaulle was no longer in office. Farmers benefited from a new regime of subsidies but consumers found that food prices rose. Growing opposition within the Labour Party meant that after it returned to power it held a referendum in June 1975 on whether Britain should stay in.

The referendum raised questions not only about British sovereignty but also about the self-sufficiency of the Welsh and British economies. Supporters like the *Western Mail* pointed to the potential benefits to Wales of Europe's regional policies, while the 'yes' campaign told people to vote for a better future of their children: 'Vote No and you'll get a lonely Britain: a troubled Britain, a Britain with more jobs at risk and the danger of shortages of all kinds.' In contrast, the secretary of the Wales Trades Union Congress (TUC) claimed that 50,000–65,000 Welsh jobs would be at risk if Britain stayed in. On the day of the vote, the 'no' campaign drummed up support with an advertisement that declared 'Keep Your Children Off The Dole!'[46] No wonder then that many ordinary voters were rather perplexed. In Cardiff an elderly lady told the press she was voting 'yes' because Prime Minister Harold Wilson had said to and that was good enough for her. Another eighty-four-year-old lady from the city was voting 'no' because 'We won the war. I don't see why we should be dominated by foreign people.' Some, however, felt they did not understand the issue and even feared starving if Britain was cut off from Europe. On referendum day a cartoon in the *Western Mail* showed a voter flipping a coin in the voting booth and both sides feared there were more 'don't knows' than committed voters for either case.

The paper claimed that many ordinary voters would have voted 'no' before the campaign but now felt they 'had no choice but to vote, unenthusiastically but not without bewilderment, Yes'. The economic arguments for staying in were simply more persuasive. In the end, 64.8 per cent in Wales voted 'yes', compared with 68.7 per cent in England. The 'no' vote was highest in Mid Glamorgan, where it reached 43.1 per cent. The 'yes' vote was strongest in rural areas where people knew the advantages of Europe to agriculture. It reached 74.3 per cent in Powys.[47]

In a context where the Welsh economy was both in trouble and becoming more entwined with the wider world, the likelihood of Welsh nationalism growing was remote. If Britain was unable to stand alone economically then the chances of Wales doing so were very slim. The Scottish National Party (SNP) could point to North Sea oil in its argument that Scotland was a viable economic nation but Plaid Cymru had no such fallback and its support remained concentrated in Welsh-speaking areas. At the February 1974 general election the party took Merioneth and Caernarfon and came within three votes of taking Carmarthen, a seat which it then took in the October election that year. But, overall, Plaid Cymru lost twenty-six of its thirty-six deposits in that election and took just 10.8 per cent of the vote. Even in the Rhondda Plaid Cymru only took a few hundred more votes than the Tories.

Although Labour had offered some form of elected national council for Wales in its 1970 election manifesto, the failure for any nationalist threat to emerge at that election seemed to push the issue down Labour's agenda. At the first of the two 1974 general elections both the Conservatives and Labour were vague on devolution. The Tory manifesto said they were studying the report of the Royal Commission on the Constitution (see chapter 8), while Labour ignored it, despite having commissioned it in the first place. In Scotland, the backlash was clear when the SNP won 22 per cent of the vote and seven seats. By the October election Labour was offering a Welsh Assembly and the Tories, while not offering the indirectly elected assembly they offered Scotland, promised increased powers for the Welsh Secretary of State.[48] The SNP success ensured that devolution was firmly on the agenda, especially since the incoming Labour government needed the support of nationalist MPs. Despite some grassroots pressure within Labour and the elevation of committed devolutionist and Welsh speaker John Morris to Secretary of State of Wales, the Labour government's support for devolution remained half-hearted and support among its Welsh MPs was ebbing too.[49] A referendum of the kind used for the EEC question offered a solution that could avoid a divide within the Labour Party by passing the decision to the electorate. For the government, a devolution bill was thus a matter of political expediency rather than political principle. Many English MPs were, however, hostile and during the bill's committee stage, at the suggestion of a Scotsman sitting for a London constituency, an amendment was inserted requiring at least 40 per cent of the electorate to vote in favour for devolution to be enacted.

There was some administrative sense to the idea of devolution. From its creation in 1964, the Welsh Office's responsibilities had grown in a gradual but *ad hoc* fashion through the 1960s and 1970s. Initially it was responsible for roads, housing, tourism, heritage and local government but health was added to its remit in 1969, school education in 1970 and industry, agriculture and higher education between 1974 and 1979. This was not the result of public pressure but rather how the Welsh Office made no administrative sense unless it actually had discrete powers. It thus moved away from coordinating and lobbying other government departments to ensure Welsh interests were represented, to governing Wales itself. In doing this it was assisted by a growing number of publicly funded bodies such as the Welsh Arts Council (established 1967), the Wales Tourist Board (1969), the Sports Council for Wales (1971), the Land Authority for Wales (1975), the Welsh Consumer Council (1975), the Welsh Development Agency (1976) and the Development Board for Rural Wales (1977). By 1975 the Secretary of State for Wales was making 628 appointments to local, regional and national nominated bodies.[50] None of this was particularly democratic, given that the Secretary of State was appointed on the basis of UK-wide election results and not support within Wales. Nor, as a small department, was the Welsh Office always able to stand up for Welsh interests when they competed with those of a rival Whitehall department, something only too obvious in the wranglings that came in the wake of the Aberfan disaster (chapter 9). But the creation of the Welsh Office and other national bodies did at least signal the beginnings of something resembling a Welsh state, something which other organizations began to respond to. *The Times* appointed a Welsh correspondent in 1968 and the BBC created its first Welsh political correspondent in 1970. The Conservative Party began to hold an annual conference in Wales from 1972.

Popular opinion was less certain and the government was making a mistake in believing otherwise.[51] In the 1960s opinion polls had suggested that perhaps 60 per cent of the Welsh electorate supported the creation of a Welsh Assembly. But the polls revealed little sense of oppression or that Wales had lost out because of the union. They also suggested that even nationalists thought it was more important to improve standards of living than to change the governance of Wales.[52] A 1970 investigation for the Royal Commission on the Constitution found that support for political devolution away from London existed but was much the same in Wales as it was in English regions. In its Welsh survey 64 per cent of respondents thought Wales would be run more efficiently if it had more say in its own affairs but 30 per cent thought Wales would be run less efficiently. The motivations of respondents who supported devolution were as much about economic interests and efficient administration as the symbolism of self-governance. Just 9 per cent of respondents said they supported devolution if it was going to mean Wales would be worse off financially. Thirty per cent of respondents did not know about the existence of the Welsh Office and a quarter did not even appear to agree that Wales should have its own sports teams for international events.[53] The questions in the survey had been chosen to avoid showing strong support for devolution but another independent poll that year concluded, 'a good many Welsh nationalists do not want complete independence and doubt the economic benefits'.[54] This was worrying for advocators of devolution because it meant that in the worsening economic climate of the 1970s the soft support for more Welsh powers would slip away amid doubts about cost and whether any Welsh assembly or parliament could reinvigorate the economy. As a letter to the *Aberdare Leader* put it during the 1974 crisis over power supplies, economics had to come first and 'Separation, in any form, must wait for happier days'.[55]

When devolution became a serious political proposition after 1974, many of the arguments against it focused on its economic impact. Neil Kinnock was one of six Labour MPs in Wales who campaigned against devolution and his arguments centred on a belief that it would harm the interests of his working-class constituents. Kinnock told Parliament in 1976 that the £12 million annual running cost would pay for four hospitals, ten comprehensive schools, ten miles of motorway or two Welsh-language television channels. He argued, 'We do not need an Assembly to prove our nationality or our pride. This is a matter of hearts and minds, not bricks, committees and bureaucrats.' He maintained that his opposition came not from being anti-Welsh but 'fundamentally because we are Welsh' and want to protect Welsh interests.[56] But such arguments did not stop the reappearance of the old divisions over what being Welsh actually meant. As the devolution bill passed through Parliament, Kinnock claimed (wrongly) that children in Anglesey were being prevented from going to the toilet unless they asked in Welsh.[57] Leo Abse argued that an Assembly would represent 'xenophobia and nineteenth century nationalism'. He spoke of 'a packed gravy train' steaming out of Cardiff, with the 'first-class coaches marked "For Welsh speakers only"'.[58] Others used more mundane arguments. Tom Hooson, the prospective Tory candidate for Brecon and Radnor, announced in the press that an Assembly would not only take power further from the people but lead to more dangerous rural roads in the winter.[59] Aware that defeat was a real possibility, the government chose St David's Day 1979 for the referendum, which Nicholas Edwards MP (Conservative, Pembroke) suggested was intended 'to build up an Arms Park atmosphere and to smother fact and argument in a simple appeal to Welsh loyalty'.[60] In response, opponents played on British patriotism. 'Keep Wales united with Britain', declared a full-page advert from the 'no' campaign in most of the Welsh papers on the day of the vote.

Political and cultural nationalists were uncertain what to do. The Welsh-language press was supportive of the measure but Dafydd Wigley MP (Plaid Cymru, Caernarfon) thought there was a lack of leadership on the issue, claiming 'At the dawn of one of the most important milestones in Welsh history, the nationalist movement is unsure of itself, is afraid and nervous. It is like a child preparing for an important exam, but refusing to acknowledge its importance in case he fails it.'[61] Cymdeithas yr Iaith Gymraeg decided not to campaign for a 'yes' vote, noting the absence of any provision for the use of Welsh in the Assembly. Indeed, Angharad Tomos, one of its prominent members, thought the scheme 'a Labour conspiracy' to tame nationalists.[62] Saunders Lewis did weigh in with a letter to the *Western Mail* that argued the question was really whether Wales was a nation or not. He pointed out, perceptively as it turned out, that if the answer was 'no' a general election would follow and the government would try to tackle inflation. This mattered because 'In Wales there are coal mines that work at a loss; there are steelworks what are judged superfluous, there are still valleys convenient for submersion. And there will be no Welsh defence.'[63]

Amid all the arguments there appeared to be widespread apathy and some confusion. Once the details of the exact form of devolution being proposed were known, opinion polls never showed support for an Assembly at higher than 34 per cent. Things were perhaps not helped by the fact that, unlike Scotland, Wales was being offered an Assembly with no legislative powers. There was no rationale for this differentiation beyond the need to placate the nationalists and the tradition of administrative devolution both being stronger in Scotland. In Abergele the *Daily Post* found 'a tidal wave of indifference'.[64] A bricklayer from Ely (Cardiff) told a writer, 'I don't know what it's all about. I'm not really interested. It'll make no bloody difference to me one way or the other. I hear some of them talking Welsh in the other bar and it means nothing to me. They're foreigners to me.'[65] Not a single elector attended one devolution meeting in Merthyr during the campaign. The hostile *South Wales Echo* noted on the day before the vote: 'There are many people in Wales who are thoroughly sick of being bombarded with the views and counter-views. After all, it was an issue that the Welsh did not want in the first place.'[66]

Apart from lukewarm support from the *Western Mail*, which saw devolution as an issue of democracy and accountability rather than cost, language and separation, 'yes' campaigners found little support from the press in Wales. (The *Western Mail* had actually nearly supported full law-making and tax-raising powers but the deputy editor persuaded an ambivalent English editor otherwise, fearing that if he was seen as a closet nationalist it would harm his own chances of ever running the paper.[67]) The *South Wales Echo* played the fear card throughout the campaign, with editorials claiming that a majority of people would vote 'no' because 'they are afraid of being hived off from the rest of the country. They are right to be afraid.' The *Daily Post*, meanwhile, played on north–south tensions, claiming in its referendum-day editorial that Wales 'deserves better than this half-baked folly … a pretentious little super council, housed in a Cardiff backwater, trifling endlessly with minor governmental issues and failing to achieve anything of primary importance'.[68] The most widely read papers, however, were based in London (the *Sun* and the *Daily Mirror* alone accounted for over 40 per cent of all English-language newspapers sold in Wales) and they paid scant attention to the vote, thus contributing directly to the confusion and apathy. Television was not much more helpful considering perhaps 35 per cent of people tuned to English rather than Welsh transmitters and both the BBC and ITV refused to broadcast the Welsh devolution programming on those English transmitters.[69]

At the end of a decade when Welsh rugby had suggested a confident, even aggressive national identity, only 11.8 per cent of the electorate voted in favour of the creation of a Welsh Assembly (table 10.1). It was an emphatic result or, as John Morris, the Secretary of State, put it: 'When you see an elephant on your doorstep, you know it is there.'[70]

Whereas just under 12 per cent of the electorate actually voted 'yes', from 1975 to 1978 opinion polls had consistently shown at least 27 per cent of people said they would vote that way. By the time of the actual referendum, political circumstances had swung firmly against a 'yes' vote. Devolution was being proposed by a struggling Labour government that seemed to have lost control of the unions and the country. It came at the end of a 'winter of discontent', when strikes seemed to have crippled the nation. In the background were lingering doubts about the quality of Labour

Table 10.1 Results of the 1 March 1979 referendum on Welsh devolution

	Percentage of electorate voting 'yes' (% of turnout)	Percentage of electorate voting 'no' (% of turnout)
Clwyd	11.0 (21.6)	40.1 (78.4)
Gwynedd	21.8 (34.4)	41.6 (65.6)
Dyfed	18.1 (28.1)	46.5 (71.9)
Powys	12.2 (18.5)	53.8 (81.5)
West Glamorgan	10.8 (18.7)	46.7 (81.3)
Mid Glamorgan	11.8 (20.2)	46.7 (79.8)
South Glamorgan	7.7 (13.1)	51.0 (86.9)
Gwent	6.7 (12.1)	48.7 (87.9)

'Yes' votes: 243,048 (20.3 per cent of turnout; 11.8 per cent of electorate).
'No' votes: 956,330 (79.7 per cent of turnout; 46.5 per cent of electorate).
Turnout: 58.3 per cent.

politicians likely to dominate an Assembly and continued fears about levels of public spending in an inflation-ridden economy. Moreover, the government seemed unenthusiastic and it had not produced its own campaign literature. One poll a couple of weeks before the vote even suggested that 12 per cent of Plaid Cymru voters were going to vote 'no'.[71] Although the result was a comment on the political circumstances of the day, it was also unavoidably about nationality. In an opinion poll the week before the vote, 61 per cent of 'no' voters said they were motivated by the Assembly's cost, 43 per cent by the fear of another level of bureaucracy and 40 per cent by wanting to preserve the union.[72] The 'no' campaign's arguments that devolution would mean the southern English-speaking majority being ruled by a Welsh-speaking clique from the north and that it would ultimately lead to the breakup of the United Kingdom hit home. One writer of a letter to the press feared, 'It's another case of jobs for the boys, with higher rates and taxes when England pulls out.' After the result, a cartoon on the front page of the *South Wales Echo* showed a lady sitting down with a map of Britain on her wall, saying, 'There's lovely – still in one piece'.[73] Cymdeithas yr Iaith Gymraeg's magazine concluded that the referendum had 'shown clearly that this last decade has not resulted in any loosening of the British knot in Wales'.[74] Thus, despite the specific political issues of the day, it is difficult to avoid the conclusion that the 1979 referendum also marked the majority of Wales asserting its satisfaction with remaining within the UK, even among those whose sense of Welshness overrode any feeling of being British. In the 1979 Welsh Election Survey, 59 per cent of respondents said they were

Welsh rather than British or English but only 22 per cent of this group voted 'yes', while 42 per cent voted 'no'. Those with a higher involvement in Welsh culture – be it through language, chapel, schooling or using the Welsh media – were most likely to have voted 'yes'.[75] This explained why the 'yes' vote was highest in rural areas but everywhere in Wales, despite, and perhaps because of, the mess that the UK seemed to be in, there was little widespread appetite for leaving it.

DONALD ANDERSON MP (Labour, Swansea East), an opponent of devolution, wondered whether the message of the referendum was 'that the main loyalty in Wales, in political terms, is to Britain and thereafter to the local community within Wales, rather than to Wales itself'.[76] The surveys that showed that people prioritized their Welshness over their Britishness were misleading because they forced people to choose between two identities that were in reality entwined and inseparable for the majority. An academic survey in 1981 suggested that the percentage (86) of people in Wales who felt proud of being British was exactly the same as in England and Scotland, and 54 per cent said they were 'very proud'.[77]

The ties of the welfare state, the pull of trade unions that worked across the UK and the memories of the shared experiences of the Second World War were still strong but Britishness was a popular emotional sentiment too, just in the way Welshness was. This very real sentiment showed itself twice more in the early 1980s. In 1981 Wales, like the rest of Britain, became besotted by the marriage of Prince Charles and Lady Diana Spencer. After the engagement was announced, Welsh hairdressers reported a big demand from customers for a Lady Di cut and highlights. Roger Thomas, the Labour MP for Carmarthen, even asked the government if the M4 could be renamed 'Welshway' to commemorate the wedding. Not everyone was quite so impressed of course. The Cardiff Labour Party voted that the city council should not give the couple a wedding gift because of strains on public expenditure, an act which one paper called 'miserable and petty'. The councillors, however, were more in tune with popular opinion and decided not to follow their party's instructions. For the wedding itself, the *Western Mail* thought that its readers would not only study the colour pictures in its forty-page souvenir edition but also keep it and maybe pass it on to their grandchildren. The paper reported that in Wales the wedding day was:

> a bumper celebration for old and young alike, as the sun shone down on a fairytale land of streets decked out in red, white and blue.

> Miles upon miles of bunting strewn from rooftop to rooftop fluttered in the breeze. Below, hundreds of street parties signalled the joy of the royal occasion.
>
> City centres turned into ghost towns as estates and suburbs took part in an orgy of paper hats, flags, jelly and pop. It was a day for the children – and a night for the adults, as beer replaces squash and ox roasts replaced crisps.

There were 300 street parties in Cardiff alone.[78] When Charles and Diana toured Wales in October 1981 they were given a warm, even rapturous welcome. In Pontypridd, for example, they were cheered by a crowd of 20,000, who had lined the streets in torrential rain to welcome them. There were a few voices of dissent in Bangor, where there were scuffles as nationalist protestors hurled stink bombs at the couple and one woman sprayed paint on their limousine, but this was out of keeping with a genuine enthusiasm that was more than simple patriotism. There was an element of a fairy tale about a pretty and seemingly ordinary girl marrying a prince. As a *Western Mail* editorial pointed out, 'millions of British girls have identified with her through a still living belief in real life romance'.[79]

Few people probably knew where the Falklands were before they were invaded by Argentina on 2 April 1982 but Union Jacks were again being waved in Wales when Thatcher sent a taskforce to recover the islands. One Welsh Guard looked back on his departure, noting 'The patriotism stirred you on. You felt as if you were ten feet tall.'[80] A Gallup poll in April 1982 suggested that 67 per cent of the UK population agreed with the British response.[81] The Council of Churches for Wales expressed concern about the 'jingoistic and militaristic spirit among the people of Britain and their leaders'.[82] For the Labour Party the conflict thus presented a difficult position. Its natural inclination was to oppose it on both pacifist and imperial lines but to do so was to risk being seen as unpatriotic. Like so often in the early 1980s, Labour ended up failing to offer any realistic response to Thatcher's actions.

For Welsh nationalists the situation was similarly exasperating. Just three years after the referendum, the war was further evidence of how wedded Wales was to the British system, not just politically but emotionally too. But there was a different twist to their position. Part of Argentina was Patagonia, where a Welsh-speaking community had been established in the nineteenth century and which still survived, albeit in diluted terms. This meant that there were men in the Argentinean army with names like Milton Rhys and Carlos Eduardo ap Iwan. There have even been claims that Radio Cymru listeners knew of the conflict before anyone else thanks to a Welsh-speaking Patagonian, who was also used to give an Argentinean view on what was happening during the conflict.[83] There were also, both at the time and later, stories of Welsh speakers from both sides meeting, although there is no evidence that this actually ever happened.[84] Welsh was actually regarded as old-fashioned by young Patagonians and few people raised after 1950 still spoke the language. Moreover, in 1976 the Argentinean dictatorship had made it illegal to give children Welsh names.[85] Nonetheless, the hypothetical possibility of Welsh speakers fighting each other added to the strong anti-war feeling that could be found in parts of the cultural establishment.

There was some awareness among Welsh troops about Patagonia and the possibility of Welsh speakers on the other side but these were not dwelt upon. As one soldier from Anglesey put it, 'You don't think about it, because you'd be the dead one if you did'.[86] And people did die. On 8 June 1982 the *Sir Galahad*, loaded with ammunition and members of the Welsh Guards, was in the wrong location, had no air cover and was exposed in the daylight. It was bombed by Argentine planes. The ammunition exploded and fifty people were killed. The conflict may have lasted less than three months but it cost 655 Argentinean and 255 British lives.

IN THE WAKE of the referendum, the devastating recession of the early 1980s, the election of Thatcher with a third of the Welsh vote and such evidence of an overt British patriotism, the idea of a distinctive Welsh politics seemed to be in retreat. In one survey after the 1979 referendum there was stronger support for both Welsh devolution and independence in the north of England and the West Midlands than there was in Wales. *The Times*, *Guardian* and *Financial Times* all did away with Welsh correspondents in the 1980s.[87] A deep sense of pessimism emerged among those who thought about Wales. In 1982 Dafydd Elis-Thomas MP (Plaid Cymru, Meirionnydd) claimed 'virtually all Welsh people ask themselves today what it is to be Welsh and what Wales is'.[88] That was an exaggeration but the 'no' vote has been seen as 'one of the most painful events in Welsh history' by two historians who claim that a 'collective depression – almost a form of political post-traumatic stress disorder – set in'.[89] There was certainly something of a sense of standing on the edge of a precipice, with the danger that Wales might fall over and into oblivion. Even the fortunes of the national rugby team collapsed and Wales lost twenty-one of their forty matches in the Five Nations tournament over the course of the 1980s. A Scotsman who moved to Wales in 1983 to run the Welsh Development Agency recalled, 'I had never met a people so apparently intent on talking themselves down into terminal disaster'.[90]

This was particularly clear in Welsh-speaking circles. The referendum left Plaid Cymru 'confounded, dazed and numb'.[91] Everything it had worked for and stood for had essentially been rejected. As one Welsh-language newspaper concluded after the result, it was 'a simple and plain vote about Welsh nationalism' and the 'voice of the people must be accepted'.[92] Subsequent surveys suggested that while voting in favour of devolution had been much stronger among Welsh speakers, more than half of those who did turn out still probably voted 'no'. The 1979 Plaid Cymru general election manifesto devoted just two sentences to Welsh self-government.[93] Attention shifted to the erosion of Welsh-speaking communities as English incomers bought up cottages and farms, often just to holiday in. An archdruid told the 1979 National Eisteddfod that 'If the people of Gwynedd allow the Welsh language to be lost, the Welsh will deserve to be considered the filth of humanity'.[94] Such fears were reinforced when the 1981 census showed the number of Welsh speakers had fallen by 6.3 per cent in a decade, the smallest fall since the war but still a fall. The general frustration was evident in Angharad Tomos' novel *Yma o Hyd* (*Still Here*, 1985). It centred on an imprisoned language protestor whose frustration for her country had escalated from defacing road signs to the violent smashing up of a shop. For her, language protests had become a ritual that would achieve nothing and she became detached from her roots, seemingly more at ease in an alien prison than with the pain of contemporary Wales. Such anguish raised its head again when the question of the seventh centenary of the English conquest of Wales arose. In Ruthin, plans to celebrate the awarding of the town's 1282 charter by Edward I caused a public outcry. One councillor argued that 'A lot of people think we are celebrating the death of a nation'. After a public meeting, it was decided that there should a celebration of the town's history rather than the awarding of the charter.[95] The Welsh Tourist Board did decide to hold a festival to celebrate the centenary of the building of Edwardian castles around north Wales. The fact that these castles were symbols of the conquest of Wales meant the plans deeply annoyed nationalists, especially when one of the associated slogans (apparently added by the British Tourist Authority) was 'Wales is a country worth defending. That's why we have so many castles.'[96] But the anniversary did not have to be about just remembering the defeat and some schools used the occasion to study the survival of Wales and the defiance of the princes. Gwynedd County Council made much of the centenary and its chief executive wrote to *The Times* celebrating the last native prince's 'vision and valour'.[97]

Such scraps of optimism were less common in industrial Wales, where there was also a sense of national decline among people like the historian

Dai Smith, who claimed in 1985 that Mid Glamorgan was the 'most Welsh place in Wales'.[98] Its industrial communities were passing away, at least in their traditional form, as steel and coal closures gathered pace in the early 1980s. Preserving something of that way of life before it disappeared suddenly became a major concern and there was much talk of mining museums and retaining landmark pitheads and coal tips. By the late 1980s even the Welsh folk museum began to incorporate industrial history into its exhibits by including a row of miners' cottages. Lewis Merthyr colliery, closed in 1983, was turned into the Rhondda Heritage Park, which opened in 1989. It was envisaged as having clear economic benefits, both through the employment of former miners and by attracting tourism to the area. But such projects created a sense among some that the present and future were being given up on. One writer complained about the theme parks, heritage trails, industrial museums and cultural centres 'springing up everywhere – what was once the world's biggest workshop is rapidly being transformed into its biggest museum'.[99]

Academic writing encapsulated the sense of despair for the future. In 1985 historian Gwyn A. Williams wrote that some saw nothing in the future 'but a nightmare vision of a depersonalized Wales which has shrivelled up into a Costa Bureaucratica in the south and a Costa Geriatrica in the north; in between, sheep, holiday homes burning merrily away and fifty folk museums where there used to be communities'.[100] Using the 1979 Welsh Election Study – which asked people 'Do you normally consider yourself to be Welsh, British, English or something else?' – Denis Balsom argued that there were three Waleses: Y Fro Gymraeg (essentially Gwynedd and most of Dyfed), British Wales (Clwyd, Gwent, Powys, South Glamorgan and south Pembrokeshire) and Welsh Wales (Mid and West Glamorgan). In Welsh Wales and Y Fro Gymraeg, 63 and 62 per cent said they were Welsh, whereas in British Wales it was just 51 per cent. The fact that half of respondents in his 'British Wales' chose Welsh before British showed the limitations of Balsom's concept but it was influential nonetheless.[101] Yet divisions over Welshness were hardly surprising given the makeup of the Welsh population. By 1981 there were 468,000 people living in Wales who were English born and 21,000 who were Scottish born. Some of the English born were just residents of mid and north-east Wales whose nearest maternity hospitals were in Shrewsbury and Chester but nonetheless the Welsh population was diversifying with unknown consequences. What the 573,000 people living in England but born in Wales thought about their nationality was even less clear.

National pessimism was hardly unique to Wales in the 1980s. At the start of 1980 a *South Wales Echo* editorial pointed to the Russian invasion of Afghanistan, rising prices and unemployment and a reluctance to buy British because of people's perception of quality, but it urged

> We should not be so ashamed of ourselves. We should have no need to knock our own products. National pride and self respect have become unpopular concepts yet it is fashionable to praise the abilities of other countries.
>
> We need to learn to love Britain a bit. It is, by and large, country of hard, honest workers with a talent for self-improvement and invention. If we do not look after ourselves we cannot expect anyone else to do it for us.
>
> Yet we carp and complain, we allow ourselves to become depressed, we see nothing but blackness beyond us. Let us cuddle Britain, let us cuddle ourselves.[102]

In 1975 a north Wales manufacturer and exporter of filters replaced 'Made in Britain' with 'Made in Wales' because British products were associated with late deliveries.[103] But this was an isolated sentiment. The scale of the economic problems of the 1970s and early 1980s meant that people in Wales tended to speak of promoting Britain and British jobs. The size of the problem was simply too great to see any solution on a Welsh level.

The ever-present fear of nuclear war added to people's pessimism. The cold war intensified in the 1980s and stocks of nuclear weapons were growing, making the impact of any conflict all the more terrible than when a war had seemed more likely in the 1960s. Leaflets that recommended hiding under the stairs or a table in the event of an attack increased the fear and made people realize how vulnerable they were. 'Would ANYONE survive?', screamed a 1980 headline of the *Daily Mirror*, the second best-selling newspaper in Wales. It identified Cardiff, Swansea and Holyhead as being on a nuclear hit-list. A 1982 British survey found that 70 per cent of people were worried about a nuclear war and 38 per cent were certain that one would occur. A 1984 survey showed that 70 per cent of British teen-agers thought a nuclear war in their lifetime was unavoidable.[104]

In the 1970s and 1980s government nuclear policy seemed to be more about upholding British prestige and the veneer of being a world power than defence. Gwynfor Evans thus denounced the Trident missile as an 'evil weapon which is a badge of British nationalism rather than a weapon of military defence'.[105] Despite such sentiments and the involvement of trade unionists in the peace movement, in rural areas the Campaign for Nuclear Disarmament (CND) in Wales was often associated with English incomers, perhaps unsurprisingly since many had come to live more sustainable and peaceful lives. This did cause some tension and there was some annoyance that Welsh dissidents and intellectuals were more involved in the cultural and nationalist movement. One incoming CND campaigner remarked that if there was a nuclear war there would not be 'much left to say in any language'.[106] She was one of forty women, four men and a few children who marched from Cardiff to the US Air Force base at Greenham Common in 1981. When they got there they demanded a debate with the government about the cruise missiles destined to be housed there. They did not get one, so four women from Wales chained themselves to a gate. A camp was made and it remained there for nineteen years, becoming, in the words of one historian, the 'most powerful and persistent symbol of confrontation with the state'.[107] The Greenham camp inspired other peace protests, including one at the Royal Ordnance factory in Llanishen, where, to some Welsh shame, parts for nuclear weapons were being manufactured.[108] That factory rather undermined the local-government declaration of Wales as a nuclear-free country in 1982, as did the existence of two nuclear power stations in Gwynedd. One woman who lived near the Trawsfynydd reactor remarked, 'I think all the time of the children's health and their safety if something happened. The power station has divided families around here. It's like a civil war between those who support it and those who hate it.'[109]

Concerns about nuclear power owed much to people's uncertainty about its environmental impact. The environment had emerged as a political and popular concern in the 1970s. Earlier signs of that concern had been evident in the overarching themes of despoliation in the enduringly popular Welsh industrial novels *How Green Was My Valley* (1939) and *Rape of the Fair Country* (1959). But, within Wales, the key driving force for change was not so much the green agenda but safety. Following the Aberfan disaster, a programme began to clear coal tips and other pieces of derelict land in industrial communities. Between 1966 and 1991, some £170 million was spent on the reclamation of 17,000 acres of derelict industrial land in Wales for both new employment and public amenities. It was a slow process but the visual impact was immense and many valleys literally became green again, a state achievement as significant as any since the war.[110] It was not just land that people were worried about. Industry had severely polluted many of Wales' rivers, something exacerbated by local residents throwing their own rubbish in. In 1951 it was calculated that some 200,000 tons of coal and coal dust were being carried down the Taff every year, turning it black and killing anything that tried to live at its bottom. The National Coal Board did begin to recover coal from rivers and by 1960 there were brown trout in the Taff near Cardiff, perhaps for the first time in eighty years. But there was still much to be done, as people were increasingly coming to realize in the 1970s. Typical of the growing concerns was a 1974 newspaper article about the river Ebbw. Local industry had stopped putting slag chemicals into the river but it was still 'in a state of chemical distress, pungent and deeply discoloured, and with no signs of incipient life'. Thanks to the drains of the local steelworks and run-offs from nearby coal tips, the river bed was lined with oil and tar, while the water was sulphurous and acidic.[111] Air pollution, meanwhile, was declining everywhere in Britain because of the growth in smokeless fuels but, in the south of Wales at least, it had never been anything like the problem it was in industrial England because of the low sulphur content of local coal. In fact, air quality was often better in industrial south Wales than it was in rural England.[112] Medical studies showed that pollution was more than just an aesthetic issue. The lower levels of atmospheric pollution meant that nearly everywhere in Wales the prevalence of lung cancer was lower than the British average but, in north Wales in 1947–53, stomach cancer was 50–100 per cent above the national average, which may have been due to untreated acidic water supplies and pollution from old metal workings.[113] By the 1980s there were new concerns. Acid rain was another consequence of industry and was felt to be poisoning rural waters and forests.[114] It did not recognize national borders and was further evidence that some problems could not be tackled at a national level, something that was reinforced when popular concern about global warming emerged towards the end of the 1980s. The vulnerability of the Welsh environment to external forces became less abstract in 1986, when a Soviet nuclear reactor exploded. The radioactive contamination from Chernobyl reached as far as Snowdonia, leading to fears and even panic about the safety of nuclear power stations there. The Green Party's support never topped the 99,546 Welsh votes it won at the 1989 European election (when it outpolled Plaid Cymru in every constituency except North Wales) but environmental issues still worried many people, adding to the climate of pessimism of the 1970s and 1980s, even if few seemed prepared to compromise their living standards in the name of sustainability.

No matter what dangers Wales faced in the 1980s, political, economic or environmental, there was no reason why its national despondency had to be permanent. In an echo of what many had said in the 1960s, the *Daily Telegraph* commented after the 1979 referendum:

> Nationalism in Scotland and Wales is essentially a heart-cry against the excessive power of the modern state. If that power is not sharply and swiftly diminished then the fortunes of SNP and Plaid Cymru will soon revive and next time there may be no stopping short of the full disintegration of the United Kingdom.[115]

Such arguments were right that nationalism was not dead but wrong in their interpretation of its causes. Anger at the political actions of Labour had contributed to the growth in support for Plaid Cymru in the 1960s but the power of the British state also offered a safety net to the Welsh working class. During the economic turmoil of the 1970s and early 1980s that safety net drew people to Britain rather than repelled them from it. But both national identity and political and cultural nationalism were not just reactions to the British state and the state of the economy. For both Welsh and English speakers, they had distinctly emotional sides too that were not always, or even mostly, political or politicized. This was true of both Welsh and British sentiments in Wales. If Welsh separatism was to grow then what would have to happen was a politicization of the emotional patriotism that was only too evident at a Welsh rugby international.

Notes

1 *The Times*, 10 Mar. 1969.
2 B. John, *The Barry John Story* (1975), 32. *The Times*, 15 Mar. 1977.
3 A. Richards, 'The drop-out' [1973], in J. Davies and M. Jenkins (eds), *The Valleys* (1984), 101–2.
4 J. Taylor, *Decade of the Dragon: A Celebration of Welsh Rugby, 1969–1979* (1980), 18–19.
5 G. Davies, *An Autobiography* (1979), 15.
6 J. Davies, *A History of Wales* (1993), 644. J. Davies, *Broadcasting and the BBC in Wales* (1994), 319.
7 P. Bennett, *The Autobiography* (2003), 33. G. Price, *Price of Wales* (1984), 154.
8 Davies, *An Autobiography*, 18. *Guardian*, 2 Feb. 1993.
9 C. Williams, 'J. P.R. Williams', in H. Richards, P. Stead and G. Williams (eds), *More Heart and Soul: The Character of Welsh Rugby* (1999), 112.
10 G. Williams, 'Fields of praise', *Pl*, 14 (1972), 15.
11 T. Fishlock, *Wales and the Welsh* (1972), 7.
12 M. Billig, *Banal Nationalism* (1995).
13 D. Butler and D. Kavanagh, *The British General Election of October 1974* (1975), 159. G. R. Jones, 'Dewin y Bêl', translation from G. Williams, 'Postponing death: sport and literature in Wales', *New Welsh Review*, 36 (1997), 44.
14 *Guardian*, 3 Jan. 1975. Fishlock, *Talking of Wales* (1976), 33.
15 Davies, *Broadcasting and the BBC*, 354. D. Balsom, P. Madgwick and D. Van Mechelen, 'The political consequences of Welsh identity', *Ethnic and Racial Studies*, 7:1 (1984), 160–81.
16 Fishlock, *Talking of Wales*, 25. R. Bourhis and H. Giles, 'Welsh is beautiful', *New Society*, 4 Apr. 1974, 15–16.
17 D. W. Howell, *Taking Stock: The Centenary History of the Royal Welsh Agricultural Society* (2003), 233.
18 G. Humphreys, 'What are we?', in P. H. Ballard and E. Jones (eds), *The Valleys Call* (1975), 78. D. L. James, 'The rise of the bilingual secondary school', *Pl*, 16 (1973), 33–40.
19 G. Williams, E. Roberts and R. Isaac, 'Language and aspirations for upward social mobility', and C. Thomas and C. Williams, 'Linguistic decline and nationalist resurgence in Wales: a case study of the attitudes of sixth-form pupils', both in G. Williams (ed.), *Social and Cultural Change in Contemporary Wales* (1978), 193–205, 166–92.
20 Fishlock, *Talking of Wales*, 107.
21 Davies, *Broadcasting and the BBC*, 347–8.
22 BBC Broadcasting Research, *Listening and Viewing in Wales, December 1982* (1983).

23 N. Coupland and M. J. Ball, 'Welsh and English in contemporary Wales: sociolinguistic issues', *CW*, 3 (1989), 18.
24 R. Jones, *Cofiant Ryan* (2002), 96.
25 On Welsh television see P. Hannan (ed.), *Wales in Vision: The People and Politics of Television* (1990).
26 A. Richards, *Home to an Empty House* ([1973] 2006), 169, 206.
27 *WM*, 5 Aug. 1978.
28 Davies, *Broadcasting and the BBC*, 358.
29 C. Davies, *Welsh Jokes* (1978), 21. *HC Deb*, 1 Mar. 1978, vol. 945 cc. 507–8.
30 *Daily Post*, 12 Jan. 1977. *The Times*, 17 Jan. 1977.
31 Fishlock, *Talking of Wales*, 85.
32 *WM*, 2 July 1998.
33 Commission on the Constitution, *Devolution and Other Aspects of Government: An Attitudes Survey* (1973), xv, 81.
34 *WM*, 4 June 1975. G. C. Wenger, *Mid-Wales: Deprivation or Development. A Study of Patterns of Employment in Selected Communities* (1980), 122. *WM*, 9 June 1975.
35 C. Davies, *Permissive Society: Social Change in the Sixties and Seventies* (1975), 217.
36 Fishlock, *Talking of Wales*, 86. Commission on the Constitution, *Written Evidence 7: Wales* (1972), 83.
37 *Aberdare Leader*, 8 Feb. 1974.
38 For a literary exploration of such tensions see R. G. Jones, *Triptych* (1977).
39 G. C. Wenger, 'Ethnicity and social organization in north-east Wales', in Williams (ed.), *Social and Cultural Change*, 120–32.
40 Fishlock, *Talking of Wales*, 117. *HC Deb*, 12 July 1973, vol. 859, cc. 1923–8.
41 P. Clayton, 'Domain and register in the use of Welsh', in Williams (ed.), *Social and Cultural Change*, 206–18. G. H. Jenkins and M. A. Williams, 'The fortunes of the Welsh language, 1900–2000', in G. H. Jenkins and M. A. Williams (eds), *'Let's Do Our Best for the Ancient Tongue': The Welsh Language in the Twentieth Century* (2000), 19.
42 B. Thomas, 'The riches of the past? Recording Welsh dialects', in Jenkins and Williams (eds), *'Let's Do Our Best'*. B. Thomas, 'Here today, gone tomorrow? Language and dialect in a Welsh community', *Folk Life*, 36 (1991–2), 84–95.
43 D. Morgan, 'The Welsh language and local authority planning in Gwynedd, 1974–1995', in Jenkins and Williams (eds), *'Let's Do Our Best'*, 582–4.
44 Clayton, 'Domain and register', 214. *HL Deb*, 27 Apr. 1978, vol. 390, cc. 2501–2WA. Williams, Roberts and Isaac, 'Language and aspirations', 205. *HC Deb*, 12 July 1973, vol. 859, cc. 1923–8.
45 *Welsh Farm News*, 27 Oct. 1962.
46 *WM*, 29 May, 4 and 5 June 1975.
47 *Guardian*, 6 June 1975. *WM*, 5, 3 and 9 June 1975.
48 D. Butler and D. Kavanagh, *The British General Election of February 1974* (1975), 57. Butler and Kavanagh, *British General Election of October 1974*, 76.
49 J. G. Evans, *Devolution in Wales: Claims and Responses, 1937–79* (2006), 146, 137.
50 *HC Deb*, 12 Dec. 1975, vol. 902, cc. 414–17W.
51 I. McLean and A. McMillan, *State of the Union: Unionism and the Alternatives in the United Kingdom* (2005), 185–6.
52 A. Edwards and D. Tanner, 'Defining or dividing the nation? Opinion polls, Welsh identity and devolution, 1966–1979', *CW*, 18 (2006), 57–9.
53 Commission on the Constitution, *Devolution and Other Aspects of Government.*
54 Edwards and Tanner, 'Defining or dividing the nation?', 59, 64
55 *Aberdare Leader*, 1 Feb. 1974.
56 Evans, *Devolution in Wales*, 178, 189. Quotes from R. M. Jones and I. R. Jones, 'Labour and the nation', in D. Tanner, C. Williams and D. Hopkin (eds), *The Labour Party in Wales, 1900–2000* (2000), 257.
57 *HC Deb*, 2 Mar. 1978, vol. 945, c. 704. *The Times*, 6 July 1978.

58 Quotes from Jones and Jones, 'Labour and the nation', 257, and Evans, *Devolution in Wales*, 190.
59 Quoted in *Arcade*, 32 (19 Feb. 1982).
60 *HC Deb*, 22 Nov. 1978, vol. 958, c. 1385.
61 Quoted in translation in Edwards and Tanner, 'Defining or dividing the nation?', 61.
62 H. P. Jones, 'The referendum and the Welsh language press', in D. Foulkes, J. B. Jones and R. Wilford (eds), *The Welsh Veto: The Wales Act 1978 and the Referendum* (1983), 169–83. R. Evans, *Gwynfor Evans: Portrait of a Patriot* (2008), 379–80.
63 *WM*, 26 Feb. 1979.
64 Edwards and Tanner, 'Defining or dividing the nation?', 65. Quote from *Arcade*, 32 (19 Feb. 1982).
65 J. Tripp, 'Views from the taverns', *Pl*, 47 (1979), 20.
66 Evans, *Gwynfor Evans*, 381. *SWE*, 28 Feb. 1979.
67 J. Humphries, *Freedom Fighters: Wales's Forgotten 'War', 1963–1993* (2008), 157–8.
68 *SWE* editorial, 22 Feb. 1979. *LDP* editorial, 1 Mar. 1979.
69 J. Osmond, 'The referendum and the English language press', and G. Talfan Davies, 'The role of broadcasting in the referendum', both in Foulkes *et al.* (eds), *The Welsh Veto*, 153–68, 184–96.
70 *WM*, 3 Mar. 1979.
71 D. Balsom, 'Public opinion and Welsh devolution', in Foulkes *et al.* (eds), *The Welsh Veto*, 197–215.
72 Evans, *Devolution in Wales*, 196.
73 *SWE*, 28 Feb., 3 Mar. 1979.
74 *Tafod y Ddraig*, quoted in translation in J. Osmond (ed.), *The National Question Again: Welsh Political Identity in the 1980s* (1985), xxxvii.
75 G. Evans and D. Trystan, 'Why was 1997 different?', in B. Taylor and K. Thomson (eds), *Scotland and Wales: Nations Again?* (1999), 100–1. D. Balsom, 'The three-Wales model', in Osmond (ed.), *The National Question Again*, 1–17.
76 D. Anderson, 'Reconciling socialism with community', in Osmond (ed.), *The National Question Again*, 176–7.
77 R. Rose, *National Pride: Cross-National Surveys* (1984), 4.
78 *WM*, 9 Apr. 1981. *Arcade*, 15 (29 May 1981). *WM*, 13, 14 Apr., 28 and 30 July 1981.
79 N. Crickhowell, *Westminster, Wales and Water* (1999), 113–14. *The Times*, 28 Oct. 1981. *WM*, 29 July 1981.
80 *The Past Master*, BBC Radio Wales, 3 June 2007.
81 A. King, *British Political Opinion, 1937–2000: The Gallup Polls* (2001), 333.
82 Quoted in Noel A. Davies, *A History of Ecumenism in Wales, 1956–1990* (2008), 180.
83 D. Iorwerth, 'Battleground: the politics of language', in BBC Wales, *Defining a Nation: Wales and the BBC* (nd), 25.
84 G. Williams, 'Don't mention the war? Interpreting and contextualizing the Falklands/Malvinas War', in C. Williams and M. Cragoe (eds), *Wales and War: Religion, Society and Politics in the Nineteenth and Twentieth Centuries* (2007), 204–29. G. Cullen, 'The real war', *Pl*, 58 (1986), 30–40.
85 G. Williams, *The Welsh in Patagonia: The State and Ethnic Community* (1991), 256.
86 I. Roberts, *Rhyfel Ni: Profiadiau Cymreig o Ddwy Ochr Rhyfel y Falklands/Malvinas* (2003), 122, reproduced in translation in Williams, 'Don't mention the war?', 215.
87 McLean and McMillan, *State of the Union*, 204. D. Skilton, 'More words and pictures in the air', in D. Cole (ed.), *The New Wales* (1990), 188.
88 *Marxism Today*, Mar. 1982.
89 Edwards and Tanner, 'Defining or dividing the nation?', 55.
90 D. Waterstone, 'The incomer's view', in Cole (ed.), *The New Wales*, 235.
91 J. Davies, 'Plaid Cymru in transition', in Osmond (ed.), *The National Question Again*, 144.
92 *Yr Herald Cymraeg*, quoted in translation in Jones, 'The referendum and the Welsh language press', 181.

93 Balsom, 'The three-Wales model', 8. K. O. Morgan, *Rebirth of a Nation: Wales, 1880–1980* (1981), 406.
94 Quoted in K. J. Bernard, *Visible Welshness: Performing Welshness at the National Eisteddfod in the Twentieth Century*, PhD thesis, Swansea University (2004), 375.
95 *Free Press and North Wales Times*, 24 Sep., 10 and 24 Dec. 1980.
96 For clippings and leaflets on this see 'The Welsh patriot', at http://welshpatriot.blogspot.com/2009/06/festival-of-castles-1983-revisted-back.html.
97 *The Times*, 3 Nov. 1981.
98 *WM*, 25 Mar. 1985.
99 R. Mason, *Museums, Nations, Identities: Wales and Its National Museums* (2007), ch. 3. B. Dicks, *Heritage, Place and Community* (2000). J. Evans, *How Real Is My Valley? Postmodernism and the South Wales Valleys* (1994), 20.
100 G. A. Williams, *When Was Wales?* (1985), 303.
101 Balsom, 'The three-Wales model'. D. Balsom, P. Madgwick and D. VanMechlelen, *The Political Consequences of Welsh Identity* (1982).
102 *SWE*, 2 Jan. 1980.
103 *Guardian*, 25 Jan. 1975.
104 *Daily Mirror*, 6 Nov. 1980. L. James, *Warrior Race: A History of the British at War* (2001), 737.
105 G. Evans, *The Fight for Welsh Freedom* (2000), 160.
106 *Arcade*, 20 (7 Aug. 1981).
107 R. Colls, *Identity of England* (2002), 185.
108 A. Rolph, 'Greenham and its legacy: the women's peace movement in Wales in the 1980s', in T. Robin Chapman (ed.), *The Idiom of Dissent: Protest and Propaganda in Wales* (2006), 97–122.
109 Quoted in A. Bailey, *A Walk Through Wales* (1992), 217–18.
110 G. Griffiths, 'Regaining the wastelands', in D. Cole (ed.), *The New Wales* (1990), 61–8.
111 *The Times*, 1 June 1960. *Gwent Gazette*, 18 Jan. 1974.
112 *National Survey of Air Pollution, 1961–1971, Vol. II* (1972), 79.
113 G. M. Howe, 'Geographical distribution of cancer mortality in Wales, 1947–53', *Transactions and Papers (Institute of British Geographers)*, 28 (1960), 199–214.
114 For example see the Welsh concerns in *The Times*, 1 Nov. 1983.
115 *Daily Telegraph*, 3 Mar. 1979.

11

'Adapt to the future.' The Tory remaking of Wales, 1979–97

> As in England and Scotland, so in Wales, the Conservatives are the Party of the future. It is we who bring the new industries to the Valleys. It is we who bring new opportunities to families to do the best for themselves and for their country. And we bring a new chance to the nation to fulfil its destiny – a free people, a great people, proud of their past, ready to adapt to the future.
>
> Margaret Thatcher, speech at Cardiff, 23 May 1985[1]

> It surely cannot be contended that the Welsh are so untalented a nation that they are unable to produce one person capable of performing the function of Principal Minister in the Welsh Office?
>
> *Radical Wales*, 16 (1987)

IN THE SPRING OF 1980 Gwynfor Evans announced that he would begin a hunger strike in October and keep it up until the government agreed to implement its manifesto commitment to create a Welsh-language television channel. Few had any doubts that Evans would starve himself to death if necessary. It was an opportunity for him to make the ultimate sacrifice for Wales, to compensate for the failures of the referendum and what he and others took as his personal failing to make a final stand for Tryweryn (chapter 8).[2] After the trauma of 1979, this was a galvanizing moment for Welsh nationalists. Welsh Office minister Wyn Roberts thought Evans had 'a martyr complex' but he also expressed a real fear that Evans' death would 'inspire a less able breed to violence'. He wrote in his diary that Evans' life would be equated with 'the life of Wales, the nation and its people' and that the fight would be seen as symbolic of the government's 'heartlessness and obduracy'.[3]

Among English monoglots at least, anger about Welsh-language programming had actually receded somewhat during the 1970s. The development of televisions where channels could be changed by pressing a button rather than delicately turning a dial had made switching over easier, and new remote controls meant that some people did not even have to leave their chairs to do it. Such developments encouraged channel hopping and people were becoming less accustomed to studying channel listings, less aware of what the fifteen weekly hours of Welsh programmes were replacing and less annoyed when they did appear. Nonetheless, even Welsh speakers complained about the rescheduling of programmes like *Dallas* to make way for Welsh-language content. Yet, as television's hold on popular culture tightened, a dedicated Welsh-language channel came to be seen by some as the only answer to improving the quality and reach of Welsh-language television. Substituting an existing television channel for a new Welsh one would not be popular and arguments over the need, financing and practicalities of a Welsh-language fourth channel waged through the 1970s, complicated and politicized by the possibility of devolution and Cymdeithas yr Iaith Gymraeg targeting and vandalizing television offices and transmitters. Callaghan's Labour government accepted plans put forward by the 1974 Crawford Committee for a Welsh fourth channel but then put them on hold because of the cost.[4] Amid the financial crisis of the late 1970s, an expensive Welsh-language television service was not a priority but both Labour and the Conservatives committed themselves to creating one in their 1979 election manifestos, perhaps with an eye on not alienating Welsh sentiment after the referendum debacle.

The Conservatives repeated that commitment after winning the 1979 election but then changed their minds. Home Secretary William Whitelaw's autobiography attributed this to 'colleagues in Wales' thinking the number of Welsh speakers was not worth the cost of a special channel. Internal government papers, however, suggest that the decision to reverse the policy came from the Home Office, which presented it to the Welsh Office as something of a *fait accompli*, much to the initial disgust of the Secretary of State and his civil servants.[5] There was some rationale to the decision to keep Welsh on the BBC and HTV rather than create a separate channel. Estimates put the cost to the public purse of a new channel at £15–£20 million more than sharing out Welsh programmes between HTV and the BBC. There was some support for the government's u-turn from the higher echelons of BBC Wales and particularly HTV Wales. After all, it did not involve diluting the amount of Welsh television and it was a way of dealing with the financial and technical problems of creating a new channel. Within the Welsh Office, Welsh-speaking officials and a Minister of State offered further support, fearing a separate channel would ghettoize the language.[6] Moreover, the Welsh Office saw that while a new channel would win the attention of those committed to the language, a greater problem 'in keeping the language alive' was 'the massive indifference of many of the people who, by sheer accident of birth, happen to speak the language'.[7] Such arguments also won some support among Welsh-language newspapers. *Y Faner* agreed that the channel would ghettoize the language by reducing the contact the English-speaking population of Wales would have with it. *Yr Herald Cymraeg* thought Evans' threatened fast meant the debate 'bade farewell to caution and knowledge and judgment'. It supported more Welsh at peak times on the main channels rather than a financially insecure separate channel which fewer people would watch.[8]

The u-turn still brought a storm of protest. After the tragedy of the referendum, this seemed to be a step too far for many cultural and political nationalists and some regarded it as part of a pattern of English treachery that dated back to the Blue Books of 1847. There were renewed direct actions, including switching off a transmitter, and 600 people refused to pay for their television licences. A can of petrol, detonator and timing device were placed on a window sill, eighteen inches from the head of the Secretary of State for Wales' sleeping teenage son. Both Labour and Conservative MPs from Wales lobbied Nicholas Edwards, the Secretary of State, for a change of position. The Welsh Office believed much of the criticism was because people thought the original plan had been for the fourth channel to be entirely in Welsh, whereas some offpeak English programming had always been envisaged.[9] But even if the criticism was misinformed, the cause became a rallying call and a point of principle that Wales was a nation with rights however its people had voted in 1979. And it was a principle that Gwynfor Evans, no longer an MP but still the leader of a mainstream political party, appeared willing to die for.

Nicholas Edwards told the Home Secretary that

> he had no wish to exaggerate the problem but Mr Gwynfor Evans was serious, determined and obstinate. If he went ahead with his proposed fast there would be very unpleasant consequences indeed. The decision to abandon the Manifesto commitment seemed right at the time and but for Mr Gwynfor Evans there would be no need to review that decision; moreover it still seemed right and many people in Wales agree with this although few were willing to say so in public.[10]

Edwards appealed to Evans on the basis that the fast could lead to violence but to no avail. He wanted a single channel which would have peak-time viewing in Welsh so a continuous audience could be built up by allowing people to know where Welsh was on and to stick with it. The Welsh Office tried to ride out the storm but came to the conclusion that while it might win the argument in the House of Commons and in the wider country, that would not 'stop Gwynfor from seeking the martyr's crown'.[11] The threat of violence that his death might engender was not limited to Wales. The Home Secretary worried about the impact any concession might have on Northern Ireland, rightly so as at it turned out, since Evans did unintentionally inspire hunger strikes there.[12] The lobbying of moderates like the Archbishop of Wales increased pressure on the government but it also allowed the possibility of another change of mind without being seen as just giving in to threats.

Given the apparent weight of support for a Welsh channel within the whole Welsh establishment (rather than just its Welsh-speaking constituents) and the possibility of defeat in the Lords, the government was in a difficult position. Nicholas Edwards told the Prime Minister that although the original decision was probably right, he was 'taken aback by the strength of feeling' in Wales, which was now 'fostering intolerable consequences'. With her blessing, the initial commitment was reinstated and Evans' place in Welsh mythology was guaranteed.[13] Edwards told the press, 'If you have the support of moderate opinion then you can resist violence – but without that support it would be quite wrong to risk it'.[14] Evans himself was actually a little disappointed the government had given in so quickly, as the situation had been winning more support for Plaid Cymru all the time. Of course, not everyone was happy. A letter to the *Wrexham Leader* complained that the channel would be dominated by the south and asked when Cardiff's 'broadcasting moguls' would 'get it into their tiny heads that dialects and geography make North and South Wales as dissimilar as chalk and cheese'.[15] Nonetheless, it was still a historic moment. Welsh threats and opinion had forced a change of heart in the British government. Perhaps now anything was possible.

Sianel Pedwar Cymru (S4C; Channel 4 Wales) launched on 1 November 1982. It broadcast twenty-two hours a week of its own programming and filled the rest of its schedule with English material from Channel 4. Research suggested that 53 per cent of Welsh speakers regularly watched the channel, with the news and soap opera *Pobl y Cwm* attracting audiences of up to 150,000. This may have been small compared with the Welsh audiences for BBC1 and ITV but it still meant 30 per cent of Welsh speakers were watching at once.[16] The language used in the news, according to one historian, made large numbers 'conversant with a mode of expression in which traditional standards were respected'. Of course, it also made others just switch channel, unable to comprehend the formal and technical Welsh of the newsreader. A letter writer to the *Western Mail* complained: 'I am sure too that many of the news items could be in simpler Welsh. Words are often used that would not normally be heard in a lifetime in Wales. We are not all Welsh preachers and professors.' While some found much of the news incomprehensible, others complained about the use of English words in popular shows or in interviews with people whose 'spoken language was woefully corrupted'. But that was how many people spoke Welsh. It was perhaps little wonder then that programmes found it difficult to persuade 'countless' first-language Welsh speakers to appear on screen, because they were afraid their Welsh was 'not good enough'.[17]

There were other problems too. Some worried that S4C was taking people away from writing serious literature and into scripting soaps and documentaries.[18] It perhaps also took some people into a media career who might otherwise have devoted themselves to nationalist politics. The realism of some programmes, meanwhile, was rather questionable; there was an amazing amount of north Walian accents in the Carmarthenshire village where *Pobl y Cwm* was set, while urban communities in the south were often portrayed as if the English language did not exist. Making Welsh versions of popular English genres such as the quiz show or light entertainment did not always go down well either. Young viewers were proving hard to attract and by 1986 one academic was complaining that the bulk of programmes 'appear dated, conservative and stereotyped'.[19] Another writer complained in 1991 that S4C was unfunny: 'It's as if Welsh speakers are expected to laugh only at village idiots and the humour of the tŷ bach [toilet]'.[20] The channel was thus caught between wanting to preserve the language and its culture and making shows that reflected what most of the audience wanted and the reality of the bilingual and colloquial society that people lived in. Even a former head of the channel remarked, 'For a minority the Welsh language is a political activity but they tend to forget that the majority speak Welsh because they are Welsh'.[21] And that meant making programmes that were entertaining, even if it offended highbrow critics who wanted something more substantial.

THE CREATION OF S4C marked the beginning of a period when the idea of Wales was reconstructed after the debacle of the 1979 referendum. After the economic problems of the 1970s and early 1980s had created a strong sense of decline in traditional industrial Wales, economic restructuring finally began to gather pace in the mid-1980s, leading the government to claim it was turning Wales into a land of hi-tech factories. The reality was more complex but, as more pits were closed by a government with no Welsh majority, people in industrial Wales began to reconsider whether their sense of nationality should have any political significance. Yet, while the Tories took away with one hand, they gave back with another. To compensate for the scale of economic upheaval that its policies were inflicting, the governments of 1979–97 enacted a number of changes that did much – indeed more than any previous administration – to buttress the fortunes, status and legitimacy of the language. Not only did Welsh gain its own television channel, it was also given equal status in law and a place on every schoolchild's timetable. In its last year of office, the 1974–9 Labour government had given £350,000 in aid and subsidies to the Welsh language; in 1984–5 the Conservatives gave £2.6 million.[22] The powers of the Welsh Office were also extended, while a host of new quangos were set up to monitor and govern Margaret Thatcher's free market state. These created new tensions between the Welsh establishment and the wider working class but they also helped modern Wales become a more defined nation than ever before. Under Thatcher and John Major, administrative devolution reached such proportions that it was not misleading to talk of the emergence of a Welsh state.

This all indicated that Wales was not without influence in the Tory administrations of 1979 to 1997. Indeed, Thatcher's cabinet actually had three prominent Welshmen within it, even if all were removed from their roots. Born in Port Talbot, Chancellor of the Exchequer Sir Geoffrey Howe was a symbol of the social mobility revered by much of Wales. His grandfather had been a metal worker and his father a solicitor; Howe himself went to a Welsh prep school and then an English public school before becoming a wealthy barrister. Seemingly less conscious of being Welsh, Michael Heseltine was the son of a Swansea steel manager, educated at a leading English public school before making a fortune in publishing. Nicholas Edwards, meanwhile, was a public-school-educated merchant banker whose family came from Powys. Later, under John Major, Michael Howard, a product of Llanelli grammar school, was Home Secretary. And yet, despite the presence of Welshmen in her cabinet and the half million Welsh votes she received in each of the 1979, 1983 and 1987 general elections, Thatcher's relationship with the people of Wales was never easy. Nicholas Edwards, Secretary of State for Wales between 1979 and 1987, felt that she was uncomfortable in the 'alien territory' of Wales. Her visits could see crowds jeering, throwing eggs and stones and fighting with the police. After being booed and gestured at in Cardiff she told Edwards, 'what dreadful people, we are really wasting our time – what is the point of all your efforts if they appreciate them so little'.[23]

The advances made in the status of Wales were fought for – by protestors, the Welsh political community and by forces within the Welsh Office – rather than being simply granted by a benevolent London government. Nonetheless, perhaps because the result of the 1979 referendum had suggested that Wales was not a threat to the union, the government was content to allow administrative devolution to continue its *ad hoc* advance. In 1979 the Select Committee for Welsh Affairs was set up within Parliament and in 1980 the Welsh Office was allowed to negotiate directly with the Treasury over the size of the block grant for Welsh local authorities. In the latter year the Welsh Office opened a large new building in the centre of Cardiff, making it more of a reality in the popular mind. It also gained new powers in the early 1990s over higher education funding and employment training. By 1995 it was responsible for approaching £7 billion or 70 per cent of public expenditure in Wales.[24] Key to its operation was the Welsh-speaking north Walian Wyn Roberts, who held a ministerial post there from 1979 to 1994. He had deep traditional Welsh sympathies and ensured the language had someone with its best interests at heart at the centre of the Welsh Office. Some even regarded him as something of a Welsh autonomist. A special adviser in the Welsh Office noted that whenever John Major was asked about Welsh issues he always asked 'Does Wyn think it's important?'[25] Roberts worked with a series of Secretaries of State who, in different ways, ensured that the Conservative government was seemingly more interventionist than Thatcher's natural antipathy to state action. Edwards claimed that Thatcher mostly gave him a 'remarkably free hand' to follow his own policies, using public agencies such as the Welsh Development Agency (WDA), which 'she did not much favour'.[26] Edwards' successors, Peter Walker (1987–90) and David Hunt (1990–3), also claimed they followed far more interventionist strategies than might have been expected of a government that was supposedly reeling back the state. They were perhaps allowed to champion their 'wet' Conservative ideals in Wales because Thatcher was little interested in what happened there. The post of Secretary of State for Wales seemed to have been given to Walker as a way of marginalizing him without actually having to sack him from the cabinet. Walker himself said he took the post only after being assured by Thatcher that he 'could do it my way', which meant increasing public expenditure.[27] That certainly happened, as the Welsh Office increased its responsibilities at a time when many other government departments were scaling back. In 1976–7 public spending per head in Wales had been 6 per cent higher than in England; by 1992–3 it was 19 per cent higher. That was partly because social security spending was higher but between 1979 and 1997 the Welsh

Office's budget (which did not include social security) rose by 151 per cent in real terms.[28]

There were a series of schemes which suggested that substantial sums of money were being spent on the regeneration of Wales' shattered economy. A second Severn bridge opened in 1996, Cardiff docks started their £2.4 billion transformation into Cardiff Bay, trunks roads were upgraded (notably the A55 and A470, ensuring faster road access into north Wales and Cardiff), the south Wales section of the M4 was completed and more than fifty bypasses were built.[29] There was also a £500 million Valleys Initiative that involved derelict land clearance, road improvements, factory building, training schemes and new hospitals. Yet these substantive schemes brought the government little credit. Critics complained that the Valleys Initiative was style rather than substance and involved £300 million being redesignated within the Welsh budget rather than adding to it.[30] It did not solve unemployment but it did help create and safeguard some 24,000 jobs, saw 2,000 acres of land cleared and improvements carried out on 7,000 homes. Although the government was willing to spend to kick-start regeneration, attracting private investment remained at the heart of its economic policy, just as it had been for all governments since the war. To achieve this, the Welsh Office worked closely with local authorities, trade unions and quangos like the WDA to proactively court investment. Whereas there was often conflict between central government and Labour-run English councils, Welsh local authorities and trade unions worked pragmatically with the WDA and Welsh Office, creating a consensus of sorts that was not present in England.[31] Although this impressed investors, the global recession meant Wales still faced an uphill task, something people were only too aware of. Therefore, as well as providing an infrastructure to attract new investment, the Welsh Office prioritized improving the image of Wales and overcoming the deep prevailing pessimism. Walker was particularly upbeat about the Welsh economy, sending out a stream of optimistic press releases about the situation in Wales and even arranging for the Welsh Office to have its first ever Christmas cards without black clouds on. Such was Walker's positive outlook that Rhodri Morgan MP (Labour, Cardiff West) claimed that he would sell the Third World War 'as a great opportunity for the Welsh undertaking profession'.[32]

During Walker's three years as Secretary of State, Wales secured 22 per cent of UK inward investment. Even over the longer period 1979–89, Wales attracted, on average, 13.3 per cent of the total overseas investment in the UK.[33] Wales was thus winning proportionately more inward investment than any other part of the UK and it developed the biggest concentration of

Japanese companies in Europe. By the middle of the 1980s more jobs were finally being created than were being lost. After a net loss of 146,000 jobs between 1979 and 1986, the following two years saw employment grow by 63,000. Annual unemployment fell from 13.7 per cent in 1986 to 6.7 per cent in 1990.[34] This all brought much talk, from the media, politicians and academics, of a Welsh economic miracle based on modernization, diversification and attracting hi-tech investment from overseas. After becoming Secretary of State for Wales in 1993, John Redwood claimed that 'As other countries have been consumed by the fire of recession, Wales has been a defiant phoenix'.[35]

Such perspectives were rooted in just how bad things had got in the late 1970s and early 1980s; after that, even a small amount of economic growth could seem remarkable. They were also exercises in public relations and the presentation of selected statistics. By 1985 Welsh gross domestic product (GDP) had fallen slightly, to 84 per cent of the UK figure, and that figure changed little over the next decade.[36] A faster economic upturn in England meant that by 1986 Wales had the lowest average weekly male earnings in Britain. Many of the jobs created were concentrated in Clwyd (its GDP went from 15 per cent below the Welsh average in 1981 to 11 per cent above it in 1995) and the M4 corridor east of Bridgend, exacerbating the wealth divide that had opened with the first phases of post-war deindustrialization in the 1960s (chapter 3) and indicating how economic progress came from connections with England rather than within Wales. The new jobs were, though, frequently unskilled assembly-line positions that were often taken up by women. Two-thirds of jobs created in Mid Glamorgan in 1984–9 were actually part-time.[37] A novel said of the production lines:

> I don't know how these people punching holes in plastic survive on the enterprise zones. No wonder everyone's had it by the time they get home. You can't do anything after a day of that; just sit in front of the tv, don't even listen, then go to bed. Tomorrow same thing, go to bed.[38]

It was the availability of a workforce willing to work in such conditions for low wages that helped attract foreign investment in the first place; trade unionists and Labour MPs began to complain of companies wanting a 'coolie economy' and using 'samurai management'.[39] Moreover, some of the private investment was secured only at significant cost to the public purse. A new £20 million industrial estate in Baglan was supposed to create 5,000 jobs but two years after opening only one factory had been occupied, meaning its jobs had been created at a cost of £2 million each.[40]

Despite the upbeat rhetoric from the Welsh Office, the 1990s brought another recession and employment in manufacturing fell by nearly 32,000

between 1990 and 1994, while unemployment rose by 39 per cent. This was not the same scale of decline witnessed in England but it was hardly an economic miracle. By 1995 there were 11,000 fewer people in the Welsh workforce than there had been in 1979. In the same period the male workforce had shrunk by 89,000. Higher unemployment and lower wages meant that personal disposable income in Wales had fallen from 91 per cent of the UK figure in 1980 to 86 per cent in 1996. In 1997 'real' unemployment, as opposed to the number of claimants, was worse in Wales than in any other UK region. In Mid Glamorgan nearly a quarter of men and half of women aged between sixteen and retirement age were not economically active. Wales had three of the six UK districts with the highest rates of unemployment, including Merthyr, where, at 33 per cent, real unemployment was worse than anywhere else in Britain.[41] As those who lived in the post-coal Valleys knew only too well, the Welsh economic miracle of the late 1980s and 1990s was a mirage.

If there was one place where there was a more genuine revival, it was Cardiff. From the mid-1980s onwards, the local authorities there began to shift their aspirations and policies away from the kind of traditional industrial jobs that had been lost with the closure of East Moors steelworks in 1978 or the Rover car plant in 1983, to focusing on building the service sector. As happened in most the UK's major cities, the city centre was physically regenerated and there was some success in attracting investment in the retail, financial, legal and business services sectors. In 1984–91, the number of jobs in South Glamorgan increased by three times the national average and what had been a fading industrial city began to look more like a modern capital. Cardiff pulled away from the rest of Wales, becoming more like the south of England in terms of earnings and house prices. By 1995 South Glamorgan's GDP was the eighth highest in the UK and 35 per cent above the Welsh average.[42] This success owed much the willingness of the government to inject huge amounts of public money into the Cardiff Bay project. The development was actually kick-started by the Labour-run South Glamorgan County Council deciding to build its new headquarters in the middle of industrial wasteland near the city docks. The government took forward the vision and ploughed £496 million of public money into the Cardiff Bay Development Corporation, which led a regeneration project centred on residential and commercial developments.[43] The scale of the commitment was evident in the fact that £197 million of the money was for a barrage that did nothing but damn two tidal rivers to attract investors who would apparently not come unless they had a nice waterfront to look at. Successive Secretaries of State were important to ensuring that Wales got additional money for the project, showing that the Welsh Office had a degree of political clout. Thatcher and Major were brought to visit the Bay to ensure their personal support. Nicholas Edwards even threatened to resign unless money was forthcoming from the Treasury.[44] But even with such developments, Cardiff had its problems. Deprived estates on the city's fringes remained physically and psychologically removed from the developments and there were serious riots in Ely in 1991. Retail may have been a visible sign of regeneration but its jobs tended to be low paid. The banking and financial sector was not as diverse as it should be for a city of the European pretensions Cardiff had, while the public sector, with over 35 per cent of the city's jobs in 1995, was too dominant in an era where public spending was always under pressure.[45] Here Cardiff summed up the central weakness of the whole post-war Welsh economy: it was reliant on the state and Thatcherism did nothing to change that.

What was happening in Wales was not only not as successful as its political masters made out, it was not as unique either.[46] The Welsh Office was a fairly small Whitehall department and its Secretary of State was a junior cabinet minister (although Walker had more clout than the others). Its size and lack of influence curtailed its financial autonomy and its economic policies. Even though councils, unions and business found it easier to gain access to ministers and officials in Cardiff than they did in Whitehall, general policy remained directed from London and there was no escaping the fact that the Welsh Office was the arm of the British government in Wales. As two political scientists pointed out, the Welsh Office undertook 'the humdrum business of implementing policies decided elsewhere and introducing modest variations where they can to suit the needs and idiosyncrasies' of Wales.[47] Thatcher's government was actually fairly interventionist in seeking investment everywhere in the UK, although not always with the support of local authorities and unions that it received in Wales. The key difference in Wales was that the Welsh Office boasted about intervention rather than hid it. But even then the truth was that government expenditure on regional assistance to industry in Wales fell by 58 per cent between 1980–1 and 1990–1.[48]

It is the relentless pressure on public services that destroys the idea that Tory governance in Wales was different. Total public expenditure in Wales may have been on the up but there was a constant strain on budgets, not least in local government, which seemed expected to bear the brunt of the pressure on the public purse. Spending cuts had actually begun under Labour in the late 1970s as Callaghan's government shifted its priority from fighting unemployment to fighting inflation. The impact was felt at a very local level. By 1976 South Glamorgan County Council, for example, had dispensed with its garden party and chairman's dinner. More importantly, there were cuts in frontline services, notably in social services, whose director complained that it was no longer possible to provide services as quickly or as often as needed. Day centres for the elderly increased their charges for meals and were shut on Saturdays; staff training and grants to voluntary organizations were cut. After the 1979 general election the squeeze tightened. South Glamorgan again had to reduce grants to voluntary groups, nurseries and playgroups; it cut back on maintenance and equipment in children's homes, social services and employment centres, and introduced new charges for some previously free services.[49] When Labour returned to power in the county in 1981 it tried to maintain services by imposing a new supplementary rate and raising domestic rates by 36 per cent. But Thatcher's apparent dislike of local government meant that such supplementary rates were made illegal in 1982 and domestic rates were capped after 1983. This not only hurt the independence of local authorities but also made yet more cuts inevitable. Across local government there were redundancies and a general mood of gloom. Service delivery itself did not deteriorate drastically but the maintenance of the supporting infrastructure did, something only too evident in the deterioration of council housing. In South Glamorgan the annual resurfacing of a sixth of all the county's roads was abandoned and school buildings declined as maintenance budgets were cut. The press ran horror stories about children sitting in classes under crumbling roofs, while schools found money so tight that they started using sums earmarked for repairs for the purchase of teaching equipment. The National Health Service in Wales suffered too. Total Welsh Office spending on health quadrupled because of inflation, rising wages, higher staff numbers, new hospitals, health promotion programmes and far more people using the service but there was never enough money to go round. In 1985, for example, East Dyfed Health Authority laid off ninety-six low-paid ancillary and clerical staff to meet a £2 million budget deficit. It was little wonder then that there was a strong sense in the 1980s that the quality of public services was being eroded.[50]

Individuals were also hurt by changes to the benefit system, which the government sought to cut the value of by removing earnings-related supplements and not always raising payments in line with inflation. Thus, at a time when average earnings were growing beyond inflation, unemployment benefit fell in real terms by 4 per cent between 1978 and 1988, widening the gap between those in and out of work.[51] This figure disguised the immediate impact of some of the reforms. A sixty-one-year-old constituent of Ann

Clwyd MP (Labour, Cynon Valley) wrote to her after his weekly benefit was cut by £1.26 because of a change in mortgage interest rates. This meant he was left with £7.57 a week after he had paid his bills. He wondered how he was supposed to buy food on that amount:

> I do not eat meat. I can't afford it. A small tin of tuna, 57p is made to last three days and frozen kippers with frozen vegetables the rest of the week. I had been giving myself a treat of fish and chips £1.10 on Saturdays that will now have to go. I don't know what to give up next. I sold my car and my motor-bike years ago, and gave up drinking and smoking when I became redundant. I no longer have a social life and have virtually become a hermit.[52]

He had been out of work for nearly eight years.

The attacks on local government's power and its ability to alleviate such cases contributed to the idea that the Conservatives' governance of Wales was undemocratic and unaccountable. Over the course of the 1980s commentators started speaking of a 'democratic deficit' in Wales. The Secretary of State for Wales was appointed by Downing Street and four of the five men who held that post between 1979 and 1997 did not represent Welsh constituencies. Gwynfor Evans claimed they wielded 'the enormous powers of a colonialist governor-general'. On his first day in the job, Walker handled criticisms about the fact he was English by agreeing that it was 'absolutely appalling' but the fault lay with his mother.[53] The concerns did not necessarily reflect popular opinion. A 1997 survey suggested that 56 per cent of Welsh voters did not feel angry that it was English voters who decided who governed Wales. But it was perhaps significant that 20 per cent said they were very angry.[54] Concerns about accountability and democracy were, however, deepened by the growth of quangos, state bodies whose managers were appointed by the Secretary of State to oversee and govern various parts of Welsh life. Between 1979 and 1991 the number of bodies officially recognized as quangos in Wales doubled to eighty; if appointed local bodies and advisory committees are included there were 350. The combined budget of the eighty official quangos was £1.8 billion and they employed over 57,000 people. By 1996 there were 1,273 councillors in Wales but around 1,400 quango appointees.[55] David Hanson MP (Labour, Delyn) spoke for many when he claimed that the quangos were 'overstuffed with white, male businessmen, lawyers and accountants, with a sprinkling of establishment figures for good measure. The pattern of appointments represents the face of the Conservative Party and their sympathizers, not the people of Wales.'[56] When a Cardiff backbench MP could be voted out of Parliament but then appointed into the more influential position of chair of the county health authority, it was not surprising that even a historian claimed the Tories 'began to look like a foreign army of occupation'.[57] Despite their reputation for 'jobs for the boys', Sir Glanmor Williams said his experience of quango boards was 'very different. I found them to be composed of people who worked hard and conscientiously in return for no payment except for the reimbursement of expenses'.[58] That was probably true but the occasional scandal did not exactly engender faith in quango Wales. In the early 1990s the WDA and Development Board for Rural Wales were involved in a series of scandals that centred on unauthorized and irregular payments to members and employees. It even turned out that the WDA's marketing director was a convicted fraudster.[59] Most controversies were far less serious. A year after former Secretary of State Nicholas Edwards joined the board of Allied British Ports, 160 acres of prime development land owned by the company were excluded from a compulsory purchase order in Cardiff Bay. A local Labour MP described what he saw as the company's preferential treatment as 'an example of government sleaze of the kind with which we have become all too familiar'.[60]

Whatever the doubts over the nature of governance in Wales, the growth of quangos and the profile of the Welsh Office encouraged charities, unions and other bodies to develop their own Welsh branches. This all meant that Wales was slowly developing a civil society that was more delineated from England than ever before. By 1984 there were 466 'associations, movements, bodies, committees and institutions' based on and in Wales. It was increasingly becoming possible to argue that Welsh identity could be defined by such institutions and that a meaningful proto-state was being created.[61] Moreover, quangos may have been unelected but they were often more amenable to developing a specifically Welsh agenda than the local councils whose power and responsibilities they were accused of usurping.[62] But this all had little impact on the consciousness of ordinary Welsh people. It was a world of appointments, plush offices and decent salaries, a middle-class world that, no matter how well intentioned its members were, had little direct contact with the wider population. Of course, the same was true of government in London, but at least the electorate got to vote for that.

THE GROWTH OF public bodies governing and serving Wales did create job opportunities that allowed talented Welsh people to stay in Wales and further developed the Welsh-speaking establishment that had first started to emerge with the foundation of the BBC in the 1920s. Many of its members had nationalist sympathies, even if these were often cultural rather than political. Indeed, the emergence of this establishment perhaps held back a more radical nationalism, since these were people with an interest in the status quo and removed from the deprivation that might feed more drastic action. Even the once Marxist Dafydd Elis-Thomas MP (Plaid Cymru, Meirionnydd) joined the House of Lords in 1992. Although this actually increased the influence of nationalism, some still saw it as hypocrisy or betrayal. A more genuine case of double standards was R. S. Thomas, an acclaimed and fervent nationalist poet who said, 'Britain doesn't exist for me, it's an abstraction forced on the Welsh people'. Yet he spoke English to his son and sent him to an English boarding school.[63] The contradictions or pragmatism of the Welsh establishment were no different to the dilemmas of Wales itself, something evident in the novel *Y Llosgi* (1986). The hero is a public relations officer for the Welsh Development Council who has to sell Wales as modern and dynamic to foreign investors and old fashioned and quaint to tourists.[64]

As some of the tensions in that novel show, by joining the establishment such figures became increasingly resented and removed from some parts of the communities that they were supposed to serve. Some of the resentment was predictable and old hat; Labour complained that Plaid Cymru got too much attention on the Welsh news and that it had 'infiltrated' the BBC. As they had in previous decades, some of those who did not speak Welsh complained that the language was a kind of 'old Etonian tie' that gave its speakers access to jobs but left others feeling 'a stranger' in their 'own country'.[65] But resentment of this Welsh-speaking establishment began to extend to other Welsh speakers too. Within the Welsh-language rock scene there were complaints that it was dominated by middle-class and middle-aged patrons, 'a narrow group of like-minded bureaucrats and bosses for whom the medium (Welsh) is the whole message'.[66] That resentment found one of its most powerful expressions in the song 'Cân i Gymry' ('Song for the Welsh-speaking Welsh'), by the band Datblygu. It told of people who complained that Wales was oppressed and were anti-Britain enough 'to sound like Sieg Heil'. Yet they only, the song claimed, had to work from one to three for the BBC, had freemason friends and enjoyed a 'lifetime ticket on the gravy train'.[67] Yet there was a good deal of myth in the idea that simply speaking Welsh got you a good job. In South Glamorgan just 10 per cent of Welsh speakers had unskilled or semi-skilled jobs but this was because the language in Cardiff was concentrated among people who had moved to the city precisely because of their professional jobs. In rural Wales speaking Welsh was actually far more common among lower-grade occupations.[68]

Across the nation, the size of the Welsh establishment, whatever language it spoke, was actually rather small. This was clear in the failure of an attempt to create a serious Sunday broadsheet for the Welsh middle classes, a group who seemed to prefer what was produced in London. *Wales on Sunday* began publishing in 1989 but its circulation after six months was just 44,000 and it relaunched as a tabloid centred on celebrities and sport.[69]

Despite the growth of a Welsh establishment, Welsh speakers continued to feel that their culture was not valued by the Thatcher or Major governments. This was not entirely fair. After a long period of the issue being unresolved by previous administrations, Nicholas Edwards had instigated an inquiry into the potential hazards of Welsh coming first on road signs. It concluded there were none, so in 1980 he allowed county councils to make their own decision on which language took precedence. Further financial support was also introduced for voluntary bodies that supported the language but Edwards declared that he did not support enforcing universal bilingualism. His view was that the language would survive or die according to the personal choice of people.[70] This willingness to even contemplate the death of the language created a storm. Encouraged by the success over S4C, demonstrations against the Welsh Office and its representatives became the norm at the National Eisteddfod, despite the fact that the Office's grants were central to the Eisteddfod's viability. More seriously, Cymdeithas Yr Iaith Gymraeg began vandalizing post boxes, telephone kiosks (which both had English-only signage) and the Welsh Office itself (where the signs were bilingual). Such actions led to 289 individuals appearing in court between 1981 and 1990 and thirty-four imprisonments.[71]

Once again, breaking the law worked as a form of political protest and, after Walker replaced Edwards at the Welsh Office, an advisory Welsh Language Board was created in 1988. The Board concentrated its efforts on facilitating the use of Welsh as a community language rather than increasing the numbers of speakers. It strove to 'normalize' bilingualism so that 'it is possible, convenient and normal for everyone, in every situation where a public service is provided, to choose which language he or she wishes to use'. To achieve that goal it proposed legislation.[72] The Welsh Office sensed the difficulties of getting Thatcher and the cabinet to accept the idea; indeed, she told the BBC: 'If people love the Welsh language why do you need compulsion?' Wyn Roberts, who had his own doubts over whether the law could protect the language and who was deeply unimpressed by the pressure he was being placed under by protestors, was instrumental in getting the government to support legislation.[73] His reasoning seemed to centre on the benefits of isolating the extreme nationalists and winning over moderate support. The legislation introduced required the public sector to treat Welsh and English on an equal basis when providing services in Wales. Bilingualism was being enforced on the public sector in its dealings with the public, creating new jobs for translators and increasing paper usage and printing costs as every public document produced by the state in Wales now appeared in two languages. The 1993 Welsh Language Act was unpopular before it was even passed but not because of the costs it created. There was no absolute right for people to be able to use Welsh and exclusions could be claimed on practical grounds, arbitrated over by the Secretary of State. Gwynfor Evans called it 'lamentably weak'.[74] Its confinement to the public sector was also criticized but was perhaps understandable given the state of the economy and the huge costs compulsory bilingualism would impose on small businesses. The exclusion of banks and public utilities from the Act was a more understandable complaint, although they, like other large companies such as supermarkets, voluntarily shifted to using Welsh in their more prominent signage. Other criticisms included the failure to require Welsh-speaking juries for cases involving Welsh or to allow damages for those adversely affected by breaches of the Act. But perhaps most upsetting for critics was the Act's failure to make a symbolic and definitive statement that Welsh was an official language. Civil servants were uneasy about inserting any such point of principle into law without knowing what the consequences might be. Moreover, a Home Office civil servant wrote to one Labour Lord: 'my main reservation about a declaration of official status is that it would enforce upon Wales a bilingualism which had no regard to the varying circumstances and practicalities which exist in Wales'. John Major ended up telling the Commons that Welsh was already an official language but there was still no insertion of such a statement into the legislation.[75]

Faced with the criticisms, Wyn Roberts told Lord Cledwyn that it had been hard enough to get the bill past various government departments 'as it was'. Plaid Cymru MPs voted against the third reading, while Labour abstained. Roberts recorded in his diary, 'We produce a sound bill, which will mean the investment of a great deal of money in Welsh-speaking Wales. And Welsh MPs turn it down! So much for their professed love of the language and their concern for the best interests of their people.'[76] Whatever the problems of the Act, it cemented bilingualism into Welsh public life. Most people may have automatically turned to the English side of the form but the very existence of a bilingual form in the first place reinforced their consciousness of Wales. Novelists might make cheap jokes about signs that used to say Taxi but 'now said Taxi/Tacsi for the benefit of Welsh people who had never seen a letter X before' but no one who used a public sector service in Wales, which was everyone, could now be unaware that they were in a nation with two languages.[77]

Probably the most significant thing that the Conservatives did for Wales as a nation was give Welsh a statutory place on the new national curriculum, introduced by the 1988 Education Act. Before then, despite the 1960s and 1970s growth of Welsh-medium education (chapter 7), there was no universal policy on teaching the language and much remained up to not just individual local authorities but individual schools too. In 1984 there was no Welsh taught in 98 per cent of primary schools in Gwent, 37 per cent in South Glamorgan and even 10 per cent in Dyfed. By 1988 over 80 per cent of secondary school pupils were taught Welsh in their first year but only 28 per cent were still taking the subject in their fourth year.[78] Not unusual was the situation in Llangollen, where children were forced to choose between Welsh and computer studies in their third year. Plans to reform English education provided an opportunity to strengthen the position of Welsh in schools and, thanks to the powerful influence of Wyn Roberts and lobbying from education and Welsh-language bodies, plans for a Welsh version of the new national curriculum were drawn up.[79]

Thatcher was quite prepared to let the Welsh Office have its own way on Welsh-medium schools but she was suspicious of how a Welsh national curriculum would impact on English-language schools. In an argument with Roberts, she revealed some of her attitudes. Wales and Scotland, she thought, were holding England back. 'You have nothing! You contribute nothing!' she told Roberts; the 'only Conservatives in Wales are the English who moved in'.[80] Roberts, quite rightly, objected, although there were many Welsh socialists who probably would have agreed with Thatcher on this last point. Eventually, she gave way to the Welsh Office. The place of Welsh on the new national curriculum was not the only difference to what was enacted in England. Welsh history was also included and, as the curriculum developed, its limited divergence from English provision became officially accepted as a means of giving children a sense of Welsh heritage and identity.[81] The requirement that children be taught (some) Welsh from the ages of four to sixteen did create problems and implementation was staged, with some schools initially allowed to opt out. Established primary schoolteachers found themselves having to learn some basic Welsh quickly, sometimes staying only one step ahead of the children. It was 1999 before all schools were teaching Welsh. But it appeared to have an impact. At the 2001 census, 40.8 per cent of children aged five to fifteen were recorded as Welsh speakers, a dramatic rise on the figure of 25.9 per cent in 1991.

Despite such advances, Welsh still faced significant problems. English in-migration into the rural Welsh-speaking heartlands continued apace, undermining the language's numerical and practical hold there. Even Welsh speakers were not united in their support for the language. In a 1994 survey of Welsh speakers in Gwynedd, 9 per cent of respondents thought that Welsh had no place in the modern world and 11 per cent thought it unsuitable for business and science.[82] Elsewhere, researchers found bilingual teenagers across south Wales who saw English as fashionable and Welsh as representing an older style of life and cultural values. They formed different social groups according to their linguistic preferences but the dynamics of their language use were complex. The teenagers switched between English and Welsh according to the situations they found themselves in and what was being discussed; under 30 per cent preferred to use English for discussing college work and greeting people but over 60 per cent preferred it for discussing sex, music and cars.[83] Welsh, meanwhile, also remained much stronger in its spoken form than in its written form. At the 1981 census, only 363,116 of the 503,549 who said they spoke Welsh said they could read and write the language. Even fewer actually bought things to read in Welsh. Subsidies, which reached £600,000 by the mid-1990s, ensured a wide range of publications in Welsh but any novel that sold 2,500 copies could be regarded as a 'sweeping success'.[84] Paperau bro – short, locally produced community news-sheets – did have a combined readership of around 70,000 but the more conventional newspapers were struggling. In the early 1980s *Y Cymro* had a circulation of 8,000 and *Y Faner* just 1,800. *Y Faner* had been founded in 1843 but it folded in 1992 after losing its subsidy. In 1982 *Sulyn*, the first Welsh-language Sunday paper, was launched; it lasted fourteen issues. In contrast a survey in 1989 suggested that the *Sun* and *Daily Mirror* had a combined readership of 1,199,000 in Wales.[85]

The 1991 census recorded that 508,098 people spoke Welsh. This represented 18.7 per cent of the population, a slight fall from 1981, although the total number of speakers had risen by 4,549. When the data were examined more closely, it was clear how perilous the position of the language was. In only 14 per cent of households did all adults and children over three speak Welsh. Only 54 per cent of households with Welsh speakers in them were wholly Welsh-speaking, while 43 per cent of wholly Welsh-speaking households had no dependent children in them. The children did not speak Welsh in 42 per cent of households with children and some adults who spoke Welsh. Worse, there were 2,215 households where all the adults spoke Welsh but none of the children did. There were thus still people who spoke the language but were not passing it on. More encouraging, however, was the 9.8 per cent of homes of English-speaking adults where all the children spoke Welsh.[86] A later Welsh Office household survey, designed to give more detailed data than the census, produced further worrying signs. It suggested that Welsh was the mother tongue for just 56 per cent of the people who spoke the language. For people aged over sixty-five, the figure rose to 79 per cent but for those between three and fifteen it fell to a mere 27 per cent. Moreover, only 62 per cent of fluent Welsh speakers said they spoke the language most of the time.[87] No matter how much the Conservatives had done to bolster the official status of the language, its future as a community tongue remained uncertain.

THE 1980S DID SEE the rehabilitation of the Welsh language among English monoglots near completion. The traditional and suffocating Nonconformist life that some associated with Welsh was now beyond many people's personal memories, enabling the language to be embraced and respected. This reinforced the trend that had become apparent in the 1970s when the decline in traditional industry had created an interest in the Valleys' specifically Welsh history. Evening classes in Welsh boomed and Welsh-medium education continued to grow in urban districts, where it was seen as a badge of identity and as offering children distinct career advantages in the emerging Welsh civil society. In 1979 there were fifty-three bilingual primary schools in predominantly English-speaking areas, with a total of 9,892 pupils; by 1988 there were sixty-seven, catering for 12,112 pupils.[88] One result was that Welsh-speaking among three- to fifteen-year-olds rose between 1981 and 1991 in Gwent by 81 per cent and in Mid Glamorgan by 64 per cent. While this may have indicated a more positive view of the language, it had a very limited impact on the creation of Welsh-speaking communities. Indeed, there was probably a tendency for parents to exaggerate their children's fluency on census forms. Children at Welsh-medium schools in the south typically made limited use of Welsh outside the classroom, whether that was in the playground or through reading or watching television at home.[89] The situation typical of the late nineteenth century, where people spoke Welsh at home but English at school, had now reversed for many in urban south Wales 100 years later.

Whether new Welsh speakers were actually using the language much or not, popular attitudes to Welshness were clearly changing from something sentimental that fired the passions only when insulted, ignored or stoked on the sporting field, to something more central to how people thought of themselves. This owed much to how class structures and communities were changing. A sociologist argued that in the post-mining Valleys of the early 1990s there was a reformation of identities, with Welshness stepping into the void left behind by working-class consciousness and the end of mining. This was, he maintained, a reassertion of community distinctiveness in the face of economic decline. He found that people had a strong sense of Welshness that they often linked back to their roots, especially any Welsh-speaking ancestors. They may have been defensive about being English monoglots and resentful of the economic benefits Welsh speakers were perceived to have, but people still felt a sense of ownership of the Welsh language and blamed their failure to speak Welsh on a historic oppression by the English. An unemployed man in his twenties claimed: 'it's *our* language isn't it. We didn't have it at school, we had French, but not our own language. I might not have been interested – *but it wasn't even offered*'. But none of this extended to political nationalism because, in a climate of mass unemployment, there were doubts about whether the economy could support independence.[90]

The dismantling of the traditional industrial communities of Wales was a long-term process but in the 1950s and 1960s it had been seen as almost inevitable and the anger was turned to resignation by the availability of other kinds of jobs or the option of moving to wherever a pit had not shut. In the 1970s the economic options open to those displaced from the mines were more limited and the tensions heightened. In that decade much of the resentment was still channelled into traditional class politics. In the 1980s, however, as the working class fragmented and the labour movement seemed to offer little hope, the anger began to adopt something of a national angle, especially since it was easy to see the Tories as a government imposed on Wales by the choices of an English electorate. As graffiti in Caerphilly declared after the 1987 general election: 'we voted Labour, we got Thatcher'.[91] Adding a national dimension to the sense of political anger was a way of putting pressure on the government to recognize that de-industrialized Wales had its own special needs but the politicization of working-class Welshness ran deeper than that.[92] In 1980, amid fears for the future of the steel industry, *The Times* reported a growing 'bloody English' attitude towards London-based decision makers. Workers felt Wales had been singled out for redundancies and their 'bitterness and anger' was 'nurturing a new brand of awakened identity'. One union organizer at Port Talbot thus argued that the steel closures were 'an anti-Welsh decision aimed against the Welsh people and they won't stand for it'.[93] In 2008 Dafydd Elis-Thomas, then presiding officer of the National Assembly for Wales, claimed that the 1984–5 miners' strike was 'when it all really began'.[94] Within the National Union of Mineworkers there was a sense of having discovered community in the strike, not just where people lived but a wider Welsh community too. During the strike, union leader Emlyn Williams suggested that, had there been an Assembly, then the Welsh workers would have had a voice. Welsh iconography, from dragons to Welsh ladies, was common on the banners and posters of the strike and some activists began to make links with other groups across Wales. There was even some feeling that there was a Welsh way of conducting the dispute, with less violence needed because Welsh miners were more disciplined and loyal to union.[95] Moreover, even if the rest of Wales did little about it beyond putting loose change in collecting buckets, it did watch on as the government strove apparently not just to beat but to destroy the miners. Once the government won, then any serious hope that the labour movement could protect Welsh workers was shattered and another bastion of Britishness lost some of its residual appeal. Meanwhile, two successful primetime television history series – *Wales! Wales?* (BBC, 1984) and *The Dragon Has Two Tongues* (HTV, 1985) – increased people's knowledge of the Welsh working-class past.[96] Precisely what impact they had is difficult to determine but among some viewers at least they fed a sense that Wales had a history beyond the language, Nonconformity and medieval princes. The outcome of this complex process of politicizing working-class Welsh identities was evident when the Tower colliery was bought out by its workers in 1994. One old miner remarked, 'This is better than 1947. Then the Government became the owners but now it's the miners at last. Then they flew the Union Jack over Tower but now we are flying the red dragon of Wales'.[97]

The fact that a Welshman was leader of the opposition from 1983 until 1992 should have meant that Welsh working-class interests carried some weight in London but the way Neil Kinnock was treated further suggested to many, whether they agreed with his politics or not, that Wales was marginalized within the UK system. Whereas being Welsh did not stop Heseltine, Howe and Howard holding senior Tory cabinet jobs, they had all done so without a Welsh accent. Kinnock's voice, in contrast, clearly marked him as a product of south Wales. Canvassing suggested this counted against him in southern English constituencies and he was the victim of sustained attacks on both his abilities and his accent by much of the London press. Kinnock could be verbose but repeatedly calling him a 'Welsh windbag' or 'bumbling boyo' seemed to suggest that his Welshness was some kind of personal flaw. Even the rhetoric of senior Tories – Heseltine mimicked his accent for example – seemed to suggest that they thought a Welsh 'boyo' was not fit to be Prime Minister. If anyone had doubts that the attitudes were more about Kinnock than Wales then there was always some other bigot in the London media to illustrate English prejudices. Bernard Levin, writing in *The Times* in 1990, thought the modern terms inserted into Welsh were absurd and that public bilingualism was 'comic' and 'idiocy'. He suggested that Welsh-medium education would turn Wales into 'a kind of Third World satrapy'.[98] For those who did not read broadsheets there were comedy characters like Shadwell on *Naked Video* (BBC2, 1986–91) or Denzil and Gwynedd on *Absolutely* (Channel 4, 1989–93) to suggest that the Welsh were seen as bumbling idiots and that maybe it was time to reconsider how Wales was governed.

THE GRADUAL POLITICIZATION of people's sense of Welshness did not translate into support for nationalism. Plaid Cymru's appeal remained firmly rooted in Welsh-speaking areas and it won just 8.9 per cent of the vote at the 1992 general election, almost 2 per cent less than in 1974. That owed much to people's desire to get rid of the Tories, something which meant voting Labour. Welsh anger at the government reached an apogee not with the miners' strike but with the introduction of the community charge, something which affected far more people. Better known as the poll tax, it was supposed to create more equitable local taxation by charging individuals rather than properties. Those living alone in large homes benefited but houses with adult children or shared by groups of low-paid young people were especially hard hit. Unease was increased by how much the tax varied: in 1990–1 the average personal bill in Clwyd was £269, whereas in Powys it was £178.[99] Some low-income families were already struggling to live. Unable to afford food and housing, let alone a holiday, a colour television or new clothes, they now might have to struggle with their annual household bill increasing from £100 in rates to nearly £400 in poll tax, even with rebates. The new tax was thus simply unaffordable for some and it was no wonder that up to 20 per cent of voters (and thus poll-tax payers) disappeared from the electoral register in some urban wards, adding to the financial strain on already stretched local authorities.[100]

The sense of injustice was strong. In one Welsh drama, a woman who cannot afford to pay asks:

> But is it our fault? We didn't get into debt because I was spending money on clothes or what have you. I was just running the house … I mean was it John's fault he lost his job? Was it my fault that it got harder and harder to keep the house looking nice? And it's not our fault we can't pay this stupid tax that nobody agrees with.[101]

She and her husband saw themselves as 'decent working people' and yet had the bailiffs at the door. In 1990–1 nearly a quarter of people registered for the charge in England and Wales had summonses issued against them for non-payment. There were claims that one in three in the Rhymney valley were not paying. However, the resistance was short-lived. By the end of 1990 English and Welsh councils had collected 73 per cent of what they were due and were estimating that they would have 91 per cent by the end of the financial year.[102] People instead resorted to other means of disruption, such as writing cheques or demanding correspondence in Welsh, paying in low denominations and applying for rebates they knew they were not entitled to. The furore contributed to Thatcher's downfall and the charge was quickly replaced by John Major's new government with the council tax, which charged properties but gave discounts for those living alone. When it was introduced in 1993–4 the average council tax bill (per dwelling) in Wales was £276.[103] Those in homes with more than one adult thus made significant savings.

The poll tax hit hard because of how little financial security some people had. In 1986 nearly a half of Welsh households had no savings. Even in 1994–5 over a fifth of Welsh households did not have a current account at a bank or building society.[104] But the government also seemed unable to deliver economic stability to those who were better-off. House prices had risen through the 1970s and most of the 1980s but from late 1988 they began to fall in some places for a year or so, the first property crash since the Second World War. Between 1989 and 1990 average prices fell by 6.4 per cent in South Glamorgan and 9.7 per cent in Gwynedd. Some people found themselves in a position where they owed more on their mortgage than their home was worth. The falls, however, were not universal across Wales or long lasting. The average house price in Wales in 1992 was 45 per cent higher than in 1988. What hurt people was not house prices but the rising cost of mortgages. Interest rates hit 15 per cent in 1989 and by August 1991 seventy houses a week were being repossessed in Wales, 8,000 people were six to twelve months in arrears and another 3,000 were more than a year in arrears.[105] The property-owning dream was turning sour for those who had taken out mortgages they could only just afford and they increasingly blamed the government.

After Thatcher's ejection, the Conservatives won the 1992 general election, taking 28.6 per cent of the Welsh vote, not that much of a fall from the 32.2 per cent highpoint of 1979, and secured with a bigger total of actual votes than it had in 1983. Tory support may have been more stable than is often thought but opposition to the party was solidifying. Tactical voting and the collapse in support for the Alliance meant that whereas the Conservatives had won fourteen Welsh seats in 1983, by 1992 they only had six. This reinforced the idea that the government was being imposed on Wales. After 1987 the Conservatives drafted in English MPs to maintain their majority on the Welsh Affairs Select Committee and by 1995 just two of the six Tories on it represented Welsh constituencies.[106] Facing internal dissent without a large majority or a clear philosophy, John Major's wayward government struggled and in Wales he committed a huge blunder in appointing John Redwood, the MP for Wokingham, as Secretary of State in 1993. Redwood appeared to have little feeling for Wales or its people and was an instinctive Thatcherite and advocate of free enterprise. He did continue investing in roads and ordered a major upgrading of the Heads of the Valleys A465. But, unlike his predecessors, he stopped stressing the distinctiveness of Welsh Office policy and even had the red dragon flying on the WDA's European centre replaced with a Union Jack. He cut central government expenditure on the WDA from £69.5 million to £25 million a year and tried to champion spending cuts by handing back to the Treasury £112 million from the Welsh Office budget.[107] With a deprived Welsh economy, that was perhaps unforgivable, but more damaging to his public persona in a political culture where image was becoming everything were embarrassing television pictures of him pretending to sing the Welsh national anthem at a Conservative conference. He seemed to think that Welsh was a ruse to deceive the English and refused to sign official letters and documents in Welsh because he did not know what they said. Redwood said the wrong things too. He even claimed that 'If an Englishman enters a shop in Welsh-speaking parts of Wales, the locals are likely to switch promptly to speaking Welsh. Thus the Englishman cannot be sure whether they are talking about him.'[108] After a visit to St Mellons in Cardiff, Redwood offended locals by claiming people there 'had begun to accept that babies just happen' and they had 'no presumption in favour of two adults creating a loving family background for their children'.[109] He upset Welsh Tories too with his abrupt manner and by pointing to defects in Wales. Wyn Roberts recorded that his boss did 'not know the people he governs'. He had encouraged Redwood to write speeches that said he enjoyed being in Wales but no to avail. By 1994 Roberts was noting that Wales was 'being reduced to a backwater in the multi-ethnic, multicultural sea that is modern Britain' because it produced no political return for the Tories.[110]

Alex Carlile, the Welsh Liberal Democrat leader, remarked, 'The people of Wales are sick of being treated like a colonial outpost. The new viceroy Mr Redwood is the last straw.' In 1994 a political commentator observed,

'One of John Redwood's main achievements in Welsh politics may turn out to have been assisting Welsh Labour politicians to rediscover their national roots'.[111] The Labour Party was indeed slowly coming back to the idea of devolution and it was back on the party's manifesto by 1992, although neither Kinnock nor the shadow Secretary of State for Wales seemed enthusiastic.[112] Once John Smith replaced Kinnock as Labour leader in 1992, the party became more serious about the proposition, even if its grassroots remained cautious. A radical reorganization of local government in 1996 removed another barrier by dispersing power from eight large county councils to twenty-two small unitary authorities, neutering the argument that a devolved Welsh Assembly would be too similar to existing government structures and minimizing the influence of localized opposition within Labour. Smith's new shadow Secretary of State was Ron Davies, a keen advocate of a Welsh Assembly and not just for political reasons. He reflected the views of much of the Valleys when he told the 1994 Labour Party conference: 'Like the Scots we are a nation. We have our own country. We have our own language, our own history, traditions, ethics, values and pride.'[113] There was, however, still no groundswell of support for utilizing that sense of nationhood to deliver devolution. Yet an elected Welsh body mattered more than ever because the development of the Welsh Office and associated quangos meant administrative devolution was proceeding regardless.

It is one of the ironies of Welsh history that it was a Conservative government that did more than any other before it not just to bolster the official status of Wales and its language but also to encourage people to think about their nationality in more political terms. Of course, promoting a politicized Welshness was never the intended outcome of enhancing the role and profile of the Welsh Office or of economic policies that dismantled Wales' traditional industrial base, but it happened all the same. Moreover, such was the extent of the social and economic dislocation that traditional campaigners for Welsh issues were also meshing their own politicized Welshness with wider issues in a far more meaningful sense than ever before. This was clearly evident at the 1984 National Eisteddfod at Lampeter. Permission to hold a demonstration against apartheid was refused and members of the Campaign for Nuclear Disarmament formed a ring around the main pavilion in protest at the archdruid's refusal to pass a vote of sympathy with the people of Hiroshima. Meanwhile, there was a demonstration by feminists against a satirical magazine for its portrayal of women and Cymdeithas yr Iaith Gymraeg tipped milk over the floor of the Welsh Office's stand in support of dairy farmers and the striking miners. The old causes were still there too and members of the society also threw English textbooks at the stand of the Welsh Joint Education Committee and threatened action against anyone who broke the National Eisteddfod's Welsh-only rule. In the same year a farmer angry at the changes in milk quotas dumped a dead cow on the Welsh Office's doorstep. His daughter said he had wanted to do it at 10 Downing Street but thought 'the security would be too great and so he settled on the Welsh Office'.[114] The policy he was angry at actually originated in Brussels but the incident was further evidence that the Welsh Office was now a more accessible and accepted face of government, even when people knew real power lay elsewhere. Quite how far a sense of Wales and a wider political outlook had come together by the mid-1990s remained very unclear. Certainly some people were still worrying about what Welsh identity meant, how unified it was and how the rest of the world saw Wales. Yet, amid such musings, one historian claimed, 'Allow me to let you into a secret known by the man on the Cardiff omnibus but not by your average Welsh intellectual. Most of the Welsh never talk about Wales.'[115] Even if people were thinking of their Welshness in more political terms, the absence of any popular demand for devolution suggests they were not always sure what their nationality should mean in practical terms. What was certain was that the priority for the majority of the Welsh electorate had become getting rid of the Tories. After all, being a nation was one thing but, given the poverty that remained in some places, there were more basic things in life to worry about.

Notes

1 Document 105332, at www.margaretthatcher.org.

2 R. Evans, *Gwynfor Evans: A Portrait of a Patriot* (2008), 401.

3 Lord Roberts of Conwy, *Right from the Start: The Memoirs of Sir Wyn Roberts* (2006), 131–7.

4 G. Talfan Davies, *At Arm's Length: Recollections and Reflections on the Arts, Media and a Young Democracy* (2008), 69. A. Tomos, 'Realising a dream', in S. Blanchard and D. Morley (eds), *What's This Channel Four? An Alternative Report* (1982), 37–53. *Guardian*, 20 Feb. 1976.

5 W. Whitelaw, *The Whitelaw Memoirs* (1989), 217. Internal briefing note, 16 July 1979, N. Edwards to Whitelaw, nd, NLW, 2371/1/2.

6 NLW, 2371/1/17. Evans, *Gwynfor Evans*, 396–7. N. Crickhowell, *Westminster, Wales and Water* (1999), 19.

7 Government proposals on the fourth channel, 29 Oct. 1979, NLW, 2371/1/5.

8 R. Smith, 'Journalism and the Welsh language', in G. H. Jenkins and M. A. Williams (eds), *'Let's Do Our Best for the Ancient Tongue': The Welsh Language in the Twentieth Century* (2000), 304. Evans, *Gwynfor Evans*, 403.

9 Evans, *Gwynfor Evans*, 400, 416. Crickhowell, *Westminster, Wales and Water*, 25, 20. Briefing note, 28 May 1980, NLW, 2371/8.

10 Note of meeting between Home Secretary and Secretary of State for Wales, 7 July 1980, NLW, 2371/13.

11 Meeting between Secretary of State and G. Evans, 21 July 1980, and briefing note for Secretary of State for Wales, 9 Sep. 1980, NLW, 2371/15, 26.

12 Evans, *Gwynfor Evans*, 418. T. P. Coogan, *The Troubles: Ireland's Ordeal, 1966–1996, and the Search for Peace* (2002), 271.
13 Notes of meeting at 10 Downing Street, 10 Sep. 1980, NLW, 2371/1/1.
14 *Daily Mirror*, 18 Sep. 1980.
15 J. Davies, *Broadcasting and the BBC in Wales* (1994), 344. *WL*, 22 Aug. 1980.
16 Davies, *Broadcasting and the BBC*, 379–80.
17 Smith, 'Journalism and the Welsh language', 339–40. *WM*, 8 Apr. 1981. E. Rhys, 'Living in a language', in J. Gower (ed.), *Home Land* (1996), 44.
18 R. G. Jones, 'Of poetry, paradoxes and progress', in D. Cole (ed.), *The New Wales* (1990), 153.
19 M. Ryan, 'Blocking the channels: tv and film in Wales', in T. Curtis (ed.), *Wales: The Imagined Nation. Essays in Cultural and National Identity* (1986), 186. Smith, 'Journalism and the Welsh language', 338.
20 M. Stephens, *A Semester in Zion: A Journal with Memoirs* (2003), 239.
21 Quoted in K. Williams, 'Whose life is it anyway?', *PI*, 108 (1994–5), 19
22 C. Butler, 'The Conservative Party in Wales: remoulding a radical tradition', in J. Osmond (ed.), *The National Question Again: Welsh Political Identity in the 1980s* (1985), 165.
23 *LDP*, 12 Dec. 1980. Crickhowell, *Westminster, Wales and Water*, 51.
24 J. B. Jones, 'Changes to the government of Wales, 1979–1997', in J. B. Jones and D. Balsom (eds), *The Road to the National Assembly for Wales* (2000), 19.
25 J. Snicker, 'Strategies of autonomist agents in Wales', in H. Elcock and M. Keating (eds), *Remaking the Union: Devolution and British Politics in the 1990s* (1998), 140–57. H. Williams, *Guilty Men: Conservative Decline and Fall, 1992–1997* (1998), 46.
26 Crickhowell, *Westminster, Wales and Water*, 49.
27 P. Walker, *Staying Power: An Autobiography* (1991), 202.
28 I. McLean, 'Getting and spending: can (or should) the Barnett formula survive?', *New Economy*, 7 (2000), 76–80. R. M. Deacon, *The Governance of Wales: The Welsh Office and the Policy Process, 1964–99* (2002), 110.
29 On roads see Welsh Office, *Roads in Wales: Progress and Plans for the 1990s* (nd).
30 K. Morgan and G. Mungham, *Redesigning Democracy: The Making of the Welsh Assembly* (2000), 65.
31 K. Morgan, 'Reviving the valleys? Urban renewal and governance structures in Wales', in R. Hambleton and H. Thomas (eds), *Urban Policy Evaluation: Challenge and Change* (1995). J. England, *The Wales TUC 1974–2004: Devolution and Industrial Politics* (2004), 76–7.
32 Crickhowell, *Westminster, Wales and Water*, 35. 'North Wales is on the move', *LDP*, 21 Oct. 1987. Walker, *Staying Power*, 206. *HC Deb*, 23 June 1988, vol. 135, c. 1300.
33 Walker, *Staying Power*, 204. D. Griffiths, *Thatcherism and Territorial Politics: A Welsh Case Study* (1996), 85.
34 J. Lovering, 'Southbound again: the peripheralization of Britain', in G. Day and G. Rees (eds), *Regions, Nations and European Integration: Remaking the Celtic Periphery* (1991), 16. *DWHS–3*, 141.
35 J. Redwood, *Views from Wales* (1994), 8.
36 *DWHS-3*, 26. Mid Glamorgan County Council, *Mid Glamorgan: Issues for the 1990s* (1992), para. 4.17.
37 J. Morris, 'McJobbing a region: industrial restructuring and the widening socio-economic divide in Wales', in R. Turner (ed.), *The British Economy in Transition: From the Old to the New?* (1995), 59. *DWHS-3*, 27. J. Morris and B. Wilkinson, *Divided Wales* (1989), 15. *Regional Trends*, various editions.
38 L. Davies, *Work, Sex and Rugby* (1993), 90.
39 England, *The Wales TUC*, 89. A. Williams (Labour, Swansea West), *HC Deb*, 23 June 1988, vol. 135, c. 1297.
40 R. Fevre, *Wales Is Closed: The Quiet Privatisation of British Steel* (1989), 47.
41 J. Lovering, 'Celebrating globalization and misreading the Welsh economy: the "new regionalism" in Wales', *CW*, 11 (1998), 12–60. Select Committee on Welsh Affairs, *Minutes*

of Evidence, at http://tiny.cc/gmp4j. *DWHS-3*, 137, 141. *DWS* (1998), 223. Mid Glamorgan County Council, *Mid Glamorgan*, para. 4.23.

42 South Glamorgan County Council, *Cardiff: Towards a Euro-Capital* (1994), 10. P. Gripaios, 'Cardiff: a regional perspective', *Welsh Economic Review* (autumn, 1998), 4. *DWHS-3*, 27.

43 Cardiff Bay Development Corporation, *Renaissance: The Story of Cardiff Bay* (2000).

44 Crickhowell, *Westminster, Wales and Water*, 48–9.

45 South Glamorgan County Council, *Replacement Structure Plan* (1995), para. 3.3. For a wider critical discussion see A. Hooper and J. Punter (eds), *Capital Cardiff, 1975–2020: Regeneration, Competitiveness and the Urban Environment* (2006).

46 For claims of distinctive policy see *The Dragon Awakes: A Decade of Development* (Conservative Party, 1992).

47 J. G. Kellas and P. Madgwick, 'Territorial ministries: the Scottish and Welsh Offices', in P. Madgwick and R. Rose (eds), *The Territorial Dimension in United Kingdom Politics* (1982), 29. Griffiths, *Thatcherism and Territorial Politics*. D. Griffiths, 'The Welsh Office and Welsh autonomy', *Public Administration*, 77:4 (1999), 793–807.

48 K. Morgan and A. Price, *Rebuilding Our Communities* (1992), 10.

49 *WM*, 14 Jan. 1976 and 7 July 1981. Glamorgan Archives, South Glamorgan County Council Policy Committee, *Report of the Director of Social Services* (9 June 1977).

50 Welsh Office, *Welsh Local Government Finance Statistics* (1982/3), 33. *Cambrian News*, 28 July 1985 and 2 Aug. 1985. *DWHS-3*, 38.

51 R. Lowe, *The Welfare State in Britain since 1945* (2005 edn), 342–3. I. Gilmour, *Dancing with Dogma: Britain under Thatcher* (1992), 147.

52 Quoted in *HC Deb*, 23 June 1988, vol. 135, cc. 1314–15.

53 J. Osmond, *The Democratic Challenge* (1992). G. Evans, *The Fight for Welsh Freedom* (2000), 165. Walker, *Staying Power*, 204.

54 R. M. Jones, *From Referendum to Referendum: National Identity and Devolution in Wales 1979–1997*, PhD thesis, University of Wales, Aberystwyth (2003), 195.

55 J. Osmond, 'Living in quangoland', *Pl*, 110 (1995), 27–36. J. Bradbury, 'The devolution debate in Wales during the Major governments: the politics of a developing state?', in Elcock and Keating (eds), *Remaking the Union*, 126. Morgan and Mungham, *Redesigning Democracy*, 56.

56 Quoted in Osmond, 'Living in quangoland', 29.

57 R. Vinen, *Thatcher's Britain: The Politics and Social Upheaval of the Thatcher Era* (2009), 211.

58 G. Williams, *A Life* (2002), 120.

59 Deacon, *The Governance of Wales*, 169–70.

60 Rhodri Morgan in the *Independent on Sunday*, 5 Feb. 1995.

61 R. M. Jones, 'Beyond identity? The reconstruction of the Welsh', *Journal of British Studies*, 31 (1992), 354–5.

62 Snicker, 'Strategies of autonomist agents in Wales', 147.

63 B. Rogers, *The Man Who Went Into the West: The Life of R. S. Thomas* (2006), 12, 35.

64 R. Gruffudd, *Y Llosgi* (1986).

65 T. Wright and J. Hartley, 'Representations for the people? Television news, Plaid Cymru and Wales', in Curtis (ed.), *Wales*, 205. A. Richards, *Days of Absence: Autobiography, 1929–1955* (1986), 34. A. Richards, *Carwyn: A Personal Memoir* (1984), 2.

66 *Arcade*, 24 (16 Oct. 1981).

67 From the album *Libertino* (1993).

68 J. W. Aitchison and Harold Carter, 'The Welsh language, 1921–1991: a geolinguistic perspective', in Jenkins and Williams (eds), *'Let's Do Our Best'*, 82. J. Aitchison and H. Carter, 'Language and social class in Wales', *Pl*, 105 (1994), 11–16.

69 K. Williams, 'What Wales wants is *Wales on Sunday*', *Pl*, 102 (1993–4), 7–11.

70 Crickhowell, *Westminster, Wales and Water*, 30, 65. Welsh Office, *The Welsh Language: A Commitment and Challenge: The Government's Policy for the Welsh Language* (1980).

71 Cymdeithas Yr Iaith Gymraeg, *Deddf Iaith Newydd: Yr Hanes, 1983–1989* (1989). D. Phillips, *Trwy Ddulliau Chwyldro? Hanes Cymdeithas yr Iaith Gymraeg, 1962–1992* (1998), 68.

72 Welsh Language Board, *The Welsh Language: A Strategy for the Future* (1989).
73 Roberts, *Right from the Start*, 223, 235.
74 Evans, *The Fight for Welsh Freedom*, 166. *Golwg*, 11 Jan. 1993.
75 R. Ferrers, Home Office, to Baroness White, 16 Feb. 1993, NLW, Cledwyn Hughes papers. *HC Deb*, 13 July 1993, vol. 228, c. 827.
76 Translated from W. Roberts to Lord Celdwyn, 25 Jan. 1993, NLW, C. Hughes papers. Roberts, *Right from the Start*, 273.
77 K. Amis, *The Old Devils* (1986), 44.
78 W. G. Evans, 'The British state and Welsh-language education, 1914–1991', in Jenkins and Williams (eds), *'Let's Do Our Best'*, 367.
79 R. Arwel Jones (ed.), *Hyd Ein Hoes: Lleisiau Cymru* (2003), 13. Deacon, *The Governance of Wales,* ch. 9.
80 Roberts, *Right from the Start*, 220–1.
81 G. E. Jones and G. W. Roderick, *A History of Education in Wales* (2003), 211–12.
82 D. Morris, 'The Welsh language and local authority planning in Gwynedd, 1974–1995', in Jenkins and Williams (eds), *'Let's Do Our Best'*, 598.
83 H. Gruffudd, 'Young people's use of Welsh: the influence of home and community', *CW*, 10 (1997), 200–18.
84 D. Ll. Jones, 'Croesffordd cymuned: i ba gyfeiriad?', in D. Morris and H. G. Williams (eds), *Bywyd Cymdeithasol Cymru: Trafodion Economaidd a Chymdeithasol, Urdd y Graddedigion, Prifysgol Cymru 1997–2000* (2001), 100. D. R. Thomas, 'Welsh-language publications: is public support effective?', *CW*, 9 (1996), 40–55.
85 I. Hume, 'The mass media in Wales: some preliminary explorations', in I. Hume and W. T. R. Pryce (eds), *The Welsh and Their Country: Selected Readings in the Social Sciences* (1986), 342, 344. D. Skilton, 'More words and pictures in the air', in Cole (ed.), *The New Wales*, 187.
86 J. W. Aitchison and H. Carter, 'The Welsh language', 103–4.
87 J. Aitchison and H. Carter, *A Geography of the Welsh Language, 1961–1991* (1994), 108–10.
88 *Statistics of Education in Wales*, various editions.
89 Aitchison and Carter, 'The Welsh language', 91, 95. Aitchison and Carter, *A Geography of the Welsh Language*, 82.
90 B. Roberts, 'Welsh identity in a former mining valley: social images and imagined communities', *CW*, 7 (1994), 77–95. Emphasis in original.
91 R. Davies, *Devolution: A Process Not an Event* (1999), 4.
92 Roberts, 'Welsh identity', 82–3.
93 *The Times*, 22 July 1980. *Daily Mirror*, 14 Mar. 1980.
94 Quoted in H. Francis, *History on Our Side: Wales and the 1984/5 Miners' Strike* (2009), 55.
95 Kim Howells, 'After the strike', *Pl*, 51 (1985), 6–11. J. Osmond, 'The dynamics of institutions', in J. Osmond (ed.), *The National Question Again: Welsh Political Identity in the 1980s* (1985), 253. Francis, *History on Our Side*, 54–71. S. Morgan, *Men on Strike: Masculinity and the Miners' Strike of 1984–5 in South Wales*, PhD thesis, Swansea University (2007).
96 C. Thomas, '"The end of history as we know it": Gwyn A. Williams as a television historian', *Llafur*, 7:3–4 (1998–9), 5–19.
97 Quoted in Francis, *History on Our Side*, 86.
98 J. Thomas, '"Taffy was a Welshman, Taffy was a thief": anti-Welshness, the press and Neil Kinnock', *Llafur*, 7.2 (1997), 95–108. *The Times*, 30 Aug. 1990.
99 Calculated from Welsh Office, *Welsh Local Government Financial Statistics*.
100 D. Jones, 'The state of the working poor', *Pl*, 82 (1990), 63–9.
101 *Can't Pay, Won't Pay*, Dir: Wyn Mason, 1989, National Screen and Sound Archive of Wales, 1224.
102 R. Bellamy, 'The anti-poll tax non-payment campaign and liberal concepts of political obligation', *Government and Opposition*, 29:1 (1994), 22–41. NLW, Rhymney Valley Campaign Against the Poll Tax papers. R. Barker, 'Legitimacy in the United Kingdom: Scotland and the poll tax', *British Journal of Political Science*, 22 (1992), 522.

103 Welsh Office, *Welsh Local Government Financial Statistics.* Averages calculated from all districts within the counties.
104 Welsh Office, *Welsh InterCensal Survey 1986*, 71. *Regional Statistics*, 31 (1995), 127.
105 *WM*, 2 Jan. 1991. 'Housing market: simple average house prices, by dwelling type and region, United Kingdom, from 1986', www.communities.gov.uk/documents/housing/xls/140990.xls. *WM*, 16 Aug. 1991.
106 Bradbury, 'The devolution debate in Wales', 126.
107 Deacon, *The Governance of Wales*, 11–12. Williams, *Guilty Men*, 188. Morgan and Mungham, *Redesigning Democracy*, 66.
108 Quoted in Williams, *Guilty Men*, 100.
109 Redwood, *Views from Wales*, 71.
110 Roberts, *Right from the Start*, 291, 294, 298. Williams, *Guilty Men*, 36, 101.
111 J. Osmond, 'A viceroy on the make', *PI*, 105 (1994), 3, 7.
112 K. Morgan and G. Mungham, 'Unfinished business: Labour's devolution policy', in Jones and Balsom (eds), *The Road to the National Assembly*, 28–49.
113 Quoted in R. M. Jones and I. R. Jones, 'Labour and the nation', in D. Tanner, C. Williams and D. Hopkin (eds), *The Labour Party in Wales, 1900–2000* (2000), 260.
114 W. J. Lewis, *A History of Lampeter* (1997), 141. B. Jones, 'The Welsh Office: a political expedient or an administrative innovation?', *Transactions of the Honourable Society of Cymmrodorion*, 66 (1990), 281–92.
115 T. Williams, 'Pobl Pontcanna chatter away democracy', in *Where Wales? The Nationhood Debate* (1996), 18.

12

'Who's happy?' Social change since 1970

> They've seen huge changes in a world where there was work for everybody, where local pubs and shops thrived. They're closed now. They see their children leaving the area, they see their children going to colleges and unable to get jobs back in the area. They see this opencasting ravaging the environment. They see houses for sale everywhere and nobody buying them. They see ruins; they see the ruination of a community around them.
>
> Community worker, Cwm Gwendraeth, 1995[1]

> Pwy sy'n hapus? Dwi ddim, ti ddim.
> [Who's happy? I'm not, you're not.]
>
> Jess, 'Pwy sy'n hapus?', from the album *Hyfryd i Fod yn Fyw* (1990)

ON THE DAY Margaret Thatcher became Britain's first female Prime Minister, the *South Wales Evening Post* ran an article which complained that women in television advertisements were

> all too often seen in one of three ways: wearing an apron, a G-string or a confused expression.
>
> The sexist stereotypes of housewife or harem girl are still trotted out, as though equal pay, women's lib and sex discrimination laws had never existed.
>
> Whether they are selling cigars or soap powder, breakfast cereals or bath salts, the ad-makers use women only as sock-washers or bed-warmers – or, occasionally mere decoration.[2]

Few people probably voted Conservative in 1979 just because they wanted to enhance the position of women in British society but there had been a strong hope that Thatcher would bring changes that extended beyond politics. Before urging readers to vote Tory, the *Western Mail* had argued: 'The nation needs more radical solutions, needs to be jerked out of the gloomy lethargy that seems to have enshrouded it throughout the decade, needs a fresh atmosphere of change and of challenge'.[3] Such arguments were rooted more than anything in the economic situation, a situation that actually got worse rather than better under Thatcher, exacerbating people's fears about old problems such as crime and the loss of community. But, throughout the economic gloom of the 1970s and 1980s, there was much to suggest that Britain and Wales were becoming more prosperous and tolerant places. Social changes that first reached widespread public attention in the 1960s began to take off in the 1970s and became social norms of sorts in the 1980s and 1990s. She may not have been a feminist but Thatcher showed many women that their sex could do anything. The last hang-ups about divorce and sex outside marriage all but disappeared. Tolerance towards people who were somehow 'different' slowly became the norm. There was also the long-term onward march of the consumer society, where owning things, and being seen to own things, mattered to people. Consumer goods that were once luxuries became essentials of life; owning a house became an expected right. Such trends were slower in Wales than in most of the UK but they happened nonetheless and meant that, in so many ways, the Wales of 2000 was unrecognizable from the Wales of 1970. As one returning exile noted, 'Who would have thought, thirty years ago, that one day you would be able to walk into the Co-op in Ammanford and buy a perfectly drinkable bottle of claret'.[4]

IN 1966 AN OLD WELSH MINER complained with indignation: 'the women, God only knows, are regularly bringing more money into the home than the men'.[5] His discomfort came from how the decline of traditional heavy industries, the growth of the service sector and the rise in the number of men who were unemployed or on incapacity benefits were feminizing the workforce. This was a trend that gathered momentum over the next three decades and was perhaps the most significant social change of its time. In 1971 just 47 per cent of women of working age were economically active, compared with 90 per cent of Welsh men. By 2006 the figure for men had fallen to 79 per cent but for women it had risen to 72 per cent.[6] Women entering the world of work had profound impacts that extended beyond the economy. Quite apart from how it could change traditional family routines and arrangements, it made domestic life easier by simply raising family incomes. It also encouraged some women to compare their lives with those of their husbands rather than mothers, contributing to their awareness and sense of gender inequality and thus furthering the process of the wider feminist advance.[7] Yet this trend was restricted by some significant inequalities hidden by the bare statistics on the number of women working. Many of the women entering the labour force did so in part-time jobs. Thirty-five per cent of working Welsh women were in part-time employment in 1974 but by 1996 this had risen to 48 per cent. Rather than highlighting inequality, this often meant that women who worked just did not see their careers as equivalent to men's. Women were also struggling to break through into senior positions and, in 1981, less than a quarter of people with managerial jobs in Wales were female. Even a decade later, the figure was less than 30 per cent. This was partly the result of male prejudices. Some employers were reluctant to train or promote women because they were felt likely later to leave to 'have babies'.[8] Nor were they always keen on the equal pay legislation that was introduced in 1970 and firms often tried to sidestep the law through the technicalities of job definitions. Women did fight back in a series of factory strikes in the late 1970s and early 1980s but some employers defended their position by claiming, often quite rightly, that male workers objected to equal pay.[9] This was evident in 1981, when a trade union at Hoover's Merthyr plant insisted that a forthcoming round of redundancies should be applied to women before men. Under union pressure, Hoover agreed to make female canteen workers redundant and to transfer semi-skilled women from other parts of the factory into the canteen. The women called in the Equal Opportunities Commission and the company backtracked.[10] Five years after the 1970 Equal Pay Act women were earning on average 30 per cent less than men. Among those who worked part-time the differentiation was 42 per cent. In 1978 a sociologist suggested that in mining villages such inequalities were partly due to women's reluctance to commute to places where pay was better. Similarly, a 1975 survey found that many housewives were ignorant about wage rates and quite prepared to work for low pay because they were bored at home. But the bigger problem was not women being paid less to do the same job but their concentration in unskilled occupations where everyone was poorly paid. Even in 2005, an estimated three-quarters of Welsh women in work were employed in cleaning, catering, caring, call centres and customer services. This meant that the pay gap between men and women was still 30 per cent for full-time workers and 32 per cent for part-time workers.[11]

Some of the blame for women's concentration in unskilled labour lay with the education system. In secondary moderns there had been little emphasis on preparing girls for a career and instead a future of marriage and homemaking was encouraged. Teenage girls, enduring adolescent anxieties and the scrutiny of peers, were unlikely to challenge such expectations in numbers. Nor did the shift to comprehensives seem to bring about much change. This was evident in how some school subjects remained doggedly male. Between 1967 and 1987 the proportion of maths A-levels taken in Wales by females increased from 14 per cent to just 35 per cent. For physics the figure rose from 14 per cent to 23 per cent. The failures of the educational system to help girls were also evident in the numbers going to university. In 1957, of undergraduates at the University of Wales 31 per cent were female. The figure had risen only to 39 per cent by 1977 but the pace of change was gathering momentum and, by 1987, there were marginally more female than male full-time university students in Wales.[12]

Educational opportunities may have been growing but getting married remained at the heart of most women's life expectations in the 1970s and 1980s, something encouraged by how traditional images of femininity still dominated schools, religion and the media. The extent of this mindset was clear in 1981 when 86 per cent of women in their thirties living in Wales were married. Yet young women's expectations of what marriage should be like had changed. There had been a growing emphasis in books and magazines of the 1950s and 1960s on marriage as a happy source of 'emotional companionship and sexual intimacy', something which also probably helped legitimize pre-marital sex in loving relationships.[13] A rural study at the start of the 1960s noted that romantic ideas about marriage were becoming more common thanks to films, magazines and more contact with English people in general. People courting openly and young married couples drinking together in pubs were becoming more frequent sights.[14] Studies of Swansea in the 1960s also found a growing emphasis on companionship in marriage. Young working-class husbands were helping a little with the chores and sharing decisions over the children and money. They were also increasingly staying at home in the evenings or taking their wives out with them. Yet, even when couples were at the pub together, they often spoke to other friends of the same sex rather than each other or even sat in different rooms, with the men in the bar and the women in the lounge.[15]

Women's penetration of bars and clubs, which seemed to go hand in hand with the rise of female employment, was a very visible symbol to men that their old world was fading away, but their reaction also illustrated how slow the change in gender roles was. Even young males could be reactionary and a teenage column in the *Wrexham Leader* in 1970 claimed that a 'woman who considered herself equal to a man could not expect to be treated with the courtesy men show other women'.[16] Women's equality was a recurrent source of both male humour and male anxiety in the 1970s and into the 1980s. There were efforts to protect male sanctuaries by creating explicit men-only rules to replace what once had been an unspoken assumption. A married woman in Cardiff was cross enough about men-only bars to write to the press in 1976 pointing out that she and most of her friends could 'wield a pint glass in a public bar as well as any man (and a good deal better than some I've come across)', and that 'the swear-words used by many women make men's language sound about as obscene as little Noddy'. Although women who did this were branded unfeminine, she concluded that 'now is the time to shake themselves out of their passive stupor and prove' their equality with men.[17] That some men would take more convincing was evident in 1980, when a Newport pub was subject to a complaint to the Equal Opportunities Commission because the barman had refused to serve women with pint glasses. Such men could at least take refuge in the fact that much of the 'system' was rather traditional too. At the start of the 1970s husbands could even be barred from the birth of their own children, leading one mother to write to a local paper saying 'You would have thought I had asked for the moon when I insisted on this'.[18] Not until the 1980s did it become the norm for men to be present at the birth of their children.

At the end of the 1960s one Swansea housewife said:

> I don't expect [my daughter-in-law] to slave all her life as I have. They don't nowadays. All my life has been giving to people; spoiling the menfolk. I love it. But you can't expect the young folk to do what I've done. I've carried a heavy burden all my life. Don't expect it now.[19]

Yet many women's own attitudes towards gender roles actually remained remarkably stable. In the mid-1970s there were still Welsh women who believed that females were not biologically equipped to be the breadwinner but had a 'divinely given responsibility to bear and bring up children'.[20] Change was slowest in working-class families. Because their wages were lower than men's, most working-class women regarded their own employment as a matter of supplementing the family income rather than forging their own career. A survey of newly married couples in Swansea in 1968–9 found that, despite the growing emphasis on companionship, most drew a distinction between the money each partner earned. The man's wages were normally for housekeeping, while the woman's were saved or used for furniture and the like. It also noted how women expected to give up work after having children, how they did nearly all the childcare and housework, and how after marriage they seemed quickly to spend less money and time on their appearance. They sometimes cut their hair, stopped dying it blond, wore longer skirts and less make-up and maybe put on weight.[21] Such traditional gender patterns were very durable in working-class communities. Even in the mid-1980s the wife of a former steelworker at Port Talbot could remark, 'If there was any way that I thought giving up my own job would help him get one I'd do it like a shot. It's hard on any man to be out of work.'[22] In a 1982 study of the families of former steelworkers in that town, just over half the sample operated a traditional system where the man handed over his wages or benefits to his wife for housekeeping and received back an amount for his own personal spending. This was especially common where the man was out of work and control over the household budget was a source of stress, not power. It put the women under pressure, making them worry and fret about making ends meet. Some of the sample had more equal arrangements but over a quarter saw the man control the family's finances, with his wife given an allowance or having to ask for money every time she needed it. Even where money was tight and the women were in control, their needs did not take precedence. As one put it, 'I don't mind going short. I manage somehow. But I don't like to see him without money in his pocket. He's worth it. If they're the squandering type then bugger 'em. But if he's not wasting it then OK.' Rather than being dependent on spending money, the wives' social lives were based on talking to neighbours and contact in the street. One wife remarked: 'I never go out myself, except for a special do. But men need to really don't they. It's different for a woman, she sees her friends anyway. If he couldn't go out he just wouldn't see anyone.'[23]

Such attitudes and arrangements illustrated how the 1970s 'women's lib' movement had made little headway in Wales. In 1976 a female journalist concluded,

> We in Wales still lag behind other parts of Britain. Women have very much chosen to be kept in their place in Wales. Even women I consider as fairly liberated still do so much for their husbands even though they have jobs of their own. They still feel their husband should be able to collapse into his chair in front of the television when he comes home from work. Women have been their own worst enemies, too ready to kill themselves and do all the work.

It was not entirely unfair that, at the end of the 1970s, a running *Two Ronnies* sketch, about a future English tyrannical state run by women, portrayed Wales as offering a refuge to those who wanted a return to normality. Nonetheless, one female writer who accepted that Welsh men saw themselves as superior denied that women saw themselves as inferior. She thought they knew their worth and spoke their minds. They might not use 'women's lib' language like 'sisterhood' but they had always offered each other mutual support in times of hardship.[24]

For some families it was the miners' strike of 1984–5 that broke the traditional patterns, bringing women out, in the words of one Llanhilleth wife, 'from behind the kitchen sink'.[25] But rather than the gender revolution being something that happened to individuals, it was more a gradual process that developed over the generations. This was illustrated by a study of families in the early 1990s. Those born before the Second World War defended the domestic sphere as a woman's place, while for their daughters and granddaughters there were clearly evolving ideas of exactly how much a man should do in the home.[26] That gradual shift in attitudes was also evident in women's dress. What had begun with shorter skirts in the 1960s shifted to trousers in the 1970s and then lower-cut tops. This was one challenge to gender conventions that few men probably minded. By 1996 a story about Cardiff factory girls could declare: 'we like things that are sexy, real sexy I mean, we're not afraid of flaunting ourselves because we always sticks together, so we're always safe'. That acknowledgement of the potential dangers illustrated the limits of women's freedom and the story also had one husband being regarded as 'some sort of new man' because he let his wife have weekly nights out with her friend; but even he resorted to hitting her when she was late back one night.[27] By the 1990s research was noting that working-class teenage girls in Wales had higher expectations than their mothers, wanting some form of career and financial independence and rejecting idealistic romantic visions of marriage. Yet their career aspirations tended to be rooted in their own class and they were still aware, from their own experience of school and family, that gender equality could be a mirage.[28] Men might be increasing the amount they helped around the house, such as general tidying, playing with the children and washing dishes, but that did not mean they were taking responsibility for it. This was clear in the fact that in 1994 just 16 per cent of married and co-habiting women with children under sixteen worked full-time and only another 36 per cent worked part-time.[29] When mothers did work they often had to cope with a sense of guilt that they were not spending enough time with their children, a feeling the older generation did not always discourage. Cleaning the house and ironing in particular also usually remained female domains. One study found this was, at least partly, due to women judging their partner's housework as not being up to scratch. In 1991 an opinion poll suggested that 40 per cent of Welsh men did not take an equal share of the household chores, while 37 per cent thought that it was up to their partner to look after the children.[30] Even these figures probably overestimated the true male domestic contribution, with many men no doubt embarrassed or deluded about how much they actually did around the house. As one historian noted, 'Feminist views triumphed in theory, but translating them into practice was more a war of attrition than a *blitzkrieg*'.[31] Being a woman in Wales (and indeed, most of Britain) in the early twenty-first century was still likely to mean earning less than men, having fewer opportunities for advancement and, at the end of the day, having to do more housework.

THE SNAIL-LIKE ADVANCE of feminism was evident in how working-class humour was imbued with more than a streak of sexism, such as the one about the man who left his wife on their wedding night after finding out she was a virgin. His mother heartily approved: 'If she's not good enough for the rest of the village she's not good enough for you'.[32] In a world where such jokes were funny it was not surprising that in 1975 the Abercwmboi Institute and Social Club could introduce strip shows on Sunday mornings.[33] Mining communities like Abercwmboi centred on a traditional masculinity, embodied in the physical nature of work but also expressed in sport and, for some, fighting over issues of personal dignity and reputation. The importance of work to men's conception of themselves thus ran deeper than just providing for a family: it proved their hardness and their independence and could even be exhilarating. As a character in a novel about a steelworks put it, 'Nothing like it to make you feel good.... You can't beat fucking hard work.' Some men had specifically become miners because of the masculine status it gave them. A fifty-six-year-old miner said of his work: 'As much as I hate it, I wouldn't have any other job. Down there, you swear at the bosses, you don't have to snivel up to anyone. You are a man, working with men.'[34]

The introspective nature of mining communities reinforced such male solidarity. Another miner remembered:

> everyone gets up in the morning at 6, all the lights going on, the first hooter that would ring around the village in Seven Sisters, very few cars, catching the bus, coming home same time, play rugby with the same boys, have a pint with the same boys, very community orientated, everyone knew everything about everybody else.[35]

As such pictures became rarer with the rundown of heavy industry, the character of masculinity changed too. A night out with the boys perhaps became more important in compensation. The wife of an unemployed steelworker said of a local pub in the early 1980s: 'They all look after each down there. If you go in and you're out of work the boys will buy you a drink.... Even if they go in with no money it's a good night.'[36] But the support of your mates could only go so far. The end of work still meant a lost sense of dignity that many men struggled to come to terms with, especially when it was a job that was so obviously manly. Former miners who ended up in factories found that the women there had created their own forms of camaraderie and banter but many still struggled to accept their new jobs as masculine or to adapt to having women as workmates. One former miner remarked after getting a job in a Pot Noodle factory: 'Four weeks earlier I was a coal miner shovelling with big hairy men built like brick shithouses. Now I'm bent over a line *souping* with two women. Putting *square* sachets into *round bloody* pots.'[37] To maintain their masculine dignity, such men continued to think of themselves as ex-miners long after leaving the pits, even when they found jobs that were more pleasant and more rewarding than working underground. Yet more and more men had never had the experience of heavy industry at all and their sense of masculinity was less traditional, something evident in the growing popularity of male grooming products and the slight redistribution of domestic chores.

One group of men who clearly did not conform to the traditional gender values was Wales' gay population. How big it was is impossible to estimate with any degree of certainty, not least due to questions of definition and male homosexuality's illegality before 1967. Estimates of the proportion of the UK population who are practising homosexuals vary from 2.6 to 6.0 per cent, while in a 1991 survey 3.3 per cent of Welsh male respondents said they had had a homosexual experience.[38] Before its legalization, homosexuality had a slightly unnatural, sometimes even sinister tone for most people. This was largely unspoken but it was evident in homosexuality's portrayal in popular culture. In the novel *The Civil Strangers* (1949), the sexuality of the teacher is never made explicit but he leered at boys, making them feel uncomfortable and think that there was something 'queer' about him.[39] Discomfort with the idea did not always mean outright hostility. In England, there was some tentative evidence that working-class communities in the 1950s and 1960s could be more tolerant than the middle classes. Leo Abse's sponsorship of the 1967 Sexual Offences Act did not appear to do any damage to his huge majority in Pontypool. In 1969 a thirty-three-year-old gay man from Cardiff remarked, 'Most of our friends know what our relationship is, accept it as normal and I don't think I have heard any stupid comment for a long time. There used to be a few people who thought it was funny or clever to make the sort of two-sided comment which sets the ignorant rolling around with smutty laughter, but I think that, at last, people are beginning to grow up.'[40]

Yet complete tolerance remained some way off, even if there was not widespread open hostility. On the day homosexual acts between consenting adult males in private were legalized, the *Western Mail* made no comment on it. Legalization was certainly not the result of any popular demand and attitudes remained cautious and prejudiced. Even the medical establishment was 'treating' some gay men with electric shock treatment in the mid-1970s.[41] Gay teenagers in the Valleys could endure extreme bullying at school and the embarrassment of their parents and friends. 'What will the boys say down the club?', worried one father. His son became an entertainer in the 1970s and was asked to urinate in the dressing room sink at one local club because 'some of the lads' were not 'partial to poofs' around them.[42] Public stigma was still driving some men to 'cottaging' to fulfil their sexual needs. In 1975 the Bishop of Llandaff resigned after being charged with gross indecency with a man in a public toilet. In his defence a psychiatric report claimed the situation may have been caused by a medical condition.[43] Seeing being gay as some sort of disorder was becoming more unusual but, as with the advance of notions of gender equality, the liberalization of attitudes was a slow, uneven process. Attitudes were slowest to change in small towns and rural areas, which contributed to the formation in the late 1970s of a society for Welsh-speaking homosexuals. Even at the start of the 1980s Clwyd County Council had a policy of barring gays from being employed in children's homes and some other jobs involving the young and elderly. After the AIDS panic of the late 1980s, outright hostility towards openly homosexual people seemed to increase. A Cardiff hotel even cancelled a gay conference in 1990 for fear of publicity that would damage its reputation. A year later an official survey suggested that more 70 per cent of Welsh men and 60 per cent of women thought that sex between males was wrong.[44] None of this made being homosexual easy but in 2001 Rhondda elected an openly gay MP, a small but significant sign that Wales was becoming more tolerant.

Had such public prejudices been racial then they would never have been so accepted. Yet Wales remained overwhelmingly white and did not experience any large-scale immigration from outside the UK. In 1971 there were 17,045 people living in Wales who had been born in the Commonwealth. By 1991 this had risen to only 28,063. At the 2001 census 97.9 per cent of the Welsh population were classified as white. Even in Cardiff, the most multicultural part of Wales, 92 per cent of people were white. How exactly the lack of ethnic diversity affected racial attitudes is unclear. Charlotte Williams, who grew up in Llandudno's only black family in the 1960s, was rarely called 'darkie' or anything more sinister, but instead endured the 'polite racism' of unspoken assumptions of inferiority when race was addressed or was 'relieved of the onerous impoliteness of being black' by being told that no one had noticed her colour or that she was actually brown. In the 1970s the future sportsman Nigel Walker was one of three black children in his year at a Cardiff school. He had to endure racial taunts and being greeted one day with 'Niggers Out' painted in two-foot high letters on the gym wall. Yet other black Welsh people argue they have never once suffered any racial prejudice.[45] They were probably just lucky. In a 1980s study in Swansea, 38 per cent of respondents thought it wrong that a black person should be given a council house if there were whites on the waiting list, 17 per cent said they would move if a black family moved in next door and 42 per cent said they would not send their child to a school where the majority of children were black. Given such casual prejudices it was unsurprising that black people were more likely to be unemployed than their white peers and that others could feel isolated and frustrated by life in Wales.[46]

There were more extreme beliefs too. One commentator even suggested in 1981 that Wales was 'one of the most comfortably racist parts of a poisonously racist island'. Yet at the 1979 general election the National Front's five candidates in Wales won fewer than 2,500 votes between them.[47] In the mid-1980s the party launched a branch called NF Cymru. Its symbol was a Celtic cross and it claimed that 20 per cent of its membership was Welsh-speaking. Alongside its more obvious call for 'white power' was a streak of Welsh nationalism. One of its members, a Cardiff student, told a reporter, 'We are totally against English imperialism. We want the Welsh to rule themselves, but within a British family of nations.' He wanted rid of the Union Jack because it did not depict Wales.[48] In the twenty-first century too, the British National Party combined an anti-immigrant rhetoric with claims of standing up for Welsh nationality and culture. At the 2007 Welsh Assembly election the party won 4.3 per cent of the regional votes cast.

A novel about a teenager from a deprived Valleys estate claimed 'he'd been brought up to piss on them. On their difference. And the fact they were in his country. But not many on the estate had even met one. Niggers were the unknown who lived down in Cardiff.' Although the same novel noted that 'Pakis' were 'tolerated, more or less, for their food and generous opening hours', the most virulent attitudes did seem aimed at Asians rather than blacks.[49] A study in Torfaen in the 1990s found that black people with Welsh connections were accepted in a way that Asians were not. In such communities there was some resentment of Asian doctors and complaints that people could not understand them. One Muslim woman in Cardiff remarked that racism was rarely spoken but was present in the way 'they look at you, the way they talk to you, their behaviour and attitude'.[50] The impact of the most extreme prejudices was clear in 1990, when the Swansea press reported claims that nearly all the 300 Asians in the Hafod area had been victims of racist attacks. These varied from being beaten up to having stones thrown through their windows and lit cigarettes pushed through their doors. Even children were spat and sworn at on their way to school. In 1994 south Wales had the third highest number of recorded racially motivated incidents in Britain. That year an Asian man died after being hit on the head with a brick during a racist attack on his shop near Neath.[51] There were genuine shock and outrage at that event, which, like so much of the extreme racism, was down to a tiny minority. But, however much the Welsh liked to think of themselves as a tolerant people, the drift towards genuine social equality was just that, a slow drift.

WHILE EVERYONE WHO was black, female or gay was slowly finding Wales a more tolerant place, teenagers were increasingly being demonized. As in the 1950s and 1960s, the blame for much petty crime and anti-social behaviour was, quite fairly, placed on the shoulders of teenagers. Half of all persons found guilty of indictable offences at Welsh magistrates' courts in 1981 were under twenty-one.[52] However, the mistrust of young people in the 1970s and 1980s was as much to do with their popular culture as it was with their crimes. Long hair may have become ubiquitous enough in the 1970s that it was no longer shocking even on businessmen or rugby players but there were plenty of new concerns, like Mohicans, punk music and even the danger to passers-by caused by the skateboarding craze.[53] When the Sex Pistols played Caerphilly in 1976 there was an angry demonstration of churchgoers who seemed to think the band was the devil incarnate. Punk even found its own Welsh-language controversy with Y Trwynau Coch (The Red Noses), who released provocative songs like 'Niggers Cymraeg', 'Mynd i'r capel mewn Levis' and 'Merched dan 15'. But, like so much English punk, there was an element of simply wanting to shock in songs that compared the Welsh to slaves and celebrated wearing jeans in chapel and underage girls.[54]

More serious than how teenagers behaved in the 1970s and 1980s was the fact that many could not get a job. Youth unemployment was becoming so pervasive that some teenagers were now growing up with few aspirations. Sociological research on male teenagers in Ely in Cardiff in the mid-1970s found they tended to leave school with little idea of what they wanted to do and there was social pressure on those who did want to learn because it was not cool to be clever. They hung around in public spaces to escape their cramped houses and the gaze of their parents and frittered away any money they had on cigarettes and drink. One of them later looked back on that time: 'I just wanted to enjoy myself. It was the same with most of the Boys. I'd just pick up a bit of work here, a bit of work there – just go drinking and having so much fun. There was no plan, nothing at all.' When the sociologist revisited them in 1999–2000 he found that some of the boys had drifted in and out of work and prison. They had suffered from drink problems and some were dead. But others had eventually settled down into normal stable lives as they aged: they got married, had children and held down jobs.[55]

Although the Ely research suggested that a lack of aspiration among the young was not necessarily a barrier to later leading fulfilling adult lives, it also showed the potential costs. The pattern of young people on council estates like Ely having no expectation of making a better life for themselves or even finding steady employment continued into the 1990s and beyond. Indeed, people who had left school in the 1970s and failed to get a job now had their own unemployed children, creating a sense of downward spiral and despair. The semi-autobiographical novel of one young Rhondda woman noted:

> Hendrefadog teenagers followed their parents to the dole queue, making us a notch lower than working class. My generation, the products of unemployed parents, divorce and downright poverty, tried desperately to find satisfaction in joyriding and class B drugs (which were barely affordable); cider drinking in lanes and underage sex.[56]

A minister on Rhondda's Penrhys estate claimed that locals felt powerless and impotent at what was happening to their young people. He complained that drugs there had become a 'way of life'. People burgled, stole cars and shoplifted to pay for their habits. Others bought the stolen goods cheaply and asked no questions. Fear or family ties stopped those who knew what was going on from speaking out. Unemployment on the estate in the early 1990s was around 80 per cent and of those who did work half were in part-time jobs. Rhondda social workers estimated that the estate accounted for 90 per cent of their cases but only 2 per cent of the local population. Those who could move away did, reinforcing the sense of isolation of those left behind, who nicknamed the estate Alcatraz or Colditz. One-third of the population changed every year and the total number of residents on the estate was estimated to have halved in the previous ten years. Yet, despite such problems, the local minister also found community and humanity among residents, bolstered by family networks of support, resilience and compassion.[57]

Two social scientists argued that the main concerns of the young unemployed were a lack of income and structure in their lives. They were isolated, bored and lacking in status and independence because they had to live at home. Having a baby was one way to at least gain adult status and a place of your own.[58] But it was no easy solution. The benefit payments motherhood brought offered little more than subsistence. Teenage boyfriends and difficult financial circumstances were hardly recipes for long-lasting relationships. Moreover, the council homes many teenage mothers were given were often on the estates they were trying to escape. That might help ensure some family support but it did little to create more diverse communities on those estates, reinforcing their poor reputations. Indeed, for those on the right, single teenage mums became a symbol of all they thought wrong with society: the lack of aspiration, the breakdown of conventional families and a dependency on the state. Perhaps it was a realization of how hard it could be that meant that teenage pregnancy was never quite the problem that was imagined. One Welsh survey found that just 6.4 per cent of women reported losing their virginity before the age of sixteen and that the median age of first sexual intercourse was seventeen for men and eighteen for women.[59]

The education system was failing those who did see pregnancy as a way out. It was not doing much to end Welsh economic problems either, as it turned out large numbers of unqualified school-leavers and prepared others for a higher education that would lead many to leave Wales. The high status that education once enjoyed in Wales also seemed to be falling away. In 1966 whereas 17 per cent of seventeen-year-olds in Wales were still at school, in England the figure was just 12 per cent. By 1977 the gap had narrowed to 22 per cent in Wales and 19 per cent in England. However, whereas only 16 per cent of school-leavers in England in 1975–6 had no formal qualifications, in Wales the figure was 26 per cent. The education system in Wales thus appeared to serve the able relatively well but the academically poor very badly. There were also significant variations in educational attainment within Wales. Rural counties tended to see higher achievement in terms of qualifications. Thus, in 1976–77, 23 per cent of boys and 24 per cent of girls in Gwynedd left school with no qualifications but in Mid Glamorgan the figure was 38 per cent for both sexes.[60] It was concerns about the academically weak rather than the academically strong that had led to moves to abolish grammar schools. Anglesey ended the eleven-plus in 1952 but other counties moved towards comprehensive education more gradually, by opening new schools and developing fluid organizations within segregated 'bilateral' schools that were attended by both grammar and secondary modern children. The first official comprehensive in Glamorgan opened in Port Talbot in 1958 and by 1961 there were twenty-two such schools in

Wales. Encouraged by both Labour and Conservative governments, their number grew rapidly over the course of the 1960s and early 1970s. By 1976 there were just eighteen grammar schools left in Wales, compared with the 202 comprehensives that were now educating 89 per cent of secondary school children in the state system in Wales. Not all local authorities liked this idea and more than half the remaining grammar schools were in Dyfed, with the rest in Gwent and Mid Glamorgan.[61] Milford Haven, the last grammar in Wales, 'went comprehensive' in 1988.

Although it often meant the end of single-sex education, the shift to comprehensives was not as radical as it first seemed because classes were often 'streamed' according to ability, something which was more widespread and happened at a younger age than in England. Thus pupils remained segregated by ability in the same way they had in the old grammars and secondary moderns. A 1978 Welsh Office report bemoaned that lower-ability pupils were being neglected, even left for several lessons a day to copy out passages from books they did not understand.[62] The level of attainment did notionally improve in the 1980s and, by 1995–6, 37 per cent of male and 48 per cent of female Welsh school-leavers had five GCSEs at grade C or above. But this was lower than the equivalent figures for both England and Scotland and it generated new debates about falling standards.[63] Leaving school with no or few qualifications, especially in an era of economic problems, did not bode well for the future. In 1986 income support was withdrawn for sixteen- and seventeen-year-olds, in the hope of forcing them into work or training schemes. But such schemes did not offer much hope either. A man from Oakdale (Gwent) who left school in 1985 remembers becoming 'increasingly disillusioned' with the training he received as he moved from factory to factory: 'For the two years I was on the schemes, never once was I offered a full time job. I hated working the eight-hour shifts in the full realisation that when the time came to be either taken on or let go, I would end up back at the job centre only to be sent on to another factory.'[64]

One inequality at least was falling away and higher education was becoming more accessible. A survey at the start of the 1960s had found that 26 per cent of sixth-formers in Wales who attained the basic qualifications for university failed to obtain a place.[65] In the wake of such concerns, the British university system underwent significant expansion following the Robbins report of 1963. This led to St David's College in Lampeter and the College of Advanced Technology in Cardiff joining the University of Wales, and to Glamorgan College of Technology becoming a polytechnic. The number of students at the University of Wales rose from 8,279 in 1963–4 to 14,678 in 1970–1. By 1990 the university had over 23,000 students.

The student body, however, was changing, as more English students sought university places in Wales and more Welsh students went to England. The percentage of Welsh students at the University of Wales dropped from 84 per cent in 1951 to 37 per cent in 1971 and 28 per cent in 1990. Although, theoretically, higher education was open to everyone with the ability to get in, actually going to university remained far more likely among the better-off, even in the 1990s. But that decade did see a huge increase in the numbers going to university, partly just because there were more universities after 1994. In 1991 there were 13,202 Welsh students at UK universities. By 1998 the figure was over 45,000.[66] Some wondered if this had been encouraged just to keep the young off the dole but, regardless, it did broaden horizons, better job chances and expand the middle class.

While the young were becoming better qualified, the elderly were becoming more numerous. In 1971 there were 379,005 people aged over sixty-five in Wales (13.9 per cent of the population); by 1991 this had risen to 490,612 (17.3 per cent). Old age also increasingly meant an end to work. In 1959 there had been 2,425 men aged sixty-five and over employed in south Wales mines. But working beyond sixty-five was becoming less common. In agriculture retirement off the farm with an associated move to a local village was becoming the norm, whereas before the war old farmers had remained in charge, even dominating sons in their thirties and forties.[67] Even for those who had not yet reached sixty-five, retirement was sometimes coming quicker than they wanted. Middle-aged men could struggle to find employment, especially if they needed light jobs because of health problems from working underground. Manufacturing companies appeared reluctant to take on older men because they might be ill more and would not give as long service as a younger man, especially one who already had a family and was thus less mobile.[68] The result was that many middle-aged people felt old and consigned to the scrapheap long before they thought they should be.

It was among the old that poverty was probably worst. They often endured the worst housing and their pensions were undermined by inflation, especially during the era of rapidly rising prices of the mid-1970s. In 1976 a report suggested that a quarter of elderly people living on their own in Wales were in houses without indoor sanitation. The price of television licences and cost of public transport were particular causes of concern and some pensioners felt they were unable to afford to go to shops or see relatives because of the price of local buses. Even the very basic essentials of life were not always affordable. The Pensioners Protection Party claimed in 1990 that there were elderly people in Wales forced to eat pet food because of their financial position.[69] One Rhondda pensioner summed up what seemed to be an existence rather than a life: 'I'll scrape by from day to day. I might put the odd 50p in the gas meter, and I wrap myself in a blanket when I watch TV.'[70] The depth of pensioner poverty, of course, depended on whether it was compared with the society they lived in or with what had gone before. It was certainly far short of contemporary living standards but in 1978 one resident of Mountain Ash argued, with some good reason, 'I derive intense pleasure from sitting in a ladies' hairdressers and hearing the contented chatter of a couple of old-age pensioners in pastel-coloured cardigans who are splurging on a not-infrequent shampoo and set and a touch of the blue rinse because they are going out somewhere that will make it worth their while to dress up, and I think of their grandmothers at the same age, shrivelled and broken with toil, clad in shabby black and waiting to die – don't ask me to weep for the good old days.'[71]

People did weep for the old days, but for their social rather than material conditions. The elderly were increasingly becoming isolated as life became more privatized and the character of communities slipped away from traditional neighbourliness. With people living longer and families being more mobile, it was becoming more common for the elderly to be left living alone. In 1991 there were 174,049 single-pensioner households, whereas in 1971 there had been just 103,120.[72] In the 1990s an ex-steelworker from Cardiff, born in 1935, said his working-class neighbourhood had 'changed horrendously. The old neighbourliness has gone.... It was a very close community – you could spot a stranger coming in, it was that close, and it was a very caring community.... But now you could drop dead in the street and they'd walk over you.'[73] An elderly Newport man remarked that it was not hours or days he went without seeing anyone but weeks. The sense of isolation was not helped by how different the elderly could feel from the young. R. S. Thomas, admittedly something of a grumpy old man, recounted the time he heard the name Branwen, a woman of great beauty from Welsh legend. He turned and saw 'a stupid, mocking slut, her dull eyes made blue by the daubings of mascara – a girl for whom Wales was no more than a name'.[74] Even if the elderly did not mind changes in public standards of behaviour and appearance, there were plenty of new irritants, such as how the interests of the young dominated television or indeed how televisions were becoming more complicated to even use. Technology was one thing but even money changed. Decimalization in 1971 confused and upset many elderly people. A seventy-five-year-old told a Wrexham paper, 'It's a nuisance. A load of bumkin. I don't understand it at all.'[75] Young people were not always very understanding, failing to see or understand the lives of the elderly or even to appreciate they had been young once. Some elderly people thus felt ignored and even invisible. Angharad Tomos' novel *Si Hei Lwli* (1991) captured that psychological gap between the generations. The family of the elderly lady at the centre of the story have no real conception of her past life and emotions, while she has a strong sense of fear and resentment about being put in 'a home'. Families may have felt guilty about dispatching their elderly relatives in such a way but in a world where both partners increasingly worked and people were less willing to endure cramped houses it was perhaps inevitable. Some elderly people did, in contrast, enjoy strong networks of support from family and neighbours but they also feared being a burden and wanted to maintain their independence and autonomy, even if that meant enduring discomfort and hardship.[76] If a society is judged by how it treated its elderly then too much of Wales was not a particularly caring place.

FOR SOME OF THE ELDERLY, the idea of the good old days was rooted in their disapproval of modern morals. The 1960s government reforms to the death penalty, homosexuality, divorce and birth control had not been driven by popular opinion. Social surveys had suggested there was widespread antipathy across the social spectrum for both the liberal social reforms and wider issues such as immigration, student protest and the commercialization of sex. They may not have always been particularly popular at the time but the reforms did lay the basis for a gradual social revolution.[77] In Wales, however, perhaps because the lasting influence of religion, social conservatism was stronger than in much of the UK. In the late 1960s James Callaghan, Home Secretary and a Cardiff MP, feared that liberalizing the law on issues like pornography would lose Labour support 'in the back streets of Cardiff'.[78] He was probably right. Surveys in the 1970s and 1980 suggested that around 70 per cent of Welsh respondents thought pornography was too readily available, while over three-quarters supported capital punishment. In a 1980 *Western Mail* survey, 48 per cent of viewers wanted all nudity and explicit sex on television to be banned, 33 per cent wanted violence outlawed completely in films and 13 per cent even wanted it removed from news and current affairs programmes.[79]

Public opinion had once been a powerful weapon against transgressions of accepted behaviour but greater mobility and the fracturing of traditional social networks based on work and chapel lessened the censure possible in a world where everyone did not know everyone. Thus the number of abortions had by single women in Wales rose by 153 per cent between 1974 and 1995; the annual number of marriages fell by 31 per cent in the same period, while the percentage of births that took place outside marriage rose from 8.3 to 38.1. Whereas at the start of the 1970s living together and having a baby outside wedlock were still surrounded by social embarrassment and disapproval, twenty years later, while not a norm, they were hardly a matter of comment. A 1991 survey suggested that fewer than one in twenty in Wales thought sex before marriage was wrong. In contrast, other behaviours like drink driving or violence within marriage were rapidly gaining in censure, even if they did not disappear. In 1974 in a case where a 'cultured gentleman' in England was being tried for kicking his wife, the judge, Sir Neville Faulks, remarked, 'If you had been a miner in South Wales I might have overlooked it'. The *Western Mail* was unimpressed with what the judge thought of the Welsh but more insulting was his view of the rights of working-class wives not to be kicked.[80] In 1985–6 a total of 1,151 women were given refuge from physically or mentally abusive partners in Welsh Women's Aid shelters. More women probably just accepted the abuse. Wives were, however, increasingly unwilling to tolerate unhappy marriages, whatever the cause of tension. One cause was the growing awareness of women's sexual potential, something which created frustration when it was not met, whereas in the past little had been expected.[81] Individual happiness increasingly became more important than protecting the sanctity of marriage and divorce was losing its stigma at gathering pace. The number of divorced women in Wales stood at 7,481 in 1961 and 14,365 in 1971. In 1981 the figure was 43,013 and it was 81,220 by 1991.

For many people conservative social attitudes were interlinked with religious belief and the gradual retreat of both went hand in hand. The liberal reforms of the 1960s were a clear sign of Christianity's diminishing influence on public culture, although belief in God still remained the norm.[82] In rural areas active religious practice was still relatively strong in the 1970s. A survey of Machynlleth and Newtown in the middle of that decade suggested that 37 per cent of the population were regular church- and chapel-goers, 28 per cent occasional attendees, while 35 per cent never went except for weddings and funerals.[83] But that picture was being eroded at frightening speed. By 1982 an extensive survey suggested that while 523,100 people (24 per cent of the adult population) were members of churches or chapels, only 280,000 (13 per cent) actually attended and 45 per cent of this group was aged over fifty.[84] Between 1970 and 1995 the Baptist Union of Wales saw its membership fall by 58 per cent, while the Union of Welsh Independents suffered a 49 per cent drop. Bolstered by English in-migration, the rate of decline in the Church in Wales was less sharp but nonetheless it saw its number of Easter communicants fall by 37 per cent between 1970 and 1995. A 1991 survey of the Church suggested more than a third of congregations were aged over sixty-five and less than a quarter were aged between sixteen and forty-four. By 1995 the most frequently reported congregation size was just ten.[85] By then surveys in Wales were suggesting that among men religious attendance was less common than attending professional sports events or the cinema and significantly less common than activities like DIY and gardening. Among women religious attendance was almost twice as strong as among men but far less popular than home-based leisure activities or going to the pub. By 2000 just 7.5 per cent of the Welsh population were active church- and chapel-goers. The upkeep of ageing religious buildings was increasingly a drain on the resources of ever-decreasing congregations. In urban areas it was not uncommon for buildings designed to hold up to 1,000 people to have congregations of just fifty. It was little wonder then that 731 churches and chapels in Wales closed between 1982 and 1995. By the 1990s chapel buildings had become everything from pubs, cinemas and factories to shops, community centres and libraries. One was even a strip club.[86]

Organized religion was partly to blame for its own decline. The remaining Nonconformists were spread thinly over different denominations that refused to come together, thus further weakening their religion to such an extent that its death seemed a real possibility. Some churches and chapels were deeply conservative and refused to change the staid aspects of their worship that were putting newcomers off. Unmarried families could even be told by ministers that they had to choose between each other and coming to church. In such cases organized religion was quite simply falling out of step with dominant social values. The decline in religious attendance was also the product of the wider drift away from communities that were forged around shared institutions. As people moved around more, worked and socialized in more varied and dispersed places, and thus experienced lessened emotional ties with their neighbourhood, places of worship, which were always as much social as spiritual institutions, inevitably declined.[87] Moreover, the rise in privatized communities also lessened any social pressure on people to attend church or chapel, just as it freed people to get divorced, live together without getting married or to formalize their union before the state but not God (the proportion of marriages that were civil ceremonies rose from 38 per cent to 61 per cent between 1971 and 2004).[88] The decline in religious observance and belief should also not be divorced from a social climate where pain and suffering were becoming less common. The need to believe that there was something better coming in an afterlife was diminished. As a character in a short story reflected: 'I've always felt I didn't need God. He was for people who didn't have much, people who couldn't cope.'[89] Nonetheless, Christianity remained part of the culture of Wales. At the 2001 census just 18.5 per cent of people said they had no religion, while 71.9 per cent recorded theirs as Christian. This was more than just ticking a box. At the start of the 1990s over half of Welsh children were being christened, while 95 per cent of burials were Christian affairs.[90] Most people may have turned their backs on religion in their day-to-day lives but they still came back to it when those lives came to an end.

Funerals and weddings (although not normal Sunday services) were two of the few places outside work where suits and ties remained the norm. The decline of formal dressing was one of the most significant changes in popular attitudes in the 1970s and 1980s. Wearing a tie to leave the house was something not even most middle-aged men did anymore and jeans had changed from being the trousers of the young to the something worn by nearly everyone without a pension, male or female. Hats as normal attire were long gone, although the baseball cap was becoming popular among some young people, a sign of American cultural influences. Again, some saw informal attire as a mark of declining public standards but it made for a more comfortable life, if one more vulnerable to ever-increasing shifts in fashion. People now changed their wardrobes not when things fell apart but when they wanted a change or something more modern.

People still usually dressed up to go out, even if it was not in a smart skirt or a shirt and tie. A night in the pub remained important in popular culture and was one source of continuity in a period of cultural change. Newport alone had 142 pubs in the mid-1990s. Drinking was an important source of comfort and relief, but the formal and informal sociability that pubs offered were as attractive as the liquid pleasures within them. Yet excess alcohol always had the potential to spill over into unsociable violence. At the end of the 1990s Gwent had the highest level of violent crime of any county in England and Wales and much of the blame was attributed to the centre of Newport, where there were over fifty pubs and clubs, which would be visited by 8,000 drinkers on a Friday night.[91] This was nothing new. In a novel about 1977 Merthyr, one character remarks of the town centre: 'It's the bloody Wild West, innit? All them kids out to make a reputation for themselves. It's got worse too. There was always fighters, but nowadays, it's like the whole bloody town has gone stark raving mad.' Elsewhere the novel notes: 'Used to be that if you stayed away from certain pubs, you never had to worry. The fighters knew where to go if they wanted to fight, and decent people stayed in their own pubs. Now, you can't feel safe even in your own home.'[92] The concerns over violent crime that had abounded in the 1950s and 1960s (chapter 4) intensified in the 1970s and 1980s. A 1981 opinion poll suggested that 83 per cent of UK residents thought violent crime was the country's main social problem. Football hooliganism had become a particular source of popular concern but rugby was not exactly peaceful either. In the 1970s Cardiff was said to be increasingly rough on international days, with 'hordes of rampaging youths'.[93] Statistics seem to confirm the perception that violent crime was in steep ascension. Between 1974 and 1994 violent crimes against the person in Wales increased by 283 per cent. However, the rise was partly due to better reporting and many incidents were probably not actually physically damaging but rather minor fights that in the past would not have been reported. Moreover, violent crime and robbery were less frequent than in England.[94] The gap between the reality and perception of violent crime was evident in the statistics for sexual offences, which rose by just 8 per cent between 1974 and 1994. Many rapes probably did go unreported but the statistics do not bear out the anxieties that existed.

Although people worried more about violence, other kinds of crime were a far bigger problem. Recorded crime in Wales rose by 147 per cent between 1974 and 1994. Burglary rose by 98 per cent in the same period. In 1989 around one household in nine in south Wales was the victim of a serious property offence such as theft or criminal damage. Vandalism and graffiti remained persistent concerns and criminal damage grew from 3,512 reported incidents in 1974 to 50,732 twenty years later, a staggering 1,345 per cent rise. Despite these escalating statistics, many crimes were actually going unreported and thus unrecorded, especially vandalism, petty theft and minor assaults, where unreported levels could be 50 per cent or higher.[95] These crime levels were generating such anger and frustration that they led to threats of vigilantism. Perhaps this was no wonder when the impact of criminal damage is considered. At one point in 1971 twenty-two of the fifty telephone kiosks in Wrexham were not working due to vandalism. In 1978 the press reported that an old people's complex in Cardiff was a nightly target for vandals who pelted windows with mud, ripped fencing apart, painted swastikas on buildings and stole milk. The residents had been 'attacked, robbed and harassed' and were said to live in 'nightly fear'. It was the elderly who felt most vulnerable to rising crime and they increasingly stayed at home behind locked doors. Their fears were partly due to the frequent portrayals of violent crime on television but they also drew on personal experience and a third of respondents to an Age Concern survey in Barry in 1982 had lost property or been attacked in the previous year.[96]

Yet crime rates in Wales as a whole were generally lower than the English average, although they were higher in south Wales, especially for burglary and theft. This suggested that the causes were rooted in social conditions such as unemployment. Welsh surveys identified a pattern where juveniles committing crimes were typically from low-income and unstable families, especially on council estates, where there were few opportunities and aspirations. Crime was certainly lower in affluent areas. In 1986, for example, the Swansea suburb of Killay had 16 recorded crimes per 1,000 people, whereas working-class Llansamslet had 374. The design and demography of post-war council estates were part of the problem. The provision of open space should have been a positive factor in theory but it was easily vandalized, difficult to maintain and allowed teenagers and young people, who made up a disproportionately large share of council-estate populations, to gather, threatening others. Yet it would be wrong to simply dismiss the large estates as dens of crime and many of those arrested in Penrhys in the Rhondda, for example, came from just one small group of streets and families.[97]

JUST AS IN THE 1950s AND 1960s, one reason for the continuing growth of crime was the continuing rise in consumerism. There was more to steal and a greater desire to own things. At the start of the 1970s consumerism was still not as evident in parts of Wales as it was in metropolitan England. Visitors to towns like Merthyr noted the lack of eating places, laundrettes and garages and how more men wore ties and more women had hats on than in most places.[98] The consumerism that undermined such pictures is often seen rather derogatorily but it did improve people's lives. This was evident in the changes in what people ate. In 1973 a welfare officer in Cardiff had complained that families in his service's care 'eat baked beans and chips all the time and never think of fresh veg which would be healthier and cheaper'.[99] But a wider national survey in the early 1970s suggested that people in Wales ate more bread and butter than the British average, slightly more fruit and vegetables and slightly less meat. By 1984–5 government statistics implied that the Welsh were spending 6 per cent more than the British average on alcohol, 18 per cent more on tobacco but 8 per cent less on fruit and 9 per cent less on meat.[100] But whatever the variation with the rest of Britain, there was a long-term for eating less red meat and fat and more fruit and vegetables. Diets were also slowly becoming more interesting. A 1976 cookery book, based on recipes that had appeared in *Y Cymro*, outlined 'simple' and 'plain' foods for 'normal girls'. Despite such claims, a mark of how much things were changing was the fact that it included guacamole, ratatouille, moussaka and hochzich kucha.[101] For those who did not have time for even simple recipes there were new convenience foods in the 1970s such as Angel Delight, instant potato and dehydrated curries. These not only saved housewives time but also seemed terribly modern. Rising disposable incomes also enabled people to eat out more. Over the course of the 1970s Indian and Chinese restaurants opened in small towns, further diversifying people's tastes, although their menus suggested that local preferences were still quite conservative. As well as curries and sweet-and-sours, Indian and Chinese restaurants also served chips and other traditional British delights. When, in 1974, an Italian became Mountain Ash's first cordon bleu chef, he promised, rather cautiously, to 'stimulate Welsh appetites with something just that bit different'. McDonald's opened its first Welsh outlet in Cwmbran in 1986 and quickly became very popular, combining the familiarity of chips with the allure of American hamburgers. That year a novel was remarking of Gower: 'not so long ago it had been hake and chips, bottled cockles, pork pies and pints of Troeth bitter, these days it was cannelloni, paella, stifado, cans of Foster, bottles of Rioja'.[102] But there were limits to such cosmopolitanism. In 1985 a survey of Newport noted there was nowhere in the town 'to eat first-rate food'. A Welsh cookbook claimed in 1980 that in most working-class homes tea was still served in flowered china cups with gold rims and came with homemade cakes, scones and jam, while shops still met traditional Welsh tastes by selling 'cawl meat', coarse-cut sausages, Welsh cakes, bara brith, laverbread, cockles and old-fashioned boiled sweets.[103]

However cosmopolitan Welsh tastes were, thanks to intensive farming and competition between supermarkets, food was becoming relatively cheaper. In 1973–4 Welsh households spent an estimated 27 per cent of their expenditure on food. By 1994–5 the figure had fallen to 19 per cent.[104] Yet only those with transport were able to take full advantage of the falling prices competition between stores created. Thus in Cardiff, research in the early 1980s found that retired households were making less use of chain stores than younger shoppers.[105] The lack of access the elderly and poor had to the cheapest shopping was exacerbated by the growth of out-of-town retail parks. The UK's first hypermarket was opened by Carrefour outside Caerphilly in 1972. It had 55,000 square feet of selling space and 950 parking spaces. It aimed to undercut prices in the local town centre by 8 per cent and when it first opened demand was so great that the store had to ask people to stay away. After a year, a report noted the hypermarket had taken a 'distinct' proportion of the local food trade. Such effects meant that smaller high streets suffered significantly from the rise of the supermarket, even if large regional shopping districts, like the centres of Cardiff and Swansea, boomed in the consumerist climate.[106]

Even amid the high unemployment of the early 1980s there was still evidence of a consumer boom, something clear in the *Western Mail*'s regular lifestyle supplement, which was full of articles about fashion, cars, furnishings and holidays. Shopping was increasingly becoming a leisure pursuit in itself. In 1981 a new Debenhams opened in Cardiff. Its interior designer, a former farmer from near Llanelli, tried to achieve 'a sense of theatre':

> Every department had been individually styled, coloured, lit and decorated. Even the clothes models have faces copied from individual, real-live model girls. The lingerie department is done out in deep cyclamen pink velvet. Menswear is in tobacco brown with natural wood and chrome. The toy department is in red with space-age metal mesh fitments. Books are displayed against a deep peach background with library shelving. Cosmetics are reflected in a department of white, silver and mirrors.

Eighty-three per cent of Debenhams customers were female and the designer claimed, 'I think the woman gets a rough time. It may be her bank manager, her husband, the kids, her feet. It is so nice for her to walk into a store and see that somebody loves her.' Walking there was obligatory because Queen Street, where the store was located, had been pedestrianized

Figure 12.1 Annual personal disposable income in Wales (adjusted for inflation to 2008 prices), 1974–95.

Personal income less taxes and social-security contributions. Non-adjusted data from *DWHS*-3, 28.

Table 12.1 Ownership of consumer durables (percentage of households), 1970–91

	1970–1		1980–1		1990–1	
	Wales	UK	Wales	UK	Wales	UK
Central heating	24	31	52	58	82	81
Washing machine	69	65	81	77	88	87
Refrigerator	59	67	91	93	na	na
Television	92	91	98	97	99	98
Telephone	24	37	67	73	84	88
Deep freezer	na	na	50	47	85	82
Tumble dryer	na	na	23	22	44	47
Dishwasher	na	na	2	4	11	13
Microwave	na	na	na	na	59	52

na = data not available.
Source: *Regional Trends*, 18 (1983), 100, and 28 (1993), 108.

in 1975, another step in improving the shopping experience and one that was soon repeated around Wales. By 1993 Queen Street was the fourth most profitable shopping site in the UK.[107]

What enabled the growth of the retail sector was the long-term rise in disposable incomes, something which increased by 49 per cent in real terms in Wales between 1974 and 1995 thanks to rising wages and falling direct taxation. Although there were short-lived falls in periods of high unemployment, the inescapable trend was upwards (figure 12.1). One impact of this rise in disposable income was the onwards march of consumer durables (table 12.1). Such goods all helped make life more comfortable and more entertaining and should not be underestimated as significant social advances. Refrigerators reduced the need for constant shopping, while telephones ensured people did not become disconnected in the more privatized lives that television continued to encourage. The development of the video-recorder – by the start of the 1990s two-thirds of households had one – made watching television even more common, since it freed people from the limitations of scheduling. By 1992 the average number of hours watched a week by someone in Wales was twenty-five but among people aged over sixty-five this rose to over thirty.[108] Perhaps the most important of the consumer gains was the spread of central heating. It could push up the rateable value of a home but it allowed people to use their whole house in the winter rather than huddling close to the fire, although this was perhaps to the detriment of family life, since it enabled children to spend more time in their bedrooms rather than the lounge. If people did not have the money for durables they could always borrow it and the consumer boom was partly built on credit. Hire purchase continued to be important in giving people access to larger goods but credit cards and bank loans were also becoming significant and people were both more able and more willing to go into debt in search of a better lifestyle. Important here was the 1974 Consumer Credit Act, which allowed women to borrow without a male guarantor. Rather than being associated with the shame of debt, owning a credit card became a status symbol in itself in the 1970s. By 1986 around a third of Welsh adults were estimated to have one.[109] But some were spending beyond their means and consumer debt emerged as a real problem. By 2002 one in five Welsh households reported they were having financial difficulties, while the average debt of clients of the Citizens' Advice Bureau in Wales was £11,000.[110]

At the end of the 1960s there had still been houses with no running water, front rooms that were rarely used in two-up two-downs and children who slept more than one to a bed. In 1971 only 85 per cent of Welsh households had their own baths and showers, while just 80 per cent had inside toilets. The fact that nearly 442,000 people in Wales were unable to go to the toilet inside their own homes was a clear sign of how far there was to go for modern housing conditions to become near universal. But there were very significant improvements in housing infrastructure over the course of the 1970s and 1980s, not least due to the 1971 Housing Act, which allowed individuals to claim grants of up to 75 per cent of the cost of central heating, bathrooms, rewiring and other improvements. By October 1973 over 43,000 housing improvement grants had been approved in Wales.[111] By the 1990s it was an oddity not to have an inside toilet. Even after people had the basics of a bathroom and central heating, there was still much that could be done. A description of a policeman's house on a new estate in the Valleys captured many people's aspirations:

> He had worked hard to imprint his personality on it, hanging horse brasses and a brace of reproduction flint-locks over the fireplace which did not have a fire. It was made of blue and puce stone, with a television and video housed in the grate recess. He had been the first person on the estate to have a video. Outside the garden was a miniature version of a country estate he had once been called upon to police. An ornamental pond held oversized, ornamental fish and was bordered with carefully layered rocks. A mix of infant trees lined the garden wall.[112]

The general demand for property and the strength of people's spending power were evident in house prices, which rose beyond inflation in Wales by 26 per cent over the 1970s and 29 per cent over the 1980s.[113]

Property ownership was one area where Wales was ahead of UK averages and an economist commented in the early 1970s that Wales was closer to the ideal of a 'property-owning democracy' than any other part of Britain.[114] In 1971 55 per cent of households were owner-occupied; by 1991 the figure had risen to 71 per cent. That increase owed much to the right to buy council houses, introduced in 1980, for tenants who had lived in their home for three or more years. The price they had to pay diminished according to how long they had lived there and some people were able to pay less than a third of the market value. The wealthier working class, usually middle-aged couples in skilled jobs who were able to get a mortgage, were the key beneficiaries. By the end of 1991 a total of 83,994 council houses in Wales had been sold to their occupiers under the scheme.[115] Labour-controlled authorities were often deeply unhappy at this. In Wrexham the council even drew up a leaflet warning people of the pitfalls of owning their own home. But property owning was something to aspire to, especially as more and more were achieving it, and it would have been higher if people had had the means. A 1986 government survey showed that 46 per cent of Welsh renters would have liked to have been owner-occupiers.[116] In 1980 a Port Talbot steelworker told a journalist of his property-owning plans: 'It's an investment, something you can pass on to your children. I'm not being snobbish about council houses, but I just want something better than the place I was brought up in. It's only natural isn't it?'[117]

Some people were being left behind by the changes in housing. This was clear in the fact that nearly 20,000 Welsh people still did not have an inside toilet in 1991. The most vulnerable to poor housing were those who neither owned their own home nor were able to get a council property. Whereas just 3 per cent of owner-occupied homes were classified as substandard in the late 1980s, the figure for furnished privately-rented homes was 30 per cent.[118] More and more people were finding themselves trapped in poor rented accommodation, as council houses were sold off and waiting lists for public housing grew. In 1980 there had been some 56,000 people on council house waiting lists in Wales. A decade later there were 90,000. In 1992 there were even 10,270 households classified as homeless, an 82 per cent increase on the figure ten years earlier. Few actually slept rough but there were also an invisible number of people sleeping on friends' floors, those evicted from private accommodation or forced to leave home or care.[119]

Although the homeless and those stuck in damp flats, grotty bedsits and houses without toilets and baths should not be forgotten, the overall significant improvement in housing conditions is an important reason why concentrating on unemployment and economic problems gives a misleading impression of Wales in the 1970s and 1980s. Moreover, consumerism continued to define how many thought about their lives. In the 1950s and 1960s consumer goods like televisions and fridges were status symbols; by the 1970s and 1980s it was video-recorders and holidays abroad. As early as 1974–5 nearly 100,000 people were flying from the airport near Cardiff for holidays in the summer and 20,000 were in the winter. In 1995 an estimated 27 per cent of Welsh adults took a holiday abroad. Cars were another status symbol that were becoming more attainable and the number of private licences rose from 705,200 in 1974 to 1,085,900 in 1996. This meant there was more than one vehicle per three people and it created no end of parking problems in urban areas.[120] Material goods were even beginning to define time. The *Abergavenny Chronicle*, for example, noted at the end of 1981 that it had been the year of 'Space Invaders, Rubik's Cube, disco skates, stereo head phones, videos and CB radio. And some of it even penetrated to this neck of the woods!'[121] Many of these goods were for children and teenagers and it was the young whose lives were most shaped by consumerism. As well as the ever-ubiquitous pop music, by the 1980s being young had become a whiz of branded bicycles, toys and sweets. One Cardiff woman remembered her adolescence:

> I loved the 80s! Seeing ET in the cinema and crying at the end! Being madly in love with Simon le Bon and wanting to be like Madonna, riding around on a battered BMX, watching Live Aid on telly, Marathons in a selection box every Xmas, drinking Quantro and trying to get drunk on Top Deck.[122]

Amid such consumption there were killjoys complaining that childhood was losing some of its simplicity and innocence but the real victims were perhaps those children whose families could not afford such treats.

IN THE 1980s a steelworker noted that while he had been brought up before the war in a slum with an outside toilet and a cold water tap in the yard, he could not now envisage life without a car and a fridge. He told a journalist: 'in the old days you felt differently. There are no poor people if you're all poor people. It's only when you see the rich that you realise "God, I'm poor" and in those days in Port Talbot you never met them.'[123] But in the 1970s and 1980s those who were rich, at least in the sense of owning a house full of nice consumer goods, lived in the same communities as the poor, undermining the sense of working-class unity in places like Port Talbot. For the rising number of unemployed in particular, there was thus a strong sense that they were being left behind in a culture of rising affluence, especially in the 1980s, when the government spent much time trumpeting that affluence. Unemployment meant Wales never shared in the consumer boom to quite the same extent as some parts of England. In 1974 Welsh per capita consumer expenditure stood at 92 per cent of the UK figure. By 1995 this had fallen to 88 per cent. This meant that it was nearly £1,000 lower per head in Wales.[124] Indeed, for those out of work or in low-paid jobs, the consumer boom could seem rather distant. A survey in Newport in the early 1980s found that 16 per cent of households said they could not make ends meet, 58 per cent were not saving any money, 47 per cent were not spending money on holidays and 31 per cent were not even spending anything on leisure and entertainment.[125] The kind of dire deprivation that led to the establishment of the welfare state had disappeared but such surveys showed that poverty certainly still existed. With Thatcher's government chipping away at the value of benefit payments, commentators on the left increasingly worried that an underclass was being created and that Britain was becoming a deeply divided society. The Council of Churches for Wales became vexed about the 'increase in long-term unemployment, in poverty, in divided families and communities, in conflict between allies and colleagues, in the erosion of hope, in the feeling of powerless and despair'.[126]

Such problems were most associated with the former coalfields. Reeling from the loss of mining and manufacturing jobs, by the early 1990s Mid Glamorgan had the lowest gross domestic product and the lowest average household incomes in the UK. Low incomes meant low demand for goods and services, which then reinforced the weak economy, creating a vicious circle. The lack of jobs meant that the long-term migration away from the Valleys continued. While the Welsh population rose by 5.4 per cent between 1981 and 2006, Merthyr endured a fall of 8.3 per cent, Blaenau Gwent 8.4 per cent, Neath Port Talbot 4 per cent and Rhondda Cynon Taff 1.9 per cent. Most people who left were under forty five years old and the number of five- to twenty-four-year-olds in Mid Glamorgan fell by more than 16,000 between 1981 and 1991, while the number of people over seventy-five increased by 4,600.[127] The communities left behind in the Valleys were increasingly caught in what was widely perceived to be a downward spiral, especially those smaller places where a pit had dominated or those further up the Valleys and too far for an easy commute down to the M4 corridor. With the closure of mines in such places, other amenities such as shops, pubs, taxi services and libraries could eventually go too, a process exacerbated by the wider trend towards out-of-town retail parks. The town centres that were left behind were often tired and tatty, overloaded with charity shops and fast-food joints, and with boarded-up chapels and working men's clubs to remind people of better times. Local-authority estates, meanwhile, were often poorly maintained by cash-strapped councils, with accumulating rubbish, rodent infestations and an appearance that stigmatized the people living there.[128] The people themselves were not always in much better health either, thanks to the effects of heavy industry, poor housing and low incomes. By the 1990s an estimated 47 per cent of Mid Glamorgan males were overweight, 40 per cent smoked and nearly half drank more than the recommended alcohol limit. People in the county also ate less fruit and vegetables and more fat and salt than the Welsh averages. In 1991 fifteen of the twenty local-authority wards in Britain with the worst rates of limiting long-term illnesses were in industrial Wales. By 2001 30 per cent of the population of Merthyr had some form of limiting long-term illness. Life expectancy there was five years less than in Ceredigion, the healthiest part of Wales. There was nothing new in any of this – in the mid-1960s mortality rates in the Glamorgan valleys had been nearly 30 per cent higher than the England and Wales average – but the fact that people had to live with the consequences of industrial work long after they stopped being paid for it added to many people's sense of anger at what was happening.[129]

And there was anger. One investigation argued that, after the collapse of mining, communities had experienced an acute sense of loss and even went through a period of grieving as they struggled to come to terms with the disappearance of their economic *raison d'être*.[130] People complained that the old solidarity and togetherness were lost after an industrial closure. Poverty may no longer have meant going hungry but it undoubtedly involved a loss of status. That meant there was much talk of social breakdown and a loss of hope and community. An article in *The Times* described part of the Rhondda in 1992, a year after its colliery closed:

> These people of Maerdy are dying in a long, hard season of crime, poverty and fear. Since the pit closed they have lost everything. They have lost their wealth, their health, their faith, their jobs and, most important of all, their dignity. They do not have a single thing going for them.... people sit bewitched by their televisions as the dogs of lawlessness howl outside every home. They drink too much and their marriages are breaking down. Only their depression and confusion reminds them that they are still alive as they now all wait, with some impatience, to die.[131]

Although this smacked of exaggeration, in the Cynon, Neath, Rhondda and Rhymney valleys over the period 1985–91 criminal damage rose by 102 per cent, theft by 40 per cent and violence against the person by 44 per cent.[132] A lack of optimism was encouraged by the poverty trap that many people found themselves in, where low incomes were compounded by having no access to a good school, a bank account, gas and electricity on credit or even a cheap supermarket. A fashion developed in the 1990s for novels, films and plays depicting how bad life in urban Wales was: the lack of hope, opportunity and stable family life.[133] One captured how even the politically sympathetic could despair. In Richard John Evans' *Entertainment*, an English community worker encounters aggressive locals and claims, 'You could get stabbed here for just standing in a queue.… How far did you have to dig to find the community here?'[134]

Yet community was far from dead in working-class areas. Despite the migration of many people, at the start of the 1990s more than half of Mid Glamorgan households had lived at that address for more than ten years. This created a strong sense of community and continuity.[135] A 2002 study of Swansea found that working-class areas often had a stronger sense of community because of a lack of geographical mobility and high levels of marriage between local families, even if people did feel that community had declined over their lifetimes because outsiders had moved in. One forty-one-year-old woman from a deprived estate in the city claimed, 'I wouldn't move out of here for nobody'. A fifty-five-year-old man on the same estate said: 'All right you get a few families who cause a bit of trouble, but overall, it's one of the nicest and safest places to live'.[136] By the turn of the twenty-first century one large survey suggested that a fifth of people felt there had been a decline in community in the Valleys, with rising crime, poor amenities and people becoming more private. Yet 85 per cent of respondents still felt that there was an acceptable, good or excellent level of community spirit where they lived, and nearly 60 per cent said this made the Valleys different to the rest of Wales. In the much-maligned estate of Penrhys only 6 per cent said the community was poor, compared with 15 per cent in the overall survey. A closer reading of the survey, however, suggests that what people thought represented a good community was probably very different from their grandparents. Only 54 per cent of respondents said they had at least weekly contact with neighbours and almost half of people aged over forty-one did not feel safe in their neighbourhood after dark. As two academics claimed in a commentary on the Valleys, 'over-romanticised notions of community' were sometimes obscuring 'the unpalatable facts of everyday life'.[137] The reality was that, no longer united by manual work let alone by a single industry, Valleys communities were as fragmented as those everywhere else. People with jobs were increasingly, socially, economically and even physically distanced from the unemployed and low paid, who, by the 1980s, were being described as an 'underclass'. Deprived estates like Penrhys were as much stigmatized by others in the Rhondda as they were by people outside the area, as suggested by the fact that people there did not use it as an address when applying for local jobs. Sociologists noted deep psychological divisions between people on what were regarded as respectable private estates, those on council estates of more questionable respectability and the clearly unrespectable local youths who hung around on street corners.[138]

Social and economic divides were thus everywhere. Through the 1970s, 1980s and 1990s Wales was poorer than England and the Valleys were poorer than the M4 corridor but such broad geographic divisions are inevitably far too simplistic. There were people who were relatively rich and relatively poor everywhere, just in varying levels of concentration. It was perhaps because society was so obviously divided that research suggested that class remained a powerful identity in people's minds. A large 2002 survey of Swansea found that 32 per cent of people said they were middle class, 43 per cent said they were working class, while 14 per cent said they did not know and 11 per cent gave different answers, disliking the idea of class because of its associations with snobbery or because it might undermine their own status. When pressed on why people chose these categories, family backgrounds seemed as important as current occupations, which meant that the label people gave themselves might not reflect their own social mobility. Thus in another 1997 Welsh survey less than one in five labelled themselves middle class but more than half could be objectively put in that in category.[139] Deindustrialization, the rise of the service sector and expanded higher education all meant the middle class was undoubtedly growing: the proportion of economically active heads of Welsh households in categories now usually classified as middle class (those with professional, intermediate/managerial and non-manual skilled jobs) rose from 28 per cent in 1971 to 46 per cent in 1991. But the division was misleading in a world where the classes' lifestyles and even incomes had converged. A survey in the mid-1990s found ABC1s (middle class) and C2DEs (working class) shared the same five top leisure activities (going to the pub, sport, DIY, gardening and country/seaside trips) and in the same order of popularity. Specific types of consumption – the size of your house, the car you drove, the holidays you took and even which supermarket you shopped at – were all important symbols of status but they could cut across class, especially in a world where skilled manual trades could pay more than middle-class professions.[140] The money that could be made from rising property prices had further blurred traditional class boundaries, as had the 'gentrification' of some traditional urban working-class areas by young professionals buying their first homes in these more affordable districts. Moreover, in 1999, while up to half of people had experienced upwards social mobility (measured by comparing their occupation with that of their parents), approaching a third had moved down that occupational ladder.[141] There were still cultural tastes, such as reading matter and diet, that might be thought of as middle and working class but these were rooted in differences in education rather than income and were thus easily transcended.[142] Even if cultural tastes were the markers of class then there were poor middle-class and wealthy working-class people. And then there was the gulf that had opened up between the comfortable working class and those on low pay or benefits. Aspirations, political outlooks and material conditions divided groups that were once easily described as the working and middle classes but were now far too diverse to easily describe at all

THE POPULAR IMAGE of late twentieth-century Wales was one of economic gloom. Contemporaries certainly felt it, whether they were looking inwards or outwards. As the mayor of Brynmawr remarked to her local paper:

> Apart from the Royal Wedding, 1981 gave us little to enthuse about. Unemployment reached three million, many being youngsters who currently see no hope in the future. One-third of the world's people are starving; hundreds of millions are to be spent on new nuclear weapon systems, and once again Poland is being ground under the heel of an aggressive dictatorship.[143]

Poverty was very real, especially in communities that had lost pits. Yet economic problems did not dominate the atmosphere of the 1970s, 1980s and 1990s. These were decades when it became easier to be black, female or gay, even if real equality was still a mirage. The permissiveness that first gained attention in the 1960s finally became the norm in the 1980s. Divorce and sex outside marriage became accepted as normal behaviours. Housing improved; food got more diverse, cheaper and healthier. Disposable incomes continued on their general long-term upward curve, paid holidays grew longer and working hours shorter and there was continued talk from the 1960s of the emergence of a leisure society.[144] People even lived longer, primarily thanks to advancing medical care and a growing awareness of the dangers of smoking and poor diet. Life expectancy in England and Wales rose from 69.0 for men and 75.3 for women born start of the 1970s to 74.1 and 79.4 respectively for those born in the middle of the 1990s.[145]

Meanwhile, from disco and flowery shirts in the 1970s to pastel colours and New Romantics in the 1980s, there was a background of cultural vibrancy, driven forward and promoted by the continued growth of consumerism. From 1994, those who could not afford lavish or even modest material rewards could always dream with a flutter on the National Lottery, a game which quickly became ingrained in popular culture. By 1995, 77 per cent of Welsh adults (compared with 67 per cent in Britain) were buying lottery tickets or scratch cards, spending an average of £2.63 each a week. Critics called it a tax on the poor, since it was they who spent the most on it, and worried that it was a sign of how obsessed society was becoming with wealth. The odds of a jackpot win were tiny but people enjoyed speculating what they would spend the money on and 109 Welsh people did win prizes of £1 million or more in the Lottery's first decade.[146]

Despite the emergence of a more tolerant society and a more comfortable one, it is questionable whether people in Wales were actually any more content than their predecessors. Life was certainly far easier than in the pre-war days, when poverty meant going cold and hungry, but across the western world there was little to suggest that the increased wealth of the post-war period had made people happier. The general instability of the economy perhaps made it difficult to enjoy the fruits of affluence. People struggled with what one 1973 novel called 'Bad luck, ill health, a tightening of credit … the high tensions of overdraft living'.[147] They worried about crime, violence and the young. Such insecurities were hardly new but there were other problems developing in modern life that unsettled people and replaced the more fundamental concerns of the past. One historian has suggested that growing affluence was breeding an impatience for further material reward and personal gratification, a feeling which then undermined general well-being.[148] Diseases of prosperity were replacing those of poverty, not so much because there was something inherently unhealthy about affluent lifestyles but because the longer people lived, the more likely they were to get cancer or heart disease. Quite simply, in the past other things tended to kill people first. For some, technology could make life as frustrating as it made things easier for others. A 1993 Welsh survey suggested that 44 per cent of people were uncomfortable programming a video-recorder and 21 per cent would like to use typewriters rather than electronic keyboards. There were other new annoyances, like junk mail, the subject of an angry 1970 editorial in the *Wrexham Leader*.[149] The reorganizations of local government in 1974 and 1996 even changed where people lived, leading one novel to proclaim: 'The bastards, they won't even leave the names you've always known things by alone'. Within the new 1974 county of Dyfed there was strong local support for continuing to use the old names of Pembroke, Carmarthen and Cardigan.[150] There was also the continuation of concerns from the 1950s and 1960s about crime, morality, the emptiness of modern life, family break-up and the decline of community. Fewer and fewer people were falling back on the belief in a god and afterlife that might make up for problems in this life. When AIDS became a popular worry in the 1980s it was even seen by some as the logical outcome of a world of promiscuity.

Owning property and consumer goods and worrying about health focused people's minds inwards on their homes rather than outwards on their community, something which perhaps denied people a sense of solidarity and belonging. In 1971 one journalist noted that the British mostly led a 'withdrawn and inarticulate life', spending their free time 'mowing lawns and painting walls, pampering pets, listening to music, knitting and watching television'.[151] That trend intensified over the next two decades. One 1973 Welsh novel suggested that concerns about violence and other problems encouraged people to become more self-centred:

> You turned the telly on, there was a limb in the gutter, somebody's house gone up in smoke, four-figure numbers of dead every week, towns, villages, homes, lives all expendable somewhere or other. You couldn't invent a dirty trick that wasn't somebody's policy, all high-level stuff. So what did you do but opt out unless you were some kind of crank? Unless it was bread and butter, ordinary people didn't bother any more, just escaped, building private forts against the general dismay.[152]

Over a decade later, miners' families were similarly remarking how everyone had grown more cynical after the 1984–5 strike, concentrating on looking after number one. When people did pull together – for example during the 'big snow' of 1982 – then it became a topic of comment. But even in that example there was looting of stranded cars.[153]

For some on the left, the large numbers of Welsh people voting Conservative was one outcome of such processes but this trend did not mean that society had become more selfish or that people had given up completely on the communal ethos so important to Labour. After all, Labour did remain Wales' biggest party. The Tories themselves, meanwhile, continued to support the principle of the National Health Service, while state assistance for economic development remained a central plank of their policy, despite their free-market rhetoric. The majority of people probably disagreed with Thatcher's denial in an interview with *Woman's Own* of an abstract concept called society but they also lived their lives in accordance with the prioritized principle she espoused in the same interview that 'It is our duty to look after ourselves and then also to help look after our neighbour … life is a reciprocal business'.[154] Moreover, her repeated advocacy of the importance of individuals working hard to improve themselves was no different to the traditional Welsh value of using education to move up the social ladder. There were other signs that Conservative governance did not mark or bring a revolution in popular thinking and attitudes. Privatization was generally accepted rather than well liked, with Welsh surveys suggesting a majority wanted neither more nor less of it.[155] Given that by the 1970s nationalization did not seem to have brought any long-term benefits to the likes of coal or steel, some loss of faith in state ownership should not be interpreted as a sign of a collapse in collective thinking. The enterprise culture that, to some, symbolized greed above communal responsibility was also something of a mirage. A 1990 survey suggested that 18 per cent of adults in Wales owned shares in a company but this seemed to be concentrated among the middle-aged middle class; thus the people who made money from this popular capitalism usually had money in the first place.[156]

The reality was that, like government policy after 1979, popular attitudes were actually rather contradictory, a mix of nods towards the collective good and prioritizing the individual. A 1987 survey suggested that 93 per cent of the Welsh electorate supported government expenditure to get rid of poverty. But that did not mean they wanted to pay for that action themselves and only 54 per cent said they supported government action to redistribute income and wealth, while 45 per cent supported better levels of welfare benefits. Interpreting such data is not easy and there is some belief that people give opinion pollsters socially responsible answers in the knowledge that they will not have to be acted on. Perhaps the respondents who did favour more left-wing action were those who felt they would be the beneficiaries rather than the ones paying. But if Britain did become a more selfish society under the Conservative governments of 1979–97 then it is hard to explain why annual charitable giving doubled across the UK in real terms during the same period.[157] Nor did the value people placed on community die; indeed, it was widely celebrated, even if rather romantically, in popular culture and political rhetoric. But perhaps this, like putting a few pounds in a collection tin, just made people feel better without having to endure the greater personal expense a socialist shift to fairer communities would bring.

One change that was far clearer was that more people were living on their own. The rising number of elderly widows, divorcees and affluent young people meant that single-person households rose from 9 per cent of the Welsh total in 1951 to 26 per cent by 1994. That did not mean this was a permanent state and many younger ones would have expected to find a partner and have children. For older people, living on their own could be a conscious affirmation of independence. Moreover, the statistic also shows that three-quarters of people did not live on their own. For all the claims that traditional family life was disintegrating, family remained at the heart of society, something recognized and championed by the Conservative governments of the 1980s and 1990s and the Labour administration that succeeded it. Families, with the rise of divorce and same-sex couples, might have become more complicated structures but they remained, as one historian has noted, 'central to the lives of most people'.[158] More comfortable homes, more equal gender relations and fewer community activities led fathers to spend more time with their nearest and dearest, although women still remained likely to be at home when the children were not at school. Moreover, women also performed important caring roles for elderly parents, without which the welfare system could well have collapsed. Indeed, as people lived longer, extended families grew and four generations were not uncommon. But the continued importance of family perhaps also contributed to the privatization of lives, by ensuring that people were less reliant on neighbours for support and social interaction.

For all the accusations that family life had broken down on estates and among the poor, it was in the working class that the concept of family was strongest. Social mobility and careers meant that the middle-class extended families were often dispersed. The car and the telephone could compensate for that but the working-class extended family seemed much stronger. Frequent contact remained the norm and parents offered their adult children financial and emotional support, not to mention childcare support. A 2002 survey in Swansea found that over two-thirds of adults' parents lived in the city and over 30 per cent of respondents' parents lived in the same part of Swansea as them. Thanks partly to rituals such as Sunday lunch, 79 per cent of partnered daughters had seen their mothers in the last week and 41 per cent in the last twenty-four hours; 64 per cent of partnered sons had seen their fathers in the last week.[159] It was in such ways that a strong strand of continuity remained across the social, technological and cultural changes of the 1970s, 1980s and 1990s. And it was in such relationships that people found a happiness and emotional reward that could more than compensate for the stresses, disruptions and inequalities of modern life.[160]

Notes

1 Quoted in T. R. Chapman, *Encounters with Wales* (1995), 34.
2 *SWEP*, 4 May 1979.
3 *WM*, 1 and 2 May 1979.

4 G. Talfan Davies, *At Arm's Length: Recollections and Reflections on the Arts, Media and a Young Democracy* (2008), 18.
5 K. Nurse, *Footsteps to the Past: A Welsh Quest* (1998), 81.
6 Calculated from *Census 1971: Economic Activity, Part 1* (1973), 81, and WAG, *Statistical Focus on Wales and the UK* (2007), 66.
7 C. Rosser and C. Harris, *The Family and Social Change* (1983 edn), xv.
8 *DWHS-3*, 140, 135. T. L. Rees, 'Changing patterns of women's work in Wales: some myths explored', *CW*, 2 (1988), 119–30.
9 See for example the film *So That You Can Live* (Cinema Action, 1982).
10 J. England, *The Wales TUC, 1974–2004: Devolution and Industrial Politics* (2004), 94.
11 Equal Opportunities Commission in Wales, *Changing Wales: Thirty Years of Progress Towards Sex Equality*, press release, 2 Dec. 2005. S. W. Town, *After the Mines: Changing Employment Opportunities in a South Wales Valley* (1978), 72. *WM*, 3 June 1975.
12 D. Beddoe, *Out of the Shadows: A History of Women in Twentieth Century Wales* (2000), 152–4. P. E. Jones, 'Some trends in Welsh secondary education, 1967–1987', *CW*, 2 (1988), 99–118. *Statistics of Education: Further and Higher Education*, 4 (1990), 8. *Statistics of Education in Wales*, 4 (1979), 82.
13 J. Benson, *Affluence and Authority: A Social History of 20th Century Britain* (2005), 127–8. *Census 1981: Sex, Age and Marital Status* (1983), 14. C. Haste, *Rules of Britain: Sex in Britain, Word War I to the Present* ([1992] 2002), 227–35.
14 I. Emmett, *A North Wales Village: A Social Anthropological Study* (1964), 112.
15 Rosser and Harris, *The Family and Social Change*, 184–5. D. Leonard, *Sex and Generation: A Study of Courtship and Weddings* (1980), 79.
16 V. Griffiths, 'Gilfach Goch', *Pl*, 5:6 (1971), 39–44. *WM*, 5 Jan. 1976. *WL*, 9 June 1970.
17 *WM*, 7 Jan. 1976.
18 A. Roderick, *The Pubs of Newport* (1997), viii. *WL*, 29 Jan. 1971.
19 Leonard, *Sex and Generation*, 59.
20 *WM*, 5 June 1975.
21 Leonard, *Sex and Generation*, 241, 249, 264, 269–70.
22 C. C. Harris, *Redundancy and Recession in South Wales* (1987), 137.
23 L. D. Morris, 'Redundancy and patterns of household finance', *Sociological Review*, 32:3 (1984), 492–523.
24 *WM*, 2 Jan. 1976 and 18 Jan. 1982.
25 *Channel 4 News*, 3 Mar. 1985.
26 J. Pilcher, 'Who should do the dishes? Three generations of Welsh women talking about men and housework', in J. Aaron, T. Rees, S. Betts and M. Vincentelli (eds), *Our Sisters' Land: The Changing Identities of Women in Wales* (1994), 31–45.
27 S. James, 'Happy as Saturday night', in *Not Singing Exactly* (1996), 201, 202.
28 H. L. Yewlett, 'Marriage, family and career aspirations of adolescent girls', in S. Betts (ed.), *Our Daughters' Land: Past and Present* (1996), 241–58.
29 T. Rees, *Women and Work: Twenty-Five Years of Gender Equality in Wales* (1999), 27.
30 Harris, *Redundancy and Recession*, 142–3. *WM*, 18 Feb. 1991.
31 C. Williams, 'On a border? Wales, 1945–85', in G. E. Jones and D. Smith (eds), *The People of Wales* (1999), 214.
32 C. Davies, *Welsh Jokes* (1978), 32.
33 *Aberdare Leader*, 21 Feb. 1975.
34 C. Meredith, *Shifts* (1988), 97. *WM*, 3 Dec. 1973.
35 S. Morgan, *Men on Strike: Masculinity and the Miners' Strike of 1984–5 in South Wales*, PhD thesis, Swansea University (2007), 138.
36 Morris, 'Redundancy and patterns of household finance', 519.
37 J. Hunt, *From Despair to Where? Coal, Capital and the New Economy*, PhD thesis, Cardiff University (2004), 144, 33.
38 A. Rosen, *The Transformation of British Life, 1950–2000* (2003), 188. Health Promotion Wales, *Sexual Attitudes and Lifestyles in Wales: Implications for Health Promotions* (1995), 19.

39 C. Hughes, *The Civil Strangers* (1949).
40 A. Jivani, *It's Not Unusual: A History of Lesbian and Gay Britain in the Twentieth Century* (1997), 120. *WM*, 17 June 1969.
41 J. S. Jones, *Crawling Through Thorns* (2008).
42 C. Needs. *Like It Is: My Autobiography* (2007), ch. 4, 82.
43 *The Times*, 29 Oct. and 19 Nov. 1975.
44 *LDP*, 13 Dec. 1980. *WM*, 5 Dec. 1990. *Sexual Attitudes and Lifestyles in Wales*, 29.
45 C. Williams, *Sugar and Slate* (2002), 49–50. A. Llwyd, *Black Wales: A History* (2005), 159, 164.
46 V. Robinson, 'Racial antipathy in South Wales and its social and demographic correlates', *New Community*, 12:1 (1984–5), 116–23. C. Williams, 'Social inclusion and race eqaulity in Wales', in C. Williams, N. Evans and P. O'Leary (eds), *A Tolerant Nation? Exploring Ethinic Diversity in Wales* (2003), 139–59.
47 *Arcade*, 24 (16 Oct. 1981) and 16 (12 June 1981).
48 G. Davies, 'National Front Cymru', *PI*, 65 (1987), 109–11.
49 R. Granelli, *Status Zero* (1999), 191, 21.
50 C. Williams, 'Passports to Wales? Race, nation and identity', in R. Fevre and A. Thompson (eds), *National, Identity and Social Theory: Perspectives from Wales* (1999), 83. *Welsh Way of Life: Healthy, Wealthy and Wise*, BBC 1 Wales, 2 Oct. 2006. T. Threadgold, S. Clifford, A. Arwo, V. Powell, Z. Harb, X. Jiang and J. Jewell, *Immigration and inclusion in South Wales* (2008), 52.
51 *SWEP*, 23 Nov. 1990. C. Williams, '"Race" and racisms: some reflections on the Welsh context', *CW*, 8 (1995), 113–31. *Guardian*, 26 Oct. 1995.
52 *DWS*, 28 (1982), 35.
53 For sustained concerns about skateboarding see *SWE*, Jan. 1978.
54 S. Hill, *'Blerwytirhwng?' The Place of Welsh Pop Music* (2007), 77–8.
55 H. Williamson, *The Milltown Boys Revisited* (2004), 34.
56 R. Trezise, *In and Out of the Goldfish Bowl* (2000), 66.
57 J. Morgans, *Journey of a Lifetime* (2008), 543, 112, 438, 532, 540, 563. J. Osmond, 'When dignity can grow from despair', *PI*, 101 (1993), 55–9.
58 T. Rees and V. Winckler, 'Last hired, first fired', *PI*, 57 (1986), 38–43.
59 *Sexual Attitudes and Lifestyles in Wales*, 17.
60 G. Rees and T. L. Rees, 'Educational inequality in Wales: some problems and paradoxes', in G. Rees and T. L. Rees (eds), *Poverty and Social Inequality in Wales* (1980), 89, 74–8.
61 D. Rubinstein and B. Simon, *The Evolution of the Comprehensive School, 1926–1972* (1973), 87. *Statistics of Education in Wales*, 1 (1976), 31.
62 Rees and Rees, 'Educational inequality in Wales', 83. *Guardian*, 24 Aug. 1978.
63 G. Rees and S. Delemont, 'Education in Wales', in D. Dunkerley and A. Thompson (eds), *Wales Today* (1999), 242.
64 Hunt, *From Despair to Where?*, 3.
65 Labour Party, *Signposts to the New Wales* (1962), 19.
66 G. E. Jones and G. W. Roderick, *A History of Education in Wales* (2003), 164. *Statistics of Education in Wales: Further and Higher Education*, 5 (1991), 57, 62. *DWS* (1999), 145.
67 L. Jones, 'Coal', in B. Thomas (ed.), *The Welsh Economy* (1962), 98. C. LeVay, 'The family farm', *PI*, 33 (1976), 44–51.
68 Town, *After the Mines*, 93, 73.
69 *Guardian*, 20 May 1976. *WM*, 3 June 1975 and 17 Mar. 1990.
70 Osmond, 'When dignity can grow from despair'.
71 *WM*, 5 Aug. 1978.
72 *Census 1971: Persons of Pensionable Age*, 140. *1991 Census: Report for Wales (Part 1)*, 384.
73 H. Williams (ed.), *The Century Speaks: Voices of Wales* (1999), 12.
74 B. Dumbleton, *'Help Us, Somebody': The Demolition of the Elderly* (2006), 72. R. S. Thomas, *Selected Prose* (1983), 159.
75 *WL*, 2 Feb. 1971.

76 Williams, *The Century Speaks*, 55. G. C. Wenger, 'Old women in rural Wales: variations in adaption', in Aaron *et al.* (eds), *Our Sisters' Land*, 61–85.
77 D. Sandbrook, *White Heat: A History of Britain in the Swinging Sixties* (2006), 190–1, 319, 322.
78 Quoted in A. W. Turner, *Crisis? What Crisis? Britain in the 1970s* (2008), 145.
79 I. Crewe, N. Day and A. Fox, *The British Electorate, 1963–1987: A Compendium of Data from the British Election Studies* (1991), 442, 410. *WM*, 24 June 1980.
80 *DWHS-3*, 14, 18, 20. *Sexual Attitudes and Lifestyles in Wales*, 27. *WM*, 31 Jan. 1974.
81 L. Dee and K. Keineg (eds), *Women in Wales: A Documentary of Our Recent History* (1987), 20. Haste, *Rules of Britain*, 227–35.
82 C. Brown, *The Death of Christian Britain: Understanding Secularization, 1800–2000* (2009).
83 G. Day and M. Fitton, 'Religious organization and community in mid-Wales', in G. Williams (ed.), *Social and Cultural Change in Contemporary Wales* (1978), 242–52.
84 D. D. Morgan, 'The Welsh language and religion', in G. H. Jenkins and M. A. Williams (eds), *'Let's Do Our Best for the Ancient Tongue': The Welsh Language in the Twentieth Century* (2000), 395.
85 P. Chambers, *Religion, Secularization and Social Change in Wales: Congregational Studies in a Post-Christian Society* (2005), 17. C. Harris and R. Startup, 'The Church in Wales: a neglected Welsh institution', *CW*, 7 (1994), 97–116. Bible Society, *Welsh Challenge to Change: Results of the 1995 Welsh Churches Survey* (1997).
86 *DWHS-3*, 296. Chambers, *Religion, Secularization and Social Change*, 17, 46. D. D. Morgan, *The Span of the Cross: Christian Religion and Society in Wales, 1914–2000* (1999), 275. A. Jones, *Welsh Chapels* (1996), 131.
87 Morgan, *The Span of the Cross*, 265. Chambers, *Religion, Secularization and Social Change*, especially 69.
88 WAG, *Wales's Population: A Demographic Overview, 1971–2005* (2007).
89 J. Stephen, 'The other side of summer', in J. Davies (ed.), *The Green Bridge: Stories from Wales* (1988), 248.
90 D. P. Davies, 'A time of paradoxes amongst the faiths', in D. Cole (ed.), *The New Wales* (1990), 211.
91 Roderick, *The Pubs of Newport*. *Independent*, 3 Jan. 2000.
92 D. Barry, *A Bloody Good Friday* (2002), 95, 145.
93 M. Garnett, *From Anger to Apathy: The Story of Politics, Society and Popular Culture in Britain since 1975* (2008), 142. G. Williams, 'Fields of praise', *Pl*, 14 (1972), 20. *SWE*, 19 Mar. 1979.
94 Calculated from *DWHS-3*, 275. D. J. V. Jones, *Crime and Policing in the Twentieth Century: The South Wales Experience* (1996), 116, 72.
95 Calculated from *DWHS-3*, 275. Jones, *Crime and Policing*, 159, 8.
96 *WL*, 15 and 26 Jan. 1971. *SWE*, 6 Jan. 1978. Jones, *Crime and Policing*, 4.
97 Jones, *Crime and Policing*, 72, 81, 93, 95. A. Power, 'Housing, community and crime', in D. Downes (ed.), *Crime and the City* (1989), 206–35.
98 M. Jones, *Life on the Dole* (1972), 82–3.
99 *WM*, 15 Nov. 1973.
100 Samuel Knight Publishers, *The Wales Yearbook, 1974–5* (1974), 86. M. Savage, 'Spatial differences in modern Britain', in C. Hammett, L. McDowell and P. Sarre (eds), *The Changing Social Structure* (1989), 263.
101 R. Williams, *Bwyd i Bawb: 88 o Risebau Syml Sydyn* (1976).
102 *Aberdare Leader*, 18 Jan. 1974. K. Amis, *The Old Devils* (1986), 54.
103 Gwent College, *Roll on Friday: A Photographic Survey of Leisure in Newport* (1985), 9. B. Freeman, *First Catch Your Peacock: A Book of Welsh Food* (1980), 40.
104 *Regional Statistics*, 11 (1975), 198. *Regional Trends*, 31 (1995), 130.
105 C. Guy, 'The food and grocery shopping behaviour of disadvantaged consumers: some results from the Cardiff consumer panel', *Transactions of the Institute of British Geographers*, New Series, 10:2 (1985), 181–90.
106 *The Times*, 23 Sep. 1972, 28 Feb. and 1 Nov. 1973. R. D. F. Branley and C. J. Thomas,

Retail Parks, Enterprise Zone Policy and Retail Planning: A Casestudy of the Swansea Enterprise Zone Retail Park (1987).

107 *WM*, 8 Apr. 1981 and 6 Dec. 1993.

108 *Regional Trends*, 28 (1993), 108, and 31 (1996), 133.

109 J. Benson, *The Rise of Consumer Society in Britain, 1880–1980* (1994), 196. *DWHS-3*, 298.

110 The Poverty Site, 'In financial difficulty', at www.poverty.org.uk/w07/index.shtml.

111 *Census 1971: Housing, Parts II and III* (1974), 86-7. *HC Deb*, 22 Oct. 1973, vol. 861, c. 367W.

112 R. Granelli, *Dark Edge* (1997), 7.

113 Calculated from 'Table 515. Housing market: simple average house prices, mortgage advances and incomes of borrowers, by new/other dwellings, type of buyer and standard statistical region, from 1969', at http://tiny.cc/kval0.

114 G. L. Rees, *Survey of the Welsh Economy*, Commission on the Constitution research paper (1973), 52.

115 *DWHS-3*, 257–8. R. Vinen, *Thatcher's Britain: The Politics and Social Upheaval of the Thatcher Era* (2009), 203.

116 *WL*, 31 Oct. 1980. Welsh Office, *Welsh InterCensal Survey 1986*, 30.

117 I. Jack, *Before the Oil Ran Out: Britain in the Brutal Years* (1997), 84.

118 *DWHS-3*, 268–9. C. C. Harris, 'Changing social conditions', in Cole (ed.), *New Wales*, 224.

119 *Arcade*, 14 (15 May 1981). P. Stead, 'Political power', in R. Jenkins and A. Edwards (eds), *One Step Forward? South and West Wales Towards the Year 2000* (1990), 68. J. Osmond, 'Living in quangoland', *Pl*, 110 (1995), 35. M. Liddiard, 'Young, free and homeless?', *Pl*, 86 (1991), 83–8.

120 *Wales Yearbook, 1974–5*, 145. *Regional Trends*, 31 (1996), 133. *DWHS-3*, 108.

121 *Abergavenny Chronicle*, 31 Dec. 1981.

122 A. Andrews at 'More 80s memories', at http://news.bbc.co.uk/1/hi/magazine/6752387.stm.

123 Jack, *Before the Oil Ran Out*, 83.

124 *DWHS-3*, 28.

125 J. Miller, *Situation Vacant: The Social Consequences of Unemployment in a Welsh Town* (1982), 30, 36.

126 Quoted in N. A. Davies, *A History of Ecumenism in Wales, 1956–1990* (2008), 133.

127 *Regional Trends*, 40 (2008), 72. Mid Glamorgan County Council, *Mid Glamorgan: Issues for the 1990s* (1992), para. 2.2.

128 D. Adamson, 'Poverty and social exclusion in Wales today', in D. Dunkerley and A. Thompson (eds), *Wales Today* (1999), 51.

129 Mid Glamorgan County Council, *Mid Glamorgan*, para. 3.13. Rees and Rees, *Poverty and Social Inequality*, 294–6, 101. County census profiles, 2001.

130 P. Michael and C. Webster (eds), *Health and Society in Twentieth-Century Wales* (2008), 300–2.

131 *The Times*, 15 Oct. 1992.

132 K. Morgan and A. Price, *Rebuilding Our Communities: A New Agenda for the Valleys* (1992), 30.

133 For example Trezise, *In and Out of the Goldfish Bowl*.

134 R. J. Evans, *Entertainment* (2000), 146.

135 Mid Glamorgan County Council, *Mid Glamorgan*, para. 2.16.

136 N. Charles, C. A. Davies and C. Harris, *Families in Transition: Social Change, Family Formation and Kin Relationships* (2008), 202–4, 208.

137 D. Adamson and S. Jones, 'Continuity and change in the valleys: residents' perceptions in 1995 and 2001', *CW*, 16 (2003), 1–23. Morgan and Price, *Rebuilding Our Communities*, 30.

138 J. Scourfield and M. Drakeford, 'Boys from nowhere: finding Welsh men and putting them in their place', *CW*, 12 (1999), 11–12.

139 Charles *et al.*, *Families in Transition*, 84–7. G. Evans and D. Trystan, 'Why was 1997 different?', in B. Taylor and K. Thomson (eds), *Scotland and Wales: Nations Again?* (1999), 98.

140 *DWHS-3*, 154, 296. Benson, *Affluence and Authority*, 50–2.

141 L. Paterson and C. Iannelli, 'Patterns of absolute and relative social mobility: a comparative study of England, Wales and Scotland', *Sociological Research Online*, 12, 6 (2007), at www.socresonline.org.uk/12/6/15.html.
142 N. Abercrombie and A. Wade, *Contemporary British Society* (2000), 159.
143 *Abergavenny Chronicle*, 31 Dec. 1981.
144 A. Beckett, *When the Lights Went Out: Britain in the Seventies* (2009), 417.
145 Benson, *Affluence and Authority*, 57.
146 *Regional Trends*, 31 (1996), 134. *WM*, 1 Nov. 2004.
147 R. Layard, *Happiness: Lessons from a New Science* (2005), 3. A. Richards, *Home to an Empty House* ([1973] 2006), 13.
148 A. Offer, *The Challenge of Affluence: Self-Control and Well-Being in the United States and Britain since 1950* (2003).
149 Benson, *Affluence and Authority*, 67–71. *WM*, 21 Sep. 1993. *WL*, 27 Mar. 1970.
150 D. Bush, *Glass Shot* (1991), 1. *Cardigan and Tivyside Advertiser*, 20 Sep. and 4 Oct. 1974.
151 A. Sampson, *The New Anatomy of Britain* (1971), 427.
152 Richards, *Home to an Empty House*, 24–5.
153 *Can't Pay, Won't Pay*, Dir: Wyn Mason, 1989 (National Screen and Sound Archive of Wales, 1224). *WM*, 20 and 12 Jan. 1982.
154 Transcript of interview, 23 Sep. 1987, Margaret Thatcher Foundation, doc. 106689, at www.margaretthatcher.org/document/106689.
155 Vinen, *Thatcher's Britain*, conclusions. Crewe *et al.*, *The British Electorate*, 333.
156 *DWHS-3*, 298. Vinen, *Thatcher's Britain*, 200. M. Pugh, *State and Society: British Political and Social History, 1870–1992* (1994), 321–3.
157 Crewe *et al.*, *The British Electorate*, 405. M. J. Oliver, 'The retreat of the state in the 1980s and 1990s', in F. Carnevali and J. Strange (eds), *20th Century Britain: Economic, Cultural and Social Change* (2007), 275.
158 Harris, 'Changing social conditions', 222. *Regional Statistics*, 31 (1995), 223. P. Thane, 'Population and the family', in P. Addison and H. Jones (eds), *A Companion to Contemporary Britain, 1939–2000* (2005), 55.
159 Charles *et al.*, *Families in Transition*, 63–4. Chambers, *Religion, Secularization and Social Change*, 108.
160 On families and friends as sources of happiness see M. Argyle, 'Subjective well-being', in A. Offer (ed.), *In Pursuit of the Quality of Life* (1996), 18–45.

13

'They don't belong here.' The countryside since 1970

They don't belong here. They would be all right if they were part of the community, spoke Welsh. But they live as if they were still in England.

Resident of Devil's Bridge[1]

[W]e are to keep quiet, admire the view, and not impose our alien culture upon local inhabitants. We are to have no say in the education of our children, although of course, we must pay rates and taxes.

Letter to *Cambrian News*, 2 January 1970

IN 1973 MEMBERS of Cymdeithas yr Iaith Gymraeg began a short campaign of filling the locks and daubing the windows of holiday homes owned by English families in Welsh-speaking communities. Protestors claimed they had the assistance and sympathy of locals but one neighbour told a reporter, 'It was Welshmen who sold these houses to the English because no Welshman in his right mind would want to live in them'. Most locals were, she felt, utterly opposed to 'this kind of nonsense'.[2] Regardless of how much support they enjoyed, the actions marked a shift in the language campaign from the legal status of Welsh to the danger it faced in its own heartlands. Here, what was once regarded as a curious trickle of English in-migration was now thought to be turning into a flood of colonization. While the English were moving in, either for good or for just a few weeks a year, the Welsh were still moving out in search of better jobs and better wages. Once, the fear had been that the countryside would be emptied altogether, but now people worried that it would just be emptied of Welsh speakers. The depth of anger became apparent in December 1979, with the beginning of a campaign of arson attacks against holiday homes.

Although a number of groups claimed responsibility, focus concentrated on the name Meibion Glyndŵr (Sons of Glyndŵr). Over the next decade the campaign broadened to include attacks on estate agents and Conservative Party offices and then, in 1990, to letter bombs, including one sent to a Dolgellau café owner who had changed the name of his premises from Y Sospan to 'Allo 'Allo.[3]

Many were horrified at such 'fanaticism'. The police claimed the arsons were the work of an isolated minority, while Peter Walker, Secretary of State for Wales, even attributed them to one family, although the timings and wide geographical spread of the attacks suggested otherwise. At other times, the press and police reported links with the National Front and the IRA. On top of a £50,000 police reward, the *Western Mail* decided to offer its own £30,000 incentive to 'flush out these cowards' and restore 'the name of Wales as a land of peace and goodwill'.[4] Others, however, focused on the arsonists' motivation. In the midst of the campaign, *Yr Herald Cymraeg* declared:

> For too long we have deliberately ignored the constant in-migration which is drowning our villages. The price we are paying for this is that we are fast becoming strangers in our own land.... Unless we do something about the foreign influx, all the concessions that have been won for the Welsh language during recent years will be worthless, and all the campaigns in its favour will have been totally in vain.[5]

In 1981 a Gwynedd letter writer claimed 'those of us with a modicum of sense coupled with patriotism realise that we are witnessing genocide by substitution'. Such sentiments meant the arsons were greeted with sympathy as well as condemnation and the *Western Mail* printed a letter which concluded, 'It's about time people realised that the "cowardly minority" and the "terrorist bombers" are our heroes, our last and only hope'.[6] Students and sixth-formers wore t-shirts and badges that declared 'Taniwch dros Gymru!' (Light for Wales!) and 'Ta ta tŷ ha' ha ha' (Bye bye, summer house, ha ha). More seriously, a Plaid Cymru councillor resigned from the party after one of its MPs called for more police resources to catch the arsonists. R. S. Thomas, Wales' leading living poet, even asked what one English life was compared with the destruction of a nation. Many more were ambivalent, supporting the cause but not the means. Surveys gave contradictory evidence on how far this extended. One poll in Welsh-speaking areas suggested that 56 per cent of people did not support the motives, with 33 per cent not knowing. However, another survey put support for the campaign's aims at 57 per cent.[7] The fact that there was any suggestion at all of widespread support for the cause led to very real fears that the situation could escalate into further violence. The chairman of Gwynedd County Council wrote to the Secretary of State for Wales: 'sooner or later an innocent neighbour, fire officer or owner is likely to be maimed or killed. Once that happens, Welsh politics could well enter a chilling new dimension.'[8]

The arson campaign came to an end in 1992 but not before nineteen English families were sent letters telling them to leave Wales or be burnt out. In all there had been 134 attacks in Gwynedd, forty-three in Dyfed and Powys and twenty outside Wales. The sole injury was to a fireman who was hurt when a staircase collapsed at an attacked London estate agent.[9] Despite the involvement of MI5, the only person convicted was twenty-one-year-old Sion Aubery Roberts. He was imprisoned for twelve years in 1993 for possessing explosives and sending incendiary devices to police officers, a Welsh Office minister and a Conservative Party agent. Roberts was seven years old when the campaign had begun.

THE NUMBER OF holiday homes had been growing since the early post-war years, as rising disposable incomes in England allowed people to take advantage of lower house prices in the depopulating Welsh countryside. Some people could sell up in England, pay off their mortgage and still buy somewhere bigger in Wales with what was left. By 1991 just over 10 per cent of households in Gwynedd were officially second homes but the proportion was as high as one in three in some communities in the county. Such places became winter ghost towns, with local shops and services completely undermined. During the 1990s rising house prices made it more difficult for people to buy second homes and in the decade up to 2001 there was nearly an 11 per cent decline in the number of such properties in Wales. In Gwynedd the fall was almost 23 per cent.[10] Concerns instead shifted to those who were settling permanently. After decades of depopulation, the rural population had begun to grow in the 1970s, as English migration into picturesque villages and seaside locations gathered pace. Between 1971 and 2001 the counties of Dyfed, Gwynedd and Powys experienced a net migration of more than 130,000 people.[11] This figure disguises the sheer scale of in-migration because it takes into account the tens of thousands, mostly the young and educated, who were moving out each year. In the mid-1980s there were as many as 50,000 people coming into Wales each year and one social scientist calculated that a million individuals had moved in and out of Wales in a decade. Despite an ageing population, rural Wales thus enjoyed levels of population growth two to three times the national

Welsh average between 1981 and 2006. In Ceredigion the contrast was even greater. By 2006 the county's population had grown by 26.1 per cent in the previous quarter century, compared with a 5.4 per cent increase in Wales as a whole. The traffic was not just with England; in 2000–1, for example, 41 per cent of people moving into Welsh rural areas came from other parts of Wales. But the cumulative effect of the movement meant that by 1991 only 60–70 per cent of the population of most wards in rural Wales were born in Wales. In some villages the proportion of incomers was even said to have reached 80 per cent.[12]

A drift from the urban to the rural was hardly unique to Wales or even the UK. People sought to replace the stresses, crime and congestion of city living with a slower-paced life in more beautiful and relaxed surroundings. Many also hoped they would find a sense of community that had by-passed them in urban settings. A few were even openly seeking a refuge from racial tensions in English cities.[13] Others were looking to replace the rat race with a more sustainable, greener life, sometimes courtesy of other people's taxes. Some of these 'hippies' (as they were often labelled) were also attracted to Wales by ideas of Celtic mysticism and farmers found young men and women trampling over their land in search of 'magic' mushrooms and stone circles. This respect for folklore would have been approved of by past Celtic scholars but it also led to incomers being associated with contemporary social ills such as drugs.[14] However, most migrants were rather more traditional in their lives and aspirations and many came because their employers relocated them, the distance to their urban jobs was commutable or they saw an opportunity to set up their own business.

The biggest concerns surrounded those who moved to rural Wales to retire. They were perceived to be placing demands on local welfare services without giving much back. Thus, in 1989, the chairman of Dyfed County Council complained that rural areas were becoming a home for the old aged.[15] This was a common view but it was not entirely fair since the British population as whole was ageing and many rural incomers were of working age. Between 1981 and 1991 there was a 7 per cent decline in the number of sixteen- to twenty-four-year-olds in rural Welsh counties but this was actually slightly smaller than the fall in this age group in Wales as a whole. Among twenty-five- to forty-four-year-olds in the same period, half of rural counties saw a rise broadly in line with the Welsh average of 9 per cent, although Anglesey, Monmouthshire, Pembrokeshire and Powys all saw 7 per cent falls. In terms of the proportion of population in rural counties, there were rises in the numbers of sixteen- to twenty-four-year-olds between 1991 and 2001 and a fall in the numbers aged sixty-five and over, a complete reversal of the 1981–91 trend.[16] Nearly everywhere in rural Wales, from 1999 migration began to add to the population more people under fifteen years of age than those aged sixty-five and over. However much the demographic structure belied simple description, by 2001 rural counties did have a lower proportion of under-forty-fives and a higher share of older people than the Welsh averages. Moreover, by 2006 the number of people over sixty-four in rural counties had increased by 10 per cent since 1991, compared with a 5 per cent growth in Wales as a whole.[17] It was on the north Wales coast that the elderly were arriving in the largest numbers. In Conwy in 2001 as much as 23 per cent of the population was sixty-five and over, compared with 17 per cent in Wales as a whole. Nearly a third of households in the county were pensioners and just 54 per cent of its population was Welsh-born.

The most contentious impact of the population changes was on the housing market. Although maybe a majority of the holiday homes were actually renovated derelict cottages, their growth in number, along with the rise in permanent in-migration, was thought to be responsible for inflating house prices, creating a perception that locals were being excluded from finding homes in their own communities. This resentment, however, was far from universal and one 1970s survey suggested that in most villages just under half of residents had no objection to local second homes.[18] An internal 1980s Welsh Office ministerial memo claimed that beyond Plaid Cymru MPs, Gwynedd County Council, the media and the arsonists, 'the evidence of general dissatisfaction with the second/holiday home position is thin. My constituency mail on the subject is non-existent and our Ministerial correspondence is not voluminous.'[19] Feelings were, however, intensifying, as council house tenants' new right to buy reduced local-authority housing from 25 per cent of the total rural stock in 1981 to 15 per cent in 1991. Planning restrictions on new builds in National Parks further reduced the housing supply, while a lack of jobs and public transport also reduced people's options over where they lived. It was these wider issues more than the growth in second homes that was driving the young away. Indeed, there were actually more empty houses in rural Wales than there were second homes. By 2001 only 2.6 per cent of rural households were second homes, while 4.3 per cent were vacant.[20]

Rural Wales was not so much suffering from a general shortage of properties but from a lack of affordable housing, a problem that beleaguered much of the UK during the period of excessive house price inflation that began in the mid-1990s. In Wales as a whole, average house prices rose by 73 per cent between 1997 and 2003, but in rural areas external demand contributed to an 83 per cent increase. This made the average 2003 house price in rural Wales nearly £10,000 higher than the Welsh figure. In 2003 36 per cent of rural wards had mean house prices more than four and a half times higher than average household incomes, compared with 21 per cent in Wales as a whole. Thus those who had grown up in picturesque villages – those that were popular with incomers and subject to National Park planning restrictions – found it difficult to settle in their own communities. House prices in the most accessible and prettiest parts of rural Wales may have escalated well beyond the reach of the local working class but the same was also true of the suburban and fashionable districts of urban Britain. With property becoming so expensive everywhere, there was little evidence that people left rural Wales completely just to buy or find a house, especially since there were variations in costs within the rural west; prices in Gwynedd, Anglesey and Carmarthenshire, for example, were still below the Welsh average in 2003. Rural house price inflation was, however, greater than in urban areas and prices continued to rise steeply until 2007, exacerbating the difficulties. By then Ceredigion had emerged as the county with the worst problem. The average house price was around £200,000, an approximate 270 per cent increase on a decade before and nearly ten times average earnings in the county. In the face of such costs young people were residing longer with their parents or turning to the private rented sector. Worse, official figures for the number of homeless people in rural Wales increased by 309 per cent between 1978 and 2005, almost two and half times the corresponding rise in urban areas.[21]

Rural house prices were unjust and probably unsustainable but young people were leaving rural Wales to get work or an education rather than to find an affordable house.[22] Professional opportunities in rural areas were distinctly limited, meaning many university students, who were becoming more and more common, were unlikely ever to return to the rural communities where they grew up. In the villages they left, even manual jobs were neither plentiful nor well paid, which further encouraged migration away. A large 1970s survey in mid-Wales suggested that more than a quarter of sixteen- to twenty-four-year-olds planned to leave the area. By 1981 the census was suggesting that less than half of mid-Wales school-leavers stayed in the area.[23] However, the decision to move away did seem to become harder in the 1970s. Being Welsh was coming to be valued more and, as tourism and in-migration grew, some young people also started to see the positives of living in rural Wales before the negatives. This outlook was encouraged by the ongoing growth of television and the media, something which increased young people's understanding of the outside world, enabling much stronger comparisons with their own lives than earlier generations had been able to make. Some young people thus consciously decided to return home or not move away at all, often in order to be part of a Welsh-speaking community, even if that did mean lower wages or taking a job below their level of education.[24] However, in the 1980s the growth of a Welsh state (chapter 11) meant that young rural Welsh speakers had more professional opportunities open to them in Cardiff, a place that did not require them to leave Wales. This eased the psychological upheaval of moving away and reaffirmed the drift from the countryside.

THE FACT THAT even a few young people were placing being part of a Welsh-speaking community above their personal economic situation owed much to the growing awareness that rural in-migration was undermining the Welsh language. The county language statistics (table 13.1) disguised the extent of change in some communities. In 1981 in Penmachno (Gwynedd) 37 per cent of houses were second homes and the proportion of Welsh speakers had fallen to 70 per cent from 84 per cent just a decade earlier. In the same period the proportion of the population of Llangeitho (Dyfed) able to speak Welsh fell from 83 per cent to 55 per cent.[25] Once the Welsh-speaking population in any community fell to such levels then English would inevitably become the dominant language in local public life. One small example of this came in an inspection of a primary school in Llandrindod Wells which noted how Welsh-speaking children frequently spoke English because they did not want to be different to the majority of children at the school. Mixed marriages also became more common and in one survey of rural communities in the early 1990s just two-thirds of Welsh speakers spoke Welsh at home.[26] In-migration also created significantly varying levels of Welsh-speaking within relatively small areas. On Anglesey in 1977, for example, 76 per cent of pupils at Llangefni secondary school

Table 13.1 Percentage of Welsh speakers in rural counties, 1971–91

	1971	1981	1991
Dyfed	52.5	47.0	43.7
Gwynedd	64.7	63.0	61.0
Powys	23.7	20.5	20.2
Wales	20.8	18.9	18.7

Source: *DWHS-3*, 12.

spoke Welsh as their first language, whereas at Holyhead it was 25 per cent. Such a mosaic made the notion of the Fro Gymraeg, the Welsh-speaking heartland, problematic. Geographers compared it to a pool drying out: no longer one single accumulation of water but scattered patches that were themselves in retreat. Even some of the physical traces of the Fro Gymraeg were being obliterated as a few incomers changed the names of their new homes into English.[27] It was thus with good reason that in-migration became the primary cause of the Welsh-language campaigning community in the 1980s, filling the void left by the victories over road signs and the S4C television channel (chapter 11).

In 1986 the chairman of Gwynedd County Council wrote to the Secretary of State maintaining that people were welcome to move to Wales but what caused resentment was 'the sheer scale of immigration, the arrogance of some immigrants and the ease with which some unemployed people from the conurbations can live in comfort on our coast at the taxpayer's expense'.[28] That arrogance was perceived in how some incomers had not even been aware they were moving to a different country and thus ended up surprised at how many people spoke Welsh and how much the language mattered. Any delusions of having just moved to another English county were soon shattered as incomers found the Welsh language all around them, sometimes leading them to feeling excluded and even ostracized. One woman who settled in the Conwy valley in 1965 summed up, 'if you come up around these parts you will be made strongly aware that English is a foreign language'. She accepted that she was a foreigner and there on sufferance.[29] Others were less tolerant and attracted public hostility by campaigning against Welsh-medium education or even trying to stop their employees speaking Welsh at work. More common were less formalized tensions. A woman in Anglesey reported, 'They keep you out of everything here by insisting on having Welsh; they're just being bloody awkward', while another said, 'I hate going into the village because everyone speaks Welsh. It's not right, this is the UK and everyone should speak English.' Some even claimed there was an '"English-go-home" attitude' among local officials who were supposed to help them find employment.[30] A Prestatyn woman complained to the Race Relations Board in 1975 about language requirements for jobs: 'I know it is always described as "Welsh-speaking" and not just Welsh but is it right that British people should be discriminated against because they only speak English in their own country?' In response to a complaint that even adverts for factory workers specified Welsh speakers, the Board expressed suspicions that language was being used for selection but it concluded that such discrimination was not illegal because it was not based on ethnicity, nationality or race.[31]

The feeling that local authorities could be rather hostile to incomers was not entirely misplaced. In the early 1970s Llŷn Rural District Council illegally denied home improvement grants to second homes. Bala Town Council responded to in-migration by deciding in 1975 to record its minutes in Welsh rather than in English.[32] In the 1980s local-authority hopes of restricting incomers buying or building residences in Gwynedd were halted by the limitations of planning legislation and Welsh Office objections. But lobbying, not least from Plaid Cymru, led the Welsh Office to concede in 1988 that protecting the language could be considered in planning decisions, a criterion some authorities then used to restrict new builds likely to attract incomers.[33] Such planning issues, like Gwynedd County Council's requirement of Welsh for many low-grade jobs, added to the politicization of in-migration but political representation itself was also being affected by migration patterns. Incomers had helped the Conservatives take Anglesey's parliamentary seat in 1979 for the first time since the eighteenth century, but concern surrounding in-migration was also boosting support for Plaid Cymru and it won Anglesey in 1987 and Ceredigion and Pembroke North in 1992, giving it four of the six parliamentary seats where more than 50 per cent of the population spoke Welsh.

A 1988 letter in the *Bangor and Anglesey Mail* spoke for many incomers when it drew parallels between local attitudes and Nazism: 'Why not in fact start by giving all the immigrants a yellow star – or a red rose or a Scottish thistle before putting them in cattle trucks', the writer asked.[34] Given the cottage burnings, anti-English graffiti and incidents of windows being broken and eggs being thrown at houses, such parallels were not surprising. By the 2000s people were becoming more aware of such incidents as the local press in the north-west repeatedly focused on Welsh–English tensions to stimulate debate and sales.[35] Rising house prices may have slowed the levels of in-migration but the debate often grew nastier, emotionalized by the accusations of racism thrown at those who objected to English in-migration. One incomer remarked, 'It's like living in an inner city estate. I'm moving back to England.'[36] In 2001 even a former chair of Welsh Water and the Welsh Language Board could be found calling in-migrants a human form of foot-and-mouth disease.[37] Yet hostility was not a universal experience and most incomers found that open antagonism came from only a minority. In one survey of in-migrants in the north-west a fifth of respondents expressed 'feelings of isolation and alienation from their local community' but a third spoke of 'an atmosphere of friendliness' and a 'good community spirit'. When asked about the worst aspect of living in the area, only 11 per cent said anti-Englishness, the same figure as nominated the weather.[38]

Such levels of satisfaction might be incomers being unaware of how the issue was viewed or just preferring to say the right thing in public. As in England, at least some of the local resentment of rural change remained hidden from the public arena. The impact on the Welsh language was certainly profoundly unsettling for those who had grown up in a completely different linguistic environment to the one that had emerged. One example was a Cwm Rheidol (Dyfed) woman who was born in 1908 and who could not speak English after leaving school. Yet now, as an old woman, she felt she had to speak that language in shops in nearby Aberystwyth because she did not know whether she would be understood in Welsh.[39] Concern about incomers, however, ran far deeper than just the language, hence a couple who moved to Maenclochog (Dyfed) became known as the foreigners who spoke Welsh. Whatever language incomers spoke, they were changing the character of rural communities. Even in the 1970s there were still villages where there were enough local services that they were essentially self-sufficient and where everyone knew not just everyone else but their family histories too. It was thus easy for people to regard their village as the 'centre of the universe'.[40] Established residents, however, increasingly felt such tight-knit neighbourly communities were disappearing, as their villages were swamped by unfriendly strangers from outside. It did not help that some incomers did not properly pronounce their neighbours' names or even their own addresses. The discomfort was, however, tempered by a parallel awareness that, after decades of depopulation, villages and their economies were being revitalized and local schools were being protected from closure by a reverse in falling pupil numbers. In the late 1960s Cwmystwyth (Dyfed), for example, had a population of seventy-three in forty-seven houses and just fourteen school-age children. Twenty years later there were 124 people and seventy houses, only three or four of which were new builds rather than restorations.[41] An awareness that in-migration both helped and undermined rural communities created very varied and deeply divided opinions on the issue. Surveys in different communities suggested that opposition among established residents to population changes ranged from around one-third to nearly three-quarters, while anything from a fifth to nearly half did not know or held no strong opinions either way. One respondent to an early 1990s survey unintentionally represented the views and behaviour of many when they voiced opposition to English in-migration in principle but said that this did not affect how they treated incomers.[42] Being openly hostile or rude to individuals was, quite simply, unusual.

Even if people accepted that in-migration had benefits, that did not mean incomers were just accepted into local communities. Those who tried to join in and contribute to village life could be accused of wanting to take over, while those who kept their distance were criticized for being unsociable. One incomer wrote in 1975, 'in spite of the unstinting friendliness shown to us, we have no illusions of "belonging". We live alongside these people, but we are not of them.' A Llandeilo (Dyfed) café owner claimed that you could live in the town for thirty years and still not be regarded as 'from these parts'.[43] At the heart of such feelings was the barrier that the language represented in daily life. An incomer in Gwynedd noted, 'You never feel one of them – because of the language. To be accepted I think you do have to have the language.' Not every migrant might have noticed this but it was largely right. Nearly half of the respondents to a north Wales survey of incomers in the mid-2000s had tried to learn Welsh. Forty-two per cent thought the language would bring some improvement to their lives and open social and employment doors. But half thought that being able to speak Welsh would make no difference to their lives since everyone spoke English.[44] Some of those who did learn Welsh 'went native' and giving their children Welsh names was one conscious attempt at integration. Adults spoke of finding comfort and solace in learning the Welsh language and literature but there were limits to what could be achieved. Learning Welsh was never easy, not least because its system of mutations made translating with a dictionary very difficult. Many learners felt their efforts were unappreciated. They often found people preferred to speak English to them and some were told they had learnt 'posh Welsh'. Few incomers thus became proficient enough in Welsh to take part in community entertainments or to read the community papers.[45]

This, together with the sheer scale of in-migration, ensured the creation of loose separate social networks based around language, which in itself lessened incomers' need to learn Welsh. In a study of an Anglesey village, for example, nearly every local Welsh speaker belonged to a church or a chapel, whereas only a third of English-monoglot incomers did and none of those attended a place of worship in the village itself. The result was very significant variations between the number of people whom locals and incomers actually knew. There were, however, large cultural and economic variations among the in-migrants, which meant there was nothing like a 'settler society' but rather a series of loose social groups of incomers. There were also strong variations among Welsh speakers but the language did provide a bond that united people and gave them a common sense of purpose. Such situations led one man to describe Welsh speakers in his village as a community within a community.[46] Social contacts did, of course, cross linguistic divides. Neighbourliness was widely regarded as an important value, regardless of what language your neighbours spoke. Among farmers, cooperation between neighbours was essential, again regardless of who they were. Schools were perhaps the most important focal point in rural communities and had an important role in bringing the different linguistic groups together. They also offered a route for the children of incomers to integrate and regard themselves as Welsh, although they were not always accepted as such and were sometimes bullied because of their background.[47] In the 1970s there were complaints that most incomers' children were not learning Welsh but as local authorities developed Welsh-medium education, partly in response to in-migration, this became less common. Concern about the impact on children's English skills meant there was some opposition to increased teaching through the medium of Welsh among both locals and incomers. One incomer in Dyfed even claimed in the press that English families were being driven out of villages by Welsh-medium education. But most were more accepting, aware perhaps that local attitudes towards incomers were often determined by whether they were happy for their children to learn Welsh.[48] By 2001, 17 per cent of people in Gwynedd who were born outside Wales could speak, read and write Welsh. Across Wales as a whole there were more than 46,000 people born outside Wales but able to read, write and speak Welsh and more than 50,000 others with some skills in Welsh. But education could be as divisive as it was unifying. Secondary schools in Welsh-speaking areas could be divided, both formally and informally, into Welsh speakers, Welsh language learners and English monoglots.[49] Such divides deepened when schools were formally designated by language. When, in 1991, Ysgol y Preseli in Crymych (Dyfed) was converted to a bilingual school (where all pupils were taught in both languages) it became impossible to receive an English-medium education without leaving the immediate area. The replacement of a linguistic streaming system within the school meant the loose linguistic divide within the community was reinforced and those with no or weak Welsh were bussed off to schools elsewhere.

It would be deeply misleading to view rural society in the 1970s solely in terms of nationality and language. The same regretful feeling that in-migration was undermining community cohesion and neighbourliness could be found in English villages. Some of the opposition to incomers in both England and Wales was simply a cultural gulf between rural and urban lifestyles. While incomers could complain about agriculture's noises and smells, some rural people just did not understand why urban migrants wanted to be on their own rather than be sociable.[50] Similarly, one farmer remarked, 'I cannot understand all these people coming to a place like this every summer. What is there to see? I've lived and worked here most of my life, and I know every inch of this ground, and for me it spells endless struggle. Where's the beauty in that?'[51] Incomers provided convenient scapegoats for modern problems such as drug use, violence, a reliance on social security and the decline in traditional notions of community. This meant that more common neighbourly disputes became entangled with notions of incomers' impact on the community and even their curtains and gardens could be sources of general complaint.[52] This resistance to 'townees' and their ways could be found across rural Britain but the language issue spiced it up, made it angrier and raised the stakes. However, as some incomers quickly came to regard themselves as locals, the dynamics of communities were further complicated. Such converts could be just as opposed as any established resident to further in-migration, new housing developments or even anything that might endanger the language. As in the 1950s and 1960s, some of the tensions framed in terms of nationhood were also interwoven with issues of class and there were complaints that incomers showed off about their possessions and professions.[53] Despite the influx of 'hippies' there was also a strong perception that most incomers, whether working or retired, were wealthy and this was not entirely unfounded. Buying a second home required considerable capital. Even the tourist industry was being largely developed, found a study of Anglesey, by English in-migrants. Manufacturing firms that came to rural Wales employed local labour but generally brought their own (often English) managers. At the 1991 census 29 per cent of Welsh speakers in Gwynedd held professional, managerial or technical jobs, whereas 41 per cent of non-Welsh-speaking, non-Welsh-born workers in the county did. Incomers also tended to choose to move to the picturesque villages rather than the poorer rural towns, adding a spatial dimension to the linguistic pattern. The most deprived areas of Anglesey were 77 per cent Welsh-speaking in 1981, whereas the least deprived were 48 per cent Welsh-speaking.[54] It is thus impossible to divide the concerns about nationality and culture from the less emotive topics of class and status, especially since people were aware that those with power over rural Wales – the government, the Milk Marketing Board, supermarkets and large companies – were often from England. Thus the rural class struggle, as Emmett argued in the 1980s just as she had in the 1960s, 'manifests itself in nationalism'.[55]

CLASS TENSIONS EXISTED in rural Wales because local job opportunities tended to be low paid, low skilled and have low prospects. In the 1970s average wages in rural Wales were some 10 per cent below UK averages. By the mid-1990s this had increased to around 20 per cent.[56] Comparisons with the rest of Wales were not much better. In 2003 Carmarthenshire, Anglesey, Pembrokeshire and Gwynedd all had mean annual household income averages below the average for the Valleys. Even in Monmouthshire, Wales' richest county, 15 per cent of households were on low incomes. The result was real deprivation and one rural survey in the early 1990s estimated that around a quarter of households were in or on the margins of poverty.[57] The ongoing decline in public transport, local shops, welfare services and educational facilities added isolation to the problems of those on low incomes, with around a third of rural Welsh households having no car in 1991. Their poverty was not as visible as in urban Wales, where the absolute numbers of people on low incomes were much higher and their distribution was more concentrated. Nor was it as obvious as in much of rural England, where the numbers of high earners meant that affluence and deprivation existed side by side.[58] Consequently, it was not uncommon, even among those officially classified as being on low incomes, to deny that poverty existed in rural Wales.[59]

One obvious cause of rural poverty was unemployment, which in some pockets hit levels worse than in the Valleys. In March 1977, for example, male unemployment was running at 26.5 per cent in Tenby, 22.4 per cent in Cardigan and 19.9 per cent in Rhyl. A mid-Wales survey that year found that more than three-quarters of sixteen- to twenty-four-year-olds and nearly a third of twenty-five- to forty-four-year-olds had experienced unemployment.[60] Problems intensified in the early 1980s with the general economic downturn. A 1988 study of local economic performance found that Holyhead was the lowest-performing area in the whole of the UK, while Cardigan and Pembroke were the fourth and fifth lowest. Neath was the only Welsh industrial area in the UK's lowest fifteen.[61] Parts of Dyfed had been badly hit by defence cuts which led to the loss of 1,600 jobs in the 1980s and early 1990s. By 1992 South Pembrokeshire, Cardigan and Haverfordwest had the second, third and fourth highest rates of unemployment of any travel-to-work area in Wales.[62] It was towns like Cardigan and Pembroke in the south-west and Blaenau Ffestiniog and Rhyl in the north that had become the focal points of rural deprivation. This was not just because of unemployment but because they were where the bulk of local rented and council housing was. North coast resorts were also attracting unemployed people from north-west England, simply because it was nicer to be out of work by the sea. By 2008 three of the five officially most deprived areas in Wales were within Rhyl.[63]

Not all rural towns were so deprived, and conditions could vary even within small areas. In 1989 unemployment was 8 per cent in Carmarthen, a town which enjoyed good transport connections with south Wales and the M4; meanwhile, in Cardigan, just thirty miles away but without rail or dual carriageway links, 26 per cent were out of work.[64] In the east of Wales, rural areas also benefited from their proximity to larger centres of population. Communities near the English border were 'suburbanized', as people with well paid jobs elsewhere moved in and commuted, a trend that had begun to be seen near Cardiff and Swansea in the 1950s and 1960s but gradually spread into Powys and Clwyd. By the twenty-first century, the lifestyle there was unrecognizable from not just the rural poverty of the early post-war years but also from the scattered deprivation that still existed further west. The border village of Holt (Wrexham) was thus described in 2007: 'New four-by-fours, twenty grand at least, draw up on the pavement; jumpered, tousle-haired thirtysomething dads climb out to collect their order of duck for the weekend, and to pick up the *Saturday Telegraph* from the corner shop. It's a colour supplement come to life. This is the kind of place where "game" means pheasant not football.'[65]

This was a far cry from when such villages had been dominated by agriculture. As coal symbolized the economic problems of industrial areas, it was agriculture that represented the transformation of rural Wales. Ongoing mechanization, increasing imports and the shift of the production of some foodstuffs like cheese and butter from farm to factory were all making agriculture less labour intensive and reducing its importance to food production. The industry was becoming more productive thanks to scientific breeding and the growing use of pesticides and herbicides but, like so much of the British economy, it was also still being propped up by the state.[66] Milk producers were legally obliged to sell their product to the Milk Marketing Board in return for a guarantee of the average market price. After the UK's entry into the European Economic Community (EEC) in 1973, agriculture became even more reliant on subsidies: by the middle of the 1980s some 70 per cent of farm incomes came from state and European subsidies. Nonetheless, two economists could still conclude that for lowland cattle and sheep producers in Wales, 'incomes can only be described as miserable'.[67] Low incomes and the availability of subsidies consolidated the long-term process of small farms being bought up and merged, and the number of holdings of ten to thirty hectares fell from 16,772 in 1974 to 8,002 in 1995. Farmers increased their holdings by borrowing money, something which proved costly because their reliance on the state left them as vulnerable to external interests as the miners were. In 1984 milk quotas were introduced to limit how much milk farmers could sell. The result of the reduction of the subsidized milk market was significant hardship and anger, especially since many farmers were struggling with large mortgages at a time of rising interest rates. The excess milk farmers were not allowed to sell was poured down the drain, an emotive sight at a time when the world was waking up to famines in Africa. It was estimated that quotas led to the loss of 2,000 jobs in Welsh farming and another 800 in supply industries.[68] In 1989 the incomes of farmers in west Wales were 35 per cent lower than they had been in 1980. Things then got worse after the milk market was deregulated in 1994 by a Conservative government that believed in the benefits of market forces. Supermarkets replaced the state as the main dictator of prices and farmers' incomes were undermined once again. By 2009 there were fewer than 2,000 milk producers in Wales. In 1974 there had been almost 12,000.[69]

Even with subsidies, half of Welsh farms by 1986 were unable to support full-time work for one person. Gone was the expectation that the son would take over the family concern and even that the wife's occupation would be on the farm. As a Carmarthenshire farmer noted, those 'who have been brought up to the drudgery, monotony and penury of small scale family livestock farming often want none of it'.[70] In 1961 agriculture had made up 16.7 per cent of employment in Dyfed, Gwynedd and Powys. By 1991 this had fallen to 8.8 per cent, meaning some 20,000 jobs had disappeared in thirty years.[71] Worse was to come. A ban on the sale of British beef after the 1996 BSE crisis was a devastating blow, adding to the deep sense of decline in the industry. One farmer in the Brecon Beacons noted that when he began agricultural college in 1995, milk was 25p per litre, a bull calf cost £100 and a dairy cow £1,500. Just five years later he was getting 15.5p per litre of milk, cows were worth practically nothing and bull calves were being sent to hunt kennels to be fed to the hounds. He concluded, 'all common sense seems to have disappeared'.[72] Then, in 2001, there were 118 confirmed foot-and-mouth cases in Wales. One and a quarter million Welsh animals were slaughtered and the countryside was effectively shut to visitors for six months. The sight and smell of their herds burning was deeply traumatic for farmers and the most conservative estimates of the cost to the Welsh economy were £140–220 million, of which £70–100 million was borne by tourism. Others, however, calculated that Welsh rural tourism enterprises endured an average 75 per cent loss of turnover during the crisis, costing them £596 million. Whatever the exact figures, it was a financial and emotional catastrophe at both a collective and an individual level, and a devastating one for a failing industry. Between 1997 and 2001 total annual agricultural income in Wales fell from £210 million to £46 million.[73] Yet public sympathy for the farmers (always much less than that for their slaughtered animals) never matched that given to the miners in the 1980s and the protests against the shipment of live farm animals in 1994–5 demonstrated the gap that was opening up between farmers and the wider public. By 2001 agriculture, hunting and forestry accounted for just 3.5 per cent of total male employment in Wales. In Ceredigion the figure was nearly 12 per cent but even in Wales' sparsest populated areas the sector accounted for half as many jobs as manufacturing and construction.[74] What once was the mainstay of the rural economy was now an unloved and often forgotten industry, despite the fact that it still shaped the landscape and everyone ate its produce. A teenager from near Builth Wells who wanted to be a farmer encapsulated the frustration: 'I don't ask to be rich or powerful but just to be given a chance. A chance to be allowed to earn a decent living doing the job I enjoy and caring for the countryside in our area for future generations, as previous generations have done for us. Is this too much to ask?'[75] Yet there were glimmers of hope. Organic produce became fashionable in the 1990s, offering better incomes to some farmers. House prices also pushed up land prices and suddenly old bits of land and barns were worth a decent sum of money if planning permission could be gained. By 1999 there were as many as 3,761 people in Wales who owned land worth over £1 million.[76]

As they did in industrial areas, successive governments saw manufacturing as the solution to rural economic problems. Although it rarely created well paid skilled jobs, economic policy centred on encouraging small-scale industrial developments in rural towns by offering grants and loans and building advance factories. This was given an impetus by the Development of Rural Wales Act 1976, which set up a development board covering Ceredigion, Powys and Meirionnydd, a recognition that these areas had economic needs similar to the Valleys. By the middle of the 1980s nearly 500 factories had been built and manufacturing was providing around 15 per cent of employment in rural Wales. Yet many of the jobs were unskilled and poorly paid; indeed, companies were partly attracted to rural Wales precisely because of low wages. Much of this development was in Powys, which was near the English border and the West Midlands.[77] Further west, the scattered population and distance from English markets made services and transport expensive, meaning new industry would never develop in any significant volume in Gwynedd and Dyfed. Indeed, without the public funding it was given there may have been next to no manufacturing in rural Wales.

A more successful industry was tourism, which continued to benefit from rising disposable incomes, improved roads and the powerful image rural Wales had as a beautiful place. That image was stronger within Britain than beyond and Wales struggled to attract overseas visitors. Nonetheless, in 1997 at total of 41.8 million tourist-nights were spent in Wales by UK visitors and another 6.4 million by overseas visitors. Tourism was directly employing 60,000 people and indirectly supporting another 30,000 jobs. It thus accounted for nearly one in ten Welsh jobs and contributed as much to the gross domestic product of Wales as it did in Greece or Spain.[78] Even in the post-industrial Valleys, much hope was invested in tourism and there were desperate marketing attempts to overcome the outdated image of a coal-scarred environment and replace it with one that reflected the green mountainous landscape that actually now existed. Yet tourism's impact on local economies was not as significant as might be expected. A majority of the jobs it created were low paid and seasonal; many were part-time too. Sometimes developments did not even create jobs. The parishes of Llanllugan and Llanwyddelan (Powys) had four caravan camps in 1977 with a capacity of over 300. The caravan owners tended to bring their own food and petrol because prices were cheaper back in the Midlands. The main impact on the wider local community was congested lanes and trespassing.[79] There was thus some vague resentment that the countryside was being treated as a playground for urban visitors. Locals and outsiders also complained about the environmental and aesthetic impact of tourism. The writer Bill Bryson described the north Wales coast as looking 'like holiday hell – endless ranks of prison camp caravan parks standing in fields in the middle of a lonely, windbeaten nowhere'. Others complained that this 'hideous expanse' was 'scouse in speech and sentiment'. Tourism was widely criticized as an agent of Anglicization, bringing English entrepreneurs, casual foreign workers, second homes and retirees. In 1991 only 40 per cent of those working in Gwynedd hotels and catering could speak Welsh, compared with 60 per cent of the county's wider workforce; among those who owned tourist businesses it was just 24 per cent. Even some places of worship introduced English into their services to cater for tourists. The 1972 Cymdeithas yr Iaith Gymraeg manifesto thus argued that 'the flood of the tourist industry is destroying the villages as surely and completely as the waters covered Capel Celyn'.[80] A surveyor for the Camping and Caravanning Club argued in 1986 that most Welsh local authorities paid lip service to tourism for economic reasons, 'whilst wishing that the "foreigners" could be turned back at the frontier, preferably leaving their money behind them first'. But it was rare to find complaints about tourism from those young people who worked in a café or a shop and who did not have the education to find alternative employment. More common than the nationalist view was an ambivalence which saw tourism as a 'necessary evil', as the general secretary of the Farmers' Union of Wales put it.[81]

Tourism contributed to the dominance that the service sector came to have over the rural economy. By 2001 it accounted for 69 per cent of all employment in rural counties, compared with a Welsh average of 65 per cent. In some tourist destinations like Betws-y-Coed, the service sector accounted for more than 80 per cent of employment. Within the service sector the state was the biggest employer, especially local councils and health authorities. By 2006 well over a quarter (28 per cent) of the rural workforce was employed by the public sector and in Gwynedd and Carmarthenshire this rose to a third, a figure comparable with Cardiff.[82] In places like Aberystwyth and Bangor, where the growth of higher education created secure and well paid jobs for locals and incomers, there were clear economic benefits that dented any simplistic picture of poverty in the rural west. But there were always critics, and one right-wing historian saw Aberystwyth, where 88 per cent of the workforce was employed in the service sector in 2001, as a symbol of all that was wrong with Wales: reliant on the state and happy to live off grants rather than entrepreneurship.[83] Others complained that the state's economic aspirations threatened the preservation of the rural countryside. Government-sanctioned developments, such as the building of power stations in Snowdonia or oil refineries at Milford Haven, were certainly bigger threats to the National Parks than any small-scale private development. But those who objected were minority voices. As with the encroachment of RAF Brawdy onto National Park land in Pembrokeshire, the benefits of these developments for the local economy were simply too great for any serious local objection.[84]

THE RELIANCE ON the public sector showed how far rural Wales had become integrated with the wider world. As the post-coal Valleys were 'greened', it was not even so clear where rural Wales was anymore. In the traditional rural areas of Dyfed, Gwynedd and Powys, the motorcar, media and telephone had broken down rural isolation, villages were now home to commuters and old countryside traditions had been consigned to history, replaced by a lifestyle not dissimilar to that in urban areas. As early as 1969 an incomer to Newtown found that life was not all that different from his native Birmingham. One of his neighbours was a fellow 'Brummie', there was bingo for his wife and pop concerts for the children. He missed the cricket but not his fifteenth-floor flat. He liked the people, the countryside and the sense of community, noting that 'strangers say "good morning" to me as though they mean it'. He also pointed out that there were those in Birmingham who liked to keep Sunday special too.[85] The referenda on

Sunday drinking provided a continued marker of the retreat of traditional rural culture. Three more districts went wet in 1975 and another four did in 1982. This left just Ceredigion and Dwyfor dry. By 1996 all Wales was wet and a century-old tradition was at an end. Now able to take advantage of weekend custom, the landlord of the Coach Inn in Clynnog Fawr remarked, 'It's good to have come into the 20th century'.[86]

Others were less impressed with such developments and a sense that life was getting worse was common across rural Britain. This ran far deeper than concern at how incomes were falling further behind national averages. Now that rural housing had been improved, many thought the modern world had little to offer. Instead, it seemed to present a multi-faceted onslaught. The practice flights of low-flying jet fighters over upland areas became one particular bugbear.[87] Far more serious were the ninety-four incidents between 1973 and 1998 of oil pollution that extended for more than a mile on Welsh shorelines. Even the sheep were not safe from pollution after radioactive fallout from the 1986 Chernobyl disaster hit Snowdonia, with some restrictions on the sale of sheep from there still being in place in 2009.[88] Anti-social behaviour was another worry that was felt to be alien to rural traditions. From the early 1980s there was increasing concern about 'drunkenness, hooliganism, and pilfering' at the Royal Welsh Agricultural Show. A decade later there were worries about drugs at the National Eisteddfod. One Carmarthenshire farmer remarked in the mid-1990s, 'Twenty years ago I never bothered to lock my house, ten years ago I would leave the keys in my motor at the mart in case anyone wanted to move it to get by. This year I have put locks on my tool shed and paid for a week's welding and woodwork to make secure barn doors.'[89] Nor was the landscape safe from external pressures. Wind farms were dramatic additions to the landscape brought about by the wider energy crisis. By 2009 there were thirty-three in Wales and another forty being planned. They became as controversial as in-migration and debates raged about noise levels, the aesthetic impact and whether they were actually environmentally friendly or not.[90] Some even saw them as foreign impositions, with one writer describing them as 'monsters … marching across the hills of Wales like the most determined of invading armies, ripping up ancient landscapes and industrialising them'. A campaigner claimed, 'They've taken the water; they taken the coal; they've taken over farming through the European grants system.… And the last thing we have left is the beauty.'[91]

Whatever the critics said, wind farms were simply not numerous enough to have radically transformed the Welsh landscape. Instead, the changes were more subtle. The percentage of Welsh land that was woodland increased from 9.7 in 1965 to 11.9 in 1992. Derelict cottages all but disappeared, while bungalows slowly but steadily changed the look of nearly every Welsh village. Scientists calculated in 2007 that the amount of snow on Snowdon had fallen by around a third in ten years because of climate change.[92] Farmers had been removing hedgerows and trees, draining fields, ploughing old grasslands and putting chemicals and effluents onto the land and into rivers. Beyond the visual impact, birdlife suffered from the consequent loss of habitat, compounded by the impact of pesticides on their food sources. The shift towards making wet silage also reduced the wildlife in fields, especially field mice, which in turn hit the owl population. Yet other species thrived, and foxes, magpies and crows in particular benefited from the continued development of upland forestation.[93] Within the fields themselves, the short-horns, Herefords and Welsh blacks that dominated during the early post-war years were replaced by the more productive black-and-white Friesians, a breed which by the end of the century had become ubiquitous. The number of sheep in Wales rose from 6.3 million in 1974 to 11.2 million in 1995 before falling by more than a quarter in the decade after 1998 as prices stagnated and farm subsidies shifted away from production to conservation. That policy did, at least, encourage the restoration of hedgerows and the growth of fodder crops that benefited wildlife.[94] But this change was simply an attempt to reverse the environmental damage done by agriculture's own modernization.

Changes to agriculture and the environment could divide communities but opposition to local authorities' attempts to rationalize primary school provision rarely did. The number of primary schools in Wales fell from 1,958 in 1974 to 1,527 in 2007 and many of these losses were in small rural villages. While there was no evidence to suggest that children suffered educationally by not being taught in their own villages, schools were at the heart of village life and their events were ones for whole communities rather than just parents. When Llanfyrnach in the Brecon Beacons lost its fifteen-pupil school in 1989, the vicar claimed 'village life seemed to dissipate'. Some commentators even claimed that the loss of a local school weakened children's connection with their village, contributing to rural depopulation.[95]

The extreme frustration people felt at the loss of a local school encouraged the feeling found across the British countryside that rural communities were neither in control of their own destiny nor being looked after by those in authority. In a national democracy, rural communities, rich or poor, had become a minority interest. By 2008 around 85 per cent of Welsh land may have been agricultural, forestry or common land, but only around 20 per cent of the Welsh population was officially classified as broadly rural, although a third of the population did live in predominantly rural counties. Rural county councils might sometimes have felt that central government was interested only in urban areas but, as the closure of schools demonstrated, the more remote countryside voices could go unheeded within rural authorities too. Even on Gwynedd County Council more than half the councillors represented urban wards. National Park authorities were another source of tension and there was often a strong sense that these bodies were not accountable to the communities within the Parks.[96] Feelings of rural powerlessness intensified after Labour took office in 1997. The 2005 banning of fox hunting became an emotive symbol of urban values being imposed on the countryside. Royal Mail, meanwhile, shut a number of rural post offices in the name of efficiency, dealing another body blow to traditional ideas of rural community. Even devolution got off to a bad start when, in 1999 and to much anger in the farming community, Labour appointed a female vegetarian as Welsh agriculture minister. The Countryside and Rights of Way Act 2000, which gave people the right to roam over open land, was another source of resentment. A Carmarthenshire farmer noted that antipathy towards ramblers was not about loss or damage but power over what happened in the countryside. Quite simply, the ramblers and conservationists were not 'one of us'.[97] Similarly, people's desire to assert some control over their destiny lay as much at the heart of the resentment of in-migration in rural communities as any concern over language and culture. This was why some people found the easiest way to assimilate was to say nothing. Nonetheless, the drift of government policy could also bring incomers and established residents together, unified by rural causes against the urban 'other'. In 2006 the press reported cooperation in the Welsh countryside between farmers of different nationalities in dealing with foxes in the wake of the hunting ban. One observer told a newspaper, 'it doesn't matter where you are from, we are in this together'.[98]

Rural frustration perhaps owed something to a realization that many of the problems were self-inflicted. Small towns had their congestion relieved by much sought-after by-passes but then complained when trade by-passed the centre of towns for nearby supermarkets. Village shops became symbols of the community but also struggled against people's preference for supermarkets. A 1997 survey of Llanfihangel-yng-Ngwynfa (Powys) found that less than 4 per cent used the local shop for their main weekly shopping.[99] Unemployment was a problem but surveys showed strong opposition to the building of factories because of the impact on rural life. Despite the shortage of affordable housing there was often strong opposition from existing homeowners to new buildings in villages, making planning and development the most common source of discord in a community.[100] Opposition, which came from both locals and incomers, was often framed in terms of preventing traditional villages losing their character and being swamped but it also meant that the 'haves' were harming the 'have-nots'.

For all the deprivation and the constant sense of unease at the direction in which modern rural society was heading, surveys suggested that people in the countryside were generally happier with their lives than those in urban areas. They liked the beauty of their surroundings, the lack of pollution and crime, the friendliness of the community and the calm pace of life. They still, however, bemoaned the lack of jobs, transport and leisure facilities. Significant new concerns were emerging too, such as over broadband access and mobile telephone reception in more remote areas. Nonetheless, in one 2009 investigation of small rural communities, as many as 94 per cent of respondents rated their quality of life as either 'very good' or 'fairly good'.[101] People may have been happier in rural areas but their experiences had much in common with other communities. Social ills such as poverty, the loss of community, crime and environmental despoliation were hardly unique to rural communities. Nor were concerns over migration; the whole of Wales rather than just the rural districts was suffering from a loss of young and skilled people.[102] Although few liked to admit it, especially when the issue was raised in racial terms, there were also parallels between the complaints that rural culture was being destroyed by incomers and opposition to overseas immigration into towns and cities on the basis that it was endangering traditional English working-class culture. Indeed, in 2007 the assistant chief constable in north Wales claimed that some Welsh people in the north-west felt as vulnerable as Muslim communities and that English–Welsh tensions accounted for 20 per cent of hate crimes.[103] Even if the question of whether English–Welsh differences were racial is dismissed, there was a substantive difference within the parallel. Rural Welsh-speaking Wales was not underpinned by a wider cultural hegemony; it was itself a minority within both Wales and the UK and was thus vulnerable when incomers came from that wider position of power and did not surrender it when they arrived.[104] Rural Welsh-speaking communities were thus like a sandcastle slowly being washed away by an incoming tide. The same was true of rural England and the Welsh borderlands. There, too, villages had lost their sense of unity and traditional culture. They were no longer defined by agriculture, or even tourism, and instead had been absorbed into wider urban ways of life and economic patterns. Even the landscape – the mountains, hills, fields, rivers and lakes that made up the countryside – was slowly altering, in the name of both conservation and progress. But it remained at the heart of what people inside and outside the nation imagined Wales to be. No matter what was happening to Wales politically, or to its people in the towns and villages, for many, Wales remained a land of mountains and countryside.

Notes

1 Quoted in P. Cloke, M. Goodwin and P. Milbourne, *Rural Wales: Community and Marginalization* (1997), 149.
2 *LDP*, 31 Dec. 1973. *Guardian*, 3 Dec. 1973.
3 A. Gruffydd, *Mae Rhywun Yn Gwybod* (2004).
4 R. Greary, 'Meibion Glyndŵr: folk-devils or folk heroes?', *PI*, 92 (1992), 39–44. *WM*, 23 June 1990.
5 Quoted in translation in R. Smith, 'Journalism and the Welsh language', in G. H. Jenkins and M. A. Williams (eds), *'Let's Do Our Best for the Ancient Tongue': The Welsh Language in the Twentieth Century* (2000), 303.
6 *Arcade*, 20 (7 Aug. 1981). *WM*, 2 July 1990.
7 B. Rogers, *The Man Who Went West: The Life of R. S. Thomas* (2007), 283. *Wales on Sunday*, 8 July 1990. J. Humphries, *Freedom Fighters: Wales's Forgotten 'War', 1963–1993* (2008), 186.
8 Letters, 15 Oct. 1986 and 9 May 1986, NLW, ex 2371/3.
9 *Independent*, 7 Feb. 1993. Humphries, *Freedom Fighters*, appendix A, 160.
10 J. W. Aitchison and H. Carter, 'The Welsh language, 1921–1991: a geolinguistic perspective', in Jenkins and Williams (eds), *'Let's Do Our Best'*, 74. N. Gallent, A. Mace and M. Tewdwr-Jones, 'Dispelling a myth? Second homes in rural Wales', *Area*, 35:3 (2003), 271–84.
11 Net migration is the difference between the number of immigrants and emigrants. Calculated from *DWS*, 40 (1994), 8, and Wales Rural Observatory, *Population Change in Rural Wales: Social and Cultural Impacts*, research report 14 (2007), 26. This figure is approximate because of boundary changes in 1996. It is inflated by the inclusion of the county of Conwy, which encompassed parts of Clwyd.
12 G. Day, '"A million on the move?": population change and rural Wales', *CW*, 3 (1989), 137–60. Office for National Statistics, *Regional Trends*, 30 (2008), 72. WAG, *The Role of the Housing System in Rural Wales* (2006), 34. Aitchison and Carter, 'The Welsh language', 98. N. Jones, *Living in Rural Wales* (1993), 18.
13 G. C. Wenger, *Mid-Wales: Deprivation or Development. A Study of Patterns of Employment in Selected Communities* (1980), 149.
14 T. R. Chapman, *Encounters with Wales* (1995), 115.
15 Dyfed County Council, *Prospects for Rural Prosperity*, report of a conference, 6 and 7 Apr. 1989.
16 Rural counties defined as: Anglesey, Carmarthenshire, Ceredigion, Conwy, Denbighshire, Gwynedd, Monmouthshire, Pembrokeshire, Powys. WAG, *The Role of the Housing System*, 28.
17 WAG, *The Role of the Housing System*, 33. Office for National Statistics, *Patterns of Migration in Wales* (2006). WAG, *A Statistical Focus on Rural Wales* (2008), 67.
18 G. Harbour, 'Housing', in K. D. George and L. Mainwaring (eds), *The Welsh Economy* (1988), 77. C. Bollom, *Attitudes and Second Homes in Rural Wales* (1978), 77.
19 NLW, ex 2371/3.
20 P. Cloke, M. Goodwin and M. Milbourne, *Rural Wales: Community and Marginalisation* (1997), 34. Gallent *et al.*, 'Dispelling a myth?' Dyfed County Council, *Prospects for Rural Prosperity*, 4. WAG, *The Role of the Housing System*, 52.
21 WAG, *Role of the Housing System*, 76–7, 80. Welsh housing statistics. Joseph Rowntree Foundation, *Rural Housing in Wales* (2008).
22 WAG, *The Role of the Housing System*, 121.

23 Wenger, *Mid-Wales*, 137, 143. *WM*, 1 July 1981.
24 I. Emmett, 'Place, community and bilingualism in Blaenau Ffestiniog', in A. P. Cohen (ed.), *Belonging: Identity and Social Organisation in British Rural Cultures* (1982), 202–21. Wenger, *Mid-Wales*, 91.
25 Aitchison and Carter, 'The Welsh language', 67, 74.
26 J. R. Webster, *School and Community in Rural Wales* (1991), 226–7. Cloke *et al.*, *Rural Wales*, 20.
27 D. Morris, 'The Welsh language and local authority planning in Gwynedd, 1974–1995', in Jenkins and Williams (eds), *'Let's Do Our Best'*, 586. E. G. Bowen and H. Carter, 'Preliminary observations on the distribution of the Welsh language at the 1971 census', *Geographical Journal*, 140:3 (1974), 432–40. J. Davies, *The Making of Wales* (1999), 145.
28 Chairman of Gwynedd County Council to Secretary of State for Wales, 15 Oct. 1986, NLW, ex 2371/3.
29 H. Davis, G. Day and A. Drakakis-Smith, 'Being English in north Wales: migration and the inmigrant experience', *Nationalism and Ethnic Politics*, 12:3–4 (2006), 642–55. E. West, *Hovel in the Hills: An Account of the 'Simple Life'* (1978), 159.
30 D. Phillips, 'We'll keep a welcome? The effects of tourism on the Welsh language', in Jenkins and Williams (eds), *'Let's Do Our Best'*, 546. *Y Cymro*, 10 Oct. 1990. D. Morris, 'A study of the language contract and social networks in Ynys Môn', *CW*, 3 (1989), 107. West, *Hovel in the Hills*, 129.
31 'Discrimination on the ground of language: Asian and Welsh languages', NA, CK 2/264.
32 Bollom, *Attitudes and Second Homes*, 9. Wenger, *Mid-Wales*, 122.
33 Morris, 'The Welsh language and local authority planning', 591–7. B. Newman, 'Local authorities and the Welsh language', *Local Government Studies*, 19:1 (1993), 108–20.
34 Quoted in R. Fevre, J. Borland and D. Denney, 'Nation, community and conflict: housing policy and immigration in north Wales', in R. Fevre and A. Thompson (eds), *Nation, Identity and Social Theory: Perspectives from Wales* (1999), 142.
35 A. Drakakis-Smith, G. Day and H. H. Davis, 'Portrait of a locality? The local press at work in north-west Wales, 2000–05', *CW*, 21 (2008), 25–46.
36 Davis *et al.*, 'Being English', 589.
37 J. E. Jones, 'Buches a Buchedd', *Barn*, July–Aug. 2001, 59.
38 Davis *et al.*, 'Being English', 589–90. G. Day, A. Drakakis-Smith and H. H. Davis, 'Migrating to north Wales: the "English" experience', *CW*, 21 (2008), 111.
39 Day *et al.*, 'Migrating to north Wales', 121. H. Newby, *Green and Pleasant Land? Social Change in Rural England* (1985), 171. Jones, *Living in Rural Wales*, 23–4.
40 H. Wyn (ed.), *Mam-gu, Siân Hwêl a Naomi: Hanes a Hudoliaeth Bro Maenclochog* (2006), 438, 427–8.
41 P. Cloke, M. Goodwin and P. Milbourne, '"There's so many strangers in the village now": marginalization and change in 1990s Welsh rural life-styles', *CW*, 8 (1995), 47–74. Cloke *et al.*, *Rural Wales*, ch. 7. L. Shankland, *Buying and Running a Small Holding in Wales* (2008), 15–16. Jones, *Living in Rural Wales*, 18.
42 Cloke *et al.*, *Rural Wales*, 22, 25. Wales Rural Observatory, *Population Change in Rural Wales*, 95.
43 E. James, 'Research on your own doorstep: Welsh rural communities and the perceived effects of in-migration', in C. A. Davies and S. Jones (eds), *Welsh Communities: New Ethnographic Perspectives* (2003), 49–79. West, *Hovel in the Hills*, 162. A. Bailey, *A Walk Through Wales* (1992), 95.
44 Davis *et al.*, 'Being English', 593, 590. D. Balsom, 'The smoke behind the fires', *Pl*, 73 (1989), 16–19.
45 J. Seymour, 'Living in Wales', *Pl*, 8 (1971), 36–40. Llanfihangel Social History Group, *A Welsh Countryside Revisited: A New Social Study of Llanfihangel yng Ngwynfa* (2003), 137. G. Hill, 'English voices', *Pl*, 64 (1987), 14–19. Jones, *Living in Rural Wales*, 36, 20.
46 Morris, 'A study of the language contract'. R. A. Jones (ed.), *Hyd Ein Hoes: Lleisiau Cymru* (2003), 32.

47 M. Löffler, 'The Welsh language movement and bilingualism', in Jenkins and Williams (eds), *'Let's Do Our Best'*, 516.
48 *Y Cymro*, 27 Sep. 1977. *WM*, 14 Oct. 1990. Wenger, *Mid-Wales*, 149.
49 Löffler, 'The Welsh language movement', 517.
50 A. Howkins, *The Death of Rural England: A Social History of the Countryside since 1900* (2003), 179. N. Jones, 'Village voices', in J. Gower (ed.), *Home Land* (1996), 85–99.
51 Jones, *Living in Rural Wales*, 247.
52 Newby, *Green and Pleasant Land?*, 174, 191. Wales Rural Observatory, *Population Change in Rural Wales,* 103. Cloke *et al.*, *Rural Wales*, 150.
53 James, 'Research on your own doorstep'.
54 Aitchison and Carter, 'The Welsh language', 102. Morris, 'A study of the language contract', 116.
55 I. Emmett, '*Fe godwn ni eto*: stasis and change in a Welsh industrial town', in A. P. Cohen (ed.), *Belonging: Identity and Social Organisation in British Rural Cultures* (1982), 172.
56 P. Wilding, 'Income and wealth in Wales', in G. Rees and T. L. Rees (eds), *Poverty and Social Inequality in Wales* (1980), 40. G. Day, *Making Sense of Wales* (2002), 170.
57 WAG, *The Role of the Housing System*, 48. Wales Rural Observatory, *Poverty and Social Exclusion in Rural Wales*, research report 6 (2005), 49–50. Cloke *et al.*, *Rural Wales*, ch. 6.
58 S. D. Nutley, 'The extent of public transport decline in rural Wales', *Cambria*, 9:1 (1982), 27–48. Cloke *et al.*, *Rural Wales*, 80, 119–20.
59 Wales Rural Observatory, *Poverty and Social Exclusion*, 49–50.
60 Wilding, 'Income and wealth', 36. Wenger, *Mid-Wales*, 83.
61 P. W. Daniels, 'The geography of economic change', in P. Addison and H. Jones (eds), *A Companion to Contemporary Britain, 1939–2000* (2005), 217–18.
62 D. H. Blackaby, D. Hall, P. L. Latreille, D. N. Manning, P. D. Murphy, N. C. O'Leary and F. Sumner, 'Defence cuts, redundancies and future employment prospects in west Wales', *CW*, 6 (1994), 49–72.
63 Welsh Index of Multiple Deprivation 2008.
64 Dyfed County Council, *Prospects for Rural Prosperity*, 3.
65 G. Davies, *Real Wrexham* (2007), 164.
66 Howkins, *The Death of Rural England*, 152.
67 K. D. George and L. Mainwaring (eds), *The Welsh Economy* (1988), 147, 152.
68 *DWHS-3*, 67. J. Osmond, 'The modernisation of Wales', in N. Evans (ed.), *National Identity in the British Isles* (1989), 77.
69 G. Howells, *Rural Wales in Crisis* (1991), 10. *DWHS-3*, 86. Dairy Development Centre, *Wales Statistics*, formerly at www.ddc-wales.co.uk.
70 P. Dobbs, 'Farming through the decades: a personal view', in Gower (ed.), *Home Land*, 18. C. LeVay, 'The family farm', *Pl*, 33 (1976), 44–51.
71 G. Hughes, P. Midmore and A. Sherwood, 'The Welsh language and agricultural communities in the twentieth century', in Jenkins and Williams (eds), *'Let's Do Our Best'*, 554.
72 S. Brook (ed.), *Where We Belong: Life in the Beacons, Then and Now* (2000), 41.
73 A. Scott, M. Christie and P. Midmore, 'Impact of the 2001 foot-and-mouth disease outbreak in Britain: implications for rural studies', *Journal of Rural Studies*, 20:1 (2004), 1–14.
74 2001 census. WAG, *A Statistical Focus*, 42.
75 Erwood Women's Institute Working Group, *Hills and Sunny Pastures: Life in Erwood and Its Surrounding Parishes* (2001), 145.
76 K. Cahill, *Who Owns Britain: The Hidden Facts Behind Landownership in the UK and Ireland* (2001), 13.
77 Day, *Making Sense of Wales*, 156. Dyfed County Council, *Prospects for Rural Prosperity*, 3. R. Thomas, *Industry in Rural Wales* (1966). G. Day and M. Hedger, 'Mid Wales: missing the point', *Urban Studies*, 27:2 (1990), 283–90.
78 Phillips, 'We'll keep a welcome?', 538.
79 Wenger, *Mid-Wales*, 49.

80 B. Bryson, *Notes from a Small Island* (1996 edn), 248. Phillips, 'We'll keep a welcome?', 542, 544. *Cardigan and Tivyside Advertiser*, 22 July 1966. H. Webb (trans.), 'Cymdeithas yr Iaith: the manifesto', *Pl*, 26/27 (1974–5), 77–136.
81 Phillips, 'We'll keep a welcome?', 529–30.
82 WAG, *The Role of the Housing System*, 44. Cloke *et al.*, *Rural Wales*, 59, 60. Wales Rural Observatory, *The Significance of Public Sector Employment in Rural Wales*, research report 8 (2006), 7.
83 *Cymru Hywel Williams: Y Economi* (S4C, 19 Nov. 2009). Workforce statistics based on Aberystwyth community.
84 J. Burchardt, *Paradise Lost: Rural Idyll and Social Change in England since 1800* (2002), 184. C. Witham, 'Sheep, subs and showcases: the American military in Brawdy, 1974–1995', *WHR*, 24:4 (2009), 168–86.
85 *Montgomeryshire Mercury*, 3 Oct. 1969.
86 *Independent*, 11 Nov. 1996.
87 Howkins, *The Death of Rural England*, 206. *Y Faner*, 21 May 1976.
88 *DWS* (1999), 267. Jones, *Hyd Ein Hoes*, 37–8. *Guardian*, 7 May 1986 and 12 May 2009.
89 D. W. Howell, *Taking Stock: The Centenary History of the Royal Welsh Agricultural Society* (2003), 234. *Golwg*, 11 Aug. 1994, 10–11. Dobbs, 'Farming through the decades', 17.
90 British Wind Energy Association statistics at www.bwea.com/statistics. M. M. Hedger, 'Wind energy: the debate in Wales', *CW*, 7 (1994), 117–34.
91 M. Parker, *Neighbours from Hell? English Attitudes to the Welsh* (2007), 100. Campaigner against wind farms in Chapman, *Encounters with Wales*, 155.
92 W. Linnard, *Welsh Woods and Forests: A History* (2000), 217. 'Scientist's fear for Snowdon snow', 16 Jan. 2007, at news.bbc.co.uk/1/hi/wales/north_west/6264931.stm.
93 W. Condrey, *The Natural History of Wales* (1981), 11–12. Llanfihangel Social History Group, *A Welsh Countryside Revisited*, 44–5.
94 *Daily Post*, 9 July 2009. *DWHS-3*, 56.
95 *DWHS-3*, 171. WAG, *Key Education Statistics 2007*. Brook, *Where We Belong*, 53. R. Nash, 'Perceptions of the village school', in G. Williams (ed.), *Social and Cultural Change in Contemporary Wales* (1978), 81.
96 WAG, *A Statistical Focus*, 9. Dyfed County Council, *Prospects for Rural Prosperity*. Nash, 'Perceptions of the village school', 77. Chapman, *Encounters with Wales*, 45.
97 Translated from Dobbs, 'Farming through the decades', 17.
98 *WM*, 10 Jan. 2006.
99 Llanfihangel Social History Group, *A Welsh Countryside Revisited*, 147.
100 Day, *Making Sense of Wales*, 157. Wales Rural Observatory, *A Report on Living and Working in Rural Wales* (2004).
101 See for example Wenger, *Mid-Wales*, 125–6, 135–6. Wales Rural Observatory, *Deep Rural Localities* (2009), iii.
102 S. Drinkwater and D. Blackaby, *Migration and Labour Market Differences: The Case of Wales* (2004), at http://ideas.repec.org/p/sur/surrec/0604.html.
103 BBC News, internet and Radio Wales, 12 July 2007.
104 T. Webb, 'Y Fro Gymraeg Declaration', *Pl*, 169 (2005), 63–7.

14

'A nation once again.' 1997–2009

He pointed to the west, 'Over there, they have grants for *everything*!'
'I don't agree.'
'Everything's free in Wales – free prescriptions, free car parking, free bus passes. . . .'
I tried irony in an attempt to stop his flow, 'A land of milk and honey. . .'
'Yes! Paid for by me!'

Gareth Wheatley, *On an Offa Bus* (2009), 109

–I'm telling yew, mun, its fuckin happening. It's gonna come. A nation once again. It's on the fuckin way boy, nothing fuckin surer.
–My arse.
–I'm telling yew. I saw it on-a telly before I came out like. Fuckin devolution, boy. Plans're being made, for the election like. National fuckin assembly.
–Ah yeh, an how many punters yew reckon're going to turn out to vote then? Twenty, thirty percent of-a population? Remember 1979?
–No. I was six.
–Same thing'll happen. Apathy. Can't-be-fuckin-arsed-ness. That's what wrong with this fuckin country mun, the general fuckin apathy of its inhabitants. Nothing fuckin moves em. Nothing fuckin gets em off eyr arses. Telly an beer an-a takeaway curry an they're happy. . . .

Niall Griffiths, *Sheepshagger* (2002), 74–5

IN SEPTEMBER 1997 Tony Blair visited Wrexham to campaign for Welsh devolution. The *Guardian* noted:

Ton-ee! Ton-ee! They shouted, not just the girls waving from above Marks and Spencers, but the young lads as well. Sometimes they chanted like a football crowd; other times they were more ragged. All the time the sound bounced off the walls and boomed around the shops. This is a new phenomenon in British politics: the Prime Minister as rock star.[1]

Four months earlier, eighteen years of Conservative government had come to an end. Labour had taken 54.7 per cent of the Welsh vote and thirty-four out of the forty Welsh seats. The Conservatives failed to win a single constituency and achieved just 19.6 per cent of the vote, a fall of 9 percentage points from 1992 and their lowest share since 1918. More than 200,000 fewer people had voted Conservative than in 1979. The desire for change was not rooted primarily in policy. Devolution seemed to be the only radical thing New Labour was offering and that issue had taken a backseat during the election campaign. In contrast, from privatization to curbed union powers, many of the mainstays of Thatcherism had become political orthodoxies. This failure to offer much that was radically different perhaps contributed to the Welsh turnout being 73.5 per cent, a fall of 6.2 percentage points from the previous general election. Among those aged under twenty-five years, the UK turnout was estimated to be less than 60 per cent.[2] For all the claims of rock-star-like popularity, the reality was that only 40 per cent of the Welsh electorate had voted New Labour.

Devolution was one of the first things on the new government's agenda but the push for this came not from Wales or Blair but from Scotland, where the majority of the establishment had come to regard a Scottish Parliament as a democratic necessity after years of governance by a Conservative Party that they had not voted for. In Wales there had been virtually no public debate on whether devolution should take place or what form it might take. Within parts of the Labour Party, however, there was a strong belief in the need to democratize what Ron Davies, the new Welsh Secretary of State, called the 'substantial administrative devolution' that had already taken place.[3] The decision to achieve that by following the example of 1979 and offering Wales only an Assembly without law-making or tax-raising powers was an internal party decision that had no obvious rationale beyond what its advocates thought the rest of the party and the electorate might support. Nevertheless, had political expediency alone been their guide then Wales would never have been offered devolution at all, since there was no popular groundswell of support for it. Labour's 1997 manifesto had not mentioned a referendum on the issue but the decision was taken after the general election to hold one to give devolution legitimacy and undermine opposition to its introduction. The electorate, however, was unprepared and uninformed about the issues, resulting in confusion and apprehension. After attending early Welsh focus groups, one of Labour's polling experts told the party's London headquarters: 'There is a lot of emotional resistance to the Assembly. People in Wales feel vulnerable and uncertain both on a personal and national level. They do not want things to start going wrong and are suspicious of change.'[4]

As the referendum campaign got going that suspicion did not alter but it was not taken advantage of because the 'no' campaign was something of a shambles, hampered by financial restraints and too dependent on the Tories, who were demoralized after the general election and feared their unpopularity might undermine the 'no' vote.[5] In contrast the 'yes' campaign managed both to keep most of the opponents within Labour quiet and to minimize the public role of Plaid Cymru, which might have associated devolution with nationalism. The arguments that devolution would deliver democratic accountability and improved services were inspired by the experience of Conservative governance but they failed to excite and lacked the emotional pull of a case based on Welsh patriotism, something that had been discounted as vulnerable to accusations of nationalism. The 'yes' campaign could, however, draw on the trust and hope placed in Blair and his new government. The simple fact that the government advocated a 'yes' vote was a powerful persuader.

Twenty days before the referendum Diana, Princess of Wales, was killed in a car crash. Campaigning was suspended amid what television depicted as a mass outpouring of grief. A Cardiff woman recalled:

> All those people, all those flowers, all those people waiting to sign the book [of condolence], it's unbelievable and very, very moving.... When I felt my reaction to Diana's death I did not dream that so many people felt like I did. I felt I was so silly to feel this way about someone I never knew.... Now I know that I wasn't stupid, the majority feel the same.

One reporter even told viewers on the day of the funeral: 'Perhaps it's really in this principality that the community will feel the severe loss hardest.... No-one can really believe what they're seeing all around the country but particularly in Wales where they hold her in such great esteem in their hearts.'[6] Yet the majority of people did not watch Diana's funeral on television. Some were working but others were not interested or disapproved of the monarchy and Diana's Welsh title. She was, after all, 'England's rose' as Elton John's song put it. Within the BBC in Wales there were senior discussions about whether its coverage was creating or responding to the public's reaction, but even if the media did dictate the idea of a nation united in grief, it was a moment that showed that profound cultural ties did extend across the English border. Nick Bourne, a leading Welsh Conservative, later suggested that Diana's death 'evoked a strong sense of Britishness' in Wales, something which some Welsh people deeply touched by her death also noted.[7] Whether this was true and whether it impacted on the referendum is impossible to tell. It may well have dissuaded some from voting to undermine British unity but Diana's death also prevented a week's campaigning for the 'yes' side, a side whose arguments were more cogent and sensible than those who fell back on claiming devolution would be a waste of money that might break up Britain.

The early hours of 19 September 1997 were dramatic. With the 'no's some 16,000 votes ahead, the chief executive of Carmarthenshire County Council, the final local authority to declare, announced in rather faltering Welsh that the 'yes' majority in his county was 22,996. For the first time in its modern history, Wales would be, at least partially, self-governing. But amid the jubilation this generated were all the old uncertainties. The majority was just 6,721 and the turnout a mere 50.1 per cent (table 14.1). In eleven of the twenty-two Welsh counties more people had voted 'no'

Table 14.1 Results of the 1997 referendum on the establishment of a Welsh Assembly, by county

Local authority	Turnout (%)	Yes	%	No	%
Blaenau Gwent	49.3	15,237	56.1	11,928	43.9
Bridgend	50.6	27,632	54.4	23,172	45.6
Caerphilly	49.3	34,830	54.7	28,841	45.3
Cardiff	46.9	47,527	44.4	59,589	55.6
Carmarthenshire	56.4	49,115	65.3	26,119	34.7
Ceredigion	56.8	18,304	59.2	12,614	40.8
Conwy	51.5	18,369	40.9	26,521	59.1
Denbighshire	49.7	14,271	40.8	20,732	59.2
Flintshire	41.0	17,746	38.2	28,707	61.8
Gwynedd	59.8	35,425	64.1	19,859	35.9
Merthyr Tydfil	49.5	12,707	58.2	9,121	41.8
Monmouthshire	50.5	10,592	32.1	22,403	67.9
Neath and Port Talbot	51.9	36,730	66.5	18,463	33.5
Newport	45.9	16,172	37.4	27,017	62.6
Pembrokeshire	52.6	19,979	42.8	26,712	57.2
Powys	56.2	23,038	42.7	30,966	57.3
Rhondda Cynon Taff	49.9	51,201	58.5	36,362	41.5
Swansea	47.1	42,789	52.0	39,561	48.0
Torfaen	45.5	15,756	49.8	15,854	50.2
Vale of Glamorgan	54.3	17,776	36.7	30,613	63.3
Wrexham	42.4	18,574	45.3	22,449	54.7
Ynys Môn	56.9	15,649	50.9	15,095	49.1
Total	50.1	559,419	50.3	552,698	49.7

than 'yes', allowing the media to produce maps of a nation divided. Voting patterns were actually far more complex than this and individual counties were irrelevant when the result depended on cumulative totals. The capital was lamented for voting 'no' but there were more 'yes' votes there than in any other area except Carmarthen and Rhondda Cynon Taff. Carmarthen, the supposed saviour of devolution, supplied more 'no' votes than Monmouthshire, the county where the 'yes' vote was weakest. But if the idea that the west and the Valleys won it could be rejected, the narrowness of the margin could not. The slender majority allowed an organizer of the 'no' side to claim, 'another £10,000 and we could have done it'.[8] In 1998 the Committee on Standards in Public Life suggested that 'a fairer campaign might well have resulted in a different outcome'.[9]

Political scientists got down to the job of analysing the result by surveying how people voted. Their research suggested that those under forty-five were significantly less likely to have voted than older people but if they did turn out they were more likely to have voted 'yes'. There seemed to be no change from 1979 in the voting patterns of supporters of Plaid Cymru (strongly 'yes') and the Conservatives (strongly 'no') but there was a strong rise in Labour voters saying 'yes', although they were less likely to turn out than supporters of other parties. As in 1979, those who spoke Welsh fluently or prioritized a Welsh identity over a British one were more likely to have both turned out and voted 'yes'. There was no evidence to suggest that the 'yes' result was due to any significant rise in Welsh national identity, just as its rejection in 1979 was not a decision rooted primarily in perceptions of national identity. But there did seem to have been a conversion to devolution among Labour voters who saw their national identity as primarily Welsh. It was not the numbers of Labour voters who identified themselves as Welsh that had changed significantly but rather the political consequences of making that identification.[10] This was clear in how the 'yes' vote had increased since 1979 by, respectively, 36, 39 and 30 per cent in what had been the industrial counties of Mid Glamorgan, West Glamorgan and Gwent, a remarkable change in political opinion. No matter how close the overall result, that shift had taken place everywhere and averaged out at 30 per cent across Wales. Even at its smallest, it was 19 per cent in Gwynedd and 20 per cent in Clwyd.[11]

Why that happened was less clear. It certainly did not seem to be the fine detail of what was on offer and just 16 per cent in one survey answered questions about the proposals correctly. The devastation of trade unionism had removed a powerful voice for British unity and policies, while the end of the cold war and its nuclear threat meant the potential breakup of Britain, however remote that might be, was no longer quite as frightening as it had been in the 1970s. Scotland's 'yes' vote a week earlier may have eased some fears and encouraged people to demonstrate Wales' equality. Most importantly, Welshness had become more political under the Conservatives as the traditional industrial base was dismantled, with little being put in its place. That had happened without the electoral consent of the Welsh majority but had also been accompanied by a growth in Welsh quangos and in the Welsh Office, delivering a form of administrative devolution that encouraged people to think at a Welsh level (chapter 11). Adding a democratic executive to that process was thus a logical next step, especially since it would lessen the chances of Conservative governance again.

Sensing that, the *Western Mail* and *Daily Post* had both been supportive of the 'yes' campaign, although they maybe reached only 12 per cent of households between them. The evening papers, such as the *South Wales Echo* and *Evening Post*, were better read collectively but they avoided making a recommendation either way, although they did urge people to vote. Of Wales' two best-selling newspapers, the *Mirror* had produced a special Welsh edition encouraging people to vote 'yes' but the *Sun* wondered what the Assembly Members (AMs) could possibly talk about and asked its readers to 'imagine sixty Neil Kinnocks in one room'.[12] Seventy per cent of people, however, used television rather than the press or radio as their main source of news. Although there was heavy coverage on the Welsh stations, 35 per cent of the population could choose to watch English regional stations, while the British news programmes seemed uninterested and gave the campaign fairly minimal coverage.[13] It is thus difficult not to conclude that the media's key influence was encouraging the low turnout by failing to properly inform the electorate about the arguments of either side.

EIGHT MONTHS AFTER the referendum, the first election for the new National Assembly for Wales (NAW) was held. It failed to generate any real excitement and less than half the electorate voted. But the results were more interesting, thanks to the new electoral system that combined traditional constituency representation with a regional vote for a party. It was a system designed to add to devolution's legitimacy by giving limited recognition to the plurality of Welsh political opinion but without harming Labour's chances of a majority. But the Labour architects were too confident and Plaid Cymru turned out to be the immediate beneficiary (table 14.2). Despite surprising many people by announcing that it had never supported independence, the party won Islwyn and Rhondda in Labour's heartland

Table 14.2 National Assembly for Wales election results, 1999–2007

	1999		2003		2007	
	Share of vote (%)	Number of seats	Share of vote (%)	Number of seats	Share of vote (%)	Number of seats
Con	16.2	9	19.5	11	21.9	12
Lab	36.5	28	38.3	30	30.9	26
LibDem	13.0	6	13.4	6	13.3	6
PC	29.5	17	20.5	12	21.7	15
Other	4.9	0	8.3	1	12.2	1
Turnout (%)	46.3		38.2		43.5	

and almost tripled its share of the vote from the general election two years earlier. Labour, in contrast, won 18 percentage points less of the vote than in 1997 and seemed to be paying the price for its drift towards the interests of 'middle England'. Without an overall majority, the party was left in shock. A senior Labour figure asked, 'what sort of an election is it where we hold Cardiff North but lose the Rhondda?' On seeing the result Tony Blair reputedly retorted 'Fucking Welsh'.[14]

With a divided Assembly and the narrow 'yes' vote still fresh in the memory, building a consensus became a priority. Ron Davies, the Welsh Labour leader, had been advocating the importance of this since the referendum but he had resigned before the election after apparently being robbed while looking for a homosexual encounter on Clapham Common. Tony Blair, overlooking that devolution was supposed to be about reducing the influence of London, then helped engineer Alun Michael's election as the new Welsh Labour leader by gathering the bloc vote of the unions to outweigh the preference of individual party members. This undermined the talk of inclusive politics and after the election Michael's leadership of the Assembly never overcame the idea that he had been imposed from outside. In 2000 he resigned ahead of a 'no confidence' vote; a month later he quit as an AM, cementing the impression that his loyalties lay elsewhere despite his place in history as the Assembly's first First Secretary.[15]

His replacement as Labour leader and First Secretary (a position soon rechristened First Minister) was Rhodri Morgan. Rhodri, as everyone called him, had the reputation of being a man of the people, despite being very much part of the establishment: a Welsh speaker, the son of an academic, educated at Oxford and Harvard and married to an MP. He was also a little eccentric; when asked if he wanted to be First Minister, he was reputed to have answered, 'Do one-legged ducks swim in circles?' At a time when UK politics was increasingly viewed as cynical and manipulative, Morgan was what was needed and under his leadership devolved politics eventually settled down. His first administration was a formal Labour–Liberal Democrat coalition, something which marked a new direction from the party's instincts in London. Aware of the probable causes of Labour's disastrous 1999 election, Morgan stressed his desire to place 'clear red water' between Wales and English New Labour and he even changed the party's name from Labour Party Wales to the Welsh Labour Party. Despite this symbolic statement of difference and nationality, the fact that Morgan was in the same party as the UK government helped him immensely, not least when he secured additional Treasury monies to ensure Wales was granted European Union aid that was dependent on match funding.

Under Morgan, Welsh Labour's popularity recovered slightly but the 2003 NAW election still left it one seat short of an overall majority. The party decided to govern alone anyway, encouraged by Plaid Cymru's problems. Beyond constitutional issues, Plaid had struggled to offer a distinctive programme and was damaged by losing the popular Dafydd Wigley as leader in 2000. The party lost five seats and nine percentage points of its vote in the 2003 election, leaving it with just one more seat than the Conservatives, for whom devolution was providing something of a renaissance. Their share of the vote may have remained under 20 per cent but the electoral system gave them the Welsh representation they had failed to win in the 1997 and 2001 general elections. As the Tories grew in confidence again, they also began to redefine themselves locally as a specifically Welsh party, committed to devolution and Welsh issues and divorced from the old Thatcherite image of an English party in Wales.[16] The presence of LibDems, meanwhile, meant Wales also had a fourth main party, although it struggled to find an identity. Welsh Labour's popularity, however, was more affected by what its own side was doing in London than by what its opponents were doing in Wales. The decision to go to war in Iraq alienated many core Labour voters and Blair's government seemed to be running out of domestic steam and ideas. By the 2007 NAW election, Labour's share of the vote had collapsed to less than a third, while ten of the party's seats were won with majorities of less than 1,600, including two with majorities of less than 100. To the horror of some party loyalists and MPs, Labour was forced into a coalition with Plaid Cymru. Had the other parties been able to bring themselves to work together then Labour would have been out of office all together. By 2008 Labour held just two councils in Wales. At the 2009 European elections the

Tories took more votes in Wales than any other party and Labour failed to top the poll for the first time since 1918. Even at the more important 2010 general election, Labour secured just 36 per cent of the Welsh vote, although Britain's skewed electoral system still gave it 65 per cent of the seats.

Despite the failure of any one party to secure an overall majority in the NAW, the inclusive and open brand of politics initially envisaged never quite developed. Central to this was the decision in the first term to separate the Assembly's legislature, as represented by its members and presiding officer, from its executive, what became known as the Welsh Assembly Government (WAG). This was to avoid any impression among the public or media that decisions were coming from the whole Assembly, something neither the parties in power nor the opposition wanted. However, the shift to a cabinet method of government encouraged more adversarial party politics, limited the influence of individual AMs and necessitated high levels of lobbying.[17] Within the NAW, personal point scoring and arguments over budgets and the detail of policy became incessant. Even though it ran (or at least dominated) the executive, Labour struggled to accept that it could not control Welsh politics in the ways of old and its traditional suspicions of anything perceived as nationalism were hard to kill, especially among its MPs, who were now left with little influence over Welsh domestic policy and uncertain of what their role was in the new devolved settlement.[18] One area where the NAW could claim some success in inclusion was in its gender balance. With half of AMs being female from 2003 to 2007, Wales was one of the most equal democracies in the western world.

However much politicians claimed otherwise, beyond Plaid Cymru's rediscovery of a commitment to independence (something not obviously shared by all its AMs, let alone all its voters), there was actually little substantive policy divergence between the four main parties. They all supported the broad concentration on social justice and equality policies that characterized the first decade of devolution. This focus was evident in the creation of a children's commissioner, consulting minority interest groups on all major policy developments, and the emphasis on healthier communities when English health policy centred on tackling illness. Other social-justice policies, such as free bus travel for the over-sixties and free school milk for the under-sevens, may have been acts more akin to a pre-Thatcher local council but they mattered nonetheless.[19] Lower fees for Welsh students studying at Welsh universities was more ambitious, although the policy was expensive, left universities in Wales underfunded and was abandoned in 2009. Free prescriptions from 2007 were popular but of limited impact when more than 80 per cent were already given away for nothing.[20] There were also symbolic rejections of English developments, such as school league tables and testing for seven-year-olds, when they were felt to be at odds with notions of social justice. The impetus for all this was from within WAG rather than from the electorate, which had broadly similar values and expectations to its English peers and even seemed to prefer policy uniformity within the UK over key issues.[21] Ministers, in contrast, wanted to do things differently and civil servants felt under pressure to develop specifically Welsh policies.[22] Developing transport links within Wales was one such aspiration, although finances prevented this developing much beyond a subsidized air route between Anglesey and Cardiff. Academics thus began to interpret WAG's policies as containing more than a hint of nation building. As Morgan himself put it in his 'clear red water' speech, 'we can now make our own social policy in Wales, for Wales', based on 'a Welsh version of the so-called post-war consensus'. Elsewhere he claimed, 'we have to use devolution to bind Wales together'.[23] Yet there was little that was Welsh about WAG's social policies. Indeed, some, such as free bus travel for the over-sixties and the banning of smoking in public places, were actually part of UK-wide developments, even if they were implemented in Wales before England.

How much difference any of this made to the lives of people in Wales was a recurring source of criticism. A 2006 BBC survey suggested that 43 per cent thought things had got better since devolution, 18 per cent worse and 36 per cent no difference.[24] By the end of 2008, free prescriptions and lower university tuition fees were starting to be valued and official research suggested that 52 per cent were satisfied with what WAG was doing, although that still meant nearly half were not.[25] By then, some were arguing that standards in education and health were actually falling behind England, perhaps because of the lesser emphasis placed on meeting external targets.[26] Whether this was actually happening depended on which measures were used but those who criticized the lack of difference devolution was delivering probably had expectations that were too high. Changing the course of any democracy is so slow that few passengers notice that the captain is actually pushing the tiller in any particular direction. Moreover, the reality of life in the UK held back aspirations. This was evident in the development of a Welsh baccalaureate, which was meant to replace A-levels but was curtailed by how it might disadvantage Welsh people seeking jobs or university places in England where it probably would not be understood. Nor did the electorate actually seem to want anything too radical. An official 2007 Welsh survey found that less than a third of respondents agreed government should redistribute wealth.[27] Popular socialism was dead.

Its limited powers provided the Assembly with a suitable explanation for why policies had not been more radical or decisive. The speed with which devolution had been delivered meant the new system was complex and not always very rational. In the early days there was confusion inside and outside the NAW over what precisely its powers were and what might be done with them.[28] The NAW had taken over the Welsh Office's areas of responsibility but those had grown haphazardly since the 1960s, with no clear rationale, and the Assembly was thus left dealing with anomalies such as not being responsible for S4C because broadcasting was not a devolved issue. The 2001 foot-and-mouth crisis (chapter 13) illustrated how this was more than an abstract problem. Agriculture was a devolved issue but the NAW did not have the power to implement its own solutions and thus Welsh farmers ended up subject to heavy-handed policies decided in London.[29]

Money, inevitably, was another problem. Without tax-raising powers and dependent on a block grant set in London, the NAW's options were curtailed. This was clear when WAG faced a choice between cutting services or asking London for more money in order to be able to provide the match funding required to secure Objective One grant aid from the European Union. Worse, the Barnett formula that calculated increases to Wales' block grant had started to become more problematic. It had always overfunded Wales according to its share of the UK population and underfunded it according to its social needs but after 1997 the implications of its design to converge public spending across the UK became apparent. The formula achieved this convergence by increasing spending in Wales, Scotland and Northern Ireland by the same absolute number per head as England (rather than on a percentage basis). This was less noticeable under the Conservatives, who had been both more willing to sidestep the formula and less prone to raising spending. In contrast, after 1997, the Labour government both increased public spending in England dramatically and stuck more rigidly to Barnett. The net result was that public spending per head in Wales (discounting social security and agriculture) fell from 13 per cent above the UK average in 2002–3 to 8 per cent above in 2007–8, despite the fact that the wealth gap between Wales and England had grown. Nonetheless, these figures still meant that public spending per head was more than £500 per annum higher in Wales than in England and that Welsh services were being subsidized by English taxpayers.[30] This meant it was possible to argue that the UK was giving Wales both too much money (on a per head basis) and too little (on a needs basis).

The Assembly's problems meant that, despite how close the decision to implement devolution had been in the first place, debate quickly arose about extending its powers. The UK government did not seem opposed to modest incremental increases, as evidenced in it giving the NAW powers over transport strategy. The aspirations of AMs were also encouraged by how quickly the Welsh electorate came to accept devolution as the status quo. Opinion polls consistently suggested that, by 2008, opposition to devolution had fallen to around 15 per cent, with about 40 per cent supporting a Welsh parliament and maybe 10 per cent in favour of independence. A little unexpectedly, the 2006 Government of Wales Act allowed law-making powers to be transferred to the NAW should a referendum be held on the issue. That Act also allowed the NAW to pass laws before such a referendum was held, via 'Assembly measures', which had first to be approved by the Secretary of State for Wales, a post which until then had seemed to some a little superfluous in an era of devolution. It was a complex system and meant that a government elected by England still had some power over Welsh domestic policy (and was willing to use it), but it did allow laws to be enacted in Wales for the first time since the medieval period. The system, however, was short-lived and in 2011 a referendum conferred on the NAW the right to make its own laws in devolved areas. Although the turnout was only 35.6 per cent, 63.5 per cent of people voted in favour of the change and only in Monmouthshire were the 'no' votes in a majority. The low turnout meant talk of a nation coming of age was rather over the top but it was a sign that devolution was here to stay.

ONE THING DEVOLUTION did deliver was the development of a Welsh civil society that would have seemed remarkable thirty years before. Those involved in public life now thought more at a Welsh level and had a confidence that policy could be made and delivered in Wales. The voluntary sector in particular began developing more specifically Welsh institutions. By 2004 more than thirty organizations had appointed Assembly liaison officers to lobby for their charities and interest groups.[31] Many AMs themselves had backgrounds in the public and voluntary sector, reinforcing their willingness to listen. The actual impact of this civil society was less straightforward. Some trade unionists claimed they lost influence because instead of relying on close informal contact with individual Labour politicians they now had to build up researched cases to sway policy.[32] Organizations with limited resources struggled to exert influence or even respond to the constant WAG consultation exercises. Groups concerned with radical action, especially for the Welsh language, lacked influence simply because their aims were unappealing to those in power.

The voluntary sector had its own problems in voicing radical solutions and representing interest groups while simultaneously receiving funding from an Assembly that it had no wish to alienate by being too critical or too different to existing policy preferences.[33]

This civil society also remained something of a closed network to ordinary voters and it made little impact on the consciousness of the majority of people. Indeed, an impression developed that the Assembly simply served the needs of a small political class in Cardiff. Events in devolution's history had fed such cynicism. The Labour leadership's parachuting in of Alun Michael or enforcing female candidates on local parties did little to create a sense that the Assembly was either independent from London or particularly democratic. A sham-like exercise over where in Wales the NAW should be located (it was always destined for the capital), the public money still going into the Cardiff Bay redevelopment and the escalating cost of the £67 million Senedd built to house the Assembly did not help either. In 2004 one inquiry noted, 'We have been struck by the contrast between the enthusiasm of those actively in contact with the Assembly, and a seemingly wider public indifference'. The Assembly's presiding officer said in 2006, 'we are not really loved out there by the Welsh public'.[34] Polls suggested that people in north Wales felt ignored and neglected by the Assembly. Even some northern AMs perceived and resented a southern bias in power and the allocation of resources.[35] Less than a quarter of respondents to a survey for the 2007 Welsh Life and Times Study thought that WAG looked after all parts of Wales more or less equally. To overcome such resentment and distribute the economic benefits of devolution, Welsh government offices were moved to Aberystwyth, Merthyr and Llandudno Junction, but the feeling of disengagement was so profound that it could even be found in Butetown, the traditional docklands on the Assembly's very doorstep. One resident complained to Radio Wales that while the Senedd was meant to be open to the community it actually showed its arse to Butetown. Perhaps such resentment was not surprising when part of Butetown was officially classified as the most deprived area in Wales in 2005.[36]

People's lack of engagement with devolved politics was evident in the fact that turnout fell some way short of 50 per cent at the first three NAW elections. In Swansea East turnout was as low as 35 per cent in 2007. Among the young, turnout was even smaller and perhaps fewer than one in five people under thirty-five voted in 2003.[37] People did not vote for a variety of reasons but some of the most powerful explanations could be seen in a campaign that appeared in Cardiff in 2007. An anonymous leaflet urged people to 'vote nobody, because nobody cares'. It maintained that people did care about issues but that voting made no difference because all parties always just served themselves, the rich and big business. It quoted one young mother as saying, 'All politicians are liars – they'll all keep privatising everything and crapping on ordinary people'.[38] Here, the Assembly's problems were part of a wider trend that could hardly be blamed on devolution, a trend where people felt removed from, disillusioned with and distrustful of mainstream politics. In 2009 that disillusionment turned to anger after press revelations about the extent of MPs' expenses. The electorate's cynicism was evident in how the Welsh turnout at UK general elections fell from 79.7 per cent in 1992 to 62.4 per cent in 2005. Within that period, mainstream parties had themselves encouraged cynicism by placing more attention on media manipulation and 'spin', which itself encouraged the media to snipe, question and rarely give anyone credit for anything. The failures of Blair's government to deliver on the optimism that greeted its election did not help either. But the popular disillusionment with politics was also rooted in the social transformations that began to take grip in the 1970s and which undermined the old British system of class politics, in which many had a natural alliance to one party. In a world where people did have not an automatic or emotional affinity to a party it was easier to have no faith in any of them. Nonetheless, Welsh parties could at least claim nationhood as an affiliation that united them with the electorate and a 2007 survey suggested that 72 per cent trusted the NAW to govern in Wales' best interests most of or nearly all of the time. Only 35 per cent had the same level of trust in the UK government.[39]

Defenders of the Welsh political system preferred to think that people were disengaged from politics more out of ignorance than apathy. It was certainly true that many people did not even know who was running the NAW. Rhodri Morgan was the only Welsh politician with any kind of popular profile but in a 2007 poll only 43 per cent of people could name him. Worse, only 7 per cent could name the Plaid Cymru leader and just 6 per cent could name the Tory and LidDem leaders. Despite the survey being conducted in the run-up to the NAW election, half of respondents were unaware that a poll was to take place.[40] People might not know anything about WAG ministers but surveys showed that the majority had a grasp of the basic principle that the Assembly had limited power. What those powers were, however, was less understood and a 2008 survey suggested that 32 per cent thought the NAW could raise income taxes and 14 per cent thought it had power over defence policy.[41]

The blame for such ignorance was often laid at the feet of the media.[42] The Welsh newspaper industry was struggling to survive in an age of instant television and internet news. By 2009 the *Western Mail* was selling fewer than 33,000 copies, while the *Daily Post* had a circulation of just 34,000. The London press, meanwhile, was just not interested in the goings on in Cardiff Bay. In the 1970s seven London-based newspapers had permanent correspondents based in Wales. In post-devolution Wales none had. The *Sun*, Wales' biggest-selling newspaper, reported the 2007 NAW election results in just thirteen words.[43] With the press offering such poor coverage, it was television that was the most important source of political information and those who watched BBC Wales were more likely to vote. But UK-wide television could be condescending and patronizing in its limited coverage of the NAW.[44] Devolution had been undermined in its infancy by the BBC's decision not to grant the wishes of its Scottish and Welsh sections to abandon a UK-wide version of the six o'clock news in favour of different broadcasts that combined national and international news from the UK's capitals. The separation of the Welsh news from the main news left the former with the air of a local newspaper, concentrating on mundane human-interest stories or whatever Welsh angle it could squeeze out of UK and international events. Any casual observer of the media in Wales thus struggled to develop any real appreciation of devolved politics. Yet the media alone could not be held responsible for apathy or ignorance. UK-wide research showed that public knowledge of Westminster was hardly any better than Welsh knowledge of the Assembly, despite the much larger and more politically conscious London media.[45] Perhaps the root cause of the lack of engagement with Assembly politics was that what the Welsh government was talking about simply seemed rather trivial in a world where the planet was dying, where multinational corporations were growing ever more powerful and where terrorists were hijacking aeroplanes and then murdering innocent people in their thousands. Compared with this, localized social justice policies were neither exciting nor likely to solve the big problems facing the world.

SOME FIVE MONTHS after the 1997 referendum, the Welsh band Catatonia released their *International Velvet* album. The chorus of its title track proclaimed 'Everyday when I wake up I thank the Lord I'm Welsh'. The rest of the lyrics suggested a sense of irony but that did not stop it being latched onto by those who wished to champion Wales. It provided the climax of the Assembly's opening concert, was used by the BBC in sports trailers and was employed by academics and commentators as an illustration of a post-referendum national confidence. For a brief period Catatonia was one of the UK's most successful bands and, to the delight of the Welsh media, singer Cerys Matthews openly championed her Welshness, even emphasizing her accent with rolled 'r's on one of the album's hit singles. In and outside Wales the media began to talk of 'Cool Cymru', as a number of other bands achieved success in the UK. Most notable was the Manic Street Preachers, who twice won both best band and best album at the British music industry awards. They referenced Welsh history in their songs and sleeve notes and draped a Welsh flag on their kit at concerts. In 1999 the *Western Mail* declared: 'Call Cool Cymru a cliché but our rugby team is riding high, our musicians and actors dominate the charts and the big screen, our language is enjoying a renaissance and our new devolved politics means Wales is taking control of its own destiny.'[46]

Cool Cymru smacked of media exaggeration but the connections drawn between devolution and a popular sense of nationhood never went away. In 2009 Peter Hain, the Welsh Secretary of State, claimed that with devolution Wales had been 'transformed very much for the better. More self-confident. More vocal. More democratic.... Welsh identity is flourishing as never before.'[47] He was far from alone in feeling this but if it was true it was not a one-way process and political scientists argued that devolution had become the settled will of the majority because it offered political recognition to the Welsh nation. Social psychologists certainly found that people across the nation strongly valued Wales and Welshness.[48] Given how, since the early 1990s, the national curriculum had been relating subjects to a Welsh context, encouraging children to appreciate their national history, geography and culture, this was perhaps not surprising. A sense of Welsh identity was more obvious in daily life in the post-devolution period than at any other time since the war. Clothing, car stickers and other ephemera emblazoned with a red dragon or other national emblems became fashionable. Wales was often still near invisible on UK television but the few Welsh shows that were broadcast to England enjoyed success and a degree of 'coolness', something evident in the sitcom *Gavin and Stacey*, *Torchwood*, a sci-fi series set in Cardiff, and BBC Wales' revival of *Doctor Who*.[49] The modern landscape of Cardiff Bay, which featured prominently in *Torchwood*, provided a symbol of a renewed Wales. Central to this was the splendour of the Millennium Centre, with its giant writing (that few quite understood) on a huge Welsh slate facade. In the nearby city centre, the Millennium Stadium, opened in 1999, became another icon of Welshness and a genuine source of pride for many Welsh people, whether they liked sport or not. Its hosting of the Rugby World Cup final in 1999 and the FA Cup final from 2001 to 2006 brought both Wales and its capital to a global audience. Even the national rugby team itself found success again, with Grand Slams in 2005 and 2008, their first since 1978. The BBC's coverage of international rugby was a clear illustration of a popular sense of nationhood. Even if people did not watch the matches themselves, it was difficult to miss the frequent patriotic trailers. In 1999 one even centred on a rock star singing 'As long as we beat the English, we don't care'. After his band, the Stereophonics, sang the same song to a patriotic fervour at a stadium concert in Swansea, a London music magazine asked 'Is Wales the new Germany?'[50]

This popular sense of Welshness had always existed but it was clearly becoming more prominent. Sociologists found that elderly people were becoming more aware of their own Welshness because of the education of their grandchildren and the constant 'flagging' of Wales all around them. As one woman put it, 'being Welsh is everywhere'.[51] Children themselves had a pronounced sense of Welsh nationality, although it was often confused and had limited points of reference beyond accent, sport and language.[52] With in-migration changing the make-up of the rural west, it was in the industrial south that the sense of Welshness was most widespread. In the 2001–2 Labour Force Survey, respondents were asked to choose between different national identities; all five counties where the proportion of people selecting Welsh was 80 per cent or higher were in the former coalfield. In Denbighshire and Flintshire in the north-east and in Conwy, where in-migration was very strong, the 'Welsh' proportion was below 50 per cent. The survey also affirmed suggestions that Welshness was stronger among the young: 71 per cent of sixteen- to twenty-four-year-olds chose Welsh, compared with 62 per cent of those aged sixty-five and over.[53] Other large surveys produced less definite evidence of a dominant Welshness, with the 2007 Welsh Life and Times Study recording 33 per cent of people choosing British, 55 per cent Welsh and 8 per cent English as their primary national identification. That these labels mattered to people became evident when there was a media storm after the Office for National Statistics refused to have a Welsh ethnicity box in the 2001 census, first through an oversight and then seemingly because of concerns about cost and whether it would lead to similar demands in England. In the absence of a box to tick, 418,000 people chose of their own accord to write 'Welsh' on their census form. There were, however, regional variations (ranging from 27 per cent of residents in Gwynedd to 6 per cent in Flintshire) that again pointed to how the importance placed on being Welsh varied across Wales.[54]

In north-east Wales, people's sense of national identity was complicated by how the patterns of daily life criss-crossed the border. Some Flintshire families saw their children born in England simply because Chester had the nearest hospital. In 2008 more than a quarter of the county's workforce had jobs in England. Local accents and postal and telephone codes that failed to distinguish between England and Wales, a constant movement of people, the popularity of north-west football teams and the proximity of Welsh-speaking north-west Wales all encouraged a sense among north-east residents that they were somehow less Welsh. But this did not mean they did not feel Welsh and the fact that they were not always treated as such, by both their compatriots and the English, was a source of genuine grievance.[55] In some ways devolution intensified their national consciousness because being in Wales now had a greater impact on ordinary life, through free prescriptions and lower university fees, something which also created some resentment among people who lived just over the border.[56] Yet there was a strong sense that Welsh politicians did not take the north-east seriously or wanted to impose on it some external definition of Welshness, something evident in this letter in the *Daily Post*:

> Hain and his cronies seem determined to produce a Welsh elite, a sort of cast culture where, for example, those living in north east Wales who don't speak Welsh, shop in Chester, support Liverpool, never watch rugby, fly on holiday from Manchester and consider Welsh Assembly debates about as intellectually stimulating as a Vicar of Dibley parish church meeting, are considered lower cast untouchables.[57]

Similar feelings of both pride and resentment could be found in Monmouthshire and Powys. At the 2007 NAW election an English Democrats party even took 1,867 votes on a manifesto of making Monmouthshire part of England. Yet a Powys woman in her late fifties who lived just inside Wales remarked, 'no-one takes much notice of the border. There's no need to really for things are more or less the same in Wales or England – except for health of course.' She appreciated her free prescriptions. But that was not a unanimous feeling. The author of a travel book about nationality along the border summed up: 'I had met people who were obsessed by it and others who never thought of it. Some people buried it away and only brought it out with great reluctance, while others wore it as a badge of pride.'[58]

The absence of an official category for Welsh ethnicity at the 2001 census was followed by a series of public attacks on the Welsh character from minor writers and celebrities that led to angry reactions and demands for prosecutions for inciting racial hatred. After people failed to find the EU leaving Wales off a map of Europe funny, the *Guardian* even talked of a Welsh 'chippiness'. Some of the comments were ignorant but when the reaction included the police spending £1,656 on investigating Tony Blair for swearing at the Welsh in private there was something ludicrous going on. One academic argued that the sustained attention given to slights that should have been quickly forgotten was evidence of a vacuum in political thinking.[59] It certainly showed how shallow any notion of Welsh confidence was. Here was a nation that seemed unable to step above the petty prejudices of publicity-seeking celebrities. There was plenty of other evidence that the old insecurities had not gone away just because Wales now had an Assembly. While some in the south learnt Welsh to affirm their patriotism and overcome what they perceived as a history that had stolen the language from them, there were plenty of others for whom encounters with Welsh speakers could lead to an embarrassment and defensiveness about their own Welshness. Nor had the belief quite disappeared that Welsh-language policy was 'a trick by a middle-class clique to monopolise the best jobs in the public sector'.[60] This was not surprising when sociologists had no problem finding people who regarded the language as a prerequisite of being Welsh. As a resident of Bangor put it, 'The Welsh person who can't speak Welsh is no different to the English'. Even a prominent academic upset much of Welsh public life by telling AMs that 'to be Welsh is to speak Welsh'.[61]

Such brashness disguised the sense of insecurity that still surrounded the language. The 2001 census had recorded the first ever increase in the percentage of Welsh people claiming to be able to speak the language: 20.8 per cent said they spoke Welsh (up from 18.7 per cent), while 16.3 per cent said they could read, write and speak Welsh. There were slight declines in some rural parts of the Welsh-speaking heartland but some big growths in the urban south. The teaching of Welsh in schools was fundamental to these rises and 40.8 per cent of five- to fifteen-year-olds were recorded as Welsh-speaking. Welsh-medium education had also continued its growth. By 2007 a fifth of primary school children were receiving a Welsh-medium education and more than 15 per cent of eleven- to sixteen-year-olds were taught Welsh as a first language. Yet Welsh-medium education was a false dawn because language ability was not the same as language use. English was still often the dominant language of the playground at Welsh-medium schools in the south. Less than a third of fluent speakers aged three to fifteen spoke the language at home all of the time. Even in the classroom just 10 per cent of GCSEs were taken through the medium of Welsh in 2007–8, some 5 percentage points less than the overall proportion of children taught Welsh as a first language at secondary school.[62] Beyond education, there were continued signs that official bilingualism remained rather symbolic. At the 2001 census 1,720,000 Welsh-language forms were printed but just 43,800 were returned. In 2005 only 3.4 per cent of marriages, 8.2 per cent of births and 4.4 per cent of deaths were registered in Welsh. Such figures can be explained by surveys that suggested only 58 per cent of Welsh speakers considered themselves fluent. Welsh was not even the main language used in 39 per cent of households where everyone spoke Welsh.[63] Welsh may have had more official status and more visibility than ever before but as a living, everyday language it remained weak. Social psychological research suggested that people placed more importance on the symbolism of the language than on its use.[64] But perhaps the best indication of Welsh as the language of life was the fact that in 2007 just 7.6 per cent of primary school pupils spoke fluent Welsh at home. Moreover, new threats were emerging. According to one historian, the internet was 'an agent of cultural imperialism' serving English-speaking masters.[65] Welsh certainly struggled to fit in with the abbreviations beloved of teenagers' electronic communication, while all Welsh speakers found it quicker to text in English.

Welsh identity was thus a curious mix of the confident and the insecure, although the scales were tipping in the direction of confidence. These contrasting tensions were, of course, nothing new. Survey evidence demonstrated that national identity in Wales was actually remarkably stable during devolution's first decade, at least in terms of the labels that people used to describe themselves (table 14.3). With a quarter of the Welsh population being born outside Wales, it is perhaps not surprising that Welsh residents were very divided in how they labelled their nationality. Such data are also difficult to interpret because they do not reveal what people thought that nationality meant or how important it was to them. One indication of whether the younger half of the adult population prioritized their nationality came from the names they chose for their children. There were just three Welsh names among the thirty most popular chosen for boys in Wales in 2008; among girls there were four. This was little different to the picture ten years earlier and Dylan and Megan were also in the twenty most popular names chosen in

Table 14.3 Self-description of national identity in Wales (%), 1992–2007

	1992	1997	1999	2001	2003	2007
Welsh not British	28	13	17	24	21	22
More Welsh than British	20	29	19	23	27	21
Equally Welsh and British	30	26	36	28	29	31
More British than Welsh	7	10	7	11	8	10
British not Welsh	14	15	14	11	9	10
None of these	1	7	7	3	6	5

Source: C. Bryant, *The Nations of Britain* (2005), 5. *Welsh Life and Times Study* (2007).

England. Thus, while some people appeared to be making conscious statements about nationality in their naming of their children, the majority were not, and devolution had made no difference to that.[66]

What is striking about national identity surveys or naming fashions is how they undermined those who claimed devolution was killing a sense of British identity. Certainly some of the old pillars of Britishness – the nationalized industries, trade unions, the memory of the Second World War and the popularity of the Royal Family – had faded. But the generational shift this involved was not as stark as some made out. In 1997 one survey found that while more than 90 per cent of people over sixty-five included Britishness in their self-described identity, so did 78 per cent of those under twenty-four, a generation that had grown up after the traditional bastions of Britishness had lost their importance.[67] In a 2003 Welsh survey three-quarters of respondents said they were either very or somewhat proud of being British, a similar figure to English results. The strength of their attachment to Wales was stronger but a widespread sense of Britishness was very clear.[68] This was because so much of daily life, the realm where people understood who they were, was no different in Wales to England, creating a common sense of British citizenship. In this the legal system and the welfare state were important, although maybe less so than in the past, as their reputations were jaded by scandal, familiarity and a lack of appreciation. The emerging policy divergences in health and education had not fundamentally altered the experience of going to school or being treated in hospital in Wales from that in England. People also moved back and forth over the border for entertainment, work and education. In 2007–8, a third of Welsh students had chosen not to go to university in Wales (although 42 per cent had made the same decision a decade earlier, when there was no financial incentive to stay in Wales).[69] London continued to exert a powerful pull on everyone Welsh with ambitions in popular culture, the arts and business. Nor did they find doors shut there and even the BBC's main newsreader was a first-language Welsh speaker from near Llanelli. Welsh-speaking farmers were affected by British agricultural crises and took part in 'Buy British' campaigns. The armed forces remained widely respected and recruited heavily in Wales, while the conflicts in Iraq and Afghanistan raised their importance and profile. The Welsh and English spent the same money and shopped in the same chain stores. Most of them shared many of the same broad values and cultural norms, such as a general public politeness evident in queuing and unselfish driving. Youth culture was another powerful shared experience where national distinctions were mere window dressing in a broader pattern of music, clubbing, drinking and partying. Most importantly, Welsh people of all ages watched the same television as the rest of Britain. A 2003 study suggested that just 6 per cent of Welsh airtime on BBC1 and 7 per cent on ITV were specific to Wales.[70] While a sense of Welshness was certainly promoted in some of that programming, the most popular shows were soaps set in England or were in the new genre of reality television, where the 'British public' were judge and jury. Television assumed and developed a common identity, speaking to the audience as fellow Britons and situating them within a national calendar and culture. As it had done since the 1950s, it generated shared hopes and fears, interests and outlooks. The result of all this was the polls in devolved Wales that consistently suggested that at least 60 per cent of people felt both Welsh and British. Moreover, in a 2007 survey just 28 per cent of respondents said they had more in common with Welsh people from a different class than English people from the same class as them.[71] Enjoying the same television programmes, shopping in the same shops with the same money, claiming the same benefits, being subject to the same laws, none of these things stopped people being Welsh. Indeed, through pride in Welsh accents on television, buying 'Made in Wales' products at a British supermarket or just getting annoyed when the London media ignored Wales, British experiences could simultaneously act as forums to recognize Welsh nationality. Thus, as the novelist John Williams put it, 'to come from Wales is to be at once part of the mainstream British culture and yet at the same time significantly other'.[72] But the extent of Welsh 'otherness' should not be exaggerated. Perhaps the best illustration of this was the cross-border sitcom *Gavin and Stacey*, where different ways of speaking and a pride in where you came from could not disguise the fact that people from Barry and Essex held the same essential values, lived the same essential lives and could, quite easily, fall in love.

ECONOMICS REMAINED CENTRAL to that process of locating Wales within Britain. The NAW neither sought nor was able to create anything resembling an economy that was remotely separate from England. Nor was it or the London government able to rescue the Welsh economy from its long-term problems. The closure of the steelworks at Brymbo in 1991 and Ebbw Vale in 2002 illustrated how the last remnants of traditional heavy industry were heading towards oblivion. Nearly 2,000 employees lost their jobs but there was little wider fuss, a sign of how far the deindustrialization of Wales had come to be regarded as inevitable. Manufacturing also had been given up on, at least in terms of ever creating large numbers of jobs. Whereas once low wages had helped attract factories to Wales, now jobs were being lost as companies relocated to Asia and eastern Europe, where workers could be paid even less. In New Labour's first decade, some 50,000 factory jobs in Wales disappeared.[73] This was offset by the continued growth of the service sector and Wales developed a particular reputation as a home for call centres, although they were often not pleasant places either to work in or to telephone. The new Welsh economy was evident in the fact that more than 30,000 people worked for the four main supermarket chains in Wales, a figure greater than that for coal before the 1984–5 strike. Above all, the Welsh economy continued its post-war dependence on the British state, something devolution intensified. By 2008–9 public spending accounted for 61.6 per cent of Welsh gross domestic product (GDP), compared with 51.1 per cent in Scotland and 41.8 per cent in England. Moreover, almost a quarter of Welsh employment was in the public sector, compared with less than a fifth in England.[74] The question of whether the state was willing and able to sustain that was a dark cloud on the horizon that threatened to unleash a deluge on the Welsh economy.

Wales remained the poorest part of the UK if the government's preferred measure of wealth, GVA (gross value added), was used. Indeed, under New Labour and devolution the gap with the rest of Britain widened, with Welsh GVA standing at just 74 per cent of the UK equivalent in 2008, a fall of 6 percentage points since 1997.[75] One in five Welsh men of working age were neither in work nor looking for it, a higher proportion than in Scotland and every English region. Disposable income was lower than in Scotland and every English region except the north-east. Comparisons with the rest of Europe were not much better. Wales had 95.8 per cent of the EU average for GDP per head, while the UK as a whole had 121.8 per cent.[76] Significant wealth divides remained within Wales too. In 2008 whereas just 4 per cent of wards in Ceredigion were in the 30 per cent most deprived wards in Wales, the figure for Merthyr Tydfil was 72 per cent. In the part of Rhyl that was officially Wales' most deprived area, 64 per cent of the adult population of working age was claiming some form of 'key benefit', compared with 19 per cent in Wales as a whole. One reason was that 47 per cent of people there aged sixteen to seventy-four had no qualifications. In contrast, in the part of Heath in Cardiff that was Wales' least deprived area, just 7 per cent of working-age adults received a key benefit and only 14 per cent had no qualifications.[77] Wales thus remained a deeply divided society.

Yet, as the *Western Mail* summed up of Blair's decade as Prime Minister, things had got 'a little better'.[78] Crime fell and Wales did get wealthier; it was just that England got even wealthier even quicker. Actual unemployment in Wales stood at 8.1 per cent just before Labour took power in 1997. By mid-2004 it was down to 4.2 per cent and the UK government was enjoying a reputation for having delivered stable economic growth. The number of people claiming unemployment benefits was even lower, and dipped to 40,735 in 2004, a fraction of the 180,578 post-war peak in 1985. Low unemployment, along with the UK government's tax credits policy, helped reduce the number of people living in households with incomes below the poverty threshold from 27 per cent (1994–7) to 22 per cent (2004–7). This meant there were some 150,000 fewer people in poverty.[79] The biggest improvement was among the elderly. Whereas 26 per cent of Welsh pensioners in the mid-1990s were in low-income households, only 19 per cent were a decade later. Yet the fact that more than one in five of the Welsh population lived in households below the poverty threshold was a damning statistic. Among children the figure was one in three.[80]

None of this went unchallenged, even if it sometimes had an air of inevitability about it. Most notably, the EU's designation of west Wales and the Valleys as an 'Objective One' area from 2000 to 2006 led to the investment of £1.5 billion in improving infrastructure and creating jobs. There was some success in helping people find work and raising local incomes but not enough to stop the area falling further behind the rest of Britain in wealth terms.[81] More successful was the improvement in the built environment, where streets, public buildings and private residences were done up with EU money, erasing some of the shabbiness that beleaguered the face of too many of Wales' poorest areas. Yet some residents felt even the new developments such as retail parks were not for them because, as individuals, they were too old or too poor.[82] While WAG sought to fight poverty by empowering community projects, the UK government concentrated on providing opportunities for people to work, which it increasingly felt people had an obligation to undertake, whether they wanted to or not. This policy, like the government's reputation for economic stability, was destroyed when a banking crisis brought recession in 2008. The Welsh number on the dole came close to doubling between 2007 and 2009, with actual unemployment reaching 9 per cent in the middle of 2009, the worst rate of any of the UK nations. As always, there were significant disparities within Wales, with the annual rate in 2010 varying from 16.4 per cent in Blaenau Gwent to 5.2 in Conwy.[83]

That poverty was not one of the defining features of the age owed much to how, even within deprived areas, older house-owners were able to build up significant personal assets thanks to the property boom brought about by low interest rates, a lack of new builds and the cultural desire to own rather than rent. With more than 70 per cent of Welsh homes owner-occupied, getting on to the property ladder became most young adults' key aspiration but it was increasingly difficult as the average cost of a house bought by a first-time buyer in Wales rose by 170 per cent between 1997 and 2007.[84] The property obsession not only helped minimize popular concern about poverty, it also contributed to conspicuous consumption becoming ever more important to people. Lifestyle shows dominated the airwaves as people sought inspiration or just an opportunity to look down on or up to other people's tastes. Ironically, as consumer spending continued its upwards trajectory, people increasingly spent their money on the same things. Welsh homes, with their gadgets, neutral colours and neat rectangular furniture, became not only indistinguishable from the those in the rest of Britain but from those in the rest of the western world too. Of course, there were still variations of taste but for those under fifty everything became rather uniform, even safe. It was what a historian of homes called 'blandification'.[85]

The obsession with lifestyle was further evident in how even minor celebrities became trend setters. Celebrity was perhaps the defining feature of the age's popular culture. It was the reason why the death of Diana had drawn such a strong reaction and it firmly rooted many Welsh eyes on the wider world of Hollywood, tabloids and television. It also gave Wales new icons such as Swansea actress Catherine Zeta Jones, who married one of the world's most famous movie stars, had Welsh lamb, Caerphilly cheese and Brains beer at her wedding (which a magazine paid £1 million to cover) and named her son Dylan.[86] The singer Charlotte Church was another patriotic celebrity about whom much of the media obsessed. She grew up from being a cute child with the 'voice of an angel' to a teenager who argued with her family, got drunk and misbehaved in public, before falling in love with a Welsh rugby star and settling down to become a loving mother. In some of this she was actually rather typical of the lifecycle of most young people but what made celebrity culture so captivating was that it mostly involved normal people living extraordinary lives. This made people believe fame was attainable for anyone and, with the growth of reality television, it was. Critics sneered at the shallowness of this world of 'celebs' but it was really no different from what earlier forms of popular culture had given people: an escape from the humdrum of everyday life.

In 2007 the clothing manufacturer Burberry decided to close a factory it owned in Treorchy in the Rhondda. The decision and the reaction epitomized contemporary Wales' economy and culture. The factory employed 309 workers and production was being moved to China, where shirts could be manufactured for half the price. Rather than striking, workers and the local community fought a vigorous media campaign against the closure, with the backing of celebrities and local politicians. Their campaign mixed Welsh imagery with a demand to 'keep Burberry British'. Burberry was embarrassed enough to improve redundancy payments and give the building, its machinery and £1.5 million to the community, but it closed the factory nonetheless. A Burberry representative claimed that Wales had been damaged because companies would be reluctant to invest there now.[87] Even with celebrity endorsement, a Welsh community and its politicians were powerless in the face of the realities of the free-market global economy.

DEVOLUTION IS THE MOST significant development in post-war Welsh history but it is an irony that Wales achieved a degree of self-governance at a time when nations had less control over their independence than ever before. This extended far beyond the influence of a global economy and popular culture. An energy shortage loomed, while global warming threatened the future of the human race (although environmental concerns still rarely won when they came up against economic interests). Islamic terrorism was a concern that both made immigrants in Wales feel unsafe and led, at least indirectly, to twenty-six Welsh-born troops dying in Iraq and Afghanistan by February 2010.[88] The proliferation of channels that digital television brought, meanwhile, undermined the media that had previously been so important in sustaining both Welshness and Britishness. By 2008 the five main channels had an audience share in Wales of just 63 per cent, a fall of 13 percentage points in five years. The web was also drawing people away from the shared experience of television and more than half of Welsh households were online by 2008, with adults with access using the internet for an average of eleven hours a week.[89] While the internet offered some opportunity for Welsh speakers, ex-pats and political aficionados to come together, it was also a space where, despite an unsuccessful campaign for '.cym' web addresses, Wales had no clear identity and which gave its citizens memberships of new virtual communities based on shared interests and hobbies that extended far beyond the nation. Who those citizens were had even diversified more than ever, as Wales experienced its first wave of significant immigration from overseas with the arrival of more than 16,000 migrant workers from eastern Europe in 2004–7.[90]

In such an outward-looking context, the NAW was always going to struggle to engage and involve the Welsh people, a majority of whom chose to not even vote in its elections. Much of Welsh politics thus resembled a private game, carried on in corridors and on websites inhabited and read by a few, overlooked even by the mass of Wales' own media. Post-devolution, most people's lives in Wales simply carried on much as before. The NAW existed on the peripheries of their vision, coming into focus only at certain times, such as when their son or daughter went off to university or when an election leaflet dropped through their letterbox, although even then it might go straight in the bin. Before the advent of devolution, Ron Davies, its key architect, had argued that it would 'only succeed if it can deliver a better quality of life and higher standards of living'.[91] He was wrong. For all the limited impacts of its policies and the general apathy that surrounded its workings, with astonishing speed devolution became an accepted part of Wales and a symbol of Welsh nationhood, one that stepped into void left by the disappearance of older symbols like coal and religion. Moreover, the popular legitimacy that the NAW gained was remarkable when set in the context of post-war history. Gone were the old arguments over what Wales meant or whether the language mattered or even whether Wales could enjoy a modicum of self-government and still survive. Some of this may have been at the expense of Wales' cultural uniqueness, but it was to the benefit of Wales' nationhood and more of the Welsh people felt Welsher than ever before. But that did not imply that the nation meant the same thing to everyone. It was still a very personalized identity, based on individual experiences and outlooks, but it was much easier to feel part of a nation that was not too closely defined or indeed defined at all. The Welsh nation was still part of a wider British and global civic and cultural space, but it was a nation in its own right too. In the twenty-first century that might seem a rather odd thing to say but it has to be set against the previous seventy years of history, when Wales' survival could not always be taken for granted. Moreover, Wales now had a political function and a political meaning as the creation of the NAW gave everyone in Wales a democratic citizenship. They might not have noticed or have even cared but it happened all the same.

Notes

1 *Guardian*, 17 Sep. 1997.
2 E. Phelps, 'Young voters at the 2005 British general election', *Political Quarterly*, 76:4 (2005), 482–7.
3 Letter from R. Davies, 22 July 1997, at http://webarchive.nationalarchives.gov.uk/20090409223949/http://www.walesoffice.gov.uk/foiarchive/2005/foi_20050429_2.pdf.
4 Quoted in K. Morgan and G. Mungham, *Redesigning Democracy: The Making of the Welsh Assembly* (2000), 97.
5 J. B. Jones, 'The "no" campaign: division and diversity', in J. B Jones and D. Balsom (eds), *The Road to the National Assembly for Wales* (2000), 70–95.
6 J. Thomas, *Diana's Mourning: A People's History* (2002), 162, 107.

7 G. Talfan Davies, *At Arm's Length: Recollections and Reflections on the Arts, Media and a Young Democracy* (2008), 129. N. Bourne, 'Devolution: a view from the right', in T. R. Chapman (ed.), *The Idiom of Dissent: Protest and Propaganda in Wales* (2006), 126. Thomas, *Diana's Mourning*, 162.

8 Jones, 'The "no" campaign', 95.

9 Committee on Standards in Public Life, *The Funding of Political Parties in the United Kingdom*, fifth report, Cm 4057–I (1998), 163.

10 R. W. Jones and D. Trystan, 'The 1997 Welsh referendum vote', and G. Evans and D. Trystan, 'Why was 1997 different?', both in B. Taylor and K. Thomson (eds), *Scotland and Wales: Nations Again?* (1999), 65–93 and 95–117.

11 D. Balsom, 'The referendum result', in Jones and Balsom (eds), *The Road to the National Assembly*, 159.

12 K. Williams, 'No dreads, only some doubts: the press and the referendum campaign', in Jones and Balsom (eds), *The Road to the National Assembly*, 96–122. H. Mackay and A. Powell, 'Wales and its media: production, consumption and regulation', *CW*, 9 (1996), 8–39.

13 I. Bellin, 'Television and the referendum', in Jones and Balsom (eds), *The Road to the National Assembly*, 123–32.

14 Quotes from V. Roderick, 'Assembly huge Labour own goal?' (2009), at http://news.bbc.co.uk/1/hi/wales/wales_politics/8033814.stm, and 'Complaint over PM Welsh "insult"' (2005), at news.bbc.co.uk/1/hi/wales/4290624.stm. D. Balsom, 'The first Welsh general election', in Jones and Balsom (eds), *The Road to the National Assembly*, 212–28.

15 Morgan and Mungham, *Redesigning Democracy*, postscript. For an entertaining view of some of the early controversies of devolution see P. Hannan, *Wales Off Message: From Clapham Common to Cardiff Bay* (2000).

16 Bourne, 'Devolution: a view from the right', 136.

17 E. Royles, *Revitalizing Democracy? Devolution and Civil Society in Wales* (2007).

18 C. Fowler, 'Nationalism and the Labour Party in Wales', *Llafur*, 8:4 (2003), 97–105.

19 A. Cole, *Beyond Devolution and Decentralisation: Building Regional Capacity in Wales and Brittany* (2006), 71.

20 J. Osmond, 'Wales', in A. Trench (ed.), *The Dynamics of Devolution: The State of the Nations 2005* (2005), 56.

21 C. Jeffrey, 'Devolution and divergence: public attitudes and institutional logics', in J. Adams and K. Schmuecker (eds), *Devolution in Practice 2006: Public Policy Differences Within the UK* (2005), 10–28.

22 Cole, *Beyond Devolution*, 78–9.

23 Quoted in G. Mooney and C. Williams, 'Forging new "ways of life"? Social policy and nation building in devolved Scotland and Wales', *Critical Social Policy*, 26:3 (2006), 616. R. Morgan, *Ten Years of Devolution: Reflections of a First Minister* (2009), at www.llgc.org.uk/fileadmin/documents/pdf/darlith_rhodri_morgan.pdf.

24 *WM*, 1 Mar. 2006.

25 GfK NP Social Research, *Research to Support the Work of the All Wales Convention* (2009), 22.

26 M. Drakeford, 'Health policy in Wales: making a difference in conditions of difficulty', *Critical Social Policy*, 26:3 (2006), 543–61.

27 *Welsh Life and Times Study (Welsh Assembly Election Study)* (2007), at www.esds.ac.uk/findingData/snDescription.asp?sn=6293.

28 Cole, *Beyond Devolution*, ch. 4. Hannan, *Wales Off Message*, 68.

29 Cole, *Beyond Devolution*, 73.

30 I. McLean, G. Lodge and K. Schmuecker, *Fair Shares? Barnett and the Politics of Public Expenditure* (2008), 5.

31 J. Osmond, 'Nation building and the Assembly: the emergence of a Welsh civic consciousness', in A. Trench (ed.), *Has Devolution Made a Difference? The State of the Nations 2004* (2004), 71.

32 J. England, *The Wales TUC, 1974–2004: Devolution and Industrial Politics* (2004), 110.

33 Royles, *Revitalizing Democracy?* G. Day, 'Chasing the dragon? Devolution and the ambiguities of civil society in Wales', *Critical Social Policy*, 26:3 (2006), 642–55.

34 *Report of the Richards Commission: Commission on the Powers and Electoral Arrangements of the National Assembly for Wales* (2004), 255. R. W. Jones and R. Scully, 'Welsh devolution: the end of the beginning, and the beginning of...?', in A. Trench (ed.), *The State of the Nations 2008* (2008), 69.

35 *Daily Post*, 1 Mar. 2004. A. Halford, *Eeks from the Back Benches* (2007).

36 *Good Morning Wales*, BBC Radio Wales, 2 May 2007. 2005 Welsh Index of Multiple Deprivation, at http://wales.gov.uk/topics/statistics/theme/wimd/?lang=en.

37 *Daily Post*, 1 Mar. 2004.

38 *Vote Nobody*, NAW election (Cardiff West) leaflet (2007).

39 *Welsh Life and Times Survey* (2007).

40 'Half voters 'unaware' of election' (2007), at news.bbc.co.uk/1/hi/wales/6405943.stm.

41 'The National Assembly for Wales: public attitudes 2008', www.assemblywales.org/abthome/abt-nafw/abt-commission/about_us-public_attitudes_2008.htm.

42 D. M. Barlow, P. Mitchell and T. O'Malley, *The Media in Wales: Voices of a Small Nation* (2005), 61.

43 Circulation data from www.abc.org.uk. BBC Wales, *Defining a Nation: Wales and the BBC* (nd), 7. Talfan Davies, *At Arm's Length*, 299.

44 R. Scully, R. W. Jones and D. Trystan, 'Turnout, participation and legitimacy in post-devolution Wales', *British Journal of Political Science*, 34:3 (2004), 519–37. *Wales on Sunday*, 13 Aug. 2000.

45 S. Kalitowski, *Parliament and the Public: Knowledge, Interest and Perceptions* (nd).

46 R. Edwards, '"Everyday, when I wake up, I thank the Lord I'm Welsh": reading the markers of Welsh identity in 1990s pop music', *CW*, 19 (2007), 142–60. *WM*, 12 July 1999.

47 Speech by Peter Hain, 29 Oct. 2009.

48 R. W. Jones and R. Scully, 'The political legitimacy of devolution in Scotland and Wales', paper delivered at the annual meeting of the American Political Science Association (2008). N. Coupland, H. Bishop, B. Evans and P. Garrett, 'Imagining Wales and the Welsh language: ethnolinguistic subjectivities and demographic flow', *Journal of Language and Social Psychology*, 25:4 (2006), 351–76. N. Coupland, H. Bishop and P. Garrett, 'How many Wales? Reassessing diversity in Welsh ethnolinguistic identification', *CW*, 18 (2006), 1–27.

49 On Wales being 'cool' see *The Times* 22 Apr. 2008.

50 *NME*, 21 Aug. 1999.

51 A. Thompson, 'Temporality and nationality', *CW*, 19 (2007), 138.

52 J. Scourfield, A. Davies and S. Holland, 'Wales and Welshness in middle childhood', *CW*, 16 (2003), 83–100.

53 Office for National Statistics, Annual Local Area Labour Force Survey, 2001–2.

54 *Welsh Life and Times Study* (2007). J. Humphries, *Freedom Fighters: Wales's Forgotten 'War', 1963–1993* (2008), 192–8. 'Welsh' on census form, formerly at www.statistics.gov.uk/cci.

55 WAG, *Statistics on Commuting in Wales, 2008*. D. Evans, '"How far across the border do you have to be, to be considered Welsh?" National identification at a regional level', *CW*, 20 (2007), 123–43.

56 Wheatley, *On an Offa Bus* (2009), 109.

57 *Daily Post*, 12 Jan. 2006.

58 Wheatley, *On an Offa Bus*, 50, 80.

59 *Guardian*, 8 Oct. 2004. BBC Radio Wales news, 12 July 2007. K. Williams, 'Living in Room 101: the wider significance of Anne Robinson's remarks', *PI*, 147 (2001), 42.

60 *Analysis*, BBC Radio 4, 25 Oct. 2007. Thompson, 'Temporality and nationality'. N. Charles, C. A. Davies and C. Harris, *Families in Transition: Social Change, Family Formation and Kin Relationships* (2008), 94–6. B. Davies, 'Welsh identity without illusion', in T. G. Williams (ed.), *Welsh Identity* (2004), 57.

61 A. Thompson and G. Day, 'Situating Welshness: "local" experience and national identity', in R. Fevre and A. Thompson (eds), *Nation, Identity and Social Theory: Perspectives from Wales* (1999), 35. *WM*, 25 Oct. 2001.

62 WAG, *Welsh in Schools 2007*¸ SB 63/2007 (2007). Welsh Language Board, *The Welsh Language Use Surveys of 2004–6* (2008). WAG, *Schools in Wales: Examination Performance 2008* (2009), 31.

63 General report on the 2001 Census in Wales, formerly at www.statistics.gov.uk/census 2001/2001_ciw_report.asp. WAG, *Wales's Population: A Demographic Overview 2009* (2009), 63. WLB, *Welsh Language Use Surveys of 2004–6*.

64 N. Coupland, H. Bishop, A. Williams, B. Evans and P. Garrett, 'Affiliation, engagement, language use and vitality: secondary students' subjective orientations to Welsh and Welshness', *International Journal of Bilingual Education and Bilingualism*, 8:1 (2005), 1–24.

65 WAG, *Welsh in Schools 2007.* G. H. Jenkins, 'Terminal decline? The Welsh language in the twentieth century', *North American Journal of Welsh Studies*, 1:2 (2001). D. Iorwerth, 'Battleground: the politics of language', in BBC Wales, *Defining a Nation*, 23.

66 Boys' names (2008): Dylan 2nd most popular name in Wales, 19th in England; Rhys 4th Wales, 55th England; Morgan 14th Wales, 116th England. Girls' names (2008): Megan 3rd Wales, 19th England; Seren 5th Wales, 277th England; Ffion 8th Wales, 454th England; Cerys 24th Wales, 137th England. Source: Office for National Statistics. Various charts formerly at www.statistics.gov.uk/statbase/Product.asp?vlnk=15282.

67 R. M. Jones, *From Referendum to Referendum: National Identity and Devolution in Wales 1979–1997*, PhD thesis, University of Wales, Aberystwyth (2003), 206.

68 *Welsh Life and Times Study* (2003). *British Social Attitudes Survey* (2003). Both available online via www.esds.ac.uk.

69 Calculated from Higher Education Statistics Agency, *Students in Higher Education Institutions* (2007–8 and 1997–8).

70 Barlow *et al.*, *The Media in Wales*, 144.

71 *Welsh Life and Times Study* (2007).

72 J. Williams (ed.), *Wales Half Welsh* (2004), 3.

73 'Job exodus abroad "will continue"' (2007), at news.bbc.co.uk/1/hi/wales/6677855.stm.

74 Centre for Economics and Business Research (CEBR), *Public Spending as a Share of GDP by Country/Region* (2009), at www.cebr.com. *Agenda* (spring 2010), 44.

75 WAG, 'StatsWales', at www.statswales.wales.gov.uk, table 114.

76 WAG, *A Statistical Focus on Wales and the UK* (2007 edn).

77 Welsh Index of Multiple Deprivation, 2008, at http://wales.gov.uk/topics/statistics/theme/wimd/?lang=en Office for National Statistics, Neighbour Statistics, www.neighbourhood.statistics.gov.uk.

78 *WM*, 10 May 2007.

79 Data taken from www.statswales.wales.gov.uk. Actual unemployment is officially known as the ILO level. Poverty threshold is 60 per cent of median British household income minus housing costs. Numbers of claimants given are not seasonally adjusted.

80 'Children in low-income households', at www.poverty.org.uk/w16/index.shtml.

81 'EU grant areas "falling behind"' (2007), at http://news.bbc.co.uk/1/hi/wales/6384305.stm.

82 T. Threadgold, S. Clifford, A. Arwo, V. Powell, Z. Harb, X. Jiang and J. Jewell, *Immigration and Inclusion in South Wales* (2008), 40.

83 Data taken from www.statswales.wales.gov.uk, tables 014383, 000430.

84 'First-time buyer survey region-by-region' (2008), at http://news.bbc.co.uk/1/hi/business/7351275.stm.

85 D. Cohen, *Household Gods: The British and Their Possessions* (2006), 210.

86 P. Stead, *Acting Wales: Stars of Stage and Screen* (2002), 181.

87 For an overview see *Observer Magazine*, 25 Mar. 2007.

88 'UK military deaths in Afghanistan and Iraq', at http://news.bbc.co.uk/1/hi/uk/7531254.stm. Threadgold *et al.*, *Immigration and Inclusion*, 42–3.

89 Ofcom, *The Communications Market 2008: Nations and Regions. Wales* (2008), 46, 23, 29, 34 (including C4).
90 WAG, *Statistics on Migrant Workers in Wales* (2007).
91 R. Davies, 'The economic case for a Welsh assembly', *Welsh Democracy Review*, 2 (1996), 6–7.

Conclusion. Wales 1939–2009

'You ain't a foreigner, are you sir?'
'Yes and no, I'm from Wales.'

Jack Jones, *Lucky Lear* (1952), 162

For too long Wales has been the nearly nation. Our past is littered with heroes of whom we can say 'Almost, but not quite.' Even as they lifted the cup of success to their mouths to drink, they found it dashed from their faltering fingers.... The new Wales stands on the threshold of an exciting era. For the first time for nearly 600 years, since Glyndwr and his Parliament slipped into the shadows of history, we have a government whose sole responsibility is to shape the destiny of Wales.

Western Mail, 26 May 1999

AFTER A DECADE of devolution Wales could no longer be called a nearly nation. Not only did it have a degree of self-government, its people were more conscious of being Welsh than at any time in the previous seventy years. Yet that did not happen because of devolution. It was a much longer-term process, with two inter-related causes: the actions of the state and the actions of individuals.

The Second World War changed how both the electorate and politicians thought about the role of the state. The crisis demanded state intervention in every facet of life if Britain was to win and survive. Once that had happened, the scale of reconstruction and the bitterness of the memories of the depression meant there was no going back and the state set about building a new country. It may have been inherently conservative in its attitudes towards the traditional foundations of society but there was an undeniable attempt to create a fairer society within the existing class hierarchies. State intervention in directing the economy and providing a broad safety net became political orthodoxies that were not challenged until the financial crises of the 1970s. This raised questions about how Wales should be represented within the extended powers of the state. There were some who saw the issue as an irrelevance, a bringing in of sentiment into far weightier matters, but there were others who feared Welsh interests being lost within the wider panoply of competing demands and such voices did find sympathetic ears in the highest echelons of both the Conservative and Labour parties. Thus unease about Welsh fortunes set in motion a chain of events that saw Wales become formalized as a political unit through an advisory council, a minister representing its concerns and then a full Secretary of State in the cabinet. The importance of the Welsh Office was much extended in the 1980s and it gained a degree of fiscal and political autonomy. That administrative devolution laid the basis for the political devolution that arrived in 1999. In making these changes the British state may have been reactive but it did not have to be, especially since the pressures for devolution were from a minority rather than a majority. In granting first administrative and then political devolution, the state showed it was willing to concede that the British nation was a plural place, with different cultures, and that was why Britain survived. This did not mean Welsh interests always won through – there were after all other interests and demands on resources too – but it did mean that Wales became more than just an abstract patriotic sentiment.

But the growing power and reach of the state also led to disillusionment. A generation grew up who had not known the harshness of life before the welfare state. They were unappreciative of what politicians did do and prone to see the state as impersonal and far away, something that created huge bureaucracies that took little interest in them or created inconveniences and annoyances in everyday life. It was, after all, not some abstract concept but something that had a human face like the Post Office clerk giving out the pensions, the doctor seeing patients or the local manager from the National Coal Board.[1] These faces were not always accessible, on time or popular. Some on the right had thought and resented that since the very earliest days of the welfare state but it was a feeling that extended to the working classes in the 1960s, a decade when the economic benefits of state support were not always apparent to those in the mines being closed or unable to find a job at all. The state also became a scapegoat for many of the social ills people saw around them, such as the decline in traditional communities, the rises in crime and the fading of the Welsh way of life. In England one product of such anger was a backlash against rising immigration. In Wales it contributed to rising concern about first protecting the Welsh language and culture and then about protecting industrial Wales. Both perspectives centred on thinking that London government was not doing its best for Wales.

Another reaction was an increased emphasis on individualism, especially among the young. This was evident in their dress, their music and their behaviour. It was also evident in Welsh-language culture. By singing pop songs and by writing and talking about sex in Welsh, by creating new terms for computers and televisions, by seeking careers in the media rather than in the pulpit, some Welsh speakers took the language into the modern world, shedding its traditional values. That upset many but, alongside the passing of the chapels' grip on communities, it freed Welsh from the old-fashioned image that had distanced people from their nation. Wales itself could not be reinvented until the language at the heart of its difference was. With the language no longer seen as a remnant of past times, and with the oppressive Welsh way of life gone, English monoglots now felt more able to see their own Welshness as something more substantive than just a sentiment in the back of the mind, brought out to be celebrated in the sporting arena, at the school concert or after a few drinks. In this they were also encouraged by the growth of the Welsh media and the increasing smattering of Welsh many received at school.

The updating of Wales was not always carried out consciously but at times it was. The language protestors who broke the law and those who employed violence were the most obvious examples. Although they created situations where conceding to their direct demands was difficult, they cumulatively put the Welsh nation on the political agenda and the fear that they might be the tip of an iceberg of patriotic protest was instrumental in the state's receptiveness to Welsh issues and Welsh nationhood. There were others who worked more quietly behind the scenes, lobbying ministers and corporations, presenting the respectable face of Welsh interests that showed the extremists did have moderate support for their cause, if not their means. There were those in government who did their bit too. James Griffiths was instrumental in leading the Labour Party to create the post of Secretary of State for Wales that he was the first holder of, while Wyn Roberts was a tireless persuader for the Welsh language within the Conservative Welsh Office. Wales, thus, did not survive by accident. The history of the nation after 1939 was not an inevitable march towards devolution and perhaps beyond. Wales survived because people fought for it.

That was the choice of individuals. No one made them do it but they did it in conditions that were not of their own making. None of these processes can be divorced from the economic picture and their causes and successes were rooted in wider economic trends. The language and the Welsh way of life were endangered by people's desire for a better standard of living, away from the countryside, and by similar aspirations for their children, who could be freed from wasting time on Welsh at home or at school. Of course, there was a cultural side to this too – people also wished to escape the moral restrictions of the chapel – but it was the desire to get on that mattered most of all. Despite the constant concerns about economic decline and realignment, material conditions were improving in the 1950s and 1960s and the victory against the basic needs of hunger and housing allowed some attention, notably among the young, to be diverted into thinking about Wales. Over the course of the 1970s, economic dislocation brought political tensions, as many people resorted to striking to exert their rights and interests. When that failed, they turned away from a belief in the post-war consensus and its associated labour movement and towards an appreciation that being Welsh might have political salience after all. The 1970s and 1980s also brought a generational change as the last people who had been of working age before the war retired. Those who took their place had less emotional investment in the state and the labour movement. They might still vote Labour rather than Plaid Cymru because the economic promise of separatism was unappealing but some had a more prominent sense of being Welsh and they were more willing to consider different political arrangements within the union. That shift may have initially been small and uncertain but it was enough to turn the 'no' vote of 1979 into the 'yes' vote of 1997. Once devolution proved not to be an economic disaster or the end of the UK then that shift also underpinned the widespread acceptance of the Assembly and Wales as a legitimate level of government.

Economic patterns also undermined localism, causing people to relocate in search of work or to commute to jobs in communities other than the ones they lived in. Rising disposable incomes also enabled greater travel for leisure and allowed people to engage more with the cultural outputs of the wider world. Although this encouraged people to look beyond Wales, it also broke down regional variations within Wales, something further encouraged by the growth of the national media. The end result was that the psychological gaps between north and south, east and west, town and country, all lessened, making Wales more of a coherent nation. Like all nations, it still had multiple meanings that ranged from Wales simply being where you lived to it being almost why you lived. Most people were somewhere in-between, increasingly aware and increasingly proud of being Welsh but also bearing an allegiance to family, neighbourhood and town, and to Britain.

If the Wales of 2009 is compared with the Wales of 1939 then society was undoubtedly wealthier. Fewer had to struggle to pay their bills and feed their families. People had more money for small luxuries and entertainment. They were more likely to have the sense of security and status that owning a home could give. But when compared with the rest of the UK then Wales had fallen behind and become the poorest British 'region'. Within Wales there were profound wealth divides too. The psychological barriers between regional and linguistic communities might have faded but material divides within Wales were growing more profound, as the middle class expanded and the working class fractured. The boundaries between the workers and middle classes may have blurred to such an extent that they were difficult to draw but the gulf between skilled workers and the unemployed or low paid widened to a chasm. In day-to-day life such divisions were far more meaningful than any notion of national unity.

The Welsh economy retained all its old weaknesses, lacking in domestic enterprise, dependent on the British state. If taxpayers, not least in England, were content for that to continue then there was no reason to worry but the global financial crisis than began in 2008 suggested that public spending was entirely unsustainable at the levels that had emerged. That crisis was further evidence that concern about economic decline was far from unique to Wales. The transformation of the Welsh economy, with its shift from producing goods and materials to providing services, was mirrored across Britain, just as was the feminization of the workforce. Alongside this, while the Welsh worried about falling behind England, the wider UK worried about falling behind the rest of the world.

The economy was also central to keeping Wales within the UK. The fear of standing alone undermined the arguments of those who said London governance had not been good for Wales. Patriotism was not enough to line one's pockets. The cultural ties that kept the UK united, though still strong, had faded but the economic ties had not. Europe once promised an alternative safety net to Westminster but, after the enlargement of the EU to take in much of eastern Europe, Wales could no longer expect so much from its sharing out of wealth and so the UK remained as important as ever.

The people of Wales, meanwhile, continued to live their lives, worrying more about their families, social lives, bank balances, bodies and prospects than about their nationality or how they were governed. But that did not mean Wales was unimportant to them. In the 2003 Welsh Life and Times Study six out of ten respondents said they felt very proud on seeing the Welsh flag and another fifth said they were a bit proud. A further fifth may have been indifferent but less than 1 per cent said they were hostile to the flag.[2] If anyone had asked such a question in 1939 they might have got a not drastically dissimilar result, but the difference was that Welshness had become something more than a matter of simple pride. By 2009 Wales was acknowledged as the level at which many political decisions should be made at, especially those that governed the everyday existence that people's mental outlook was dominated by. And that was a rather remarkable change. Indeed, it might even be said to be an appropriate outcome of the war fought seventy years earlier, a war for freedom and the right to choose. But the majority also exercised the choice to remain British too, meaning the Welsh could still answer 'yes and no' to an English question of whether they were foreign. That did not make Wales 'a nearly nation', since nationhood in the UK was not a choice between two competing countries. In the decades after the Second World War, Welsh identity did become more confident, more noticeable and more political but Wales had never been a nearly nation.

Notes

1 L. Black, M. Dawswell, Z. Doye, *et al.*, *Consensus or Coercion? The State, the People and Social Cohesion in Post-war Britain* (2001), 3.

2 *Wales Life and Times Study (Welsh Assembly Election Study)* (2003), at www.esds.ac.uk/findingData/snDescription.asp?sn=5052.

Index